Ordeal of the Union

Sectional "Pacificator": HENRY CLAY

Ordeal of the Union

VOLUME I...
**FRUITS
OF
MANIFEST
DESTINY
1847·1852**

by ALLAN NEVINS

*" Political history, to be intelligible and just,
must be based on social history in its largest sense "*
LETTERS OF JOHN RICHARD GREEN

New York · CHARLES SCRIBNER'S SONS · London

ACKNOWLEDGMENTS

SHENSTONE, writing his classic lines about the traveller who found his warmest welcome at an inn, knew nothing of the hospitality which the modern historical scholar receives among the keepers of libraries and archives. A host of pleasant memories crowd upon the present writer as he sets down the names of a few of the many who have aided him to rifle part of their stored treasures. Kirke Mechem of the Kansas State Historical Society and James Malin of the University of Kansas; Walter P. Webb, E. C. Barker, J. Frank Dobie, Llorena Friend, and Winnie Allen of the University of Texas; Mrs. John Trotwood Moore of the Tennessee State Historical Library; Robert J. Usher of the Howard Memorial Library in New Orleans; W. D. McCain and Charlotte Capers of the Mississippi Department of Archives and History; Edwin Adams Davis and W. O. Scroggs of Louisiana State University; Mrs. Marie Bankhead Owen of the State Department of Archives and History in Alabama; Paul M. Angle and Jay Monaghan of the Illinois State Historical Library; Christopher B. Coleman of the Indiana Library and Historical Board; J. H. Easterby and Miss Ellen Fitzpatrick of Charleston College and the Charleston Society Library; W. J. Van Schreeven of the Virginia State Archives—these are but half of those who should be listed. The author will not soon forget the unselfishness with which Dr. Robert L. Meriwether of the South Caroliniana Library, J. G. De Roulhac Hamilton of the University of North Carolina, Avery Craven and W. T. Hutchinson of the University of Chicago, and Professor Charles S. Sydnor of Duke University laid aside their own work to assist him. He can never forget the kindness with which some librarians gave him free access to their stacks, let him work there into the small hours of the night, and even gave him a key on Sunday. He must always treasure the profitable hours of counsel he received at the Massachusetts Historical Society from Allyn B. Forbes, whose untimely death removed a rare scholar.

To some friends the author owes an incalculable debt for aid, counsel, and encouragement. To Frank E. Hill, whose keen critical sense and artistic talents improved the book at every stage; to Henry Steele Commager, who read it all and strengthened many parts; to Margaret Clapp, who gave months to research and contributed much invaluable material; to Louis M. Hacker, who furnished many stimulating suggestions; and to Basil Rauch, who reviewed the sections on foreign affairs, special thanks are owed. Mr. Oscar Zeichner and Miss Margaret Rossau helped verify material and search for errors. At a distance accomplished scholars kindly read portions of the book: Charles S. Sydnor, E. M. Coulter, Holman Hamilton, George Fort Milton, Merle Curti, and James G. Randall. My colleague, Dr. Reinhard Luthin, of Columbia University, generously undertook responsibility for the index, and gave the author throughout the benefit of his exact scholarship. To these, to various advanced students who lent a helping hand, and to many others who furnished assistance, warm thanks are tendered. Finally, the author must specially thank his family, without whose help in manifold ways the work could never have been undertaken.

Material aid was generously furnished by two organizations. The Rockefeller Foundation made a grant which permitted the author to stretch a sabbatical half-year for research into a full year; while the American Philosophical Society made another to defray some of the costs of travel and copying. Their assistance is deeply appreciated. To Columbia University must also go a special word of thanks for the facilities it has furnished in office space and adjustment of teaching duties.

New York, April 1, 1947

PREFACE

IN COLLECTING materials for this work the author, during intervals of wartime service abroad, wandered widely in the United States. His labors carried him from New England to California. But the happiest of his memories have to do with the South, and all its amenities of scenery, winter climate, hospitality, and social picturesqueness. The sedate dignity of the old residential streets of Raleigh and Nashville; the classic grace of the capitol at Montgomery, its marble pillars gleaming amid noble trees; the legendary atmosphere which quivers in the sunshine of Savannah's statued squares and melts in the tones of Charleston's bells; the contrast of Old World and New in the streets that look out over the crescent river at New Orleans; the haughtiness of the Natchez mansions and the breezy independence of Austin—all this offers a timeless beguilement. While the hustling modern South is much in evidence, it has merged with rather than submerged the older era. Certain heroic qualities appertain to both. The heroism of 'the voice that rang through Shiloh's woods, and Chickamauga's solitudes, the fierce South cheering on her sons,' finds echo in the voice of Southern leaders demanding stern adjustment to changed conditions, and Southern liberals exhibiting more thrust and constancy than their Northern brothers.

But in any prolonged Southern sojourn, it would be an insensitive visitor who did not catch in the multitudinous accents of the region an insistent overtone: the overtone of a grim indictment. At every turn the traveller sees some physical wreckage left by the sweeping hurricane of the greatest of the world's civil wars. On every side he finds some reminder of ardent hopes blighted and rising enterprises cut down. In newspaper items and social converse he catches glimpses of cultural and spiritual losses still felt. From sedgegrown field, abandoned plantation house, impoverished church, and struggling college rises the indictment. The myriad cemeteries of Union and Confederate dead catch it up. It is sustained and deepened by answering notes still vibrant in the North and Northwest; for though their scars have better healed, they also had their losses, retardations, and tragedies. To attentive hearers the Civil War, if we listen for a deeper chord than its clangor and fanfare, speaks an undying reproach. In part the indictment is simply of man's fate:

> The Sinister Spirit sneered, "It had to be";
> But still the Spirit of Pity whispered, "Why?"

In greater part it is the indictment of a generation of political leaders, and behind them, of a whole nation, its spirit and civilization.

vii

When the republic was founded near the close of the eighteenth century, its people hoped that, sundered from the passions, false ideas, and feudal vestiges of the Old World, and given a rich empty continent to exploit, it might escape serious disaster. Hardships and vicissitudes would be plentiful enough; they would be needed, indeed, to sharpen America's mind and toughen its spirit. But such terrible calamities as had almost overwhelmed one older country after another—these it might totally escape. Those who took this view were too optimistic. Twice in a century and a half terrible calamities came; twice a failure of statesmanship if not of national character cost the country far more than it could afford to pay. The Civil War and the Second World War should have been avoidable. Because the people and leaders of the United States did not act with determination and sagacity in solving the problems of slavery, sectional irritation, and a right adjustment of races, part of the country was half ruined for generations, and all of it set back by decades. The subsequent failure to consolidate the victory won in the First World War—the refusal to help set up a system of collective security and to play a manly, farsighted part in the world community—imperilled the very existence of the republic. Only colossal effort and the sacrifice of a vast part of the national wealth saved it. Such errors can in time be largely retrieved. But they cannot be forgotten or forgiven, and their lessons should be driven home.

These two volumes begin a series in which the author hopes to write the history of the Civil War era. It will be primarily a narrative history; only a careful narrative can lay bare the inner meaning of the crisis, as only an ordered story can do justice to the suspense, drama, and human passion of the era. But room will be found for purely analytical and descriptive elements, and the whole civilization of the country will be brought under examination. In most works of this sort the chapters on social, economic, and cultural life are set off from the political narrative, and treated as separate compartments; here an effort will be made to integrate them, or at least to suggest that an integration existed. These volumes aim at objectivity, and at equal fairness to North and South, East and West. But they aim above all at rendering an impression of the tremendous upheaval of American life, and of its wild variety. It was an era of storm and lightning, of fierce passions, of tidal movements of men and ideas, of rascality and debasement, of integrity, heroism, and devotion. Senate, factory, farm, and market; pine-clad mountain, sagebrush plain, fertile prairie, and burning cotton-field; millhand, farmer, preacher, rancher, clerk, and sailor— all felt a surge as of the sea. Part of its pulse should be in every history of the time.

From the long study he has given to the years preceding the Civil War, the author has concluded that this period can best be understood if a number of dominant themes or clues are kept in mind. It seems clear, in the first place, that the conflict of North and South, of slave area and free, was part of a broader movement for the unification of the nation, and for the merging of elements both varied and conflicting into a homogeneous whole. The country felt a strong tendency to organize its energies, knit closer its economic structure, and standardize its moral and social values. Most of the forces created by science, invention, and business technology thrust toward unification. This tendency had to contend against centrifugal impulses born of the wide spaces of the land, the varied national origins of the people, and the existence of two utterly different labor systems. The slavery quarrel and the social differences of North and South were simply the most important of certain disruptive tendencies; but all were gradually being forced to yield to the powerful impulses that were making the United States homogeneous in economic life, political ideals, and social outlook. By 1860 men who gave their patriotism to region, not country, saw the handwriting on the wall. Irresistible factors were making unity triumph over sectionalism, homogeneity over heterogeneity.

Another consideration to be kept in mind is that the sectional issue is not only oversimplified but essentially misstated when it is discussed in terms of North and South alone. The Upper Mississippi and Lower Missouri valleys held one main key to the history of the era. The Southern attempt to gain Kansas, and the Southern hope that St. Louis might continue to drain most of the wealth of the Northwest toward the Gulf, represented a desperate effort to maintain a precarious sectional balance. The rise of Chicago and other lake ports, the Northwestern surge of agriculture, and the riveting of railroad chains between the upper Mississippi and North Atlantic, wrote economic laws far more powerful than any statute of Congress. Still another cardinal fact to be remembered is that the slavery question can also be readily oversimplified. The problem offered by the millions of Negroes far transcended slavery. Dominant elements North and South saw all too dimly that the one really difficult problem was that of permanent race-adjustment, that the abolition of slavery would only present it in starker form, and that the united efforts of all sections would be needed to cope with it. Had this truth been clearly grasped, the country might have struggled out of its blind drift toward disaster.

Certain other considerations are perhaps more obvious and familiar. As the sectional struggle developed, nearly all groups involved in it steadily substituted emotion for reason. They used stereotypes for facts, and epithets in lieu of cool arguments; they forgot the emollient grace of humor and the wisdom of the long view. The angry issue of slavery in the Territories, settled by the great compromise of 1850 but wantonly reopened in 1854, was practically settled again by the end of 1858. But by 1858 passions had been so deeply aroused that large sections of the population could not view the situation calmly or discuss it realistically; fear fed hatred, and hatred fed fear. The unrealities of passion dominated the hour. Had some great leader appeared, he might have broken through this emotional fabric. But the sectional tension distorted the party mechanism (none too well adjusted at best); and in three successive elections, 1848, 1852, and 1856, a nation which needed a President of penetrating vision, moral courage, and practical grasp was given three singularly incompetent chieftains. Zachary Taylor was stubbornly wrong-headed; Franklin Pierce impulsively erratic; James Buchanan timidly fumbling. It has never been sufficiently emphasized that in their weakness, these men leaned to an extraordinary degree upon groups of aides. Zachary Taylor turned to Seward, Weed, and a few others; in the days of Pierce, Jefferson Davis and Caleb Cushing swayed the sceptre; and when Buchanan occupied the White House, he was guided first by a Southern circle including Howell Cobb, Jacob Thompson, and John B. Floyd, and later, when his course had to be sharply altered, by a Northern group headed by Jeremiah Black, Edwin M. Stanton, and John A. Dix. Particularly under Pierce and Buchanan, the country was governed by a Directory rather than by a President.

Yet despite the violent climax of the era, the nation's story in the years 1846–1857 here covered was to a great extent sunny and hopeful, not dark and dispiriting. Despite all its difficulties and errors, the country was steadily growing in economic power, cultural vigor, and social stability. In letters and science, the United States was already presenting the world with fruits in which it might take pride. In its economic development, a business enterprise of identifiably American type was beginning to emerge with technologies unlike those of Europe. In a hundred other fields, the initiative, self-reliance, and optimism of the people were writing a record of almost unexampled vigor and color. Energy, versatility, progressiveness—these were the traits of the young republic.

A third volume will bring this history to the summer of 1861. This third volume, it may be said, will include chapters on the westward movement, on financial affairs (as connected with the panic of 1857), on the higher aspects of culture, including literature, and on slavery in its final phases.

Columbia University, February 12, 1947.

ALLAN NEVINS

CONTENTS

ILLUSTRATIONS

Ordeal of the Union

1

Hour of Victory

ON THE high Mexican plateau the September nights are chill. The first gray glimmer of day was appearing outside Winfield Scott's headquarters on the craggy height of Tacubaya, less than a mile from Chapultepec on its sister hill, when the sentries' challenges rang out to halt a group ascending the slope. An orderly roused the general. It was a deputation from the municipal council of Mexico City, he reported, passing through from Worth's command under the escort of Major W. W. Mackall. A few minutes later the councillors, facing the tall, heavily-built general, were pouring out their voluble information. Santa Anna and other leaders had stolen away from the capital at midnight; the remaining Mexican forces, leaderless and disheartened, wanted no more fighting; the people were eager for peace. The councillors had come to capitulate in form.

Relief stole over Scott's heavily-lined countenance even as he shook his head. The afternoon before, Quitman and Worth had fought their way inside the city walls. Some of Worth's officers (Raphael Semmes and a lieutenant of the Fourth Infantry named U. S. Grant were specially mentioned) had performed gallant exploits. The intrepid Quitman, with his tall frame, stiff graying hair, and keen eye, had seen South Carolina's palmetto flag go up as the first American banner over Mexico City. As darkness fell, with Santa Anna still holding the citadel, everybody had looked forward to another day of carnage; and Scott now rejoiced to learn that the fighting was over. But he told the councillors that he would sign no capitulation—that the city was already virtually in American possession, and that his army would enter it under no terms not self-imposed.[1]

A few minutes later the far-off noise of bugle and drum came from the

---

1 C. M. Wilcox, *Hist. of the Mexican War,* 480, 481; G. L. Rives, *The United States and Mexico,* II, 561, 562. Among officers mentioned in Scott's dispatch to Secretary of War Marcy dated National Palace of Mexico, September 18, 1847, were Captain Robert E. Lee (Engineers), Captain John B. Magruder, and Lieutenants George E. Pickett, James Longstreet, P. G. T. Beauregard, and Earl Van Dorn. N. C. Brooks, *History of the Mexican War,* 424–440.

northeast, where amid its lakes and marshes lay the gleaming city of the Aztecs, its domes, spires, and aqueducts plainly visible.[2] As dawn flushed the snowy slopes of Popocatapetl, Quitman's begrimed column left the walls, and began moving slowly toward the heart of the capital. It paused at the citadel and then pushed on. A brilliant sun was beginning to shine upon roofs and balconies crowded with silent people, the streets empty, the shops locked. Reaching the plaza, the American forces formed in battle line; a knot of soldiers disappeared inside the palace; and almost precisely at seven o'clock, the band playing and the men presenting arms, the starry flag rose on the staff overhead. Everyone waited expectantly. Presently distant cheers announced the approach of Scott, and within a few minutes he made his imposing entrance, mounted on a heavy bay horse, his powerful figure resplendent in full-dress uniform, gleaming epaulets, and nodding plumes, his aides clustered about him. Without loss of time he appointed Quitman governor of the city and moved into the palace to take up his quarters. By noon the hardjawed marines were patrolling the Halls of the Montezumas as if they were an immemorial possession.[3]

This year of 1847 had been a year of victory. The roll of triumphs had begun in February with Buena Vista, the most brilliant military feat of the war; an achievement which captured the American imagination, for Santa Anna had outnumbered Taylor four to one, and the nation had momentarily expected news that Old Zack was overwhelmed. Immediately afterwards, Scott had landed his army at Vera Cruz for an unbroken series of successes. Particularly impressive was his final march from Puebla to the capital. Setting out early in August with only 10,738 rank and file, he had traversed a difficult country, fought half a dozen pitched battles against forces which exceeded 30,000 men, stormed heavily-fortified Chapultepec, and had now taken possession of Mexico City on September fourteenth.[4] The suppression of guerrillas was the principal task left.

The war had been so rapid, easy, and glorious, indeed, that it could not fail to create martial ardor. The South was long to boast the exploits of Pierce Butler's Palmetto Regiment and Jefferson Davis' Mississippi Rifles, and the Northwest the feats of its volunteers. Pride in American strategy was general. "Sir," Stephen A. Douglas later told the Senate, "it was said with truth that the order of battle issued at Cerro Gordo a day before the engagement was a complete history of the triumph after the battle was over, so perfect were its

2 A good contemporaneous description of the country around Mexico City may be found in *To Mexico with Scott, Letters of Captain E. Kirby Smith to His Wife*; another in the diary of Captain Robert Anderson, *An Artillery Officer in Mexico*.

3 Justin H. Smith, *The War With Mexico*, II, 164.

4 When Scott finally entered the city he had fewer than 6,000 men in his army. *Cong. Globe*, 30th Cong., 1st sess., Appendix, 74, 75.

arrangements." [5] While much of this vanity was pardonable, the quick and ample gains of the conflict could not fail to excite some unhealthy appetites. Half-empty Latin American realms, the glamorous regions of peak and palm to the southward, seemed to beckon to fresh conquests; and it is not strange that John A. Quitman, leader in the assault on Mexico City, became in the next decade one of the princes of filibustering.

[I]

But the victories of 1847 neither united the American people nor shed on the Administration the luster which President Polk and his Cabinet coveted. It was one of the ironies of the war that, prolonged beyond Polk's original antici-pations, its two principal heroes were Whigs; for all the President's efforts, as the conflict lengthened, to place a Democrat in chief command had broken down.[6] It was another ironic fact that even while the war covered the army with laurels and gained the republic such rich additions of territory, the party which had made the conflict lost strength, and the party which had opposed it gained ground. One State election after another, while the voters were cele-brating the news of victory, ended in Whig successes. Polk's own Tennessee in April chose a Whig governor in place of a Democrat, and so did Connecticut in July. Iowa, holding her first legislative election since gaining Statehood, repudiated the Democratic party. As autumn came on, the eyes of Eastern politicians were fixed upon New York. Here the unhappy Democrats, broken into two factions—the Barnburners with their cry of free soil and free labor, and the Hunkers with their conservative stand on sectional issues—faced a united opposition; and the Whigs won a sweeping victory, electing a New York attorney of aristocratic family, Hamilton Fish, as lieutenant-governor, and a self-made Buffalo leader, Millard Fillmore, as comptroller.

The fact could not be denied that this victorious war, costing so little and gaining so much, was bitterly unpopular throughout great parts of the Union. Nor was the odium in which many held it at all inexplicable. It was not yet over —guerrilla warfare might drag on for weary months; its expenses seemed high; and any discussion of the terms of peace excited violent animosities. To many Southerners the war seemed certain to bring in its train tariffs, government

5 For Douglas' defense of the Mexican War, see Allen Johnson, *Douglas*, 109-112; for a specimen of Jefferson Davis' oratorical pride in the feats of the war, see his *Letters, Papers and Speeches*, edited by Dunbar Rowland, III, 340-342.

6. Representative Barrow of Tennessee accused the President of appointing only Democrats to both high and low military posts. Polk, he said, had appointed sixteen major-generals and brigadier-generals, of which number fourteen had accepted; but only one of the fourteen had been a Whig. *Cong. Globe*, 30th Cong. 1st sess., 226.

centralization, and a huge pack of hungry officeholders. To many Northerners it seemed primarily a war not for national but for sectional advantage, not to promote but to cripple free institutions; a war to spread slavery over vast new areas. Believing that it had originated in the craft of Southern expansionists, these critics were anxious to make sure that the Union, not the 'slave power,' should be the gainer. The war President had many fine and some great qualities, but no talent whatever for popularity; and he and his Cabinet proved singularly inept in uniting public sentiment behind their measures—partly because the Administration itself was far from united.[7]

An old age was dying, a new age being born; and such stormy transitions always bear harshly upon party structures. Facing the new issues which the war created, both Whigs and Democrats showed the strain. Being in power, the Democratic Party suffered the more. A few years earlier it had seemed homogeneous and closely knit. Actually, it was composed of disparate interests bound together by very loose ties and ready to quarrel the moment a sufficient motive appeared; and now the war revealed its essential lack of unity. A power-ful body of Northern Democrats, their greatest strength lying in New England and upper New York, stood opposed to any expansion of slavery. A still more powerful body of Southern Democrats, counting many Northern supporters, held that slavery had a right to spread through any areas where climate and other conditions favored it. Alongside these two bodies stood a vigorous array of Democrats, their principal strength in the Northwest, who were not un-willing to allow slavery to grow if by some compromise free soil grew with equal or greater celerity. The staunchly anti-slavery Democrats were repre-sented by Martin Van Buren of New York and Thomas Hart Benton of Missouri; the towering leader of the slavery expansionists was John C. Calhoun; and the moderate element was captained by Lewis Cass of Michigan and Stephen A. Douglas of Illinois. Any jarring new force was certain to reveal the lines which separated these three elements. Tyler's proposal for the annexation of Texas had brought them into view, and Mr. Polk's war had deepened the cleavages.

But it was not merely the new urgency of the slavery question which accounted for the growing factionalism of the Democratic Party in 1847–48. Another element was the belief of many Northwestern men that their interests had been neglected in the great territorial gain which Polk had achieved. In the

7 Polk was treated with almost uniform unkindness in our historical literature until his *Diary* was published in four volumes in 1910 by Milo M. Quaife, and his life was written with scholarly thoroughness by Eugene I. McCormac in 1922. Justin H. Smith's *War With Mexico* is also friendly in tone. A good picture of his management of his two plantations is offered in John Spencer Bassett, *The Southern Plantation Overseer as Revealed in his Letters* (1925).

Baltimore convention of 1844, they held, an implicit bargain had been struck. Texas was to be balanced against Oregon; the national boundary was to be carried to the Rio Grande on the south and to 54° 40′ on the north.[8] When the Administration wisely followed the guidance of Calhoun and his Southern lieutenants, among others, in fixing the Oregon boundary at 49°, many Northwestern leaders were resentful, and some were ready to accuse Polk and Calhoun of bad faith. Their resentment found expression in support of the movement to close all the new territories to slavery. Those who maintained this position to the bitter end shortly quit the party or were read out of it, while those who recanted were taken back into the fold.

Another cause of Democratic dissension lay in the failure of Polk and his advisers to mollify the jealousies and irritations of various party leaders. Calhoun, who had repressed but not forgotten his bitter disappointment in losing the presidential nomination in 1844, showed a dour frigidity toward the Administration. His half-hostile attitude in time engendered a fierce counter-hostility in Polk's breast. As for Van Buren, he and his followers, recalling that he had held a majority of delegates in the convention and been defeated only by the two-thirds rule, regarded the "dark horse" who had supplanted him with grim dislike.[9] Their antipathy rose when Polk virtually ignored Van Buren himself, and gave his Barnburner faction in New York only the starveling crumbs of patronage. The sharp-tongued Van Buren made no secret of his animosity, while his ablest associate, Silas Wright, who had refused the vice-presidential nomination to become governor, and who was Jacksonian in his bluntness as well as his views, denounced the Administration as imbecile and corrupt. Many Barnburners were determined to have their revenge in 1848. Another Jacksonian dissenter was the upright, large-spirited, and self-willed Thomas Hart Benton. He had opposed Polk's nomination; he had opposed the annexation of Texas without Mexican consent; he had opposed war with Mexico. Though at one time Polk had been ready to make him general-in-chief of the armies, increasing friction led to a complete breach, so that by the beginning of 1848 the two men were almost open enemies.[10]

In the background stood the party editors, prickly, discontented, and mutually jealous. Francis P. Blair, after long years in charge of the party's semi-official organ, the Washington *Globe*, had been compelled by Polk to give up that newspaper, and had yielded his place of influence to Thomas Ritchie of the *Union*. Sulkily retiring to his Silver Spring estate near Washington, he corresponded with Van Buren and Benton while meditating a possible

8 C. E. Persinger, "Bargain of 1844," *Oregon Hist. Quarterly*, XV, 137–146.
9 E. M. Shepard, *Van Buren*, 420, 421.
10 For a dignified expression of Benton's resentment, see his *Thirty Years' View*, II, 709–711.

revolt.[11] In New York the eloquent William Cullen Bryant, another Democrat of Jacksonian stamp, had indignantly spurned the Administration for its policy of war and annexation. His *Evening Post* was vibrant with denunciation. A different type of hostility was expressed in the Charleston *Mercury*, a Calhounite journal soon to pass under the part-ownership of a fanatical Representative, well known as attorney, orator, and writer, Robert Barnwell Rhett. Just as Polk had proved powerless to give unity and direction to his party, so Ritchie and the *Union* had been totally unable to furnish the Democratic press, from Maine to Louisiana, with any body of doctrine upon which its conductors could agree.[12]

Fortunately for the Democrats, the Whigs also had their sharp differences of principle and acrid personal rivalries. Such members from the slaveholding South as W. P. Mangum and John M. Berrien were sundered from such "conscience Whigs" of the North as J. Q. Adams and Truman Smith by a wide gulf. The brilliantly temperamental Clay, the Jove-like Webster, and that perennial candidate Judge John McLean, pompous but shrewd, all had a thirst for the presidency so long unslaked that it had now become desperate. Behind them stood lesser men like the mild John J. Crittenden, the three political musketeers Thurlow Weed, William H. Seward, and Horace Greeley, still fast allies, and the witty Rufus Choate, who entertained widely variant hopes and ambitions. But the Whigs were fortunate, for instead of assuming responsibility, they had only to criticize. By brazenly evading all themes of contention (that is, all principle) and fixing their eyes on nothing but the lure of office, they could temporarily preserve a superficial coherence. And this gave them a decisive advantage. Numerically the two parties were so nearly equal, both North and South, that the one which could show the greater unity and better organization was almost certain to win.

Divided parties, a divided country, an Administration which in some ways was strong and in others singularly impotent, an outlook gloomy even in victory —this was the situation as Scott marched into Mexico City. With Mexican forces still in the field, no one knew when fighting would be stopped. On every street corner, in every hotel lobby and country store, men quarreled over the proper terms to give to the enemy. Some would annex nothing, or almost nothing; that was Daniel Webster's view. Some would draw a line from the Gulf of Mexico to the Paso del Norte and take nothing beyond it; that was Calhoun's view. Some would have the United States possess itself of all or nearly all Mexico; that was Cass's and Bancroft's view. Some were for giving Polk more money and men, and some for withholding them. And in the back-

11 William E. Smith, *The Francis Preston Blair Family in Politics,* I, 216ff.
12 Smith, *War with Mexico,* II, 279ff.

ground loomed a far graver and more portentous issue, the mere thought of which frightened prescient Americans.

[II]

More deeply divisive of the nation than any question which had arisen since 1820 was the problem of slavery or free soil in the new territories, be they small or large—the problem wrapped up in the Wilmot proviso. On a hot summer evening in 1846, a portly young Democratic Representative from northern Pennsylvania, David Wilmot, had stood up in the House to move that a pending appropriation bill be amended to debar slavery from all lands acquired in the war.[13] The language of his proposal was purposely copied from the Ordinance of 1787, and its object was to extend to the new domain the great principle which Jefferson and others had applied nearly sixty years earlier to the lands northwest of the Ohio. Had he not offered this limitation, some other Northerner would have done so. It was fitting that it should come from a Jacksonian Democrat, a courageous fighter for the rights of labor, hard money, and such reforms as the abolition of imprisonment for debt. Now he raised in the skies what seemed to many Northerners a flaming beacon of hope, and to many Southerners a fiery sword threatening humiliation if not destruction. A tumult of cheers and protests at once flooded up from the nation. While one Northern State after another—New York, Massachusetts, Michigan, Vermont—passed resolutions endorsing the proviso, one Southern State after another denounced it.[14]

The Wilmot Proviso, after various vicissitudes, failed, but not before it had acted as a sharp chemical reagent upon public sentiment. To most people below the Mason and Dixon line, it seemed grossly unfair and gratuitously insulting. Their blood and treasure had helped to conquer these new additions to the national domain; were they now to be shut out of their fair share of the common possessions in the West? The proposal was "treason to the Constitution," declared Senator Andrew P. Butler of South Carolina; the South would secede rather than submit, asserted Calhoun. The Washington *Union*, assailing Wilmot

13 On Wilmot see C. B. Going, *David Wilmot: Free Soiler.* Richard R. Stenberg, "The Motivation of the Wilmot Proviso," *Mississippi Valley Historical Review*, XVIII, 535–541, dismisses some of the charges brought against Wilmot's motives.

14 Governor Brown of Mississippi wrote Governor Smith of Virginia that the South was determined to exhaust reason and argument, but if every friendly remedy failed, the section would not hesitate "to become *enemies*, and defend our rights with those means which God and nature have placed in our hands." The general tone of the South's protest was vigorous if not belligerent. *Niles's Register*, LXXII, 178; see also vol. LXXV, 73, 270, 374, 384 for the resolutions adopted in Virginia, Missouri, Tennessee, and Kentucky.

as a traitor to the Democratic faith, tried to read him out of the party. In reply, he declared that he was a better Democrat than James Buchanan, who he believed had written or inspired the article.[15] President Polk was keenly distressed by the Proviso, which he deemed a mischievous, wicked, and unnecessary agitation of the slavery question, playing into the hands of demagogues and ambitious politicians anxious to gain advancement through public excitements. He and others earnestly assured the rotund Pennsylvanian that the whole question was academic, for it was practically certain that slavery could never thrive in California or New Mexico.[16] To the President, slavery was a great social and economic fact which politicians had best leave alone, to be settled by the compromises of the Constitution. As the territorial question grew exigent, his solution was to extend the Missouri Compromise line to the Pacific, excluding slavery from all the area north of it, and letting the people to the southward decide for themselves. Condemning Calhoun as much as Wilmot, he set his face equally, as he wrote in his diary, "against Southern agitators and Northern fanatics." [17]

But Northerners of the anti-slavery faith found the Proviso a rousing expression of their deepest convictions. The issue was squarely joined, wrote Walt Whitman in the Brooklyn *Eagle;* the issue between the grand body of white workingmen, the millions of mechanics, farmers, and operatives, and the interests of a few thousand rich and aristocratic slaveowners.[18] No injustice would be done the South, argued such Democrats as Preston King of New York and Hannibal Hamlin of Maine as well as scores of Whigs, for Southerners could migrate freely to the new West without their slaves as they had migrated to Indiana and Illinois. But a very real injustice would be done to free white labor if slavery were introduced, for the sons of toil could not live without disgrace in close association with slaves. "If slavery is not excluded by law," declaimed Preston King, "the presence of the slave will exclude the laboring white man." Such statements Calhoun sharply contradicted. "The fact is not so," he told the Senate. "There is no part of the world where agricultural, mechanical, and other descriptions of labor are more respected than in the

---

15 *Cong. Globe*, 30th Cong. 1st sess., p. 304; February 7, 1848. The Proviso cut through both parties on a sectional basis. The Democrats, the Charleston *Courier* admitted, were as frightened by the "two-edged sword" as were the Whigs; Washington correspondence dated February 28, 1848, in the issue of March 3, 1848. See also Representative Benj. Hill to Buchanan, January 8, 1848; *Buchanan Papers.* But nearly all Southerners were deeply stirred. "You of the North," exclaimed Howell Cobb, "extend your territory, your government, your power, strength, and influence, day by day and year by year; but here stands the South, her limits fixed, bound hand and foot, subject to your mercy and to such legislation as you may think proper . . . to make."

16 Polk, *Diary*, II, 75, 289, 308; IV, 251.

17 See McCormac, *Polk*, 612ff, and Polk's *Diary*, IV, 299.

18 Whitman, *Gathering of the Forces*, I, 208.

South"—menial labor and the work of a body-servant alone excepted. White men could and did work in the same field or at the same bench with black men and lost no dignity. The white toilers of the South frequently ate at the table of their employers—could the North say as much? [19]

Among Northern Whigs the Proviso had emboldened a number of men to fiercer denunciation of the war and its assumed object of slavery-expansion. It helped prepare the way for that long-famous bit of invective by Tom Corwin which rang through the Senate and across the nation on February 11, 1847. Cass had said that the American nation, rising steadily toward a population of two hundred million, needed room—the word *lebensraum* was yet unknown. "This," declared the angry Corwin, "has been the plea of every robber chief from Nimrod to the present hour." Freesoil journalists were long to quote his fiercest sentences. "If I were a Mexican, I would tell you, 'Have you not room in your own country to bury your dead men? If you come into mine, we will greet you with bloody hands and welcome you to hospitable graves.'" His outburst recalled Pitt's eloquent denunciation of the Hessians—if he were an American, while such levies stood on his soil he would lay down his arms never, never, never! As Wilmot had made a name in a day, so the better-known Corwin won in an afternoon a new reputation. [20]

For the moment anti-war Whigs fancied that their party had found a new leader. "I find by all the information I can gather," wrote Charles Francis Adams, "that Mr. Corwin by his late speech has given an impetus to opinion, the force of which he did not in all probability himself foresee. A very large part of the people is ready to rally around him at once." He should hold to the path which he had marked out. "If Mr. Webster should falter or equivocate, whom have we to look to but him? Tell him that there has not been in America since the Revolution such a chance for a man to make an everlasting reputation as is now before him . . ." [21] Joshua Giddings, the spokesman for the Western Reserve in Ohio, to whom Adams addressed his remarks, was equally pleased. "Corwin is on the top of the swell of public sentiment," he wrote his son. "He is at this moment the most popular man in the nation. From all parts of New England we get letters exhibiting the high estimate in which he is held." [22] And Henry Wilson, listening to the voice of eastern Massachusetts, recorded that its demand was all for bold action. "The people are delighted with the speech of Corwin. He has touched the popular heart, and the question asked in the cars, streets, houses, and everywhere where men assemble is have you

19 *Cong. Globe,* 30th Cong., 1st sess., p. 876; June 27, 1848.
20 Josiah Morrow, *Life and Speeches of Thomas Corwin,* 49.
21 Adams to Giddings, February 22, 1847; Giddings Papers.
22 February 22, 1847; Giddings Papers. Giddings asserted that Corwin's speech followed "precisely in the tracks which I made last December."

read Tom Corwin's speech." [23] Wilmot had protested against new slave lands, Corwin against the robbery which he thought the new lands represented—and to many Corwin seemed to reach the higher moral level.

The slavery-extensionists replied to Wilmot in Congress early in 1847 with a set of resolutions introduced by Calhoun, denying the power of Congress to restrict slavery in the Territories.[24] They replied still more fiercely in Alabama, in South Carolina, and in Virginia, by legislative and party utterances. The "Alabama resolutions," passed by the State Democratic Convention early in 1848 under the guidance of William Lowndes Yancey, were especially defiant, repudiating the Missouri Compromise, declaring that slavery could not be touched in the Territories, and threatening secession if the proviso became law. One member wrote that, passed late at night after a vehement speech by Yancey, they were not understood by half the delegates.[25] It is certain that they pained such moderate Alabamians as William R. King, while they frankly horrified King's oldtime friend James Buchanan. The bland Secretary of State, eager to be nominated by his party for the presidency, had come out in the late summer of 1847 for extending the Missouri Compromise line to the Pacific. "From my first entrance into the Senate of the United States until the present moment," he wrote an Alabama correspondent, "my efforts have been devoted both in and out of that body, whenever the occasion required, to the mainte-nance of the constitutional rights of the South in opposition to all the projects of the abolitionists and quasi-abolitionists." After much thought, he had decided that the Missouri Compromise principle presented the best common ground on which Democrats of the North and South might unite. He was still certain that it would furnish the best solution of this delicate and exciting question; and "I shall most deeply regret it if the Democracy of Alabama should abandon me for this determination." [26]

Thus the contest was joined on the central issue which was to dominate all American history for the next dozen years, the disposition of the Territories. Two sets of extremists had arisen: Northerners who demanded no new slave Territories under any circumstances, and Southerners who demanded free entry for slavery into all Territories, the penalty for denial to be secession. For the

23   To Giddings, February 24, 1847, Giddings Papers.
24   *Cong. Globe*, 29th Cong., 2nd sess., p. 453; February 19, 1847. Calhoun added that the attempt by Congress to prohibit slavery in a Territory would be not only a breach of the Constitution but a subversion of the Union. These resolutions were not pressed to a vote, but they provoked an angry discussion.
25   G. W. Gayle to Buchanan, February 16, 1848; Buchanan Papers.
26   Buchanan to G. W. Gayle, February 24, 1848; Buchanan Papers. This letter was marked "confidential." "If," Buchanan wrote, "I should be repudiated by the South for adhering to the Missouri Compromise, this will be a hard measure of justice. Still neither for this nor for any other cause shall I ever cease to maintain their just rights by all honorable means in my power. . . ."

time being, moderates who hoped to find a way of compromise and to repress the underlying issue of slavery itself—its toleration or non-toleration by a great free Christian state—were overwhelmingly in the majority. But history showed that in crises of this sort the two sets of extremists were almost certain to grow in power, swallowing up more and more members of the conciliatory center.

[III]

The Thirtieth Congress, meeting for its first session in December, 1847, had to deal with all the questions raised by the continuance of the war; for Polk announced in his long message that no peace had been obtained and that the "obstinate perseverance" of the enemy shut off any immediate likelihood of one. Congress had to pass upon the President's request for more men and more money. It had to confront the slavery issue in Oregon, which awaited territorial organization, and it would certainly not avoid a fresh discussion of the issue in the still-undetermined area to be taken from Mexico. Meanwhile, its members were intent upon the impending presidential campaign, for not in decades had weightier decisions seemed to hang upon control of the government. This was the first Congress to find the American flag waving over the entire Pacific coast from Puget Sound to the Gulf of California—the first to legislate for three millions of square miles.

Seldom has a Congress mustered a more striking array of members new and old. The future seemed written in the House, the past still dominant in the Senate. To be sure, the popular chamber contained one great historic figure, for far down toward the front sat the venerable John Quincy Adams, at eighty-two palsied but still alert, anxious to use his experience for the public weal, and tenaciously and stingingly opposed to slavery. Forcible in logic, rich in sarcasm, he had an energy in debate that, as Lord Morpeth once said, "put one in mind of a fine old gamecock." But most of the other Representatives had the best part of their careers still before them. Illinois numbered among her delegation a solitary Whig, conspicuous for his gaunt, powerful frame, homely countenance, and pithy sagacity, Abraham Lincoln. On the Democratic side sat another plebeian figure, the Tennessee tailor-politician Andrew Johnson, beginning his second term. One Whig later to sit in Lincoln's Cabinet was Caleb B. Smith of Indiana, a man of rigid freesoil principles. The House had its prominent scholar in politics, the historian and theologian John G. Palfrey of Massachusetts. From Virginia came John Minor Botts, one of Clay's most devoted adherents, and like Clay, no friend to slavery expansion; from Massachusetts came George Ashmun, invincibly loyal to Daniel Webster.

Physically and morally, no member was more impressive than Joshua Giddings, whose stalwart form, massive head crowned with flowing white locks, and deeply-lined features arrested every eye. Entering Congress in the midst of the contest over the right of petition, he had followed Adams in the perils and glories of that struggle. Free-soilers had thrilled to his resignation and re-election following a vote of censure, and he had been in the thick of the subsequent battles over the annexation of Texas, the Oregon question, and the Wilmot proviso. He was a born fighter. Many vividly recalled the occasion in 1846 when, in an angry debate, he was confronted by Black of Georgia, armed with pistol and sword-cane, who threatened to chastise the anti-slavery man. "Come on!" Giddings defiantly shouted. "The people of Ohio don't send cowards here!" [27]

Yet the South had given the House two members of equal picturesqueness and greater ability, Alexander H. Stephens and Robert Toombs. Both Georgians, both Whigs, they had entered public life almost simultaneously, the Castor and Pollux of their State. Toombs, with a tall, robust figure, a handsome, sunny face, a merry eye and keen wit, was the more engaging of the two. A man of rough, coarse instincts, nobody could hit harder in debate and more quickly forget the exchange of blows. But Stephens, the product of a grimmer struggle, was a finer spirit and destined to a larger career. Born in poverty, his early years filled with farm-toil broken by brief intervals of schooling, while still a small boy he had been left a penniless orphan. By unremitting effort, with some friendly help, he pushed through the University of Georgia, beginning life with a fair education, but burdened by debt, and worse than that, with wretched health. He was so distressingly frail and emaciated in body, feeble in constitution, and melancholy in temper that men unjustly suspected him of epilepsy. Always a semi-invalid, and at times racked by disease till he stood on the edge of his grave, he struggled on until he became a brilliant ornament of the bar, an energetic, farsighted politician, a member of Congress, and finally a leader of his section. To a clear and inquisitive mind he united a kind heart, manners of great charm and gentleness, and rare integrity. He once said that ill health had been a blessing in disguise, for "it has given me a sense of entire resignation to the divine will." [28] Like Toombs, he exhibited strong convictions and independent thought, never hesitating to differ from others. Both were sincere lovers of the Union. Both were staunch believers in State rights, but not in Calhoun's theory of nullification, which Stephens in particular saw was a constitutional absurdity that would lead to the gravest conflicts.

The Senate was adorned by veterans of old renown, a galaxy of talent which

27 N. Y. *Weekly Tribune*, February 26, 1859.
28 See the sketch of Stephens in Charles Lanman, *Haphazard Personalities*, 342–364.

had lifted it to a prestige perhaps never since equalled—Webster, Benton, Calhoun, John J. Crittenden, and John M. Clayton—while among other members of experience and influence were Cass, Corwin, and Reverdy Johnson. But there were men of the future in this body too. Of the new Senators at least five, all former members of the House, were destined to an eminent place in national affairs.

The handsome Jefferson Davis, a cool, polished Southern gentleman, wearing the laurels of Monterey and Buena Vista, had been appointed to a vacancy by the governor of Mississippi with warm commendation for his services. A strong devotee of slavery expansion as well as State rights principles, Davis lost no time in making his views heard. In character half a military martinet, half an ecclesiastical precisian, he had shown his dogmatic tendency when he refused a brigadier-generalship from Polk on the ground that the President had no constitutional authority to appoint officers of volunteers. He was shortly defending the right of conquest in Mexico, attacking the Wilmot Proviso, and speaking disdainfully of "the lower grades of men." Another newcomer was his political opposite, the jovial John P. Hale of New Hampshire, a man of positive anti-slavery convictions, but far too liberal to be a fanatic. The moderate John Bell of Tennessee, and the slow, honest, sensible Robert M. T. Hunter of Virginia, a tireless worker who devoted himself especially to finance, also took their seats in the Senate. Quite the most interesting addition, however, was Stephen A. Douglas, a redoubtable champion of the Northwestern Democracy; his fighting power written in his short, thickset frame, determined jaw, and snapping dark eyes. He had come to Washington in 1843 as a prairie politician and lawyer, reckless of temper, addicted to sly party manoeuvre, and ready to make his point with any half-truth. But his views had broadened, and he showed promise of growing into a statesman.

Nominally the House was Whig and the Senate Democratic. But actually the balance of power in the House was precarious, for the three radical free-soilers, Giddings, Palfrey, and Tuck of New Hampshire, a trio who came close to being abolitionists, insisted upon extreme measures, while several Southern Whigs would have nothing to do with any proviso men. With some difficulty that lanky Whig, Robert C. Winthrop of Masachusetts, of spectacled face and serious mien, was chosen speaker. Intellectual, dignified, and able, he was too tolerant of slavery and of the war to suit many of his constituents. "Blood! blood! is on the hands of the Representative from Boston," Charles Sumner had said—with the result that Winthrop ceased to speak to him.[29] During the contest over the speakership J. Q. Adams had sent to Palfrey to ask him to drop his opposition. "If I can vote for Mr. Winthrop with a clear

29 E. L. Pierce, *Memoir and Letters of Charles Sumner*, III, 117.

conscience," the ex-President said, "I should suppose Dr. Palfrey could." But neither Palfrey nor Giddings yielded, and it was only when a Democrat with a strong personal friendship for Winthrop, Holmes of South Carolina, purposely left the hall, that the choice was made. The new speaker filled his difficult post most admirably. Elected by the general vote of his party, he did justice to both its Northern and Southern members in the choice of committees. The abuse which he received from Giddings on the one hand, Toombs on the other, testified to his impartiality. Winthrop correctly spoke of his own opinions as "uniting with that sense of the evils of slavery which is common to the free States, that respect for the Constitution and the Union which would infringe on no right of the slave States." [30]

[IV]

The first months of this session of 1847–48 were given up to a frantic but futile debate on the prolongation of the war; a debate which, as most Whigs and some Democrats attacked the Administration while party regulars rallied to its defense, became a furious mêlée. No one line of attack was followed. Some assailants were inspired by dislike of annexations, some by fear of slavery expansion, some by irritation over Polk's recent veto of a rivers and harbors bill, some by a desire for protective tariffs, some by dislike of them, some by a belief that the President was behaving arbitrarily, and some by general ill-nature.[31] War weariness was finding its voice. The disputes within the Democratic party itself over the proper boundary to be drawn in the Southwest grew daily more savage. The overworked, sad-faced President, aghast at the sudden ferocity of the sectional struggle and at the blows rained upon his head, found his defenders few and feeble.

Calhoun, speaking on January 4, 1848, drew so huge a crowd to the Capitol that an hour before the Senate convened the halls and passageways were completely blocked up. A hush of intense interest fell upon the crowded chamber when he rose to speak—as usual, without notes. He was opposed to the continued occupation of central Mexico, where he said the United States was tied to a dead or dying enemy, and to the futile expenditure of men and money in continued fighting. The American forces, he went on, should be brought back to a defensive line in the north, enclosing California and New Mexico, the only

30 R. C. Winthrop, Jr., *Memoir of R. C. Winthrop*, 71–80. Correspondence was published between Winthrop and the abolitionist trio which showed that Tuck, Palfrey, and Giddings had demanded, as a consideration for their votes, the control either of the committee on Territories or that on the District of Columbia. Winthrop had indignantly refused. Charleston *Courier*, January 1, 1848.
31 Albert J. Beveridge. *Lincoln*, I, 408, 409.

regions which we could profitably annex. To press forward with the war would mean a total overthrow of the Mexico government and the extinction of the republic; the cost of another campaign would be sixty millions; and to hold Mexico in subjection would require forty thousand men. For what object? To keep Mexico as a subject province would be contrary to the genius of our government and subversive of our free popular institutions. To incorporate the land, with its motley Indian population, into our national fabric would be still more ruinous; for "none but a people advanced to a high state of moral and intellectual excellence are capable, in a civilized condition, of forming and maintaining free governments." The attempt to conquer a peace by new battles would saddle the United States with more debt, though already he was authoritatively informed that a loan of fifty millions could not be raised at less than seven per cent interest; high tariffs would be required to pay these obligations; a heavy incubus of patronage and bureaucracy would become unescapable; and thus we would face the loss of all our ancient liberties. It was a statesmanlike speech, forcible in its general moderation of tone.

Other Democrats, though for different reasons, took their stand beside Calhoun. Thomas Hart Benton was equally critical. The venerable Albert Gallatin, always heard with respect, sent the *National Intelligencer* an essay denouncing a war of subjugation, which if continued would require a large standing army, "break down our union into separate communities, and destroy our nationality." [32]

But it was the Whig voices which were the most numerous and acrid. In the Senate, Clayton caught up Polk's statement that we required indemnity for the past and security for the future; indemnity, he said, meant one half of Mexico, security the other half! The object of the Constitution was to establish justice, "not to perpetrate injustice and robbery by indulging a love of plunder and a thirst for conquest or territorial aggrandizement." [33] Reverdy Johnson's single eye (he had lost the other in helping a friend practice for a duel) glared fiercely as he declared that the blood of the Mexican battlefields stained Polk's hands. From Webster came a repetition of his well-understood views. Holding that little or no territorial expansion was desirable, and believing that the proposed annexations would bring on a controversy which would shake the country to its center, he was for concluding peace on a liberal adjustment of boundaries and with a mutual indemnification of private claims. [34]

In the House, Alexander H. Stephens was as stinging as anyone. "The

32 February 7, 1848.
33 *Cong. Globe*, 30th Cong., 1st sess., p. 161; January 12, 1848.
34 Webster's speech supporting the resolution introduced by Senator Berrien of Georgia, March 1, 1847. See also the two resolutions previously introduced by Webster; *Cong. Globe*, 29th Cong., 2nd sess., p. 422; February 15, 1847.

principle of waging war against a neighboring people to compel them to sell their country," he said, "is not only dishonorable, but disgraceful and infamous." [35] Who had dreamed, demanded James Dixon of Connecticut, when Congress first voted to protect Taylor's forces, that when Mexico at last lay prostrate and bleeding at our feet, the President would insist that we plunge the sword still deeper into her vitals? [36] Underneath the whole debate ran an undercurrent of contempt for Polk, termed by one speaker the smallest President, with a single exception, who ever sat in the White House.

Exaggerated and even hysterical as many of these utterances were, the real object of most of the speakers, to shorten the war and to prevent limitless annexations, was sound. The position of many of Polk's advisers had become genuinely alarming. Bancroft, recent Secretary of the Navy, believed that the United States should "rescue" a large part of Mexico south of the Rio Grande from anarchy; Cass leaned toward taking the whole country, and his followers were explicitly for that course; Buchanan had caught the fever, and was writing pompously about fulfilling the destiny imposed on America by providence; the head of the Treasury, Robert J. Walker, who believed that the rich economic resources of the Mexican republic invited development, was for the most sweeping acquisitions.

A great imperialist movement was fast developing. It caught up secessionists like William Gilmore Simms of South Carolina, eager to strengthen the South; Northwestern expansionists like Senator Hannegan of Indiana; land speculators and capitalists; manufacturers hopeful of new markets; army officers who anticipated a wide new field for action; and Democrats who believed that they might win the election of 1848 on the issue.[37] Even some anti-slavery men inclined toward the absorption of Mexico on the ground that it would draw Negroes out of Virginia and the other border States, making this area freesoil. If the crescent movement were not checked, the American flag would be carried as far as Central America, and a new and perilous direction given to American destiny. The whole country should be congratulated, Tom Corwin had written, that Webster, "the ablest and wisest man alive, the greatest constitutional expounder in America, has taken the ground firmly of the *right and duty of Congress,* to withhold supplies, unless the further prosecution of the

35 *Cong. Globe,* 30th Cong., 1st sess., App., p. 163; February 2, 1848.
36 *Cong. Globe,* 30th Cong., 1st sess., p. 228; January 24, 1848.
37 Scott later declared that wealthy and prominent Mexicans had offered him a million dollars and a princely salary to help get the United States to annex Mexico. Speech delivered at Sandusky, October 11, 1852, and reported in the *National Intelligencer,* October 15, 1852. Scott's MS corrections are attached to the report of the speech in the Lieber Papers, HL. S. M. Randall told Buchanan that the people of northern Illinois "would execrate any other termination" of the war except on "the terms of an honorable indemnity of territory conquered." January 17, 1848; Buchanan Papers.

war, is shewn to be clearly justifiable." [38] And Charles Francis Adams declared that the more he reflected upon the situation, the more he was convinced that an unflinching stand was imperative. "If the Mexicans will not consent to stop the war, we must push opposition to it until the Administration be completely overthrown. It must be done too upon the slavery ground which is now exposed palpably enough." [39]

[V]

But the bitter debate was cut short when on February 22, 1848, the Senate received the treaty of Guadalupe Hidalgo, signed three weeks earlier—a product of the most curious negotiation in the history of the United States. The agent whom Polk had sent to Mexico, Nicholas P. Trist, had been officially recalled. But Trist, a middle-aged Virginian who after studying in Jefferson's law office and marrying Jefferson's granddaughter had risen to be chief clerk of the State Department, was a man of character. He ignored the recall, treated with the Mexican commissioners, made a compact (legally only a memorandum drafted by a private American citizen and a few Mexican officials), signed it, and sent it with a pert dispatch to Polk. His recall, he wrote the President, was born of ignorance as to the true situation in Mexico; the golden moment for making a treaty must be seized at once or lost forever; and the boundary to which he agreed was the best obtainable. The much-harassed Polk trembled with anger and disgust. He had already entered in his diary (January 15, 1848) that Trist was "contemptibly base," and that a previous dispatch was "arrogant, impudent, and very insulting to the government, and personally offensive." Left to himself, he would have tossed the compact into a wastebasket.

He had, however, to consider two uncomfortable facts: first, that a highly critical state of opinion was forming throughout the country, and second, that Trist was essentially right. When he laid the "treaty" before his Cabinet, four members were for acceptance; Robert J. Walker, voice of speculation, was for rejection; and James Buchanan, Secretary of State, was characteristically two-faced, talking rejection for the record, as helpful to his presidential aspirations, but making it clear that he actually believed it should be accepted. Polk finally decided to lay the treaty before the Senate.[40] After all, it conformed with the original instructions which he had given to Trist; he deeply resented the accusation that he loved war and relished conquest; and, with the dismaying prospect of a long period of guerrilla warfare ahead, Congress might actually deny him men and money. The treaty went in.

38 To Giddings, October 12, 1847; Giddings Papers.
39 To Giddings, January 27, 1848; Giddings Papers.
40 See Polk's comments in his *Diary*, III, 350. He wrote of Buchanan, February 22: "No candidate for the presidency ought ever to remain in the Cabinet. He is an unsafe adviser."

Received with a curious medley of applause and jeers, it at first seemed likely to fail. "Great Jehovah!" exclaimed young William T. Sherman, what a wretched treaty!—"just such a one as Mexico might have imposed on us had she been the conqueror." [41] That was the attitude of many army men. Some Senators thought that the treaty did not win enough territory, and some that it exacted far too much. Chairman Sevier of the Foreign Relations Committee informed the President that the committee would reject it and recommend the dispatch of an "imposing" peace commission to Mexico City. Senators of both parties and both sections were in opposition. But as the fate of the document, and with it the question of empire or republic, trembled in the balance, a sobering event befell the nation.

On February 21st, John Quincy Adams, still apparently hale and alert as ever, took his punctual seat at his desk in the House. He had recently spoken on Polk's January message with all his wonted fire and had held a crowded reception for Henry Clay, who was visiting the capital. The House was dispatching its early afternoon routine when someone lifted a startled cry: "Look to Mr. Adams! Look to Mr. Adams!" The aged statesman had fallen in a convulsion over the arm of his chair, and was grasping his desk for support. Members ran to his side and carried him to a sofa. Amid a flurry of confusion the House adjourned, and the Senate immediately took similar action. Physicians hurried in, and as they prescribed fresh air, the sofa, with the half-insensible ex-President upon it, was borne to the east doors. Then, as the air proved too cold, the dying man was carried back to the Speaker's room, to which were admitted only a doctor, nurse, Miss Adams and some women attendants, a nephew, and the towering Joshua Giddings, upon whom everyone knew Adams' mantle would fall. The night passed, and a rainy morning came on. It was Washington's Birthday, but the celebration was canceled, and when the House met, it immediately adjourned again. Giddings, sitting by the couch hour after hour, recorded for his daughter his poignant impressions.[42] "Prostrate on the couch before me," he wrote, "lay the form of the greatest statesman of the age, slowly sinking into the arms of death. I felt his feeble pulse and wiped the cold sweat from his brow." He heard Adams' breathing become more choked and labored. He saw members of Congress collect in solemn knots at the door, and turn away, many of them in tears. As night fell, some eight or ten men were waiting at the bedside. "It is my purpose not to leave him while the vital spark remains," Giddings wrote—and he was present when, on the evening of the twenty-third, the spark fled.

Like Chatham, Adams had fallen in the senate house, said his friends. His

41 Rachel Sherman Thorndike, *The Sherman Letters*, 46, 47.
42 February 22, 1848; Giddings Papers.

final words, "This is the last of earth—I am content," seemed a fitting valedictory.[43] Even in the seat of his bitterest enemies, the Charleston *Courier* courteously shrouded its columns in black as a token of respect for one who, it remarked, had given his country abundant cause for pride in his eloquence, learning, versatile brilliancy, and statesmanship. His going shed a momentary glory on the turbulent political scene, and some legislators perhaps resumed their tasks with an enhanced sense of responsibility.

But the main reason why the Foreign Relations Committee decided for the treaty was that public sentiment unmistakably seemed to want it. Reported favorably, it made a swift passage through the Senate. On March tenth, by a vote of 38 to 14, it was ratified;[44] and before May ended, the Mexican Congress at Queretaro had furnished its sanction. By the middle of June the returning troops began to arrive at New Orleans in jubilant throngs.

[VI]

The Senate's ratification made the question of territorial organization more acute than ever. What should be done with the spoils of victory, these vast new territories, with their 850,000 square miles (including Texas) of mountain, forest, desert, and rocky coast?

Few men yet appreciated the wealth which the nation had gained. Even California was so little known that most Easterners thought of it as an almost uninhabitable wilderness, fit for nomadic ranchers and nobody else. Daniel Webster had made it one of his objections to the new annexations that they must long be so sparsely settled that, years after they were carved into four States and sent eight Senators to the national capital, they would have but a tiny fraction of the population of the older commonwealths. Under the terms of the Texas admission, Congress might make that State over into five, with ten Senators; and this would give the empty Southwest eighteen Senators in all, or enough, wrote Webster, to turn the Constitution "into a deformed monster." [45] An early historian of the Mexican War spoke of California as a mere "waste" of "broken mountains and dreary wilds," and W. T. Sherman, after living there, declared that he would not trade two good Eastern counties for all of it.[46]

43 An eye-witness of Adams' collapse described him as being "pale as death, but calm, composed and serene as if perfectly resigned to his fate—indeed he has often been heard to say 'he would die at his post.' " Thomas Curry, February 21, 1848; Liddell Family Papers, Louisiana State University Archives. Some caught his last words as "I am composed."

44 As late as March 3, there had been much doubt as to the ultimate fate of the treaty. The ballots against it were equally divided between Whigs and Democrats.

45 Edward Everett, ed., *Works of Daniel Webster*, V, 271, 301.

46 E. D. Mansfield, *History of the Mexican War* (1849); M. A. DeWolfe Howe, ed., *Home Letters of General Sherman*, 108.

Yet poor as the country seemed, both North and South were eager to assert their "rights" in it; and as soon as its status became of immediate concern, sectional and party lines stiffened.

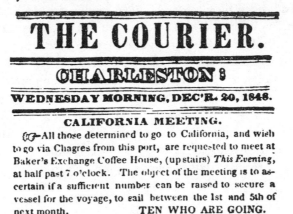

THE COURIER.

CHARLESTON:

WEDNESDAY MORNING, DEC'R. 20, 1848.

CALIFORNIA MEETING.

☞ All those determined to go to California, and wish to go via Chagres from this port, are requested to meet at Baker's Exchange Coffee House, (up stairs) *This Evening*, at half past 7 o'clock. The object of the meeting is to ascertain if a sufficient number can be raised to secure a vessel for the voyage, to sail between the 1st and 5th of next month.   TEN WHO ARE GOING.
D 20

On the Eve of the California Gold Rush.

This hardening of temper made it plain that the current session of Congress would take no decision upon California and New Mexico (the latter including present-day Nevada and Utah), but would leave them under the existing military regimes. Polk, who was eager to have territorial governments erected, sent a special message on July 6 urging immediate action. But the question of slavery stood like a lion in the path, for much of the new acquisition lay below the line of 36° 30′, and the South was as unwilling to devote this area to free soil as the North was to surrender it to possible slave occupation. However emphatically Polk, Buchanan, Douglas, and other Northern Democrats might assert that if the Missouri Compromise line were extended to the Pacific, slavery would never take root below it, a multitude of Northerners doubted that statement. Though long forbidden in California and New Mexico by Mexican law, servitude, they declared, really existed there in the form of peonage. The ignorant Mexican hands employed on some great ranches, the Indians driven to work at the California missions, and the Kanakas managed in droves on August Sutter's princely domain were indeed no better than serfs. Seeing these facts, anti-slavery men insisted that no concession be made to the hated institution. Most settlers pushing into California shared this antipathy. The San Francisco *Star* declared in the spring of 1848 that ninety-nine in a hundred of them looked upon slavery as "an unnecessary moral, social, and political curse upon themselves and posterity." [47] They did not believe that it

47 San Francisco *Star*, March 25, 1848, quoted in Charleston *Courier*, September 23, 1848.

would ever be generally introduced, but they did fear that in Southern California it might gain a sufficient foothold to deter the entry of a sober, industrious middle class of workers, and so "blast the prospects of the country." Yet to nearly all Southerners the extension of the Missouri Compromise line seemed the merest justice.[48]

The one strong effort to heal the dispute was made by Senator Clayton. On July twelfth the whole question of governments for Oregon, California, and New Mexico was referred to a select committee of four Whigs and four Democrats, representing North and South equally, of which Clayton became chairman. Six days later Clayton reported a compromise bill.[49] It provided for organizing Oregon with its existing anti-slavery laws, though with recognition of the authority of the territorial legislature to alter them; for organizing California and New Mexico with a prohibition of any action either for or against slavery by the territorial legislatures; and for referring all question of the legality of slavery in these Territories, as involving a constitutional issue, to the territorial courts, with an appeal to the Federal Supreme Court. This tribunal would decide whether slavery could or could not be excluded.

Although Clayton described the Supreme Court as a dial which shone lustrously in the gloomy hour, the debate showed that few men shared his belief in its august potency. While freesoil Senators asserted that Chief Justice Taney and his associates would certainly decide in favor of slavery, Southern Senators were equally convinced that he would betray that institution. Men plainly felt a general disbelief in the ability of the court, now that the slavery issue had become acute, to decide questions without sectional bias. Corwin declared that Congress would be enacting not a law, but a lawsuit. So fierce were the expressions of mistrust that many Whigs in the House, taking alarm, pronounced against dragging the highest tribunal of the land into a maelstrom of politics which might overwhelm it. Cass voted for the "Clayton Compromise"; so did Calhoun; so did Jefferson Davis. It passed the Senate. But in the House it failed miserably.

The territorial organization of Oregon fortunately proved feasible, but only after a further irritation of sectional feeling. When a separate bill to establish a government for this great area (including present-day Washington, Oregon, Idaho, and parts of Montana and Wyoming) came up, a protracted and quite

48 Robert J. Walker worked hard to convince Wilmot that slavery could never flourish in California; and according to Polk, Wilmot was so impressed by the argument that he declared that if he had thought of these considerations, he would never have offered his Proviso. Polk, *Diary*, February 20, 1849. Webster, typical of many Northern students of the subject, did not think it likely that slavery would find root anywhere in the Southwest— but he did not exclude the possibility. Benton, better informed than most of his colleagues, believed that slavery could very easily be introduced.
49 Text of the bill in *Cong. Globe*, 30th Cong., 1st sess., 1002–1005.

unnecessary battle began. Everybody knew that climate, soil, and the views of
the early settlers made all idea of slavery in Oregon preposterous. But those who
were determined to assert the Wilmot Proviso principles, those who wished to
shove the Missouri Compromise line to the Pacific, those who believed in the
right of Congress to legislate on slavery in the Territories, those who denied it,
those who wished to let the local legislature act, and those who flatly refused
to do so, all rushed into a wild scrimmage. We need not enter into the varied
fortunes of the combat in the two houses. It is sufficient to say that Senator Hale
of New Hampshire needlessly challenged the South by moving to extend to the
Territory the anti-slavery clause of the Ordinance of 1787—a step which some
Southerners thought unconstitutional, and others insulting. Senator Bright of
Indiana supported a proposal for leaving the slavery issue to the Territorial
legislature. Douglas, head of the recently created Senate committee on
Territories, offered an amendment declaring the Missouri Compromise line to
be "in full force and binding for the future organization of the Territories of
the United States." [50]

The debate, always heated and sometimes passionate, brought out a varied
array of views. Why make any provision at all regarding slavery? demanded
Senator Bagby. The only purpose was to create a precedent injurious to the
planting States. Calhoun felt more intensely on the issue than any other
Southerner. Never had Clay's classic description of him been more apposite:
"tall, careworn, with fevered brow, haggard cheek and eye, intensely gazing,
looking as if he were dissecting the last and newest abstraction which sprung
from some metaphysician's brain, and muttering to himself, in half-uttered
words, 'This is indeed a crisis!' " Rising to speak on a bright June day, he said
that he regarded the Missouri Compromise line as a mischievous and unconstitutional assumption of Congressional power over slavery; that the South
had never consented to it—the North had forced it upon the Southern people.
If all the inhabitants of the country were allowed to go into the Territories as
they pleased, taking their property with them, and deciding the question of
slavery or freedom when the various States were formed, then he thought the
resultant line would be somewhere near 36° 30'. In some places it would be a
bit north and in some a little south but it would be a natural, not an artificial,
line, and hence far preferable. Webster spoke against the 36° 30' line on very
different grounds. He had no doubt whatever of the constitutional power of
Congress to legislate on slavery in the Territories, but he would consent to no
extension of the area of slavery anywhere, nor to any increase of slave
representation.[51]

50 Cong. Globe, 30th Cong., 1st sess., 1048. Polk consistently clung to the same proposal.
51 George Ticknor Curtis, Life of Daniel Webster, II, 343.

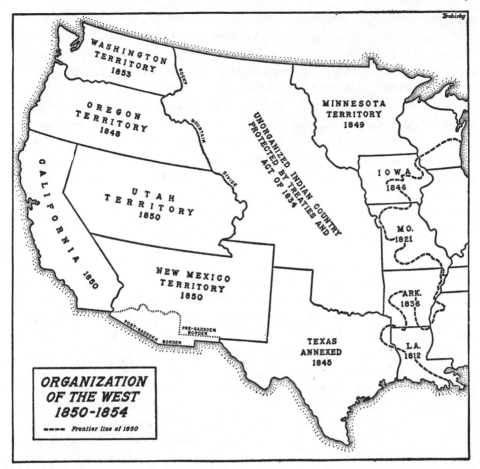

ORGANIZATION
OF THE WEST
1850-1854
---- *Frontier line of 1850*

*The original Territory of Oregon included the present State of that name,
and in addition Washington, Idaho, and part of Montana. Washington was
separated in 1853, Idaho in 1863. Present-day Arizona north of the Gila and
part of Nevada were at first incorporated in New Mexico Territory, Congress
creating Arizona Territory in 1863.*

When the Oregon bill finally passed, August 13, 1848, it was with the
slavery prohibition of 1787 (and of Wilmot) attached to it. Calhoun, resentfully returning to Charleston, declared that lamentable as was the defeat of the
South, it was still more unfortunate that it had been accomplished by the vote
of two Southern Senators. Benton of Missouri and Sam Houston of Texas had
given way. Had they stood firm with their fellows, the section would have
triumphed.[52] President Polk, in signing the bill, stated that he did so because

52 Charleston *Mercury*, August 21, 1848. As one writer put it, "The South has been beaten
by the South. If united, she would have conquered." See also issue of August 18, 1848.

Oregon imperatively needed a territorial government, and because the line of 36° 30′ (which he again urged upon the country) would exclude slavery without recourse to the objectionable proviso. Throughout the country angry feeling had been aroused by the Congressional debates, and the Lower South in particular showed the strongest animosity over the Oregon law.

Congress adjourned in mid-August with a meager record of accomplishment, but then Congress during the whole ensuing decade was to do little constructive work. In eight months it had ratified the epochal treaty with Mexico; it had organized far-off Oregon, with its few thousand of farmers, missionaries, and fur traders; it had admitted Wisconsin to the Union—and that was substantially all.

[VII]

At this point we may pause for a brief examination of the constitutional issue lying behind the question of slavery in the Territories. The Oregon debate had not only irritated both sections, but had given various schools of opinion, corresponding to different political and economic interests, an opportunity to state their views on this constitutional issue. Did Congress have power to regulate or prohibit slavery in the Territories?

Until the annexation of Texas the national leaders, with little explicit dissent, had apparently assumed that it did. As Henry Clay said, for fifty years every branch of the government, legislative, executive, and judicial, had acted on the postulate that Congress held a broad power over slavery in the common domain. In 1789 the first Congress had reaffirmed the Ordinance of 1787, including the clause which excluded slavery from the Northwest. In 1790 Congress had promised North Carolina that it would not act to emancipate slaves in the area which shortly became the State of Tennessee. In 1798 it had regulated slavery in Mississippi Territory by forbidding the entry of slaves imported from abroad; and in 1803 it had regulated slavery in Orleans Territory by three separate stipulations, the effect of which was to exclude any slave brought to America after 1798, and any slave not held by the owner for his own use. In setting up the Territories of Michigan and Illinois, Congress had reaffirmed the exclusion of slavery under the Ordinance of 1787. When the Missouri question arose, Congress did not hesitate to pass an act prohibiting slavery forever in the extra-Missouri portion of the Louisiana Purchase above the line of 36° 30′.

It is worth noting that the vote in the House on this Missouri Compromise line was three to one, and that not one of the opponents stated a constitutional objection. The Cabinet, when questioned by President Monroe, unanimously affirmed the constitutionality of the slavery restriction—and Calhoun was a member. This Missouri Compromise, as Benton later wrote, was a peculiarly solemn assertion of Congressional power, for "it not only abolished slavery where it legally existed, but forever prohibited it where it had long existed, and that over an extent of territory larger than . . . the Atlantic slave States." In 1838 Calhoun, in some fiery resolutions called forth by the Northern anti-slavery agitation, clearly assumed the power of Congress to legislate on slavery in the Territories, merely protesting against its abuse. For that matter, it could be asked whether the readiness of a host of Southerners in 1847–48 to extend the Missouri Compromise line to the western ocean did not admit the authority of Congress to deal with slavery in the new acquisitions.[53]

In constitutional theory, the freesoil contention that Congress had power to regulate or forbid slavery rested upon two main bases. One was the argument that sovereign authority in the regions acquired from France and Mexico had been transferred by those nations to the United States. As Henry Clay said: "Now I put it to you, gentlemen, is there not a power somewhere either to admit or exclude slavery from the territories acquired from Mexico? It is not an annihilated power. That is impossible. It is a substantive, actual, existing power. And where does it exist? It existed . . . in Mexico, prior to the cession of these territories. Mexico could have abolished slavery or have introduced slavery either in California or New Mexico. Now, that power must have been ceded. Who will deny that?"

The other pillar was found in a broad interpretation of Article IV, Section 3 of the Constitution, the 'ductile' provision that "Congress shall have power to dispose of and make all needful rules and regulations respecting the Territory or other Property belonging to the United States." The word territory in this section was read as meaning Territories, not mere land property. The power to make "all needful rules and regulations" was interpreted as a broad legislative power, embracing slavery. In the American Insurance Co. vs. Canter (1828), John Marshall had declared that the power of governing a Territory might be deduced from various sources, but "whichever may be the source whence the power is derived, the possession of it is unquestioned." Now Marshall did not say precisely what was bound up in his "right to govern." He did not say that slavery fell under "needful rules and regulations." But on this topic the broad constructionists could point to Congressional precedent. "I must say," Henry Clay remarked, "that when a point is settled by all the elementary authorities, and by the uniform interpretation and action of every department of our

---

53 A detailed summary of precedents for asserting Congressional power may be found in Senator Collamer's speech in the Senate, December 9, 1856, and in Justice Curtis' argument in the Dred Scott case.

government, legislative, executive, and judicial, and when that point has been settled during a period of fifty years"—then it might be taken as "fixed." [54]

Yet when the freesoilers took their firm stand behind the Wilmot Proviso, the angry slaveholders began to see the Constitution in a new light. They began to rank themselves beneath the constitutional banner which R. B. Rhett and Calhoun defiantly unfurled in the Proviso debates. Rhett, in his famous speech in the House early in 1847, declared that the States were joint owners of the Territories and "co-sovereigns" in them; that the general government was only the agent of the States in dealing with them; and that the emigration of any citizen into a Territory was "the ingress of his sovereign," the State, which was bound to protect him in all his property rights. Calhoun's appeal to fundamental law was equally uncompromising.

"But is there not a remedy in the Constitution?" the gaunt South Carolinian defiantly asked the Senate. "Ours is a Federal Constitution, of which the States are the parties, and the nation—the 'States United'—own jointly the Territories. Our whole system is based on justice and equality, and a monopoly on one side is not equality. It is utterly inconsistent with equality to pass measures which rob us of all share in the common property." Calhoun's five resolutions of February, 1847, previously mentioned, asserted that the States held joint ownership of all the Territories; that Congress had no constitutional power to pass a law by which any State should be deprived of its equal rights therein, or its citizens stopped "from emigrating with their property, into any of the Territories of the United States"; and that when the people of a Territory formed a State Constitution (but not before), they had the authority to adopt the institutions they deemed best. These resolutions aroused the fury of Benton, a Jacksonian nationalist whose belief that Congress had full power over slavery in the Territories never wavered. He denounced Calhoun's resolutions as firebrands for setting the nation aflame. "As Sulla saw in the young Caesar many Mariuses," he exclaimed, "so I see in them many nullifications." [55] But the speeches of Rhett and Calhoun effected their main purpose. They planted their constitutional seed throughout the South, where it was soon blossoming in defiant legislative resolutions.

This new Southern doctrine that the Constitution _ex proprio vigore_ legalized slavery in all the Territories, and that Congress was powerless to interfere, was more and more vigorously asserted in 1848. Its advocates cited James Madison's famous letter to Robert Walsh of Philadelphia, maintaining that Congress was impotent in such Territorial matters; they pointed to the Supreme Court decision in the United States vs. Gratiot (1840), holding that Congress had

54 _Cong. Globe_, February 5, 1850; 31st Cong., 1st sess., App., 118.
55 Benton, _Thirty Years' View_, II, 697.

authority over the Territories only as *land*—as property.[56] The before-mentioned platform drawn up by the Alabama Democratic Convention under the influence of Calhoun's disciple, William L. Yancey, in February, 1848, took the ground that the Federal Government must even remedy any failure of a Territory to protect slavery. During the spring and summer of 1848 not only Benton, but Clay, Webster, and others crossed swords on the constitutional issue with Calhoun. The most impressive intellectual battle of the session, in fact, was the debate of Webster and Calhoun; and most observers agreed that Webster's strong logic and incomparable eloquence surpassed the speeches of his quicker, more vehement, more dogmatic antagonist. Taking the stand of a moderate-minded lover of free institutions, Webster asserted with a wealth of historical and legal citations that Congress had full power to act, that its plain duty was to keep all the new Territories free, and that while a slave-holder might carry his black man with him into a Territory, he could not constitutionally take the local law which made this man a slave.

No positions could have been more antithetical than those of Calhoun and Webster, Yancey and Wilmot; and it was plain that sectional interests, with all their economic and social components, determined theory. The Constitution was interpreted by geography! This fact, at once absurd and alarming, was wittily pointed out by Tom Corwin: "It is a sad commentary upon the perfection of human reason that with but a very few exceptions, gentlemen coming from a slave State . . . have argued that you have no right to prohibit the introduction of slavery into Oregon, California, and New Mexico; while, on the other hand, there is not a man, with few exceptions (and some highly respectable), in the free States . . . but believes in his conscience that you have a right to prohibit slavery. Is not that a curious commentary upon that wonderful thing called human reason?" Senator Underwood rejoined that human reason "is regulated by a line." [57]

[VIII]

But as the two schools of extremists became more intransigent, a more moderate group of leaders began asserting a third view which gained rapid favor in the Northwest. The doctrine of popular sovereignty was clearly adumbrated by Daniel S. Dickinson in resolutions which he offered in the

---

56   14 *Peters,* 542. In this case the Supreme Court, interpreting Article IV, Section III, of the Constitution, had ruled: "The term territory, as here used, is merely descriptive of one kind of property, and is equivalent to the word lands." Madison's Walsh letter, dated November 27, 1819, took a strict constructionist view of the phrase "needful rules and regulations" in this section.

57   *Cong. Globe,* July 24, 1848; Morrow, *Corwin,* 343.

Senate in the closing weeks of 1847. Even earlier, Representative Caleb Smith of Indiana and Representative Leake of Virginia had hinted that the slavery issue might well be left to the people of any Territory for decision. The moment Dickinson presented the general idea, Calhoun blazed up and denounced it as worse than the Wilmot Proviso.[58] The first really full exposition of popular sovereignty, however, was contained in Lewis Cass' letter of December 24, 1847, to A. O. P. Nicholson of Tennessee.[59] He declared that Congress had no constitutional power whatever over slavery in the Territories; that they were entitled to complete self-government in all matters not controlled by the Constitution; that slavery, having been abolished by Mexico, did not exist in the regions gained by our arms, and that the Constitution could not carry it there; and that slavery could exist there only by virtue of legislation by the Territorial governments.

In this classic letter Cass spoke to a great extent for the Northwestern Democracy. He had been an entirely regular Democrat: a devoted follower of Andrew Jackson, a strong nationalist and expansionist, a supporter of the annexation of Texas, and a pillar of the Polk Administration. But he was also a son of the frontier. He had been the first man to receive a certificate of admission to the bar under Ohio's constitution of 1802; he had been a colonel of Northwestern troops in the War of 1812; he had grown up with Michigan, becoming its most distinguished personage. He knew the frontiersmen and declared that they exhibited by the very act of emigration a spirit of enterprise and self-reliance which proved their ability to govern themselves. Was Daniel Boone to be treated as a political minor? The ability of the Anglo-American settlers in new regions to preserve order and direct their own concerns was, he asserted, one of their salient characteristics, exhibited upon many trying occasions from Plymouth Rock to the Golden Gate.

When the slavery issue became acute, he had to reconcile his Democratic regularity with his loyalty to the free Northwest. That reconciliation was naturally effected by the popular sovereignty doctrine. We cannot say that Cass created the doctrine, for it sprang from the instinctive sentiment of a vast body of Western citizens and from a mass of vague suggestions. But he was the first to give it a clear formulation, and with Douglas, the first to defend it by well-marshalled arguments; and his biographer, after talking with men who knew Cass at the time, became convinced that it represented his sincere conviction.[60] He and Douglas maintained that the people of a Territory

58 Henry S. Foote, *War of the Rebellion*, 71–76; *Cong. Globe*, 30th Cong., 1st sess., App. 871. Caleb Smith's adumbration of popular sovereignty (January 6, 1847) may be found in the *Cong. Globe*, 29th Cong., 2nd sess., 124; Leake's statement *Idem*, 444.
59 *Niles's Register*, January 8, 1848.
60 Andrew C. McLaughlin, *Cass*, 239.

were just as capable of regulating their internal affairs as the people of the States. They were allowed to do so when they drew up their first Constitutions. Then why should Congress, during their preceding novitiate, exercise upon their domestic problems a doubtful and invidious authority? As Douglas put it, the republic had always allowed the people of a Territory to decide what kind of school system, banking system, tax system, and franchise system they should have. Then why not let them decide upon their own labor system?

The whole argument possessed much force. Not to go back into colonial days, the frontiersmen of Vermont in Revolutionary times, struggling to be free of New York and Massachusetts, had sent the Continental Congress a manifesto declaring themselves "capable of regulating our internal police *in all and every respect whatsoever,* and we have the *sole and exclusive and inherent right of governing ourselves* as in our own wisdom we think proper." They were squatter sovereigns, in Calhoun's contemptuous term!—a term that Cass repudiated, for it seemed to imply that where people did not own the land, but were mere squatters, they had no just claim to self-government. The frontiersmen of western Pennsylvania and western Virginia during the Revolution had asserted this same claim to the full right of self-determination. So had those of Kentucky and of the "State of Franklin" just after the Revolution. So did the settlers of the Cumberland Valley in 1786, using the words of Jefferson: "For ourselves we fought, for ourselves we conquered, and *for ourselves alone we have a right to hold.*" Now the settlers of California were disclosing the same eagerness to organize their own local governments, fix their own institutions, and debar all external authority. Cass, in short, could point to a long line of precedents, and could insist that self-government in embryo states was a peculiar and very proud Anglo-American doctrine.[61]

An argument of force, but one against which, as pushed to extremes, searching questions could be raised. At just what point would the settlers become numerous enough to determine their own institutions? Cass, saying that they must have "organized communities," did not state of what strength, leaving that to be determined when cases arose.[62] But the question was vital. And was it not true that while a Territory was in a state of pupilage, the general government had a right to see that it did not conduct its affairs in a manner detrimental to the welfare of the nation? A small group of settlers, looking forward to incorporation in a larger population and meanwhile dependent on that body,

61 Brodhead of Pennsylvania told the Senate that under the American system of government "Communities . . . must be left to judge for themselves what will best promote their own interests provided that in judging they do not violate the provisions of the Constitution or acts of Congress made in pursuance thereof." *Cong. Globe,* February 28, 1854.
62 See Cass's summary of his doctrine, *Cong. Globe,* February 20, 1850.

could not before incorporation took place conduct all their concerns precisely as if they formed an independent entity.[63]

[IX]

These three main views of the constitutional issue were squarely before the American people by the summer of 1848. The ambiguity and vagueness of the Constitution made it possible to defend each position. Its makers had passed over the subject of Territorial government with provoking brevity. Calhoun's school did their utmost to explain away the Congressional reaffirmation of the Ordinance of 1787 as a deed of trust with Virginia, the Missouri Compromise as a compact among the States, and other Congressional laws dealing with slavery in the Territories as departures from the true interpretation of the Constitution. They similarly whittled down the meaning of John Marshall's decision in the case of the American Insurance Company vs. Canter, which seemed to lay a broad foundation for Congressional authority in the Territories. The Cass-Douglas school, holding a doctrine which bristled with practical difficulties, made the most of their appeal to the innate American belief in self-government. But beyond doubt, the defenders of the right of Congress to legislate upon territorial slavery occupied much the strongest constitutional ground. Not only did the doctrine of implied powers sustain them, but they had at their back fifty years of varied and practically uncontested precedents.

The practical-minded American people, however, were not greatly interested in constitutional abstractions. They believed that the essential issue was to be decided by political action and by settlement. Was California, left in its painfully unorganized condition, to be opened to slavery by Congress, or to be kept shut against it? Was New Mexico, with its considerable Mormon population, to stand with gates wide or closed? With the Presidential and Congressional elections of 1848 impending, these questions would be decided primarily at the polls. Men's tempers, as they faced the issue, were growing short. Multitudes of Southerners believed that the North was trying to cheat them out of a fair share of lands which their sons had fought bravely to bring under the American flag. Multitudes of Northerners were vowing that this great new domain should never be cursed by an institution which paralyzed free enterprise, crippled cultural progress, and made America the scorn of Europe. The more apprehensive Southerners looked forward to an abolitionist domination of the republic; the more timid Northerners to an arrogant slave-

63 *Michigan Historical Magazine*, XIV, 32–37; Allen Johnson, *Iowa Journal of History and Politics*, III, 3–19.

drivers' despotism.[64] The head of the distracted nation, his health failing, his spirits low, could only hope that his successor would prove more successful than he in helping effect a rational compromise.[65]

And yet, as farsighted men knew, a mere compromise of the Territorial question would not be enough, for it would leave the deeper issues untouched. It would simply afford a foundation on which constructive statesmanship, if the nation had it, might operate to deal with slavery itself, the root of the sectional quarrel. Somehow a way must be found to teach the South that slavery offered simply a temporary and evolutionary status for the Negro; to teach the North that it must shoulder its fair share of the national burden in making the steady evolution of the colored race to this higher status possible. As yet the situation was far from implying an ultimate catastrophe.

But what prospect existed that the country would find in itself the resources of statesmanship needed? De Tocqueville had noted: "The dogma of the Republic is that the people is always right, just as The King Can Do No Wrong is the religion of monarchical states." [66] What kind of people were these, conducting their confident experiment in wider suffrage, frequent elections, and majority control? What was the popular culture, what the aspiration for change, what the machinery for registering the will of the masses and meeting problems?

64 An example of the growing extremist sentiment in the South may be found in a letter by a prominent Mississippian. Writing from Washington as the year 1848 closed, J. H. Hammonson protested that abolition was "carrying everything before it." The "insulting arrogance of these Yankees, would-be masters," angered him. "Shall we meekly bend our necks and receive their galling yoke or shall we resolutely, unflinchingly, contend for equal rights, all our rights under the constitution to the very letter?" Hammonson believed that if the South stood firm "and let the usurpers know that we will be their equals or their actual foes and will contend to the last, they will hesitate, nay will abandon their traitorous violations of the Constitution." To J. F. H. Claiborne, December 24, 1848; Claiborne Papers, Miss. Dept. Archives and History.

65 Polk was greatly harassed by the quarrels attending the end of the Congressional session. Calhoun vehemently pleaded with him at the White House on August 13 to veto the Oregon bill on constitutional grounds. Resolutely declining, Polk sent Congress a message on August 14 defending his approval. "My long confinement and great labor has exceedingly exhausted me," he wrote in his diary.

66 George W. Pierson, *Tocqueville and Beaumont in America*, 484.

2

Lineaments of a Young Republic

WHEN IN the early eighteen-fifties the United States lay basking in the sunshine of recent victory, California gold, and general prosperity, a South Carolinian and a Connecticut Yankee, each with office in view, met in a Washington drawing-room. The Southerner was William J. Grayson, future author of *The Hireling and the Slave;* the Yankee was Samuel J. Goodrich, then famous to schoolchildren as Peter Parley. Conversation in their group dealt with the supposed degeneration of the age from the Revolutionary standard of public and private morals. Goodrich, after listening for some time, turned to Grayson with the query: "Confine your attention to your own neighborhood as it was in your youth, compare its condition with that of today, and tell me which you think better, the manners and morals of the older time or the present?"

Grayson reflected for a moment on the oldtime ways and standards.

"I compared them," he tells us, "with those prevailing in my parish at the time of the conversation, and was compelled to confess that the change for the better was immense. Religion had revived. The churches were filled. Sunday was kept sacred. Schools on that day were established. Temperance prevailed. The riotous sensuality of the old times had disappeared. If immorality existed it was at least deferential enough to conceal itself from the public eye. My experience is that of every man whose memory runs back as far as sixty years, when every public day was a day of drinking, disorder, and fighting throughout the country. I replied to Mr. Goodrich by saying that so far as my own people were concerned, I was obliged to admit that the improvement of the present times over the past was incalculable. He said that he had put the same question to a great number of persons, in every part of the country, and had received the same reply everywhere." [1]

The two most vital questions to be asked of any nation are, What is its civilization, and, in what direction is its civilization tending? These questions

[1] MS Autobiography of William J. Grayson, South Caroliniana Library.

are complementary and inseparable. The level attained by a nation in material well-being, education, public health, religion, morals, recreation, and literature may be high; and yet if disruptive tendencies are undermining the whole structure, it is in an unhappier position than some neighboring land whose culture and wealth may be inferior, but the trend of whose national life is upward. The Spain of Philip II, Cervantes, Lope da Vega, and Velasquez had a civilization equal to that of Elizabethan England; but Spain had acquired a social and governmental system which was to carry her downward, while Great Britain as the generations passed grew stronger and more healthily active in world affairs. Often when a nation seems proudest and most prosperous its foot is on the descending path; often when adversity is hardening a people it begins its march upward.

[I]

By 1846 no country in the world was so interesting to other nations as the United States; none attracted so many visitors with pen in hand and an observant gleam in the eye. Since Alexis de Tocqueville's book had made such a noise on the continent of Europe and had been caught up by influential Liberals in England, the verdict had been more and more favorable. Gone were the prejudice and sneers of Mrs. Trollope's day. Travellers now arrived, like the scientist Charles Lyell, to find the bay and city of Boston beautiful; to marvel over the way in which "one flourishing town after another, such as Utica, Syracuse, and Auburn," had risen from the wilderness; to be delighted, in traversing the North, at seeing no beggars or signs of want, "but everywhere the most unequivocal proofs of prosperity and rapid progress in agriculture, commerce, and great public works." [2] They came, like the journalist Alexander Mackay, to expatiate not on the hogs in Broadway and the squalor of the Five Points, but on the pleasant residential streets of New York, with their lofty houses of brick or granite; the forest of masts along the East River, and the crowded wealth piled on the wharves; and the splendor of the banks, hotels, and exchanges. T. C. Grattan, after half a dozen years in America as consul, made the observation (later echoed by Matthew Arnold) that its life was unfavorable to high distinction, but he cordially granted that the United States "are better adapted than any country on earth for securing the greatest good to the greatest number of mankind." That all-around reformer James Silk Buckingham, detailing what he saw in eight weighty and otiose volumes, con-

---

2   Charles Lyell, *Travels in North America in the Years 1841–42*, chs. 1–3; *A Second Visit to the United States*, II, chs. 38, 39.

cluded that if the nation were preserved from luxury, intemperance, and war, "there are hardly any bounds to the expectations that may be formed of its future greatness." [3]

Till 1857 it was a nation in full enjoyment of a prolonged boom. Whether the foreign visitors landed at New York, Philadelphia, or Boston, they were struck by the bustle, enterprise, and rough-and-ready cheerfulness of the people. Men talked of money, and had it. A bright, sunshiny look distinguished New York, with its high buildings, varied architecture, free use of white marble, and glittering shop-windows. Compared with Philadelphia's handsome squares, broad shady streets, and neat red brick houses with scoured white stone door-steps, Manchester or Lyons seemed cramped, dingy, or poor. Most buildings looked new, for Americans had a way of pulling down and rebuilding every few years. Extravagant in their tastes, to European notions, the city dwellers liked everything about them handsome and stylish-looking. Hotels must offer the latest comforts; the shops must be spick and span; a man's house, furniture, and carriage displeased him if they were poorer than his neighbor's. Foreigners who asked for a one-horse cab of the sort common in London or Paris met a scornful look. The American hack was a stately, dashing vehicle drawn by two horses.

Nowhere in the world could the wayfarer rest his head in such grandeur as in the St. Nicholas Hotel, a stately pile on Broadway which, rebuilt in 1856 as the first two-million-dollar hotel in the world, boasted of its magnificent parlors, fine cuisine, and seven hundred beds. No business house in Europe was more imposing than A. T. Stewart's huge store in the same city. American women, even in the small towns, wore more silks and satins than women else-where. And how comfortably they seemed to live! Even a modest Northern hotel, where the inclusive charge was but two dollars a day, offered for dinner, besides soup and fish, six varieties of boiled meats, three of cold meats, ten entrees, six roasts, and a variety of vegetables, concluding with puddings, pastry, pineapple ice-cream, blanc-mange, and nuts and raisins.[4] Lyell saw the colored

3 Alexander Mackay, *The Western World*, chs. 3–5; T. C. Grattan, *Civilized America*, I, chs. 6, 20; James Silk Buckingham, *America, Historical, Statistical, and Descriptive*, I, chs. 3–9. Of all British books written on America before Bryce's, Mackay's was the best. Its three volumes offered not only a fairly comprehensive description of the country, but penetrating essays on education, literature, government, slavery, and the national character. For observations by foreign critics, see Henry T. Tuckerman, *America and Her Commentators*, especially ch. 6; Allan Nevins, *American Social History Recorded by British Travellers*, 139–422; and Max Berger, *The British Traveller in America, 1836–60*.

4 In hotels on the "American plan," with breakfast eight to twelve, lunch twelve to two, dinner two to six, and tea and supper six to twelve, a guest might eat all day without extra charge. The first great luxury hotel in the United States, the Tremont of Boston, had many successors. The St. Nicholas in New York displayed much marble and mahogany; the Fifth Avenue Hotel, built in 1859 with 530 rooms, was nearly as grand. The New York Hotel, erected in 1844, is said to have been the first to boast of private baths. The Continental in

servants in a Southern house supping on roast turkey, ice cream, jelly, and cakes, while in a Mississippi inn he heard the landlord (a militia general) call the guests in his dining-room to order with the stentorian remark, "Gentlemen, we air a great people!"—after which he recited the long menu. A ready hospitality, warmest in the South but evident elsewhere, seemed characteristic of most Americans. When they travelled, too, they did it with a flourish. The high-pressure steamboats might inspire a premonitory shudder, but they were beautifully appointed; the trains might lack privacy, but they were roomy, cheerful, and sociable.

All visitors quickly found, if they did not already know, that two Americas really existed: the North and the South. Most of the go-ahead spirit and nearly all the we-can-whip-universal-natur' brag was concentrated in the North; much of the leisure, courtliness, and pride in the South. Disliking slavery, heat, and inferior travel facilities, most travellers imitated Dickens in avoiding at least the cotton States. But those who, like Thackeray, pressed courageously into the lower South, usually felt well rewarded. If there was poverty, there was also picturesqueness. If the blacks were sad to look upon, the whites seemed more English in aspect and more old-world in outlook than the Northerners. Where else on the globe was a city like Charleston, with its magnolia-shaded Battery swept by sea-breezes, its sandy streets lined by rustling palmettoes, its airy-looking mansions with their bright gardens, double verandahs, and mahogany furniture, its beautiful St. Michael's and St. Philip's keeping watch over the smart business district, and its charming old schools, the Citadel and the College? As for New Orleans, travellers who approached its noble amphitheatric front by steamer thought it one of the most impressive commercial towns of the world. The river was full of gaudily-painted steamboats, ferries, barges, and keelboats, with nearly as many square-rigged ocean craft as filled the Pool below London Bridge. Three miles of massive warehouses and offices lined the levee; and what a scene the broad quays presented! A throng of merchants, ship captains, clerks, supercargoes, custom-house officials, sailors, porters, and draymen milled busily up and down the thoroughfare. From end to end the levee was piled with goods and produce. Here were pyramids of cotton-bales, rows of sugar hogsheads, stacks of sacked rice, and barrels of pork. On the other side was flour ready for export to South America. A fragrant pile of coffee bags from Rio spilled across boxes of fruit from Havana. Behind all this bustle stretched not one city but two: the old town of French and Spanish

---

Philadelphia, a six-story structure of six hundred rooms, was with the Fifth Avenue the only hotel in 1860 to possess an elevator; "a vertical railway, on a new and scientific principle . . . which will take the inhabitants of the upper stories up and down without any of the fatigue of ascending or descending flights of stairs." *Godey's Lady's Book*, LX, 465. For the whole development, see Jefferson Williamson, *The American Hotel: An Anecdotal History*.

architecture, largely stucco of lively hues, and the new town beyond Canal Street of wide paved ways, modern buildings, and showy stores.[5]

The West, too, was a world in itself, but a world in rapid transition, the rifle, axe, and saddlebag giving way to the organized civilization brought by De Tocqueville's "deluge of men rising unabatedly, and daily driven onward by the hand of God." (More prosaically, driven on by appetite for cheap land, love of wilderness freedom, and pure restlessness.) The various kinds of frontiers, and their varied modes of advance, were worth a lifetime's study by any observer. What was most significant in the early society of trans-Allegheny America, stressed by the sons of pioneers as they later wrote their recollections, was the self-sufficing character of the settlers' economy, each family producing nearly all its own food, clothing, furniture, and even crude implements. Out of the Western ideals of freedom of opportunity, social equality, and faith in the common man—with a beggar as much unknown as a mastodon, wrote Anthony Trollope a bit later from Milwaukee—arose two types of materialism. One was the git-aplenty-while-you're-agittin' type satirized in Eggleston's *Hoosier Schoolmaster;* the other an aspiring materialism passionately thirsty for Frederick J. Turner's "higher plane of existence." By the later forties the Western World of Revolutionary days, the Western Waters of the flatboat era, were becoming the Middle West of farms and shooting cities. Lyell, travelling from Cincinnati with its pork aristocracy across Ohio to Cleveland with its merchant-shippers, thought that history presented no other example of so sudden a rise of a large country to opulence and power.

The epitome of Western growth was already to be found in Chicago, which in 1847 saw the *Tribune* printing its first issue of four hundred copies, Cyrus H. McCormick choosing the city as the site of his new reaper factory, and workmen swinging picks on the Galena railroad which next year was to send the first cars of wheat to the harbor-front. It also witnessed a river-and-harbor convention, the city's answer to Polk's veto of a harbor improvement bill; a gathering which brought Horace Greeley, Thurlow Weed, Representative Lincoln, and hundreds of others to town. Year by year the frame houses stretched farther out into the tall prairie grass, where at night wolves still acted as scavengers for offal; the trains of ribbed prairie schooners, drawn by mules, horses, or oxen, rolled more thickly through State Street; and the brigs, schooners, and propelled barges on the lake grew more impressive.

It seemed but yesterday that Chicago had been only Fort Dearborn, John Kinzie's trading station, and a few shanties. Even yet it was an unpaved city, where abandoned wagons could often be seen in the mire, with a sign "No

5　The popular lecturer and song-writer Charles Mackay has left vivacious descriptions of New Orleans and Charleston in *Life and Liberty in America;* I, chs. 20–23 (1859).

bottom here." But two long piers now strode out into the lake. Swaying lighters helped load ever-greater quantities of wheat, lard, hides, and tobacco, with lead brought overland from Galena, into the lake vessels. *Hunt's Merchant's Magazine* had carried a prediction in 1843 that of Cleveland, Detroit, Chicago, and Maumee (Toledo), in half a century Maumee would be the greatest. But when in 1848 the first locks swung open on the Illinois and Michigan Canal tapping the interior, Chicagoans knew better. Merchants who bought goods in the East on credit, travelling thither twice a year, were making the city a distributing-point for the whole Northwest. Ungainly wooden warehouses sprang up, with elevators for grain, at first powered by horses and then by steam. Already the Rush Medical College was ten years old in 1847, the Young Men's Association and Library was sponsoring lectures, concerts were given, and the New Englanders who dominated the place lent marked attention to books. It was the soft-coal grime in the air, however, sent up by factories and mills, which gave the center the distinctive atmosphere of its future. "Chicago is a pretty good place," A. H. Burley had written in the year of incorporation, "for men that are in business for making money, but it is a miserable place for loafers." [6]

[II]

The one common magnet for all travellers was Washington, a city which excited mixed responses. It was but a fourth-rate town, the dullest of spots when Congress was absent and the diplomatic corps had fled from its summer heat. The Capitol and the Washington Monument both remained unfinished down to the Civil War. The parks were unimproved till in Fillmore's day the landscape designer A. J. Downing was called upon to furnish a plan, long but desultorily pursued. The straggling, dusty streets connected what looked like a half-dozen country villages; the Capitol faced the wrong way, for the city had been expected to grow in the opposite direction; Robert Mills's Treasury Building, still shinily new, spoiled the vista between White House and Capitol; the plain brick government offices were ugly; the tidal flats grew noisome under the August sun. But in winter Washington took on a liveliness which hid most of its defects.

With December and the meeting of Congress the hotels and boarding-houses filled up, the shopkeepers displayed a varied stock, and the deserted villages coalesced into a bustling town. A motley assemblage gathered in lobbies, offices,

6 Bessie L. Pierce, *A History of Chicago*, I, chs. 9 and 12; Caroline M. McIlvaine, *Chicago in the Forties and Fifties;* Caroline Kirkland, ed., *Chicago Yesterdays;* Harry Hansen, *The Chicago.*

and bar-rooms. The burly backwoodsman, the keen New Englander, the polished Southern gentleman, the pushing manufacturer and his lobbyist, the shabby-genteel office-seeker, with land-speculators, railroad projectors, and raffish adventurers, all jostled shoulders, their incongruity the more conspicuous because the place was so small. Washington 'society' in the best sense had for its permanent core such established families as those of the editor-mayor, William Winston Seaton, the banker W. W. Corcoran, Peter Force, and the Madison-Todd circle, to which were added scientists like Maury and Joseph Henry, and various military and naval dignitaries. They attracted about them the most cultivated of transient Senators, Representatives, and Cabinet members. Outside this circle, whose entertainments might be brilliant, Alexander Mackay found a "general boorishness," ranging from mere gaucherie to the vice of the Pennsylvania Avenue gaming dens.[7]

In some ways Washington seemed very backward. Gas lighting was not introduced until 1847, when by a free demonstration at the Capitol an enterprising businessman persuaded legislators to adopt it; a proper water supply and sewage system were unknown in the ante-bellum era. Music and the drama were so ill-cultivated that a third-rate vocalist or strolling troupe created a sensation. Intellectual interests were few, and the Library of Congress, an imposing room at the rear of the Capitol with a balcony commanding a fine view of the Potomac, seemed valuable chiefly to the belles for flirting. Not until Mrs. Fillmore took an interest in the matter was a good collection of books installed in the White House. Yet the capital did have three great advantages. One was its scientific coterie of men connected with the Smithsonian or government departments. One was its lively newspaper life, the staid *National Intelligencer* being consistently good while administration "organs" rose and fell. The third was the abundant political ferment, a simmering pool fed by rills from every State. Moreover, the indiscriminate mingling of men of all types, from all sections and all walks, and the lack of any barrier between the great and the insignificant, helped explain the successful workings of democracy. More than one foreigner thrilled as, walking on Pennsylvania Avenue, he saluted Polk, Taylor, or Pierce, taking his exercise without attendant or guard.

Congress was unquestionably a remarkable spectacle. Taken individually, its best members inspired high respect for their grasp and quickness of mind, their keenness of vision; viewed as a body, it was less prepossessing. The House gallery had seats for a thousand spectators, frequently so noisy with applause or dissent as to be important participants in the debate. Below were two hundred and

7 Careful observers could have found much poverty; Washington newspapers repeatedly mention destitution so widespread that many citizens could not buy winter fuel. See, for example, the *National Intelligencer*, February 12, 1856.

more guardians of the nation, separated with increasing sharpness during the fifties into two camps, the sensitive Southerners and impatient Northerners. A disorderly place the House seemed at best. In the corners were members writing, folding, and sealing letters; on the sofas were Representatives talking, reading, or simply lolling about; at the doors were buzzing groups; in the aisles restless men paced up and down. Summoned by light popping handclaps, pages raced about. Whenever a bore rose to speak, the seats emptied or a thicket of newspapers suddenly arose. On the other hand, moments of intense excitement became more and more frequent. One British visitor, who saw Haskin of New York, in some violent gesticulations, drop a pistol from his coat-pocket, while several Southern members who thought he was about to use it rushed forward to meet the fancied attack, expressed a preference for the manners of Parliament. The Senate, still small enough to be truly deliberative, had usually a sedate dignity. But that Congress in the fifties was nearly always intensely interesting could not be questioned.[8]

The foreign observer was not always certain about the stature of the President. That officer spent an undue amount of time in the favorite American pastime of shaking hands; on stated days the White House was thrown open, and he greeted everybody from the Indian chief to the Baltimore plug-ugly.

"Now, gentlemen," one foreign note-taker heard Buchanan announce as the reception hour struck, "I must take you by the miller's rule, first come, first served. Have the goodness to state your business as shortly as possible, for I have much to do and little time to do it in."

This was one phase of democracy. Callers on Fillmore, Pierce, and Buchanan did not find them rising in awful grandeur above the general American level; and Fredrika Bremer thought Zachary Taylor simply a kind, affable, commonplace old gentleman, distinctly worried by his burden.[9] Nobody, however, failed of due respect to the elder legislative giants, who were pronounced statesmen

8 Under the apportionment following the census of 1850, the House had 237 members; under that following the census of 1860, it had 243. *Biographical Directory of the American Congress, 1774-1927*, p. 39. For Congress see H. Reid, *Sketches in North America, With Some Account of Congress and the Slavery Question*, 76-154. Fredrika Bremer was horrified by the encounter between Foote of Mississippi and Benton of Missouri, when the latter, "a strong-built man with an expression and beak-like countenance resembling a bird of prey," bared his breast to Foote's pistol. *Homes of the New World*, I, 438, 439.

9 Yet Pierce and Buchanan lived with a certain state. The former had what the New York *Tribune's* correspondent called "a magnificent carriage," its windows of plate glass, its linings of morocco; "for beauty, richness, and uniform appropriateness" the equal of any in Mayfair. It was drawn by a team of fine large bays, their harness richly ornamented with silver, and the white driver and footman were clad in blue with gilt buttons. August 13, 1853. The *Tribune* remarked that "it is customary for great families and rich men in the large cities of the republic to dress their servants in livery." The White House as refurbished for Pierce had elegance, and the handsome furniture, silver, china, and glassware made a deep impression on Westerners like Ben Wade.

worthy of any land. Though Miss Martineau, somewhat overpowered by the austere Calhoun, had thought him stiff and harsh, Alexander Mackay, after spending much time in his society, declared that the charm of his conversation and affability of his demeanor were delightful, while the keenness of his intellect dazzled all who listened to him.[10] Henry Clay, with his animation, emotional warmth, and courtly charm, was irresistible. But it was Webster who, at least after John Quincy Adams' death, seemed to most European sojourners the statesman best worth meeting. When one of Miss Bremer's friends remarked that "nobody was so wise as Webster looked," the witty Senator Berrian responded, "Not even Webster himself!" Others disagreed. It was true that his deep, brilliant eyes seemed to open 'a catacomb full of ancient wisdom'; yet those who heard one of his speeches, delivered with calm intensity of power, often deemed him as great as he looked.[11]

In Washington and the country at large, the two salient notes of American life were energy and variety. The amplitude of the scene was matched by the rich heterogeneity of the nation's activities and the speed of its growth. Planters, gold diggers, cattle-ranches, lumbermen, and whalers; Mormons, Irish Catholics, Quakers, Unitarians, and hardshell Baptists; old-stock Virginians and Yankees mingling with Germans, Norwegians, and others of the immigrant flood; men molded by the precise conventions of seaboard towns two centuries old, or free as the rolling Mississippi and the chaotic ferment of the frontier beyond it—all went to make up America. And above the whole country a bright morning sky! It was a land, observers agreed, of better-diffused prosperity, greater social equality, and ruddier hopes, than any other under the sun.[12] All its problems save

10 Harriet Martineau's anti-slavery feeling made her hostile to Calhoun; hence, her description of "the cast-iron man who looks as if he had never been born and could never be extinguished" is to be taken with reserve, while it should be remembered that she paid tribute to "a never-failing evidence of power in all he says and does which commands intellectual reverence." *Retrospect of Western Travel*, I, 147. Mackay's estimate of Calhoun in *The Western World*, II, 191, is to be compared with Daniel Webster's tribute: "There was a charm in his conversation not often found. He delighted, especially, in conversation and intercourse with young men. I suppose that there has been no man among us who had more winning manners, in such intercourse and such conversation, with men comparatively young, than Mr. Calhoun." G. T. Curtis, *Life of Daniel Webster*, II, 435.

11 Cf. Philip Hone's comment on Webster as he gathered himself together after dinner to talk to his friends. "Then the dark brow at the head of the table became contracted; the noble intellect began to arrange itself and the bright eye to gather up its lightnings, piercing but benignant as those which irradiate the darkness of a summer evening." *Diary*, Allan Nevins edition, II, 628.

12 Wrote Charles Eliot Norton in 1857, just after returning from England: "The contrast between America and Europe never struck me so forcibly as it does now. The grandeur of our opportunities is proportionate to the immensity of our deficiencies—so that one may rejoice to be an American even while seeing how far we fall short in many ways of what is accomplished elsewhere, and how much we ought to do to make life what it ought to be and might be. But to be contented here one must work." *Letters, With Biographical Comment*, by Sara Norton and M. A. DeWolfe Howe, I, 178.

one (and that terrible indeed) seemed easy of solution. But behind this happy, inviting exterior, this pleasant façade, what were the deeper complexities of life?

[III]

Both the virtues and vices of the national character were exhibited upon a larger scale, and with more emphasis and vigor, than in the old-settled parts of Europe. How could it be otherwise in a land so vast, young, and expansive? The 23,191,876 people of 1850 (who become 31,443,321 ten years later) were for the first time occupying the whole continental domain. As they spread to the Pacific, they had at their disposal three million square miles, as against the one million eight hundred thousand which they had possessed when Tyler took his oath of office. The double frontier had made its appearance: one frontier of settlement moving west beyond the Mississippi, and another moving east from the Pacific coast, which by 1860 had about 620,000 people. The conquest of the rough continent—the exploitation of field, forest, and mineral-vein, the weaving of railroad lines, the broadcast seeding of raw villages which in numberless instances sprang overnight into uncouth little cities—was in faster swing than ever before. The variegated population, sieved from Europe by processes which for better or worse emphasized its individualism, found its strength stimulated by opportunity, its daring challenged by difficulty. Freedom from discipline, scope for adventure, what Walt Whitman called "the certainty of space, increase, freedom, futurity," brought out the best and worst in men. "Muscle and pluck forever!" exclaimed Whitman. "How beggarly appear arguments before a defiant deed!" [13]

The vitality of growth, and the constant changes wrought by a half dozen varieties of expansion—expansion westward; expansion from country to city (for the population of cities of 8,000 and more grew in the fifties from 2,897,000 to 5,872,000); expansion of social institutions; expansion of immigrant stocks; expansion of thought—gave life a vibrant excitement. Almost everything seemed permissible, almost anything possible. It was frequently noted that the analyst shocked by some gross defect could find a compensating grace registered with equal energy. America offered an appalling total of violence, yet it had the most vigorous pacifist movement in the world. It was cursed by gross intemperance in the large cities and along its borders, yet great areas proscribed liquor with inexorable severity. It seemed in some places the most licentious of lands, in others the most puritanically strait-laced. Americans were frank to confess them-

13 For a summary of Whitman's ideas on national destiny see "Democratic Vistas," in *Complete Prose*, 197-250. "I hail with joy the oceanic, variegated, intense practical energy, the demand for facts, even the business materialism of the current age, our States."

selves materialistic and addicted to money-hoarding, yet they were equally the most idealistic and philanthropic of peoples. The nation at times witnessed deplorable exhibitions of religious bigotry, but it prided itself, with justice, upon the general tolerance of its laws and traditions. The whole gamut of human failings and attainments seemed expressed with more emphasis and color than in older nations.

This fact made it easy to draw distorted sketches of the country. Most studies, as we have said, were favorable, but through error or malice, some critics of America saw only its worst side. An anonymous writer in the *Atlantische Studien* for 1853, once editor of a German-American journal, scored the violence, lynch-law, rampant speculation, intellectual superficiality, and parvenu manners of the republic. Hypocrisy and charlatanism, he thought, were national traits. Americans boasted of free speech, but no abolitionist could open his lips in the South; they bragged of their exemption from the martial law of Europe, but their vigilante law was ten times worse. They had raised humbug to a fine art: advertisements were humbugs, medicines were humbugs, religious revivals were humbugs, Barnum's shows were humbugs, half the new boom cities were humbugs. The almighty dollar was so recklessly pursued that "everything is a matter of trade, from the President to the black slave." Equally caustic was Frederick Gaillardet, founder and long editor of the *Courrier des Etats-Unis*, who, returning in 1855 to the United States after years of absence, recorded in letters to the Paris *Constitutionnel* his disappointment in the nation's tendencies. Plainness, simplicity, integrity, he wrote, were valued no more, for wealth and ostentation ruled the hour. Mexican conquests and California gold had made Americans insatiable. Force had been substituted for right; elections were decided by mob battles or brazen frauds; license in the wild Western communities was corrected by the tyranny of the rope and revolver. Meanwhile, America concerned herself not with ideas, but with gain. She nurtured no school of philosophy, but was a great trading-mart. Selfishness was the ruling principle of people and parties alike.[14]

Such assaults were not exaggerated except in the sense of being one-sided; every criticism was true, but a multitude of compensating facts were also true. Horace Greeley justly remarked that Continental observers could have no philosophic understanding of America unless they knew something of Britain, whence so many American principles, institutions, and attitudes were drawn; and he pointed to the more judicious tenor of British estimates—even those of

14 Most French and German views of America were distinctly favorable; see J. J. Ampère, *Promenade en Amérique* (1855), and J. G. Kohl's *Life in the New World* as examples. Both men met numerous famous Americans—Ampère talked with Bryant, Longfellow, Agassiz, Kent, Irving, and Jefferson Davis, while Kohl saw much of Prescott, Ticknor, Everett, Benton, Bancroft, and Sumner—and both thought highly of American institutions.

Marryat, Dickens, and Basil Hall.[15] In most countries the balance between merits and faults is nicely poised.

Most of the Continental critics, indeed, recognized this fact. Another German, A. Roesler, who became editor of the Quincy (Illinois) *Tribune*, published in 1854 a fair appraisal. The United States, he wrote, was indeed the country of mob law, where bowie-knives and Colts often served for legislation, where Congressmen swore to the peaceful character of a notorious filibuster, and where the outcome of a trial often depended on who could pay the best lawyer. It was the country of wirepullers, lobbyists, and log-rollers, of Galphin claims, of constructive mileage steals, of rivers and harbors "pork," of votes bought in Congress by patronage, and of drunken rows in State legislatures. It was the country of the lash and bloodhood, of steamboat explosions, Mississippi debt-repudiation, Wall Street speculators, and frontier land-grabbers; the country where women were whipped for teaching colored children to read, and planters sold their own flesh and blood on the auction-block. But it was also the land of Washington, Adams, and Jefferson; of ample religious toleration; of civil rights protected by the courts; of a rising interest in free schools; and of democratic institutions which really worked. Above all, it was the land of optimism, of a confident belief in a bright and happy destiny.[16] Dr. Philip Schaff, delivering two lectures in Berlin on the political, social, and religious character of the United States, declared that in spite of slavery, money-seeking, political faction, and sectarian animosities, the fundamental liberty and vigor of the nation were unquestionable. Culturally and morally as well as materially, it was sound; and it seemed to him assured of a future greatness that would make it a beacon light of the world.[17]

[IV]

The fact is that in a new, fast-growing country, great virtues have their inseparable companion in great faults; one is obverse, the other reverse, of the current coin. Rampant individualism was a dominant trait of American life. It did much to make the nation great, achieving wonders in its application to rich

15 N. Y. *Tribune*, July 8, 1853. Greeley was right, but it was not easy for any aristocrats, British or Continental, to view republican tendencies with genial eye. See Lord Acton's "American Diaries" of this period, published in the *Fortnightly Review*, vols. 110, 111 (1921), which are jaundiced in tone; and the foreign criticisms in the article on "Representative Reform" in the *Edinburgh Review*, 1857, with comment on it in the *National Intelligencer*, September 26, 1857.

16 Summarized in N. Y. *Tribune*, July 13, 1854.

17 Schaff's lectures were expanded into *Sketch of the Political, Social, and Religious Character of the United States of North America* (1855); a book in which the sections on religion and German immigration had special value.

natural resources; and such faults as competitive ruthlessness, hurry, boastfulness, and even lawlessness are not to be treated as isolated phenomena, but as the natural—if deplorable—accompaniment of a quality indispensable to progress. How could a man get to the front, on an untamed frontier or in a new industry, without developing a tendency to grab and push? How could he be a hustler without hurry? In older lands then, as in America later, brusque individualism could be considered reprehensible, but in the United States of 1850 it was on the whole a virtue. Another dominant trait was materialism. It had to be. The great urgent tasks of the time were material tasks. Prairies had to be broken, plains covered with cattle, mines opened, towns built, and factories set going before less exigent tasks could be undertaken. Was it really necessary to grow so fast, to make the republic so rich, populous, and powerful within a few generations? The years 1917 and 1940 gave the answer to that question. Materialism had its sordid as well as constructive side. It made for greed, worship of size, and a contemptuous attitude toward the arts. But in 1850 it was impossible to seize its benefits without its faults, and its benefits were invaluable.

The facility with which unrestrained individualism ran into excess was all too plain in politics, where men were ready to appeal to a "higher law" than constitutions and statutes, or dispense with law altogether; in religion, where varying opinions led to endless sectarian division; and in social thought, where new isms appeared every year. Even in their language, Americans manifested as great a taste for exaggeration as their British kinsmen showed for understatement. "Powerful," "magnificent," and "mighty" were adjectives applied to everything. A factory, a water-cure, or a Negro became an "institution." American humor was largely a humor of exaggeration, ideas being distorted by aggrandizement until they became amusing. The Southern editor commenting on a low stage of the Mississippi wrote: "The catfish are rigging up stern-wheelers." The Minnesotan trying to describe the clearness of his lakes said that, looking into them, a man might see people making tea in China. Anything that was great "beat all creation," while anything small was "the little end of nothing whittled down to a point." The land speculator puffing a new town, the orator spouting of national glory, the young poet describing Niagara, and the attorney denouncing his opponent's client, ran naturally to exaggeration, for it was a product of American individualism. When S. S. Cox, a young editor-politician, delivered a commencement address at Brown University in 1857, he correctly said that restraint was the crying national desideratum; the country needed less nervous hurry and more deliberation, less surface glitter and more substance. Why could we not have "earnestness without extravagance, imagination without wild romance, talent . . . without vehemence and rashness?" [18] Yet Cox himself became

18 *National Intelligencer*, September 8, 1857.

famous by a wildly rhetorical description of a sunset, bearing through life the sobriquet of "Sunset" Cox.

It was all very well to talk of restraint, but the genius of the land was still hostile to it. As people read of the rich copper mines of Keweenaw Point on Lake Superior, or Drake's oil-well in northwestern Pennsylvania, or the sensational discoveries of silver at Virginia City, they saw their continent oozing wealth. Population growth and the development of new areas meant rising values, so that men could take long chances in the faith that three times out of five they would win. On every hand, too, were evidences of youth and its exuberance. The Erie Railroad, the longest continuous line in the world, opening with Fillmore and his cabinet on hand to help celebrate the event; the Crystal Palace Exhibition collecting under one roof the many initial evidences of American prowess in industry and the arts; the North American Phalanx being dedicated, with a long address by W. H. Channing, to the exploration of fresh social principles; [19] new national magazines like the *Atlantic, Putnam's,* and *Harper's Weekly* being founded; California, so recently a wilderness, suddenly rising to opulence with ranches, mines, a roaring port, and two senators in Washington— all this showed that the country was still in the gristle, still changing overnight.

Social stability, with a slow growth of standards and traditions, is essential to restraint, and in America nothing seemed stable. Rich untouched resources, a high ratio of land to population, a consequent buoyancy in wage-rates and interest rates, special stimulants to invention, and a heavy stream of immigration, strengthened the venturesome qualities of the people. A special rôle, too, was now being played by the frontier, and a different rôle from that of earlier periods. Individualism of the dynamic type, while strong enough in the rising industrialism and in profit farming or planting, reached its natural apogee on the frontier. Till that frontier was closed, from 1845 to 1895, the pioneer regions would draw closer to the Atlantic belt than ever before.

Communications were in fact transforming the frontier. The growth of railroads, telegraphs, and waterways brought the coarse fringes of the nation ever closer to its fine-textured seaboard areas. In the first decades after settlers poured across the Appalachians, days and weeks of weary travel had lain between the log cabin and the cobbled street. But now, with through eastern trains about to roll into Chicago and St. Louis, the frontier was overnight from the urban center. The railroads which soon veined and branched the central valley drained life away from many old districts, so that New England and Virginia more visibly than before lost their old stock. It created frontier communities of novel

19 Channing, nephew of William Ellery Channing, and an impassioned advocate of Fourierism, had rallied a little group including George Ripley, Albert Brisbane, Francis G. Shaw, and others in 1847 in a Religious Union of Associationists. See O. B. Frothingham, *Memoir of William Henry Channing.*

type, so little primitive that the men read eastern newspapers and the women copied New York fashions. It kept the two zones in close touch, so that each vitally affected the other.[20]

The early frontier had been jealous and suspicious of the urban East. This new frontier, though jealous too, was eager to take on the higher organization, culture, and prerogatives of the original States, and before 1860 partly did so. The infant St. Paul and Madison, Dubuque and Kansas City, Little Rock and Austin, far from feeling themselves wilderness outposts, strove for an elaborate social and economic life—for schools, churches, clubs, shops, and general polish. This took money and energy. Their frenzied effort, as young John Fiske observed, helped give American life "the aspect of a life-and-death struggle for mastery over the material forces of that part of the earth's surface upon which it strives." [21] Equally important was the effect of the mores and standards of the West upon the older settled regions. The Western individualism which expressed itself in saltiness of speech, exaggeration of humor, crudity of manners, and untrammeled directness of action was no longer a faraway, curious thing, but a part of the texture of national life.

[V]

Meanwhile, the materialism and optimism of American life, always salient traits, had become more marked than ever. As the nation rounded out its domain to the Pacific, accumulated capital, and made movement easier, life became freer and its prizes more glittering. Greater fortunes could be made, and made more quickly.

The mobility of American life, one element in the situation, had now been quickened in striking degree. Immigration was great, the westward movement was constant, and a thousand cross-currents and counter-eddies were discernible. In Great Britain, a man born in Yorkshire was likely to remain there, but in the United States the roving tendency was so keen that the country became a huge mixing-cauldron. Hence the importance of the hotel and boarding-house in America. Countless people made not one move but dozens, and a considerable element was always on the wing. Horace Greeley, crossing the plains in 1859

20 For a succinct contrast between the old westward migration of gradual growth, the migration that began at Plymouth and Jamestown and continued down to the railroad age, and the new migration which leaped swiftly from settled communities to raw new lands, see F. L. Paxson, *History of the American Frontier*, 437ff.

21 *The Unseen World and Other Essays*, 395ff. The impact of urban influence on the rural South was also the subject of comment. A Southern planter reported with little regret that country dress, manners, and ideas were fast disappearing in the cotton States, and everything was becoming "redolent of city life." "Prospect and Policy of the South, as Seen by a Southern Planter," *Southern Quarterly Review*, October, 1854, p. 449.

to the new mining camps about Denver, was struck by the nomadic habits of the people. Among a dozen settlers in Iowa and Kansas, he would usually find natives of five or six States and two or three foreign countries. It was still more remarkable that among any dozen men in Colorado, two or three had probably spent a year in California, three or four had taken up land in Kansas, and at least one had sojourned in Texas. The most varied occupations, from banking to fur-trapping, were represented. One rough station where Greeley slept was kept by a former Cincinnati lawyer and his wife, a former Bowery actress. A later generation was to note how many Easterners, like Richard H. Dana, Jr., Thomas B. Reed, Philip D. Armour, and Isaac J. Wistar, had tasted California life, and how much it had modified their outlook.[22]

An equally important element in generating both materialism and optimism was the development of the new industrial frontier. This opening world of factories, iron-mills, and machine-shops promised fresh avenues to endeavor and new titles to wealth. It was as wild and free as the land frontier, and shook out gold from a larger cornucopia.[23]

A significant social effect of the new industrialism, as manufacturing began to offer a challenge to mercantile employments, was the change it bred in ideals of success. Americans had always dearly loved a success story, and especially a story of toil, thrift, and uncorroded virtue illustrating the Protestant ethic. That Stephen Girard had begun life as a cabin-boy; that Gideon Lee, later so wealthy, was often sent through the snow before daybreak on winter mornings to milk the cows, and found it a luxury to warm his bare feet in their beds; that Samuel Appleton had been an ill-paid schoolmaster in a little New Hampshire town; that the merchant Thomas Eddy, "the American Howard," had been a penniless apprentice to a New Jersey tanner—such beginnings had a wide appeal. Americans had once liked to learn that their wealthy men had gained riches not by rash speculations, cornering a market, or taking advantage of a war, but by slow, steady accumulations. The men celebrated in Freeman Hunt's *Lives of*

22 Greeley, *An Overland Journey From New York to San Francisco in the Summer of 1859*. Various estimates have been made of the value of an able-bodied migrant to the country in which he established himself. Sir William Petty calculated in 1690 that an able-bodied young man was worth on an average £80 to England. The figures of modern economists vary between Alfred Marshall's $2,237 (1895) and Nicholson's $13,895 (1891). No precise statistics are possible; it can only be said that migrants have a hard cash value over and beyond their intangible worth. This movement of population in one sense enriched the West at the expense of the East; but the East recompensed itself by immigration from Europe. It was the South which felt the net loss most heavily.

23 Few Americans of the time foresaw the speed with which the nation would be urbanized. Greeley, travelling in Illinois in 1859, wrote in the *Weekly Tribune* (May 28, 1859): "Doubtless the child is born who will see here a State of Ten Millions of People, One Million of them inhabiting her commercial emporium." He was near the mark in his estimate of total population growth; far from it in his estimate of the future population-ratio between Chicago and down-State Illinois.

American Merchants, published in the middle fifties, had all followed the safe road. They had never been eager for sudden gains and had never followed dubious courses. Somebody once tried to interest Thomas Handasyd Perkins in a speculation in coffee, which had fallen to fifteen cents a pound. He rigidly declined any such enterprise, but accurately predicted that coffee would fall much lower, that many plantations would be abandoned, and that it would then rise to a high price. Gideon Lee, importuned to sell his country home during a period of real-estate speculation, did so; but he took precisely what it had cost, refusing to accept speculative gains. Peter C. Brooks would never consent, under any circumstances, to receive more than the legal six per cent for his money. These men of mercantile training, though remarkably resourceful and enterprising, were all sober, conscientious, and to some degree altruistic; more altruistic than the textile manufacturers who made 30 per cent a year while paying girls two dollars a week.

Very different were the traits of the ascendent business heroes of the new period of the forties—Cornelius Vanderbilt in transportation, Cyrus H. McCormick in manufacturing, Jacob Little and Daniel Drew in finance. More different still were the ablest of the young business leaders, such as Carnegie, Rockefeller, and Collis P. Huntington, getting their start in the fifties.

These men thought in larger terms, moved with greater velocity, and battled with more pitiless weapons. The rapid growth of the country had placed its mark upon them; they all began as poor and restless boys. Most of them, like McCormick, Carnegie, Rockefeller, and Huntington, were associated with the westward movement, and they pushed forward fast. Behind them, the minor business leaders were increasingly made of the same stern stuff. To subdue the wilderness, to wrestle with competitors for the title to raw wealth, to overcome the obstacles of distance and rough terrain, to adjust trade to a fast-growing social environment—all this made American businessmen alert, strenuous, and brusque. They accepted David Harum's maxim about doing unto others as they would do unto you and doing it fust, not always qualifying it by David Harum's innate kindliness. Yet businessmen, like others, felt the exhilarating optimism of the country. If the path was stony, the air was sparkling and the sun bright. European and Asiatic peoples toiled in a gloom that could not exist in a land so rich, so largely empty, and so resplendent with opportunity. The essential difference was that in the Old World laborious talent stood two chances in three of failure; in the New, two in three of success.[24]

24 Speculation in land and commodities was an old American pursuit; speculation on the exchanges was newer and seemed more reprehensible. Denunciation was frequent in Eastern journals; see the editorial, "A Growing Evil," New York *Evening Post*, August 3, 1857; article, "Stock Gambling in New York," *National Intelligencer*, August 11, 1857. W. W. Fowler's exposé, *Ten Years in Wall Street*, begins in 1857, when Jacob Little was the most famous stock-market operator.

[VI]

Alongside the dominant traits of individualism, materialism, and optimism ran a fourth characteristic in which Americans took uncritical pride, their democracy. Few men paused to reflect that the four attributes were not wholly harmonious; that even in Jefferson's day a conflict between equality and liberty had been visible. In both economic and political spheres, individualism and materialism were allying themselves to place fetters on democracy. Admiration of wealth, love of power, and the tradition of free economic enterprise led naturally to the growth of plutocracy. The industrial revolution had made England the classic land of huge inequalities of fortune, but now America was taking her place. Even in 1845 Moses Y. Beach's directory of wealthy New Yorkers filled thirty-two double-column pages of fine print, ranging from August Belmont's $100,000 to John Jacob Astor's $25,000,000. In Albany, Trenton, Harrisburg, and other capitals rich corporations were acquiring a pernicious influence over political affairs. Meanwhile, the national optimism had its unhealthy results in the governmental sphere. Engendering a blind faith in the future, it tempted Americans to drift when they should have rowed against the stream. Assuming that the glorious principles and institutions inherited from the fathers would meet any test, they devoted much less thought and labor to government policy than was proper. They were effortlessly confident that Jefferson's and Jackson's handiwork would endure even while it was being sapped by new oligarchies.

Though social democracy fared better, it was less pure and vigorous than most Americans believed. It was commonly assumed that no class lines existed, but they did. In the North two, of very different character, might be discerned. One divided manual workers from the great middle class of professional men, tradesmen, and small capitalists. William Dean Howells testifies that even in democratic Ohio in the fifties this line was so emphatic that it was seldom crossed. The brain-worker was loath to have a mechanic at his table, and Howells, as a printer working at his case, was debarred from homes that welcomed him when he became an ill-paid journalist.[25] The second line, found in large Northern cities, divided the very rich from the middle classes.[26] It was vague, and easy for talent

25 *Years of My Youth*, 173.
26 Family lineage also played an important role in many communities. Charles Godfrey Leland writes in his *Memoirs*, p. 192, of Philadelphia circles: "The lines of demarcation in 'society' were as strongly drawn as in Europe, or more so, with the enormous difference, however, that there was not the slightest perceptible shade of difference in the intellects, culture, or character of the people on either side of the line. . . . Very trifling points of difference, not perceptible to an outsider, made the whole difference between the exclusives and the excluded." The Boston society described in Henry Adams's *Education* differed in its emphasis on family from the New York society described in Mrs. John Sherwood's *An Epistle to Posterity*, which emphasized wealth.

to cross. The richest Bostonian or New Yorker was usually glad to make an honored guest of the poor but distinguished writer, architect, Senator, or general. It was the slightness of this upper social line which made it easy for Americans to delude themselves into believing that no stratification whatever existed. But the laborer and mechanic knew better, and their wives better still; in the new semi-industrial towns many people lived on the wrong side of the tracks. Jarring economic antagonisms of class interest lay close to the surface. As for the South, the class-structure of slaves, poor whites, overseers, small farmers, professional men, and rich planters, a hierarchy of half a dozen grades and much complex overlapping, was patent and oppressive.

The best test of social democracy is freedom of opportunity, the career open to all the talents. To that test American life rang fairly true. In every field opportunity was free. An analysis of the careers of Americans prominent in the generation 1850-90 would show that the overwhelming majority began life as very poor boys—if not as poor as Lincoln, Rockefeller, and Mark Twain, still poor enough.[27] This was true not only of business and political leaders, but of figures prominent in the professions and arts. The variety of opportunities in the plastic new society, and the general antipathy to any form of privilege in job-getting helped keep the ladders open. But the relatively low standards of preparation in law, medicine, divinity, journalism, and literature also played a part in opening paths to preferment. Talent counted for more, training for less, than in Europe. No Jude the Obscure need wear his heart out gazing at an unattainable profession; he could gain admittance to the bar, as Thomas B. Reed did in California, by an examination that approached farce. The social tradition that any man had a right to aim at any height was also of indispensable value. In some fields, notably politics, a son of the backwoods might more readily aspire to the greatest prizes than a Cabot of the Back Bay or a Randolph of the Tidewater.

The country gave nearly every native freeman a chance; but this did not mean that it gave everybody his best chance or even a good one. In the judgment of numerous foreign observers, social democracy made for mediocrity. A fairer and more penetrating statement would have been that it permitted a serious waste of human talent. It encouraged everyone to rise to a certain commonplace level, but as yet devoted little thought or energy to the fullest utilization of social resources. Just as the country was careless of forests, minerals,

27 Interesting illustrations of this fact may be found in the numerous sketches of philanthropic Chicagoans in T. W. Goodspeed's *University of Chicago Biographical Sketches*, I and II. One of these wealthy men, E. Nelson Blake, had gone to work at twelve for fifteen cents a day; another, Silas B. Cobb, was bound out as a shoemaker's apprentice while he still had next to no education; another, LaVerne Noyes, had lived as a boy in Iowa with his parents in a covered wagon until they could move into an empty log schoolhouse; still another, H. W. Thomas, had plaited his own hats of rye straw on his father's farm.

and soil, it was careless of its people. All nations are guilty of criminal human wastes, and Europe, with her old feudal abuses, standing armies, and heavy military expenditures, was a far more serious offender than America. But the United States had a system which left a great deal of brains and energy ill-utilized, the losses being heaviest in the South and just behind the frontier.

One great source of human waste lay in the inefficiency and immaturity of the educational system. Free school systems were overspreading the West, Wisconsin, Indiana, Ohio, and Illinois making provision for them in 1848, 1852, 1853, and 1854 respectively; part-free systems characterized most of the Northeast.[28] But no State except Massachusetts had a compulsory attendance law. In New York and other States where parents were required to pay a school tax in proportion to the number of their children taught, many needy families were too proud to confess their inability to pay and therefore kept their youngsters at home. The rate-bill system lasted till 1867 in New York, till 1868 in Connecticut and Rhode Island, till 1869 in Michigan, and till 1871 in New Jersey. The South was still generally wedded to private schools and academies, though North Carolina carried on a brave effort to set up a public school system, and in other states and some cities the beginnings of public education were evident.[29] In great areas, particularly in the South and West, the buildings were poor, equipment was scanty, and salaries were so low that good teachers deserted to other occupations. The average youngster of the fifties got no education beyond the common school; of the three hundred and twenty-one public high schools in 1860, more than half were in Massachusetts, New York, and Ohio. As late as that year, only eight of the thirty-one States had a state teachers' college.[30]

Equally indicative of human waste was the inadequacy of higher education. The entire South below Virginia, and the whole trans-Allegheny region, had no university and no technological school worthy of the name. Indeed, no institution in the country could be compared with the best British, French, and German universities. Harvard, like Yale, Columbia, and Princeton, was simply a higher school for boys, wherein for some years to come the guiding principle (which Emerson called the Granny system) was that ironically stated by an educational specialist: "Hold your subject fast with one hand, and pour knowledge into him with the other." Little true research work was yet pursued anywhere. In many respects the best university of the country during the fifties

28 Arthur C. Cole, *The Irrepressible Conflict, 1850–1865*, pp. 205–208.
29 E. W. Knight, *Public School Education in North Carolina, passim*. It will help us understand the intellectual equipment of Americans in 1848–60 for dealing with political problems if we bear in mind that according to the census of 1840, four-fifths of the children did not go beyond the primary grades, and only three-fourths of one per cent went to college. But America at least had a public school system; Europe did not.
30 E. P. Cubberley, *Public Education in the United States*, 198.

was Michigan, where Henry P. Tappan applied European methods and ideas, opened in 1857 the nation's first chemical laboratory, and established an efficient civil engineering course. The lack of more such technological schools as Rensselaer (reorganized in 1850 as a general polytechnic college), the Lawrence Scientific School (for which Abbott Lawrence made his generous gift in 1848), and the Sheffield Scientific School (not established until 1860), meant that few technicians were available to give impetus to industry. The multiplicity of weak church schools, competing in a fashion which prevented the emergence of really strong colleges, helped stifle higher education of real quality.[31]

The absence in vast areas, but especially the South, of a fair balance between agriculture and manufacturing, meant that much human talent was lost along with important commodity values. Many men were ill-fitted for farming; their bent was for industrial labor, management, or trade. It was sheer waste to keep them on the land, but they had nowhere else to go. Had industry taken firm root in the South—had there been more textile mills like those established by William Gregg in South Carolina and Daniel Pratt in Alabama, more iron foundries, and large meat-packing and tobacco-processing plants—the section could have made better use of its human energies. Indeed, every step toward a variegation of employment was a step toward the fuller use of talent. The substantial debarment of women from higher education, business, and most professions, too, meant a deplorable waste of ability. A republic which prided itself on progressivism and which had constant frontier object-lessons in the all-round capacity of women should have been further ahead of Europe in this field.

Much might be said also of the wastes connected with the neglect of public health, though here reform had to wait on the progress of science. But in one respect remedial measures might have been taken. The national diet, by general consent, was not what it should have been. Americans ate too much meat and hot-breads, and swallowed too much coffee and ice-water, while they paid too little attention to vegetables and fruits. The New York *Tribune* complained in 1854 that most people lived on a round of meat, bread, and potatoes. In the cities this was costly, and everywhere it was bad for the health. Why should they not buy hulled cracked maize, called samp, hominy, or grits, available for three

31 C. M. Perry, *Henry P. Tappan;* B. A. Hinsdale, *History of the University of Michigan.* George Palmer Putnam, visiting the Crystal Palace Exhibition in London in 1851, was staggered. "I cannot help imagining," he wrote, "that our people have jumped somewhat too hastily to the conclusion that they can do everything a great deal better than the rest of the world." A careful look at the Great Fair, he pursued, required the admission "that we have a vast deal yet to learn; that we have boasted almost as much as we have performed; that we have been, nationally speaking, too well contented with the go-ahead-any-way-will-do system; and, in short, that it is more than questionable whether Europe, and especially England, has not, in a large proportion of all important and useful arts, actually travelled faster during the last ten years than the great American Republic itself." George Haven Putnam, *George Palmer Putnam, A Memoir,* 206.

or four cents a pound, and excellent with milk or gravy? Why not more beans, peas, and rice? Sylvester Graham, who died in 1851, had conducted a lifelong battle for the wider adoption of vegetable food. His recommendation of whole-wheat bread, fruits, vegetables, rough cereals, looser and lighter clothing, open windows, and cold showers brought upon him an avalanche of criticism. Emerson spoke of him as the "poet of bran bread and pumpkins." But his lectures and books made a wholesome impression, and his adherents became so numerous that Graham flour and Graham boarding-houses were familiar terms. In new parts of the country the diet was likely to be worse than in long-peopled areas. F. L. Olmsted had a monotonous encounter in Texas with fried salt pork, corn pone, and unspeakable coffee, while young Rutherford B. Hayes mentions a typical Baptist meal there as burned hoe-cake, fried pork, and black coffee without sugar. The fried-steak belt was already well established in the upper Mississippi Valley.

It may be added that tobacco-chewing continued to be one of the most universal habits of American life. Dickens, looking out of his train window, had supposed that men in the forward cars must be tearing handfuls of feathers out of pillow-cases. All public buildings were crammed with spittoons. Stoves in railway cars, inns, and groceries were ringed with boxes of sawdust. In stage-coaches, theatres, and courtrooms men ground away at plug-tobacco and steadily relieved themselves. We find an advertisement of a lecture by H. W. Beecher in Rome, N. Y., praying the audience not to void tobacco-juice on the floor, for the ladies were proud of the carpet they had bought. A Yankee in Paris noticed a compatriot, visiting Notre Dame, obviously in discomfort as he looked for a receptacle, and finally, to the horror of a verger, expectorating full into the holy-water font! Verily, wrote Greeley, Americans were "the filthiest of peoples." Yet chewers were more and more on the defensive. Critics of Stephen A. Douglas could make it a reproach that his lips were tobacco-stained, and in Eastern cities few who called themselves gentlemen cared after 1850 to spit in public. That chewing was pursued to the detriment of health and efficiency was obvious.[32]

The nation was wasteful, finally, in its employment of leisure. A hardworking country, it nevertheless had a good deal of spare time, for Sundays were rigorously observed, the farms had their off-seasons, and the towns their slack

---

32 Frederick Law Olmsted, *A Journey Through Texas,* 49, 61; Rutherford B. Hayes, *Diary and Letters,* I, 252, 253 (but Hayes, complaining that Texans are essentially carnivorous, speaks of frequently seeing seven different meat dishes on the table at once); N. Y. *Tribune,* March 21, 1854, for the Rome advertisement. According to old letters of Governor James Sullivan in the N. Y. *Weekly Tribune* of August 28, 1858, John Hancock had chewed tobacco to the serious detriment of his health, while John Adams had twice given up the habit, once when minister to Holland and once when minister to England, with no small hardship.

periods. Yet the man with time on hand was usually without books, theatres, debating societies, artistic materials, incentives to writing, or other means of cultivating himself. Lacking the better forms of recreation, many turned all too readily to rowdy occupations. The prevalence of violence, from the rough and tumble fighting along the frontier to the gang battles of Eastern cities, was partly traceable to sheer lack of better diversions. Theodore Roosevelt two generations later thought that the best deterrent to street-fighting and juvenile criminality in New York would be the formation of boxing clubs, while later still H. L. Mencken suggested a brass band in every Southern town as a cure for lynching. Boredom meant vice or violence. The most rudimentary provision for leisure was that furnished by the debating society, the village library, and the athletic club, but outside New England and the North Atlantic States few communities had them. Here too democracy was wasteful because too immature to have organization.[33]

Yet with all its deficiencies, the social democracy of the nation (we speak of political democracy elsewhere) was the most healthful on the globe. When an aristocratic Frenchman, Xavier Marmier, published a book hostile to America, the New York *Tribune* pointed out the essential elements of democratic vigor in the republic. The good Xavier had found greed in Pearl Street and bad manners on the steamboats. But if some divinity were to diffuse a sudden comfort over France equal to that reigning in the western land, give every Gallic child a rudimentary education paralleling that of the ordinary American lad, and prompt the young people themselves to aspire after every human dignity and advance, "would M. Marmier expect the emancipated peasantry to put on at once the manners of the Tuileries?" [34]

[VII]

Among general intellectual interests in this land of strenuous individualism and materialistic aims, politics easily stood foremost. Probably no people on earth was quite so political-minded as the Americans. A full half-dozen factors produced this result. The democratic basis of government, enlarged in the

33 When Jackson entered the White House, hours of labor in America had averaged twelve and a half a day. By 1850 at least a third of the population were working only eleven hours a day. One student who has investigated the question of vacations concludes that very few enjoyed such a luxury in this period. Fashionable folk went to Saratoga, Newport, Old Point Comfort, and the Virginia springs; but plain people took only one-day outings—a picnic, a steamboat excursion, a short train trip. Edgar W. Martin, *The Standard of Living in 1860*, 346. Thomas Low Nichols wrote in *Forty Years of American Life:* "In no country are the faces of the people furrowed with harder lines of care. In no country that I know of is there so much hard, toilsome, unremitting labour: in none so little of the recreation and enjoyment in life." P. 206.

34 N. Y. *Weekly Tribune*, May 10, 1851.

Jacksonian era to include every adult male; the emphasis on representative institutions; the existence of three distinct spheres of political activity, local, state, and national; the lingering influence of the burning political discussions which had accompanied the Revolution and the making of the Constitution; and the fact that in America political battles took the place occupied in Europe by international complications—all these played their part. In country taverns, on steamboats and trains, in hotels and barrooms, any knot of men not discussing business would be talking politics. The ubiquity of newspapers ministered to this appetite. Whereas one Frenchman in five, or one Englishman in two, read newspapers, all Americans seemed to devour them. William Chambers noted that at breakfast in his New York hotel every man had a paper, and asserted that no respectable workingman failed to buy one several times a week. The New York *Sun*, a penny journal which had a circulation of more than fifty thousand copies a day in 1848, boasted for a time of the largest clientele in the world, and the New York *Tribune* (counting weekly and tri-weekly editions) succeeded to that claim. Though actually the per capita circulation of newspapers was small by modern standards, a well-edited sheet was then handed round until scores had seen it.

What theology was to a Scot and military affairs to a Prussian, politics was to most Americans. Enter a farmhouse in the evening, wrote Alexander Mackay, and the owner would be engrossed in a political article. Converse with him, and you would find him full of strange expertise on the tariff, slavery, and the latest veto. "The markets and a few other topics may receive passing attention, but the grand theme is politics; and you will be surprised by the sense and readiness with which he speaks on the most intricate national questions." This was true; everyone knows the wide-flung appeal of the daily or weekly editions of Greeley's *Tribune*, Samuel Bowles's Springfield *Republican*, Bryant's *Evening Post*, and Seaton's *National Intelligencer*. But only less potent were the *Picayune* and *True Delta* of New Orleans, the *Tribune* of Chicago, the *Free Press* of Detroit, the *Atlas* of Boston, and dozens more. Stump-speaking, too, was in its triumphant vogue. The higher oratory of Seward and Lincoln, Douglas and Jefferson Davis, was assured of intent audiences, able to follow the intricacies of debate on slavery as their fathers had followed the Bank question.[35]

35 Frank M. O'Brien, *The Story of the Sun*, 168; William Chambers, *Things As They Are in America* (1854), 203, 204; W. E. Baxter, *America and the Americans* (1855), 82. The English educator Hugh S. Tremenheere was horrified by the chauvinism and manifest-destiny expansionism preached by a large part of the press. Travelling in the United States during the period of the filibustering expedition of Quitman and Lopez against Cuba, he found Democratic journals cheering on the aggression, and even Whig journals excusing it. Who could expect Americans to take a sober view of international affairs, he asked, under the daily stimulus of the spreadeagle press, "flattering their vanity, pandering to their passions, and striving to fill them with exaggerated notions of their self-importance?" *Notes on Public Subjects in the United States and Canada*, 126ff.

At the climax of a national campaign the violence of party excitement grew explosive. Newspapers attacked each other with ferocity; rival speakers bellowed the direst warnings; the country seemed on the brink of a catastrophe. But the day after election a truce ensued and quiet reigned. It was only as the slavery issue aroused a deepened passion that fearful men came to wish that party animosities could be abated.

Ranking close behind politics, and with women preceding it, was the national interest in religion, which at various times and places became all-engrossing. In certain areas, to be sure, deism, other forms of free-thought, and even atheism had made inroads upon the traditional piety. William Dean Howells, growing up in Hamilton, Ohio, heard nightly debates in the village drugstore upon the existence of God and the immortality of the soul, both earnestly denied. He thought the community "prevalently irreligious," and the young people "irreverent to mocking in matters of religion." But this, if true, was unrepresentative. When he removed to Columbus he found that "everybody went to church," and that opinion was so strict that it almost condemned the mild latitudinarianism of Holmes's *Autocrat* papers.[36] In rural areas North and South the church was a powerful organization; innumerable city congregations were rich and influential; Henry Ward Beecher in the middle fifties preached regularly to more than three thousand. Protestant church magazines found an immense following. Every district had its forceful laymen who, like Salmon P. Chase and T. J. Jackson, made religion almost an obsession. That representative middle-class diarist George Templeton Strong, a busy lawyer and vestryman of Trinity, was occupied (apart from his practice) chiefly with music and religious activity. Even if the country had less piety than was supposed, it was so religious that keen-eyed travellers (Mrs. I. L. Bishop, of *The Englishwoman in America*, in the middle fifties, like Lord Bryce a generation later), pronounced it equal to Scotland and superior to other European lands in its fervent faith.[37] Once during

36 *Years of My Youth*, 106, 160.
37 One observer concluded that "the New England States are the most moral, perhaps the most religious portion of the world"; *Aspects of Religion in the United States*, by the author of *The Englishwoman in America* (1859). Rey, in *L'Amérique Protestante* (1857), was impressed by the religious fervor of the nation, declaring: "The places of worship in the United States are much more attended than those of Europe, and are very numerous." I, 117, 120. The Eighth Census showed that the country had one church for every 580 people, the churches had facilities for seating three-fifths of the population at one time, and the average value of each church was nearly $3,200. *Mortality and Miscellaneous*, 497ff. Of the nation's denominations, the Methodists were the most numerous and the richest; the Baptists second, and the Presbyterians third in numbers, but the Presbyterians second in wealth. See article in *National Intelligencer*, April 7, 1855. The Catholics apparently fell into fourth place in numbers, but immigration was rapidly swelling their ranks. For an interesting review of Catholic growth in this period, with attention to the influence of such converts as Isaac T. Hecker, who founded the order of the Paulists in New York in 1858, see James Parton, "Our Roman Catholic Brethren," in *Topics of the Times*, 132–198.

the fifties, in 1857–58, a strange and intense revival swept suddenly over half the country.[38]

To many religion was a matter of mere emotion, without intellectual excitation. But in many more it released currents of mental energy, quickening even the unconverted—as Walt Whitman proved in such bits as his notes on Elias Hicks. The voice of William Ellery Channing had been stilled by death in 1842, but its echoes were still ringing. Channing's Unitarianism had struck its special note in his insistence upon the "ray of divinity" in man, upon human dignity and worth—a very American note. This divine ray in the midst of

Theodore Parker Preaching at the Tabernacle in New York, 1853.
From a drawing by Eyre Crowe, A.R.A., for *With Thackeray in America*.

imperfect things held up a goal of perfection, commanding men to receive all truth, however it might war with their pride, and to do justice, however it might conflict with their interest. Nothing icy or narrow could be found in Channing's version of Puritan idealism. And with what an array of topics, from National Literature to Fénelon and Milton, did his essays illustrate his doctrine! His idea of the importance of religion to liberty as deepening the respect for human nature allied itself with Jeffersonian theory on one side and modern Catholic teaching on the other.

Beside him as liberators of the spirit stood two religious leaders whom the

38 See the description in *National Intelligencer*, March 20, 1858.

fifties found in their very prime, Horace Bushnell and Theodore Parker, and a third just rising to power, Henry Ward Beecher. Bushnell, a graduate of Yale and a much-beloved pastor of the North Congregational church in Hartford, had struck a powerful blow against narrow and barren theology in his *Christian Nurture*, published in 1846. Christianity, he taught, should not merely convert or redeem men, but should help them develop, and should pour vitality and beauty into the life of the masses. Then in his *Nature and the Supernatural* (1858) he expanded this doctrine, affirming that the segregation of the natural from the spiritual was an artificial distinction, and that man himself is primarily and essentially a supernatural being. Theodore Parker was a lusty, exuberant crusader for a broad natural faith, thoroughly radical in his temper—and he was one of the great practical reformers of his time.[39] Beecher, who was more evangelistic in spirit than Bushnell or Parker, being indeed the greatest preacher of the era, also poured a new idealism and philanthrophy into religion. Reared in what he called the "alleviated Calvinism" of his father, Lyman Beecher, he condemned the old doctrines of election and reprobation in favor of a broad-minded assertion of faith.[40]

Unitarianism was at the very height of its influence during this period. It dominated New England thought; Channing, Ezra Stiles Gannett, the two Frothinghams, and Parker reached thoughtful Americans by the pen rather than the voice, and their intellectual authority was felt throughout the nation. Emerson's tribute to Nathaniel Frothingham, who continued to write after his retirement from the pulpit in 1850, summed up the feeling of New Englanders. "Nothing vulgar is connected with his name, but, on the contrary, every remembrance of wit and learning, and contempt of cant. In our Olympic games we love his fame." [41] His son Octavius Brooks Frothingham, destined to a larger renown, early in the fifties broke with a Salem congregation on the slavery question, and took pastorates first in Jersey City and then New York. So radical were the convictions of this intellectual heir of Theodore Parker that he left many aghast.[42] Ezra Stiles Gannett, throughout this period pastor of the Arlington Street Church in Boston, tenaciously opposed the transcendentalism of Emerson and Parker. But his powers of logic, clarity of style, eloquence, and

39 William Warren Sweet, *The Story of Religion in America*, 373ff.; John White Chadwick, *William Ellery Channing*, 248, 249; Henry Steele Commager, *Theodore Parker, passim*; John Wright Buckham, *Progressive Religious Thought in America*, 3–54.
40 A. C. McGiffert, *Rise of Modern Religious Ideas, passim*; Paxton Hibben, *Henry Ward Beecher*, 120ff; Beecher, *New Star Papers, or Views and Experiences on Religious Subjects*.
41 Ralph Waldo Emerson, *Journals*, IV, 272. "But that fame," Emerson added, "was bought by many years' steady rejection of all that is popular with our saints, and as persevering study of books which no one else reads. . . ."
42 See his delightful *Recollections and Impressions, 1822–1890*.

intense feeling, made him a mighty battler for a dozen good causes: a sanely liberal religion, temperance, peace, education, and the gradual abolition of slavery. Beyond Unitarianism lay Universalism. Hosea Ballou, who died in 1852, had conducted a trenchant crusade against that doctrine of eternal punishment that Jonathan Edwards had made so terrible; his doctrine seemed extreme to countless Americans, but it too was a liberalizing influence.[43]

In the Middle States and much of the South, the Episcopal Church held that position of leadership which Unitarians took in New England; commingling social and intellectual influences, and owing as much to powerful lay members as to the clergy. It, too, made its steady contributions to national idealism. The Oxford movement shook the church to its centre. A meeting of the general convention in Philadelphia just after Newman's conversion to Catholicism heard so excited a debate that gallery visitors brought their lunches in order to retain their seats for the day. Fear was expressed that various divines would follow Newman's example, but the discussion ended with a determination to trust the conservative sense and recuperative power of the church to heal all schisms.[44] Among its men of intellectual power was Dr. Stephen H. Tyng, rector of St. George's in New York, a low-church leader who wielded an unsurpassed influence on the platform. Alonzo Potter, who had been raised to the episcopate of Pennsylvania, was a practical church administrator who believed that organized religion had large duties in education and humanitarian work, and who strove to bring theological training into harmony with the needs of the age. Just as the fifties ended, a young minister destined to become the brightest ornament of Episcopalianism for a long generation began to attract listeners to the Church of the Advent in Philadelphia—Phillips Brooks. Like Beecher, he held the rapt attention of large congregations, and even more than Beecher, he tipped his pen with creative fire.[45]

As much might be said of Presbyterianism, Methodism, the Baptists, and other sects which displayed a peculiar vigor in seeding the West and the newer South with faith and ideas. On the frontier the pulpit often had a unique influence. If its occupants were not book-learned, they were mighty in the Scriptures and often vigorous in native thought. Milburn's account of the pioneer minister William Burke, who died in the mid-fifties after a lifetime of such toil that there was hardly a settlement in the Ohio Valley where he had not

43 G. W. Cooke, *Unitarianism in America;* G. G. Atkins, *Religion in Our Times;* Maturin M. Ballou, *Biography of Hosea Ballou.* An illuminating view of the conflict between the older and newer theology is furnished in chapters 6, 7, and 8 of Lyman Abbott's *Reminiscences;* he holding ideas which in the fifties many regarded as heretical.

44 Bishop Thomas M. Clark, *Reminiscences,* 89, 90.

45 A. V. G. Allen, *Life and Letters of Phillips Brooks;* Bishop William Lawrence, *Phillips Brooks.*

preached or a cabin where he had not stayed, his pockets empty, his clothes patch upon patch, but his mind full, might answer for many a fellow.[46]

[VIII]

It was largely because of the continued strength of religion that the code of morals in most American communities remained extremely rigid. The Catholic Church, now strong in the large cities, and producing its first eminent leader in John Hughes, who became archbishop in 1850, was a strict guardian of conduct. The Methodists, Baptists, Presbyterians and other denominations scrutinized behavior sharply. They counselled the drinker, rebuked the swearer, admonished all vice, and expelled any persistent wrongdoer. Employers who were church-members usually imposed their moral standards upon subordinates. Most Protestant bodies showed a strong hostility to habitual tippling, and several sternly reprobated the sale and use of liquor in any quantity. They all maintained an unbending code in matters of sex-relationship. Toward business dishonesty, as being harder to detect, they were less censorious.

Social observers agreed that young people, who usually held their parties in blissful unconsciousness that any such thing as chaperonage existed, were free from blame or scandal. Elizabeth Stuart Phelps relates that in Andover, Massachusetts, an austerely intellectual town, a spirited girl of exceptional beauty was kissed one night by her daring escort. She cried all night and the next day—indeed, she did not stop crying for twenty-six hours; her teachers condoled and her schoolmates raged; "we were a score of as astonished and indignant girls as ever wept over women's wrongs." [47] Foreigners were invariably impressed by the prudish tone of society. It struck some of them as curious that in a land so puritanical, men and women should bathe together at ocean resorts—even though the women wore voluminous red frocks over white trousers.[48] American fiction reflected the general severity. When vice was portrayed it was in terms which echoed some old-world novelist. Henry James tells us that New Yorkers of the fifties tried hard to convince themselves that G. W. Curtis's *Potiphar Papers* was a trenchant satire. "We liked to think that, on our reduced but still respectable scale, we were ripe, socially ripe, both for satire and for the fine degustation of it. We liked to think that we too had our wicked worldly side, our types and our hierarchy, our great people and our less great, our raddled dowagers behind their fans, our Major Pendennises at their club windows, our snobs and parvenues, in fine, our themes for the easy moralist, our amiable

46 W. H. Milburn, *The Pioneer Preacher*, 59ff.
47 *Chapters From a Life*, 28.
48 Charles Mackay, *Life and Liberty in America*, I, 103.

vices. Our vices in the *Potiphar Papers* will have been, I surmise, of a really childlike amiability." [49]

The existence in the larger cities of a great army of prostitutes might itself be taken as one evidence of the general austerity of sexual morals. Since the great mass of women were implicity respected, and since the keeping of mistresses met the fiercest social condemnation, it was inevitable that prostitutes should do a heavy business. Estimates of the number in New York ran as high as ten thousand, and when William W. Sanger, physician of the Blackwell's Island Penitentiary, prepared the book on the social evil which he published in 1858, he questioned two thousand such women. *Harper's Weekly*, defending this exposé, remarked that at dusk every omnibus going uptown had its harlot inside, and that "we cannot walk the streets in the evening without meeting hundreds of the fallen plying their trade." The cities abounded in fast young men, and the revelation in the famous Nathan murder case that young fellows of wealth led a disreputable night life could have shocked few sophisticated people. But in one point of view this host of prostitutes might be held to indicate the general purity of American womanhood. A double standard of morals was taken for granted. Nearly all well-reared women were virtuous, many well-reared men were not. Moreover, the very rigidity of the moral code imposed on women, when accepted by harsh parents, thrust not a few seduced girls into the streets. The unhappy facts were that as cities grew and immigration brought in many unattached people of both sexes, the ancient trade grew also; and that underpayment in domestic service, the needle trades, and other occupations for women helped to furnish recruits.

It was undeniable that the prostitution which flourished in all large cities was a menace to health as well as morals. Walter Kerr of the Blackwell's Island penitentiary declared that the institution, which in the summer of 1853 held some eight hundred women, was little else than the great venereal hospital of the city. The resident physician described the life which most of them led. While nominally they paid three to five dollars a week for a wretched room, actually every shilling they gained, averaging perhaps six or eight dollars a day, was wrenched from them by the voracious madam conducting the house. When they became diseased, they were thrown on the streets and took refuge at the island; when cured, added the physician, they returned to their trade—but he did not define 'cured.' Sober Philadelphia and easygoing Washington were equally full of prostitution. The Barbary Coast of San Francisco was well established by the mid-fifties. Chicago by that date was well on its way toward the largest red-light district in the country—and the most depraved; one shore-front area, the Sands, being a haunt of the vilest criminality. As the Republican

49 James, *William Wetmore Story*, I, 305.

national convention of 1860 met, a well-timed raid ordered by Mayor John Wentworth netted a considerable body of delegates. In one costly new establishment alone three Ohio members were caught![50]

A population eager to make money, voracious in exploiting the raw wealth of the continent, highly competitive in temper, and as yet little bound by established traditions, was naturally a population of low commercial morality. To be 'sharp' was a general ambition. Bryant's partner Isaac Henderson, who was said to have made $125,000 in a real-estate deal by getting title to a two-inch strip that a lot-owner had neglected to survey, was a common type. Charles Godfrey Leland listened one day in these years to two businessmen. One honestly owed the other a large sum, but thought he had a legal way to escape payment, while the other differed. "So they argued away for a long time. There was not a word of reproach; the creditor would have cheated the debtor in the same way if he could; the only point of difference was whether it could be done." Newspaper stories of cheating were so common that only instances of the cheater cheated attracted much attention. One such occurred in Wall Street in 1851. Some promoters established a joint-stock Bank of the Metropolis with a capital of two millions, but to avoid taxation failed to file notice with the Controller. Other sharp operators discovered this neglect, organized a shoestring bank with the same name, filed it with the Controller, and thus obtained its exclusive use. The original bank had to change its name or close up its affairs; but the change of title required unanimous consent of the stockholders, and one of the originators of the new bank possessed a block of stock in the old! The new company won praise for its neat holdup game.

Sharpness ran innumerable threads through the tissue of business public and private. Leonard W. Jerome and William R. Travers, founding their Wall Street firm in 1856, gave a new sharpness to brokerage operations. Sharpness marked the westerners who illegally or semi-illegally exploited public lands, and who in Arkansas in 1854, after a year of wholesale timber-cutting, actually gathered a mob to defy the Federal Marshal. Sharpness guided the newspapers which, by puffs at one time and detraction at another, manipulated stocks to the profit of the editors. We find Edward Everett in 1857 commenting in his diary on the New York *Herald's* blackmailing campaign against the New York Central; it had "devoted a quarter of a column almost daily to the systematic abuse of this stock, affectedly classing it at all times with the broken concerns." The New York *Tribune* declared that most people never dreamed of the extent

50 *Harper's Weekly*, November 27, 1858, on Sanger's critics. Sanger's book, published by Harper's under the title *A History of Prostitution*, was a notable piece of early sociological work. See N. Y. *Tribune*, August 31, 1853, for Kerr's statement; Herbert Asbury's volumes on the underworld of various cities; and the Bangor, Maine, *Daily Whig and Courier*, May 21, 1860, on the Chicago raids.

to which articles of universal use were adulterated and falsified. "From the groceries we daily consume to the medicines which we consume more rarely; from the apparel with which we cover our bodies to the paint with which we cover our houses, we are constantly embroiled in a network of frauds, such that our whole commercial experience is very little else than a series of impositions." [51]

The most flagrant defect of American morals was the violence which seamed the land. It was seemingly inseparable from the outward thrust of the frontier and the rapid growth of the cities, while it was fostered in the South by slavery and a special code of personal honor. Obviously, it had its relation to the general carelessness of life peculiar to young countries, which filled the republic with railroad wrecks, steamboat explosions, and industrial accidents. [52] In the West, the violence of highwaymen and gunmen was seldom of an organized and persistent character, being sporadic, individual, and fitful. In various cities, however, the activities of gangs like the Bowery Boys, rowdy political clubs, blackmailing fire companies, and organized thieves, sometimes made people feel that they were treading on a social volcano. "Our columns," remarked the New York Sun in 1857, "are daily filled with the dark records of hideous crime, committed with circumstances of unusual atrocity. There seem to be in our midst bands of desperadoes, who have cast off all regard for law, human or divine." The Baltimore Patriot had recently congratulated citizens that Thanksgiving had passed over without any "lawless outbreak of serious nature," though sixty pistols had been taken from suspicious persons. [53]

Chicago, Philadelphia, New Orleans, and even Washington were disgraced during the fifties by bloody mob-outbreaks. "Turn where we will," declared the Cincinnati Times in 1857, "we find by every mail intelligence of riots, murders, and other outrages of the most flagrant character." [54]

In the North, violence was commonest among the ignorant and im-

---

51 Leland, Memoirs, 207, 208; Edward Everett, MS Diary, December 16, 1857; N. Y. Tribune, September 12, 1854. Various books already dealt with adulteration: Normandy's Handbook on Commercial Adulterations, and the works of Aecum and Mitchell. But on British commercial morality, see Dickens' Hard Times.

52 "Toujours la négligence Américaine!" exclaimed Ampère as he noted a shower of burning cinders falling on cotton bales piled high on a steamboat. The toll of life and limb taken by steamboats and trains every year ran into appalling figures. M. F. Maury computed that in 1854-57 inclusive more than eight hundred lives had been lost on the Great Lakes. A midwestern newspaper observed that "there is no country in the world in which there is so little regard for human life as in the United States." Cincinnati Columbian, July 19, 1856.

53 N. Y. Sun, November 21, 1857.

54 The violence in Washington reached such a pitch that Congress warmly discussed the subject; N. Y. Weekly Tribune, May 1, 1858. After a bloody riot in Hoboken between German picnickers and Irish ruffians, the N. Y. Tribune exclaimed that undeniably "there ferments in the bosom of our American society a mass of wanton and obstreperous brutality which does not exist elsewhere." May 31, 1851.

poverished, with certain immigrant groups usually prominent, but in the South hot words and hair-triggers were a mark of the gentleman. By 1850 duelling had fallen into disrepute in the Northern States, as in Great Britain, and the laws reinforced public sentiment. In the Far West and South it persisted. The year 1847 saw the publication in Baltimore of a volume called *The Code of Honor* by "a Southron," while in 1850 John L. Wilson of South Carolina issued a more elaborate treatise, which went into a revised edition in 1858. These books prescribed what Thomas Hart Benton would have called "high-toned" rules for duelling, but in actual practise some encounters were of ferocious brutality. Richmond, for example, was shocked in 1846 by the death of the noted editor J. H. Pleasants at the hand of Thomas Ritchie, Jr. Ritchie deliberately provoked the meeting; he fired heavy ball, though Pleasants used only blank cartridges, and shot at least eight times; and the horribly mangled Pleasants lingered two days in great agony. "Never was there a more singular duel if such it may be called," wrote Dr. Hoge, a Presbyterian minister who knew the facts. "Never since the burning of the theatre, a more mournful tragedy in Richmond." [55]

But the Southern code of honor went much further than the formal duel. It gave license to any "gentleman" who thought he had suffered a slight from an "underling" to kill the offender with little ceremony. Several incidents of the fifties attracted national attention to ideas which gave constant rise to what one Southern historian called "shocking, unregulated encounters" [56]—to hotblooded shootings, retaliatory murders, and family feuds. The idea that an insult found its only atonement in death made homicide on a point of honor as excusable as in Spain; and Spain was frankly medieval, while the South was not. The unwritten law had broad scope, and could be pleaded so successfully before courts of law that one Mississippi attorney was able to boast that he had defended more than two hundred men charged with murder, and saved every one from hanging.[57]

A peculiarly outrageous affair took place in Kentucky in 1853. A Louisville teacher, William H. G. Butler, corrected a pupil belonging to the prominent Ward family. Though the teacher had merely done his duty, an older son named Matthew F. Ward visited the school next day, had words with Butler before a roomful of children, and drawing a pistol, mortally wounded him. Public indignation was intense. But the eminent John J. Crittenden, Senator, Governor, and twice Attorney-General of the United States, was an oldtime

55 MS Journal of Dr. J. D. Hoge, Huntington Library. An almost equally savage duel near Charleston in 1856 resulted in the slaying of William R. Taber, an editor of the Charleston *Mercury*, by Edward Magrath, who had been incensed by articles in the *Mercury* attacking his brother Judge Magrath. Seconds vainly tried to stop the encounter after two shots. *Mercury*, September 30, 1856.
56 H. R. Ravenel, *Charleston: The Place and the People.*
57 Reuben Davis, *Recollections of Mississippi and Mississippians*, 77.

friend of the Wards. This rich family, supported by others of the ruling class, strained every resource. The trial was transferred to the rural village of Elizabethtown, and a simple country jury impanelled. Along with Crittenden, other able counsel were retained. It was given out that Crittenden was too noble to defend any but the innocent, and he did not correct the impression. Ward was acquitted; but to the credit of Louisville, the greatest mass meeting in the city's history denounced the outrage, rebuked Crittenden, and called upon the Wards to remove to their Arkansas estates.[58]

Such incidents were far too common in the South. The mild-mannered, flame-tongued William L. Yancey of Alabama had killed an uncle—without penalty. The temperamental Louis T. Wigfall of South Carolina met a friend, was invited to his wedding, walked down the street with him, quarreled, killed him—and went to Texas to become a Senator. On August 2, 1854, Dr. R. H. Graham of New Orleans, who had been drinking, roused a New York hotel at five in the morning by ringing all the bells. When another guest, whose wife was an invalid, expostulated, Graham fatally stabbed him with a sword cane. Greeley's *Tribune* called the crime "one of those brutal murders which seem peculiarly to belong to the institution of slavery," a statement which came with ill grace from a city notorious for its murders.[59] The Southern press was always irritated by Greeley's citation of Jefferson's *Notes on Virginia* with reference to the "boisterous" passions bred by slavery. Not long afterward a Southerner named Herbert, who had become a Representative from California, breakfasting at Willard's Hotel in Washington, was enraged by an Irish waiter and incontinently slew him. The Dutch minister, just arrived, was eating his first meal at the hotel. He phlegmatically finished his coffee, walked into the lobby, and meeting a friend, exclaimed: "What a beoples! If they do such tings at breakfast, what won't they do at dinner?"[60]

Though frontier violence was usually unregulated by code, California was the scene of many duels as well as plain murders. In San Francisco nine duels were fought in the single year 1854, while one Sacramento editor engaged in four within three years. Secretary of State James W. Denver, whose name is borne by a great city, killed the editor of the *Alta California* in 1852 because the journalist had criticized Denver's management of supply trains which the legislature had voted for the assistance of overland emigrants. The famous Broderick-Terry encounter of 1859 was fought between representatives of two groups specially given to violence. David Broderick had risen from the Irish element in New York, with a Tammany and volunteer fire-company

58 N. Y. *Tribune*, May 1–5, 1854; *National Intelligencer*, May 18, June 3, 1854; Mrs. Chapman Coleman, *Life of John J. Crittenden*, II, 60–110.
59 N. Y. *Tribune*, August 3, 1854.
60 *National Intelligencer*, May 17, 1865.

background, to be one of California's senators; David S. Terry, an able but arrogant Southerner who had lived in Kentucky, Mississippi, and Texas, had become California's chief justice. They quarreled, met at dawn just outside San Francisco, fired pointblank—and Broderick was carried away mortally wounded.[61] But the ordinary California affray and Colorado hold-up were less disturbing than the gang warfare of New York or the Southern feud; they were marks of an immature civilization, while no such excuse could be made for the violence rampant in many older communities. In the same way, the prominence of lynch law on the frontier was far less sinister than its occasional appearance in long-settled areas; in Indiana, Iowa, and the South.

[IX]

The sources of violence were many, and the hopeful fact was that some were plainly evanescent. For frontier regions, James Parton correctly though incompletely listed them as "Abundance—Idleness—Indians—Africans—Isolation—Whiskey!" He listed also the hardhitting temper which Highlanders, Ulster Scots, and Irish brought from Europe; the influence of the Revolution, with its civil strife of Tory and Whig; and the love of combat aroused by Indian-fighting.[62] We have noted that many communities rated bloody encounters as an amusement. W. H. Milburn informs us that a happy frontier market-day was enlivened by a political harangue, a sheriff's sale, numerous horse-swaps, and "half a dozen free fights." Both Peter Cartwright and Davy Crockett in their autobiographies give wonderful pictures of Tennessee fighting as a diversion and a proof of manhood. The "fighting class" followed the frontier westward to become the wild men of Montana and Nevada in later decades. In the Eastern cities, too, many immigrant groups often looked upon personal encounters as a spirited amusement. In 1854 the notorious New York pugilist John Morrissey had a drunken quarrel with the gang leader Bill Poole, which ended in Morrissey's wager that he could whip Poole on the Amos Street dock at seven o'clock on the morning of July twenty-seventh. The news flew through the dens of the city, bets were multiplied, and a huge crowd gathered. "They go," declared the scandalized *Tribune*, "to the very center of one of the most populous wards of the city, accompanied by five hundred thieves, burglars,

61   Jeremiah Lynch, *A Senator of the Fifties: David C. Broderick of California*, 213-226. Terry was indicted after the duel, but his case was transferred to another county and dismissed. After the Civil War he became enraged against Stephen J. Field, associate justice of the Supreme Court, for a verdict involving Terry's wife, assaulted the bailiffs in Field's session of the circuit court, and was jailed for six months. The next year, when Field returned to the State, Terry attacked him, and was shot dead by Field's bodyguard. Carl B. Swisher, *Stephen J. Field: Craftsman of the Law*, 328-354.
62   Parton, *Life of Andrew Jackson*, I, 33, 155, 295ff.

thimbleriggers, pickpockets, and 'gentlemen' sympathizers; deliberately arrange their plans, fall upon each other rough and tumble, and fight, strike, bite, scratch, kick, gouge, and gnaw each other like dogs for three quarters of an hour, without the shadow of an officer to interfere!" Morrissey was led off temporarily blinded.[63] Yet this was less shocking than the gang battles which sometimes left a dozen dead.

An important element in the high homicide rate was the ease with which deadly weapons were procured, and the general fashion of bearing them. Particularly in the South and the farther West, most of the male population went constantly armed. A British visitor in New Orleans was astonished to observe in shop windows the variety of lethal implements for sale: poniards, cutlasses, bowie knives, revolvers, swordcanes, and the like. An old resident, pointing to the crowd in the streets, declared that seven men out of every ten were carrying some kind of weapon.[64] "The practise of going armed with concealed and deadly weapons," remarked the *National Intelligencer*, "has well nigh become one of our social habitudes. The only conceivable object . . . is *to kill;* the violent, that they may perpetrate their misdeeds with impunity, the peaceful under the plea that the habit . . . has become a dire necessity under the reign of license and disorder." [65] In the Southwest some bravoes armed themselves with "devil's claws," which, quickly donned, would at one blow leave a man's face in bleeding shreds. The time came in the late fifties, as we shall see, when practically every member of Congress bore a deadly weapon. Even theological students carried them, and in Virginia one theologue killed a man in a Sunday School affray![66]

But if the sources of lawlessness were many, its main taproot was clear: it was the ease with which punishment was evaded. Had the machinery of American justice possessed the efficiency of the English system, violence would rapidly have diminished. But lawbreakers found the chances heavily in their favor. In some cities political protection gave thugs assurance of safety. Recorder Smyth of New York in a grand jury charge of 1857 declared that crime was "fearfully on the increase" because the political desperado felt immune from punishment. "The experience of the past has taught him that political influence would shield him from the penitentiary, particularly if his outrages had been perpetrated for and in behalf of those who held place and power." [67] Criminals who lacked a protector could count on the carelessness of public prosecutors, the

63 N. Y. *Tribune*, July 28, 1854. For assorted examples of gang violence in New York and other cities, see the *National Intelligencer*, August 31, 1852; November 8, 1853; December 6, 1856.
64 Henry Ashworth, *Tour in the United States, Cuba, and Canada* (1861).
65 October 6, 1857.
66 *Ibid.*, June 20, 1857.
67 *National Intelligencer*, June 4, 1857.

technicalities of the law, the wiles of attorneys, and the sentimentality of juries. "It seems to be quite sufficient for the common people if the burglar, or murderer, or defaulter is arrested," growled the New York *Commercial Advertiser*. "They care little or nothing whether punishment follows crime." [68] But even arrest was often difficult. Municipal police forces were universally inadequate, and no state constabularies existed. The middle fifties found New Orleans with a police force of two hundred and fifty men, a number insufficient at all times, but flagrantly inadequate in winter, when tens of thousands of strangers arrived and the city swarmed with vagrants, bullies, and assorted criminals. [69]

Looking toward the future, men perceived that if only the taproot could be cut, half the violence and crime would disappear. Eventually, courts could be improved; police forces could be reorganized and strengthened. The example set by New York, where Mayor James Harper in the middle forties had given the police uniforms and a stricter discipline, was gradually followed by other cities. In Baltimore, for example, the police system was renovated in 1857, and Mayor Thomas Swann that year reviewed the entire force of four hundred men in its natty uniforms of blue cloth and brass buttons. Now and then a public prosecutor won renown by his efficiency. Now and then the courts vindicated themselves nobly. [70]

The most memorable criminal case of the time was the trial of Professor Webster of Harvard for the murder of Dr. Parkman. Taking place early in 1850, it divided public attention with the Compromise debates and aroused more discussion than any case since the Duke of Praslin had been arraigned for murdering his wife. Thoughtful people looked forward to the trial, one Bostonian wrote, as to an earthquake. [71] Few men liked Webster, who had seemed a great overgrown, vulgar boy. "He was noisy, officious, meddlesome, and in pecuniary matters loose, reckless, self-indulgent, and even dishonest." But the evidence against him at first seemed weak; his position was high and his connections were important; Chief Justice Lemuel Shaw was a close friend. When he was swiftly convicted, Massachusetts felt that her system of justice had been spectacularly vindicated. Robert C. Winthrop put his finger on the main significance of the verdict. "It is indeed an appalling thing that such a man as Dr. Webster should have been doomed to the gallows. But I honestly think that a verdict of 'not guilty' would have been ten times more appalling . . . Upon the whole, I regard the result as the highest triumph of law and justice over influence, position,

68 Quoted in the *National Intelligencer*, August 27, 1857.
69 *Report*, New Orleans Police Department, May-October, 1855.
70 See H. O. Sprogle, *The Philadelphia Police, Past and Present*; J. J. Flinn, *History of the Chicago Police*; L. V. Harrison, *Police Administration in Boston*; R. B. Fosdick, *American Police Systems*.
71 George S. Hillard, January 29, 1850; Lieber Papers, Huntington Library.

partiality, and artifice, and almost everything that could be arrayed against them." [72] All the New England States could boast of an efficient system of justice; New York had her tradition of Kent, and other parts of the Union that of equally great jurists. The violence which stained American society need not after all be taken as a permanent defect. With the disappearance of the frontier, the growth of settled habits and traditions, the improvement of police systems, and the strengthening of the law, it could be abated—though it would long leave its mark.

[X]

The strain of idealism in American life had been marked by every observer from the days of those very practical idealists Benjamin Franklin and Thomas Jefferson. It had been implanted by the founders of American institutions; by William Bradford and Roger Williams, the noble Penn and generous Oglethorpe. It had found a favoring environment in the kindly economic conditions of the country and the egalitarian passion of many communities. Above all, it had been nurtured by religion: by the Puritan church, by the Quakers who produced in John Woolman a 'schöne Seele' typifying the purest essence of idealism, by the Methodists with their fervent evangelism stemming from Wesley, Whitefield, and Francis Asbury, by the independent-minded Baptists and the humane Episcopalians. It had not been neglected by the Catholics. The two main expressions of American idealism lay in a broadfronted reform movement, of which we shall say more elsewhere, and in philanthropy.

The vital spirit of Protestantism in America was an idealistic and philanthropic spirit. The chief denominations since the beginning of the century had filled the West and Southwest with missionaries. A single agency, the Home Missionary Society, representing the Presbyterians, Congregationalists, and Dutch Reformed Church, by 1855 had more than a thousand men employed in twenty-seven States and Territories; while other agencies strewed missions over the pagan world.[73] Publication for religious ends had been given a sturdy basis. Not merely did the American Bible Society and the American Tract Society scatter the Scriptures, with religious books and innumerable pamphlets, all over the country, but the larger sects all had publishing houses. By 1855 the Tract Society employed 659 colporteurs who that year visited nearly a thousand families apiece.[74]

Particularly were the religious bodies active in education. When the

72 To John P. Kennedy, March, 1850; Kennedy Papers, Peabody Institute.
73 William Warren Sweet, *Story of Religion in America*, 361–363.
74 *National Intelligencer*, May 12, 1855.

American Sunday School Union celebrated its twenty-third anniversary in 1857, its officers declared that the previous year they had covered the nation with their agents, who had organized more than eighteen hundred new schools with eighty thousand children.[75] Theological seminaries had multiplied, the Protestant sects establishing no fewer than twenty-five between the founding of Andover Seminary in 1808 and the year 1840. Small denominational colleges were being sprinkled all over the West and South. While the Presbyterians and Congregationalists had led the way, other denominations had followed with crusading zeal. A band of workers from the Yale Divinity School had founded two colleges of exceptional merit, Illinois at Jacksonville, Ill., and Iowa at Grinnell, Iowa. The Baptists established colleges all the way from Colby in Maine to Baylor in Texas, the Methodists from Wesleyan in Connecticut and Randolph-Macon in Virginia to Asbury in Indiana and McKendree in Illinois.

But if idealism found the church its principal stay and reinforcement, it drew strength from many other sources. Emerson has enumerated them. The writings of Schelling, the generalizations of Goethe, the prophet utterances of Coleridge and Carlyle, the poetry of Wordsworth, the finer impulses of German scholarship, the influence of science, all played a part. It was hardly possible for Emerson to include his own writings and those of Margaret Fuller and Thoreau, but they were important. So were the teachings of Swedenborgianism. Idealism, in fact, was a clean, bracing wind blowing throughout the world; the world of the long peace from Waterloo down to Sebastopol and Solferino.[76]

Philanthropy was so much the handmaiden of idealism that by the mid-century Americans had earned the reputation of a remarkably freehanded people. "They love to give, even as they love to acquire," wrote Fredrika Bremer.[77] The principle of tithing was accepted by many hard-fisted businessmen. Young Rockefeller, going to work on a tiny salary in Cleveland, gave money generously to the poor in the church, the Five Points Mission, the mite-society, and other good objects. Three of the most admired of American businessmen were Peter Cooper, George Peabody, and Amos Lawrence; admired because their ability in getting was matched by their liberality in giving. The fifties saw Cooper open in New York his nobly-conceived Union, an institute for adult education which from the outset proved magnificently effective.[78] George Peabody's benefactions to Baltimore won him, when in 1857 he revisited the scene of his early struggles, a reception which might have flattered a ruling prince. "You have proved, sir," John H. B. Latrobe said at a banquet in his

75 National Intelligencer, May 16, 1857; M. C. Brown, Sunday School Movements in America, 45ff.
76 Oliver Wendell Holmes, Emerson, 148ff.
77 Homes in the New World, I, 357, 358.
78 Allan Nevins, Abram S. Hewitt, With Some Account of Peter Cooper, 169–191.

honor, "that politics and diplomacy are not the only field on which may be won an honorable renown." [79] Amos Lawrence was likened to the Medicis. His death in 1852 awakened heartfelt expressions of sorrow, for his biographer could show that in the last twenty-three years of his life his known benefactions had totaled $640,000, and his unknown gifts had added much more. Hardly less honored was his brother Abbott Lawrence, whose gift to Harvard for a scientific school we have noted. Both men gave from a religious impulse; "our talents are trusts committed to us for use, and to be accounted for when the Master calls," Amos wrote his brother.[80]

In number, variety, and strength, American philanthropies were equalled only by those of Great Britain. Figures were published in 1857 on the budgets of various organizations holding annual meetings in New York. The American Tract Society the previous year had expended $420,000; the American Board of Foreign Missions, $323,000; the Presbyterian Board of Foreign Missions almost $220,000. The Female Guardian Society and the Magdalen Society had a combined budget of about $50,000. The Seamen's Friend Society had spent almost $30,000. The expenditures of the American Anti-Slavery Society were $34,000, and those of the American Abolition Society $6,000. The missionary department of the American Sunday School Union had spent nearly $85,000. Theodore Frelinghuysen, presiding over the American Bible Society, declared that its receipts of $442,000 had enabled it to distribute 772,500 volumes, including its first New Testaments in Ojibway and Hawaiian. Of agencies for relieving the poor there were scores, while hospitals and asylums were liberally sustained. The New York Association for Improving the Condition of the Poor did a useful work in exploring the causes of poverty as well as in relieving it.[81]

[XI]

To home and foreign observers alike, the main tendencies of American life seemed sound. "We cannot look on the freedom of this country, in connection with its youth," wrote Emerson, "without a presentiment that here shall laws and institutions exist on some scale of proportion to the majesty of nature." He thought that the heterogeneous population crowding from all corners of the world would make the nation more catholic and cosmopolitan than any other. "It seems to be easy for America to inspire and express the most expansive and humane spirit; new-born, free, healthful, strong, the land of the laborer, of the

79 *National Intelligencer*, March 21, 1857.
80 W. B. Lawrence, ed., *Diary and Correspondence of the Late Amos Lawrence.*
81 *National Intelligencer*, April 30, May 16, May 19, 1857; "American Benevolent Societies," *Harper's Weekly*, May 16, 1857.

democrat, of the philanthropist, of the saint, who should speak for the human race. It is the country of the Future . . . a country of beginnings, of projects, of designs, of expectations." [82] Of coarseness and mediocrity, spittoons, Colt's revolvers, and bogus stock there was too much. But the main tendencies seemed as sound as Cooper had found them in his *Notions of the Americans*. J. M. Philippo, publishing his book on the country in 1857, made the shrewd prediction that by 1900 the country would be approaching a hundred millions and would be almost indubitably the most powerful on earth. There seemed no limit to her growth, and no possible check to her rise except internal dissension. He found the government sane and liberal; he eulogized the humanity of the laws, the freedom of the press, and the simplicity of manners, though stamped with a republican roughness. "I can conceive of no spectacle, exhibiting in a greater degree the elements of grandeur," he declared, "than twenty-three millions of men, educated, intelligent, and industrious, enjoying the freest political power, and yet without the presence of a standing army." [83]

The only grave doubts as to American tendencies sprang from Southern institutions. That slavery should exist in fifteen States was in itself a saddening fact. As an inherited system, deeply intertwined with the economic life of the section and rendered formidable by the race problem with which it was connected, it might dishearten any beholder. But the readiness of a great part of the Southern people not merely to defend it as a temporary necessity, but to extol it as a positive and permanent good—this was a portentous omen.

82 *The Young American* (1844).
83 *The United States and Cuba*, quoted by Nevins, *British Travellers*, 289, 290.

3

Culture of the Masses

IN HIS *Remarks on the Manners, Government, and Debt of the United States* (an odd combination of topics), Noah Webster said of Americans that "having raised the pillars of the building, they ceased to exert themselves, and seemed to forget that the whole superstructure was then to be erected." American culture in 1847 was essentially democratic. Its characteristics were breadth rather than depth, diffusion rather than intensity, humanity rather than austerity. It might be regarded as a plateau, highest along the eastern seaboard and gradually declining toward the West and South, but being slowly raised there by broad subterranean forces.

At three points only did it lift a peak of real eminence to catch the transatlantic gaze. About Boston a variety of social, economic, and intellectual factors had united to produce a foundation for high literary talent. One was the inherited wealth of the old families, the Lawrences and Lowells, the Everetts and Prescotts, permitting leisure. One was the tradition of intense interest in learning and letters stemming back to the Mathers. One was that accumulation of books and allied materials which had enlisted the energies of Thomas Prince and Jeremy Belknap. Among the other stimulants were facilities for foreign travel, a high moral idealism derived from Puritanism and Unitarianism, the fertilization of Anglo-American ideas by German, French, and even Oriental thought, and an ambition to raise America to a place in world culture. All this played a part in what Charles Francis Adams, Jr., was the first to call the flowering of New England. In New York, the seat of another peak, Fenimore Cooper, Irving, and Bryant had their associates and successors. Meanwhile, Washington provided a center for another type of eminence. There government enterprise and patronage aided in the rise of distinguished scientific activities, represented by such names as Joseph Henry, M. F. Maury, and J. D. Bache.

What might this new American culture be expected to express? Would it reflect the practical spirit that had subjugated a continent in little over two centuries? Would it echo the hammer chorus that had forged the world's most chal-

75

lenging instrument of democratic government? In concrete terms, it might be expected to prove fertile in works of exploration and travel, books on husbandry and the mechanic arts, newspapers devoted to practical needs, agricultural magazines, political oratory, treatises on government, and lectures on utilitarian subjects. Religious interests, too, would find due expression. While all these required no intensity, no genius or inspiration, their relation to culture was direct and important.

[I]

The country was not rich in original ideas, nor did it keep its stock of borrowed ideas brightly up to date. The prevalent intellectual climate was still that created by writers and thinkers active between 1775 and 1830. Political thought was dominated by the fathers of the republic, with some Jacksonian modifications; economic thought by the school of Adam Smith and Ricardo; literary taste by the British and French romantics; and religious belief, in so far as old dogmas were broken down at all, by Deism, Unitarianism, and Swedenborgianism. Because Europe was far away, because communications everywhere were slow, because journals devoted to ideas were few, and because many communities were highly conservative, thought seldom had much velocity. Utopian Socialism got transplanted by 1840, when Albert Brisbane published his *Social Destiny;* but other new doctrines came slowly.

In this era and later the sway exercised by Walter Scott over the South was frequently noted. Down to Sumter countless Americans debated the theology of Butler, Paley, and Chalmers, and Virginians compared them with the works of their own fervent theologian Archibald Alexander, who was equally old-fashioned.[1] The most influential American economist was Francis Wayland, who trod largely in the footsteps of the great British pioneers. Greeley lamented in the *Tribune* the fact that although Henry C. Carey had published his *Principles of Political Economy* in 1837–40, seventeen years later his ideas were less known in America than in Europe. He had developed a great new principle in his book *Past, Present, and Future*, issued in 1848, but not one American in a thousand could name it. "After a while, it may be that our own colleges will take courage from the example of the foreign schools, to look for original thinkers at home for textbooks in this department of instruction." It was only

---

1 "The new school of writers—Goethe, Emerson, Channing, George Sand, Hawthorne—were not in our libraries." Moncure D. Conway, *Autobiography, Memories, and Experiences,* I, 67. For the influence of Scott in the South and a tribute to its healthy character, see Ludwig Lewisohn, *Up Stream: The Making of an American,* 61. Hugh Blair Grigsby wrote W. C. Rives April 11, 1866, comparing Alexander at length with older writers; Rives Papers.

on the eve of the Civil War that Carey made a convert of that brilliant young student of economics, David A. Wells.[2]

When Comte died in 1857, the tone of the obituary notices showed that his name had little general currency. He had published his great work on the positive philosophy half a generation earlier, he had found a translator in Harriet Martineau, and he had strongly colored George Eliot and other English writers. Naturally visitors to France knew his theories, and one American admirer, dying in Paris in 1853, left a hundred dollars a year to the needy thinker.[3] The brilliant Julia Ward, returning from Europe in 1851, made an earnest effort to acquaint herself with the philosophy. "I do not like it!" she would tell Theodore Parker, who read everything worth reading.[4] The *Methodist Quarterly Review* had published a series of able articles upon him. But Americans at large knew only that he was regarded as one of the world's intellectual innovators, a second Lord Bacon, and did not discuss his ideas. Even the elder Henry James, who read him with acute interest and wrote about him in the New York *Tribune* 1855–56, merely lumped him with Fourier and Saint-Simon as a naturalistic Utopian whose views were censurably irreligious. The curious Parke Godwin, a young man who liked to rummage in bookstores, penned an article in *Putnam's Monthly* (June, 1854) in which he gave three reasons for the neglect of Comte: the aridity of his style, the distrust aroused by his bold generalizations, and the conflict of his principles with the reigning theology. The work of Buckle was happily better known, its sweep arousing immense admiration, heightened by his tragic death.[5]

But in theology, the advanced criticism of Europe provoked discussion only in tiny circles. The currents of thought represented by Strauss and Baur, with the lesser swirl typified by Newman's *Development of Christian Doctrine*, might well have been known in the late forties, as Renan's work soon after; but

2 N. Y. *Tribune*, March 23, 1854. For the connection of the two Careys with Whig ideas, and their contributions to American economic thought, see Kenneth W. Rowe, *Matthew Carey: A Study in American Economic Development*; C. H. Levermore, "Henry C. Carey and his Social System," *Political Science Quarterly*, V, 553ff; and Joseph Dorfman, *The Economic Mind in American Civilization, 1606–1865*, II, 789–825. This issue of the *Tribune* reviewed two foreign translations of Henry C. Carey's *Principles*, one Swedish and one Italian. Wells, reared on Wayland, wrote Carey May 1, 1858, that he was now shaping all his teachings on Carey's principles; Carey Papers. For Bastiat's appreciation of Carey, see *National Intelligencer*, April 6, 1858.

3 This was Horace Binney Wallace; MS Diary of Edward Everett, May 1, 1854.

4 Julia Ward Howe, *Reminiscences 1819–1899*, 205, 206.

5 Austin Warren, *The Elder Henry James*, 121; N. Y. *Weekly Tribune*, February 16, 1856; R. L. Hawkins, *Positivism in the United States*. A lengthy review of Comte's philosophy was published in the *National Intelligencer*, March 2, 1854; a shorter one in the N. Y. *Times*, April 30, 1855. Parke Godwin republished his article on Comte in *Out of the Past: Critical and Literary Papers*, which also contains an article of 1855 on Strauss' *Jesus*.

it was not until Tennyson's *In Memoriam* appeared in 1850 that the idea of a deeper inquiry into religion, historical and exegetical, began to take popular root. The free-thinking of the time was primarily that inspired by Paine and Jefferson. One reason why new ideas made progress slowly is suggested by one of John Fiske's early letters. The troubled grandmother of the precocious lad showed the pastor his library, which included Humboldt, Lewes, Buckle, Schlegel, Theodore Parker, Strauss, Comte, Grote, and John Stuart Mill, asking his opinion; "his only response was to shake his head." Julia Ward's father, picking up a translation of *Faust*, shortly came to her exclaiming:

"My daughter, I hope you have never read this wicked book!" [6]

In science, the same time-lag was visible, and the same tendency of theory to follow old-fashioned channels. Abroad, the bold advance of scientific thought was rapidly reshaping the intellectual map; at home, the practical work of Henry, Agassiz, and Maury seemed more important. Darwin's *Origin of Species* was produced in 1859 on the basis of a general advance in ideas which made it natural that another British thinker, Alfred Russel Wallace, should almost simultaneously hit on the same thesis, and that champions like Huxley, Hooker, and Tyndall should immediately spring into the lists. But in America this general advance was dimly perceived. One of the most delicious bits of scientific myopia in all history is surely that to be found in an unpublished letter of Francis Bowen, professor of moral theology at Harvard, to the editor of the *North American Review*. Dated January 27, 1860, it remarks that "Darwin's book on *The Origin of Species* is making a great sensation," and that Bowen could furnish an article "of moderate length" for the April number. "But the interest in such a matter so quickly passes away, and the book is so sure of being reviewed at an early day in all the leading periodicals, that it will all be used up before July, and it would hardly be worth while to recur to it then." Darwinism would die within six months! [7]

The scientific writer best approved by the general public was probably the Scottish geologist Hugh Miller. When his *Testimony of the Rocks* was issued in 1857, it sold eighteen thousand copies in America in six months. So popular was his *Old Red Sandstone*, an earlier book on the geological history of his native Cromarty, that for fifty years it exercised a spell over the American imagination. Mary Austin, growing up in southern Illinois, heard it mentioned, thought the title had "a calling sound," and found in it the inspiration of some of her most characteristic books. [8] Miller, writing with force and passion, evoked a sense of the ancient grandeur of the earth, the spacious beauty of its

6 Ethel F. Fisk, *Letters of John Fiske*, 31; Julia Ward Howe, *Reminiscences*, 59.
7 Bowen to A. P. Peabody; Chamberlain MSS, Boston Public Library.
8 *National Intelligencer*, October 22, 1857, on Miller's sales; Mary Austin, *Earth Horizon: Autobiography*, 104, 105, on her debt to him.

pattern, which impressed the American mind more than Thoreau or Audubon; to dwellers in the most grandly sweeping of nations he showed the unfolding history of the globe. Two other British scientists found wide audiences. Charles Lyell's *Principles of Geology* became something more than a standard book; Robert Chambers' *Natural History of Creation* was equally famous. Both, like Miller's work, had passages comforting to old-fashioned piety; both, though soon antiquated, were admirably written; and both cleared the ground of some old prejudices. But Miller and Chambers belonged to a school of thought which England was rapidly relegating to oblivion.[9]

The sway of an older school was equally firm in the social field. In an elementary sense, a good deal of social thought was visible in Thoreau and Channing, Cooper and Bryant, Francis Lieber and Hugh S. Legaré. But of distinguished social theorists the United States was singularly destitute; it had no Carlyle, Mill, or budding Ruskin. The Puritan and Quaker consciences were amply exemplified in social and humanitarian activities, while a Benthamite impulse was also discernible. Socialism of various sorts—Owenite, Fourierist, transcendental (as in the early phase of Brook Farm), and mystical (as in John Humphrey Noyes's experiment at Oneida) flourished and faded. But newer forces were not yet to be found. Doubtless one reason lay in the fact that American life was still too elastic and hopeful, its horizons too wide and its social problems too ill-defined, to make the cultivation of social theory a necessity. No Henry George appeared because no need for one existed. Another reason was that the great snake, slavery, swallowed up the smaller snakes.[10]

But it is obvious that one defect of American letters in this period was its lack of sociological content. The grim depression in England at the beginning of the forties produced Carlyle's flaming *Past and Present;* the American de-

9 Oliver Elton in *A Survey of English Literature 1830–1880*, I, 65ff, notes that Lyell's other writings down to and including his *Antiquity of Man* in 1863 were temporarily equally influential. "He told by the mass and strength of his reasoning, and by the extreme cautiousness, noted by Darwin, of his mind; and his orthodox belief, set forth at the conclusion of the *Principles*, doubtless aided in reconciling prejudice." For his influence on one alert young American, see *The Education of Henry Adams*, ch. 15. The rudimentary nature of American scientific thought in the fields explored by Darwin, Wallace, and Huxley is evident in James Dwight Dana's *Thoughts on Species* (1857), which assumed an immanent element in the evolutionary process.

10 "I have endeavored in this work to lay the foundations at least, leaving it for others to raise the superstructure, of an American system of Political Economy, and for this purpose have subjected to a rigorous examination the leading doctrines of the science as taught by English writers. . . ." Francis Bowen, *The Principles of Political Economy Applied to the Condition, the Resources, and the Institutions of the American People* (1855). But this book too was elementary. Young Americans interested in building a science of society naturally took their basis in Comte and Buckle, and naturally went abroad to study; cf. Harris E. Starr, *William Graham Sumner*, 47ff. For early land reformers see Dorfman's *Economic Mind*, II, 684ff.

pression after the panic of 1837 produced nothing. The economic frictions rife in Britain during the forties and fifties gave the island a sheaf of memorable sociological novels: *Alton Locke, Yeast, Hard Times, Coningsby, North and South, It is Never Too Late to Mend*, and so on; in the United States they had no counterpart. Not until Rebecca Harding in 1861 published her *Life in the Iron Mills*, a harshly realistic story of the overworked, underpaid millhands of Pittsburgh, was the sociological note struck clearly and artistically. It is not astonishing that the slavery problem, a fierce djinn that hovered over every bed to produce nightmare dreams, inspired *Uncle Tom's Cabin;* what is noteworthy is that this book stood practically alone as a strong imaginative effort to treat social problems—and even it was read rather for its sentimentality than its social content.[11] America was not on the same level of hardship (or maturity) as Europe.

[II]

One of the channels through which Old World ideas reached America was travel. A trip to Europe in this generation cost much in money and discomfort, but it was an experience which intellectual Americans eagerly courted. It is interesting to compare the views expressed in the travel letters of three representative Yankees: George Ticknor, Theodore Parker, and Charles Sumner. Ticknor was the cultivated, tolerant man of the world, whose letters abound in social gossip and records of the talk of Macaulay, Lyell, and Milman; Sumner was the earnest student and moralist, almost insatiably concerned to meet eminent people, of whom he gives well-limned pictures; and Parker was the keen inquirer into social conditions, his letters full of statistics and other facts. All three were lovers of literature, versed in the great British authors particularly. They all brought home much which not only enriched their lives but stimulated others. Sumner, giving six hours a day to linguistic studies, mastering French and German, and writing home two years after he sailed that "there is no Italian which I cannot understand without a dictionary; there is hardly a classic in the language of which I have not read the whole or considerable portions,"[12] was the most laborious of the three.

11 For weaknesses of most fiction in this period see Herbert R. Brown, *The Sentimental Novel in America 1789–1860;* Fred Lewis Pattee, *The Feminine Fifties*, 50–67, 110–125. "America," wrote Hawthorne in 1855, "is now wholly given over to a d—d mob of scribbling women, and I should have no chance of success while the public taste is occupied with their trash—and should be ashamed of myself if I did succeed." His ire was specially roused by Maria S. Cummins's *The Lamplighter* (1854), the work of a twenty-seven-year-old girl of Hawthorne's own Salem, which sold forty thousand copies in eight weeks. Caroline Ticknor, *Hawthorne and His Publisher*, 141, 142.
12 Edward L. Pierce, *Memoir and Letters of Charles Sumner*, II, 118.

But all were transmitters of European culture. Even such resolute Americans as Stephen A. Douglas and Horace Greeley thought a foreign tour important, though Douglas was too stiffly convinced of republican superiority to imbibe much knowledge. People avidly perused volumes of travel that the next generation found tame, and if Bayard Taylor's books, Mrs. Stowe's *Sunny Memories of Foreign Lands,* and other descriptive works lacked intellectual content, they nevertheless did enlarge the national horizon.

Sumner made the illuminating observation that many British institutions were better known in America than at home, and many British ideas had their fullest impact in the New World. "We judge English authors better than the English themselves," he wrote a Cambridge friend. "The magazines and reviews are not read here with half the avidity they are in America; and when read are not judged with the same dispassionate fairness." [13] In a single issue the New York *Tribune* could publish three columns of correspondence on letters and art in England.[14] When Appleton's brought out the first volume of Buckle's *History of Civilization,* the *National Intelligencer* devoted almost the whole of one of its huge pages to a critique of perhaps five thousand words. Unquestionably the British reviews, republished in New York by Leonard Scott & Company, exercised as much influence in America as at home. The *Quarterly, Edinburgh, North British, Westminster,* and *Blackwood's* all had admirers. Any one of the five could be had for $3 a year, the four reviews for $8, and the four with *Blackwood's* for $10 [15]—and few libraries or reading rooms were without them. The great Victorians were reaching the apex of their power, and new books by Dickens and Thackeray, Tennyson and the Brownings were as eagerly seized in American as in British bookstores. We might distrust the memories of men who, like Andrew D. White, have described how these writers moulded their minds. But there is no discounting the fervent enthusiasm of the diarist George Templeton Strong as each new book of Ruskin's appeared in the fifties; there is no minimizing such comments as Edward Everett's in his journal for 1854— "Finished the first volume of Carlyle's *History of the French Revolution;* a work of tremendous power and equal literary ability." [16]

Our own New England school was also reaching the height of its fame and influence. A significant bit of reminiscence has been left us by Henry Howard Gratz, of the well-known Philadelphia mercantile family. Resident in the fifties

13 *Idem,* II, 18.
14 N. Y. *Tribune,* July 22, 1854. On July 18 the *Tribune* had given four columns to a careful review of Grote's monumental work on Greece. For the activities of its literary editor, see Octavius Brooks Frothingham, *George Ripley,* 202ff.
15 See advertisement in *National Intelligencer,* January 6, 1859.
16 Strong's huge MS diary, 1835–1875, is being prepared for publication by the author; Everett's note is in his MS journal June 5, 1854.

on the Missouri border, he became infatuated with Carlyle, read everything by
and about him, and in Gilfillan's *Literary Portraits* lighted upon a sketch of
Carlyle's friend Emerson. This roundabout discovery was less remarkable than
it seems; Moncure D. Conway tells of a Virginia kinsman who similarly knew
Carlyle before Emerson. Procuring the essayist's works, Gratz found them
admirable. In 1859, while a guest of Francis P. Blair in Washington, he heard
of the Burns centenary dinner in Boston and decided to attend. Arriving, he
found that all the tickets had been sold; got the secretary to issue him another
for six dollars; and when the dinner began, he bribed a waiter to seat him near
the speakers. Placed opposite Emerson, Holmes, and N. P. Willis, he requested
Emerson to join him in a glass to the health of Carlyle. Then he asked the *Globe*
reporter for the manuscript of Emerson's speech and Holmes's poem; and by
visiting the composing room at two in the morning, got both. Holmes was
there correcting proof, and the delighted young man was able to walk back
to his hotel with the poet. Seeing in the morning paper that Emerson was to
lecture in Providence the next evening, Gratz took the proper train, found a
seat beside the lecturer, and talked with him about literature all the way down.
They found the church overcrowded, and Emerson kindly took Gratz with
him to the platform.

"In speaking of the lecture," Gratz records, "I told him that it was *so*
loaded with thought and references that no one could remember a tithe of what
he said. He replied that he did not expect his hearers to remember all that he
said, but that a thought or allusion would cling to memory here and there and
thus influence character and make an impression." [17] All this was one indication
of the worship of the New England immortals that was pervading much of the
the land, and of the ways in which their influence was diffused.

For the immediate purposes of a democratic culture, Emerson, Hawthorne,
and Longfellow were much more effective than Walt Whitman (whose *Leaves
of Grass* was widely but suspiciously reviewed in the spring of 1856), Thoreau,
or Herman Melville. Their books sold effortlessly; their personalities laid a
sharp imprint on the nation. "*Hiawatha* is the rage just now," declared the
National Intelligencer a few weeks after it had attacked Whitman's volume for
its "transcendental sinuosities of thought," [18] adding that it bade fair to remain
so. "Poetical mothers christen their children by the unchristian names of
Hiawatha and Minnehaha; shipbuilders name their crafts by the same euphonious
titles; and last of all, adventurous ladies . . . recite *Hiawatha* in Indian costume,
with a background of wigwams and forest scenery, and crowds gather to hear

17   MS reminiscences. Gratz Papers, Missouri Historical Society Library.
18   Whitman was reviewed in the *National Intelligencer*, February 19, 1856.

the strange and novel performance." [19] When crowds met to listen to recitations, poetry was a democratic force.

Of Longfellow's several contributions to the intellectual endowment of common folk, one has remained inadequately appreciated. It is well understood that he imported ideas, themes, and verse-forms from Europe, familiarizing readers with much in Scandinavian, German, French, and Italian thought and art that would otherwise have remained unknown to them. But it is more seldom recognized that he clothed the bare, rocky landscape of the American past with flowers which few would have believed could grow there.

Most people would have felt that the story of the Pilgrims, while heroic, was too stern, sombre, narrow, and full of hardship to be made the subject of a brilliantly colored narrative. There was much in the history of Old Plymouth which spoke of duty and courage; little that spoke of beauty. But in *Miles Standish* Longfellow drew a succession of pictures, of which some were grimly picturesque—Standish striding on his martial errands; some were charming— Priscilla singing from her psalmbook at the spinning wheel, the carded wool like a snowdrift at her knee; and some fragrantly beautiful—the bridal procession riding through the bright Plymouth woods. Most readers of Indian legends would have pronounced them monotonous and prosaic. In his romantic ballad of *Hiawatha*, Longfellow proved that they could be wrought into a tale of bold imagination and glowing fancy, full of grace and essential poesy. A writer of the day compared him with Agassiz: one searched hill and forest for fossils, the other delved into the past of the race for primitive romance and mastodon histories of supernatural heroes.[20] The audacity with which Longfellow reached into European letters, or American legend and history, for his subjects helped give him his unequalled appeal to the popular imagination.

[III]

American oratory was in its golden prime in 1850, and at its best might challenge comparison with any in the world. To its touch on mind and emotion the people were then singularly susceptible. Not merely did the country possess a long list of political orators, from Webster and Clay down to regional luminaries like Rufus Choate in Massachusetts and W. L. Yancey in Alabama.

19 *National Intelligencer*, March 29, 1856. On the day that *The Song of Hiawatha* appeared, November 10, 1855, Longfellow wrote in his journal that "more than four thousand out of the five of the first edition are sold." Samuel Longfellow, *Life of Henry Wadsworth Longfellow*, II, 292.
20 The comparison with Agassiz appeared in the review of the *The Song of Hiawatha*, *National Intelligencer*, November 24, 1855. "What the greatest poets have done for their lands," the reviewer exclaimed, "Longfellow has done for his."

Careful attention was paid to literary discourse, pulpit oratory, and the half-informative, half-inspirational lecture.

William Cullen Bryant's commemorative addresses upon Cooper and Irving, delivered in the fifties, were shaped with classic touch. George William Curtis, in his speech of 1856 to Wesleyan students on "The Duty of the American Scholar," began a series of orations expounding the special civic responsibilities of educated men. Edward Everett, of the musical voice, magnetic presence, learning, and a rich command of language, dwelt upon patriotic themes and the national idea. He had won his spurs by his brilliant Phi Beta Kappa address at Harvard in the presence of Lafayette; he had developed his talent during five terms in Congress; and when he entered the Senate in 1853 he was regarded in some sense as the successor of Webster. No man was more unwearied in travelling to far parts of the nation. The sermons of Theodore Parker, James Freeman Clarke, and Henry Ward Beecher gave the pulpit distinction. Much oratory of the period was rhetorical and some of it flatulent; but the sinewy, close-knit argumentation of the best part of the Lincoln-Douglas debates, the lean, hard, shrewd legal arguments of Choate and Samuel J. Tilden, and the compressed passion of Wendell Phillips exhibited another side of spoken discourse.

Much that gives oratory its power over one generation can be for the next only a tradition. For all the high offices that Edward Everett held—Senator, Governor, president of Harvard, Secretary of State—he is now remembered chiefly as the man who also spoke when Lincoln appeared at Gettysburg! Yet he was the imposing Ciceronian figure of his day. Many a listener, writes Holmes, had his enthusiasm fired by "his full-blown, high-colored, double-flowered periods, the rich, resonant, grave, far-reaching music of his voice." [21] His oration on Washington was delivered 129 times before Fort Sumter, often before auditories packed from floor to dome. When he visited New York in 1856, thousands were turned away from the Academy of Music; when he went to Richmond, two thousand of the best citizens crowded the capitol; at Charleston a gathering of equal size crammed Institute Hall. There was much of the actor in Everett; his orations were full of Demosthenian "action" which left him exhausted at the end of his stated two hours. It was hard to believe, said the *National Intelligencer* in 1859, that the staid man of sixty-five who slowly ascended the platform was the impassioned, vivacious figure, now humorous, now pathetic, who soon swayed every hearer.[22] He constantly freshened his discourse, throwing into the "Washington" by 1858 telling references to Florence Nightingale and to the heroic sea-captain's widow, Mary Patton, who,

21 Holmes, *Emerson*, 147, 148.
22 *National Intelligencer*, January 6, 1859.

though newly bereaved, under twenty, and pregnant ("overshadowed by the sacred primal sorrow of woman") quelled a mutiny and bossed an ignorant crew from Cape Horn to San Francisco. It was said of his oration on Charity that no hearer would ever forget the pleasure derived from the interesting narrative, beautiful imagery, and eloquent appeal, presented with faultless grace.

What is certain is that Everett's oratory really had much of the power that Emerson attributed to it. The most distinguished people flocked to hear him. "A flowing stream of convincing wisdom," wrote one Richmond hearer. Our audience, a Charlestonian assured John P. Kennedy, was stirred "to the point of rapture." He added that Everett's sentiments had "given much strength to the Union in this quarter," and that he was generally admitted to surpass such Carolina orators as H. S. Legaré. "Learning, and taste, and genius, and profound and faithful meditation, with illustrations from all the arts and sciences, and travel and history, blend their wealth to make up the grand whole . . ." [23] Everett resented the charge that his school had more manner than matter. "My 'school' has mostly dealt with historical, biographical, and occasional anniversary subjects, and if it has erred either way it has been in the redundancy of matter," he wrote.[24] But he insisted that he was no whit superior to Choate, who had an oration on the eloquence of Revolutionary times, or Robert C. Winthrop, who was always felicitous and instructive.[25]

Equal activity was displayed by Theodore Parker. In one winter, travelling from Maine to Wisconsin, he spoke to eighty thousand people. "Hour after hour," declared one admirer, "the great audience would listen; held by the tread of a masterly and clear argument; enlivened, indeed, not infrequently by flashes of wit, and touches of poetic description." Whereas Everett spoke as a lover of the Union and went to all sections, Parker spoke as champion of the oppressed and confined himself to the North. "His end was to revolutionize public opinion; to beat down, by terrible blows of logic and satire, the cool defenders of inhuman wrong; to pour floods of fiery invective upon those who opposed themselves to the progress of a great cause; . . . to raise up those who are bowed down, and to break every yoke." [26] Much the same could be said of Wendell Phillips and the youthful T. Starr King.

Webster and Clay spoke in their prime to "acres of men"; and after they were dead, speakers in Faneuil Hall and Metropolitan Hall, at Western picnics

23 *National Intelligencer*, March 6, 22, 1856; George S. Bryan to John P. Kennedy, April 20, 1858; Kennedy Papers, Peabody Institute.
24 Everett's MS Journal, July 31, 1857. A critic had charged that in Everett's " 'school of oratory' there is the least amount of thought which will bear the greatest superstructure of oratory."
25 Everett's MS Journal, February 26, 1857; Everett, November 1, 1855, Kennedy Papers.
26 James Freeman Clarke, *Memorial and Biographical Sketches*, 124, 125.

and Southern barbecues, still enchained huge followings. In rural areas impromptu speaking was an art. O. H. Smith, an Indiana politician, relates that in 1853, making a trip to Memphis, he unexpectedly came upon a huge barbecue with which Henderson, Kentucky, was celebrating the commencement of a railroad. The chairman invited him to a seat on the platform, and as he took it announced that a distinguished son of Indiana, "a general," would address the throng. "I was taken wholly by surprise," relates Smith, "entirely unprepared, but there was no backing out, and I went ahead with an extemporaneous speech of some hour and a half." [27] Lawyers were valued in many areas according to their forensic powers, and the greatest ministers were those who held the largest congregations by their gifts of speech. Beecher, emotional by nature, his compelling personality schooled to unconventionality by his work in semi-frontier Indiana, had gone to Plymouth Church in 1847. He was soon attracting such audiences that the seating capacity had to be enlarged to hold three thousand people. "If you want to hear Beecher," ran the popular saying, "take the ferry to Brooklyn and then follow the crowd." When Virginia unveiled her grand equestrian statue of Washington in Richmond, the work of Thomas Crawford, a gathering of fifteen thousand heard R. M. T. Hunter pronounce a swelling discourse.[28]

The lyceum was a response to three separate forces: the democratic delight in the spoken word and the personality of an eminent man; the enlargement of men's interests by common school education; and the improvement in transportation. By the early fifties the system, though still unorganized on a nation-wide commercial basis, flourished so broadly that it was dubbed the "people's college." As Edward Everett noted, the most impassioned and radical views were those which the North liked best.[29] The growing excitement over the slavery issue helped give the lyceum vigor. Wendell Phillips, asked his terms by a committee, replied that for a literary lecture he would expect a hundred dollars, but for an anti-slavery address he would pay his own expenses and charge nothing.

The lyceum speakers included writers—Emerson, Holmes, E. P. Whipple; editors—Greeley, Curtis, Bayard Taylor; ministers—Beecher, Starr King, Henry W. Bellows; advocates of women's rights—Lucy Stone, Antoinette Brown; and scientists—E. L. Youmans. At its worst the institution was dull and perfunctory. "To be received at a bad inn by a solemn committee, in a room with a stove that smokes but not exhilarates, to have three cold fishtails laid in your hand to shake, to be carried to a cold lecture-room, to read a cold lecture to a cold

27 O. H. Smith, *Early Indiana Trials and Sketches,* 200.
28 *National Intelligencer,* February 23, 1858.
29 Everett, MS Journal, February 10, 1857.

audience, to be carried back to your smoke-side, paid, and the three cold fish-tails again—well, it is not delightful exactly." So Lowell wrote from the capital of Wisconsin in 1855.[30] But there was a better side. Greeley lectured with unfailing gusto. So did Joshua Giddings, who spent the winter of 1859–60 before large audiences in New England, the North Atlantic States, and the Middle West. Nearly sixty-five, the old freesoil warrior delivered his twenty-third lecture at Poughkeepsie after an exhausting December ride of thirty miles over frozen ground, and wrote his son that he felt as sore as if he had been riding a trip-hammer for a fortnight. But he was exhilarated, for he spoke out truths in plain language; "I think I am doing something for the cause and a little for myself." [31]

Discerning people found a lecture by Emerson unforgettable. "It was not a sermon nor an oration, nor an argument; it was the perfection of talk; the talk of a poet, of a philosopher, of a scholar. Its wit was a rapier, smooth, sharp, incisive, delicate, exquisite. The blade was pure as an icicle. You would have sworn that the hilt was diamond. The criticism was humane, lofty, wise, sparkling; the anecdote so choice and apt, and trickling from so many sources, that we seemed to be hearing the best things of the wittiest people." [32]

[IV]

The same impulse that dignified oratory lifted the newspaper to special importance. A people occupying a common level of education and busy with adventurous tasks and controversial issues will pay well for their journalism. Except England, no other country possessed dailies which purveyed intelligence so intelligently as the best sheets in the larger American cities. In display of news, no journal equaled the New York *Herald;* as an organ of opinion, fought in all its departments as a captain fights a battleship, none was so trenchant and effective as the New York *Tribune.* Yet as we have said, not a few other dailies might be placed near these two. The Boston *Atlas,* the Chicago *Tribune,* the Philadelphia *Public Ledger,* the New Orleans *Item,* all had their merits. "For more than forty years," Edward Bates wrote Joseph Gales in 1851, "I have been a reader (more or less attentive) of the *National Intelligencer,* and have derived from that paper more political knowledge, in fact and doctrine, than from any other source—perhaps from all other sources. During

---

30 J. R. Lowell to Miss Norton, April 9, 1855; *Letters,* edited by C. E. Norton, I, 224. Lowell's experiences were not always so dreary. "Sometimes," he admitted, "one has very pleasant times, and one gets *tremendous* puffs in the local papers."
31 See the letters from Clairmont, N. H., November 26, 1859, and from Poughkeepsie, December 11, 1859. Giddings Papers.
32 George William Curtis, *From the Easy Chair,* 25, 26.

that long period the prominent facts that constitute our public political history have all been recorded, and the biographical history of the country (so to speak) has been preserved for all of us. And still more important, almost every branch of constitutional law has been discussed and explained in its practical bearings upon public principles and private interests." [33]

It was a time of great editorial personalities, the fame of Greeley, Bryant, Henry J. Raymond, Samuel Bowles, Thurlow Weed, John W. Forney, W. W. Seaton and others filling the land; but the role of the journalistic chieftains is easily exaggerated. For two reasons the great editors were less important than they seemed. Each of the larger journals was managed by a group, not a dictator. The New York *Tribune* represented not Greeley alone, despite the cracker-barrel impression that he wrote all of it, but by Charles A. Dana, James S. Pike, George Ripley, Sidney Howard Gay, Bayard Taylor, Solon Robinson, and others of a gifted staff who (as Greeley complained) often overrode the editor. The *Evening Post* was nearly as much John Bigelow's paper, and to some extent Parke Godwin's, as Bryant's. Even the imperious James Gordon Bennett leaned heavily on able lieutenants, men like Isaac Pray possessing capacities that he signally lacked. The rule held for many smaller dailies; the picture Howells gives us of his cooperative relationship on the *Ohio State Journal* with its editor, Henry D. Cooke, a group of Republican chieftains in the background, suggests as much.[34]

Moreover, the metropolitan journals did not really dominate the national scene. It is true that in 1860 the New York *Weekly Tribune's* circulation of 200,000, and the *Herald's* daily circulation of 60,000, were rightly considered remarkable. [35] Even in the tensest days of the Crimean War, the London *Times* had attained a circulation of only 70,000. But three great factors, the huge extent of the country, the importance of local and sectional interests, and the spread of the telegraphs with their rapid transmission of news, limited the field of the metropolitan press. By 1860 the republic had three thousand and more newspapers, twice as many as in 1850.[36] Hundreds of cities were proud of their

33 Letter dated October 28, 1851, Charles Lanman Papers.
34 James S. Pike, *First Blows of the Civil War*, emphasizes the fact that the *Tribune* was managed by a group in which Greeley was simply *primus intra pares*. For Bryant's unwillingness to override his associates on the *Evening Post*, see John Bigelow, *William Cullen Bryant*, 76, 77; Margaret Clapp, *Forgotten First Citizen: John Bigelow*.
35 Frank Luther Mott, *American Journalism*, 303. The *Tribune* claimed in 1854 that it had a daily circulation of 150,000, and boasted that the circulation of its weekly edition was 110,000 copies, *Tribune*, May 19, 1854.
36 Cole, *Irrepressible Conflict*, 228. The Associated Press was formed by representatives of six New York newspapers meeting in the *Sun* office in May, 1848, and the election of that year was its first major assignment in news distribution. Correspondents were rapidly found in most major centers, and in 1856 bureaus were established in Washington and Albany. Oliver Gramling, *A.P.: The Story of News*.

dailies, and an arresting amount of talent, personality, and conviction was poured into sheets like the Cleveland *Plain Dealer*, Toledo *Blade*, Louisville *Courier*, and Charleston *Mercury*. A courageous small-town editor—for example, that staunch South Carolina Unionist, Benjamin F. Perry, with his Greenville *Mountaineer*—could then as later gain national reputation. The Richmond *Examiner* from the late forties onward was known as "John M. Daniel's paper" and read far and wide. Witty, relentlessly partisan, and full of brilliant literary as well as political articles, it filled Virginia with talk until the press could hardly supply the demand. "At every table, at every street-corner," later recalled Moncure D. Conway, "the subject was Daniel's last article." [37]

The press of the large Eastern cities had the most elaborate organization of reporters, special correspondents, telegraph facilities, and editorial specialists; but for the most striking example of courageous crusading by a newspaper in this period we must go to the Pacific Coast. The fight which James King of William conducted against corrupt and lawless elements in California offers one of the most stirring chapters in the history of all journalism. When he founded the San Francisco *Bulletin* the city was populated, as that paper said, by two classes of immigrants—the workers and the thieves. In government, the thieves, who included saloonkeepers, gamblers, and crooked politicians, had gradually gained the upper hand. By a series of masterly movements they had secured every avenue of public remonstrance and reprehension. They had gained the ballot boxes, for their minions filled nearly all offices of trust and profit. The press was theirs, for no editor dared expose their villainy. The political arena was theirs, for no man could get a nomination without giving them promises, and no candidate could obtain his election without taking from their ranks a partner in plunder. In personal combat they were irresistible, for they were crack shots and adepts in stabbing. Thus entrenched, they gained strength and boldness, until by 1855 "the theatres were filled with their mistresses, the public offices reeked with their toadies, the streets were stained with the blood of their victims."

King declared a one-man war on the regime. "At first he was scoffed at as a madman, then pitied as an enthusiast, then respected for his courage, then applauded for his independence, then beloved for his purity, his self-sacrifice, and his noble magnanimity." Finally he stood forth as the acknowledged champion of morality, the vindicator of reform, and the decent elements of the State rallied behind him. Though San Francisco admired him, his principal support came from the interior valley and mountain settlements. Not content

37 For a vivid portrait of this passionate editorial pontiff, who made the London *Times* his model and thundered like Delane, see the essay "John M. Daniel's Latch-Key" in George W. Bagby, *The Old Virginia Gentleman and Other Sketches*, 166–216.

with generalities, he denounced corrupt groups and individuals with blunt specifications. The *Bulletin* rose to a daily circulation of 5,800. Feeling the power of the rising movement, the corrupt element retaliated in familiar fashion; a felon named Casey shot King in cold blood. The indignant public uprising which followed; the reorganization of the vigilante committee to take an iron grip upon the city; the dramatic scene as King's tremendous funeral procession began its march, amid tolling bells and firing cannon, at the very moment that Casey was hanged; the general purgation of San Francisco which ensued—all this was one of the most striking episodes of the time. In its demonstration of the power of a fighting journal it was one of the most heartening.[38]

The public spirit and enterprise of the best newspapers heightened their cultural importance. Greeley, anxious to increase the influence of his journal, deliberately plowed all its profits in 1850 into an effort to increase its circulation. He spent money lavishly for new type and telegraph tolls. "Just see how we thrashed the United States this morning," he exulted to Schuyler Colfax, "in a column of news a month later from California made up for us in San Francisco by Bayard Taylor and telegraphed direct from New Orleans. . . . That hit was worth $500 at least. The whole town rings with it." [39] At two cents, the *Tribune* was the first New York paper to exceed a hundred thousand in circulation; and not only did its weekly edition go all over the North, but it published frequent special editions for Europe and for the Pacific Coast.[40]

The worst side of the press, shocking foreign visitors, was its sensational news. The Webster-Parkman murder, the Forrest divorce case, the Burdell mystery, Dan Sickles' shooting of his wife's paramour, and similar melodramas were played up with spicy detail. But special articles, written leisurely for the mails, were both fuller and better than the superficial telegraphed news which later succeeded them. Many of the best papers printed important lectures in full, gutted new books in reviews which summarized their main content (the *Tribune* gave three columns to Parkman's *Conspiracy of Pontiac*[41]), and

38 For a summary of the story see the article by "Caxton" on "The Freedom of the Press" in the San Francisco *Daily Evening Bulletin,* May 16, 1856, and the issue of May 19. Stewart Edward White deals vigorously with King's work in *The Forty-Niners,* chs. 13–16.
39 Greeley to Schuyler Colfax, January 10, 1850; Greeley-Colfax Papers, New York Public Library. A year earlier Greeley told Colfax that he was determined to build up the paper's circulation so that its influence would be felt "in future struggles"; letter dated April 1, 1849.
40 Greeley to Colfax, March 17, 1850; Greeley-Colfax Papers.
41 N. Y. *Weekly Tribune,* September 27, 1851. A week before the paper devoted some two columns to the fifth volume of Hildreth's *History of the United States.* Six months later the *Tribune* gave almost the entire first page to a review of Bancroft's fourth volume. See issues of September 20, 1851, March 27, 1852. The Ashtabula *Sentinel,* published after January 1, 1854, by the father of William Dean Howells, regularly subordinated ordinary news to literature. Excerpts from the poetical and prose works of prominent British and American authors were frequently and prominently displayed in the *Sentinel.* See E. H. Cady, "William Dean Howells and the Ashtabula *Sentinel,*" *Ohio Arch. and Hist. Quarterly,* Vol. 53, pp. 40–41.

offered serials by important authors. The Washington press gallery contained men of stature. Their dean was Nathan Sargent, who continued writing even after he became a Federal office-holder in 1849, and the others included at various times Greeley, Pike, Dana, Ben: Perley Poore, Henry Villard, Joseph Medill, and Whitelaw Reid. Though the "interview" remained practically unknown, officially inspired news articles were common.

The newspapers, like other cultural agencies, distributed their benefits unevenly. Their mobility was remarkable; they quickly followed settlers into the West, and the London *Athenaeum* commented that the American troops in Mexico had published a daily newspaper though British troops in the Crimea had none.[42] But sparsity of population and poor communications kept their Southern currency small. The total sale of all dailies below the Potomac just before the Civil War was less than that of the New York *Herald* and *Tribune*. New York City, indeed, had a newspaper circulation more than double that of all the slave States. A larger proportion of Southern than Northern newspapers, moreover, were strictly attached to party; neutral and independent journals enjoyed about two-thirds of the Northern circulation, but less than half of that below the Mason and Dixon line. For the conclusion that the Southern masses were less thoroughly and impartially informed than Northerners, much evidence could be assigned.[43]

[V]

If the newspaper press was worthy of the young republic, the periodical press was not. Magazines of force, trenchancy, and high literary merit, written for and by people who were in earnest, were few indeed. The number of magazines was legion, nearly six hundred being issued just before the Civil War, while some of them sold in great quantities—the *New York Ledger* four hundred thousand copies a week, *Harper's Monthly* two hundred thousand, and *Godey's Lady's Book* one hundred and fifty thousand.[44] But quantity and quality were largely antithetical; and it is impossible not to agree with the critics who declared that twenty million white people engaged in the most hopeful enterprise of social and political progress that the world had yet seen deserved fresher, bolder, livelier magazines, fuller of the spirit and impulse of the age.

One ponderous organ had come down from an earlier generation. Of secular

42 Quoted in the *National Intelligencer*, October 9, 1855.

43 Warsaw, Ill., *Bulletin*, June 20, 1859. Yet James D. Davidson, who in 1836 found that the Southerner's interest was monopolized by politics and cotton, records that everyone seemed to read the newspapers, and it appeared to him that the people were "well informed on political subjects." "A Journey Through the South in 1836; Diary of James D. Davidson," ed. by Herbert A. Kellar, *Southern Historical Review*, I, 345-377.

44 Frank Luther Mott, *A History of American Magazines*, II, *passim*; Edgar W. Martin, *Standard of Living in 1860*, 318ff.

quarterlies the *North American Review*, learned, polished, and timid, alone had a place of importance; and while it was venerable and respectable, no better adjective could be applied to it. Unlike the leading British quarterlies, the *Edinburgh* or *Westminster*, it had no strong conviction or salient character. It expounded intelligently the conservative view of politics and morals, and discoursed pleasantly of new books and recent scientific discoveries; but nobody looked into it for profundity, startling theories, or highly original ideas. That it was inferior to its British compeers was generally admitted. It lacked vivacity. looked too much to the past and too little at the present, and recruited its writers too much from men who inhabited libraries, not life. What was worse, it cautiously skirted those unpleasant issues and facts which stirred up controversy and enemies. Lively journalists longed to take its essayists by the collar and shake them into consciousness of the hot history all about them. In some respects it was surpassed not only by the *Southern Quarterly Review*, excellent while it lasted, but by two religious reviews. The *Methodist Quarterly*, widely read outside its own denomination, carried the best philosophical articles in the country. *Brownson's Quarterly* was even better; full of absurdities, conceit, and prejudice. but full also of logic and forcible polemics. Begun as a radical Unitarian review, it became a conservative Catholic magazine, and in both capacities its editor, who had something to say and said it manfully, gave it force and energy.

Of the literary monthlies the country had but one which it could regard with pride; from 1853 to 1857 *Putnam's*, and from 1857 onward the *Atlantic*. George Palmer Putnam founded his magazine to print nothing but original American material, published work of almost all the eminent New Englanders and New Yorkers, and attained a circulation ranging from twelve to twenty thousand copies. It had independence, variety, and a democratic Americanism of spirit, while its literary merit was attested by the number of books reprinted from its pages. Unidentified with any party, it discussed public questions intrepidly. Good judges thought it superior to any foreign monthly save *Blackwood's;* its fiction was below the British level, but its political essays, social discussions, travel sketches, and scientific papers were not excelled anywhere. An efficient editorial staff—Charles F. Briggs, George William Curtis, Parke Godwin—gave it animation and point. But the year of the panic was too much for it. Fortunately, the *Atlantic* was immediately ready to take its place. Founded by the publisher James T. Fields, whose personal charm, liberality, and keen literary judgment had drawn to his side most of the eminent New Englanders, it was assured of a long list of the best American contributors. The first issue contained Holmes' "Autocrat," Emerson's "Brahma," and Longfellow's "Santa Filomena." Far more than any other magazine, its history from the outset was intended to be, and became, part of the history of American literature.[45]

The enormous circulation of *Harper's Monthly*, which travelers found in the rudest cabins of the West, was attributable to its abundant illustrations, cheapness, varied table of contents, and assiduous presentation of Dickens, Thackeray, Bulwer, Trollope, George Eliot, and other popular Victorians. In select circles its influence was small. Everybody knew that at least half its minor articles were lifted without credit from such foreign periodicals as *Fraser's, Cornhill, Household Words*, and *Chambers' Miscellany*. They might be fragmentary or garbled and were certainly not original. The aroma of piracy that hung around the magazine and the fact that its pictorial interest largely submerged the literary made it vaguely disreputable. Yet it was almost unfailingly interesting, some original articles were genuinely excellent, and its English fiction often had classic value. It was no mean agency in popular education—and as it gained vigor, it improved.[46] *Harper's Weekly*, established in 1857, also prospered. It "now circulates 93,000, and is very thoroughly read," wrote George William Curtis with pride in 1859.[47] But till the war gave it conviction and purpose, it was primarily a picture book, a weak imitation of the *London Illustrated News* and nothing more.

The announcement late in 1858 that Robert Bonner of the *New York Ledger* had engaged to pay Edward Everett, in behalf of the Mount Vernon Association, ten thousand dollars for a series of articles, brought to notice the most striking story of magazine success in the period. A poor young man, just graduated from the Hartford *Courant*, Bonner had paid a trifle in 1848 for a small commercial weekly, the *Merchants' Ledger*, issued at fifty cents a year. He transformed it into a family paper, raised the price first to a dollar and then to two dollars, enlarged it, and began to buy such popular authors as "Fanny Fern," Mrs. E. D. E. N. Southworth, and Sylvanus Cobb, who engagingly combined the moral with the melodramatic. Its clientele grew till in 1858 it exceeded three hundred thousand, and in 1860, four hundred thousand. "The sum of its influence being instructive, elevating, and in the best sense improving to the great body of its readers," said the Springfield *Republican*,[48] "there is abundant reason for rejoicing in its great circulation." Undoubtedly many read it who would otherwise have read nothing; and if they let their attention stray from Cobb, they might see occasional contributions by Dickens and Tennyson, Long-

45 M. A. DeWolfe Howe, *The Atlantic Monthly and Its Makers*, 20-49; George Haven Putnam, *George Palmer Putnam*, 171-191. A good summary of magazine literature in the United States may be found in the N. Y. *Weekly Tribune*, January 17, 1857.
46 In 1852 the *Monthly* boasted that it was distributing 75,000 copies a month. N. Y. *Weekly Tribune*, March 6, 1852.
47 Edward Cary, *George William Curtis*, 120.
48 Quoted in the N. Y. *Weekly Tribune*, December 18, 1858.

fellow and Bryant, Greeley, Beecher, and Bancroft. With its eight power presses running twenty-three hours daily, its reputed profits of $125,000 a year, and its mass prestige won by Bonner's diligent advertising, this eight-page folio weekly, well printed and bearing one good woodcut in each issue, was a peculiarly American product.[49] The fact that it paid a hundred dollars for a short article was not without significance to authorship.

For all purposes of popular enlightenment the numerous and widely scattered religious and agricultural magazines were more potent than the 'national' periodicals. Sectarian journals were published in scores. The South alone had twenty-eight in 1850, and thirty-five in 1860. Edited usually by the most talented men in the denomination, they had their unfortunate side in the zeal with which they heightened sectarian antipathies, their happier aspect in their battle against drinking, duelling, gambling, and other vices, and their occasional bits of literature. An old postmaster's account book of the period, kept for Bennettsville, South Carolina, throws a ray of light upon the taste of a rather superior Southern town in magazines.[50] Religious periodicals constituted the largest single group taken: the *Southern Presbyterian Review*, the *Missionary Herald*, the *Baptist Magazine*, and others. Next in popularity came the *Southern Cultivator*. The local "Sans Souci Library" subscribed for *Blackwood's*, the *Southern Quarterly Review*, the *North American Review*, and the *Southern Literary Messenger*; while scattering residents took in *Graham's*, *Putnam's*, *Harper's*, *The Eclectic*, and *Godey's Lady's Book*. But church magazines had the strongest hold upon the town. It is a significant fact that during the fifties thirty-eight new religious periodicals were founded in the South, and though many died, the average circulation more than doubled.[51] At the North, the *Independent*, which, with Beecher first as contributor and then as editor, discussed social and political questions as well as religion, attained a circulation of 35,000 before the War.

As for agricultural periodicals, the best contained a great variety of materials that had nothing to do with farming. When the *Southern Field and Fireside* was founded in 1858, it was with three editors, one agricultural, one horticultural, and one literary; and its projectors announced that the most distinguished Southern authors—Augustus B. Longstreet, William Gilmore Simms, John P. Kennedy, John Esten Cooke, Paul H. Hayne—would lend their pens.[52] Much of this promise was fulfilled. Nearly all farm journals North and South con-

---

49 See the article in the Hartford *Daily Press*, December 11, 1858.
50 Gregg Account Book, 1853–1855, South Caroliniana Library. The identification of Bennettsville is not complete, for the book contains no specific mention of any town's name; but the families listed fit Bennettsville of the period.
51 For an analysis of religious publications in the Old South see Henry S. Stroupe, *The Religious Press in the South Atlantic States 1802–1865*, MS doctoral dissertation, Duke University, 1942.
52 John D. Wade, *Augustus B. Longstreet*, 330–332.

tained biographical essays, travel articles, book reviews, and bits of fiction. The *Cultivator*, which Jesse Buel had founded at Albany in 1843, and which various successors carried on; the *American Agriculturalist*, to which the original-minded Orange Judd gave distinction; and the *Prairie Farmer*, maintained by John S. Wright, were typical of many more.[53]

In Wright, agricultural journalism produced an editor who became a broad cultural leader of the Northwest. A manysided man, he promoted Chicago's first real-estate boom; built the city's first schoolhouse; became secretary of the state educational and agricultural societies; proposed the Chicago park system; urged the licensing of teachers and the opening of a normal school; supported Western railroad building; and opposed land and timber monopolies. Gifted with a contagious enthusiasm, he showed equal zeal in combating slavery and in urging adoption of the osage-orange hedge as the poor man's fence. But above all, he made his *Prairie Farmer* a popular educator for hundreds of thousands of prairie dwellers. It was a practical paper, full of readable matter supplied by nearly three hundred correspondents scattered over the West. But it made room for an educational department, printed general essays and short stories, and undertook a crusade for various important objects, including an industrial university. The reading-room that Wright maintained in Chicago for visiting farmers contained agricultural books and a wide array of farm journals. With its shrewd editorials on politics, its campaign for good schools, and its demands for a more scientific kind of farming, the *Prairie Farmer* brightened the West.

In popular impact, no publishing activities of the time produced a greater effect than those of the government. The political education of the country was largely derived from that quasi-official journal, the *Congressional Globe*. So liberally did Congress support it that in 1852 the publisher, J. C. Rives, was able to announce that he would deliver full sets of both the *Congressional Globe* and the *Appendix* for the year, containing the proceedings, debates, "the written-out speeches," the President's messages, the reports of departmental heads, and the laws of the session, for only three dollars.[54] By a law of this year the *Globe*

53 Lloyd Lewis, *John S. Wright, Prophet of the Prairies*. Other writers in agricultural periodicals had a great influence upon their respective sections; Edmund and Frank G. Ruffin in the South, Andrew J. Downing in New York, M. H. Batcham and Warren Isham in the Middle West. A fuller discussion is reserved for the subsequent chapter on agriculture. Albert L. Demaree in *The American Agricultural Press, 1819–1860*, emphasizes the broad educational influence of farm journals. They tried to avoid politics, but poetry, short stories, and news items were numerous, educational articles abounded, and they offered much discussion of social, economic, and moral problems. Demaree, 235, 236. One Southern planter, Ravenel of Hampton Hill, South Carolina, on the eve of the Civil War was taking the *Southern Cultivator, Horticulturist*, two other agricultural journals, three newspapers, *The Spirit of Missions*, and *Silliman's Journal;* Ravenel Diary, South Caroliniana Library.

54 The price went up a few dollars in later years; in 1856 and 1857 the cost of the *Congressional Globe* and the *Appendix* was $6.

passed through the mails free of postage. No other nation offered its parliamentary proceedings at so low a rate; and diffuse and partisan though many Congressional debates were, they had vast utility in supplying information and sound opinion to the people.

"It is very rarely, sir," said Senator John P. Hale in 1858, "that a debate in the Senate is intended to influence the action of members here, but it is made to enlighten the country." [55] This was precisely what the best speeches did. The Washington *Globe* had been founded in 1830 by Francis P. Blair, Kentucky banker and planter, had gained young John C. Rives as partner and business manager in 1833, was continued by them until 1849, and was conducted by Rives and his family until Rives died in 1864, when his son Franklin took it over. The plan of reporting Congressional debates fully and impartially had been originated by Rives in 1833. The years between the treaty of Guadelupe Hidalgo and the firing on Fort Sumter were a period of the keenest public interest in Washington discussions. The magnitude of the issues, the intensity of party feeling, and the forensic ability of the leaders, conspired to create a wider if not deeper concern in governmental affairs than in any other nation.

After the famous triumvirate of Calhoun, Clay, and Webster had passed away, the speeches of Seward, Sumner, Douglas, Jefferson Davis, Slidell, and Lyman Trumbull, to mention Senators alone, were followed with the closest attention. The amount of dependable economic information contained in the debates of the two houses was always noteworthy. Probably no other generation would have bought Benton's sixteen-volume *Abridgement* of Congressional debates 1787–1856, on which he labored while dying of cancer, as this one did. It was one of his unfulfilled wishes that Congress should purchase and distribute a thousand sets. Great numbers of Congressional documents were constantly franked out over the country. In the first five months of the winter session 1857–58, with its exciting controversy on Kansas, Senators of the free States distributed 680,000 copies of speeches, and those of slaveholding States 130,000 —while the House was equally busy.[56]

[VI]

That Americans read more books than any other people on the face of the earth was a fact cordially granted by foreign visitors. The literary tastes of New Englanders were already proverbial, and William Chambers was told by a Boston publisher that every Yankee mechanic had to possess a small library of his own. "People read enormously in America," wrote the Count de Gasparin.

55　*National Intelligencer*, August 17, 1858.
56　N. Y. *Weekly Tribune*, May 22, 1858.

"There is a library in the meanest cabin of roughly-hewn logs, constructed by the pioneer of the West." Anthony Trollope, after travelling all through the North, concluded that the people were the most conspicuous consumers of literature on earth. Whereas an English publisher contented himself with an edition of thousands, an American turned out tens of thousand. In Europe a porter, coachman, or farm laborer was proud of reading; in America such men took it as a matter of course. After visiting numerous homes of manual laborers, Trollope declared that he had never examined the rooms of an American without finding books or magazines in them.[57] Actually, the production of all books, including school texts, seems not to have exceeded a dollar's worth for every adult each year, but that was sufficient to support the most flourishing book-publishing industry in the world.[58]

One characteristic of the industry was its decentralization; for while of about three hundred book publishers active in 1856, three-quarters were found in Boston, New York, Philadelphia, and Baltimore, vigorous houses were at work in Albany, Auburn, Buffalo, Louisville, St. Louis, and other cities.[59] Nashville, issuing religious books and school texts, had a remarkable publishing trade. To an increasing extent, however, New York and Boston drew to the front, and the former boasted in the middle fifties that it was the principal seat of book production in the world.[60] Another characteristic of the business was its rapidity of growth. The dollar value of books printed was tripled between 1850 and 1860. Immense mechanical progress had been made since the days when James Harper and Thurlow Weed as poor lads worked together in a New York printing office in 1817, and Peter Force acted as president of the New York Typographical Society. Improvements continued to be made, and the invention of electrotyping in particular, a New York discovery which effectively supplanted stereotyping about 1850, greatly cheapened all book publishing.

Of the half-dozen leading New York publishers, Harper & Brothers had been established by John and James Harper, who began to print books in 1817; Appleton & Company had been founded by Daniel Appleton, then owner of a bookshop in Clinton Hall, in 1831; Robert Carter & Brothers, whose trade was chiefly in reprints, had gone into publishing in 1834; George P. Putnam & Co. (originally Putnam & Wiley) looked back to 1840 for its beginnings; and Baker

57 Chambers, *Things as They Are in America*, 219; Gasparin, *Uprising of a Great People*, 60, 61; Trollope, *North America*, ch. 19.
58 Martin, *Standard of Living*, 325.
59 See the article on "Booksellers and Trade Sales," originally printed in the Baltimore *American* and reprinted in the *National Intelligencer*, February 5, 1856. The handsomest edition of Borrow's *Bible in Spain* yet published came from a Cincinnati press in the fifties; a copy is in the Dartmouth College library.
60 N. Y. *Tribune*, March 23, 1854.

and Scribner had commenced business in 1846, Charles Scribner succeeding to the whole concern in 1850.[61] The house of J. S. Redfield had also attained prominence, publishing the books of Halleck, Alice Cary, William Gilmore Simms, and Bayard Tuckerman; while J. C. Derby, an enterprising businessman, had recently come from Auburn. In Boston, Charles C. Little and James Brown had united in 1837 to publish, import, and sell books, taking over from an earlier house the writings of Jared Sparks and George Bancroft. The old Boston firm of Ticknor, Reed & Fields in 1854 became Ticknor & Fields, to grow famous under that name during some of the most productive years of mid-century writing and publishing.[62]

The scope of the business of some firms was decidedly impressive. Appleton's conducted a bookstore on Broadway which in amplitude, convenience, and beauty challenged comparison with any in London or Paris. They had invested $800,000 in their business, and in the middle fifties sold a million dollars' worth of books a year. Harper & Brothers counted themselves in 1853 second only to Brockhaus in Leipzig. They were employing six hundred persons and had fifteen hundred titles on their list when on December tenth of that year their establishment in Cliff Street burned down with the loss of half their assets. But their plates had nearly all been preserved, and within a week presses from Boston to Cincinnati were renewing their stock of books. The year 1856 found them turning out three million volumes. Several publishers besides Ticknor & Fields prided themselves upon their long list of native authors. Thus Putnam, a largely self-educated native of Maine who rose to be a notable force in the literary life of America and Britain, and who wrote books himself, was pleased to be known as the publisher of Cooper, Irving, Bryant, Lowell, Bayard Taylor, Caroline Kirkland, and Susan Warner. Scribner's by 1854 had sold some 200,000 copies of J. T. Headley's popular histories, some 75,000 of Donald Grant Mitchell's works, and large numbers of N. P. Willis' scribblings, with the books of R. H. Dana and Washington Allston.

But the great Victorians held first place, the appetite for Dickens, Thackeray, Lytton, Reade, Willkie Collins, the Brontës, and others being insatiable. Reli-

---

61 See *The House of Harper; One Hundred Years of Publishing 1837–1937;* Grant Overton, *Portrait of a Publisher, and the First Hundred Years of the House of Appleton, 1825–1925;* George Haven Putnam, *George Palmer Putnam;* and Roger Burlingame's *Of Making Many Books.* A good contemporary summary of book publishing in New York city appeared in the N. Y. *Tribune,* March 17, 1854.
62 A shelf of books is required to do justice to Ticknor & Fields in American letters. The more important volumes include James T. Fields's *Yesterdays with Authors;* his *Underbrush;* his *Biographical Notes and Personal Sketches,* compiled posthumously; Annie Fields's *Authors and Friends; Memories of a Hostess* (Annie Fields), edited by M. A. DeWolfe Howe; and Caroline Ticknor, *Hawthorne and His Publisher,* of which pp. 1–112 relate particularly to Ticknor's publishing activities. Houghton, Mifflin succeeded to the literary heritage of Ticknor & Fields.

gious titles sometimes attained a great vogue, and several houses, such as Stanford & Swords (chiefly Episcopalian), and M. W. Dodd (chiefly Presbyterian) were devoted mainly to them. Carter & Brothers by 1854 had sold more than 150,000 copies of D'Aubigne's work on the Lutheran Reformation, which Andrew D. White rated later as one of the books which awakened his mind.[63]

Book agents had long been ubiquitous, and such catch-dollar publications as *New York by Gas-Light, The California Gold-Mines,* and Solon Robinson's *Hot Corn* were peddled in tens of thousands. But the primary agency in distributing books was the semi-annual trade sale to bookstores. This, modelled on the annual book fairs of Frankfort and Leipzig, had been originated early in the century by Matthew Carey, carried on for a time by an organization headed by Hugh Gaine, then the oldest printer-bookseller in the country, dropped, and finally revived and matured by Henry C. Carey, head of the Philadelphia house of Carey, Lea & Carey.[64] Various firms, acting as agents for American and British publishers, received the booksellers and auctioned off huge lots of volumes. In New York, Bangs, Brother & Company in Park Place was credited in the early fifties with holding the largest trade sales in the world; they were agents for several London publishers and handled the popular Bohn Library.

In 1855 the new Publishers' Association began supervising the regular trade sales of its members. Practical details were put in the hands of Leavitt, Delissier & Company, who owned a large and comfortable salesroom, and the catalogue was distributed to two thousand booksellers. All catalogued books were sold without reserve, and special discounts were given varying with the number purchased.[65] If Harper's, or Appleton's, or Little, Brown disposed of fewer than a hundred thousand volumes at a semi-annual sale, they felt gravely disappointed. Even in the spring just after their fire, Harper's distributed more than 200,000 volumes at the sales in New York and Philadelphia.[66]

The best publishers showed a highly commendable degree of enterprise. Little, Brown began in the fifties the fullest, cheapest, and most convenient edition of the British poets yet presented anywhere, with Francis J. Child of

---

63 N. Y. *Tribune,* March 17, 1854; White, *Autobiography,* I, 21. "Are you aware of the enormous sales of books in this country, beyond all precedent?" G. S. Hillard inquired of Francis Lieber on March 1, 1854. "Such a book as *Hot Corn* sells 40,000, Grace Greenwood's tour of Europe (perfectly trashy and worthless) 8,000, already, Mrs. Mowatt's autobiography (pleasant and graceful) 10,000, and so on. . . . The book trade in our country is to be as novel and unprecedented a thing as our political system or our social life." Lieber Papers.

64 See N. Y. *Tribune,* March 23, 1854, for a history of early book-auctioning.

65 See the article "Booksellers and Trade Sales" and the advertisement of Leavitt, Delissier in *National Intelligencer,* February 5, 1856.

66 N. Y. *Tribune,* March 18, 1854.

Harvard as general editor. He made use of Pickering's Aldine edition, but added many new volumes, and arranged for much fresh editorial material; Lowell, for example, contributing the prefatory memoir upon Shelley. Child himself furnished the series the best edition of Spenser then known, while he brought out in 1857–58 the eight-volume collection of British ballads, which, as later enlarged and revised, was to be the enduring monument to his name. Little, Brown also gave the world the first collected edition of Thomas De Quincey's widely scattered works. It announced in 1856 an edition of Shakespeare by Richard Grant White, who issued the first volume the following year. As an editor White was acute, learned, and brilliant, and though his version unfortunately coincided

The Historian George Bancroft Lecturing to the New York Historical Society.
From a drawing by Eyre Crowe, A.R.A., for *With Thackeray in America*.

with the epochal work of Clark, Glover, and Wright on the Cambridge edition, it had permanent merit. It was Little, Brown, too, which published Judge B. R. Curtis's twenty-two volume edition of the Supreme Court reports, with notes and a digest, and which issued the *Life and Works of John Adams*, edited in ten volumes by his grandson Charles Francis Adams.[67]

By a happy inspiration Charles Scribner proposed to two literary journeymen of New York, Evert A. and George L. Duyckinck, the *Cyclopaedia of*

67 See advertisements of Little, Brown in *National Intelligencer*, December 27, 1855, January 25, 1856.

American Literature which they brought out in two volumes in 1855. "We happened then to be free," writes Evert, "our weekly paper, *The Literary World*, having been recently brought to a close, so we entered heartily upon the new undertaking and were both of us engaged upon it without interruption for about two years." [68] A first edition of two thousand sets rapidly selling off, it was three times reprinted by 1868. An equally impressive compilation, this time by one man, was William B. Sprague's nine-volume *Annals of the American Pulpit*, begun in the late fifties by a learned Albany clergyman; and another was Samuel A. Allibone's *Critical Dictionary* of British and American literature, the first volume appearing in 1858. [69]

The most notable evidence both of publishing enterprise and the general advancement of American culture, however, was the commencement in 1857 of Appleton's *New American Cyclopaedia*, the first creditable work in the field. Its conception is credited to Dr. Francis L. Hawks, a man of omnivorous mind who was perhaps the ablest student of church history in his time. [70] Its original editors were Charles A. Dana and George Ripley; they found competent writers and supervised their work with rigor; and the sixteen large volumes were issued with punctuality, the last appearing in 1862. The fact that a venture of such scope should be originated in a year of panic, and pursued through all the convulsions of secession and civil war, was highly creditable to the publishers. Selling tens of thousands of sets by house-to-house canvassing, they gave the American public the first serious rival of the *Britannica*. [71] In 1860, with the work more than half done, Appleton's also brought out the first of their indispensable annual cyclopaedias.

Great quantities of the best British books, since no international copyright existed, were constantly sold in cheap editions. Most American authors and editors, led by Bryant and Greeley, denounced this piracy as a crime. Campbell and Moore had lived in straitened circumstances, declared the *Tribune*, when six cents a copy on American sales would have made them independent; Thomas Hood had left his family to charity though his books sold a hundred thousand copies in the United States. Cruikshank in 1854 sent fifteen thousand copies of one of his humorous books to America, paying $125 duty, and when some New York publishers instantly brought out cheap copies, the consignment had to be

68 Evert A. Duyckinck to J. W. Dean, May 20, 1868; Chamberlain MSS.

69 George W. Childs, Philadelphia publisher, encouraged Allibone, and issued the first volume through Childs & Peterson.

70 Frothingham, *George Ripley*, 218, 219; but Grant Overton, *The House of Appleton*, 45, declares that the idea originated when W. H. Appleton and Charles A. Dana, attending the opening of the Chicago & Rock Island Railroad, were "struck with the thought that such events should have preservation in an informative work." Hawks was for a time employed as editor; *Dictionary of American Biography*.

71 *House of Appleton*, 45

sold for waste paper. Early in 1853 Edward Everett inspired President Fillmore
to take up the subject of copyright conventions with Britain and France, but
though John P. Kennedy supported the idea, it came to nothing.[72] Henry Carey,
in fact, opposed an international copyright law and was backed by such journals as the Hartford *Times*. Many British authors received $500 for a review
article, declared this paper; some editors got $8,000 a year for three articles a
week; the novelists received $10,000 for a book which might occupy them only
a few months. Yet they had "the meanness and the impudence to come before
the Senate" and ask for royalty protection! [73]

Thackeray Offered a Copy of One of His Own Books by a Train Boy, 1853.
From a drawing by Eyre Crowe, A.R.A., for *With Thackeray in America*.

It should be said, however, that reputable American publishers did pay
British writers a partial due. For *Great Expectations*, Harper's sent Dickens
£1250, and for *The Virginians* it remitted £480 to Thackeray, while the firm
within a dozen years paid Macaulay £650 for his *History*.[74] Putnam had organized an international copyright association, and until his death always hoped
that Congress would act "next year." Nor was the situation wholly one-sided,
for British publishers sold increasing quantities of Yankee books. The two most
successful titles of 1852–53 in the British market were *Uncle Tom's Cabin* and
The Wide, Wide World. Of Mrs. Stowe's book, various publishers up to midsummer in 1853 had issued about 1,200,000 copies, supposedly the largest circulation ever attained within an equal period by any work, native or foreign, while

72 Everett to Kennedy, January 10, 1853; Kennedy Papers.
73 Quoted in N. Y. *Tribune* January 20, 1854.
74 *House of Harper*, 114.

Susan Warner's sentimental romance had sold 300,000 copies.[75] Poe, Longfellow, and Whittier among poets, and William Ware and Hawthorne among romance writers, were highly popular in England. The lack of copyright, in fact, operated in both nations as a means of bringing much good literature within popular reach at very low prices.

[VII]

The flourishing bookshops of Appleton and Putnam in New York, and the "old corner bookstore" of Ticknor & Fields so beloved of Boston authors, had counterparts in Cincinnati and St. Louis, Charleston and New Orleans, and scores of smaller cities. Russell's bookshop in Charleston was literary forum, social club, and birthplace of the Southern rival of the *Atlantic*, *Russell's Magazine*, all in one. Chicago by the middle fifties had three large bookshops. That of A. B. Cooke & Company, the greatest in the West, occupied a five-story marble structure for which it paid $8,000 a year. In the early fall of 1856 they boasted that they had sold seven thousand campaign biographies of Frémont, more than three thousand copies of *Hiawatha*, and three thousand sets of Macaulay's *England*. They also did a thriving trade in schoolbooks, a single fall order upon A. S. Barnes & Company for texts coming to almost sixty thousand volumes. The bookstore of S. C. Griggs & Company drove nearly an equal business.[76] In far-off San Francisco, Hubert Howe Bancroft arrived in 1852 to set up a bookstore destined to become both lucrative and famous.

Large and valuable private libraries were now commonplace, for it was a day when gentlemen prided themselves upon their private collections. Perhaps the most remarkable was that of the venerable Peter Force, which Charles Lanman called "the sunniest spot in Washington." It filled seven large rooms of a dingy old brick building adjoining Force's home. While an apprentice printer in New York early in the century, Force had regularly expended his savings at the auctions of a bookseller near the Tontine Coffeehouse, and as the years passed he had gone on acquiring rarities—first editions, black-letter folios, unique pamphlets, and manuscripts. He had large numbers of unpublished letters of Washington and other Revolutionary leaders, while one of his treasures was the

75 *National Era*, quoted in N. Y. *Tribune*, July 21, 1853. Miss Warner at first used the pseudonym Elizabeth Wetherell. She shortly perpetrated another sentimental romance, *Queechy*, which (with 245 gushes of tears in 574 pages) also sold enormously. Down to 1851, Joseph Holt Ingraham of the blood, thunder and religion school was responsible for 70 titles, and T. S. Arthur for 50! Lyle H. Wright, *Huntington Library Quarterly*, II, 309–318.

76 See the article, "Growth of Chicago—The Book Trade," in the *National Intelligencer*, October 9, 1856. The Cooke company not only received orders from scattered places in Illinois, but from Iowa, Minnesota, Indiana, Wisconsin, Michigan and Kansas. Its annual sales were close to $200,000.

copy of the Federal Constitution submitted to the committee on revisal. No catalogue existed, but Force was said to know the position of every one of his nearly fifty thousand items. The government made one of its best bargains when in 1857 it purchased the collection to add to the Library of Congress.[77]

Within narrower range, an equally notable collection was that of Thomas Dowse, the Cambridge leather dresser who in 1856 died at the age of eighty-four. When a young man too pinched to own shoes he had bought books. Then while accumulating a fortune, largely through the sale of legal bindings to Little, Brown, he spent much of it in acquiring some five thousand volumes, many of them rarities. Edward Everett pronounced his the most complete English library within his knowledge. On his death Dowse gave it to the Massachusetts Historical Society. Prominent among the best Boston collections were that of Edward Everett and the more specialized collection of George Ticknor, two of the intellectual jewels of the city. When Philip Hone died in 1851, the catalogue of his library showed how extensive had been that delight of his leisure hours; ranging from translations of the classics to Voltaire, from McKenny and Hall's *History of the Indian Tribes* to first editions of American authors.[78] Scattered over the South were hundreds of private libraries which emphasized ancient writers, the English classics, and politics. One fine Virginia collection has fortunately been preserved to use precisely as it stood when the storm of civil war drew the owner from its shelves.[79]

It was public libraries, however, which best showed the infectious interest of the period in books. The Astor Library in New York opened its doors in 1854, the Boston Public Library the same year, and the Peabody Library of Baltimore in 1857. The first had a national influence for the simple reason that it was under the superintendence of an expert who had made librarianship a professional study. "In the history of similar collections," an expert wrote in 1853, "there is nothing to compare or compete with the gathering of the Astor Library in New York." [80]

At the death of John Jacob Astor in 1848, funds for the library were placed in the hands of Dr. Joseph G. Cogswell, an educator and editor who early in life had been librarian of Harvard and had later become Astor's literary adviser. Cogswell drafted careful plans. He drew up lists of all the primary

---

77   Cf. Charles Lanman, *Haphazard Personalities*, 160–167; John Spencer Bassett, *American Historians of the Middle Period*. Lanman supplies a description of the collection as it stood in the fifties, visited only by friends of the proprietor, scholarly members of Congress, and literary pilgrims, and guarded by a large assortment of dogs and cats.

78   A catalogue of the Dowse collection was published in 1870; one of Hone's library by the auctioneer.

79   M. H. R. Garnett's, now at the University of Virginia.

80   Charles C. Jewett, *Smithsonian Institution Report*, December, 1853; see also the matter in H. M. Lydenberg, *History of the New York Public Library*.

books needed; then, on visits to Europe, he purchased about sixty thousand carefully selected volumes without regard to cost. For practical utility, fairness of balance among the departments of knowledge, and choice of editions, this small initial collection might challenge comparison with any of its size in the world. When opened, the library had seventy thousand titles, and its catalogue formed a guide to correct acquisition which other libraries unhesitatingly followed. By the summer of 1858 the shelves held more than a hundred thousand books, and Cogswell wrote that numerous as was the range of Buckle's citations, his learned history might easily have been written with the aid of the Astor Library. [81] Cogswell labored throughout the decade, not resigning until the close of 1861, when a new building had been opened with space for 300,000 volumes. While too new to be compared with the old institutions of Europe, the library was, as its head remarked, one of the noblest tributes that wealth had yet paid to learning.

Yet as such a tribute it was not unique. George Peabody, endowing his Institute in Baltimore, directed that it should contain the best books on every field covered, and should be maintained for free daily reference and study.[82] When Peter Cooper founded his Union, he provided for a free library which became one of the most intensively used in the country. A number of generous citizens cooperated with the municipal authorities of Boston in erecting the public library of that city. Robert C. Winthrop somewhat boastfully wrote in 1855: "I am building a Public Library, setting up a statue of Franklin, presiding over the great charitable association of the city, superintending with others the course of things at Cambridge, helping along the affairs of Trinity Church, presiding over the Historical . . ." [83] Actually, Everett's influence, George Ticknor's unremitting work, and a gift of $50,000 by Joshua Bates were more important than Winthrop's activity.[84] The various State libraries had become indispensable. That at Albany, which by 1858 had some 50,000 volumes, then ranked eighth in the country.[85] It was the State library in Springfield which supplied Lincoln with books, while Howells has described how his editor-father brought home volumes from the Ohio collection.[86]

81 See Cogswell's interesting article for the New York *Evening Post* quoted in full in the *National Intelligencer*, September 25, 1858.
82 Peabody's letter of donation is printed in the *National Intelligencer*, February 19, 1857.
83 Winthrop to J. P. Kennedy, April 17, 1855; Kennedy Papers.
84 Anna Ticknor, *Life, Letters, and Journals of George Ticknor*, II, chs. 15, 16. Ticknor was determined to make the library free and popular. "That the appetite for reading can be very widely excited," he wrote in 1851, "is plain, from what the cheap publications of the last twenty years have accomplished, gradually raising the taste . . . up to the excellent and valuable works of all sorts which now flood the country, and are read by the middling classes everywhere, and in New England, I think, even by a majority of the people." II, 30.
85 N. Y. *Weekly Tribune*, June 12, 1858.
86 Howell, *Years of My Youth*, 128.

Precisely how many public libraries the country possessed in the fifties, it is difficult to say. The census reported more than ten thousand at the end of the decade, with a total of nearly eight million volumes. But to these had to be added nearly fifty thousand school and Sunday School collections, with another eight million books.[87] According to a specialist who gave several years of study to library activities, there were eight libraries in the summer of 1858 with more than fifty thousand books; Harvard standing first, with 112,000, the Astor second, the Athenaeum of Boston third, the Library Company of Philadelphia fourth, and the Library of Congress fifth. He computed that Massachusetts, with 635,000 volumes in her public libraries, New York with 617,500, and Pennsylvania with 425,000 (all exclusive of school collections) stood far in advance of other States.[88] The South was particularly ill-furnished. Indeed, below the border States, only South Carolina had as many as a hundred thousand volumes in its public libraries. In the Northwest, small library associations were fairly common. Altogether, Americans probably had fuller access to books than any other people.

[VIII]

The darker side of the cultural scene included a widespread illiteracy which frequently allied itself with frontier vulgarity to produce appalling results. Edward Eggleston's reproduction of a backwoods sermon in *The Hoosier Schoolmaster* might be deemed exaggerated if we did not have veracious reports to confirm it. Two young women of South Carolina who visited Mississippi in the middle fifties, for example, set down the discourse of an itinerant flatboat preacher. His peroration contrasted the different sects: the highflying Episcopalians, like buzzards, the Methodists leaping from one degree of grace to another, like squirrels in a tree. "And then, my brethering, thar's the Baptists-ah, and they have been likened unto a possum on a 'simmon tree-ah, and the thunder may roll, and the earth may quake, but that possum clings thar still-ah! You may shake one foot loose and the other's thar-ah, and you may shake all feet loose and he laps his tail round the lim' and he clings forever-ah!"[89] Senator C. C. Clay of Alabama, visiting Tampa for his health in 1851, wrote back of the ignorance of the "cowdrivers" or settlers of the Florida frontier. His guide, the postman, asked him what "Presbattery" was, saying that "Pason Knight come

---

87 Eighth Census, *Mortality and Miscellaneous*, 505.
88 W. J. Rhees in the N. Y. *Weekly Tribune*, June 12, 1858. In 1853 the Mercantile Library in New York City had about 4,000 members and close to 40,000 volumes. N. Y. *Tribune*, September 12, 1853. In San Francisco the rooms of the Mercantile Library were opened in December 1856. Readers could choose from a collection of almost 6,000 volumes, 200 newspapers from all over the world, and a rich selection of magazines. San Francisco *Evening Bulletin*, December 13, 1856.
89 MS Poems and Prose by Kate and Carolina Hopkins, South Caroliniana Library (1850).

over the word a heap of times in the samon he preached," and that the school-master and a mechanic had quarreled over its meaning; the mechanic contending that it was a machine for grinding sugar, and the schoolmaster, an implement for killing Indians. When Clay explained that it was an assembly of church elders, the postman was thunderstruck at the error of the schoolmaster, who like the dominie of Goldsmith's village had been considered infallible.[90] Col-porteurs for the American Tract Society travelling in the hilly regions of the South found communities where illiteracy seemed the rule, books and papers were almost unknown, and ignorant preachers inveighed against schooling as inimical to morals.[91]

The darker aspect of culture included reactionary forces like that repre-sented by one delegate in the Kentucky constitutional convention of 1849, who protested vehemently against a State law library. In good old times, he said, a wheelbarrow or two would have carried all the law books the judges had to

90 Clay, March 19, 1851, to his wife; Clay Papers, Duke University Library.
91 A colporteur in a very destitute field in Virginia reported in 1856: "Among 35 families with an aggregate of 140 souls, I could not find a member of a church; many never go to preaching oftener than once in three or four years, and some not at all. Not more than one in ten could read, but the young people were very anxious to get books; and although they could not read a word they would sit with delight and hear me read. There are many such places to be found. These families are generally in poor circumstances, not able to buy books. The only way they can be reached with the word of Life is by the Colporteur, for a missionary preacher never visits them. Some live on the mountain top almost inaccessible; others in deep ravines."
  A colporteur in North Carolina who during the quarter found 68 of 454 families he visited without the Bible and 185 destitute of all other religious books, sent a report full of painful interest respecting the people he visited, "the great mass of whom are under the influence and prejudices of the 'Hardshell Baptists,' who oppose all denominations but their own, and also the Bible, Tract, and Temperance Societies together with all other benevolent institutions and schools of higher grade. A preacher of this sect refused to buy books saying there were too many books in the country and that books were an evil. Looking at the title page of one he said 'Published by the American Tract Society—now that word is not in the Bible—it is human invention calculated to do much evil.' Another would not allow such books to go into his house, as he said they had an evil tendency. I was ready to make allowance for his conduct, for he had a still house in his yard. A prominent member of the church would have nothing to do with the Tract Society saying that its object was evil, and in a few years it would join the Temperance Society and overthrow the government. One family had attended preaching but once in five years; there were five children but not a book in the house. Neither the parents nor the children knew the alphabet. When I pro-posed prayer the mother consented, saying it was something only two of the children had ever heard."
  An agent in North Carolina reported that "in travelling through sixteen counties, several intelligent and responsible persons gave me facts of their own knowledge showing a degree of ignorance, destitution, and belief in witchcraft of a highly startling character to the Christian & Patriot. A physician of high standing and extensive acquaintance told me he had good reason to believe that nearly half of the poorer class in his county were in this condition. A prominent clergyman told me that he spent a night with a magistrate who had no book except a small copy of the New Testament, which had never been read at all, as he thought it a book which all magistrates were furnished with simply to swear witnesses on!" Unsigned MS statement dated Tract House, New York, July 24, 1856, in E. D. Morgan Papers.

consult; they reflected more and read less in forming their decisions—and they wrote shorter, pithier, better decisions. [92] The dubious aspects comprehended the vogue of novels dealing in saccharine vein with home, children, church, and reform, a form perfected for such master-sentimentalists as T. S. Arthur to use in *Ten Nights in a Bar-Room*. They comprehended the inanities of Peter Parley, the historical simplifications of John S. C. Abbott, and the melodramatic fiction that, becoming wildly popular in the hands of Sylvanus Cobb (*The Gunmaker of Moscow* and scores of other tales), in 1860 flowered out into a new genre, Erastus Beadle's dime novels. This was the decade of Joseph Ingraham's *Prince of the House of David*, combining lurid thrills with Christian piety, and of the virtuous inanities of Fanny Fern. Examples of chromo culture were scattered thickly over the decade.[93]

Yet a systematic attempt to assay the culture of typical American communities would have revealed more that was hopeful than was disheartening. Behind an unpromising exterior often lay growing forces of promise. In Tom Taylor's absurd comedy "The American Cousin" the clownish Yankee rustic, Asa Trenchard, was presented as a native of Brattleboro. James Parton indignantly remarked that visitors would be as likely to find a Tony Lumpkin at Windsor Castle as an Asa Trenchard at Brattleboro.[94] No village was more advanced. "They have a club there for taking the periodicals of Continental Europe, such as the *Revue des Deux Mondes*, the numbers of which circulate from house to house. They have a Shakespeare Club, which assembles on winter evenings to read and converse upon the plays of that poet, each member of the club taking a part. They form other winter clubs to study a language in common under the same teacher. They have an endowed library . . ."

A young New Yorker who went to Vicksburg in 1854 to teach formed an initially unfavorable impression of that thriving commercial city. To be sure, the professional men were thoroughly educated and one of the lawyers had the best library, legal, theological, and general, that the visitor had ever seen. But popular culture was low. "There is not a reading room or public library or Literary Association of any kind in town. No public lectures upon literary or scientific subjects are delivered here." On longer acquaintance he found more

92 *Debates and Proceedings*, Ky. Const. Conv., 237.
93 "Give me Vesuvius' crater for an inkstand," wrote Herman Melville, looking across Berkshire vales to Greylock as he penned *Moby Dick* (1850–51). Some bad elements in the spirit of the age—hatred of restraint, pseudo-German romanticism, cloudy mysticism, intellectual naïveté—affected even proud Melville and grave Hawthorne; see the psychological writhings of *Pierre* and the creaky mysteries of *The Marble Faun*. The shoddy magazine element had been strong in Poe, and the shoddy journalistic touch was frequent even in so great a book as *Leaves of Grass* (1855), which Whitman tried to saturate with "audacity of freedom."
94 *Topics of the Time*, 52

to praise. including a steady advance in the standards of the public schools.[95] As a matter of fact, investigation shows that Vicksburg in 1850 had a public library of five hundred volumes, and ten years later a newspaper reading-room as well; that a number of public lecturers appeared in the fifties, including Henry Hughes of neighboring Port Gibson, who has been called the first American sociologist; that Ellen Tree, Edwin Forrest, and the elder Booth acted Shakespeare; and that the free graded public school system, which an energetic Yankee superintendent, Dr. J. G. Holland, had briefly taken in hand in 1848, was one of the best in the South. Behind its rather rowdy, slipshod façade, Vicksburg had elements of true culture.[96]

Quite as much may be said for Memphis, growing in the fifties from 8,840 people to 22,620; spending money on street improvement and railroad subscriptions until its debt exceeded a million; replacing the frame buildings of its business district with brick and stone; absorbing numerous English and German artisans. As river and rail traffic made it the metropolis of western Tennessee, it ceased to be the crude, frowzy Memphis of the flatboat era and became a hustling, ambitious little city. Of its six newspapers, two, respectively Whig and Democratic, were ably edited. It had two medical schools, one of high standards. Several boys' academies existed, two seminaries for women, and a Mechanics' Institute which offered a library, free lectures, and a night school with technical courses. A historical society was organized in 1857. To the New Memphis Theatre came Jenny Lind, Edwin Booth, English and Italian opera companies, and troupes giving Shakespeare and other dramatists. The Germans in 1860 organized a Philharmonic Society. Though Memphis had no public library, though it produced no writer, artist, or musician of consequence, though it spent far too little on its free schools (of which it had twenty-one in 1860), it also was not without vigorous elements of culture.[97]

Mrs. Trollope had drawn a scathing picture of Cincinnati at the time of her residence there in 1828–30; but when we turn to Moncure D. Conway's description of the city as he found it when he became minister of the First Congregational Church in 1856, the colors have changed. It was noted for its jurists: George Hoadly, afterwards governor, Alphonso Taft, later Attorney-General of the United States, and Stanley Matthews, in time Justice of the Supreme Court. A congenial literary club which met every week for essays, conversation, cigars,

95 MS Diary of Edward E. Welles, entry under date January 23, 1855; Miss. Dept. of Archives and History.
96 On the Mississippi school system see F. L. Riley, *School History of Mississippi*; and on Hughes see *Social Forces*, XV, 154–176.
97 Gerald M. Capers, *The Biography of a River Town*, ch. V. Nashville, however, was the cultural center of the State. It boasted a good public school system, and its university had more than 14,000 books on the shelves by 1860. The city was also the medical center of the middle South. See F. G. Davenport, *Cultural Life in Nashville 1825–60*.

and Catawba counted among its members A. R. Spofford, a future librarian of Congress, and Rutherford B. Hayes, a future President. The city library was well stocked, and a lyceum attached to it gave lectures by Emerson, Holmes, Agassiz, Beecher, Wendell Phillips, and others of repute. Pike's Opera House furnished frequent musical entertainments, including an annual season of opera or operatic concerts. Fair stock companies, playing good Anglo-American drama or melodrama, kept two theatres prosperous. Conway himself courageously attacked those ministers who denounced theatre-going, and even defended the ballet, entertaining actors and dancers at his house. Fanny Kemble gave some of her readings, James H. Hackett offered Shakespeare, and Charlotte Cushman produced a marked impression in her various character-parts.[98] The poet Clough applied to teach in the city schools.

At "The Bazaar" which Mrs. Trollope had erected to encourage the employment of women in mercantile establishments, a female medical college had sprung up. Adherents of George Rapp's "Harmonist" colony, of Robert Owen's cooperative village and workshops, and of Fanny Wright's settlement for free Negroes in Tennessee had drifted into Cincinnati, helping to stir an intellectual ferment there. One German lady kept a portrait of Rapp surrounded with evergreen as a shrine, while admirers of Fanny Wright made regular pilgrimages to her tomb near the city. Much was being heard of the experiment in coeducation at neighboring Antioch College, whose president, Horace Mann, was sometimes seen thoughtfully strolling the streets. The Lane Seminary, a Presbyterian institution, and the Jewish weekly *Israelite* founded by the learning and piety of Dr. Isaac M. Wise, brought in men of intellectual distinction and diffused an interest in ideas. Wealthy businessmen (Conway's own congregation was said to represent ten million dollars!) were collecting examples of European masters, the Catholic cathedral owned Benjamin R. Haydon's picture of Christ's entrance into Jerusalem, and an English painter had formed an artistic club which held weekly meetings. Among the newspaper workers were four men, Whitelaw Reid, Donn Piatt, Murat Halstead, and Junius Henri Browne, of distinguished abilities. Book publishers were to be found, and one of them brought out Conway's first volume. Altogether, Cincinnati was more than a centre of pork-packing and the river trade; it was a city of much light and beauty, where not a few cultivated people delighted in each other's society, in the cosmopolitan spirit imparted by British, French, and German elements, and in the tolerance befitting a border city which looked east and west, north and south.

But even younger Western cities had their graces. When Schuyler Colfax of the South Bend *Register* visited Jacksonville, Illinois, in 1859, he was

98 Conway, *Autobiography*, I, 251-364.

fascinated by the atmosphere of that offshoot of New England.[99] It had its sturdy young college—Illinois, planted by the Yale Band. It had its farm leader, grim-faced, warm-hearted Jonathan B. Turner, battler for better tillage and a chain of land-grant universities for the "industrial classes." Here lived Porter Clay, brother of Henry Clay, and here the gallant John J. Hardin ("our best Whig man," said Lincoln) had practised law till he gave up his life at Buena Vista. Here had grown up the celebrated blind preacher W. H. Milburn, long chaplain of Congress. Here Peter Cartwright often preached, and here was the home of Richard Yates, one of the best Congressmen the State ever had and its future war governor. Colfax could not know that one of Jacksonville's small boys was Edmund J. James, who would go to the University of Halle and become a leader of western education; or that Jacksonville would be the scene of William Jennings Bryan's college education and initial practice of the law.

Yet Jacksonville had no wider range of cultural interests than its neighbor Galesburg.[100] The two prairie towns were linked by the fact that Edward Beecher, brother of Henry Ward Beecher, served in both—college president in one, minister in the other. Galesburg had its able newspaper, the *Free Democrat;* its lyceum; its young men's literary club, which opened a reading room in 1855; its conservatory of music; its women's seminary; and its ten churches. At Knox College, despite financial difficulties, it had teachers of devotion and skill. It had a budding man of letters, Clark E. Carr, whose books on Illinois life and leaders would later find a large public. The first railroad train rolled into Galesburg in 1854, and four years later Lincoln arrived on a rainy October day to find an immense crowd gathering for his debate with Douglas on the morrow.

In short, centres of culture, some great, some small, were gradually being established all over America. They were created by the vitality of an idealism stretching far back into colonial days, by the accumulation of wealth, by the spread of democratic implements of culture—the newspaper, the lecture course, the public library, the literary or scientific society, the small college—and by foreign impacts brought by immigration. It was an unambitious county seat which, given a few thousand people and a fair amount of wealth, could not find a weekly or daily journal, a lyceum, a literary association, and a collection of books. The denominational college, which flourished in the South no less than the West, sprinkling its buildings from Georgia to Michigan, and following the pioneer preachers into Texas and Iowa, had both merits and defects. As we have noted, it tended to debase collegiate standards and delay the rise

99 For an account of his impressions see the Warsaw (Ill.) *City Bulletin*, August 8, 1859.
100 Ernest E. Calkins, *They Broke the Prairie*, particularly sections 5 and 8.

of true universities. Yet it did establish local centers of culture and placed a useful brake on the movement of youth toward the great cities. A newspaper and a lecture course could leaven a whole community, the former in particular reaching into rural areas and stimulating every member of literate families. In the South the intellectual atmosphere was more aristocratic than in the North; only the prosperous were likely to have access to books and advanced education. But the stratification of Southern society has been exaggerated; the middle class was much larger everywhere, and the "gentry" on one side and the "poor whites" on the other were much smaller than has been supposed. The colleges and universities of the South were full of middle class lads, and sons even of simple country farmers or storekeepers sometimes, like young J. L. M. Curry of Alabama, went on to Harvard or Princeton.

4

The Pulse of Reform

THE DAEMON of reform, Emerson called it, telling Boston at the beginning of the forties that in the whole history of the world doctrines of reform had never enjoyed such scope, that all abuses were being placed under inquest, and that the narrowest cleric, the stupidest legislator, and the sharpest money-catcher could find no fortress against the new ideas.[1] Reform was a wind sweeping throughout the world, which made the air of Manchester, Paris, and Frankfort seem to crackle with electricity. Its most dramatic manifestations appeared in the explosions of '48, when gunfire shook the continent of Europe. Perhaps England furnished it the sturdiest and most unflagging support; the England of the Chartists, the crusade to abolish West Indian slavery, the revolt against the Corn Laws, the Oxford movement, and Shaftesbury's inspiring measures of social betterment. But America was not really behind—America where Neal Dow strove for Prohibition, and Elizabeth Cady Stanton for women's rights, and Robert Rantoul for the ten-hour day, and Horace Mann for better schools, and James G. Birney for emancipation, and Greeley for free homesteads, and Theodore Parker for a purer religion; America which Jefferson had taught to believe in the indefinite perfectibility of mankind.[2]

The yeasty aspirations of countless Americans, their ardent desire to fight for moral issues or noble causes, found a typical expression in William H. Seward's speech at a university dedication in Columbus, Ohio, on September 14, 1853.[3] The country, he declared, must have a future that would be "surpassingly comprehensive and magnificent." It was to be achieved only by effort—

1 Emerson, *Man the Reformer* (1841).
2 For more than a generation the interest in reform had been rising. The diverse streams that fed it are described in C. R. Fish's *Rise of the Common Man 1830–1850;* Alice Felt Tyler's *Freedom's Ferment;* and Grace Adams and Edward Hutter's *The Mad Forties.* But the best impression of the movement is to be gained from Emerson (not neglecting his *Journals*), Thoreau, Theodore Parker, and W. E. Channing. It should not be overlooked that reform moved within strict bounds. The "chief direction of the universal activity of the age," wrote Channing in 1841, "is a conservative one, so as to render social convulsion next to impossible." *Works*, one-volume ed., 168.
3 N. Y. *Tribune*, September 16, 1853.

earnest effort. "Is the nation to become suddenly weary, and so to waver and fall off from the pursuit of its high purpose? Is paralysis to fall upon the national brain?" To these queries the answer was, Never! The republic must press on to new spiritual victories. It must do more for the progress of mankind than Greece or Rome had done. Nursed in the instructions of Milton, Sidney, and Locke, it must illustrate their ideals upon the noblest stage known to human annals. It had already produced Cooper and Irving, Morse and Fulton, but it must go on to give mankind a Shakespeare, Bacon, and Descartes. To realize its destiny, it must cultivate high aspirations, maintain a stern temper, and cherish the boldest virtues:

Now there certainly is a political philosophy which teaches that nations, like individuals, are equal, moral, social, responsible persons, existing not for objects of merely selfish advantage and enjoyment, but for the performance of duty, which duty consists in elevating themselves and all mankind as high as possible in knowledge and virtue; that the Human Race is one in its origin, its rights, its duties, and its destiny; that throughout the rise, progress, and decline of nations one divine purpose runs—the increasing felicity and dignity of Human Nature; and that true greatness and glory, whether of individuals or of nations, is justly measured, not by the territory they compass, or by the wealth they accumulate, or the fear they inspire, but by the degree in which they promote the accomplishment of that great and beneficent design of the Creator of the Universe.

Fine words!—as fine as Emerson's challenge to Americans to be poor to selfish purposes, and rich to great ends. They remind us that if the decade before the Civil War seethed with sectional and partisan hatreds, if these were the years of Know-Nothing bigotry, fugitive-slave chases, vigilante mobs, bleeding Kansas, and Congressional fistfights, it was also a time of better impulses. It was a time in which Dorothea Dix brought help to the insane, S. G. Howe gave sunshine to the blind, and Elihu Burritt pleaded for the abolition of war. Without some understanding of this zeal for reform, its ardors, successes, limitations, and failures, the era defies comprehension.

[I]

The extravagances of reform could easily be satirized. On a September day in 1853 a reform convention met at the Mechanics' Institute in the Bowery, with one John White in the chair. Its purpose was to establish a party; and to the audience White explained that numerous reforms were being agitated— anti-slavery, temperance, land-reform, protection of public school funds, stoppage of child labor—but that division prevented the advocates from accomplishing much. The time had come to fuse the various groups in one grand organization, which would advocate everything good and oppose everything bad. Resolutions were adopted declaring that a union of the whole people under one banner of clearly-defined principles offered the only salvation from current evils. At an adjourned meeting that evening trouble was encountered in suppressing a German with a new reform: every alien should be given the vote immediately on arrival. But before the session broke up "universal reform" was triumphant.

At that moment a woman's rights convention, an abolition convention, and a world's temperance convention were assembled in New York. The temperance folk met in Metropolitan Hall, with Neal Dow and Antoinette Browne prominent; the women's rights enthusiasts gathered in the Tabernacle, with Lucy Stone, Lucretia Mott, and Wendell Phillips much in evidence; and the abolitionists oscillated between the Tabernacle and Hope Chapel, where some State prohibitionists held forth. At the Tabernacle a colored woman stirred up a tempest by making a speech. At Hope Chapel two rival sets of city delegates to the State Temperance Alliance quarreled furiously. At Metropolitan Hall, Antoinette Brown, though a regularly-elected delegate, was driven from the platform and refused a hearing because she was a woman; Dr. J. McCune Smith was barred from the deliberations because a mulatto; and Wendell Phillips, after making a brief speech, was expelled on the ground that the temperance society he represented had been too recently organized. In brief, all three gatherings witnessed scenes of disorder, and the World's Temperance Convention ended in a grand row.[4] In a letter to the press Phillips fulminated against the "shameful trick" to which he had been subjected. Clearly, temperance, women's rights, and abolition did not always mix well. Hardheaded temperance leaders like Neal Dow were afraid that women in bloomers and anti-slavery firebrands would compromise their crusade.

A fringe of eccentrics, charlatans, and ignoramuses inevitably attends every general reform movement. One group of come-outers took up phrenology, which Gaspar Spurzheim had brought to America in 1832, and another set eagerly promoted mesmerism. The growth of spiritualism, which some adherents called the new religion, still better illustrated the extravagances of the time. The sensation produced by the "Rochester rappings" of Margaret and Kate Fox in 1848 spread rapidly, and when the sisters exhibited their 'occult' powers in New York in 1850, they gained hundreds of supporters. Mean-

4 N. Y. *Times*, September 7, 8; N. Y. *Tribune*, September 7, 8, 14, 1853. For three hours the crowd of angry male delegates at Metropolitan Hall shouted down every effort of Antoinette Brown to make herself heard. Although the *Times* took Miss Brown to task for her "unwomanly conduct," Greeley came to her defense. In three days of momentous achievement, he sarcastically remarked, the convention had succeeded in "crowding a woman off the platform . . . gagging her," and then finally, "voting that she shall stay gagged." N. Y. *Tribune*, September 9, 1853.

while, the mesmeric lecturer Andrew Jackson Davis, who in 1845–47 had delivered more than a hundred and fifty New York discourses in a state of trance, professing inspiration by Swedenborg and other illustrious dead, also rallied a large following. During the fifties he threw off a series of books, *The Great Harmonica, The Philosophy of Spiritual Intercourse*, and so on, which, with the exhibitions of the Fox sisters, impressed many with a belief in spirit communications. Even Greeley was half converted, while Judge John Worth Edmonds threw his great influence into the cause. Educated at Williams and Union Colleges, Edmonds had effected valuable reforms as prison inspector, sat on the highest New York bench, and compiled the standard edition of the New York statutes. Convinced of the possibility of communicating with the dead, he became co-author in 1853 of a book on spiritualism, and as late as 1859 was pouring forth articles which Greeley eagerly printed in the *Tribune*. Robert Dale Owen, an efficient reformer in various spheres, meanwhile described *Footfalls on the Boundary of Another World*.[5]

It was plain that both Transcendentalism and Swedenborgianism had done much to prepare a seedbed for spiritualism. A member of journals sprang up, Edmonds founding *The Sacred Circle*, and a former Presbyterian gaining a circulation of nearly four thousand for the *New England Spiritualist*.[6] Just before the Civil War the new sect was credited with about twenty-five thousand believers, of whom perhaps ten thousand were avowed and active supporters. Massachusetts furnished its chief stronghold, with regular Sunday meetings for a time at three Boston halls and in Cambridgeport, Chelsea, and Roxbury, much use of tracts, and even a hymnbook, *The Spirit Minstrel*. In other Eastern cities hardheaded people, including the cultivated diarist George Templeton Strong, attended seances and became convinced that while part of what they saw was fraud, part was not. Upper class intellectuals, indeed, responded more readily than workingmen, shopkeepers, and farmers. While the first flush of interest pervaded the North (little impression was made in the West and South), some orthodox churchmen inveighed with dire alarm against the craze, but the majority wisely ignored it.

Religion actually had more to fear from eccentric, rowdy, and bigoted rabble-rousers and cultists. This was the period of the antics of John S. Orr, the self-styled "Angel Gabriel," who went about the country denouncing sin and the Roman Catholics. Born in Demerara, educated in Britain, and for a time a member of the London congregation of Edward Irving, he had the fanatic temperament needed by an itinerant preacher. He attracted large crowds by

5 W. J. Stillman, *Autobiography of a Journalist*, I, ch. 9, describes typical experiments of the time. Cf. T. C. Grattan, *Civilized America*, II, 355–372. John Weiss, *Life and Correspondence of Theodore Parker*, I, 137ff., gives the attitude of hardheaded clergymen.
6 Grace Adams and Edward Hutter, *The Mad Forties*, 222ff.

Extravagances of Reform in the United States: A Meeting in New York.
Harper's Weekly, May 28, 1859.

advertising street meetings and blowing fierce blasts on his trumpet. His harangues to mixed audiences of Irish Catholics and old-stock Protestants were perfectly devised to set them fighting, and the police frequently had to interfere. Various imitators were even more provocative. Every Monday, grumbled the New York *Journal of Commerce* in 1854, just after a crowd of five thousand had been lashed to general battle by one "Moses" and a termagant female preacher, "we have the duty of recording the riotous incidents of the Sabbath day." [7] In these years the cometary flight of James J. Strang came to its lurid climax. Brilliant, audacious, unconventional, and gifted with an instinctive comprehension of mob psychology, he adopted Mormonism for personal advancement, seceded from the church when Brigham Young became its leader, and presently led a hegira to the "Kingdom of St. James" on Beaver Island in the Straits of Mackinac. Like Brigham Young, he undertook to create a planned society and a collectivist state. All its property held in common, his kingdom organized a strict central control of economic life, morals, and social activities. Strang established an imperious domination, fought off hostile mobs, repelled court attacks, and became prosperous in his new Zion with five wives. Unhappily for him, dissension reared its head.[8] Apostate followers in 1856 raised a new mob, he was assassinated, his flock was brutally dispersed, and his kingdom perished.[9]

At another of the extremes of change, the Utopianism of the communistic experimenter—one of whose essential doctrines was that a society reared on the foundation of private property finds many cardinal reforms impossible—made little real impression. One communist experiment after another broke down. Brook Farm, which was to substitute a system of brotherly cooperation for competitive greed, was decently interred as the last shots of the Mexican War were being fired. The interest of radical thinkers was then largely transferred to the predominantly French community of Icaria which Etienne Cabet (whose Utopian novel *Voyage in Icarie* had excited the enthusiasm of many French workmen) founded in 1849 by purchasing Mormon property at Nauvoo and establishing nearly four hundred colonists to operate its farm, workshops, and mills. Instead of the compulsory celibacy of the Shaker communities, its leaders sensibly adopted the rule of compulsory marriage. For a time it prospered so well that preparations were made to plant daughter colonies in Iowa and other States. But factional squabbles, the deposition and death of Cabet, the panic

7 For Orr, see N. Y. *Herald*, April 24, June 12–15, 1854; Ray A. Billington, *The Protestant Crusade*, 305, 306. For "Moses," see *National Intelligencer*, June 22, 1854.

8 Detroit *Advertiser*, June 20, 1856.

9 M. M. Quaife, *The Kingdom of St. James;* O. W. Riegel, *Crown of Glory: the Life of J. J. Strang.*

of 1857, and other troubles brought the community to complete ruin in 1859.[10] John Humphrey Noyes' Oneida community of "perfectionists," religious in origin but stamped by economic features of unusual promise—for Noyes had the qualities of a successful industrial entrepreneur—began its career in 1847 and did well when it developed certain manufactures of unique value. Its other aspects were overshadowed, however, by the extension of the community-of-property idea to community of wives, which More had expressly condemned in his *Utopia*. But true to reform ideas, the Oneida system of "complex marriage" emphasized feminine freedom of choice. As for the orthodox Fourierists led by Albert Brisbane, their movement by 1850 was passing into twilight, and one-time zealots like Charles A. Dana and Parke Godwin were becoming cynical conservatives.[11]

Though Utopian communism found in America one great favoring circumstance, the cheapness of land, its influence was in fact certain to be sharply limited by two adverse factors. It thrived best where it could gain recruits from people who felt their original lot unbearable—and such people were few in the United States; while its life seemed so commonplace, unadventurous, and even prisonlike in contrast with the eager competitive thrust and bustle outside that it constantly lost many of its younger, more ambitious followers. Public opinion was hostile to it, as the eager political use of charges of "communism" against the Republican Party in 1856 and 1860 showed.[12]

[II]

The hallmark of American reform was not eccentricity but practicality; it was essentially a pragmatic growth in a pragmatic society. In its hasty pragmatism, indeed, lay its chief defect. The American habit in treating social evils was to pay far more attention to hurried cures than to slow preventives. Very little was done to stop crime, disease, and poverty at the sources; a good deal was done to poultice such sores. This was in part because modes of prevention were poorly understood, no scientific studies of poverty, crime, and other evils being available, and in part because of the laissez faire, individualistic tradition,

10   Cole, *Era of the Civil War,* 1848–1870 (*Centennial History of Illinois,* Vol. III), 18, 19.
11   Charles Nordhoff, *Communistic Societies in the U. S.;* J. H. Noyes, *American Socialisms;* Robert Allerton Parker, *A Yankee Saint: John Humphrey Noyes and the Oneida Community.* For the business success of the Oneida group, built chiefly on the manufacture of steel traps, see Parker, 205–214.
12   When the property of the defunct North American Phalanx was sold at auction in 1855, the *National Intelligencer* made some typically smug observations about the "infatuated" experimentalists; October 9, 1855.

hostile to highly organized effort. The result was that in many fields the remedial effort just about kept pace with the growth of the evil itself. By 1860 twice as much money, pains, and labor was being given to some social problems as fifteen years earlier, but as the problems had become twice as great, the net gain was zero. While in certain areas progress was plain, in still others a loss had to be recorded. It was the old *Alice in Wonderland* situation; society had to run twice as fast to do more than keep up. There was a paucity of reformers who, in the spirit of Charles Loring Brace, active agent of the New York Children's Aid Society in dealing with juvenile delinquency, tried to probe to the taproots of great social problems.

One of the most practical reforms, the abolition of flogging in the navy, showed that even evils which arose from sheer brutality were none too easy to reach. Till 1850 the use of the cat or colt was frequent on many warships. The marines stood to their arms; the crews were herded on deck by the boatswain; the culprit was lashed by his wrists to the hammock-rail; the boatswain's mate swung the cats with all his might against the quivering flesh; at the fourth blow the purple stripes oozed blood; and after the twentieth the man's back was raw meat. Charles Nordhoff saw a score of men flogged off Rio for drinking. Some officers were notorious floggers. Captain A. S. Mackenzie of the brig *Somers*, scene of a famous mutiny, had a crew who were largely boys, yet he was forever using the cat—for noisiness, for skulking, for profanity. In one five months' period he gave 2,313 lashes to 90 persons. A statement was published in 1849 showing that aboard the brig *Independence* in a recently-completed cruise to the Pacific 44,435 lashes had been inflicted. Men were flogged in the navy yards as well as at sea. The law for naval discipline was in part copied from an act of 13th Charles II, which had been condemned even under the Stuarts as excessively severe, and from which British practice had long since deviated.[13]

When a long agitation, maintained by an untiring champion of the sailors, Watson G. Haynes, and assisted by Herman Melville's eloquent denunciation in *White Jacket*, brought about the abolition of flogging in 1850, humane men rejoiced that punishments which had scourged the manhood out of seamen no longer disgraced the flag.[14] Yet conservative naval officers raised a chorus of protest. "I venture to predict," S. F. DuPont wrote Senator Clayton, "the moment the order for the abolition of corporal punishment if unaccompanied by any other authority of power is read on board any vessel in the Pacific, that her crew will take possession of her, carry her to California, and there disembark en masse for the Gold Region, leaving the ship to take care of herself; and this will happen where corporal punishment may not have been

13 See evidence of Watson G. Haynes, N. Y. *Tribune*, March 6, 1850.
14 Charles Nordhoff, *Man of War Life*, ch. 7.

inflicted once in six months . . ." [15] Other officers asserted that when in President Jackson's time a Secretary of the Navy had recommended the use of other punishments than flogging, discipline had disappeared, and drunken, disorderly sailors had constantly insulted officers with impunity.[16] They declared that sailors guilty of misconduct stood up and took the lash like men; that it was only when they were unjustly punished that they objected to it.[17] These conservatives continued to deplore the reform. After the novelist John P. Kennedy, appointed Secretary of the Navy under Fillmore, came out in bold advocacy of flogging, so intelligent a man as Robert C. Winthrop congratulated him; [18] and numerously signed petitions flowed in to Congress for the restoration of the lash.

When some Senators supported these reactionaries, Stockton of New Jersey, who had seen the heroism of American tars in the pestilential coastal waters of Africa, among the piratical lairs of the West Indies, and in the conquest of California, uttered a fierce protest. Even felons were now spared the lash, he said. No man in the chamber would permit his dog to be thus maltreated. "There is no spot on the habitable globe known to me where a man would be permitted to seize upon a dog and lash him until he cut the flesh off his ribs, and the blood should be made to run down from his backbone to his heels." [19] Since the navy maintained the grog ration, officers would scourge men for tipsiness even while they put the bottle into their mouths. The reform stood. When the *Congress* entered New York harbor in 1853, the first warship to return to that port from a three-year cruise since the cat disappeared, the petty officers published an emphatic address to their commander. They had been treated like men, they declared; treated in a manner to lead them to respect themselves, and thus to deport themselves in a manner to earn respect.[20]

Other reforms of a highly practical cast dealt with the amelioration of prisons and lunatic asylums. This, of course, was a movement which reached far back into the eighteenth century and which would have to be carried far forward into the twentieth—for no victories could be more than partial and precarious. Dorothea L. Dix, the former Boston schoolmistress, who had undertaken to do for the American insane all that Tuke and Pinel had done in England and

15 January 24, 1849; Clayton Papers.
16 Henry A. Steel to Clayton, February 15, 1849; Clayton Papers.
17 Washington *Union*, March 3, 1850.
18 Winthrop to Kennedy, December 13, 1852; Kennedy Papers.
19 *Cong. Globe*, January 7, 1852; 32d Cong. 1st sess., 218ff.
20 N. Y. *Tribune*, July 29, 1853. Brutality continued to reign on many merchant ships. Benjamin Moran wrote President Buchanan on April 3, 1857, from the London legation: "Much has been said of late in the English papers about the brutal treatment of seamen in our merchant ships; and I regret to be obliged to confirm these reports." He thought many Yankee skippers "among the vilest villains alive." Buchanan Papers.

France—and much more—had by 1850 labored continuously for thirteen years. In that short time she had pricked the conscience of the nation to sensitivity. During a single three-year period she had traveled more than ten thousand miles, visiting eighteen State penitentiaries, three hundred county jails, and more than five hundred almshouses or similar institutions.[21] She told Congress in 1848 that she had seen more than nine thousand insane, idiotic, or epileptic persons held without proper care; a great part of them bound with ball and fetter, galled with chains, or lacerated with ropes; held up to scorn and gibes, terrified by storms of profane execrations and cruel blows; the women in some instances subjected to the most outrageous violations. Confessedly diffident and troubled with weak lungs, Miss Dix tried to avoid public appearances (though sometimes she used one to score a dramatic success, as when in 1848 her reception to North Carolina legislative leaders brought about the building of a State hospital [22]). She relied upon the press, petitions, and capable legislative spokesmen. By 1853 she had spurred the legislatures of Massachusetts and more than a dozen other States, stretching from Canada to the Gulf and from the Atlantic to beyond the Mississippi, into at least partial action. Old hospitals had been improved, new ones founded, and the crude use of bars and chains modified.[23]

Yet neglect and cruelty were giants that still devoured myriads. Not one State in 1850 afforded quarters for all its insane, or even provided properly for those whom it took in charge. Not more than a third of the lunatics of the country were in asylums, the others being held in poorhouses, public and private jails, and shelters fit only for untamed beasts. While the most populous industrial States, New York, Pennsylvania, Massachusetts, and Ohio, had four hospitals apiece, these far from sufficed for their demented, and several States lacked even one asylum. It had been abundantly proved that early and careful treatment of the mentally ill would restore half of them to health. An association of the medical officers of the various asylums, founded at Philadelphia in 1845, was steadily doing much to improve methods of treatment, while the *American Journal of Insanity*, published quarterly from the Utica hospital, drew upon the best European and American experience. Much more might have been accomplished had the government recognized the problem as demanding some national contribution, but Miss Dix's bill of 1854 for a generous land grant came to shipwreck upon President Pierce's veto. The years 1854–57 she spent largely in European travel, her work inspiring the creation of a royal commission to investigate the lot of the Scottish insane. Then she returned to resume her struggle, in which, though its first fine impulse was now lost, she still toiled

21 Francis Tiffany, *Life of Dorothea L. Dix*, 132.
22 M. C. McCulloch, "Founding the North Carolina Asylum for the Insane," *N. Carolina Hist. Rev.*, XIII, 185ff. (July, 1936).
23 Cf. Alfred S. Roe, *Dorothea L. Dix*.

doggedly. The great stumbling-block was always lack of money. North Carolina, for example, would not pay to complete its asylum; would not build a wall about the grounds, or pay the head more than $2,000 and his assistant physician more than $600; starving the young plant till the war withered it just as it gained strength.[24]

In the days of the penitentiary systems of Pennsylvania and New York, which de Tocqueville had come from France to study in 1831, America had led the world in prison reform.[25] Now the movement was making slower progress. It was directed not by one inspiring leader, but by groups and associations, among which the New York Prison Association held the most prominent place. Various State investigations, such as that conducted by the New York legislature in 1851, revealed how disgraceful were the abuses in the penitentiaries. Just before the Civil War a legislative committee in Alabama recommended a general jail-delivery of women prisoners, who were detained in such misery that "every feeling of humanity revolts at their present condition." [26] For that matter, most wardens' reports told their own story. The head of Auburn Penitentiary, for example, revealed that during 1853 more than two hundred prisoners had been subjected to the shower-bath (that is, brought to the point of drowning), and nearly a hundred to the painful punishments called the yoke or "bucking." [27] At Sing Sing the record was equally bad. "Have the days of inquisitorial tortures returned?" demanded the secretary of the Prison Association.[28] Much indignation was aroused when late in 1858 a Negro convict at Auburn was killed by prolonged immersion in the shower-bath, and *Harper's Weekly* gave two pages, with illustrations, to "Torture and Homicide in an American State Prison." The governor of New York in 1854 stigmatized the county jails of that State as nurseries of crime, and it was notorious that all over the country any investigation of them would have revealed shocking—nay, perfectly medieval— outrages.[29]

24 This was admitted by the North Carolina legislature; see McCulloch, *op. cit.*
25 America at the time of Tocqueville's visit had two penitentiary systems: the Auburn plan of social training and discipline with coöperative workshop labor, and the Pennsylvania plan of complete solitude with less severe discipline. For the superiority of American prisons to those of France, and for the European influence of American penal ideas, see George W. Pierson, *Tocqueville and Beaumont in America*, 700–717.
26 Undated paper, probably January or February, 1860; Governors's Papers, State Dept. of Archives and History. The committee also recommended that no woman be sent to the penitentiary in the future "unless under the most aggravated circumstances" and "until more suitable accommodations can be provided for them."
27 *Report*, 1854; N. Y. *Tribune*, May 11, 1854.
28 *Harper's Weekly*, December 18, 1858. A year before the authorities at Sing Sing had quelled an incipient revolt. As punishment, every participant in planned outbreak was subjected to the shower-bath treatment until half drowned. The ringleaders got special treatment: their heads were shaved, ball-and-chain were clamped on their legs, and they were put in close confinement. *National Intelligencer*, May 14, 1857.
29 N. Y. *Tribune*, January 5, 1854.

Public executions were still allowed even in some of the advanced States. On March 1, 1861, with the country convulsed by the political crisis and Lincoln about to deliver his first inaugural, eight thousand people assembled at Pekin, Illinois, to see the perpetrator of a brutal murder hanged. A Methodist clergyman seized the opportunity to address the multitude just before the trap was sprung, and the whole crowd, with prisoner and sheriff, knelt in prayer! [30]

[III]

"Our ancestors," declared Greeley's *Tribune*, "used to think that a glass of cider at breakfast, a little brandy and water or punch at eleven o'clock, half a bottle of wine at dinner, a little more punch in the afternoon, and a comfortable nightcap of hot whiskey toddy on going to bed was a very moderate and salubrious disposition." [31] Then, it added, the Temperance Movement came along.

It was true that rum and hard cider had once been universally used in New England, and whiskey in the South and West, while hospitality and wine had been synonymous. John Woolman's remarks on the general abuse of liquor and his belief that it sprang from overwork are familiar.[32] Amos Lawrence recalled how during the thirties in Ohio and Kentucky he had seen troops of travelers and farmers ride up to the country inns, take a glass of toddy, and sit in the bar till dinner was ready.[33] As times changed, Americans became too busy for the slower types of refreshment. They would take a quick glass (a Briton denounced their "damned perpendicular drinking"), but they would not loiter over wine. People at table in the city hotels and restaurants turned instead to huge pitchers of ice water.[34] Churches and temperance advocates also played their part in the change by placing liquor under a moral ban. Preachers of all evangelical sects inveighed against drink; temperance associations snowed the country under with their tracts; and essays and charts showing the baleful effects of alcohol upon the human system were scattered broadcast. The resulting social condemnation of tippling by a growing majority of farmers, shopkeepers, and professional men was not diminished by the fact that Irish im-

30 Havana (Ill.) *Squatter Sovereign*, March 7, 1861. Pennsylvania had given privacy to executions in 1834; Ohio followed in 1844. Albert Post, "The Anti-Gallows Movement in Ohio," *Ohio Arch. and Hist. Quarterly*. England, in spite of powerful protests by Dickens and Thackeray, did not abolish public executions until 1868.
31 N. Y. *Weekly Tribune*, October 27, 1860.
32 See Woolman's *A Plea for the Poor*.
33 William Lawrence, *Life of Amos A. Lawrence*, 27, 28.
34 Captain Marryat had reported a common Western greeting: "Stranger, will you drink or fight?" But when the Rev. Jabez Burns made the visit reported in his *Tour of the United States and Canada* (1848) he was astonished to find few drunken men in the large cities, and none in New England rural districts.

migrants used whiskey freely, and Germans beer; for the Celts were themselves an object of widespread dislike, while beer drinking was associated with foreign tastes and habits.[35]

It was with the aid of emotionalism—a kind of emotionalism that would perhaps have offended such early banner-bearers as Benjamin Rush and Lyman Beecher—that the temperance propaganda was now achieving its mass conversions. John B. Gough, the Kentish-born, New York reared bookbinder who descended into the valley of dissipation and delirium tremens, and then clambered up to deliver orations combining confession and exhortation in a way that enthralled multitudes, could play on every emotional chord. His Catholic counterpart was the noted Capuchin, Father Theobald Mathew, who came over in 1849 to win the Irish-Americans to abstinence, and before his departure in the fall of 1851 traveled 37,000 miles and induced half a million people to sign the pledge.[36] The "Washington" movement, meanwhile, had all the unction of a revival splurge, for the Washingtonians gave prominence to reformed drunkards, and their "experience meetings" of the forties and fifties possessed a sensationalism which appealed to common folk and made the Demon Rum seem horribly real. Other temperance enthusiasts made a specialty of joyous processions of the "cold water army," and the Sons of Temperance, with ritual, regalia, and banners, gave a martial touch to thousands of communities.[37]

Early in the fifties the main force of the temperance movement was slowly but surely converted into a campaign for prohibitory laws; for aggressive haters of drink declared that thus alone could the virtuous majority protect itself against the vicious minority. Greeley, bewailing rum-soaked New York with its six thousand licensed and one thousand unlicensed grog-shops, asserted that if the State passed a Maine law, resolute temperance men would see it executed. After experimental legislation in 1846, Maine had led the way in 1851 with a statute forbidding the manufacture or sale of drink which became a great land-

35 The connection between the drinking of lager beer in New York city and the German immigrants was pointed out in a letter printed in the Richmond *Enquirer*, November 5, 1858. According to the communication it was only ten or fifteen years since lager beer had become known "to any material extent," and yet it was already making a "complete revolution in the beverages drunk by the people."

36 In 1855 Gough returned to the States after a two years' lecturing tour in Great Britain. A great crowd greeted the reformer with "long-continued cheers" in the Broadway Tabernacle. They were rewarded with one of Gough's "telling lectures," delivered "with great effect." Newspapermen found that Gough's European tour had not dulled his ability to influence the audience. *National Intelligencer*, October 11, 1855. For Father Mathew see J. F. Maguire's *Life;* Morley's *Gladstone*, II, 192; Cole, *Irrepressible Conflict*, 161.

37 Census returns for 1860 indicate a consumption of three and three-quarters gallons of beer per capita (exclusive of home brew); and government figures estimate the consumption of wine at about one-third of a gallon. *Statistical Record of the Progress of the United States, 1800–1920*, p. 799. No figures for spirits are available.

mark of the times. Immediately Maine-law alliances were formed, State and local conventions were held, and voters were encouraged to cast their ballots for the parties and candidates most friendly to the reform. Newspapers were enlisted. P. T. Barnum, estimating that the country wasted a hundred and fifty millions a year on liquor, denounced the alliance of saloonkeeper and politician. Bankers, merchants, and manufacturers, the Corcorans, Grinnells, and Lawrences, for idealistic reasons but also realizing that drink took many a shilling from their tills, helped finance the appeal.

It was in moral New England and the Middle West that the forces of virtue and aridity carried most of their laws. For ten years the battle, swaying back and forth with variable fortunes, filled the press with news. New Hampshire was the last New England State to yield, and it fell into line in 1855. By the end of that year, most of the Northwest was also legally arid; except in Illinois, where popular vote rejected an enactment, from Ohio to Iowa prohibition stood triumphant. But in several industrial and half-urban States the struggle was doubtful. Pennsylvania passed a law after the Maine model in 1854 and submitted it to the people, who by a narrow margin defeated it. The New York legislature, in long and bitter fighting, repeatedly voted down prohibitory bills; when one finally passed, the governor vetoed it; and when his successor signed an act effective July 4, 1855, the judges quarreled over its interpretation. It was never rigorously enforced while it lasted, and its life was short. In New Jersey the upper chamber stolidly held out against the reformers, while Maryland preserved her ancient freedom in personal habits. The conservative South, the land of juleps and stingarees, was hostile to this as to other isms.[38]

In short, prohibition roared like a Khamsin wind through those Northern States which were predominantly rural, gained temporary victories in Massachusetts and New York, which were fast becoming industrialized, and was decisively checked along the Delaware River, the Chesapeake, and the Mason and Dixon Line. No slave State except Delaware became even transiently dry. The forces engaged on both sides were motley and their doctrines mixed. But in the North the mêlée revealed with some distinctness a struggle of country against city, the churches against the godless, and the native stock against the foreign-born. Once a law was passed, the question of dealing with blind pigs and bootleggers remained. While friends of the law were likely to lapse into inertia, its opponents were always sleepless. In large cities enforcement was often openly mocked. After New York's enactment of 1855 went into effect, the mayor of Albany defied it, Buffalo ignored it, and the metropolis made it a dead letter. "Hotels, saloons, eating-houses, and all other establishments where liquor has hitherto been sold sell it today as freely and as openly as ever,"

38 See John A. Krout, *A History of Prohibition, passim.*

reported the New York *Commercial*.[39] It is not remarkable that the thirteen prohibition States of the middle fifties had fallen to half a dozen ten years later.

But the moral feeling against drink persisted, and the temperance movement remained as strong as ever. As cities grew larger, the invariable partnership of drink, crime, prostitution, and poverty made the saloon a scapegoat for them all. Police Chief George W. Matsell of New York in 1852 made a report upon conditions in the metropolis during the previous six and a half years, showing that of some 180,000 arrests in that period, more than 140,000 had been for offenses (intoxication, assault and battery while intoxicated, street fighting, and the like) which were connected with the use of liquor. A majority of the 18,400 arrests for the latter half of 1851 were for drunkenness or offenses allied to it. In 1854 Matsell published more careful tables covering the eight years since the organization of his department. This showed arrests for assault and battery totalling 27,994; for disorderly conduct, 34,735; for street fighting, 4,131; for plain intoxication, 63,994; for intoxication plus disorderly conduct, 43,217; and for vagrancy, 21,115. The total of 200,000 slightly exceeded one-third of the city's population. Baldly stated, as Matsell remarked, the statistics seemed to convict New York of a frightful demoralization. But of course many persons were arrested several times, and some strangers were arrested, so that he estimated that not more than 52,000 citizens (one in eleven) had been hauled up in the eight years! The chief cause of disorder, he repeated, was liquor. At the close of 1853 the city had more than seven thousand licensed and unlicensed places selling drink, and of these more than five thousand had been keeping open to solace New Yorkers on Sundays.[40]

Descriptions of urban vice and crime usually emphasized the role of drink. The Five Points in New York, a gloomy slum quarter where five narrow streets intersected, were already internationally famous. The murky, malodorous atmosphere; the sunken, filthy pavements; the dilapidated houses; the air of sullen reckless poverty which the district represented—all this was notorious. But churches and philanthropic societies liked most to expatiate on "the dim light from drinking cellars and beer houses" and "the curses of drunken men

39 Quoted in the *National Intelligencer* July 10, 1855. A committee appointed by a religious society reported early in 1858 that it found open in New York on a single Sunday, in flagrant violation of the law, 3,408 drinking saloons. *National Intelligencer*, Feb. 2, 1858. Lord Acton in his American diary (*Fortnightly Review*, CX) was scornful of the hypocrisies bred by the prohibition law. George Combe admired the device of the striped pig. Thirsty men flocked to see this wonderful animal, paid an admission-fee equivalent to the price of a drink, and found a glass standing beside the painted china pig. *Notes on the United States*, I, 87.

40 Report for year 1853, dated February 9, 1854. The N. Y. *Tribune* took pains to collect from its own files particulars of 42 homicides publicly reported in the fourteen months ending February 28, 1859. According to the paper 28 of these crimes were committed under the direct inspiration of alcohol. N. Y. *Weekly Tribune*, March 19, 1859.

and women." The occupants of the Five Points, they said, looked sub-human as they emerged from their hovels "to throng around the doors of the groggeries." [41] However luridly overdrawn such descriptions seemed, we have the subsequent word of Jacob Riis that they did not exaggerate the scope of the evil. When George Kibbe Turner long afterward made the investigation of Chicago vice which led to the creation of that city's Vice Commission, he found that the three chief sources of underworld revenue were saloons, gambling houses, and houses of prostitution, in the order named, and that they were closely interrelated. Accounts of the worst side of city life were always being effectively used by temperance folk to arouse popular hostility to any drinking whatever. So were such exposures of rural depravity as T. S. Arthur embodied in his instantly dramatized book of 1852, *Ten Nights in a Bar-Room.*

The temperance battle, which spread from America to Europe, gaining real strength in Britain and Scandinavia, had its close relationship with other crusades. T. S. Arthur of the barroom melodrama flirted with spiritualism and Swedenborgianism, as his book *A Good Time Coming* (1855) indicated. Wendell Phillips of the woman's movement and abolition tartly rebuked a president of Harvard for serving wine at a dinner which honored a notable guest.[42] Harriet Beecher Stowe, whose anti-slavery convictions were but one part of a manysided reformative activity, refused to dine with the Atlantic Club unless they excluded liquor. Garrison was against drink and tobacco no less than slavery and war. As for Greeley of a thousand reforms, temperance was one of the causes nearest his heart. "Last spring I went West," he wrote Schuyler Colfax, "and was especially and formally invited to visit Warren, Ohio, and deliver a Temperance Address there. I did it to the best of my ability, losing three days and spending fifteen dollars therefor, of which I had to pay $8 in that village for a horse and carriage to take me out of it. About half the world would like to get the use of other people on these terms. Well, I can afford it, but it is all I can do." [43]

[IV]

The terrible cost of pauperism, and the seeming impossibility of curing it, greatly worried many reformers. America was popularly assumed to be a land of universal if crude plenty, but few assumptions could have been falser. In every city and many a rural slum, poverty was painfully conspicuous.

Philadelphia, for example, prided itself upon its general comfort. Yet in

41 Report of the Society of the Iron Man, December, 1852, in the *Ragged School Reporter.*
42 Cole, *Irrepressible Conflict*, 163.
43 March 17, 1850; Greeley-Colfax Corr.

1854 the number of its adult professional beggars was expertly estimated as fully 700, and that of vagrant begging children at 1,800.[44] The latter category included children peddling shoe-laces, matches, fruit, and the like, or picking up wood, coal, and rags along the streets and railroads. On cold winter mornings crowds of ragged women and children could be seen waiting at the rear of the principal hotels till a barrel of bones, half-consumed vegetables, and fragments of bread was thrown out to be culled over by the shrieking groups. Juvenile delinquency among vagrant children, according to the managers of a horribly overcrowded House of Refuge, was dangerously increasing. Official reports at Albany revealed that in 1855 the number of persons in New York State relieved at the public expense reached 204,000 (in a total population of perhaps 3,400,000) and that $1,379,954 was expended in furnishing this relief. The same documents asserted that during the twenty years 1831–1851 the increase in population had been 61 per cent, and the increase in pauperism 706 per cent.[45] In New York city. Charles Loring Brace, who had money, time, and the skill to do good, was much depressed in the early fifties by the immense number of girls and boys floating and drifting about the streets, with hardly any assignable home or occupation, who continually swelled the multitude of criminals, prostitutes, and vagrants.[46]

Americans have shuddered over Herman Melville's picture of a mother and children dying unregarded in a Liverpool areaway. Britons might have shuddered over a paragraph in the New York *Tribune* of February 7, 1854, relating that at dawn the previous day, the temperature near zero, a penniless woman was delivered of a child on the steps of City Hall. Few incidents of the time excited more indignation in New York than the revelation just before the Civil War that the new-born baby of a destitute woman brought into Bellevue was actually half-eaten by the rats which infested that hospital; the press rang with angry comments.

Such incidents were, of course, highly unusual, but extreme destitution, leading even to starvation, was not. Southerners noted with scorn that even in the prosperous year 1853 Massachusetts relieved some 26,400 paupers, 2,630 being children under fourteen; but the South, as we shall see, was by no means without pauperism itself. In the business depression of 1854 and still more that of 1857–58, the scenes among the poor of some large cities were harrowing.[47] From State after State came reports of crowds of unemployed clamoring for

44 Pa. *Journal of Prison Discipline*, 1853–54.
45 The report was summarized in the *National Intelligencer*, May 27, 1856. According to the report the State had one pauper to every 123 persons in 1831; one to every 24 persons in 1851; and at the time the report was made one pauper to every 17 persons. More than half of the paupers were of foreign birth.
46 *Life of Charles Loring Brace by his Daughter*, 155.
47 John Bach McMaster, *History of the People of the United States*, VIII, 296–302.

bread, denouncing the rich, and demanding legislative action. But pauperism so completely defied the reformers of the day that not one generation but several had to pass before it received even the elementary analysis given it by Charles B. Spahr, Jacob Riis, Robert A. Woods, and Robert Hunter. As yet it had not even a Carlyle to evoke in vivid scene painting the anguish of the hopelessly impoverished—"to live miserable we know not why; to work sore and yet gain nothing; to be heartworn, weary, yet isolated, unrelated, girt in with a cold universal laissez-faire." [48]

The prescriptions of the day for poverty usually included nothing more than new attacks on intemperance and a demand for checks on immigration. A few bold men suggested government schemes of employment; New York's secretary of state in 1855 proposing industrial institutions and model farms.[49] The New York State superintendent of instruction in 1856 timidly hinted at public support of all homeless children: "If the vagrants and street-beggars, if the rag-pickers and gleaners of old junk, if the houseless wanderers who sleep in coal-bins and old barrels, if the victims of starvation and nakedness, are to be gathered into the schools, the city and State must do something more than furnish them with seats, and books, and teachers." [50] New Haven, a city of about 33,000 people in the middle fifties, was one of the few communities which tried to deal constructively with pauperism. Under the leadership of James Brewster, it set up a farm in connection with its almshouse, required useful labor of able-bodied inmates, made the farm self-supporting, and restored many discouraged paupers to self-confidence and independence.[51]

[V]

The feminist movement of the period was not as yet primarily a crusade for the ballot. It was primarily a demand for equality in education, in marriage, in property-holding, and in employment. Though conservatives poured ridicule upon it, no reform movement of the time was more pressingly needed, better founded, or more gallantly led.

The stark fact was that American women were still treated as a subordinate race of beings. The middle of the century found them without adequate schools of higher instruction, with no proper rights over their persons or belongings, and with no real chance of entering most professions. Many years had passed since Emma Willard had published her *Plan for Improving Female Education*

---

48 *Past and Present.*
49 *National Intelligencer,* May 27, 1856.
50 N. Y. State Supt. of Public Instruction, *Report for year 1856.*
51 See Brewster's letter and the editorial on the subject in the N. Y. *Weekly Tribune,* January 31, 1857.

WILLIAM LLOYD GARRISON, GEORGE THOMPSON, AND WENDELL PHILLIPS

JAMES BUCHANAN

STEPHEN A. DOUGLAS

The Reformers and the Politicians

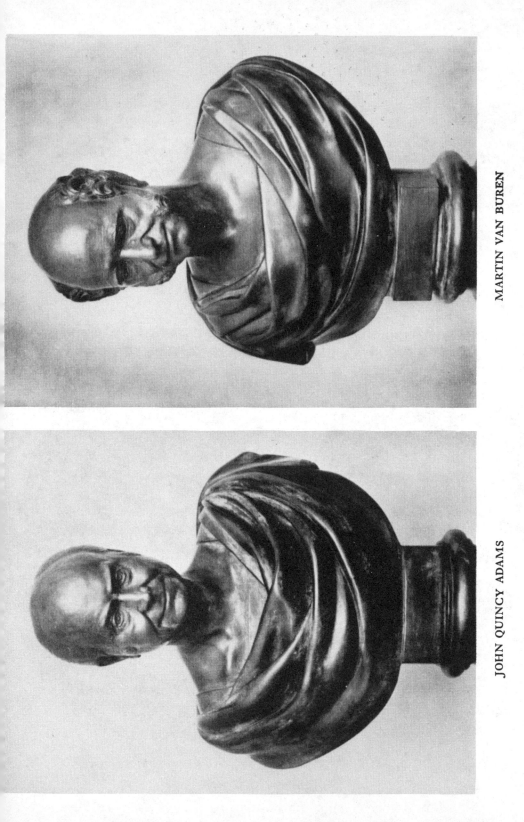

JOHN QUINCY ADAMS

MARTIN VAN BUREN

Two Surviving Ex-Presidents: 1848

(1819), since women had been admitted to Oberlin (1833), and since the first chartered women's "college" had been established at Macon, Georgia (1836). But at the beginning of the fifties Oberlin retained its unique position as the only college of real standing open to women. T. W. Higginson pointed out that if women were fitted for any education, they were fitted for all; that the true issue was, "Ought Women to Learn the Alphabet?"—but few men accepted this logic.[52] As for property, a married woman in many States could not bequeath any, though some codes provided that she could make a legal will if her husband wrote his assent upon it, or if she left everything to her husband, his assent being taken for granted! [53]

Certain cases which reached the courts were eloquent of the cruelty of various State laws upon property-holding. When a woman who fled from her husband after two months of abusive married life, taking some clothing bought by her father before her wedding, found refuge with friends, her husband sued them for the value of the clothes and compelled them to pay. Another woman also took harborage with friends; her irate husband sued them for ten thousand dollars for detaining her (though with her own consent), and recovered a large sum for the loss of her services. Though a squadron of brilliant women were distinguishing themselves in the professions, the male world believed that woman's place was the home—and the home alone.

To a great extent, women were victims not of conscious repression but of a false chivalry which masked subconscious conservatism and selfishness. They were treated as "superior" beings because men did not want the trouble of treating them as equals. In Great Britain, remarked a writer in the *Edinburgh Review*, women were regarded as sturdy, rational creatures, and expected to make due return for the respect shown them. But in America their situation was different: "There they seem to be viewed as . . . something more than mortal. All their caprices must be listened to with deference, all their whims satisfied . . . American women are, in fact, spoiled children." Francis J. Grund made the same observation. Eastern and Southern women were treated as poor helpless dependents, rather condescended to than admired. At every turn some officious man was remarking: "The ladies must be waited upon"—"the ladies must be handed into carriages"—"the ladies must have their india-rubber shoes put on." [54] Probably most women liked this attitude. "In no country," complacently

---

52 *Atlantic Monthly*, 1859. Although the older state universities of North Carolina and Michigan had refused to open their doors to women, the University of Iowa began accepting them in 1860. By the latter year the wealthy brewer, Matthew Vassar, touched by the arguments of an invalid niece, was considering a plan for the college which now bears his name.

53 N. Y. *Tribune*, September 7, 1853.

54 Grund, *Aristocracy in America*, I, 87-101.

wrote Fenimore Cooper's daughter, "is the protection given to woman's help-lessness more full and free; in no country is the assistance she receives from the stronger arm so general; and nowhere does her weakness meet with more for-bearance and consideration." [55] An increasing proportion of women, however, wanted less talk of their weakness and more of their strength; fewer friends assiduous about their rubber overshoes, and more who shared Judge Joseph Story's opinion that Jane Austen's works (his favorite novels) and other achievements proved women entitled to the fullest intellectual training.[56]

The assault upon the old common-law disabilities of women with respect to property holding, perhaps the worst of their hardships, was largely a man-made movement. The first important new legislation recognizing a married woman's right to property seems to have been passed by Mississippi in an act of 1839, followed by Maryland two years later. Then between 1844 and 1846 all the New England States except Vermont, with Kentucky and Arkansas, instituted at least a mild reform. In the next four years eight or nine other States, including New York, Pennsylvania, Wisconsin, and California in the North, and Alabama, Tennessee, and North Carolina in the South, joined the column.[57] It is clear that dissatisfaction with the common-law status of women had welled up in effective action in fully half the States before the famous convention of woman's rights leaders called by Elizabeth Cady Stanton (a pupil of Emma Willard) and Lucretia Mott met at Seneca Falls, New York, in 1848, to draw up their manifesto demanding general social and political equality. In great part a revolt against an obvious cruelty and injustice, which every man conveying property to a married sister or daughter would feel, it gained important victories in slaveholding States, which generally abhorred women's suffrage. In the North attorneys like James T. Brady and publicists like George William Curtis were shortly enlisted.

But much remained to be accomplished, notably in giving women control over their own earnings. In pursuance of a resolution of the national woman's rights convention held in New York in 1856, memorials were presented to a number of legislatures that winter. Ohio, Indiana, and Missouri passed laws similar to one recently enacted in Wisconsin, providing that if a woman were compelled through neglect or desertion by her husband to provide for herself and her children, she was entitled to her earnings and to all property bought with it; while a law of Maine gave married women full control of all wages

---

55 Susan Fenimore Cooper, *Rural Hours* (1850).
56 As a boy Story had attended the coeducational classes of Marblehead Academy; M. E. Phillips, *Reminiscences of William Wetmore Story*, 19–53. W. W. Story's work on *Contracts*, 1844, contained a protest against legal injustices to women; *Id.*, 61.
57 Henry Hitchcock, "Modern Legislation Touching Marital Property Rights," *Journal of Social Science* (March, 1881).

received for services outside the home, whether neglected by husbands or not.[58]

All feminist leaders held that if women were properly educated and were given full liberty to mingle in business and professional work, they could become infinitely more useful to themselves and to society. "Let them be sea-captains if they will," Margaret Fuller remarked—and the press was soon celebrating Miss Betsey Miller, skipper for a dozen years of the Scottish brig *Cloetus*. It was possible by the late forties to point to Harriet Hosmer, the sculptor; Maria Mitchell, the astronomer; Lucretia Mott and Antoinette Brown, the preachers; Harriet Hunt, the physician; and Jane Grey Swisshelm, the successful editor.[59] There were women merchants, women lawyers, women lecturers (Lucy Stone, Elizabeth Cady Stanton, Susan B. Anthony, and Mrs. Swisshelm were familiar platform figures), and a whole division of women writers. Few men earned more by the pen than "Fanny Fern" (Sara P. Willis); and the midsummer issue of *Godey's Lady's Book* in 1849, "the greatest number yet issued," had twelve female as against fifteen male contributors, including Mrs. E. F. Ellet, Grace Greenwood, Alice Cary, and Sarah J. Hale.

When a Western editor declared that he was against the women's movement because it might yet land a Harriet Beecher Stowe in the White House, T. W. Higginson commented that for the same reason he supported it.[60] Women had displayed notable powers of leadership in the anti-slavery and temperance movements and in philanthropy. Harriet Martineau, in her highly-colored book *The Martyr Age in the United States*, was severe upon Margaret Fuller, asserting that she and her pupils sat about talking of Plato and Goethe and fancying themselves intellectual monitors while basic human liberties were being assaulted. But among Margaret Fuller's disciples were two women who taught Miss Martineau her first lessons in abolitionism, Lydia Maria Child and Mrs. Ellis Gray Loring; one girl, Maria White, who as James Russell Lowell's wife did much to make him an abolitionist; and others who helped lead the philanthropic action of Massachusetts.[61]

About the activities of the Blackwell family an entire chapter in the history of women's rights could be written. The brilliant and indomitable Elizabeth Blackwell was one of a family of nine children who in 1832 emigrated from England. She determined to become a doctor, and supporting herself by school-teaching at Asheville, North Carolina, began reading medical books in 1845.

58 *National Intelligencer*, August 1, 1857; for the Wisconsin law, May 26, 1855. May 26, 1855.

59 See A. J. Larsen, ed., *Crusader and Feminists, Letters of Jane Grey Swisshelm*. It was possible for John S. Hart to publish a book in the early fifties on *The Female Prose Writers of America*.

60 Higginson, *Woman and Her Wishes*, Woman's Rights Tracts, No. 4, 1851

61 T. W. Higginson, *Margaret Fuller Ossoli*, 126ff.

She soon studied more systematically under a professor at Charleston Medical College, and after rebuffs in Philadelphia and New York, gained entry in the fall of 1847 to the Geneva Medical School in western New York. Regarded as either "mad or bad," she never lost courage; she took her medical degree with highest honors in 1849 and sailed immediately for Europe to study at La Maternité in Paris and St. Bartholomew's in London. On leaving the latter institution, she was admitted to English practise in all branches of medicine except pediatrics and gynecology, and received warm congratulations from Florence Nightingale and numerous English scientists of note. Returning to New York in 1850 to practise, she soon opened a private dispensary, which in the spring of 1857 was enlarged into the New York Infirmary and College for Women, a hospital and teaching institution conducted for and by women alone. By that time medical colleges for women had been established in Boston (1848) and Philadelphia (1850), and though their graduates encountered much professional as well as popular prejudice, they helped blaze the way for the ultimate establishment of medical training on a coeducational basis—a reform which Dr. Oliver Wendell Holmes had courage enough to support at Harvard.

Elizabeth Blackwell's sister Emily assisted in founding her infirmary and college. Their brother Henry became an enthusiastic adherent of the anti-slavery and women's suffrage movements, formed a friendship with the attractive Lucy Stone and in 1855 married her—the two publishing on their wedding day a joint protest against the inequalities of the marriage laws. Lucy, her militant temper ill-matched by her girlish figure, bright cheeks, and musical voice, but expressing itself in rapid, confident, and slightly saucy utterance, gave up the ridiculous, impertinent little bloomer costume she had long affected—but did not give up her maiden name.[62] Henry possessed a shrewd business talent and accumulated a considerable fortune, much of which he devoted to agricultural reform, women's suffrage, and other causes. A second brother, Samuel C. Blackwell, married Antoinette Brown, the militant feminist who, after education at Oberlin, had been ordained a Congregational minister in 1853; and he was her partner in religious and temperance endeavors, and in various branches of Civil War activities.

All of this remarkable group extended their activities through a long generation. Elizabeth Blackwell, after organizing an efficient unit of field nurses during the war, returned to England for an influential career as medical teacher and writer until her death in 1910. Henry B. Blackwell, one of the pillars of the American Woman Suffrage Association from its founding soon after the war, lived

---

62 E. M. Mesnard, *Elizabeth Blackwell et les Femmes Médecins.* For Lucy Stone's bloomer costume see N. Y. *Weekly Tribune,* March 10, 1860. Elizabeth Blackwell's *Pioneer Work for Women* is a classic human document.

until 1909, interested to the last in a wide range of reform causes, from the abolition of Russian pogroms to the promotion of free trade. Antoinette, living to be ninety-six, was till her death in 1921 a valiant fighter for women's rights and temperance, and as much could be said for Lucy Stone. Few family groups have left so deep an impress on the general liberal movement.[63]

It was not the specially talented woman, however, but the average woman, who most needed a larger sphere of opportunity; and however much the speakers at the recurrent women's rights conventions of the fifties might talk about political privileges and intellectual emancipation, it was the economic position of women which chiefly troubled them.

Money is power, wrote Elizabeth Cady Stanton to the Worcester convention in 1851. The majority of women truly supported themselves, but by working sixteen hours out of the twenty-four, and all too generally at slavish and unprofitable occupations. "If, in the pursuit of happiness, we take possession of all the post offices, daguerreotype rooms, telegraph offices, book, china, silk, lace stores, and the like, we have abundant excuse for what seems the beginning of a most aggressive warfare in the fact that we have heretofore been crowded by these lordly monopolizers almost off the footstep." The report of Paulina Davis for the committee on education complained bitterly that women were overwhelmingly restricted to the duties and drudgeries of domestic work and could never rise without a wider field of occupation—a note struck by nearly all the speakers. Health was important because it would enable women to compete with men. Education was important because it would train them to do so. A larger view of women's capacities was important because it would throw open many avenues of effort. The ballot was important because it would help women protect their earnings. But at the foundation of the whole movement lay the economic groundsill, and the look ambitious women bent on the world was preëminently the twelve-pound look of J. M. Barrie's heroine yearning for a typewriter and independence. Among the resolutions adopted at Worcester were two declaring that women must seek a new order of employments, for marriage and the needle were inadequate, and that men would have freer scope for their own mental and physical endowments if they yielded minor business and professional jobs to their sisters. "Go, get you gold by honest toil," was Mrs. Stanton's concluding exhortation to the delegates.[64]

Yet the prevalent mood of the country remained hostile, or what was worse, indifferent. It was thought that girls might temporarily find employment as factory hands, clerks, milliners, and schoolteachers, but these employments should lead to marriage, not to permanent independence. Much of the press

63 See sketches in the *Dictionary of American Biography.*
64 N. Y. *Weekly Tribune*, October 23, 1851.

never tired of sneering at the supposed Amazons who filled the women's rights
conventions. The real place of woman, ran the typical Victorian gush of the
Buffalo *Commercial Advertiser*, was as "the angel of man's home, the wife of
his heart, the mother of his children, the sharer of his joys, and the soother of
his sorrows"; if she pushed into the learned professions, worked at the bench,
and drove the engine, who then would cook the dinner, mend the clothes, and
quiet the baby? [65] James Gordon Bennett's *Herald* declared that Lucy Stone
was fit for a lunatic asylum, and that it was the fixed sentiment of America and
all other civilized countries that the rights of women, like their duties, were
bounded by the household.[66] So redoubtable a champion of higher education in
agriculture and engineering as Jonathan B. Turner, whose strenuous labors
during the fifties were one factor in the ultimate grant of land-endowments
to a long list of State colleges and universities, did not include women in his
scheme. Demanding education on a broad democratic basis for all the "industrial
classes," he thought of men alone.[67]

If slow but fairly steady progress was made it was because the incessant
labors of the women's rights advocates were assisted by natural factors in a
country of public-school co-education, frequent labor scarcity, and a type of
Western pioneering that demanded as much hardy toil and initiative of women
as of men. Of all the States, Indiana was perhaps the most progressive in its
legislation for women. This was partly because of the farsighted liberalism of
Robert Dale Owen, onetime friend of the impassioned Fanny Wright, and a
leading member of the Indiana constitutional convention of 1850, whose bust
has been placed by the women of the State in its capitol grounds. It was also
partly because pioneer life in Indiana placed a high valuation on women, and
made even its easy divorce system (the scandal of older States) seem natural.[68]
Labor scarcity had given two-thirds of the teaching positions in Massachusetts
schools by 1850 to women, who during the next ten years crowded into the
teaching field in most other States.[69]

Year by year more women were found in factories and stores; year by year
a larger number emerged as artists, authors, editors, and ministers. The shock

65 Quoted in the *National Intelligencer*, September 21, 1852.
66 N. Y. *Herald*, April 4, 1858; Cole, *Irrepressible Conflict*, 177. "I found the 'woman's
rights' spirit very intense in Philadelphia, and also a counter-spirit quite as strong," wrote
Horace Mann in 1852; *Life* by his wife, 392.
67 Mary Turner Carriel, *Life of Jonathan B. Turner*, chs. 11-14
68 On Indiana and Owen's influence on the women's rights movements in the State see
the *Nation*, July 5, 1877. On divorce see also Stanton, *E. C. Stanton*, II, 49; Cole, *Irrepressible Conflict*, 172, 173. The *National Intelligencer* of November 9, 1858, quotes Judge
Test of Indiana as saying that the dockets in every circuit were burdened with divorce
applications, "a large portion of which are made by persons who were never seen in the
States till a few weeks before the sitting of the courts."
69 Cole, *Irrepressible Conflict*, 175.

of seeing women in bloomers, at least for sports, began to wear away. Just so, the shock of seeing women plead in courts, write in newspapers, and prescribe in hospitals began to be less unnerving. Nobody could contend that such women as Mrs. Stowe, the Grimké sisters, and Dorothea Dix were less energetic and capable than men. Nobody could deny that many women were proving that outside pursuits could be combined with domestic activities and that many a household was happier if the wife enjoyed a stimulating breadth of interests.

[VI]

In a very literal sense, the anti-slavery movement had by 1850 come of age. The abolitionist agitation had begun to take on volume, energy, and fervor about the year 1829, and any young man who attained his majority in 1850 had lived his whole life under the potential influence of the radical anti-slavery movement. The sectional controversy over slavery, in its acute stage, was ten years older still; it dated from the year of the Missouri Compromise, and any man who was thirty in 1850 had lived his whole life within the possible influence of this conflict. It is worth noting that down to about 1850 the United States was governed by men who had for the most part been born in the eighteenth century, and whose formative education antedated 1820. They were under the influence, that is, of ideas dominant in the early national era. After 1850 the country began to be ruled by men who had been born in the nineteenth century and whose formative education was at least partly obtained after 1820; by Douglas, Alexander H. Stephens, Jefferson Davis, Lincoln, Sumner, and Seward, whose fundamental prepossessions on certain issues differed from those of Clay, Jackson, Polk, Cass, and Webster. But above all, it is to be noted that the emerging generation in 1850, the great body of new voters, had been exposed all their lives to a conscious and increasingly powerful anti-slavery agitation in the North, an increasingly powerful pro-slavery defense in the South.

Everyone knows that anti-slavery sentiment, rooted in the ideas of religious thinkers like John Woolman, of humanitarians like Benjamin Franklin, and of egalitarians like Thomas Jefferson and Tom Paine, can be traced far back in American history; and that it long commanded as earnest votaries in the South as in the North. The cotton gin and the cheap lands of the Southwest gave slavery vigor in one great section while it was declining in another. Within a single generation thought and prejudice below the Mason and Dixon line adjusted themselves to economic fact. The Lower South by the time Jackson became President regarded slavery as permanent; the North retained and deepened its hostility to an institution which seemed ever stranger and more distant. For just as the cotton gin strengthened slavery in the South, the economic interests of the North, revolting against the policies of the Virginia dynasty, were transmuted into opposition to the three-fifths clause and so strengthened anti-slavery sentiment. It remained to organize the radical anti-slavery thought of the North and Northwest, to make it militant, and to disseminate it until it permeated the whole population. As the 1820's ended and the 1830's opened, the time was ripe, and five striking figures, the Tappan brothers, Theodore D. Weld, James G. Birney, and William Lloyd Garrison, appeared almost simultaneously in central roles. That of these men Garrison had the intensest fire, Weld and Birney the strongest practical sense, there can be no question.[70]

Intimately connected with the sudden rise of the American movement was the triumphant conclusion in 1834 of the British crusade for colonial emancipation. Three developments had made possible the great enactment for liberating every slave under the British flag, whether in the West Indies, in South Africa, in Mauritius, or in other dependencies. One was the vigor of the general humanitarian movement in Britain, reforming the criminal law and the prisons, removing Catholic disabilities, protecting the workers, and relieving the poor. One was the serious economic decline of the British West Indies, reducing the political influence of their planters. In the era of the Napoleonic Wars, West Indian trade had been one of the main pillars of the British commercial structure, but by 1830 it sank to about five-ninths of what it had been in 1814. The third factor was the magnificent organization of British sentiment, both churches and philanthropic organizations lending their aid in a mobilization of opinion which Parliament at last found absolutely irresistible.[71]

Millions of Americans who had learned to admire Zachary Macaulay, Thomas Clarkson, William Wilberforce, and other leaders of the struggle, transferred their attention after 1834 to the sweeping change in the West Indies which one historian has summed up in half a dozen sentences: [72]

Sunset for 70,000 white men, but dawn for 700,000 black. No need for sentimentalists to gild the picture; it is certain that, though the pace presently slowed down, the progress of the Negroes continued after 1838. Some of them, of course, reverted more or less to barbarism. There were plenty of idlers and vagabonds. But, speaking broadly, the freedmen converted themselves with remarkable rapidity into a stable, contented, and not unprosperous peasant community. They congregated in "free villages" and increasingly acquired the ownership of their land. Family life became more common, and the old fall

70 See Gilbert H. Barnes, *The Anti-Slavery Impulse 1830–1844.*
71 Frank J. Klingberg, *The Anti-Slavery Movement in England,* p. 278; Reginald Coupland, *The British Anti-Slavery Movement,* 137.
72 Reginald Coupland, *The British Anti-Slavery Movement,* pp. 145–148.

of population gave place to a steady rise. The improvement in the standard of living, in clothing, housing, furniture, and the like, was reflected for a time in the doubling of the imports of manufactured goods from England. In many parts they paid for their children's education, and in some they were well enough off to contribute large sums for building churches.

In a natural effort to imitate the achievements of the British philanthropists, two wealthy idealists of New York, Arthur and Lewis Tappan, came forward in 1831 to set up a national society.[73] Arthur, a merchant who had made a fortune in importing British dry goods, had a few years earlier assisted in founding the American Tract Society, and its success encouraged him to think that he had found the secret of effective propaganda work. He and Lewis had established the New York *Journal of Commerce* in 1828. In June, 1831, they announced plans for an American Anti-Slavery Society, and after making careful preparations during the next two years, they launched it at the close of 1833. Its objects were the establishment of anti-slavery organizations in every city, town, and village; the employment of agents to lift up voices of warning, rebuke, and remonstrance throughout the land; the circulation of anti-slavery tracts and periodicals, "unsparingly and extensively"; the enlistment of the pulpit and the press; the rousing of the consciences of churches previously dumb; and the encouragement of free labor by the purchase of its products in preference to that of slaves.[74] For a time Arthur Tappan gave the Society a thousand dollars a month.

At the outset the main activity of the Society lay in the wholesale distribution of pamphlets and articles. "They have raised funds," John Quincy Adams was soon writing of it and other organizations in his diary, "to support and circulate inflammatory newspapers and pamphlets gratuitously, and they send swarms of them into the southern country, which is causing great excitement and fermentation in all parts of the Union." [75] The central British society had encouraged the formation of affiliated societies, which increased within one year from 200 to 1,300; it had circulated monster petitions; it had boldly used women speakers; it had so successfully enlisted the clergy that anti-slavery sermons became commonplace; it had brought newspapers and magazines into the crusade, among them the *Edinburgh* and *Westminister Reviews;* and it held influential conventions. By no means least, it had circulated pamphlets in great numbers. When a young Yorkshireman named Whitely came back from a short visit to Jamaica, T. F. Buxton persuaded him to put his story, with its

73 The first number of the *Quarterly Anti-Slavery Magazine*, edited by Elijah Wright, Jr., and issued by the American Anti-Slavery Society, appeared in October, 1835. The leading article, written by C. Strait, was on the "Abolition of Slavery in Great Britain."
74 Henry Wilson, *Rise and Fall of the Slave Power*, I, 257.
75 J. Q. Adams, *Memoirs*, IX, 257.

horrid details of floggings, into a booklet of which within a fortnight nearly 200,000 copies were sold.[76] All these activities, the Tappans meant to reproduce in America.

They met with some success. John Tyler, speaking at Gloucester, Virginia, on August 22, 1835, said that when he had been in Washington two years earlier the Anti-Slavery Society had been a mere handful of men ridiculed from one end of the nation to the other; but that already they had two hundred and fifty subordinate societies, with four presses in New York alone pouring out publications in large numbers.[77] It was soon plain, however, that the flood of tracts was turning no wheels.

Most of the pamphlets and articles were ineffectively written, and many of them gave sharp offense by harping upon immediate emancipation, which seemed impracticable and reckless. Actually the Society had adopted the slogan of "immediate emancipation" in a special sense, meaning that measures for ultimate emancipation should be undertaken at once; but it was difficult to make this clear. Nothing in a slogan is more important than that it should interpret itself. The first two years of the Tappans' society therefore produced little beyond a tremendous crop of hostility.[78]

How at this point Theodore D. Weld, with the aid of James G. Birney and others, gave the movement a new impulse, is a dramatic story—all the more dramatic because its details were not revealed for more than a century. Weld, born in Connecticut and reared in western New York, the son of a poor minister, and Birney, who had been a slaveholding planter and attorney in Huntsville, Alabama, were religious-minded, public-spirited humanitarians of that self-dedicated type which undertakes the maximum of work with the minimum of advertisement. At Princeton Birney had come into touch with liberal currents of thought; at Hamilton College young Weld had been deeply aroused by the preaching of the revivalist Charles Grandison Finney. Both had at first labored to promote the American Colonization Society, that futile agency whose *ignis fatuus*, the idea that the slaves might somehow be transported to another land, so long beguiled the Pliables, Ready-to-Halts, and Facing-Both-Ways among men troubled by slavery. Both grew skeptical, and they finally repudiated the colonizationists as bulwarking, not weakening, slavery.

The weeks in late 1833 which found the Tappans establishing their Anti-Slavery Society found Birney, then past forty, back in his native Kentucky

76   Coupland, *British Anti-Slavery Movement*, 137.
77   See W. S. Savage, "Abolitionist Letters in the Mails," *Journal of Negro History*, XIII.
78   Barnes, *The Anti-Slavery Impulse, 1830–1844*. In 1855 Senator Wilson of Massachusetts delivered a lecture before the New York Anti-Slavery Society. His theme was "Anti-Slavery in 1835 and in 1855 contrasted." In the former year, Wilson admitted the anti-slavery movement was "in the nadir of its weakness. . . ." *National Intelligencer*, May 12, 1855.

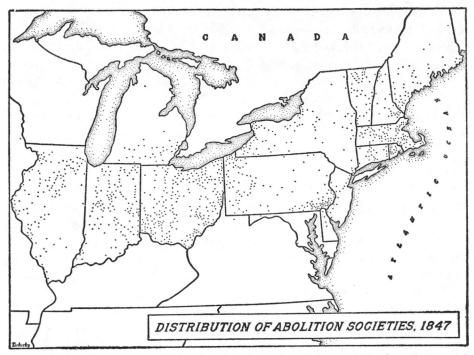

DISTRIBUTION OF ABOLITION SOCIETIES, 1847

At William and Mary College, Chancellor George Wythe—Jefferson's friend—had once given ideas to "young abolitionists." By the end of the forties, Southern feeling permitted no anti-slavery organizations. But societies had overspread the North to impart strength to an agitation more and more political.

and busy establishing the Kentucky Society for the Gradual Relief of the State from Slavery; its program precisely that of the Tappans, "immediate preparation for future emancipation." A man of handsome face, fine bearing, and oratorical ability, he brought to his task not only talent and force of character but also influential connections, for his father had been a mercantile and financial leader in Kentucky, and his wife was daughter of a Federal Judge in that State.[79] The same weeks of late 1833 found Weld, after his work for the Colonization Society and for a manual labor society, studying in Lane theological seminary in Cincinnati, of which the Tappans were liberal patrons. There he was the brilliant center of a group of tough-minded, high-spirited young men, much interested in helping the free Negroes of the city. While Birney labored to convert reluctant Kentuckians, Weld and his fellows staged their famous eighteen-day discussion: "What is our duty to the Negro race?"[80]

79 Birney's ideas on slavery at this time were fully described in his *Ten Letters on Slavery and Colonization* (1832-33).
80 On the work of the Tappans, Birney, and Weld see D. L. Dumond, *Anti-Slavery Origins of the Civil War*; and G. H. Barnes, *The Anti-Slavery Impulse, 1830-44.*

That Birney's gallant Kentucky battle failed, and his residence there shortly became disagreeable and even dangerous; that Weld's group met such disapproval among the Lane faculty and such stern condemnation from the trustees that they defiantly seceded to Oberlin, the newly founded coeducational and coracial college near Cleveland—these facts were preludes to Weld's and Birney's vigorous enlistments in the work of the American Anti-Slavery Society. The Lane rebels filled Ohio with abolitionists, a labor for which Finney's revivalism had helped prepare the way, and turned to wider fields. Becoming convinced that they should rely less on tracts and more on the spoken word, leaders of the Society determined to choose a band of devoted field-workers and asked Weld to select them. Like the Apostles of old, his picked Seventy, after brief training, went forth to speak, write, and organize. In 1837 Birney, who had been conducting a paper in Cincinnati, *The Philanthropist*, with Dr. Gamaliel Bailey as associate, was unanimously elected secretary of the American Anti-Slavery Society by its executive board. As executive officer, he was responsible for its correspondence, the employment of lecturers, the establishment of auxiliaries, and the preparation of reports.

By the late 1830's the Society, with its mid-western basis and New York headquarters, was an immense force in American life. Its *Quarterly Anti-Slavery Magazine* could boast in 1837–38 a circulation of 9,000; its monthly *Human Rights* of 189,400; and its weekly *Emancipationist* of 217,000. In the New York office, Birney's energy and conservative wisdom made him invaluable. He knew how to rebuke the callous or laodicean traits of ecclesiastical bodies without attacking the churches themselves, and to denounce what he regarded as misconstructions of the Constitution while loyally supporting that instrument. In the field, Weld continued his modest and almost anonymous work, converting men of outstanding ability to the cause, writing powerful articles, supplying organizational ideas, and more and more acting as political lobbyist. The idealism, courage, and insight of these two, the Tappans, Elizur Wright, and Joshua Leavitt must always command admiration.

They and their associates faced mobs with unflinching courage. Weld, never sustaining himself by the adulation of a special circle, correctly wrote: [81] "The anti-Abolition fury, after being pent up for a few months, is breaking out anew and with deadlier hate than ever. Let every abolitionist debate the matter once for all, and settle it with himself, whether he is an abolitionist from *impulse* or principle—whether he can lie upon the rack—and clasp the faggot—and tread with steady step the scaffold." Angelina Grimké, whom he married in 1838, the cultivated Charleston woman who, a convert to Quakerism, liberated her slaves

81 G. H. Barnes and D. L. Dumond, *Letters of Theodore Dwight Weld, Angelina Grimké Weld, and Sarah Grimké, 1822–1844.*

and wrote a touching appeal to the Christian women of the South, had won her own place in the reform field. Though a zealot for complete race equality, she saw that the Southerners were no more sinners than the Northerners—that slavery, with its manifold Northern profits, was essentially a national and not a sectional system.[82]

It was inevitable that the movement should thrust itself into the political field. Framing their indictment of slavery first upon moral grounds, many leaders were impelled by the denial of civil rights—mobbings, confiscations, destruction of presses, break-up of public meetings—to attack slavery on the ground that it was incompatible with political liberty. Slowly but steadily the proliferating anti-slavery societies of the North and West became political-minded.

The more practical leaders took the road that led to the creation of pressure groups, active in Congressional elections and well represented in State capitals and at Washington. John Quincy Adams had at first been chilly to the abolitionist agitation, but the sleeping lion in him was roused by the struggle in Congress over the right of petition, and he became a bitter sectionalist, attacking slavery at every opportunity. The controversy over the closing of Southern postoffices to "incendiary" documents deepened his feeling and that of others.[83] When Adams, Joshua Giddings, and others who constituted a virtual anti-slavery block in Congress asked Weld to come to Washington, he did so, setting up one of the most effective lobbies that the country had yet known. The redoubtable Giddings, an old Indian fighter, made himself so offensive to Southerners by his speeches and by a set of anti-slavery resolutions which he offered in 1842 that the House passed a resolution of censure, 125 to 69; he resigned and appealed to the voters of his Western Reserve district; and his overwhelming victory marked the emergence of the anti-slavery campaign into a new phase.[84] It became more aggressive politically, and was ready to accept the challenge presented by the Mexican War and its sequels. Party politics complicated the struggle over principle, the fight over the gag rule, for example, being in large part an attempt by the Whigs to thwart the program of the Democrats.

With all the circumstances of national expansion heightening the sectional

---

82 "Think ye," Angelina demanded, "that slaveholders are sinners above all men that dwell in our country? I tell ye, nay, but except ye also repent, ye manufacturers who convert the raw material into a handsome and useful fabric, and ye merchants and storekeepers who become the tempters of a vast multitude to use the product of slave labor, and ye consumers . . . ye shall all likewise be condemned, for after all the slaveholder is only one partner in a large firm, who are bound together by the strong ties of interest and whose business it is to hold man as a chattel that he may procure for them the comforts and conveniences of life." *Weld-Grimké Letters.*
83 See W. S. Savage, *The Controversy Over the Distribution of Abolition Literature.*
84 George W. Julian, *Joshua Giddings.*

conflict, it was certain that the radical anti-slavery element in Congress would grow. As hostility to abolitionism caused the old parties to avoid anti-slavery men as candidates, independent nominations for State offices and Congress became more common. The 7,369 votes that the Liberty Party gave Birney in 1840, and the 62,263 votes it gave him in 1844, were not impressive; but the stage was being set for a complete shift of scenery—for a drama in which old party allegiances would cease to control many of the chief personages.

[VII]

Meanwhile, an exemplar of the most granitic type of New England Puritanism, a man of intense convictions, of high moral elevation, of arid, colorless, and narrow mind, and of fanatical readiness to submit to any sacrifice, had taken the leadership of a more fiercely intolerant movement. William Lloyd Garrison, the son of a Newburyport sea captain and a fervently religious mother, was twenty-six when on January 1, 1831, he brought out in Boston the first number of the *Liberator*, a weekly journal which he was destined to continue for thirty-five years. A disciple and former assistant of the Quaker abolitionist Benjamin Lundy, he differed from the Tappan-Weld-Birney group, as from earlier anti-slavery workers of the time of Franklin and Jay, in his fierce disdain for gradualism, his refusal to hear the word "ultimately." His logic was simple: Slavery is wrong, and must therefore cease forthwith. To those who argued the danger to both races of loosing large numbers of slaves without preparation, he turned a stony ear. Immediately, without delay, all slaveholders should let their bondsmen leave if they wished, and pay wages to all who stayed.[85]

"I will be as harsh as truth and as uncompromising as justice"—these words of Garrison are immortal. "I am in earnest—I will not equivocate—I will not excuse—I will not retreat a single inch—and I will be heard." It has been said by Garrison's admirers that he declared a purely moral and pacific warfare and that he appealed always to the consciences of masters and their free State abetters, never to the passions of the slaves. But this is misleading. In its ultimate effects his unrelenting campaign awoke men to militant force; it appealed to the resentments, not the reason, of slaveholders; and it kindled some of the colored folk whom it eventually reached into fiery passion. Not without cause did a storm of mingled apprehension and anger sweep the South, Georgia offering $5,000 reward for his apprehension and hundreds of men sending him threatening letters.

On a dismal night in January, 1832, with a bitter snowstorm raging,

85 See the description of Garrison in James Freeman Clarke, "The Anti-Slavery Movement in Boston," Justin Winsor, ed., *Memorial Hist. of Boston*, III, ch. VI.

Garrison and eleven other men met in the Boston office of Samuel E. Sewall, a young attorney, to adopt a constitution for their special anti-slavery society. Among the group were Samuel J. May, a Unitarian minister, Oliver Johnson, later to write a history of the movement, and Gamaliel Bradford. This society had its imitators and affiliates along with the Tappans' organization. Its ideas were instantly caught up. It was upon the essential doctrine of immediacy established by Garrison that Wendell Phillips delivered his telling orations, that Whittier wrote his noble poems, that Charles Sumner carried the battle

Anti-Slavery Meeting on Boston Common, with Wendell Phillips Speaking.
Gleason's Pictorial Drawing Room Companion, May 3, 1851.

into the Senate, and that Richard H. Dana, Jr., fought the fugitive slave law. These men, like Garrison, were for instant and complete emancipation.

The Garrison who has best held the world's eye was the dauntless if homely paladin of the first desperate years. Whittier's stanzas on the almost penniless editor laboring in his mean combination of office and abode were literal truth. "Everything around it," wrote Oliver Johnson of that room, "had an aspect of slovenly decay. The dingy walls; the small windows, bespattered with printers' ink; the press standing in one corner, the composing stands opposite; the long editorial and mailing table, covered with newspapers; the bed of the editor and

publisher on the floor—all these made a picture never to be forgotten." [86]
Garrison had undergone imprisonment while Lundy's aide in Baltimore; in
1835 he bravely defied the Boston mob which dragged him through the streets
with a rope about his body. No anti-slavery polemics of the time were more
brilliant than some he penned for the *Liberator*, and his spiritual influence shone
in the utterances of far abler men. "You say that it is a merit of Theodore
Parker's letter that there is no Garrisonism in it," wrote Lowell. "Why, it is
full of Garrisonism from beginning to end." [87]

But compared with the work of Weld, Birney, and the Tappans, Garrisonism
was of mixed issue—and in some respects worse than mixed. The editor of the
Liberator had a genius for antagonizing important allies. We need not censure
him for his assaults on the Colonization Society, his brochure which condemned
that body out of its own utterances almost defying answer.[88] But his anti-
ecclesiastical position and his sharp break with New England church leaders
were unfortunate for the general cause. His flat refusal in 1840 to consent to
organized political action, on the ground that a special party would hinder
rather than help the cause of emancipation, an attitude which time soon proved
mistaken, did much to rend the American Anti-Slavery Society in twain and
impair its usefulness. He carried his own non-resistance tenets to the point of
opposing all but moral agitation.

By 1844 he was convinced that the Constitution furnished slavery its chief
support and should therefore be repudiated; and he applied to it the phrase
which Ann Lee, founder of American Shakerism, had appropriated from Isaiah
to stigmatize the institution of marriage, "a covenant with death and an agreement with hell." He and his friends called for breaking up the union of free
and slave States. He refused to vote, though when H. B. Stanton asked him
whether he thought voting a sin he replied: "Sin for me!" Such New England
abolitionists as Sumner disagreed sharply with him on the issue of political
activity, while liberal and conservative editors alike characterized his attacks on
the Constitution and demands for national disruption as seditious folly.[89] Even
admirers of Garrison's heroism grew impatient with his ideas. Lowell, who

86   Oliver Johnson, *Garrison and His Times*. See also Samuel J. May, *Some Recollections
of Our Anti-Slavery Conflict*, 15–38, for a vigorous personal portrait of Garrison; and Parker
Pillsbury, *Acts of the Anti-Slavery Apostles*, 9–27.
87   J. R. Lowell to C. F. Briggs, March 26, 1848 in *Letters*, C. E. Norton, ed., I, 125–126.
88   Garrison, *Thoughts on African Colonization.*
89   Sumner wrote to Garrison, September 9, 1860: "With you I hate, deplore and denounce
the Barbarism of Slavery. . . . In this I agree with you, and wish you God speed. But I do
not agree that the National Govt. has power under the Constitution to touch the twin bar-
barisms of slavery and polygamy. Therefore, I cannot join in your special efforts." Garrison
Papers, Boston Public Library. See also the article "Fanaticism Run Mad" in the *National
Intelligencer*, June 7, 1855, and the references to the fanaticism and folly of the abolitionists
in the issues of September 30, 1852 and May 1, 1855. Garrison informed his wife that the
Republican paper in Utica described him as an able man "but a fanatic constitutionally";
February 19, 1857; Garrison Papers.

thought him a great man with a touch of the blackguard, wrote in 1848: "I do not agree with the abolitionists in their disunion and non-voting theories. They treat ideas as ignorant persons do cherries. They think them unwholesome unless they are swallowed stone and all. Garrison is so used to standing alone that, like Daniel Boone, he moves away as the world creeps up on him, and goes further *into the wilderness*. He considers every step a step forward, though it be over the edge of a precipice." [90]

To the end the Garrisonians kept up their work of "moral agitation" while the element founded by the Tappans, Weld, and Birney, with their growing political auxiliaries, pursued broader and more fruitful paths.[91] By the establishment of Gamaliel Bailey's *National Era* in Washington in 1847, the practical groups gained an influential organ at the point where it could best support the anti-slavery block. Though Weld himself ignored Garrison, and the debate between the two wings was heated, some vestiges of cooperation were preserved. Until history becomes better able to weigh imponderables, it will be impossible either to reject or accept the assertion that Garrisonism did more harm than good to the object it was intended to promote.[92] But it is certain that by far the greater public influence was exercised by the New Yorkers and Westerners. Highly publicized in their own day, the Garrisonians were absurdly overpraised for decades to come by their special literary adherents. As E. L. Pierce wrote to George W. Julian in 1892, "Garrison has had an army of men to write him up—and his writers are unscrupulous." [93] Nothing could be more unhistorical than the New England myth that Garrison was the soul of the whole cause, the inspiration of the great plea, the man whose insight revealed the way, whose courage tempered the weapon, and whose conviction drove home the steel.[94] The true leadership of the anti-slavery movement lay in great part elsewhere.

90 Lowell to C. F. Briggs, March 26, 1848; *Letters*, ed. by C. E. Norton, I, 125ff. Lowell maintained, however, that Garrison's cast of mind was "essential to a reformer." And he predicted, quite erroneously, that posterity would forget "his hard words, and remember his hard work." Parker Pillsbury, a fanatical associate, demanded in the *Liberty Bell* of 1849: "What though [disunion] baptize the South in blood? What though smoking towns and desolated plantations should robe her in a pall black as the midnight of despair?" P. 40.

91 The slightness of the relationship between Garrison and the Weld-Birney-Tappan elements is revealed in the fact that there is not even one letter from Garrison to Weld in the entire Weld collection, and only one from Weld to Garrison. Weld receives but cold and perfunctory notice in the four volumes of *William Lloyd Garrison, 1805–1809, Told by his Children*. On the other hand, William Birney's *James G. Birney and His Times* (1890) sternly arraigns Garrison.

92 And to other objects still greater harm; cf. Avery Craven, *The Repressible Conflict*, *passim*; *The Coming of the Civil War*, 134–150. But John Jay Chapman (among others) states the case for Garrison in his brief biography with compelling force.

93 E. L. Pierce to G. W. Julian, January 14, 1892; Julian Papers, Indiana State Library.

94 Cf. the anonymous essay on "Johnson's *Garrison*," *Atlantic Monthly*, April, 1881. The subject is reviewed by Louis Filler in "Parker Pillsbury: An Anti-Slavery Apostle," *New England Quarterly*, XIX, 315–337 (September, 1946).

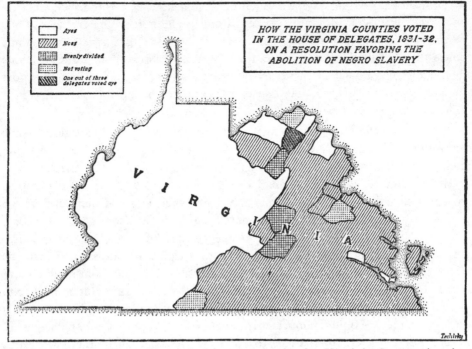

☐ Ayes	
▨ Noes	
⊞ Evenly divided	
⠿ Not voting	
▧ One out of three delegates voted aye	

HOW THE VIRGINIA COUNTIES VOTED
IN THE HOUSE OF DELEGATES, 1831-32,
ON A RESOLUTION FAVORING THE
ABOLITION OF NEGRO SLAVERY

Anti-slavery forces met a decisive repulse in the Virginia Convention just as Thomas R. Dew began composing his spirited defense of slavery on moral and social lines. At the same time Jackson's entry into the White House seemed to herald a West-South alliance in politics.

It was once accepted as a truism that the rise of the Garrisonian propaganda stirred the South into its militant defense of slavery; the old Southern view of the institution as a necessary evil being rapidly displaced by the argument that it was the ideal basis of a perfect civilization.[95] The fact is that the seeds of the pro-slavery philosophy can be found in writings of the period of Revolutionary radicalism. When the Missouri question rang the firebell in the night, the awakened defenders of the South began to develop and clarify their arguments. During the next decade, 1820–30, before Garrison founded his *Liberator*, the theory of slavery as a positive good was fully formulated; Garrison's work merely furnished an incentive for intensifying the defensive agitation.[96]

But it is unquestionably true that the radical abolitionists helped to destroy the movement for gradual emancipation in the border States from Maryland

95 See *The Pro-Slavery Argument, as Maintained by the Most Distinguished Writers of the Southern States* (1853); containing essays by Thomas R. Dew, William Harper, William Gilmore Simms, and James H. Hammond.
96 William S. Jenkins, *Pro-Slavery Thought in the Old South,* 48ff.

to Kentucky.[97] This fact was asserted by William Ellery Channing in his essay on slavery in 1835. The crusade, he wrote, had produced nothing but evil effects in the South. "It has stirred up bitter passions, and a fierce fanaticism, which have shut every ear, and every heart." It was asserted the same year by E. A. Andrews, a travelling agent for the Boston Union for the Relief and Improvement of the Colored Race, who wrote from Fredericksburg that numerous men had told him they were quietly laboring for ultimate emancipation when the abolitionists ruined their work.[98] Nat Turner's insurrection in Virginia, and the increased world demands for slave products, played their part in checking the border movement to discard slavery. But the Northern crusade, and especially Garrison's vituperative part in it, had some responsibility for the fact that whereas early in the century anti-slavery societies had been numerous in the South, by 1837 not one was left.[99]

[VIII]

If America had many radicals, it had strong conservative groups, impatient of Pythian exaltation and indifferent to the storm and stress of 1848, among whom skepticism of the extremer phases of reform remained strong. Prohibition proved a disappointment. Ten-hour-day laws were easier to enact than to enforce. When Garrison in 1855 prevailed upon the New England Anti-Slavery Convention to let John Orvis present a spiritual communication from a dead friend, while one S. S. Foster declared that every pistol fired in Kansas was music to his ears, the sober *National Intelligencer* headed its report, "Fanaticism Run Mad." [100] A widespread feeling prevailed that many reformers, like Dickens' Mrs. Jellaby, looked at distant motes while ignoring present beams. Lowell thought he would rather be an eye-witness of all the cruelty on Southern plantations than see the poor harlots flaunting up and down Broadway.[101]

"Our clergyman today," wrote Edward Everett in his journal for 1857, "both in his forenoon and afternoon services—both in his prayers and sermons—attacked slavery, which does not exist within hundreds of miles of us, and which no one who heard him in any degree favors. He had nothing to say

97 T. M. Whitfield, *Slavery Agitation in Virginia 1829–1832;* A. E. Martin, "Anti-Slavery Movement in Kentucky Prior to 1850," Filson Club Pubs., No. 29; W. F. Leftwich, *Martyrdom in Missouri.*
98 E. A. Andrews, *Slavery and the Domestic Slave Trade* (Boston, 1836); see also Hilary A. Herbert, *The Abolition Crusade and Its Consequences.*
99 S. B. Weeks, *Anti-Slavery Sentiment in the South;* L. D. Turner, *Anti-Slavery Sentiment in American Literature Prior to 1865.*
100 June 7, 1855.
101 Lowell to C. H. Briggs, August 8, 1845; *Letters*, C. E. Norton, ed., I, 92–93.

against the crying sins which do prevail all around him, and which are daily committed to some extent by half his people. He exhorted all his hearers of whatever age and of either sex to do their share to put down the great sin, recommending however nothing but 'testifying against it,' by which he appeared to mean abusing all who differed from him, as to the policy of such a course. It did not, I suppose, occur to him that there was no individual in his parish, who *practically* partakes more of the sin of slavery than himself; he

THOMPSON,
THE ABOLITIONIST.

That infamous foreign scoundrel **THOMPSON**, will hold forth *this afternoon,* at the **Liberator Office, No. 48, Washington Street.** The present is a fair opportunity for the friends of the Union to *snake Thompson out!* It will be a contest between the Abolitionists and the friends of the Union. A purse of **$100** has been raised by a number of patriotic citizens to reward the individual who shall first lay violent hands on Thompson, so that he may be brought to the tar kettle before dark. Friends of the Union, be vigilant!

Boston, Wednesday, 12 o'clock.

An Attack on the English Emancipationist George Thompson, M.P.,
Who Revisited the United States in 1850–51.
Courtesy of Oswald Garrison Villard.

smokes, he wears cotton, he drinks coffee and sweetens it with sugar and eats rice, every one of which is the product of slave labor. Every box of cigars which he buys or accepts as a gift is the payment for a slave bought on the coast of Africa for the Cuban market." [102]

Yet Reform was an inspiring force and a powerful agency in shaping America's future. Several general facts regarding its sway must strike every eye. One was its sectional character. Strongest in New England and those parts of the Northwest largely peopled by New England emigrants, not at all weak in the Middle Atlantic and border States, it possessed comparatively little strength in the deep South. Another notable trait was its close alliance with evangelical religion. Clergymen were always prominent among its votaries, and

[102] Everett, MS Journal, July 18, 1857.

many of its non-clerical leaders were, like the Tappans and Weld, sons of clergymen, or like Neal Dow, trained in church schools. Still more striking was the close interrelationship of its various branches, and the fact that they had developed common techniques. The different reformative and ameliorist societies were managed by what have well been called "interlocking directorates" of a relatively small number of clergymen, philanthropists, and publicists..[103] The various boards found it convenient to hold their annual national conventions at such times and places that they could take counsel together, the "anniversaries" in New York each spring bringing many into converse. A typical May fortnight in the metropolis witnessed sessions of the American Anti-Slavery Society, New York City Anti-Slavery Society, American Temperance Union, American Women's Educational Association, American Bible Society, American Tract Society, American Female Guardian Society, American Seamen's Friend Society, and a dozen missionary societies. The streets were crowded with reform leaders, enthusiastic delegates, and travelling agents, all experts in propaganda by voice and pen.

The international influence of American reform was great and becoming greater. We have noted the transfer of the temperance movement to northern Europe, a work in which Robert Baird had gained fame in the thirties. The peace movement of Elihu Burritt was naturally international in character, and his peace congress in Paris in 1849, with Victor Hugo presiding, seven hundred British delegates present, and a French crowd applauding, was a long-remembered event. The woman's movement, like the anti-slavery movement, was rather Anglo-American than American, for nobody can forget such English pioneers as Mary Wollstonecraft and Fanny Wright. But Lucretia Mott and the other American women who attended the meeting of the British and Foreign Anti-Slavery Society in London in 1840 gave the feminist crusade in Great Britain a fresh impulse that was long remembered; while later Fredrika Bremer brought home to Sweden from her American sojourn the idea of a comprehensive program for the emancipation of her sex. Every advance in the practical applications of American democracy was eagerly watched by liberals across the seas, where a host of men and women regarded American freedom, egalitarianism, and reform as the brightest hope of mankind.

103 See G. H. Barnes in the *Dictionary of American History*, I, 85; *National Intelligencer*, May 20, 1858, for the budgets, then running well above two millions, handled at the anniversary meetings of the religious and benevolent societies. But the budget of the American Anti-Slavery Society was less than $40,000 in 1856–57 and again in 1857–58; annual reports.

5

"For These Just Ends"

CALHOUN, DICTATING his disquisition on the Constitution at Fort Hill through the hot summer hours of 1849, had so exhausted himself and his secretary that both welcomed the idea of a stroll across the plantation. The secretary took in the evening scene with delighted eye; the stern old statesman, head bent and jaw set, seemed immersed in thought. But as they came in sight of some water-lilies glowing on the lazy little Seneca River, he roused himself. "Those will make a great impression," he ejaculated. "Yes, they are beautiful— cream and gold!" exclaimed the secretary. "Eh? What are you talking about?" demanded Calhoun. The young man pointed to the lilies. "Oh," said Calhoun, disgustedly. "I was thinking of the arguments I had dictated to you. Webster always sees such points—he will be sure to admit their force. Better send him a manuscript copy at Marshfield." [1]

As Calhoun's preoccupation showed, there were leaders of that time to whom the principles and practise of government seemed the most important matter of life. On one central point, theoretically, all parties and nearly all politicians were agreed—that the national authority should be weak. "That government is best which governs least" was a maxim publicly professed alike by Democrats, Whigs, Native Americans, and for a time Republicans.

"The government of the United States is a limited government," declared Millard Fillmore in his first annual message. "It is confined to the exercise of powers expressly granted, and such others as may be necessary for carrying those powers into effect; and it is at all times an especial duty to guard against any infringement on the just rights of the States." [2] When a Whig spoke thus, a Democrat could hardly say more. "The dangers of a concentration of all

1 A delightful account of this scene, written by Calhoun's secretary Scoville, was published in the Columbia, S. Ca., *Transcript*, August 6, 1851. Scoville declared that Calhoun was not opposed to a Southern confederacy; "on the contrary, Mr. Calhoun believed that such a result would be inevitable." He quotes Calhoun saying that if the North would only read his disquisition, "then we shall never have any more unmeaning talk about the false assertion, that the *majority shall govern.*" And he notes Calhoun's tribute to Webster: "It is a satisfaction to come into contact with a man of intellect who understands you."

2 J. D. Richardson, ed., *Messages and Papers*, V, 79.

power in the general government of a confederacy so vast as ours," warned Franklin Pierce in his inaugural address, "are too obvious to be disregarded. You have a right, therefore, to expect your agents in every department to regard strictly the limits imposed upon them by the Constitution of the United States." [3] But lip-service to the time-honored doctrines of the evils of centralized government and the importance of State rights did not necessarily mean much. Maxim and fact had quarreled badly under Jefferson, and worse still under Jackson and Polk.

Some subsequent students of history found this period marked in Europe and America by a sharp pendulum swing from left to right, and then to left again. In the middle forties free enterprise, laissez-faire ideas, and the dogma of the weak state had seemed ascendent; the Walker Tariff, the repeal of the English Corn Laws, the rise of Bright and Cobden, and in continental Europe the revolutionary movements which culminated in 1848, had all pointed in the same direction. But a profound reaction set in after 1849. The failure of the revolutionary spasm, the glittering success of Louis Napoleon in France, the energetic policies of Derby and Palmerston in England, and the growing acuteness of the slavery struggle in America, seemed to bring the principle of a strong government into repute again. Certainly the four years of Franklin Pierce exhibited some Congressional and executive measures vigorous to the point of rashness. A counter-reaction, however, soon ensued, and by the late fifties it had become strong. In continental Europe, oppressed Italy and Hungary again plucked up hope, while the French began to murmur against Napoleon III; in England liberalism once more became fashionable; and in America the government under Buchanan lapsed into inertia as the dominant party championed State rights and attacked federal interferences.

Such, according to some writers of the next generation, were the main outlines of the world movement in government; [4] and if these broad generalizations are subject to sharp qualification, some connection between American and European trends did exist.

[I]

The climate of opinion had sensibly changed since Jefferson had laid down four main conditions as requisite to the maintenance of republican liberties.

3 *Idem,* 201. For a discussion of the practical workings of the Jeffersonian "myth" see Henry Adams, *History of the United States,* I, Chs. 7ff.; Arthur M. Schlesinger, Jr., *The Age of Jackson.*
4 Charles Astor Bristed, *The Interference Theory of Government* (1867); cf. the article in the *Nation,* November 7, 1867.

He had declared against the concentration of wealth, thinking especially of landed property; but in the industrial East and Lower South a considerable concentration of riches and power had already taken place, and more was plainly on the way. He had expatiated on the importance of discouraging monopoly and promoting freedom of opportunity, pronouncing against government aid to public works and attacking State measures which favored any single class. Nevertheless, special interests had become numerous and their pressures strong. He had insisted that political power should be kept in the hands of small landowners, and that "the mobs of great cities" should not be permitted to grow numerous. Cities, however, had rapidly increased in size, and though the predominance of "cultivators" remained heavy, it was declining. Finally, placing a high value upon cultural homogeneity, Jefferson had hoped that the country would be filled by natural increase rather than immigration. In actual fact, immigration had long since become heavy, and in the late forties grew into a flood which remained torrential for a whole decade. Jefferson, like Madison, had been skeptical of the possibility of preventing a concentration of power and its arbitrary misuse—and had he lived into this period, his apprehensions would have increased.[5]

By 1850 thousands of reflective Americans were filled with doubts as to the future of the government. These doubts rested in the last analysis on the nation's lack of homogeneity; on its economic, social, and sectional heterogeneity. An instinct for unity was responsible for the clamor of the fifties in behalf of the Union, for the Native American reaction against heavy immigration, and for the desire to extrude slavery (and if possible, the Negro) as an element making for disunity. Meanwhile, a variety of groups—farmers, manufacturers, and workmen, Northerners, Southerners, and Westerners, plebeians and patricians—attempted to force their programs upon the nation. Growth economically and growth territorially were taken for granted by nearly all. But some groups believed in the idea of balance: a continued balance of agricultural as against industrial elements, and a balance of southward expansion as against westward expansion. Other groups believed in an unbalancing drive of certain elements: in a great westward movement while repressing southern imperialism, and in a drive of protected industry while agriculture remained unaided.

On the whole, the Democrats were the party of national balance—even if it was the Whigs who stood most staunchly for the Union. Most Democrats looked with benign eye upon expansion into Cuba or Central America; they favored the growth of agriculture while opposing artificial stimulants to manu-

5 Cf. J. J. Spengler, "The Political Economy of Jefferson, Madison and Adams," in David Kelly Jackson, ed., *American Studies in Honor of William Kenneth Boyd*, 3-59.

facturing, and they wished to get rid of the slavery problem by suppressing its discussion. Stephen A. Douglas, as a typical Democrat of some foresight, believed in both western and southern expansion, in carrying agriculture forward across the plains, in railroads, low tariffs, and the avoidance of quarrels about the Negro.[6] The Whig Party, followed by the Republicans, was the party of national unbalance: it favored expansion westward but not southward, while its Northern wing insisted upon the discussion of slavery. Undoubtedly majority opinion in the country was for Balance and Unity. But the situation was one in which a hard-tempered, energetic minority could await its opportunity to thrust the majority aside.

The greatest single unifying element in national life was the steady growth of communications—railways, telegraphs, and swift mails. But while communications tied the country together geographically, in one point of view they made for disunity. The huge new railway system, by 1857 the greatest in the world, created a national market on a prodigious scale. This immensely accelerated the growth of industry, helping it to outstrip agriculture. It was a Northern industry, and it left the South further and further in the rear, accentuating its sense of an inferior status. The fears born of this status inspired Calhoun's disquisitions.[7]

Governments, observed Calhoun, were formed to protect minorities, for majorities could take care of themselves. Applying a primitive theory of checks to the Constitution, he asserted an extreme doctrine of State rights and State power of nullification. The general government was in his view not at all a national government; it was a confederated government, a political union to which the sovereign confederated States were parties. The government had not been created, nor the Constitution ratified, by the people as a whole, but by the people as organized into separate States. The terms or conditions of the union were stipulated in the Constitution; and if they were violated, the parties to the compact had a right to withdraw from their engagement.

Each State, that is, was judge of the measures and limits of the general government, and if it found them transgressed, might interpose its veto against any further action. In justifying the concurrent veto, Calhoun boldly cited the very example which opponents were ready to fling in his teeth. Poland had given every member of its Diet a veto, carrying the principle to such an extent that the veto of a single member not only killed the measure in question, but prevented all others passed during the session from taking effect. And yet, wrote

6 For Douglas's ideas, see Allen Johnson, *Douglas*, 107, 108, 211–214, 311–315.
7 They also inspired his return to a program of such internal improvements as would aid the South, expressed in his famous address to the Memphis convention in the fall of 1845; R. K. Crallé, ed., *Works*, V, 293–311.

Calhoun, "this government lasted in this form more than two centuries, embracing the period of Poland's greatest power and renown." [8]

To Calhoun's Whig and Jacksonian opponents his dogma was not only bad constitutional law, but a doctrine of revolution. This asserted right of a State to refuse obedience, and to order its people to disobey the central governement, amounted to rebellion. Admit it, and the operation of the national government (for it *was* national) became impossible. There was no period of ten years in American history, declared Greeley, in which this State veto-power would not have blocked the wheels. In Pennsylvania the whiskey excise, in New England the embargo, in Virginia the national carriage-tax, in the Lower South the tariff, and in the North the fugitive slave laws, would all at successive periods have reduced the government to a rope of sand.[9] But Calhoun, intense, imperious, his chill logic unwarmed by imagination or human sympathy, insisted that his dogmas were conservative, not revolutionary. His creed was to hold both State and confederated governments, and all their departments, to their proper spheres. It was those who used the general government to encroach on the States and to trample on minorities who were revolutionary.

"I believe," he said, "that in the rights of the States are to be found the only effectual means of checking the overaction of this government; to resist its tendency to concentrate all power here, and to prevent a departure from the Constitution . . ." [10]

Outside the Lower South few theorists of government went so far as Calhoun, or even regarded him with patience. It was easy to show that this advocate of nullification and a weak general government had early in his career supported tariffs and internal improvements. In 1816, when Calhoun still believed that the South could have a flourishing textile industry, he had urged and carried a minimum duty of six cents a square yard on cotton fabrics; in 1832, when he had found that manufacturing clung to the Northeast, he denounced such a duty as unconstitutional and oppressive! His theories, said his critics, had grown out of his attachment to slavery, altering as the incompatibility of that institution with a varied, expertly-managed, and expanding system of manufactures grew plain. His disquisitions were tailored to support a permanent equality between the slave States and the free States, though the Constitution neither stated nor implied any provision for an inequality between *classes* of States, and though the free States were manifestly developing so much more rapidly than their sisters that any demand that they keep equal pace was like yoking Bucephalus and the drudge-ox. The desperation of Calhoun's last utterances on government, coupled as they were with a defense of slavery on

8   "A Disquisition on Government," Crallé, ed., *Works*, I.
9   N. Y. *Weekly Tribune*, May 31, 1856.
10   *Speech on the Admission of Michigan*, 1837. See also the discussion in William Sumner Jenkins, *Pro-Slavery Thought in the Old South*, 158ff.

grounds of right and justice, stamped them as a vain protest against the inexorable processes of nature.[11] Fact would triumph over theory in the superior growth of the freesoil areas. Fact had already won certain clear triumphs over theory in the issue of a weak vs. a strong government; as witness Jefferson's acquisition of Louisiana and application of an embargo, Jackson's enforcement of the tariff and removal of the deposits, and Polk's broad program of territorial acquisition and financial reform.

Indeed, Calhoun's own theories of hostility to governmental action implied, when analyzed, a good deal of positive intervention. He died in 1850 demanding repeal of the Missouri Compromise, which meant an exertion of government that would have rocked the nation to its foundations; and the demands of his successors culminated in the insistence of Davis, Yancey, and Slidell upon *positive* national protection of slavery in the Territories, which did much to precipitate civil war.[12] Even inaction is one type of "intervention," as monopolies and banks know when they oppose regulation, and as important economic interests knew in the fifties.

The fact that many tendencies of the time slowly but surely worked against the weak state and the classic but illusory antitheses of State rights vs. national power, strict construction vs. broad construction, and virtuous economy vs. corrupt extravagance, was recognized by intelligent observers. Some Democrats, like the tough-minded Ben Butler of Massachusetts, accepted the situation. Perceiving the conflict between Jeffersonian and Jacksonian ideas, Butler held both to be partly right. "As to the powers and duties of the government," he was a follower of Hamilton and Jackson; "as to the rights and privileges of the citizen," he followed Jefferson.[13] Other Democrats protested against the tendency. What are the dangers of the country? asked Gideon Welles in a letter to President-elect Pierce. "The most obvious is that of centralization, or the *growing* power of the federal system. If there was danger of consolidation in the time of Mr. Jefferson, when the population was only eight or ten millions, and when there were but fifteen states, how much greater must that danger be now, when there are thirty-one states and a population of thirty millions. The power of the federal government is derived from the whole of the States, and consequently the addition of every new state adds to its powers. . . . Every year the federal government more and more overshadows the States, and the people are more and more inclined to look to it as *the government*, and to regard the States as mere subordinate corporations. I am almost every day surprised at the erroneous

11 "He died the greatest reactionary of his time." W. E. Dodd, *Statesmen of the Old South*, 167.

12 The article in the *Nation*, November 7, 1867, emphasized this point. "The South," it declared, "clamored for State rights; but what it *did* was to use the powers of the central government for the spread and perpetuation of its social theory."

13 *Butler's Book*, 85.

opinions on this subject even by men of tolerable intelligence and professing to be Democrats. And we have now a large foreign element in our population who cannot well understand our system, nearly all of whom are doubtless in error on this important point and yet think they are Democrats." [14]

The tendency toward greater national power did not worry radical-minded Democrats like George Bancroft and Salmon P. Chase, who asked "Power for what?"—and were willing to use it respectively for the laboring man and the slave.[15] It worried theorists like Welles and practical Southerners who, like Alexander H. Stephens, thought the strong government an instrument for sectional exploitation. "All that we ask of you is—keep your hands out of our pockets," said Stephens.[16]

But marked as was the tendency toward an augmentation of national power, it had its ebbs and flows; and in the dozen years before the Civil War it made little real progress. These were years of weak Presidents, averse to executive leadership. Zachary Taylor in his first annual message emphasized the importance of keeping the legislative and judicial branches coordinate with the executive, attacked all tendency toward "encroachment," promised never to "dictate" measures, and engaged to use the veto with extreme caution.[17] Yet Taylor was a general trained to command, elected by the Whig party. A really strong President, as Jackson, Lincoln, Wilson, and the Roosevelts proved, must be an adept politician as well as a statesman of vision and energy. The political incapacity of Fillmore, Pierce, and Buchanan was glaring; under the two latter the presidency was controlled by a directory rather than a single leader; and if Pierce's administration was marked by showy and disastrous pyrotechnics, that of Buchanan was feeble to the point of paralysis. The nation has never seen a period in which so little was done to solve its exigent problems as in the years between Polk and Lincoln; and this was partly because the Jackson-Polk movement toward a strong government had never been "codified." [18]

At every turn the tradition of laissez faire and the distrust of federal power blocked a constructive solution of national questions. A railroad to the Pacific could not be built because sectional jealousies entrenched themselves behind the old shibboleths. Land settlement could not be judiciously promoted and con-

14 December 16, 1852; Gideon Welles Papers. President Pierce repeated this point in his inaugural address.

15 As early as 1854 Bancroft had told the New York Historical Society that since laissez-faire abandoned the workingman "to the unmitigated efforts of personal competition [it] can never be accepted as the rule for the dealings of man to man. . . ." For a full statement of the ideas in his address on "The Necessity, the Reality, and the Promise of the Progress of the Human Race," see Russell B. Nye, George Bancroft: Brahmin Rebel, 195–198.

16 Cong. Globe. December 14, 1854.

17 Richardson, Messages and Papers, II, 23, 24. Whigs of course remembered with deep resentment Tyler's use of the veto against their measures.

18 Schlesinger, Age of Jackson, 518.

trolled. Urgently needed laws to exclude unfit immigrants could not be passed. Agriculture could not be given efficient guidance. The greatest of all problems, slavery, could not even be considered in the light of constructive and far-reaching principles. Only a tremendously bold, elaborate, and costly program of action by the national government could have provided ultimate solutions for that problem without bloodshed; and though some publicists talked of gradual compensated emancipation, and others of colonizing the Negro abroad, men in responsible posts held their peace. Webster alone went so far as to say that he would gladly appropriate all the revenue from the public lands for resettlement of the Negro elsewhere.

The history of the time is incomprehensible unless its pervasive belief in the evils of strong government, its regard for local and State autonomy, and its faith in unfettered individualism as the mainspring of progress are clearly grasped. It was no Southern planter, but a prominent New York Democrat, closely associated with great corporations—Samuel J. Tilden—who proclaimed in 1855 that the dominant party intended to keep government within a highly restricted sphere: [19]

In most of the great practical questions of our time, it has opposed the interference of Government even for the best objects, and because it was solicitous for these objects, has preferred to trust them to wiser, safer, and more efficient agencies. Devoted to the rights of our American industry, which is now beginning to fill the world with the renown of its achievements, it has refused to direct its application by prohibitory or protective tariffs; preferring that each man should judge how he can make his own labor most productive, and trusting for its aggregate result to those natural laws which enable every one of our millions of city population to daily choose his own good, and yet furnish buyers for everything that has been provided beforehand. Claiming a good currency for the people, and well-regulated exchanges, it has discarded a national bank, and seeks to put these great interests under the guardianship of the laws of trade. Friendly to the modern machinery of travel and transport, which, by cheapening the interchange of products of different soils and climates, has in effect added fertility to the one and geniality to the other, it has opposed internal improvements by the General Government, and prohibited loans of State credit and money in aid of railroads. Asserting the freedom of voluntary association, it has refused special charters, and established general laws of incorporation.

[II]

With such ideas predominant, the structure of the national government remained extremely simple. The executive departments had been six in number when Washington left office; they were but seven when Buchanan quitted the

19 T. P. Cook, *Life of Samuel J. Tilden*, 50–54.

White House, the Interior Department having been set apart from the Treasury in 1849.[20] These administered the affairs of a government which, counting every village postmaster, every petty land officer and revenue agent, had at the beginning of the fifties but about twenty thousand employees; whose total annual receipts at the beginning of that decade were about sixty millions, and annual expenditures a little less; and which, then burdened (if the word be permissible) with a public debt of some sixty millions, reduced it before the panic of 1857 to less than half that sum.[21]

The State Department when William L. Marcy presided over it in 1855 was conducted with a normal staff of eighteen men: the Secretary, an Assistant Secretary, a chief clerk, twelve clerks, a translator, a financial officer, and a librarian. This small corps, toiling like beavers, not only carried on all correspondence with foreign governments, drafted and sent out all diplomatic instructions, read, filed, and answered all reports, but supervised consuls, nominated new diplomatic and consular officers, recorded commissions, issued passports, and otherwise looked after foreign relations. They had charge of the enrolled acts and resolutions of Congress, controlled their publication and distribution, took care of all Indian treaties, recorded Presidential pardons and remissions, and received and indexed all publications transmitted for copyright! The Treasury Department, then headed by James Guthrie, was considerably larger. Including the Secretary, Assistant Secretary, two comptrollers' offices, six auditors' officers, the commissioner of customs, the solicitor's office, the Lighthouse Board, and the Coast Survey, each with a retinue of clerks, it had a staff of between four hundred and five hundred men in Washington. The Interior Department, which dealt with public lands, pensions, Indian affairs, the patent office, and miscellaneous other duties, had perhaps half as many employees. But the Navy Department got along with a chief clerk, five bureau chiefs, thirty-three clerks, and a few draughtsmen and engineers, while the War Department was in much the same estate.[22]

Complaints of the evil effects of national penny-pinching were reiterated year after year by the departmental heads. The business of the country suffered in a hundred particulars from low salaries, inadequate staffs, cramped quarters,

20 The Postmaster General had not become a member of the Cabinet till 1829; H. B. Learned, *The President's Cabinet.*
21 In the fiscal year 1852–53, receipts were $61,337,574 and expenditures, $54,026,818. See the *Treasury Report, 1853.* Small as these sums seem, they aroused vehement criticism. Buchanan wrote Henry A. Wise on March 8, 1851, that the extravagant appropriations of the late Congress "ought to alarm the country," and that Democrats should bend every effort "to the reëstablishment of the truly republican doctrine of economy in the public expenditures." Buchanan Papers.
22 See the long article "Organization of the Executive Departments. . . ." in the *National Intelligencer,* June 14, 1855; A. W. Macmahon and J. D. Millett, *Federal Administrators.*

and lack of funds for special investigations and services. The Secretary of the Interior reported at the close of 1856 that since he took office the jurisdiction of the Indian Bureau had been extended over new areas of from 400,000 to 600,000 square miles, and twenty-two additional agencies or sub-agencies had been established by law. He badly wanted an inspector to visit the super-intendents, agents, and tribes, examine their affairs, correct abuses, and make detailed recommendations for improvements; for want of such a man, much maladministration went unexposed. As for the Washington office, Western settlement had within four years doubled the work of dealing with the tribes, yet the number of clerks remained stationary.[23] Secretary Jefferson Davis in 1853 pointed out not only the gross inadequacy of the little army in view of its augmented frontier duties, but the unsatisfactory state of the War Department in Washington. It needed more men; its building accommodated less than half its bureaus; it had no fireproof storage for invaluable papers. Secretary Issac Toucey complained in 1857 that the Navy Department was crippled by the stingy appropriation for testing improvements. The sum of $10,000 allotted it was not a tenth of the amount needed to search out useful innovations. Similarly, had the War Department been given decent sums to experiment with rifled cannon and to adopt good breechloaders, as its heads asked, the history of the Civil War might have been different.

The most striking instance of parsimony in executive management concerned the very interest in which four-fifths of the active population of the country was concerned. As President Taylor pointed out in 1849, the general govern-ment had given no direct aid to agriculture except by spending small sums for the collection and publication of agricultural statistics, and by making some chemical analyses; the charge being defrayed from the patent fund. Indeed, no federal moneys at all were spent upon agriculture until 1839, when $1,000 was appropriated for gathering statistics. The funds assigned to the Patent Bureau for its agricultural activities grew slowly, reaching $3,000 in 1847, $4,500 in 1850, and $5,500 in 1851. The total for the first sixty-two years of the national govern-ment was $29,000!

"Where is our agricultural department?" demanded Representative Newton of Ohio in 1852. "Pent up in the cellar of the Patent Office, and cannot be found at mid-day without a candle; and when found, a single clerk, struggling to get

23 See the report of the Secretary of the Interior in the *National Intelligencer*. December 6, 1856. The pennypinching attitude of the government affected the legislative and judicial parts as well as the executive. Congressmen protested against their low salaries; *National Intelligencer*, August 16, 1856. Judge Curtis resigned from the Supreme Court, complaining that while in Washington he had been forced to live "in such a way as neither my family nor myself have ever been accustomed to; and I must be allowed to think, in such a way as is not consistent with the dignity of the office I have held." Quoted in Nashville *Union and American*, October 10, 1857.

up the report." [24] The country was filled with State and county agricultural societies, agricultural fairs had sprung up from Maine to Texas, and New York boasted of farm journals with six times the circulation of any in Europe. Yet while several European governments generously supported laboratories, experiment stations, and agricultural colleges, Washington was inert.

A similar anomaly concerned the post office; no country, not even England, handled so much mail per capita as the United States, yet at the beginning of the fifties it owned few postoffice buildings in city or town. The annual report for 1853, after noting that 22,688 postoffices were being maintained, and that the number had grown in the past year by some 1,400, dilated upon the frequent difficulty of finding suitable rooms, and suggested an appropriation to enable the department to buy or erect suitable buildings in the larger cities. The General Land Office, charged with truly staggering responsibilities—with the survey, management, and sale of the vast public domain, and the issuance of titles to those who acquired them by purchase, special grant, bounty claim, or other means—never had adequate personnel, quarters, or funds. In 1853, a year in which nearly ten million acres were surveyed and more than ten millions were brought on the market, the commissioner complained of vexatious difficulties. He had to crowd eight or nine clerks, with their desks and tables, into rooms built for two, so that in the stifling Washington summers their health suffered and efficiency declined; valuable files being meanwhile thrust into unprotected hallways. [25]

Within the narrow limits to which they were confined, the departments operated with more efficiency than would have seemed possible in view of the small staffs, spoils appointments, frequent changes, low pay, and poor office facilities. A few devoted bureaucrats of high capacity, such as Horatio King as First Assistant Postmaster-General, and George W. Manypenny as Indian Commissioner, remained in power for sufficient periods to carry constructive plans into effect. Now and then a departmental head set a salutary example of stern discipline. When Guthrie took charge of the Treasury, for example, he issued orders requiring six hours' continuous work, nine to three; prohibiting newspaper-reading or unnecessary conversation; and punishing even a single indulgence in "ardent spirits" with instant dismissal. [26] The best department heads toiled with an intensity of application which sometimes, as with Marcy and

24 His speech is in *Cong. Globe*, April 20, 1852; *National Intelligencer*, May 6, 1852.
25 *Report*, Secretary of Interior, 1857.
26 See "Circular to Heads of Bureaus," October 1, 1853, quoted in *National Intelligencer*, October 13, 1853. The Circular was well received by the press. Typical of the reaction was the comment by the Washington correspondent of the New York *Courier* that it would inculcate "sobriety, rigid and faithful attention to duty" and would help to "enforce a salutary discipline among the employes of the Government, and at the same time to promote among them a sense of self-respect."

Kindred Spirits:

WILLIAM CULLEN BRYANT AND THE ARTIST THOMAS COLE

A painting by Asher B. Durand

Washington in Fillmore's Day, 1852

Jefferson Davis, impaired their health. Attorneys-General no longer accepted retainers in private suits, as had been done even in the forties, and publication of successive volumes of their official opinions exhibited the wide scope of their work.[27]

Nevertheless, the executive departments of the nation, by standards of later days, were loose, weak, ill-coordinated, and all too frequently slipshod. Expertness was very little valued. The census statistics of the country, for example, were a disgrace; those of 1850 collected under a law which the economist Francis A. Walker later called "clumsy, antiquated, and barbarous." Some almost incredible blunders occurred. For example, the registration of valuable letters began in 1855. But the government took no responsibility for the loss of registered mail; and hence the mark it bore simply pointed out its valuable character and, as postal officials admitted, invited depredation!

[III]

"We are going to do nothing this session, and a great deal of it," Horace Greeley, then briefly a member of Congress, confided to Schuyler Colfax in 1849. "It is not my fault. I hold my tongue most desperately, and drill, drill from day to day in favor of longer sessions, previous question, stopping debate in committee, etc., etc." [28] If the executive departments were often inefficient, Congress seemed chronically so. Copious discussion and vague purpose seemed to mark most sessions. In presidential years, notably 1852 and 1856, most of the debate bore a direct relation to the campaign. As the fifties wore on, an exhausting, exacerbating, and essentially futile conflict over slavery raged to the exclusion of nearly all other topics. It was but seldom that nationally valuable pieces of legislation, like the steamboat inspection bill of 1852 or the Atlantic telegraph bill of 1857, were carried. Throughout the dozen years after 1848, indeed, no laws except those pertaining to the slavery issue really counted; and Congress became less and less an implement for legislation, more and more simply a grand central forum for debate—a place where fears, hopes, and hatreds of the colliding parties and sections might be stated.[29]

In the first three decades of national history, when the Senate was too small to carry great weight and the House was still a truly deliberative body, public interest had centered in the lower chamber. It was in the House that Madison and Gallatin, Randolph and Webster, Clay and Calhoun, had won their first parlia-

27 See *Official Opinions of the Attorneys-General of the United States*, Vol. VI, edited by C. C. Andrews, containing the opinions of Attorney-General Cushing to October, 1854.
28 February 16, 1849; Greeley-Colfax Papers.
29 Even economic issues which should have been considered on their own merits became entangled with the sectional struggle; such as the steamship subsidy legislation defeated in 1855 largely by Southern votes. *Cong. Globe*, 35th Cong., 1st sess., 2824ff.

mentary fame. But the debates on the Missouri Compromise in 1820–21 had signalized a shift in popular attention. The Senate had by that time risen to a membership of forty-four. William Pinkney of Maryland, Rufus King of New York, and others had given it lustre, while before long Clay and Webster would enter it, and Calhoun would preside over it as Vice-President.

For the next forty years, down to the Civil War, the Senate enjoyed a much greater prestige than the House. Benton, Cass, Crittenden, and Douglas, together with the great triumvirate, lent it dignity. In size, it was almost ideal for debate, while the House, which by the fifties had nearly four times as many members, was much too large. The impossibility of doing business in the lower chamber without sharp limitations on speechmaking had led I. E. Holmes of South Carolina, recalling the Athenian regulation of the one-hour klepsydra, to induce his fellows of the twenty-sixth Congress to adopt a one-hour rule.[30] But the Senate remained free, and its standards of oratory rose while those of the House necessarily declined. Prepared speeches were often admirable, and the running debates which constantly sprang up sometimes presented fine specimens of eloquence and exhibited quick resourcefulness, thorough knowledge of the problems of the country, and statesmanlike breadth of view. When John M. Clayton of Delaware, waving aside in 1854 the suggestion that he might be nominated by the American Party, declared that he preferred his seat in the Senate to the Presidency, the country understood him.[31]

As a forum for debate, the Senate was not infrequently magnificent. But the interests which were demanding legislation grew impatient when bills pertaining to homesteads, railroads, internal improvements, and tariffs were repeatedly sidetracked or defeated. A common if superficial complaint dealt with the bad House rules which, declared the *National Intelligencer*, were not so much for the transaction of business as its stoppage.[32] Under them, bills were placed on the House

30 Isaac E. Holmes to Lieber, June 17, 1853; Lieber Papers, HL. According to Holmes the House had become impatient "under the infection of long speeches."

31 *National Intelligencer*, November 9, 1854, quoting the Buffalo *Commercial Advertiser*. This article compared the relative merits and defects of the Senate and the House of Representatives. Note Alexander Mackay's comment on the "unceasing hubbub and concatenation of all conceivable sounds in the House," where the orators sometimes fell into "a perfect screech" in the vain effort to be heard; whereas decorum and dignity ruled the Senate. *The Western World*, I, 290, 309.

32 See the article, "The Late Session of Congress," *National Intelligencer*, September 7, 1852. This was an angry condemnation of the House and the alleged "abuses" in its practices. Earlier in the year Ben Wade had observed that Congress never did what it should have been doing. He wrote his wife from Washington that had he the power, "I could put through every necessary measure in one month as well as in a year and adjourn." Wade admitted, however, that when he reflected "that every measure, before it can pass must meet the aprobation (sic), of such a multitude of minds, so hetrogeniously (sic) brought together, and representing a country extending from the frozen north to the perpetual summer of the tropics, and from the shores of the Atlantic to the Pacific, I only wonder that we are able to do anything." To his wife, March 15, 1852; Wade Papers.

calendar in the order in which they were reported from committees, with the result that insignificant measures, private claims, and the like took precedence, while important controversial bills came far down the list. Business could be taken out of due order, if a single member objected, only by two-thirds vote. Every opportunity was given to obstruction. For example, two privileged motions, one to adjourn and the other to call the yeas and nays (a process which took a half hour), were frequently used in succession to halt any measure to which a determined minority objected. Speechmaking could be strung out in an almost interminable filibuster. But the chief root of the Congressional paralysis in dealing with constructive new proposals lay far deeper than the rules. It lay deeper even than the widespread conviction that the less legislation passed, the better for the country; it lay in the increasing force and depth of sectional antagonisms.

[IV]

Industrial pressure groups, contractors, lobbyists, claim-agents, and other wirepullers infested Washington in hundreds, spending money lavishly, and creating an atmosphere in which suspicion of corruption often grew to certainty. "The Federal Government," Buchanan confided to Franklin Pierce in 1852, "for some years past has been rapidly becoming more and more extravagant in its expenditures. The hosts of contractors, speculators, stock-jobbers, and lobby members which haunt the halls of Congress, all desirous *per fas aut nefas* and on any and every pretext to get their arms into the public Treasury, are sufficient to alarm every friend of his country. Their progress must be arrested, or our government will become as corrupt as that of Great Britain." [33] This statement might be taken with salt were it not corroborated by a dozen other sources.[34] James S. Pike the same year drew a lurid picture of venal Congressmen working up petty jobs, accepting gifts, concentrating their attention on local and private bills, and neglecting national interests.[35]

33 June 21, 1852; John Bassett Moore, ed., *Works*, VIII, 453.
34 J. C. Van Dyke brazenly wrote to Buchanan, March 23, 1850: "Permit me to ask what you think of the chances of the present or the next Congress redeeming the Texas debt. There has been a great deal of money made by the improvement of 'notes' here, and I have a great inclination to enter into the speculation a few hundreds." Buchanan Papers.
35 N. Y. *Weekly Tribune*, March 20, 1852. See also the long and virulent editorial on "The Senate's Double Mileage" in the issue of October 25, 1851. The Washington correspondent of the Charleston *Mercury*, however, found that there was a tendency to accuse and condemn everybody of being corrupt. He denounced the scandal-mongers and deplored the fact that all candidates, whether for high or low offices, were no longer safe from assaults on their character. "The foul sewers of calumny," he wailed, "are emptied over honorable names, and the public, with distended nostrils, sniff in the savor." Quoted in *National Intelligencer*, January 29, 1853.

The ten million dollar payment to Texas that was part of the Compromise of 1850 formed the basis for much highly profitable speculation in Washington and elsewhere on the Texas debt; men with inside knowledge buying Texas notes for the certain rise. Veterans' legislation was already being promoted by men who expected to reap a harvest from it. The bounty land bill of 1850, granting stated amounts of public land to every veteran of the War of 1812 or the Indian wars with their widows and minor orphans, and every commissioned officer of the Mexican War, delighted the claim agents. It was expected to benefit about 250,000 people, and as the usual fee charged by these agents was ten dollars for a 160-acre warrant and five dollars for lesser warrants, there were obviously millions in it.[36]

The large claims growing out of the Mexican War and Gadsden Purchase were also a quarry upon which greedy men pounced. By the treaty with Mexico in 1848 and a subsequent act of Congress, three and a quarter millions were appropriated to liquidate the claims of American citizens against Mexico, and a commission was set up to decide on their validity. From the careless legislation and the negligent conduct of the commissioners grew the scandal of the so-called Gardiner Claim. George A. Gardiner offered documents to prove that he had owned a valuable mine in San Luis Potosi which the Mexicans had broken up. The commission had awarded him $428,750, and, thus made wealthy, he departed for Europe. But suspicion arose, the case was re-opened, and Gardiner was indicted for fraud. Sentenced in the end to ten years at hard labor, he took poison in his room. This tragic climax to a spectacular crime filled the press for days.[37] In 1854 the Senate Foreign Relations Committee was discussing the Gadsden Treaty. "Clayton says," wrote Edward Everett, "that there has been the most frightful corruption in reference to the Garay grant in connection with the Gadsden Treaty. Sixty-seven per cent of it owned by members of the Senate." [38]

36 C. C. Tucker to unknown correspondent, January 23, 1851; Wade Papers. Tucker, a claim agent in Washington, proposed in this letter to an attorney, possibly Wade, that they cooperate in preparing bounty claims, the fees to be divided equally. When another bill providing for the settlement of the claims of the officers of the Revolutionary army and their children came up in the Senate early in 1857 Senator Clay of Alabama vigorously attacked it. He charged that the real fathers of the measure were "meddlesome claim agents and lobby members who had grown into a sort of fourth estate in the legislation of Congress." *National Intelligencer*, January 15, 1857. The report of the Commissioner of Pensions for the year ending June 30, 1855, showed that nine convictions had been secured during the year for fraud in connection with land bounties, and that another nine prosecutions were pending. *National Intelligencer*, January 3, 1856. According to the Commissioner there would have been prosecutions of "many" more had there not been a two-year statute of limitations in pension and land warrant cases.

37 *Report of the Select Committee on Mexican Claims* (33d Cong., 1st sess., *Senate Report* 182). See comment in *National Intelligencer*, March 30, 1854.

38 MS *Diary*, March 30, 1854. A month earlier Everett had expressed the fear that the grant was the product of a "gross corruption"; entry under date of February 17.

The lobbyist, cheery, insinuating, and generous, was a familiar figure in capital barrooms and hotels. Frequently he had handsome quarters where he gave dinners and champagne suppers. While his activities might be innocent and in some instances beneficial, it is clear that the line of propriety was often transgressed. One of the worst types of agent was the combination newspaperman and lobbyist. Charges that improper influences had been used to pass a bill extending Colt's patent on his firearms led to the appointment of a House investigating committee headed by Letcher of Virginia, the report by which (February 23, 1855) threw much light on lobby evils. Press correspondents, regularly admitted to the floor of the House, were required to certify that they were not interested in any claim or measure, but such pledges meant little. "We find," stated the committee, "that they have been employed in many of the railroad, patent, and other schemes which have engaged the attention of Congress during the present session." Controlling Washington dispatches and thus moulding public opinion, the correspondents exercised great influence with Congressmen. For a time, the Washington columns of even the New York *Herald* had notoriously been for sale.

More prominent, however, were the professional lobbyists, men shrewd, keen, and experienced, who had seen much of the world. They arranged costly entertainments, to which beautiful women, whose interest had been engaged by presents of jewels or perfumery, were sometimes invited. Indeed, a vein of lobby influence could be traced through many of the dinners and balls of the capital.[39] Senators and Representatives who enjoyed evening parties were open to such influences as Sam Ward, the so-called king of the lobby, could expertly wield. Sam, fat, witty, and kindly, with a resounding laugh, never accepted any but legitimate undertakings, made dining an art, brought about his table gentlemen of congenial views—say Winfield Scott, Senators Mason, Cass, and Gwin, "Prince" John Van Buren and a few others—and, gently presenting his views, smoothed the way for one measure or obstructed another.[40] But other lobbyists were less circumspect. It was proved that one of Colt's agents had offered a certain Representative, an active opponent of Colt's extension bill, a "contingent fee" of $10,000 to become an advocate, and that the two men, after several conferences, had agreed on terms. Other opponents had suddenly ceased their attacks, and returning home, had kept as still as mice about the extension bill.[41]

39 C. C. Clay to his father, March 14, 1854; C. C. Clay Papers, Duke Library. One Southern lobbyist, according to Clay, resided at the National Hotel, and had plenty of "wines, liquors, and other appliances for corrupting Congresses—all at the expense of his clients." For the Colt report, see 33d Cong., 2d sess., *House Report* 132.
40 Maud H. Elliott, *Uncle Sam Ward and His Circle*, 459.
41 See summary in N. Y. *Tribune*, August 26, 1854.

Some Congressmen did not scruple to be legislators and lobbyists for private interests at the same time. One, who served as active agent for certain claimants against the government while occupying a seat for a Kentucky district, made the error of writing a newspaperman in May, 1851, from Washington, to tell how well his dual position paid. "If I could stay here a month," he confided, "I could make $5,000. As it is, I fear I shall have to hurry off without even completing the business I came on. I saw men in New York, Philadelphia, and here who want my services and are willing to pay for them, and pay well. If I can be reëlected, I can make a great deal of money. But this is between ourselves." To defeat this unscrupulous fellow, the correspondent made his shocking letter public.[42]

Other Congressmen let themselves fall into the clutches of some of the professional gamblers who ran faro games and did a bit of lobbying on the side. When late in 1858 the keeper of a famous Washington gaming establishment, one Pendleton, died, the full story of his operations came out. Large sums had been won and lost at his luxurious parlors. Though without political influence, he was a power in the lobby. He held a number of loose-living Representatives, and even a stray Senator or two, in the iron grip of pecuniary obligation, and when a fat contract was to be carried or a dubious claim lobbied through, he brought his crew up to their work with a sharp crack of the whip. His importance was attested by the fact that the crafty Commodore Vanderbilt, who was not in the habit of taking a false measure of men, had on a recent visit to Washington made Pendleton the present of a pair of carriage horses, and had eaten regularly at the gambler's table.

"A few weeks' faro, and a Congressman is cleaned up," said *Harper's Weekly*. "Where does he then dine?—at Pendleton's. Where does he drink?—at Pendleton's. When he needs money, perhaps to return home, where does he mortgage his mileage?—at Pendleton's. He belongs to Pendleton." [43]

That actual bribery sometimes took place was proved not only by the Colt investigation but also by other episodes. In the late fifties the Bay State Mills of Lawrence, Massachusetts, whose managers had been striving for a modification of the duties on wool, failed. An overhauling of the accounts showed that $87,000 had been paid into a special lobbying fund. The chosen agent, according to a stockholder's report, had gone to Washington and plied members of Congress with information and arguments. But he was told that it would be necessary for him to adopt quite another course and to be less scrupulous in the use of the means at his disposal; and he thereupon wrote home that another agent, of more pliable temper, would have to be employed. In short, it was expedient to shift

42 N. Y. *Tribune*, September 12, 1853.
43 December 4, 1858; see Helen Nicolay, *Our Capitol on the Potomac*, 284, 285, for the Pendletons' place in Washington society.

from lobbying to bribery. Another agent duly went to Washington, and $70,000 of the money he spent was never accounted for.[44]

Yet proved instances of Congressional turpitude were few, and what corruption occurred was that of individuals, not groups. In the winter of 1856–57, sweeping charges against the integrity of the House, made by the Washington correspondent of the New York *Times*, led to the appointment, by resolution of January 9, 1857, of an investigating committee. Acting swiftly, this body brought in six distinct reports, which called for the expulsion of three Representatives from New York and one from Connecticut. One was accused of taking money to get a book-purchase item through the House; one of asking a bribe for a favorable report on a claim before the Invalid Pensions Committee; one for offering to pay a fellow-member a thousand or fifteen hundred dollars to vote for a bill donating lands to Minnesota Territory; and one for urging officers of the Des Moines Navigation and Railroad Company to take corrupt steps to get a liberal interpretation of a certain land grant bill through the House. This last member, O. B. Matteson of New York, had also insulted the House by declaring that some of its members had united in a conspiracy to oppose the resolution unless they were paid off. Though he resigned his seat, a condemnatory vote was carried by a heavy majority. Three of the four men were apparently guilty; but the investigation showed that, as the committee reported, no general combinations of a corrupt nature existed.[45]

Such episodes as the Matteson affair and the Covode investigation into public abuses were faintly anticipatory of the Gilded Age and the Grant scandals. So were such instances of sharp practise as Senator John Slidell's smuggling of the Houmas Land claim through Congress early in 1860. This was a claim to title in about 180,000 acres of fertile Louisiana land. The Federal Courts had ruled that the old patent on which it rested was worthless, and Congress had blocked a direct attempt to validate it, but Slidell (who had acquired an interest in the claim) succeeded in inserting a disguised item covering the subject into a general land-claim bill referring primarily to Missouri.

The general level of Congressional conduct, however, was on a high plane

44 *National Intelligencer*, February 9, 1858. Thurlow Weed got $5,000 of the balance and David M. Stone of the New York *Journal of Commerce*, $3,500. N. Y. *Weekly Tribune*, May 29, 1858. Weed's embarrassment was acute, for while he had always preached the Whig doctrine of high tariffs, in this instance he had lobbied for a reduced rate!

45 *House Report* 179, 35th Cong., 1st sess.; *National Intelligencer*. February 21, 1857. See also Everett's comments in his *Diary* for February 21, 1857. The *National Intelligencer* for August 10, 1858, fully reviewed the affair. Substantial citizens, however, were convinced that there was a great deal of corruption in public life. See, for example, J. S. Williams to Welles, January 18, 1857; Welles Papers, New York Public Library. E. L. Huntington found some of the leading public figures were "so utterly unscrupulous" that he confessed he could no longer be surprised by any "single instance of their corruption." To Douglas, November 29, 1857; Douglas Papers.

of integrity. When Thomas Hart Benton died in 1858, it was universally pointed out that he had for many years been a public servant of the finest type. He had paid no attention in Congress to popularity, financial considerations, or personal advantage of any character, while of venality he had a tremendous abhorrence. He died comparatively poor—so poor that his daughters were shocked to find how little he had. His example, wrote Greeley, was worthy the attention of all rising public men, "who, in this budding era of corruption, are likely to be tested by severer temptations than the statesmen of the past." Such members of Congress as William Pitt Fessenden of Maine and Robert Toombs of Georgia earned equally high reputations for rectitude and devotion to duty. Toombs, for example, resolutely turned his back on private activities, toiled indefatigably, opposed extravagance even when it benefited his own section, never spoke for mere effect, constantly held principle in view, and tried to push forward the public business.[46]

The cardinal faults of Congress were two. They were the excessive weight of sectional interests and allegiances, and those defects of mechanism which in the next generation were analyzed by Woodrow Wilson and Lord Bryce—the general lack of executive influence; the tremendous power of the Speaker, too often exerted for partisan and group purposes; the excessive importance of the standing committees, which impaired the unity of the House in particular, reduced party responsibility, discouraged debate, and prevented any real attempts at comprehensive planning of legislation; and the weight given to mere seniority in committee management. These defects were plainly visible in the fifties. Battles for the Speakership aroused the bitterest feeling. Three of the men who gained the office, Robert C. Winthrop, Howell Cobb, and N. P. Banks, possessed ability and strength of will, while four, Cobb, Linn Boyd, J. L. Orr, and Banks, acted with marked partisanship. The Speaker, wrote Joshua Giddings, "exerts more influence upon the destinies of the nation than any other member of the government except the President. He arranges the committees to suit his own views." Toombs, among others, attacked the standing committees as "irresponsible juntos." The want of any general and far-reaching policy in legislation was often noted, caucuses doing little except sometimes rallying the party behind a single troublesome measure. The tendency of important Senate chairmen, such as J. M. Mason of the Foreign Relations Committee, R. M. T. Hunter of the Finance Committee, and Stephen A. Douglas of the Territories Committee, to act without due regard for the President, was often criticized.[47]

46 N. Y. *Weekly Tribune*, March 10, 1860; N. Y. *Daily Tribune*, April 14, 1858, on Benton; John C. Reid, *The Brothers' War*, 212–281, on Toombs.

47 M. P. Follett, *The Speaker of the House of Representatives*, 91–96; George W. Julian, *Joshua Giddings*, 215, 216. See also the article on "The Speaker's Committees" by "A Republican" in the *National Intelligencer*, February 19, 1856, and the article March 10, 1857. Toombs's remarks are in *Cong. Globe*, February 18, 1859.

[V]

"If there is any department of this government for which I have higher reverence than any other," Stephen A. Douglas assured the Senate in 1855, "if there is any department in the purity and stability of which I place higher hopes than any other, it is the judiciary." He was echoed by many associates. Cass deemed it "an impressive spectacle, almost a sublime one," to see nine men establishing great essential principles affecting every part of national life, and receiving implicit obedience. [48] These statements reflected the prestige to which Marshall and Taney had raised the court. There was no instance of a serious charge of corruption against any member of the Federal judiciary from the establishment of the government down to the Civil War. By the middle of the century the time had long passed when any high judge could exhibit such flagrant party animus as that for which Judge Samuel Chase had been impeached in Jefferson's day. The intellectual authority of the supreme tribunal had been lifted high by the great Virginian and kept high by the Marylander—with aid from both the decisions and the learned commentaries of Joseph Story.

Marshall had used the Supreme Court to aggrandize its own powers and strengthen the national government. Meanwhile, by holding the States to be trespassers in certain fields, he had both diminished State authority and furthered laissez faire in the economic sphere—for the Federal power seldom entered these fields. Taney had at first employed his influence to restore strength to the States, saving them from supersession by Congress. He thus gave the court a healthy shift of direction. Apart from the unfortunate Dred Scott case, however, the broad tendency of his chief justiceship did not operate to weaken the national authority. The Hamiltonian jurist and his eminent Jacksonian successor were in this respect not so far apart as they seemed. Though Taney's arguments lacked the lucid perfection of Marshall's, they were obviously the product of a powerful mind and an elevated spirit. The dignity of the court, which increasingly set itself apart from the other two branches of government, actually rose under his sway.[49]

The judicial machinery of the country, composed of a growing number of district courts (six in New England, for example), nine circuit courts (each presided over by a district judge and Supreme Court judge sitting together), and the Supreme Court (nine judges), was grossly overburdened. As the nation moved to the Pacific and the Middle West filled with population, the tribunals could not keep up with their dockets. The Supreme Court judges sat in Washing-

48 *Cong. Globe*, 33d Cong., 2d sess., 195, 298.
49 E. S. Corwin, *Twilight of the Supreme Court*, develops the philosophical implications of Taney's decisions. See also Carl B. Swisher, *Roger B. Taney*, 347–524; C. W. Smith, *Roger B. Taney, Jacksonian Jurist*. Alfred Conkling (father of Roscoe) wrote a long-standard treatise on the organization and practise of the national courts (4th edition, 1864).

ton every alternate year six months, and the intervening year three months, giving most of their remaining time to circuit duty. They were overwhelmed with business, and the middle fifties found Congress debating a variety of proposals to deal with the situation.

One, on which the Senate was almost evenly divided in opinion, was to relieve the judges from the duty of sitting in the circuits. This was opposed on the ground that the judges ought to be familiar with the laws of different States and the court procedure of various sections. It would benefit Judge Curtis of Boston, men said, to hold court for one term in Chicago and another in Charleston; it would broaden the views of Judge Campbell of Mobile to send him to Boston to hold court. Another proposal was to raise the number of Supreme Court judges and of circuits to twelve. This, it was argued, would give every part of the Union better facilities, and lessen the individual burden of circuit work. But one obvious objection was that the court would become unwieldy, and another that President Pierce would have the appointment of three Democratic judges. A third proposal, made by Chase of Ohio, was that the judges be relieved of circuit duty and be reduced in number to six. The sole act passed, however, was one for establishing a circuit court in Oregon and California, with a circuit judge who held no place on the supreme bench; a novelty in the judicial system made unescapable by the lack of rapid communication with the Pacific Coast.[50]

The only sharp antagonism to the Federal courts appeared in anti-slavery circles. When fugitive slave cases made it plain that some State courts would adopt an interfering attitude, Senator Toucey introduced a bill for transferring to the national courts any suit in a State tribunal against a Federal officer for acts performed under Federal law. In the angry aftermath of the Kansas-Nebraska Act, this bill was assailed in the wildest terms. "Sir," exclaimed Chase in language reminiscent of Nullification days, "this bill is a bill for the overthrow of State rights. It is a bill to establish a great central, consolidated national government. It is a step, let me say a stride rather, towards despotism." His colleague Wade went further, assailing the Federal judges. The bill, he told Southerners, would transfer an unlimited variety of cases from State jurisdiction "to those whom you have been feeding and pampering at this session to uphold your usurpations." His constituents would suffer death, he declared, before they would surrender their rights. It is not astonishing that Douglas, replying to Wade, declared that he had raised the standard of rebellion against the Constitution and the laws. The bill failed in the House after passing the Senate. Similarly, freesoil hostility to the court in 1855 defeated an effort to raise the judges' salaries. Repeatedly in the fifties freesoilers like Seward declared that a majority of Federal judges were named in the interests of slavery, while John P. Hale called the Supreme Court

50 Cong. Globe, 33d Cong., 2d sess., 191–198, 294–301, 604–608.

"the citadel of slavery." After the Dred Scott decision—but that is a story in itself.[51]

Yet actually the Supreme Court had repeatedly vindicated its impartiality and freedom from sectional bias, while the only judge who had mingled offensively in politics was a Northerner, John McLean of Ohio. The national tribunals, their judges appointed for life or good behavior, contrasted favorably with the State courts which to an increasing extent (as one State after another "democratized" its constitution) were rendered elective. Low pay and uncertain tenure made such judges as Lemuel Shaw of Massachusetts rare indeed.

In 1833, according to Judge Story, five out of the twenty-five States elected their judges, and elected them for only a term. In 1844, according to Judge Kent, twelve States out of twenty-nine had adopted the principle. By 1853 the judges were elective in twenty-five State out of thirty-one, and in twenty-two they were chosen for short periods only. Three States elected their judges annually! Opinion of the new system varied, some believers in unlimited popular government upholding it. J. F. H. Claiborne, the Mississippi Congressman and historian, for example, wrote that when his State adopted it in 1832 he had thought the experiment hazardous, but the experience of thirteen years had dispelled his fears, and convinced him that popular election was the best mode of choice. The general view, however, was adverse. New York had taken the plunge in its constitution of 1846. Nearly ten years later the Buffalo *Commercial Advertiser* summed up the judgment of moderate men. "Our conclusion is, that an elective judiciary is open to the arts of the demagogue and the unscrupulous partisan; that the judge must always depend for his post in a contested election on a class of men who do the dirty work of parties, and who are more frequently than any other obnoxious to law. He must make promises and pledges which he can only repay by outraging justice and violating his oath." This was an anticipation of those judicial rogues of Tweed days, Barnard and Cardozo. But the Federal bench remained untrammeled, and the Supreme Court in particular was lifted by Presidential appointment, lifetime tenure, and keen public scrutiny to a position of absolute independence.[52]

[VI]

John Stuart Mill's assertion that the spoils system was the primary defect of the American governmental system, though made in the sixties, applied equally to the preceding decade. The quadrennial scramble for office was just what

---

51 *Cong. Globe*, 33d Cong., 2d sess., App. 211–246; Charles Warren, *The Supreme Court in United States History*, 1926 ed., II, 267–269.

52 *Commercial Advertiser* quoted in *National Intelligencer*, June 12, 1855; Claiborne's unsigned letter is to J. F. Brent, March 22, 1845, in Claiborne Papers. See also article on "Representative Reforms" in *National Intelligencer*, September 26, 1857; Mackay, *Western World*, I, 316–340.

John P. Kennedy called it—sickening. When Taylor came in, the hardened John J. Crittenden warned the new Secretary of State that office-hunters would flock into Washington in such hordes that many would mistake them for the people.[53] Pierce's inauguration four years later brought to the capital another inundation. As fast as one crowd was turned away, a new levy marched up. Rival factions like the "Hards" and "Softs" of New York all but fought in the lobbies.

"Instead of the number of office-seekers diminishing," wrote an observer in late April, "they appear to be on the increase. On Friday the halls and staircases of the House were crowded with them. Today the President threw the door of his office open and admitted the crowd all at once. It was a motley assemblage, from aspirants to full missions down to messengerships, whilst some looked as if they would even be content with a suit of old clothes. They poured into the room for several hours, presenting a humiliating spectacle." [54]

The basic principle of the spoils system is often misunderstood: it was the use of public appointments not merely as rewards to members of the victorious party, but as a means of preserving equilibrium or discipline among the various factions of the organization. Fear of party chaos is a nightmare which keeps politicians sleepless; the cohesive power of public patronage is the most efficient party cement.

Personal rivalries, jealousies of country and city, and divisions produced by great public questions constantly boiled up in almost every State and all parties in schismatic tendencies. Among Democrats, Whigs, and Native Americans alike the primary difficulty of keeping the Northern and Southern wings in concert (a difficulty which all three parties eventually found insuperable) was complicated by the problems of dealing with State factions and local mutinies. Division might arise from mere desire to dominate, as in the quarrel between the Buchanan and the Simon Cameron Democrats in Pennsylvania; it might base itself upon principle, as in the fierce antipathy between "cotton Whigs" and "conscience Whigs" in Massachusetts; it might have a dozen roots, as in the battles between Hunker and Barnburner Democrats, Silver-Gray and Radical Whigs, in New York. At any rate, it was the duty of national chieftains to keep the party together, and they used spoils to recompense good behavior or punish bad. Depend upon it, Caleb Cushing in 1853 warned quarreling elements which threatened to break up the Democratic party in Massachusetts, the President will never submit to factionists, "but will set his face like flint against right-hand backslidings as against left-hand defections." [55]

53 Crittenden to J. M. Clayton, March 13, 1849; Clayton Papers.
54 Unnamed writer quoted in *National Intelligencer*, April 30, 1853.
55 To R. Frothingham, October 29, 1853; *Washington Union*, November 1, 1853, *National Intelligencer*, November 2, 1853.

In dealing with factional disputes, the President had a choice between broad lines of policy: he could distribute his favors with fair equality among the rival groups, giving just cause of complaint to none and trying to attach all to the Administration; or he could select the strongest or most loyal, give it every plum, and try to make it dominant. It need scarcely be said that the second policy was usually followed. Franklin Pierce made an effort in 1853 to ignore old divisions, accept as equally worthy all Democrats who had supported him and his platform, and scatter the offices with impartial hand. When the head of the most powerful agency of machine politics in the country, the New York Custom House, blandly ignored Pierce's desires and appointed nearly all subordinates from his own faction, the Secretary of the Treasury sent him a crushing rebuke.[56] The Collector responded with a letter so insolent that he had to be dismissed—and the fat was in the fire.[57] Meanwhile, the Postmaster-General had also departed from the President's rule in order to dismiss Democrats guilty of free-soil tendencies.[58] All in all, Pierce's policy bore such unhappy results, pleasing few and irritating multitudes, that it was universally pronounced a failure.

Other Presidents took the more logical and ruthless road. While Zachary Taylor frankly gave his favor to the Seward or radical wing of the Whigs, Fillmore reversed the ship sharply, favoring the conservative wing. Buchanan owed much to Stephen A. Douglas, whose withdrawal in the Cincinnati convention of 1856 was a handsome display of self-abnegation, and who imperiled his financial future by his generous subscription to campaign funds. Yet pressures hostile to Douglas were so strong that Buchanan from the beginning supported the Southern wing as against the Northwestern wing, and eventually used the patronage with shameless aggressiveness in an effort to crush the Douglas element.[59]

The fact is that in the phrase "the spoils system" the word *system* by 1850 deserved strong emphasis. The spoils had to be used not at random and thoughtlessly, but in obedience to an elaborate system of principles. To the general strengthening of the victorious party and the harmonization or suppression of factions was added the rule of rotation, which meant that to feed as many of the hungry as possible, four years at the public crib was generally accepted as sufficient.

Jackson had protested against long continuance in office, saying that the

56 James Guthrie, October 3, 1852, to Collector G. C. Bronson; *National Intelligencer*, October 11, 1853.
57 *National Intelligencer*, October 24, 1853.
58 James Campbell, September 28, 1853, in *National Intelligencer*, October 21, 1853.
59 The New York Democracy commended the President for showing "promptness and fearless decision" in removing all placemen who secretly or openly opposed any measure favored by the Democratic Party. *National Intelligencer*, December 19, 1857. See also the issue of June 16, 1857.

duties of all public functionaries were so plain and simple that intelligent men could readily qualify themselves for their performance.[60] It was to be expected that a Whig succeeding a Democrat, or vice versa, would make a clean sweep. Within a week after Taylor promised to look to "honesty, capacity, and fidelity" in officeholders, he was telling a Pennsylvania delegation that he would divide the places among his supporters. Approximately 5,000 postmasters received a circular stating that if they did not resign they would be displaced; and before Taylor's first year ended, 2,800 had resigned and 2,100 had been removed.[61] But even when Democrat succeeded Democrat—when Buchanan followed Pierce— the changes were sweeping. This was rotation. Jackson's dictum was patently erroneous. Long experience was invaluable in hundreds of offices, and every bureau head agreed that the innumerable blunders and negligences of the government found their chief source in the ignorance of green appointees.[62]

By 1850 the evils of the general system had become almost innumerable. It consumed the time and strength of Presidents, who in their first months were too busy parcelling out office to give any continuous thought to policy. It occupied whole cabinet meetings; it bedevilled every department head; while certain subordinates, notably the First Assistant Postmaster-General, were expected to give half their time to patronage questions.[63] The system worked innumerable personal hardships, often of tragic character. Petty officers who had toiled for years on inadequate salaries to maintain their families were causelessly turned into the street, without a penny of savings or any prospect of other work.[64]

The consul at Turin, facing removal in 1850, penned a remarkable bit of prophecy. "The time will come," he wrote to William C. Rives, "when the broken fortunes of turned out officeholders will be followed by acts of violence, terminated by despair; and then, if not before, our system in regard to the tenure of office and the general absence of morality in the action of government on the rights of individuals will be changed." [65] This was almost a prevision of Guiteau's wild shot, Garfield's death, and the swift ensuing passage of the Civil Service

60　This was in his first annual message, 1829.
61　Washington *Union*, February 5, 10, 1850. The number of those dismissed over a nine-month period aggregated four times as many as Jackson had removed in a year.
62　Cf. the letter from "Cosmopolite" in the *National Intelligencer*, June 13, 1857. "Civis" also denounced the policy of rotation. "The present system," he noted, "barely gives those who desire to do their duty time to learn before it casts them off. The public pay for the tuition, but reap none of its fruits." See issue of October 24, 1857.
63　Richard Rush advised William Trescot not to become Assistant Secretary of State, for if he did he would be hounded to death by office seekers. They would, he warned, bolt in upon him, "waiting hours and days for a chance to be heard at last, and in extenso." February 9, 1857; Trescot Papers, South Caroliniana Library.
64　"Cosmopolite" wrote that ever since the spoils system began, Washington had known of many "tales of domestic sorrow and destitution . . ." *National Intelligencer*, June 13, 1857.
65　Nathaniel Niles to William C. Rives, April 4, 1850; Rives Papers.

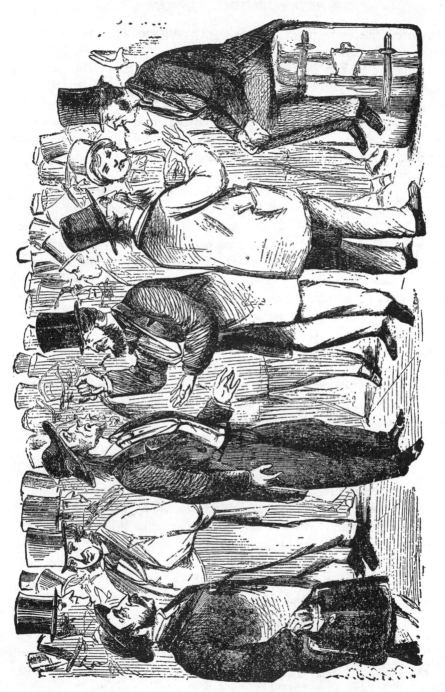

Office Seekers at Washington.
Harper's Weekly, March 16, 1861.

Act! The system filled important places not only with incompetents, but with truckling, dirt-eating sycophants. It "has converted almost the whole body of ambitious young men into political hypocrites," wrote the eminent attorney Daniel Lord, "and has resulted in filling the offices of the general government with men who in every respect injure and disgrace the country." [66]

But its worst evil was the support which it gave to the growing apparatus of bosses and machines. Of the twenty to twenty-five thousand Federal employees, perhaps a third held offices of some real value and influence. They constituted a standing political army which could be deployed with effect. Administration men in the large customhouses and postoffices, reinforced by Federal attorneys, marshals, and land officers, descended upon State conventions and frequently dominated them. They had the aid of editors who looked for a share of the public printing. They were helped by minor postmasters acting as distributors of political documents. In 1857–59 Fernando Wood headed what was known as the "custom house delegation" to Democratic conventions in New York; [67] Caleb Cushing for years could muster a phalanx of Administration officeholders in Massachusetts politics; and Isaac Cook, Buchanan's postmaster in Chicago, helped build a machine in Illinois. [68] The spoils system tended to foster a group of State bosses, cooperating with national dispensers of patronage and bulwarking the Administration.

Moreover, the system opened almost irresistible temptations to improper action. In Tyler's Administration the postmasters were called upon to peddle campaign lives of the President. A circular letter was franked out, asking each to subscribe for fifty or sixty copies, to be furnished at $50 a hundred. This circular, signed by one Abell, was accompanied by a note penned in the President's office by his son and secretary, John Tyler, Jr., who wrote: "Prompt attention and a liberal subscription will render your services still more useful." [69] Assessments for party purposes were regularly levied on many Federal employees, and Washington clerks who declined to pay, even if men of long and excellent records, were likely to be dismissed. [70] Tammany men were allowed to

66 To Secretary Clayton, March 30, 1849; Clayton Papers. A Georgia critic of the spoils system, himself a victim of a change of administration, complained that the passion to hold political office was debasing. "It soon begets an artificial behavior, a trimming policy, and more to be regretted than all, principles contracted and selfish. . . ." *National Intelligencer,* August 4, 1853.
67 D. S. Alexander, *Political History of the State of New York,* II, 249.
68 See editorial article in the N. Y. *Weekly Tribune,* July 5, 1851, and the complaint of a writer in the *National Intelligencer,* October 24, 1857, on patronage and the machines.
69 December 1, 1843; Tyler Papers.
70 Rev. Chauncey A. Goodrich to Rev. Edwards Park, August 26, 1857, Chamberlain MSS, Boston Public Library. Goodrich protested that a relative, the Rev. E. Goodrich Smith of Washington, who had occupied a minor clerkship in the Federal government for more than a dozen years, had been peremptorily turned out of his job because he had refused to contribute to Buchanan's campaign. When he was dismissed Smith was fifty-four years old, and had little to support himself.

invade the customhouse in New York to collect money, and in a typical year carried away $6,800 in sums ranging from $7.50 for night watchmen to $25 for gaugers and weighters.[71] Though Howell Cobb, as head of the Treasury, refused to allow an important subordinate leave of absence to participate in a State campaign, most department heads made no objection whatever to political activity.[72]

Closely connected with the spoils system were the printing contracts of the government and the conduct of the Administration "organ." For nearly fifteen years, 1830–1845, Francis P. Blair, conducting the Washington *Globe*, had by Jackson's and Van Buren's orders enjoyed the emoluments of departmental printing.[73] As Administrations changed, other editors came and went. Some got little, some much. Easily the most picturesque of the lot was General Robert Armstrong, a veteran of the Creek and Seminole wars, and commander of the artillery at the battle of New Orleans, who after serving as consul in Liverpool came home to take charge in 1853 of the Washington *Union*. Though he possessed some fine qualities and had been an adviser of Jackson and Polk, his best friends deplored that fact that he had "too free social habits." Edward Everett tells us that he was wholly destitute of literary culture; that he could not write a sentence, and never tried to; that it was his custom as editor to require the young men who penned the articles to read them to him; that he was an incorrigible drinker, who often disappeared from his desk for days altogether; and that according to his physician, in the twenty-four hours preceding his last fatal attack he consumed fifty-six bottles of wine.[74] He and his successors handled a great deal of government printing at handsome profits.

Indeed, late in the Buchanan Administration, Cornelius Wendell, who then had control of the field, testified that in the preceding six years the aggregate amount paid by Congress and the executive departments for public printing and binding had been approximately $3,838,000, and the profits had exceeded fifty per cent, reaching about $2,000,000. Two practical printers, in fact, had made an offer to Wendell to sublet the printing for forty cents on the dollar, for it was not uncommon to farm out the work. What had been done with these extraordinary profits? They had gone, in large degree, to support of party newspapers—the Washington *Union* (later the *Constitutionalist*), and Buchanan's home organ, the *Pennsylvanian*. But no inconsiderable sums had also been spent in the Congressional elections of 1858 in certain close Congressional dis-

71 N. Y. *Express*, quoted in the *National Intelligencer*, November 10, 1853. The Tammany men descended upon their victims on pay day when they were certain they would be able to collect. Nor did they bother to hide what they were doing, everything being done "in the most public manner."
72 Cobb's letter, dated March 30, 1857, appeared in the *National Intelligencer* April 7.
73 E. M. Shepard, *Martin Van Buren*, 163–165.
74 MS Diary, February 26, 1854.

tricts. When Wendell, finding the conduct of the *Union* a sore burden, had transferred it to another man, it was on the understanding that he should divert a fixed sum yearly out of his public printing profits to its support; and the Attorney-General of the United States drew up the legal contract to this end! [75]

Then as later, the spoils system in all its ramifications was regarded in very different lights by politicians and by cultivated outsiders of liberal tendencies. Whig editors like Greeley and Democratic editors like Bryant denounced it, while Charles Eliot Norton expressed a caustic hope that the depression of 1857 would make the governmental arrangements, if not more honest, at least less dishonest. Its more brazen manifestations now and then awakened general exclamations of disgust. When the Washington *Union* declared during the Congressional campaign of 1858 that any officeholder who did not voluntarily contribute a certain percentage of his salary to the Democratic cause should be dismissed at once, remonstrance and dissent came from many quarters.[76] Protests were numerous when that same year the head of the New York Custom House, Augustus Schell, wrote every Democratic Congressman in the city for a list of men suggested for removal, and another list suggested for appointment.[77]

But politicians in general took the system as a necessity. President John Quincy Adams, they pointed out, left most of his enemies in office, with the result that they destroyed him, and within four years he had not enough political aides to give him decent burial. "May he strike confusion to his foes!" ran the toast at a public dinner about 1827. "As he has already done to his friends!" chimed in Daniel Webster. Jackson, however, cut down his enemies and surrounded himself with henchmen, with the result that he wielded greater personal and political influence than any other President. Besides, a good shake-up made for efficiency; it got drones and sinecure-hunters out of the way. Leave the departments alone, and before long they would be full of old croakers who for ten or fifteen years had been growing fat on their high salaries of $1,200 to $2,000 a year! [78]

"Has Mr. Jordan, the Naval Storekeeper, dismissed his two Whig clerks yet?" George Bancroft, when Secretary of the Navy, asked a visitor from the Gosport Navy Yard in Virginia.

The visitor replied that he had not.

"Then tell Mr. Jordan," said Bancroft, "that if he does not dismiss those clerks

75 *Report*, Covode Committee, *passim*; 36th Cong., 1st sess., House Report No. 648.
76 *National Intelligencer*, September 23, 1858.
77 Excerpts from Schell's letter to Congressman Daniel E. Sickles were published in the *National Intelligencer*, September 23, 1858. The newspaper vehemently denounced this policy as an "organized system of mingled despotism and espionage."
78 These sentiments were expressed in a letter from George W. Ewing to Allen Hamilton, January 31, 1850; Allen Hamilton Papers, Indiana State Library.

I will dismiss him; if he lacks the moral courage, I will place a man there who has it. I have no idea of such milk and water Democrats!" [79]

In 1852 a plan was bruited for a Board of Examiners to govern the appointment and promotion of clerks in the executive departments. Daniel Webster, then Secretary of State, came out in sharp dissent, writing that the business of his department was so peculiar and various that such a scheme could easily do more harm than good.[80] When Bancroft and Webster were for the spoils system, ordinary politicians could not be expected to be against it.

[VII]

Because of the spoils system, national stinginess, and an ignorant belief that foreign affairs were neither important nor complicated, the diplomatic service of the country was dismayingly weak. A large body of Americans, as William H. Trescot remarked, believed that routine diplomatic life consisted of elaborate social trifling; that a glittering uniform, a courtly manner, some graceful gossip, and an educated taste in wine comprised most of a minister's qualifications.[81] Some prominent editors and politicians contended that three-fourths of the missions abroad might well be abolished. It is not strange that changes in important posts were incessant, that men of slight capacity or none sometimes went to the leading European capitals, that salaries were absurdly low, and that the general organization of the diplomatic and consular services was feebly ineffective.

Repeatedly the United States had sent four or five ministers to Great Britain in half a dozen years, while the same rapid changes had marked its representation in France and Russia. In 1848–53 inclusive, George Bancroft, Abbott Lawrence, J. R. Ingersoll, and James Buchanan, with Bancroft Davis as chargé, held sway in the London legation. The five men occupied four different houses, and at every change the furniture, books, archives, and current files had to be removed, with unescapable confusion and loss.[82] Changes in the leading consulates were as rapid. When a lame-duck Congressman in Pennsylvania asked for a leading consulship to restore his finances, such consulships being administered on the Leadenhall Street principle of low salaries and high perquisites, Pierce told him frankly that he had so many applications that two years must suffice.[83] By the summer of 1857 the aggregate of diplomatic and consular officers was 366.

79 Affidavit of Joseph R. Reynolds, January 25, 1859; R. M. T. Hunter Papers, Virginia State Library.

80 To Thomas Corwin, April 27, 1852; Corwin Papers, Library of Congress.

81 W. H. Trescot to A. P. Butler, *National Intelligencer*, October 5, 1853.

82 To the *National Intelligencer* this was "a striking, not to say startling 'example' of the instability of our foreign appointments"; October 5, 1853.

83 J. Glancy Jones to Buchanan, March 14, 1853; Buchanan Papers

Two ministers, those to Great Britain and France, by recent increases received $17,500 each; five were paid $12,000; and two, $10,000. Staffs were tiny, the general rule being one secretary to each mission. Indeed, with twenty-six missions and two commissionerships (to China and Hawaii), there were just twenty-eight secretaries.[84] The veteran holder of the office in London, W. B. Lawrence, wrote ex-President Van Buren in 1853 that he toiled like a galley slave and in one recent year had not left the city during eleven months; he complained that a single secretary could not possibly manage the fast-growing legation affairs—and yet he was expected to do so.[85]

Most diplomatic appointments went to men of political standing, and for obvious reasons a large proportion of the first-class posts were filled by former Senators. Not a few selections were disgraceful. The exhibition made in Berlin by a drunken lout named Hannegan, once Senator from Indiana, was long remembered by Americans abroad.[86] Hardly better in some respects was the record in Madrid of "that cheap French actor," as Henry Clay called Pierre Soulé of Louisiana. Other appointments were admirable, while the majority were simply mediocre. All envoys were handicapped by their low salaries. William C. Rives found in France during the Taylor and Fillmore Administrations that the four items of house rent, carriage hire, fuel, and subsistence more than consumed his pay; while Abbott Lawrence, minister in England at the same time, spent more than half his official income on his economical quarters and carriage.[87] These pecuniary hardships were the more sharply felt because Europe treated its diplomats generously. Sir Richard Pakenham, stationed in Washington in the middle forties, told a committee of the House of Commons that "when I have a dinner and the President a dinner, I think my dinner was rather the better of the two." [88] One American of the time never forgot the impression made upon him by his visit to the Prussian embassy in London. The marble stairways, crystal chandeliers, and handsome furniture were combined with paintings and sculptures which splendidly illustrated Prussian history from the time of Frederick; and the visitor could but think what Powers, Greenough, and Crawford might do in portraying a history not inferior to Prussia's.

But the prime defect of the American service was its inattention to system

84 *National Intelligencer*, July 25, 1857. The total appropriation for salaries exclusive of consuls was $521,750. There were 134 salaried consuls. The two most lucrative positions were in London and Liverpool; these paid $7,500, with fees additional. The next three, each of which paid $6,000, were in Havana, Havre, and Rio de Janeiro.

85 Col. F. B. Lawrence to Van Buren July 11, 1853; Buchanan Papers.

86 N. Y. *Tribune*, February 4, 1850.

87 Trescot to Senator Butler, in the *National Intelligencer*, October 5, 1853. On the other hand, Richard Rush thought that to increase salaries would be "an evil for many reasons . . ." To Trescot, October 20, 1853; Trescot Papers, South Caroliniana Library.

88 *Report on Official Salaries,* 300; cf. *Hansard,* 3d Series, XCVII, 1114–1128.

and experience. The leading British diplomatists were men of ripe training. Sir Henry Lytton Bulwer, who became minister in Washington in 1849, had begun his career in 1827, had been attaché or secretary in one important European capital after another, and had served as minister to Madrid. John F. T. Crampton, who succeeded him, had been for eighteen years an attaché and for almost ten a secretary of legation; and just before the Civil War another well-trained envoy, the future Lord Lyons, who had gone to Athens as attaché twenty years earlier, arrived. American diplomacy had both the virtues and defects (but chiefly the latter) of amateurishness. The typical American minister did not represent a fixed national policy, for none existed; he represented simply the general business of the nation, and often some special business requiring particular attention.[89] Behind him stood a State Department which, with its attenuated staff and frequent changes, had as yet no continuing tradition.

[VIII]

Campaign methods of the time bore the impress of the rural age. Party managers made industrious use of mass meetings, barbecues, open-air speeches, debates, and torchlight processions, while they freely employed newspaper editorials, pamphlets, and handbills. But the quiet organization of the voters district by district, town by town, county by county, was still in its infancy. Indeed, it was practicable only in well-settled areas, and most effective in cities. Tammany and a few other urban organizations, using saloonkeepers, gang leaders, fire companies, and ward heelers, had learned how to mobilize a well-drilled army to yell, march, vote, and if necessary, fight. In Boston, New York, Philadelphia, and Baltimore the alliance of the Democratic party with the tough elements rested upon a systematic and disciplined basis.[90] But throughout most of the country reliance was placed upon instruments of mass appeal, not personal enlistment and group drilling. After the Republican defeat in 1856, Simon Cameron wrote Thurlow Weed that the party methods must be altered. Between the State and national elections in Pennsylvania that year he and his friends had doubled the Republican vote in Dauphin County by systematic house-to-house work; and in the next battle the same system would have to be pursued throughout the State. Four years later Cameron in Pennsylvania and E. D. Morgan in New York gave to local organization and man-to-man appeals that attention which made victory certain.[91]

The essential elements of successful canvassing in the South and West re-

89 Draft of letter from W. H. Trescot to Lord Lyons, 1860; South Caroliniana Library.
90 Cf. the long article on conditions in New York: "Democratic Primary Arrangements—Scenes and Characters in the Sixth Ward." N. Y. *Weekly Tribune*, October 4, 1851.
91 The papers of E. D. Morgan at Albany throw much light on this advance.

mained in the fifties much what they had been twenty years earlier. They were almost the same in Illinois at the time of the Lincoln-Douglas debates of 1858 as in Mississippi at the time of the Henry S. Foote-Jefferson Davis debates of 1844. An effective stump speaker made the best candidate. A. G. Brown, entering a Mississippi campaign in 1853, was told that his Waterloo lay just ahead. "I made 115 speeches, travelled 3200 miles, and spent $1200," he boasted. "The cold and heat, dust and mud, sunshine and rain, were alike encountered, and for six long and hideous months I literally gave no rest to the soles of my feet. Our victory is more complete than our most sanguine friends dared to hope for."[92] Illinois crowds, yelling, "Hit him again!" as Lincoln, Douglas, or Lyman Trumbull attacked an enemy, or Indiana audiences cheering Jesse D. Bright's pugnacious oratory, were pupils in the same political school as the Missourians who alternately applauded Benton and Atchison, or the Alabamians who delightedly heard Jeremiah Clemens and W. L. Yancey exchange arguments. The paraphernalia of banners, transparencies, marching clubs, and brass bands helped to make a campaign entertainment as well as the voter's business.

Special appeals to the current political folklore were not neglected. Lincoln's rails had their parallel in Sam Houston's rough electioneering garb and panther-skin waistcoat (it was only in Washington that Houston donned his store clothes), and the trick W. R. W. Cobb of Alabama developed of singing homely songs while chewing, with great gusto, an onion and a slab of coarse corn pone.[93] By the end of this period the cities were developing their own folklore. Why vote for log cabins and rails, demanded James T. Brady when running for governor in New York in 1860. "I appeal to my friends of Irish blood whether it would not be just as good reasoning to claim that a man ought to be made President because he had once carried a hod?"[94]

In the South, as many a book of memoirs indicates, family and clerical influence counted for more than in other sections. When Reuben Davis of Mississippi made his first bid for office, he took pains to invade a hostile county, let it be known that he was the son of a Baptist preacher and husband of a most devoted Methodist wife, ingratiated himself with a minister of repute, spread word of his relationship with the May family, and made use of powerful friends. Taking all the voters he could get to a saloon, he spent a fifty-dollar bill on drinks—and carried the county.[95] It need not be said that he also made stump

92 A. G. Brown, November 15, 1853; Claiborne Papers, Mississippi State Archives.
93 On Sam Houston see the report of a Washington correspondent in the *Texas Republic* (Marshall, Texas), January 24, 1852; on Cobb, L. Dorman, *Party Politics in Alabama 1850–60*, 58, 59.
94 N. Y. *Weekly Tribune*, September 29, 1860.
95 Davis, *Recollections of Mississippi and Mississippians*, 68–71.

speeches, for Mississippians had an intense appreciation of good popular oratory. Military experience, too, carried special prestige in the South, where colonels and generals abounded. Elsewhere such men as Foote, Quitman, Jefferson Davis, and Jeremiah Clemens would have been regarded in a political light alone, but in the South their military records were never forgotten.

In the North, increasing attention had to be paid to the foreign-born vote. Of the two largest national groups, the Irish, distrusting the aristocratic element of the Whigs and attracted by the principles of Jefferson and Jackson, clung consistently to the Democratic Party. The Germans for a time held the same allegiance, and many in the middle fifties seemed confirmed in it by that Know-Nothingism which the Democrats most strongly condemned. But it had been pointed out in 1851 that their natural taste was for Whig tenets—they wanted tariffs, internal improvements, and free homesteads; and when the slavery issue became acute, the German swing to the Republican standard became pronounced.[96]

The role of fraud and corruption in party affairs was not inconsiderable. "What," asked the *Nation* a generation later, "would have been the course of our history if the Democratic repeal of the Whig registry law in New York and the Plaquemines frauds in Louisiana had not given Polk a title to the Presidency as little savory as Mr. Hayes'?"[97] Many informed Republicans firmly believed in 1856 that they were defeated by the wholesale voting of Irish laborers building railroads in Indiana and by vote buying and ballot-box stuffing in Pennsylvania. Outside Virginia, the viva-voce method of open voting had now yielded to use of the ballot. John Randolph of Roanoke had once told a London dinner party that he hoped ballot voting would never be mentioned in his State, for its adoption would make any people a nation of scoundrels if it did not find them so; and his State still clung to this view—which many old-fashioned men applauded. Not without its advantages as against secret combinations like those of the Know Nothings, it had greater disadvantages.[98] But the ballot system was highly imperfect. Many States had no registration of voters, so that impersonation and repeating were common. Official ballots were generally unknown, each party distributing its own ticket, with the result that counterfeit or spurious ballots were often palmed off on ignorant voters. The Democrats would print a supply of "Whig" ballots with names of their own candidates

96 See the editorial on "The Germans and Politics," N. Y. *Weekly Tribune*, October 4, 1851. The German immigrants, refugees from Prussian tyranny, were natural recruits for the Democratic party. Frederick Schmidt pointed out that most of the immigrants had been members of the liberal or democratic party in their native land, so that when they came here they inevitably joined "the party bearing that (Democratic) appellation. . . ." To William A. Graham, August 5, 1850; William Graham Papers, University of North Carolina.
97 *Nation*, September 13, 1877.
98 John G. Barr to C. C. Clay, May 2, 1857; C. C. Clay Papers, Duke Library.

substituted for Whig nominees, or vice-versa. Just before elections many newspapers were full of warnings against this practise.[99] They sounded warnings, too, against "colonization" schemes—the importation of voters from a safe State or district into one known to be close; against last-minute roorbacks; and against intimidation, which the use of open sheds or engine houses for voting made all too easy.[100]

Riotous battles at the polls in some large cities, notably New Orleans, Baltimore, Cincinnati, and New York, were for several years in the middle fifties rather the rule than the exception. The outright purchase of votes was far from unknown; after the Rhode Island election of 1860, in which the wealthy textile manufacturer William Sprague, running for governor, had spent money lavishly, the press declared that the price of votes had ranged from ten to a hundred dollars, and had averaged about fifty![101]

[IX]

Throughout the period most citizens were sufficiently well satisfied with their national government to spend little thought on its betterment. A blind faith in American "institutions," encouraged by every Jefferson Brick, animated a great part of the population.[102] Only a minority were discontented with what Lowell called our happy-go-lucky style of getting along and with the general want of political training, foresight, and earnestness. Such complaints as were heard, and as did not refer to superficial defects, related primarily to three subjects of disquiet. Great numbers of men, North, South, and West, agreed that Congress managed its affairs so as to produce a maximum of debate and a minimum of efficient legislative action. A smaller but growing body of opinion, concentrated chiefly in the North and Northwest, believed that the whole theory of a weak and passive central government was wrong and would have to be modified. Finally, strong groups in all sections and callings felt that something was radically wrong with the Presidency.

For twenty-five years after Jackson left the White House, no man of high abilities entered it. What was more, the country knew that no man of high

99 The Havana, Ill., *Squatter Sovereign*, November 3, 1860, for example, charged that another local newspaper had printed 2500 spurious Democratic ballots in which the names of Republican candidates were substituted for Democratic nominees, while the names of Democratic nominees were spelled wrong in every instance.
100 Quincy, Ill., *Herald*, November 3, 1860.
101 N. Y. *Weekly Tribune*, April 14, 1860. The *Tribune* editorial estimated Sprague's campaign expenses to have been $75,000.
102 Although almost every observer at the Cincinnati Convention which nominated Buchanan for President had agreed that the Convention had been a very rowdy affair, Buchanan referred to it as an example of America's "superiority over the people of other countries." *National Intelligencer*, June 10, 1856.

abilities occupied it. Calhoun, speaking to a friend in 1850 of Webster's fitness for the Presidency, added pensively: "But he is too great a man ever to be made President."[103] In 1848, and in 1856, the country was given a choice of mediocrities, neither party selecting an impressive candidate. Discontent among thoughtful men over the lack of executive leadership found one expression in a widespread denunciation of the national conventions. Walt Whitman was fierce in his condemnation of these rowdy, vote-trading, incalculable gatherings.[104] Andrew Johnson, as governor of Tennessee, proposed electing the President by direct popular vote. "That national conventions have already fallen into discredit with the people, there needs no ghost from the grave to reveal; that they are destined to be condemned, proscribed, discarded, it needs no prophet to foretell," declared the New York *Tribune* in 1854.[105] Even the patient John J. Crittenden rebelled. "Most certainly," he burst out in 1859, "it is important to the country to find some better mode of electing Presidents than the present, and some mode of making better Presidents than we have lately been blessed with."[106]

The reasons for the weakness of successive Presidents lay deeper, however, than the defects of the nominating system, for a variety of factors were involved. John Stuart Mill remarked in his essay on DeTocqueville that the main explanation for the paucity of great men lay in the fact that America needed little government. She had no wars, no powerful neighbors, no old society with a thousand abuses to reform, no half-fed, untaught millions in need of food and guidance. Society in the United States required little but to be let alone. This was essentially true when Mill wrote in 1840; it was not true ten years later, when a problem requiring great minds and iron wills had fully emerged. A time-lag in comprehending the magnitude of the issue, and the old pioneer habit of improvisation, both counted for much. The jealous readiness of petty political leaders to combine against any towering figure did something, then as later, to keep the presidency in weak hands. Pure fortuity doubtless played its role. But the chief reason why the four Presidents before the Civil War were mediocrities can be clearly traced to the torsions which the slavery contest gave to the party system. Whenever a party is closely divided by an angry issue, it instinctively moves to an uncommitted, neutral figure rather than to a bold and trenchant leader. Hence it was that the Whigs turned away from Webster in 1852 and the Democrats from Douglas in 1856; hence the demand for unknowns like Taylor and Pierce, and for trimmers like Buchanan. It was only when the parties ceased to be divided—when Northern sentiment took

---

103 N. Y. *Journal of Commerce*, quoted in the *National Intelligencer*, November 6, 1852.
104 Whitman, *Gathering of the Forces*, II, Part IV.
105 January 7, 1854.
106 To W. C. Rives, November 15, 1859; Rives Papers.

control of one and Southern conviction of the other—that bold men were called to the helm.

With a clumsily managed, hopelessly divided Congress and a series of weak chief magistrates, the country watched the national crisis grow to a point where even strong leadership could not control it. In 1860 all three parties selected strong men. Douglas, Breckinridge, and Lincoln were alike leaders of intellectual power and stalwart character. At last the country was certain of a President of statesmanlike parts—but it was too late.

6

Election of a War Hero

A FULL eighteen months before the election of 1848, public sentiment was running strongly in favor of the one military hero who had captured the imagination of the whole nation. "The probability now is, that Taylor will come in with a general rush," Webster ruefully wrote his son on April 26, 1847. He declared that he knew of no qualifications which Taylor possessed for the place, but since Buena Vista the popular demand had grown unmistakable. "General Scott," Philip Hone confided to his diary, "has a claim ten times stronger upon the gratitude and favor of the American people for services rendered to the country than General Taylor; and yet the latter chieftain, by the exercise of more discretion, and manners more popular, would beat the hero of Chippewa, of Vera Cruz and Mexico, ten to one in a contest for the presidency." [1]

Martial renown and discreet conduct, however, were not the only elements in Taylor's swift rise. The portentous cloud of sectional discord had frightened reflective people. An uncompromising frontal attack upon the sectional issue would lead straight to the disruption of the republic; evasion, conciliation, mutual concession—these unheroic expedients offered the only safety; and a presidential candidate of neutral stamp and hazy views suited the logic of the crisis.

[I]

Democratic weakness in the impending battle was patent, for not only in Washington but in one Northern State after another the party was in a chaotic condition. Had Polk possessed the political gifts of Jefferson or Jackson, he could easily have used the triumphant war to give unity and confidence to a strong central body of Democrats. The two implacable wings, the Southern Rights men under Calhoun and the radical anti-slavery Democrats who looked to Martin Van Buren, would have remained hostile, but an adroit President

---

1 Curtis, *Webster*, II, 310; Hone, *Diary* (Nevins ed.,) II, 835, 836.

might have reduced them to impotence. By skilful use of the patronage, advertisement of the Mexican victories as party triumphs, and a forceful appeal to love of the Union, he could gradually have rallied a powerful following. But the cold, narrow, conscientious President, whose ample endowment of tenacity and shrewdness was leavened by no magnetism or imagination, was politically quite inept. When 1848 opened, discontent and apprehension possessed the party. A strong new chieftain was needed. Yet as Polk prepared to retire, moderate Democrats and lovers of political fleshpots found no satisfactory leader in sight; for neither the lethargic Cass nor timid Buchanan could capture popular enthusiasm or impose a powerful will upon the rival factions.

It was in New York that Democratic demoralization was sorest and most dangerous. The followers of Van Buren, John A. Dix, and Benjamin F. Butler, sneeringly called Barnburners (a name which to some carried an allusion to the recent Dorrite incendiarism in Rhode Island, and to others recalled a current anecdote about a Dutchman who burned his barn to rid it of rats), were definitely in rebellion against the Administration. Van Buren's defeat in the convention of 1844, Silas Wright's defeat for the governorship in 1846, refusals of patronage, the war and its management—these were their main grievances. The Administration men or Hunkers (a term which at once described their hankering for offices and their stolid conservatism) seemed to be losing ground. Since the virulent schism which in the fall election of 1847 had torn open the Democratic columns and let the Whigs rush through to victory, no adequate rally had been made. Early the next year a New Yorker wrote Stephen A. Douglas that the state of the party was "horrible." The Barnburner bolt, he went on, "has created a degree of bitterness in our ranks hardly to be conceived," and "still the bolting goes on"—the rebels showing themselves "exceptionally hostile" to Lewis Cass.[2]

Similar quarrels beset the Democrats elsewhere. In Pennsylvania the Administration men were at swords' points with the Wilmot Proviso forces, and no prospect of harmony appeared. Buchanan's hopes of getting the presidential nomination rose and fell, but he lamented that no State pride united the party behind him. He and Simon Cameron agreed in keeping a platoon of party editors busy publishing the most vicious attacks on the freesoilers, but they were jealous rivals for control of the State machine. Vice President George M. Dallas, calling attention to his casting vote on the Walker Tariff, also had presidential ambitions. Early in 1848 Buchanan gained an easy victory in the State convention—but the radical freesoilers remained a menace.[3] In Ohio the

2 D. L. Seymour to Douglas, March 25, 1848; Douglas Papers.
3 The factional struggle within the Democratic party in Pennsylvania is described in Going, *Wilmot*, 245–247; L. F. Crippen, *Simon Cameron: Ante-Bellum Years*, 91–109. Letters to Buchanan reveal the strenuous efforts that his followers made to get the nomination for

anti-slavery Democrats actually ruled the hour. When the party convention met in Columbus in January, they carried a declaration that the people of Ohio, opposing slavery, felt it proper "to use all the power clearly given by the national compact, to prevent its increase, to mitigate, and finally eradicate the evil." [4] Chase, much the ablest of the radical Democrats, was so certain that the national organization would not nominate an acceptable man that he was preparing to secede. He informed Joshua Giddings early in 1848 that he hoped for a general rally of anti-slavery men behind a third-party ticket, with a platform of free principles and a candidate of the true Silas Wright stamp.

Throughout New England, too, the warfare of party regulars and anti-slavery Democrats had become truly ferocious. The radicals of Massachusetts had their young champion in Charles Sumner, who after legal study and a prolonged tour of Europe had given up a promising literary career for politics. He was as ready to quit the party as Chase. The Administration Democrats, led by Caleb Cushing, were still in the saddle, and three shrewd politicians, Benjamin F. Hallett, David Henshaw, and Charles G. Greene, editor of the Boston *Post,* controlled the State machine and divided the offices. But their hold was increasingly precarious, for anti-slavery feeling was becoming part of the very air of Massachusetts.[6] In the rest of New England, the conservative Democrats were in full retreat. The most strenuous efforts of the New Hampshire regulars, directed by Franklin Pierce, had not availed in 1847 to keep John P. Hale, so fervent a free-soiler that he had opposed Tyler's joint resolution for the annexation of Texas, out of the Senate.[7] A coalition of anti-slavery Democrats and Whigs gave him his seat. In Maine a smiliar combination was shortly to send the outspoken Hannibal Hamlin to the Senate. As for Connecticut, Vermont, and Rhode Island, in all three the Democrats were predominantly opposed to the expansion of slavery and hostile to Polk.

Some Southern observers soon concluded, indeed, that the Democratic party was fast going to pieces in the North. Robert Toombs declared that it was being "denationalized," and that if it were not for New Jersey, Pennsylvania, and the Northwest beyond Ohio, it would soon be a purely sectional party.[8]

---

him. See, for example, those of Isaac McKinley, February 15, 1848, and Henry Welsh, January 20, 1848, in the Buchanan Papers. Preparing to retire from the State Department, Buchanan this summer paid a little less than $7,000 for the neglected farm of Wheatlands near Lancaster, and had his housekeeper, Miss Parkes, select furniture for it.

4 J. W. Schuckers, *Life and Public Services of Salmon Portland Chase,* 89.
5 Chase to Joshua Giddings, March 10, 1848; Giddings Papers.
6 Roy F. Nichols, *The Democratic Machine, 1850–54,* 23.
7 Pierce, *Sumner,* III, 99; Wilson, *Slave Power,* II, 626 ff.
8 February 15, 1851; *Toombs, Stephens, Cobb Corr.,* 229.

[II]

A fortnight before the Democratic convention met in Baltimore on May 22nd, politicians en route were filling the parlors, hotel lobbies, and barrooms of Washington. A buzz of talk dealt with such possible candidates as Robert J. Walker and John A. Dix, dark or very dun-colored horses. But wiseacres of the press were assuring the public that Cass would bear away the prize. It was indispensable, they pointed out, to select a Northern man; Secretary Buchanan was too closely identified with the unpopular Polk Administration; and Cass' strength in the Northwest was too valuable to lose.[9]

These observers were correct. By the time the convention was called to order, Secretary Walker had authorized his friends to give their support to Cass, who was within sight of victory. The only excitement of the convention centered in the sharp struggle between rival sets of delegates sent down by the two New York factions. In ability, the Hunker group under Daniel S. Dickinson were outweighed by the Barnburners, whose lively contingent included John A. Dix, Preston King, the talented "Prince" Van Buren (a man of distinction as attorney, political leader, and witty social precentor in his own right, without reference to his famous father), and an incisive young attorney, Samuel J. Tilden. Anxious to conciliate each faction, the committee on credentials offered to admit both, dividing the State's vote equally between them.[10] This proposal, accompanied as it was by an effort to bind both factions to acceptance of the platform and candidate, failed to please either. The Barnburners, indeed, were violently intransigent. They made Baltimore "lurid with their wrath, frightening the delegates from the back States almost out of their wits." With New York silent, the convention on its fourth ballot nominated Cass, and then named W. O. Butler of Kentucky for Vice-President. On the territorial question the platform was the dumbest of oracles.[11]

Glowering with anger, the freesoil Democrats not only of New York but other States returned home determined to act independently, and that at once. Cass was a candidate whom all disliked and many despised. He had written a letter in 1844 favoring the annexation of Texas; he had attacked the Wilmot

9 Washington correspondence dated May 19, Charleston *Courier*, May 24, 1848.
10 Two months before the convention D. L. Seymour had attempted to find out how it would probably handle the schism in the New York Democracy. He hoped the convention would not favor the radical faction as this would read the Hunkers out of the party. To Douglas, March 25, 1848; Douglas Papers.
11 H. B. Stanton, *Random Recollections*, 162. The convention failed to make the nomination unanimous because of the objections of some Southern delegates. The day he was nominated Cass was in his Senate seat as usual, and remarked jocularly: "You who want offices are anxious, I am not." Charleston *Courier*, May 30, 1848. In the platform discussion an inflammatory resolution by Yancey was rejected by 216 to 36. It faintly foreshadowed the great Democratic split that Yancey was to engineer in 1860.

Proviso with six different reasons for its rejection; [12] and he had done more than anybody else to bring forward a popular sovereignty scheme which acquiesced in the possible extension of slavery and opened a door to numberless controversies. The platform, a bundle of platitudes which condemned all efforts to meddle with slavery or take incipient steps in that direction, was quite unacceptable to Democrats like Chase, Sumner, Preston King, and Bryant.

Cass was in fact not a man to inspire enthusiasm anywhere. In many ways he seemed a relic of the past. Born within a year after the battle of Yorktown, and a Federal officeholder under Jefferson, his career paralleled almost the whole history of the republic. Though able, upright, and rich in experience (he had been general, governor of Michigan Territory, Minister to France, and Senator), he had lost his early energy and passed into a phase of slow, phlegmatic conservatism. He had militarist tastes and an Anglophobia which might become dangerous. His portly frame, morose mouth, pendulous cheeks, and cold eyes gave him a forbidding look. In debate he was formidable, for he had a precise mind, a crushing logic, and a full mastery of constitutional law. He spoke in the Senate with magisterial authority. But he was inert and indolent, his intellect stirred to action only by some powerful appeal to self-interest, vanity, or resentment, while ever since his approval of Texan annexation, he had seemed distinctly timid in dealing with the South.[13] Lincoln, in a graphic speech in the House, ridiculed him as an ox which had backed away from the farmer's goad; he had at first seemed ready to support the Proviso, but when the cotton States grew threatening, had meekly gone back to his stall while his master ordered: "So! stand at that!" [14] All Van Buren's supporters recalled that it was Cass who in 1844, throwing his delegates to the first "dark horse," had given Polk the nomination over the ex-President. The platform declaration that Mexico had provoked the recent war, coupled with an effusive endorsement of Polk's measures, did not make the Democratic cause more pleasing.

A revolt was inevitable, and the leadership of a half-dozen brilliant New Yorkers turned it into a crushing movement. Among those actuated chiefly by a desire to avenge Van Buren's wrongs were Tilden, already gaining renown as a political strategist, who penned an indignant address to all Barnburners; C. C. Cambreleng, formerly one of Andrew Jackson's trusted lieutenants in the House; and Samuel Young, a political veteran to whom Horace Greeley later paid amusing tribute—"In his heart was no guile, in his face was no dough." Among radical anti-slavery men were Preston King, with his record as a fearless

12 *Cong. Globe*, March 1, 1847.
13 Olover Dyer, *Great Senators of the United States Forty Years Ago, 1848–49*. p. 45.
14 *Cong. Globe*, July 27, 1848. Buchanan wrote a friend that Cass (whom he made Secretary of State six years later) was lacking in moral firmness and other qualities requisite to a practical statesman; Donelson Papers, March 20, 1851, in *Tenn. Hist. Mag.*, III, 259–291.

proviso man in Congress; David Dudley Field, whose celebrated code of civil procedure was passed by the legislature this year; and William Cullen Bryant. Both groups rallied to a movement for the nomination of Martin Van Buren as candidate of all freesoilers for the Presidency.[15]

Meanwhile, a very different rebellion against Cass began to run its course in stubborn South Carolina. Calhoun was disgusted by the nomination of the chief author of the popular sovereignty doctrine. "With General Jackson," he told a friend, "I put the Congressional caucus system under foot, but I did not expect to see this monstrous system of national conventions take its place. It is far more odious than the Congressional caucus." [16] He and Rhett reached home more than half ready to oppose the Democratic nominee.

[III]

The confusion in the Democratic ranks gave the Whigs their last golden opportunity. It was more than they deserved, for, driven from their best strong-holds, they had also lost all their principles. In the spacious days of Clay's and Webster's prime a party with ideas and integrity, now they lacked any vital doctrine to give them real cohesion. They had been beaten on the tariff, on the United States Bank, and on generous national appropriations for internal im-provements; it was plain that national sentiment was against their main ideas. They had lost faith, too, in the stars of their two veteran leaders. Clay, the formulator of the old Whig tenets, the idol of multitudes all the way from the crossroad taverns of the West to the drawing-rooms of New York, was still fervently admired; so was Webster, champion of the manufacturing East, defender of nationalism, and the most eloquent voice that the New World had produced. Either, as candidate, would represent the old character of the party and revive its former integrity.[17] But neither could draw an army of new sup-

15   The address to the Barnburners by Tilden actually represented a good deal of collabo-ration. Martin Van Buren, spending the winter at Julian's Hotel in New York, one day handed Tilden a roll of manuscript, saying: "If you wish to be immortal, take this home with you, complete it, revise it, put it into proper shape, and give it to the public." Tilden, with assistance from "Prince" John Van Buren, did so, and a committee of Democratic members of the legislature unanimously adopted it. John Bigelow, *Letters and Memorials of Samuel J. Tilden*, I, 49, 50.

16   Quoted by Representative Keitt at Whippy Swamp October 2, 1858; *National Intelli-gencer*, October 23, 1858.

17   To Gideon Welles "it was plain that the Whigs had been driven from all their strong-holds and that the sentiment of the nation was clearly and unequivocally against them." Un-dated MS on the campaign in Welles Papers. Sixteen years later Welles claimed that both Lincoln and Seward considered Clay and Webster "hard and selfish leaders whose private personal ambition had contributed to the ruin of their party. . . . For years the Whig cause consisted in adulation of these two men, rather than in support of any well-established prin-ciples. In fact, principles were always made secondary to them." *Diary of Gideon Welles*, I, 507, January 8, 1864. The Boston *Herald* also asserted that the Whigs had lost the battle on all their principles, and had therefore given up principles for men; December 18, 1848.

porters into its ranks—and this was indispensable; while they were so jealous that one would sulk if the other were nominated. The party prepared to turn its back on its old faiths and captains. With a new candidate, untouched by former errors and associated with fresh hopes and nascent forces, it could march to victory. To that candidate destiny had pointed its finger.

Destiny—and some very astute politicians. It was not the elder leaders of the Whig party, but its calculating young lieutenants, who led the movement for Taylor. Webster expressed scorn for this "illiterate frontier colonel." Neither Speaker Winthrop nor any other distinguished New England Whig supported the proposal. Tom Corwin shared Webster's dislike for military candidates, feared Taylor's position on the Territories, and translated abhorrence of the war into dislike of a war leader. Clay regarded Taylor so contemptuously that it was not until it was too late that he awakened to the threat against his own primacy. It was an energetic younger group who, capitalizing upon public enthusiasm, formed their plan and carried it into swift execution.[18]

Thurlow Weed of New York, his ally William H. Seward, Truman Smith of Connecticut, "Honest John" Davis of Massachusetts, and a few others led the movement in the East. Alexander H. Stephens, who had organized a Taylor Club in Congress as early as December, 1846, was active in Washington with Toombs, William Ballard Preston, Flournoy and Pendleton of Virginia, and Lincoln of Illinois.[19] Among all these men, Weed and Stephens were perhaps the quickest to see how to use the favoring wind.

A few weeks after Resaca de la Palma, Weed chanced to meet General Taylor's brother on a Hudson River steamboat. He asked about the hero's political principles. Joseph Taylor replied that Zachary had none; that he belonged to no party and had seldom voted; and that he merely held several strong prejudices—he admired Clay, had disliked Jackson, and was so eager to protect American manufactures that he would not wear an imported garment. Such prejudices, Weed instantly declared, were as valuable as principles!—"Your brother is to be our next President." This idea the colonel termed preposterous, saying that Old Rough and Ready knew nothing of civil affairs. "When I tell you he is not as fit to be President as I am, you will see the absurdity of your suggestion." But Weed had a vision of the general learning to be President under the tutelage of himself and Seward. He was not daunted when Taylor himself modestly pronounced the idea of his election visionary. As for Stephens, he induced the Georgia Whig convention in the summer of 1847 to endorse Taylor.[20]

18 George Rawlings Poage, *Henry Clay and the Whig Party*, 152 ff., analyzes the conflict between old leaders and the "Young Indians" behind Taylor.
19 Poage, *op. cit.*, 157, 158.
20 Harriet A. Weed, *Life of Thurlow Weed*, I (*Autobiography*), 570ff; R. M. Johnston and W. H. Brown. *Alexander H. Stephens*. 224–236.

Indeed, Taylor's reluctance was quickly overcome. The Whig leaders artfully made the most of the hostility long smouldering between the general and the Administration. He had complained to Secretary of War Marcy on March 3, 1847, that the government was withdrawing its confidence from him and was apparently determined to put him in an "antagonistical" attitude.[21] It was easy to persuade him that he should help turn the rascals out. He had written a friendly politician from his camp near Monterey that he would accept the Presidency if chosen "by the spontaneous movement of the people," and on such terms that he could be chief magistrate of the whole country, not merely of a party.[22] Settled at his Louisiana residence, on April 20, 1848, he addressed a letter to the press saying that he would not refuse a Whig nomination if left free of pledges.

A considerable fragment of a 'spontaneous movement' was soon visible. Weed was joined by men who had maintained an equivocal caution until sure of the winning side: Reverdy Johnson of Maryland, George E. Badger of North Carolina, John Bell of Tennessee, and others. Even Clay's lifelong friend John J. Crittenden turned to the new luminary. His devotion to Harry of the West was undiminished, "but my conviction," he wrote, "my involuntary conviction, is that he cannot be elected." [23] Though his defection was a blow which Clay found it hard to forgive, Crittenden always insisted that his course had been wise, frank, and honest.[24] As 1847 closed, the Whig governor of Maryland, in his message to the legislature, recommended Taylor's nomination. On New Year's Day the New York *Courier and Enquirer* called for a ticket made up of Taylor and Webster—which Webster thought insulting. Immediately afterward, the Tennessee legislature by joint resolution recommended selection of the general.[25] The flowing stream was soon at flood tide.

Too late, Clay awoke to his peril. Passed over in 1840 for the infirm Harrison, and defeated in 1844 by a combination of his own errors and the misguided zeal of the abolitionists under James G. Birney, now he felt himself entitled to his fourth nomination. A great part of the rural press stood loyally behind him. In

21 Holman Hamilton, *Zachary Taylor, Soldier of the Republic*, 244.
22 The letter was to Joseph R. Ingersoll. Although written in 1847, it was not given publicity till early in 1848. W. M. Gwin wrote Buchanan January 8, 1848, that despite Taylor's refusal "to be a party candidate" the Southern Whigs would support him. To Gwin, Taylor was already "fairly in the field" for the nomination. Buchanan Papers.
23 Coleman, *Crittenden*, I, 290.
24 Crittenden to Winfield Scott, December 9, 1851; Crittenden Papers.
25 Charleston *Courier*, January 8, 1848, Washington correspondence, for Maryland; N. Y. *Courier and Enquirer*, January 1, 1848, for Tennessee. The vote in the upper chamber of the Tennessee legislature was close, but in the House it was overwhelmingly for Taylor. Charleston *Courier*, January 22, 1848. On Webster's reaction to the suggestion that he let himself be nominated for Vice-President see his letter to R. M. Blatchford, January 30, 1848; Curtis, II, 336. As early as May, 1847, Sumner and Caleb B. Smith admitted that Taylor seemed to be the most popular man in the country and would be a difficult candidate to beat. Sumner to Giddings May 24, 1847, Smith to Giddings May 21, 1847; Giddings Papers.

New York State he was the choice, as the hostile Weed estimated, of at least three-fourths of the Whigs. In the metropolis, Horace Greeley remained true. One point, Greeley told his editorial friend Schuyler Colfax, was perfectly clear: they could not with any decency support Taylor, a no-party man destitute of qualifications or principles.[26] Many influential New Englanders, shying away from Taylor, the owner of over a hundred slaves, were genuinely anxious to follow their old chieftain.[27] He had strengthened their confidence by a ringing speech at Lexington in the fall of 1847, castigating the national ambition for aggrandizement and declaring that he would never consent to acquire territory for the diffusion of slavery.[28] The Whig press of the North had hailed that speech with enthusiasm, and mass meetings in the larger cities had given it their endorsement. But now Clay suddenly perceived that his hold was weaker than he had believed—and he hastened to act.

Hearing as Congress opened in December, 1847, that he had been forsaken by many old adherents, he hurried to Washington. "Before he reached that city, however," later wrote Gideon Welles, "he learned that his most reliable supporters who were not already corrupted and seduced had become shaken. Delegates already elected to the national convention, pledged and instructed to support him, were among the most active to defeat him. His bosom friends and confidants had secretly entered into the conspiracy for his overthrow. Still, his appearance on the theater of his former renown, and among those who had for years yielded implicitly to his imperious mandates, was not without its influence. The conspirators were awed, and most of them silenced, during his presence at the seat of government. He was satisfied before he left that he had quashed the rebellion . . ."[29] Troops of friends called at his lodgings; crowds cheered him in public; and when he visited Capitol Hill, Congressmen and politicians received him with enthusiastic affection.[30] A visit to New York and Philadelphia proved, so far as outward manifestations went, equally satisfactory.

26 April 3, 1848; Greeley-Colfax Corr.
27 Writing from Washington, Caleb B. Smith maintained that most of the Northern Whigs in the city were convinced that Taylor would be a losing candidate in the North if he persisted in not committing himself. That was also Smith's opinion. He thought that if Clay were nominated he would win easily, providing the country was still at war. Smith to Allen Hamilton, February 16, 1848. See also his letter to Hamilton, dated March 26, 1848; Allen Hamilton Papers, Ind. Hist. Soc. It was the opinion of Charles Francis Adams at this time that "no union with any *heart* in it can be made upon any man excepting Mr. Clay." To Joshua Giddings, February 8, 1848; Giddings Papers.
28 Carl Schurz, *Henry Clay*, II, 292. For this speech see *Niles' Register*, LXXIII, 197–200.
29 Undated political sketch in Welles Papers.
30 Charleston *Courier*, February 15, Washington correspondence dated February 9. Several days before the paper had printed a report from Washington which emphasized the positive effect of Clay's visit to the Capital. "There can be no doubt," the report had said, "that Mr. Clay's visit to this city, and his evident health and spirits and his decided opposition to the war, have all had great influence in reuniting upon him the force of the yet powerful Whig party." Washington correspondence dated February 6, and printed February 10, 1848.

Before leaving Washington, he attended a White House dinner. Sitting next to Mrs. Polk, a woman of marked beauty and grace, he did not fail of his usual courtliness. "Madame," he said in his bland way, "I must say that in all my travels, in all companies and among all parties, I have heard but one opinion of you. All agree in commending in the highest terms your excellent administration of the domestic affairs of the White House. But"—indicating the President—"as for that young gentleman there, I cannot say as much. There is some little difference of opinion in regard to the policy of his course." "Indeed," replied Mrs. Polk. "I am glad to hear that *my* administration is popular. And in return for your compliment, I will say that if the country should elect a Whig next fall, I know of no one whose elevation would please me more than that of Henry Clay." [31] But Clay was too shrewd to be deceived by the cordialities of Washington, or even the cheers which fifty thousand spectators gave him as he passed up Broadway in a barouche drawn by six white horses. He knew the power of the ambitious new men, and doubtless returned to Lexington with a foreboding heart.[32]

[IV]

Actually Taylor was a stronger man than he seemed. A witty Democrat might satirize the heterogeneous character of his supporters by saying that they would march to "Hail, Columbia" in front and "Hark from the Tombs" in the rear.[33] Greeley might spit venom regarding "his no-party utterances, his well-understood hostility to the Wilmot proviso, his unqualified devotion to slavery," concluding: "If we nominate Taylor, we elect him, but we destroy the Whig Party." [34] But he had better qualities than his rough surface suggested.

A native of Virginia, nearing his middle sixties, Taylor had spent nearly forty years as an Indian fighter and garrison-commander at small frontier posts. He possessed little formal schooling or knowledge of the world; his foot had seldom been on a pavement. Short, thickset, roughly dressed (for he disliked uniforms and ceremony as much as Scott loved them), he was a plain, honest, hardworking soldier both in appearance and habit. He had risen by blunt sense, industry, and rigid attention to duty; he had shirked no task—strengthening border defenses, drilling awkward recruits, enduring loneliness, exhaustion, and malaria, fighting with savages. His officers respected him because he was resourceful, while his men, knowing that he was considerate and just, were always

31 The *Western Continent*, quoted in the Charleston *Courier*, March 9, 1848.
32 Welles thought that Clay returned to Kentucky "persuaded that he would be renominated and elected." Undated MS on campaign of 1848, or "Political History," Welles Papers. But Caleb Smith felt that Clay had not gained enough strength to win the nomination. And even Clay's "firmest friends" were reading the conclusion that there was not "much hope of his election." Smith to Allen Hamilton, March 26, 1848. Allen Hamilton Papers.
33 Representative T. J. Henley of Indiana, *Cong. Globe*, January 26, 1848.
34 To Colfax, April 3, 1848; Greeley-Colfax Corr.

ready to follow him with a hearty cheer for Old Rough and Ready. During the Mexican War his plebeian qualities made his troops feel a comradeship with him which no force ever felt with Scott. His record in this conflict was impressive— the record not of a great organizer or strategist, but a great captain. Like a long line of Americans from Mad Anthony Wayne to George Patton, he was a born fighter, quick-witted in moments of peril, iron-nerved under pressure, and gifted with dominating force of personality. His operations at Monterey, where he boldly and perhaps rashly divided his forces, have been severely criticized; so have his tactics at Buena Vista, which inspired Polk to record in his diary that he was responsible for a needless loss of all our brave officers and men there. But these were victories. Indeed, Taylor, however much an improviser, however lacking in foresight and profundity, was victor in the first four battles of the war, all hardfought fields.[35]

There was no lack of rude strength in Taylor; of determination, integrity, and moral and physical bravery, qualities not the less likable because commingled with naïveté and ingenuousness. Nobody ever regarded him as a man of brilliance, intellectual distinction, or learning. Ethan Allen Hitchcock, meeting him in 1820, found that about the only book he had then read was Hume's *History of England*, which he liked to discuss; nor had he found time to read much since.[36] But brilliance and scholarliness are not requisites of a good President. His principal handicaps, which made his nomination as full of risks as Webster, Clay, and Greeley believed, were his ignorance of domestic and foreign affairs, his total lack of experience in civil administration, and his unsophisticated willingness to put himself in the hands of other men (who might prove good or bad advisers) for guidance. Politically he was an amateur, and time was to disclose in him an instinct for second-rate men, or at least an unfortunate fear of being dominated by first-rate men.[37]

Weed, Seward, Truman Smith, and the other leaders in the Taylor movement managed their preparations for the Whig Convention adroitly. It was to gather June 7th in Philadelphia. On its eve they arranged a conference of numerous Whig delegates from the North at the Astor House in New York. Most of the New Englanders still preferred Webster as a candidate; most of the Ohio delegates leaned toward Winfield Scott; most of the New Yorkers and Pennsylvanians were true to Clay. Taylor, while declaring that he was "a Whig, but not an ultra one," had refused any pledges upon the slavery question in the Territories. As he was manifestly the favorite of the pro-slavery Whigs, many Northerners distrusted him. But in the New York conference, which not acci-

35 See the characterizations in George Lockhart Rives, *The United States and Mexico,* 1821–1848, II, 147, 148, and Smith, *The War With Mexico,* I, 140, 141, II, 315, 316.
36 Holman Hamilton, *Zachary Taylor, Soldier of the Republic,* 66, 67.
37 Greeley thought that Taylor "would get along tolerably well with good advisers," but he added, "it is all a lottery about that." To Colfax, May 1, 1847; Greeley-Colfax Corr.

dentally coincided with a fervent Barnburner demonstration, Weed and his friends brought forward plausible arguments. They pointed out that Clay was so repugnant to Van Buren and the Barnburners that if the Whigs nominated him, the Democratic malcontents would probably give up all idea of a third party and throw in their strength with the regular Democrats. At all costs, the freesoil Democrats must be encouraged to go forward with their independent movement. Moreover, the noncommittal Taylor could better unite the Northern and Southern Whigs than anybody else. He had no personal enemies in the party, while Clay, Webster, and the chilly, selfish Judge McLean counted them in armies.

Sentiment among Whig members of Congress also favored Taylor. The sagacious manufacturer who had done so much to establish New England's textile industry, Nathan Appleton, who was in Washington during the spring, found a general hope that the hero would be named, and a general apprehension of the result if Clay were chosen instead. Only three of the Whig Congressmen thought that Clay could carry the country, and not one believed Webster could do so. The almost universal desire, he reported, was for a ticket pairing Taylor with some good New Englander like Abbott Lawrence, Speaker Winthrop, or Truman Smith.[38] The manufacturers and merchants of whom Appleton was typical had no objection to Taylor, and in their anxiety for closing the sectional breach looked to him, a Southern slaveholder of strong national convictions, as a possible mediator. A little later Charles Sumner charged that the elevation of Taylor resulted from "an unhallowed union, conspiracy rather let it be called, between the politicians of the Southwest and the politicians of the Northeast, between the cotton-planters and fleshmongers of Louisiana and Mississippi, and the cotton-spinners and traffickers of New England; between the Lords of the Lash and the Lords of the Loom." [39] This loose talk of conspiracy was as empty as the rhetoric which garnished it was offensive. It was nevertheless true that some Northeastern Whigs who wanted less quarreling over slavery and more attention to tariffs strongly favored the general. It was also true that Abbott Lawrence had written a letter suggesting certain parallels between Taylor and Washington, and that when the Congressional committee which escorted J. Q. Adams' remains to his home was entertained in Boston, its Whig members were told by important cotton manufacturers that Massachusetts could be carried for Taylor.[40]

38 Nathan Appleton to Sumner, September 4, 1848; Appleton-Sumner Correspondence, Boston Public Library. Appleton believed that if the nomination could "be made by the members of Congress, Taylor would have been nominated by acclamation."
39 *Works of Charles Sumner* (edited by himself), II, 74ff, 303ff.
40 See Sumner's long letter to Appleton, August 31, 1848, in which Sumner discussed the reasons for his charges that there was a "combination" between the Southern cotton growers and the Northern cotton manufacturers; Appleton-Sumner Correspondence. Ten days before the Whig Convention Sumner spent an evening with Abbott Lawrence, who admitted he was

[V]

The Whig Convention, with near three hundred delegates, was full of excited rivalry. Its opening hours found Clay's adherents enthusiastic and boastfully overconfident, while the Taylor men were laboring with energy and consummate skill. Committees from the Palo Alto Club met all trains. Thomas Butler King kept the Southern delegates in line for the general, Thurlow Weed was indefatigable among Middle States delegates, and Truman Smith, converting as many New Englanders as he could, encouraged the others to vote for Webster, whose chances were nil. The first ballot gave Taylor 111 votes, Clay 97, Scott 43, and Webster 22. It was obvious that a Clay-Scott combination might have won the day. But before any arrangement could be made, the Webster delegates transferred their strength to Taylor, who was nominated on the fourth ballot. Later Webster's followers, who had mismanaged his whole effort, explained their conduct to him on two grounds: they had decided that the party could elect Taylor but nobody else, and they hoped that when Taylor went to the White House, Webster would have a real place in the Administration—while they knew that Clay would never give him one.[41] These were not elevated motives, but they were sufficiently practical.

For a brief time the defeated elements in the Whig party gave full vent to their resentment. Clay's more idolatrous followers swore, as so often before, that he had been the victim of treachery. Many delegates from Ohio and New England could not overcome their chagrin at the selection of a slaveholder of no civil training and no known convictions.[42] "The voice of the free States has been disregarded," shouted a Massachusetts delegate in the convention. Webster's position was peculiarly sad. He had just buried his beloved daughter Julia and his soldier-son who died in Mexico; his health was failing; and now he had lost his last chance of the presidency to an unqualified novice. For a time he considered coming out against Taylor, whom he thought dangerously unfit. "Keep entirely quiet until I see you," he wrote his son Fletcher.[43]

Especially significant was the anger of the freesoil Whigs. In a scene of wild disorder after the final vote, indignant delegates offered resolutions intended to place a definite platform under the candidate. In particular, they proposed to

a strong Taylor man. When Sumner expostulated and asked Lawrence to reconsider his position, Lawrence said, "What can I do? I am in up to my eyes." Sumner remarked that all the professors at Harvard were against Taylor. But Lawrence did not care how they voted. All he wanted to know was "how the truckmen will go."

41   Curtis, *Webster*, II, 338.

42   John McLean largely blamed the selfishness of Ohio's leaders for his own failure to get the nomination. "A more unprincipled set of political jugglers never lived than was found in Ohio," he wrote. F. P. Weisenburger, *Life of John McLean*, 133.

43   More than a month before the convention Sumner claimed that Webster would not support Taylor if the general were nominated. Sumner to Giddings, April 21, 1848; Giddings Papers.

commit him to the principle that slavery should not be expanded by conquest. When the resolutions were ruled out of order, Henry Wilson and Charles Allen of Massachusetts stalked out of the hall. But first Wilson declared that he could never support a candidate bound by no doctrine. "Sir, I will go home, and so help me God, I will do all I can to defeat the election of that candidate." [44] They were conscience Whigs, in revolt against the cotton Whigs. As those who remained grew calmer, the Taylor forces took steps to choose a vice-presidential nominee who would conciliate the Wilmot Proviso delegates. The wealthy manufacturer Abbott Lawrence, who had been a favorite because of a belief that he would contribute at least a hundred thousand dollars to the campaign chest, was set aside on the ground that the party could not have King Cotton at both ends of the ticket—Taylor growing cotton and Lawrence manufacturing it! [45] Millard Fillmore was notoriously sterner in his attachment to freesoil principles; so much so that Southern fire-eaters were soon assailing him as an abolitionist. At the crucial moment one of his friends, leaping to a bench, proclaimed that if he were chosen, New York would be safe. He was quickly nominated, and without adopting any platform, the convention adjourned in an uproar. [46]

A firm platform declaration on the vital issue of slavery in the Territories was actually impossible for either party. Had the Democrats adopted a proslavery attitude, or even accepted Cass' principle of popular sovereignty, they would have lost their chances in half the North. If the Whigs had declared against slavery expansion, they would have lost all their Southern chances. Evasion was the only course. It remained for the third party, the Free Soilers eagerly waiting for action, to take a stand on principle.

[VI]

For months the staunchest anti-slavery leaders, certain that neither Democrats nor Whigs would adopt a clearcut platform and a satisfactory candidate, had been preparing their own movement. [47] The letters of Chase and Giddings,

44 Wilson, *Rise and Fall of the Slave Power*, II, 136.
45 Dyer, *Great Senators*, 79; *Autobiography, of Thurlow Weed*, 578.
46 See Rhett's bitter attack on Fillmore, Charleston *Mercury*, September 29, 1848. Sumner on June 23 met Abbott Lawrence in Boston. He said: "I am glad you were not nominated for the vice presidency." "That is a doubtful compliment," said a bystander. "I would not have Mr. Lawrence's name," said Sumner, "discredited by association with General Taylor." Lawrence resented this. "Do you know where you are going?" he demanded. "You will have to support Martin Van Buren." "I am ready," said Sumner.
47 The only way, wrote Charles F. Adams early in 1848, that the anti-slavery men could avoid the difficulties arising from the struggle among the various candidates for the nomination, would be "to look beyond men to great principles." To Giddings, February 8, 1848; Giddings Papers.

Charles Francis Adams and Sumner, Greeley and Schuyler Colfax, were full of their plans; so were the columns of the Boston *Whig,* the Springfield *Republican,* Greeley's *Tribune,* Bryant's *Evening Post,* the Washington *National Era,* and other journals.

From the very beginning of 1847 Sumner, ardent, dogmatic, and intolerant, had called for uniting every possible element on an anti-slavery platform: abolitionists, Liberty Party men, anti-slavery Democrats, and freesoil Whigs. He was distressed by the quarrel between the political-minded Weld-Birney men and the fanatical Garrisonites. As his letters to Joshua Giddings show, he himself was now a full-fledged abolitionist. The freesoil Whigs did not go far enough, he wrote. "They have proclaimed slavery to be *wrong,* and have pledged themselves with force against its *extension.* It is difficult to see how they can longer sustain themselves *merely* on that ground. Their premise sustains a broader conclusion, that is, the duty of no longer allowing the *continuance* of evil anywhere within our constitutional action. They must become Abolitionists. It seems to me that our great object should be to encourage *union* among all who are against slavery. The disputes between anti-slavery men are unseemly." [48] This was confused thinking. An abolitionist test would be the surest means of fomenting a quarrel among those who merely wanted slavery excluded from the Territories, those who wanted to interpret the Constitution to abolish it everywhere, and those Garrisonians who denounced any constitutional link with slave States.

More practical freesoilers among the Whigs—Henry Wilson, Charles Francis Adams, Horace Greeley—were meanwhile urging simply a union of all who opposed the extension of slavery. Raging against the Taylor movement, honest Henry Wilson had declared from its inception that "we must not submit to it"; that "the people are opening their eyes"; that "the free state Whigs must dictate the policy of the party or the party had better be defeated and broken up." [49] Both Greeley and C. F. Adams had at first played with the idea that Tom Corwin would make a fit candidate for a new anti-extensionist party, though Greeley frankly described Corwin's timidity—"I don't know anybody more afraid of wetting his feet." [50] But Corwin soon made it clear that he would never sit in the radical anti-slavery church. Besides making speeches

48 Sumner to Giddings, January 21, 1847; Giddings Papers.
49 Wilson to Giddings, February 6, 1847; Giddings Papers. Already Wilson was determined that the anti-slavery Whigs should oppose Taylor even "if it breaks the Party to pieces."
50 Greeley to Colfax, May 1, 1847; Greeley-Colfax Corr. Greeley predicted that "the moment a cannonade" was opened on Corwin he would "duck under water and leave us in the lurch." The editor was determined that whoever was to represent the anti-slavery Whigs, it was "essential that he shall be not only right but *known* to be so—openly, avowedly, unequivocally so." To Giddings, April 14, 1848; Giddings Papers.

which indicated that he would dutifully accept Taylor, he wrote Giddings flatly that he would never countenance a disruption of the Whig Party. "We must prevent *that*. Let us divide into North and South and one of two results will follow. Either the Southern Whig wing with General Taylor will succeed, and thus make Taylor a *merely* Southern President, or the (united) Loco Foco party will elect their man over the divided Whigs. Is not this plain? Is it right to permit my name to be used with the prospect of such a result?" [51] He thought that the people were determined to make Taylor their President, and after due inquiry he convinced himself that the general would never make a Southern tool.

The freesoil men had to give up all idea of naming Corwin. But they continued to make preparations for independent action. When the tiny Liberty Party offered John P. Hale its nomination, Sumner urged him on two grounds to decline: acceptance would diminish his influence in the Senate, and "it would interfere with a broader organization which we all desire next spring." [52] However, Hale decided to consent.

Gradually, as Taylor refused to give the anti-slavery Whigs any pledges, as Corwin emphasized his party regularity, and as the Barnburner revolt within the Democratic party developed, a new conviction gained ground. [53] All the dissident groups must unite under some Barnburner chieftain. Even before 1847 ended, Barnburner emissaries were knocking at Charles Francis Adams' door to find out whether he would join with the two Van Burens in calling a Freesoil convention. The old fox of Kinderhook would not yet flatly commit himself to running on a Free Soil platform, but he would investigate the possibilities! [54] The moment Cass was nominated, the new union movement was put under way.

An enthusiastic Barnburner convention met at Utica, New York, a fortnight after Taylor's nomination. Trains from the east and the west, from New England hills and the prairies of Ohio, Indiana, and Illinois, rolled in crowded with delegates and their friends. Martin Van Buren's associates asserted positively that he could be forced to accept the nomination for President. In a

51 Corwin to Giddings, August 18, 19, 1847; Giddings Papers.
52 Sumner to Giddings, July 27, 1847; Giddings Papers.
53 At the end of February Chase expressed the hope that it would be possible to call a national convention of all the "opponents of slavery encroachments." He had opposed the nomination of Liberty party candidates in the hope that such a convention would be held. Now, he thought, Hale would be willing to have a general convention reconsider nominations. To Giddings, February 29, 1848; Giddings Papers.
54 Sumner to Giddings, December 1, 1847; Giddings Papers. Sumner urged Giddings to do all he could to further the cause of political union with the Northern Democrats. "Let the line be drawn," he wrote. "The sooner, the better." A month before Charles F. Adams was already leaning towards the idea that a Democrat should be chosen "if such can be found to lead the movement party [sic]." Adams to Giddings, November 2, 1847; Giddings Papers.

long letter dated from his Lindenwald home, and addressed to David Dudley Field and others, Van Buren certainly threw no icy water on the demand for his name.[55] He declared his belief in the constitutional right of Congress to exclude slavery from the Territories, and pronounced this exclusion a policy which had been followed with salutary results since the beginning of the government. Was it possible that "at a period when the minds of nearly all mankind have been penetrated by a conviction of the evils of slavery," the twelve million people of the free States would take so retrogressive a step as to consent to the extension of the curse? The Utica gathering nominated Van Buren by acclamation, and chose Senator Henry Dodge of Wisconsin for second place. "Prince John" gaily wrote his father that he might as well accept, for he could not prevent the new organization from voting for him.

All this was preliminary to a broader Free Soil convention which it was understood would soon assemble and make Van Buren a formidable candidate. From northern Pennsylvania the voice of David Wilmot was raised in hearty assent. From Ohio came the cheerful approbation of Chase. On June 28 a great gathering of radical Massachusetts Whigs met at Worcester under the leadership of Charles Francis Adams and Sumner. Beneath sunny skies, seven thousand men gathered in a beautiful grove. Joshua Giddings had come from Ohio, and cheer on cheer rolled from the throng as the stalwart Western leader stepped forward on the platform. The audience hung upon his words as he proceeded in a delightfully breezy exposition of his views. Before the meeting broke up, it declared for free soil, free speech, and free men, an alliteration invented by the nimble-witted Rockwood Hoar, and endorsed the principles of Van Buren's letter. "In enthusiasm, in devotion to the cause, in unanimity of sentiment, it surpassed any body which I have ever seen," wrote Sumner. "As I witnessed their determination I felt that Massachusetts was safe." [56] Giddings pushed on to carry his message to Lowell, city of textile mills, and Lynn, city of Quakers and shoemakers; and everywhere he met a royal reception. An Ohio convention had meanwhile called for a national gathering at Buffalo on August 9th.

But what of the Liberty Party men, already urging John P. Hale for the presidency, and what of the Garrisonian abolitionists? So far as Whittier could speak for the latter, he was for accepting Van Buren. "Dare! *Dare!* DARE!" he wrote Sumner, was the watchword they should borrow from Danton. Hale was for participating in the general convention called in Buffalo, but would not retire until his friends, in the light of that gathering, made their advice known. On the Barnburner side, Samuel J. Tilden and others were in favor of doing

---

55 June 20, 1848; Shepard, *Van Buren*, 425.
56 Sumner to unnamed correspondent July 2, 1848; Giddings Papers. In Boston, Giddings spoke to an immense audience. Sumner reported the effect of the speech immense.

without the firebrand abolitionists. The question was submitted to Van Buren himself by a group which Tilden, Prince John, and others took to Lindenwald. The warm affection manifested by the aging leader for his son as the two, strolling, lunching, and chatting together, hurled witty shafts at each other, delighted the onlookers. The verdict of the elder Van Buren was emphatic. The new party must be stronger before it began to pick and choose, he said. They needed every man opposed to the expansion of slavery. "Is not the vote of Gerrit Smith just as weighty as that of Judge Martin Grover?" [57]

[VII]

A heroic atmosphere surrounded the Free Soil Party Convention which opened in a huge tent in the city park of Buffalo on August 9. At least ten thousand men were present from all the Northern and three of the border States. From this concourse 465 delegates were sieved out for actual voting. Fanning themselves under the fierce sun, the crowd—freesoil Democrats, conscience Whigs, Liberty Party men, and nondescripts—listened to some of the most distinguished speakers of the day. As so often in the history of third-party gatherings, while a lofty idealism animated many participants, canny politicians were pulling wires in the rear. Men like Giddings, Preston King, and William Cullen Bryant gave the meeting elevation; men like Salmon P. Chase, who presided over a central body of "conferrees," Benjamin F. Butler of New York, who reported the platform, Tilden, and D. D. Field gave it direction. Thirty years later, Charles Francis Adams said that he had taken note of many such assemblages, "but for plain, downright honesty of purpose, to effect high ends without a whisper of bargain and sale, I doubt whether any similar one has been its superior, either before or since." [58] He did not know all that went on.

This time the platform was unequivocal, and unequivocally supported. It was summed up in its concluding words, an enlargement of Hoar's battle cry: "Free soil, free speech, free labor, and free men!" Slavery, it declared, was a State and not a national institution; the national legislature had no right to extend it; and the "slave power" should be confronted with an iron decree: No more slave States, no more slave territory, and no more compromises with slavery anywhere. In addition, the convention called for cheap postage, river and harbor improvements, free lands to actual settlers, and the abolition of unnecessary offices and salaries. Such bold planks reassured many who felt an inner misgiving with respect to Van Buren.

For Van Buren, inevitably, was the candidate. To be sure, a wide range of

57 L. E. Chittenden, *Personal Reminiscences, 1840–90,* 15–16.
58 Charles Francis Adams, Jr., *Charles Francis Adams,* 90.

nominees were discussed. Some Whigs even thought of John McLean, and some Democrats more preposterously still of Franklin Pierce. Benjamin F. Butler had urged the New Hampshire leader not to refuse if chosen, for "he who shall become the standard-bearer of the Northern Democracy in this emergency, will, in the end, have no reason to regret it." [59] The ardor of Liberty Party men for Hale threatened to result in serious difficulties. But as the confusion and uncertainty mounted, veteran politicians took control. They had a committee on nominations appointed; Butler, an adherent of Van Buren, was its leading spirit, and Chase energetically supported him. When the first unofficial ballot was taken, nearly all the Liberty men clung to Hale while the Democrats would hear of nobody but Van Buren, and conscience Whigs held the balance of power. They turned decisively toward the New Yorker.[60] On the ensuing ballot, Van Buren's nomination was made unanimous. Joshua Leavitt, the enthusiastic Garrisonian abolitionist, gained the floor to make the requisite motion, his utterance choked by feeling. "The Liberty Party is not dead," he shouted, "but translated."

Then, Ohio having been permitted to designate the vice-presidential candidate, Charles Francis Adams was named with thunderous enthusiasm; partly in veneration for his father, and partly as a tribute to his own gallant fight against the cotton Whigs of Massachusetts. As Hale withdrew, electoral tickets were put up from Maine to Virginia, from New York to Illinois. Whittier burst into song, declaring that the giant stood erect at last:

> O prisoners in your house of pain,
> Dumb, toiling millions, bound and sold,
> Look! Stretched o'er Southern vale and plain
> The Lord's delivering hand behold.[61]

In reality, this third-party movement which many participants remembered to the end of their days as a magnificent expression of crusading righteousness had its dubious and discreditable side.[62] Webster spoke acidly of the alliance between the self-seeking Van Buren politicians and the self-righteous conscience

59   June 16, 1848; Franklin Pierce Papers.
60   Charles Francis Adams, *Richard Henry Dana*, I, 137–144; on this first roll-call, 244 delegates named Van Buren, 181 named Hale, and 41 votes were scattering.
61   Though he did not expect to go openly with the Free Soil Party, Horace Greeley took an active role in the back-stage preparations for the nominations. Expressing the hope that the party would "act wisely and efficiently," Greeley suggested that many New York "friends of the movement" would favor the nomination of Judge McLean for Vice-President. Anticipating that McLean would not accept, Greeley then suggested two other possible candidates. "Please advise me," he wrote to Joshua Giddings, "for the sake of some leading Independents here who want to set the ball rolling the right way." July 15, 1848; Giddings Papers.
62   For a critical view of the third-party movement see Stewart Mitchell, *Horatio Seymour of New York*, 110.

Whigs. It would be too harsh to say that the New York Barnburners had deluded the Free Soilers into supplying a garb of reform for their political revenge upon Polk and Cass; that the gaily unprincipled Van Burens needed the respectability supplied by Charles Francis Adams' bleak, craggy face and Joshua Giddings' Old Testament fervor. Like all political groups, the Barnburners had mixed motives, and the Bryant element of Democracy was as idealistic as the Adams element in the Free Soil faction. In his letter of acceptance, a manly, well-written assertion that slavery must not pollute the new Territories, Van Buren touched a high level.

But it is certain that Sumner lost all sense of reality when he declared that the Van Buren of ten years earlier was dead, and they were supporting "the Van Buren of today—the veteran statesman, sagacious, determined, who, at an age when most men are rejoicing to put off their armor, girds himself anew and enters the list as a champion of freedom." [63] The ex-President, as time proved, was as much the Fox of Kinderhook as ever. Many other Barnburners, long athirst for revenge upon the regular Democrats, remembered with emotion that the Free Soil convention almost coincided with the first anniversary of the death of their beloved Silas Wright. The previous year James S. Wadsworth, leaping to the platform in the State convention, had retorted to the sneering remark that it was now too late to do justice to Wright: "It is not too late to do justice to his assassins!" [64] Revenge is not the most creditable of impulses, and some Barnburners combined it with selfish ambition. Young leaders like Tilden saw in the new movement a step toward the political control of New York. These men, including conservatives like John A. Dix, who was soon supporting Pierce and Buchanan in measures which gave slavery a very real chance of expansion, furnished a questionable element among the idealists.

[VIII]

As Taylor, Cass, and Van Buren thus stepped forward to ask the suffrages of the people, a host of voters, ranging from the nation's ablest statesmen to humble villagers, expressed a burning disappointment with all three. Not one had the aspect of a statesman. Webster, declaring Taylor's nomination not fit to be made, wrote Rockwood Hoar that he could never think of joining the Free Soil party. "I have no confidence in Mr. Van Buren, not the slightest. I would much rather trust General Taylor than Mr. Van Buren, even on this very question of slavery ..." [65] Clay, deeply wounded, relapsed into a gloomy silence.

63 Sumner's comments on Van Buren were addressed to Joshua Giddings July 5, 1848; Giddings Papers.
64 Stanton, *Random Recollections*, 159.
65 George Sydney Fisher, *True Daniel Webster*, 445.

He declined to say anything either to assist Taylor or to injure him. Some followers who loved Harry of the West to adulation hoped that he would let them place his name on an independent ticket, but he was too wise to court humiliation in that fashion. As for Cass, he was trusted neither in the Deep South, where thousands recoiled from his idea that the primitive settlers of a Territory could shape its future destiny on slavery, nor among a multitude of Northern Democrats. Van Buren's early associations, dubious record, and agile traits made him repugnant to numerous thoughtful anti-slavery men.

Yet in all campaigns party lines tend to harden and doubters to reënter the fold. So it was in 1848. Thomas Hart Benton was a warm friend of Van Buren, disliked Cass and his principles, and approved of Barnburner ideas. But he assented to the Democratic nomination, though coldly and perfunctorily. Invited to accompany Cass home from Washington to Detroit, he was urged to visit Van Buren en route to dissuade the New Yorker from running. Though he refused to go to Lindenwald, he did make a lukewarm speech in New York in support of Cass.[66] Two doubtful Massachusetts Democrats, Robert Rantoul and George Bancroft, similarly fell into line—though Bancroft betook himself to Europe to escape the campaign. Levi Woodbury of New Hampshire, to whom Cass sent a special emissary, loyally cleaved to the party. In the Northwest the Democrats showed surprising unity and energy.

On the Whig side, Horace Greeley had never really expected to act with the Free Soil Party, though he continued advising its leaders. He would probably have supported an independent Clay ticket. But this being impossible, with a wry face he brought the *Tribune* around to a sour espousal of Taylor.[67] As he wrote Colfax, he did so because he could not let the election be thrown to the Democratic candidate. "The country does not deserve a visitation of that pot-bellied, mutton-headed cucumber Cass!" If he could make Van Buren head of the nation he would do so, not for the man but for the principles of free soil and land reform. "I could have been the oracle of the Free Soil party, with any extent of circulation, had I chosen," he confided to his friend. ". . . I could shake down the whole rotten fabric by a bugle-blast, yet will not sound it, because some good men I love would be crushed beneath its ruins. This State would give 100,000 votes to Clay if I chose to say the word; it will give 20,000 votes though I do my best to resist it. It will notwithstanding vote for Taylor, and he will be elected . . ."[68] In a choice of evils, he took the lesser. Bryant

66 Cass to Samuel Treat, July 3, 1848. See also Treat's note on his letters from Cass and others during the campaign; Samuel Treat Papers, Missouri Historical Society. Treat believed that if Benton had used his influence, Van Buren might have kept aloof from the Free Soil movement.

67 Greeley to Giddings, July 15, 1848, Giddings Papers; N. Y. *Tribune*, September 29, 1848.

68 To Colfax, September 15, 1848; Greeley-Colfax Corr.

warmly espoused Van Buren's side, emphasizing in the *Evening Post* the economic and social aspects of the campaign. Shall the great republic, he asked, "no longer be known as the home of the free and the asylum of the oppressed, but as the home of the slave and the oppressor of the poor?" [69] But Seward, Tom Corwin, and Lincoln, all stood as party regulars with Taylor. James Gordon Bennett, who had once met Old Zack at Niagara and liked him, brought the *Herald* to his support.

The reluctant Webster knew in his heart that he too had to fall in behind the frontier colonel. Either Cass or Taylor would be elected, and while Cass would very likely help make new slave States, Taylor would probably labor to prevent this fell result. Webster's Whig friends pleaded with him; among them notably Berrien of Georgia, who sent a touching letter on the importance of New England's cooperation with the other Whig States. For weeks Webster wrestled with himself, telling his friends that he saw in the campaign no practical question of importance, for slavery would not thrive in Oregon or California, and that part of New Mexico in which slaves could be employed would probably be made part of Texas.[70] But the Douglas amendment to the Oregon bill helped bring him over, for it proved that a large body of Cass' Northern followers were ready to open all the new acquisitions south of 36° 30′ to the possible entry of slavery. New slave States might really follow Cass's triumph.

On September first, Webster delivered at Marshfield a long-awaited and much-heralded speech. Reporters had gathered from far and near; cigar-chewing politicians rubbed elbows with ruminative farmers and fishermen. Emphasizing the fact that the movement for Taylor had originated chiefly among the Northern Whigs, Webster declared that the "sagacious, wise, far-seeing doctrine of *availability* lay at the root of the whole matter." It was true, he went on, that Taylor's lack of civil experience should have caused the party to turn to some better-equipped man. But the general was upright and independent; Democratic doctrines were full of peril; and the safest course was to ensure Whig success in the election.[71]

However unenthusiastic, this declaration struck most Whigs as adequate. "Was ever anything so cold as Webster's Marshfield pronunciamento?" inquired Speaker Winthrop of the Maryland novelist John P. Kennedy. "Surely, his *North* was Nova Zembla and the frigid zone, on that occasion." Winthrop himself had faith in Taylor, whose few public utterances he thought tellingly shrewd, and he would have liked a more cordial speech from Webster. But he

69 Allan Nevins, *The Evening Post: A Century of Journalism*, 224. This year saw the able John Bigelow join the *Post* as partner and associate editor.
70 Webster to Hiram Ketchum, July 21, 1848; Curtis, *Webster*, II, 342.
71 The speech in Webster, *Works*, II, 425ff.

believed the address would do good: "A sulky support is better than opposition." [72]

[IX]

Long before the summer ended it was evident that Taylor, quietly remaining
in Louisiana and Mississippi, would be victor. It was a vacuous campaign,
significant only because obviously the prologue to momentous events. The
novelist John P. Kennedy, repairing to that happy haunt of politicians, Saratoga,
spent an August morning discussing the contest with old Francis P. Blair.
Blair's ardent sons, Frank and Montgomery, were busy founding a Free Soil
Party in Missouri, with a newspaper, the *Barnburner*, to sustain it; the father
was lukewarm in the cause.

"I understand the apathy of the voters," rapped out Blair, who detested
Cass, disliked Taylor, and though politically attached to Van Buren, had as yet
little use for Free Soilers. "The people have fallen into such a state of indifference to the presidency that they care very little who holds it. They have
tried Tyler and Polk, and yet the country has not been materially hurt. If
two such Presidents cannot injure the nation, nothing can!" [73]

But the apathy arose chiefly from lack of specific issues and the general conviction that the hero of Buena Vista would win. In Pennsylvania, its coal and
iron industries injured by the Walker tariff of 1846, Whig protectionism attracted many votes. In the critical State of New York the Van Buren ticket
cut more severely into Democratic than Whig strength. One reason why it did
so was that the elder Blair had published a letter from Andrew Jackson, dated
at the Hermitage on January 24, 1844, which he kept in his portfolio. "I cannot hope to be alive and witness the acclamation with which the people of the
United States will call Mr. Van Buren to the Presidency at the expiration of
Mr. Polk's term," Jackson had written, "but you will and I know you will
rejoice at it as the consummation of an act of justice due alike to him and to
the honor and fame of the country." It was natural for many Jacksonians to
turn to their old hero's partner. The mass of the freesoil Whigs in the North,
on the other hand, tended to support the regular nomination. For one reason,
their greatest leaders were so ringingly explicit on the territorial question that
there seemed no reason to turn to the third party. Webster had spoken in the
Oregon debate with memorable positiveness: "I shall oppose all slavery exten-

---

72 Winthrop to Kennedy, September 19, 1848; Kennedy Papers. Sumner did not think
that Webster's speech would do the Free Soil party any serious harm. Webster "was
described by those who heard him," Sumner wrote to Giddings, "as talking like a man
angry with everybody." September 3, 1848; Giddings Papers.
73 MS Diary, Kennedy Papers, August 28, 1848.

sion and all increase of slave representation in all places, at all times, under all circumstances, even against all inducements, against all supposed limitation of great interests, against all combinations, against all compromises." Seward declared at Cleveland that "freedom and slavery are two antagonistic elements of society in America," and that slavery must give way.[74]

For another reason, Taylor's own utterances won favor. The Whigs had deeply resented Polk's use of the veto and his steady employment of executive pressure to carry legislation through Congress—amounting, they thought, to an exercise of unwarrantable power. Before his nomination, Taylor had underlined these complaints by writing in a letter drafted for him (some said) by Crittenden, Stephens, and Toombs, that the President should never use his veto except in clear instances of violation of the Constitution, or manifest haste or want of consideration by Congress.[75] He thought that for years past the personal opinions of the President had been altogether too influential with the legislative branch, and threatened to pervert the American system. He did not believe in a strong President like Jackson and Polk! His promise to accept the judgment of Congress upon the tariff, internal improvements, and the currency was reassuring to old-line Whigs.[76] In such matters promise is always easier than performance; and later, when he showed that he expected his personal opinions to have very great weight indeed with reluctant Congressmen, this famous "Allison letter," as it was called, was to be remembered ironically.

In the South, and particularly in South Carolina, the canvass showed some remarkable features. There the Democrats lost many votes on the simple ground that Cass was a Northerner, Taylor a slaveholding Southerner. One irate Democrat wrote the Charleston *Courier* that the tariff and other issues became insignificant when compared with the question which an unprincipled Northern Democracy had dared to thrust upon the country. "The North has no interest whatever in that question, except so far as its agitation gratifies a malignant hostility to us, or tends to check the zeal of opposition to other oppressive and unconstitutional measures—to divert it from lesser acts of injustice and absorb it in one paramount act of insult, aggression, and treachery. It is of vital

---

74 Blair on May 18, 1848, sent B. F. Butler a copy of Jackson's letter; Blair Papers, Princeton University. Greeley predicted in October that the Taylor ticket would "do pretty fair in this State if nothing breaks—50,000 for Taylor, probably 75,000 for Fish over the next highest. . . ." To Colfax, October 2, 1848; Greeley-Colfax Corr.

75 Taylor to Capt. J. S. Allison, April 22, 1848; Poage, *Henry Clay and the Whig Party*, 176, 177. Speaker Winthrop gleefully described the letter a gem. It "will carry the country," he predicted, "if the country is to be carried." Winthrop to Kennedy, September 19, 1848; Kennedy Papers. Tyler's vetoes were also a bitter Whig memory.

76 Ewing to R. M. Corwin, June 30, 1848; Ewing Papers. But to the end of the campaign the Democrats taunted the Whigs for their lack of a platform. For example, the *Illinois State Register* published a booklet of postage-stamp size entitled "Resolutions of the Whig Convention" containing a preface saying that the authors hoped any obscurity in details would be overlooked, and then—blank paper.

importance that the South—the whole South—shall march up to this question with unbroken front, and give decisive answer. By birth, education, sentiment, feeling, association, and interest, General Taylor is one of us." [77] In other slave States numerous men took the same view.

A significant mass meeting of South Carolina Democrats in Charleston on June sixth reaffirmed the Alabama resolves. With R. B. Rhett, Judge D. E. Huger, and W. L. Yancey present, it resolved to support no candidate who did not repudiate any and all methods of excluding slavery from the Territories— that is, it would not support Cass.[78] Later that summer the two sternest leaders of South Carolina both insisted upon the necessity for a decisive effort to protect Southern interests and obtain a fair share of the Territories.

Calhoun, on a hot August night, spoke to a crowd which jammed the Charleston theater to suffocation. Gaslights flared over an eager audience in shirt-sleeves with palm-leaf fans a-flutter. When the Senator arose the gathering sprang to its feet with fervent cheers. Before them stood the sentinel of the South, their champion of spotless character, exalted abilities, and never-quailing courage. A breathless hush fell as, speaking with gestureless dignity and precise diction, he earnestly advocated the policy of holding the State aloof from the presidential canvass. The action of the North in inserting the Wilmot Proviso into the Oregon Act, said Calhoun, was a mere wanton assertion of power. The North was determined to exclude slavery from every Territory—even from Cuba, were that island ever acquired. First the injustice of the Northwest Ordinance; then the injustice of the Missouri Compromise; then the crowning injustice of excluding the slave States from any share whatever in the domain won by common American heroism. To meet this threat, Southern union was was essential. "We can rally a great Southern republican party, based on principles . . . and with such a party we can command our terms and control the North"; for the mere formation of this Southern party, said Calhoun, would evoke a Northern organization to cooperate with it. If this failed to arrest the spirit of aggression, then disunion and resistance might be forced upon them. Who was craven enough to fear the result? The South with her homogeneous population, her military prowess, her rich exports, should be more than a match for the North, with its many elements of weakness and division. While he did not court the contest, he would not shun it, and old as he was, he would willingly bear his full share in it.[79]

---

77 "A Democrat" in issue of June 20, 1848.
78 Charleston *Courier*, June 7, 1848. Someone moved that the meeting support Taylor as an independent candidate for President, but the motion was laid on the table.
79 Calhoun's speech was reported in full in the Charleston *Mercury*, August 21, 1848. Writing in the same belligerent spirit, "A True Southron" declared: "The great question before the country is not, who shall be President, but, shall the Southern States be permitted to remain in the Union on the same footing on which they originally entered it." Charleston *Courier*, September 23, 1848.

Rhett's program, unfolded in Hibernian Hall as September breezes cooled the streets, was entirely different; it was for action through the States. Let them instruct their Senators, and request their Representatives, to leave their seats immediately if abolitionism won any new triumphs in Congress. If no other State would act, South Carolina should enter the contest alone. She could force every member of the Union to take sides for or against her; she could compel every citizen to face the alternatives—respect for Southern rights, or dissolution of the Union. "Let the result be what it may," shouted Rhett, "we will at least have the consolation of having made one brave, long, strong effort to save ourselves from foul, ignominious, and dishonorable ruin." [80] While Calhoun declared that South Carolina, which had sent no delegate to any party convention, should choose no presidential electors, Rhett finally came out for Cass. Long afterward he asserted that if Cass had been elected, the Missouri Compromise line would have been extended to the Pacific and the nation saved, while Taylor's election was a calamity pregnant with future quarrels which culminated in Democratic schism and the sundering of the Union. [81]

To the last the Free Soil party, certain of defeat, fought bravely. In New England Sumner spoke almost every night for two months. The ratification meeting in Faneuil Hall was pronounced the most powerful demonstration ever seen in Boston. Van Buren's past was a heavy handicap; men recalled that John Quincy Adams had once denounced him for "fawning servility" and "profound dissimulation and duplicity"; and Sumner lamented that McLean was not the nominee—he could have swept the State easily.[82] But the meetings were so numerous, the popular feeling was so ebullient, that some Free Soil men thought that even Van Buren would carry Massachusetts. In Ohio, where Chase and Joshua Giddings labored amain, the first strong effort was made to rally German voters for the anti-slavery cause. In Indiana George W. Julian, soon to become Giddings' son-in-law, braved ridicule and denunciation. He tells us that it was a standing Whig joke that he carried a lock of Frederick Douglass' hair to revive his strength when he grew faint, and that his usual audience consisted of eleven men, three boys, and a Negro.

A light vote on election day gave Taylor and Cass each fifteen States, but Taylor (with eight slave and seven free) carried populous New York, Massachusetts, and Pennsylvania, while Cass (with seven slave and eight free) had to console himself with Virginia, Ohio, and Illinois at the head of his phalanx. Rhett had helped carry a reluctant, heart-torn South Carolina into Cass' column.

80 Charleston *Mercury*, September 29, 1848; cf. Charleston *Courier*, September 23, 1848.
81 Laura A. White, *Life of Robert Barnwell Rhett*, 98. Rhett maintained that if Cass were elected he would veto the Wilmot Proviso, but Calhoun and Senator Butler insisted that he would never do any such thing. Charleston *Courier*, September 27, 1848.
82 Sumner to Giddings, September 3, November 10, 1848; Giddings Papers.

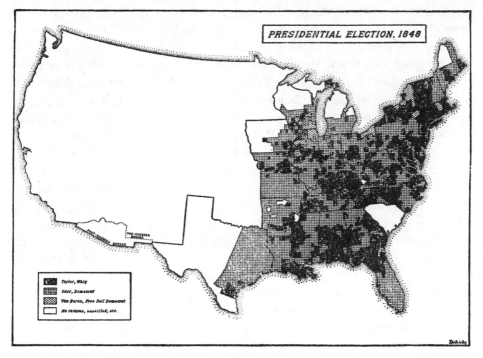

Thirty States took part in the election, Florida, Texas, Iowa, and Wisconsin having been admitted since 1844. The aggregate vote was 2,871,000.

The popular vote registered for Taylor was 1,360,000, and for Cass 1,220,000. Van Buren polled about 300,000 votes, winning no electors.[83]

What most impressed judicious observers, in scanning the general result, was the sectional coloring of the battle. One important party was purely sectional—for all the Free Soil voters in Maryland, Delaware, and Virginia, the only slave States where *any* were found, could have been assembled in a moderate-sized hall. North Carolina and Georgia, Florida and Louisiana, had obviously been carried by Taylor largely because many viewed him as a Southerner. In parts of the North sectional feeling, or at least feeling against slavery expansion, had been deeply aroused. This was notably the fact in Massachusetts, where the Free Soil party took second place.[84] It was true in Ohio, where all three parties had put forth every effort, holding incessant meetings and mustering every

83 Some 120,000 of these votes were cast in New York, and 35,000 in Ohio.
84 Sumner and the radical anti-slavery men in Massachusetts were content with the result. "If we have not reached the calculations of the more sanguine," Sumner wrote after the election, "we have disappointed all the calculations of our enemies. We have pulled nearly 40,000 votes, and taken our place before the Cass party as the *second* party." November 10, 1848; Giddings Papers.

possible speaker. "Everything that can put three words together is on the stump," Ben Wade had written his wife.[85] It has often been pointed out that the Van Buren vote threw New York to Taylor; but it was equally true that the same vote threw Indiana and Ohio to Cass. A loyal Whig wrote after the election that his party had but slender prospects in those two States until it won back most of the Free Soil voters who had deserted it. Not only had the defection cost Taylor these States, he added, but it had bequeathed a legacy of confusion and ugly passions. "We can look forward with little hope, if the Cabinet Council of General Taylor shall have no member in it from either of the great States of the old Northwestern Territory." [86]

The election unquestionably left sectional animosities swollen and sensitive. A host of Northerners were more firmly committed than ever against any expansion of slavery into the new Territories. They were more aggressive in temper, and they would have a larger voice in Congress. The Free Soil party had elected nine Congressmen, including young Julian and the redoubtable Giddings. They had gained the balance of power in the Ohio legislature, and were shortly to end a sharply contested struggle there by sending Salmon P. Chase to the Senate. [87] A host of Southerners, meanwhile, were more angrily resolved than ever to maintain their rights in the Territories and defend their peculiar institution at home.

In a contest which reflected little credit on American governmental machinery, the nation had made the best of the poor choice offered it. It had chosen an honest and sturdy—if inexperienced—man whose army training made him a nationalist, but whose Southern birth and ownership of slaves commended him to that section which distrusted nationalism. It had rejected two candidates committed to two specific modes of settling the Territorial issue, each certain to provoke heated opposition, in favor of a candidate whose hands were still free to help devise a compromise. The only question was whether Taylor's ignorance, complete lack of training in civil affairs, and intellectual slowness would not bring him to disaster. The greatest men of the republic, Calhoun, Clay, and Webster, were heartsick, but ordinary citizens remained hopeful. The nation faced a problem for which time and caution were the best solvents, and the election had at least given it a breathing spell.

85 October 24, 1848; Wade Papers. This was also true in Indiana, where George W. Julian strove to bury all old issues between Whig and Democrat and concentrate his campaign on free soil vs. slavery. The tactics of Taylor's supporters, he complained, tended to blind men "to the alarming encroachments of the slave power." June, 1849; Julian Papers.
86 John C. Wright, January 19, 1849; Crittenden Papers.
87 A. B. Hart, Chase, 104ff. Chase was elected by a fusion of Democrats, Free Soilers, and Independents, and the old Whigs never again trusted him. See A. G. Riddle, "The Election of Salmon P. Chase to the Senate, February, 1849," The Republic, IV (March, 1875), 183.

[X]

Other nations were passing through still greater difficulties. The revolutionary outbreaks of 1848 in Europe delighted the radical elements in America, disturbed some of the most conservative groups, and gave a stimulus to Yankee nationalism and bumptiousness.[88] "Europe is up to its eyes and above its eyes in trouble," wrote George Bancroft from London just after the elections. He related an anecdote illustrating the reactionary impulses of the Duke of Cambridge. At church the duke, hearing the parson reading a verse exhorting God to rise in his wrath and break the bones of his enemies, had cried out: "Capital text! Capital text to preach on and apply to the French and Germans!" Though the aristocracy, wrote Bancroft, wish the people crushed, the masses will yet triumph.[89] But the event quickly proved that he was wrong.

One by one the despots of the continent, overturned or badly shaken, recovered their power and ruthlessly crushed the rebels. If France was an exception to the general rule, it was only because France was preparing herself for a worse ruler than Louis Philippe. Bancroft, who knew Louis Napoleon very well, pronounced him "a good natured simpleton, capable of any folly." [90] Again his judgment was poor; he underrated Napoleon's capacities for mischief and repression. Millions of Americans had thrilled to the European uprising. Lieutenant Mayne Reid, who had fought gallantly in Mexico, set about mustering a battalion of Germans and Hungarians in New York (he wanted five hundred men, each with a Colt's revolver) to aid the grand struggle for freedom.[91] The press was full of libertarian articles. The hopes and fears with which the democratic masses of the New World, the old Jacksonians and the new freesoilers, regarded the convulsive uprisings in Europe, were destined to condition their attitude toward important problems of foreign relations, and to help determine the atmosphere of domestic debate.

While the European scene was swiftly changing, a kaleidoscopic transformation was taking place in the Far West. In the heat and clamor of their presidential canvass, Americans little thought that behind the veil drawn by distance a remarkable drama was being enacted in California. That far-off country, to all Easterners, still called up visions of lumbering, ranching, and

88 E. N. Curtis, "American Opinion of the French 19th Century Revolutions," *American Historical Review*, XXIX. "Every gale that floats across the Atlantic comes freighted with the death groan of a king," declared Tom Corwin; "every vessel that touches your shores bears with her tidings that the captives of the Old World are at last becoming free." Morrow, *Corwin*, 335, 336.
89 Bancroft to Buchanan, November 24, 1848; Buchanan Papers.
90 Ibid.
91 Washington *Daily Republic*, June 13, 1849; Mrs. Mayne Reid, *Captain Mayne Reid*, 97–103. But Calhoun attacked radical democracy in Europe; May 23, 1848, Donelson Papers.

general indolence. But early in 1848 Johann Sutter's sharp-eyed mechanic from New Jersey, Marshall, made his momentous discovery of the yellow specks dotting the mill-race channel that he was building on the huge semi-feudal domain of the baron of the Sacramento Valley. By the end of May, San Francisco and other coastal settlements were emptying themselves into the new Golconda. By midsummer the whole Pacific slope echoed to the cry of gold. Ships were abandoned, businesses stripped, farms deserted. First vague rumors, then authentic reports, began to reach the Atlantic cities. In the last weeks of 1848, when a naval lieutenant arrived in Washington with an official report by the military commander in California asserting the existence of enough gold to pay the costs of the war a hundredfold, and with a tea-caddy full of bright yellow dust and nuggets, the meaning of this huge new treasure-house fully dawned upon the nation.

Its meaning, that is, to the adventurers and fortune-seekers who at once lifted their cry "Ho for California!" and set California words to the merry tune "Susannah." But its immediate political implications and its ultimate economic significance were not so easily grasped.

7

The Gathering Quarrel

THE EXPIRING months of the Polk Administration in 1848–49 gave a dark augury of the storms to come. Congress no sooner met in December than the agitation of the slavery question recommenced; and even when the surface of the political sea for a few days grew calm, beneath it all was commotion and intrigue. Polk in his last annual message dwelt upon the importance of promptly supplying Territorial governments for California and New Mexico. Three modes of settlement, he suggested, were open. One, which he preferred, was to carry the Missouri Compromise line to the Pacific; another, to let the people of the Territories decide the slavery question when they applied for admission; and the third, to lay the issue before the Supreme Court. But Northern free-soilers and Southern extremists could agree on none of the three.

In token of the turmoil within the country, a new shower of resolutions from the State legislatures was falling upon the Capitol. Those from the South protested irritably against any exclusion of slaveholders from the new ac-quisitions. Some of them went further. Florida on January 13, 1849, pledged herself to join the other slaveholding States in such measures for the defense of their rights as the highest wisdom of all might devise, whether through a convention or otherwise. Inspired by John B. Floyd, Virginia followed with resolves which so emphatically threatened dissolution of the Union that moderate journals like the Richmond *Whig* sharply attacked them.[1] Nearly twenty years earlier Floyd, a young lawyer not long out of the College of South Carolina, had seen his father, the governor of Virgina, moved to perfect fury by receiving a copy of the *Liberator*, and had heard him denounce the aboli-tionists as a "club of villains, who are maturing plans for treason and rebellion and insurrection in Virginia and the Southern States." Inheriting these opinions, the younger Floyd was now a legislative leader and soon to become governor himself.[2] The Virginia resolutions declared that passage of the Wilmot Proviso, or abolition of slavery or the slave trade in the District of Columbia, would be

---

1 December 30, 1848; quoted in Charleston *Courier*, January 6, 1849.
2 C. H. Ambler, *Life and Diary of John Floyd.*

an attack upon Southern institutions to be resisted at every hazard; and that the governor, if faced by such legislation, should immediately call the legislature to consider means of redress.[3]

Northern governors and legislatures were reasserting the Wilmot Proviso doctrine. When Hamilton Fish, taking his executive chair in Albany, declared that California and New Mexico should be reserved for free white labor alone, the State rose in almost universal applause. "Even Hunkerism, at last," exclaimed the New York *Express*, "yields to the general will." [4] The New York Assembly sent Congress resolutions opposing the extension of slavery into territory already free, attacking the continuance of the slave trade in the District of Columbia, and denouncing the claim of Texas to the Rio Grande from mouth to source.[5] When presented in the Senate they provoked a tremendous uproar. Yulee of Florida declared that he would throw down the gauntlet to New York, which did not realize that the Union was tottering; Downs of Louisiana and Butler of South Carolina, agreeing that the nation was in danger of dissolution, uttered the fieriest invective. Meanwhile, the governors of Michigan, Pennsylvania, and Massachusetts asserted that slavery should never be extended into areas already free, and the Illinois legislature bade the State delegation in Congress hew to the same line.[6]

The slavery agitation, as these resolutions showed, had come to embrace several important questions lying beyond the governmental organization of the area taken from Mexico. The least difficult of these touched the slave-trade in the District of Columbia; not the right of private purchase and sale of Negroes, but the maintenance of slave-depots. Even Southerners had no liking for what Toombs called the cursed slave-pens, or for the sight of Negro gangs driven along the avenues to be auctioned.[7] The fugitive slave question was far more difficult. The existing law of 1793, undermined by the abolitionist agitation and in numerous States rendered utterly nugatory by the personal liberty laws passed following the Supreme Court decision of 1842 in Prigg vs. Pennsylvania, was inadequate, and the South loudly demanded a stronger one.

And equally thorny was the Texas boundary question. Texas had come into the Union with a statute asserting that the Rio Grande line, plus a long pan-handle extension northward to the forty-second parallel, was her western

3 *Niles's Register*, January 31, 1849. John M. Clayton denounced the Virginia resolutions as the "greatest of all humbugs." Sickened by the numerous threats to dissolve the Union, the future Secretary of State predicted that "bullying" would invite the North to some "great folly." Meanwhile, he lamented, "Crimination and recrimination will be the order of the day." Clayton to Crittenden January 23, 1849; Crittenden Papers.
4 January 3, 4, 1849.
5 N. Y. *Express*, January 22, 1849.
6 *Niles's Register*, January 24, 31, 1849.
7 *Toombs, Stephens, Cobb Corr.*, 139.

boundary. The Congressional resolution of annexation had stated that the adjustment of the boundary, at least as regarded foreign states, was reserved to Congress. Now the cession of New Mexico to the United States made the question purely internal—if it were a question at all. The freesoilers wished to cut down the area of Texas, where slavery legally existed; the Texans and their Southern supporters demanded the maintenance of the Rio Grande limits.[8]

But the most urgent question was California, where ranchmen, soldiers, sailors, clerks, and adventurers were flooding into the goldfields, with an appalling amount of disorder and license. It needed a government immediately. The normal course was to set up a Territorial organization. But as Northern and Southern extremists refused to agree on this, Douglas and others proposed forthwith to bring in the whole area acquired from Mexico as a single State, skipping the Territorial stage, and permitting the inhabitants to decide the slavery question when they drew up their Constitution. This was quite unprecedented—but then California was filling up with unprecedented rapidity. Polk saw merit in the plan, but demurred that Douglas had included too great a region in his bill. Thereupon, Douglas on January 24, 1849, brought in a substitute project for a new State covering not quite all of the old Mexican province of Upper California; New Mexico to be duly organized as a Territory. But Southern members of the Senate, led by Calhoun, flatly rejected the scheme. It was certain that California would enter as a freesoil State, and some objected to this altogether, while others wanted a quid pro quo. The project had to be dropped. With the session half ended, nothing had been accomplished.[9]

The situation was becoming serious. From California came importunate demands for a civil government which could protect life, property, and order. The previous August, Benton had advised the Californians to set up their own government. Yet Congress, the freesoilers controlling the House and the slavery element dominant in the Senate, was deadlocked.

[I]

At this point Calhoun attempted a *coup*, the gravity of which was much underrated at the time, and the purport of which has been much misunderstood since. The plan which he had sketched in his Charleston speech for a militant Southern party, to deliver an ultimatum and follow it if necessary by secession, possessed his whole mind. He watched like an eagle for an opportunity

8 Greeley angrily denounced the "swindling claim of Texas" to New Mexico. To Colfax, January 2, 1849; Greeley-Colfax Corr.

9 *Cong. Globe*, December 11, 1848, January 9, 24, 29, 1849; Polk, *Diary*, IV, 279ff; George Fort Milton, *Eve of Conflict*, 45.

to consummate it. Observers noted that he was sleepless, haggard with anxiety, stooped as with a weight of thought, quicker and more fierce of utterance than ever.

His opening came when early in January Joshua Giddings, ferociously attacking slavery as the greatest of crimes, brought up a proposal to restrict and gradually abolish it in the District of Columbia.[10] The Ohioan enlisted the more moderate Abraham Lincoln in this endeavor, and Lincoln prepared a bill which was much discussed even though it made no real progress.[11] Its salient provisions were for the liberation, under an apprenticeship system, of all slaves born after a certain date, and for government purchase and liberation of any slave in the District whose owner would accept a fair compensation. Lincoln seems to have canvassed some leading Washingtonians for their confidential opinion. Giddings, writing in his diary of an evening visit to McLean, adds: "After my return Mr. Lincoln called at my room and read to me his bill as he had amended it. He visited Mr. Seaton, the mayor of the city, and consulted with him. The mayor thought I should be opposed to it and Mr. Lincoln thinking that such an idea may be useful, did not undeceive him." [12] Though Lincoln gave notice that he would formally introduce his measure, nothing was done, and the whole subject slept until at the end of the month the District Committee reported a simple bill for the prohibition of slave-depots. The Northern Whigs had cautiously receded. But between them, Giddings and Lincoln had enraged the sensitive Southerners.

Calhoun, with his sectional party in view, gathered these incensed Southerners into caucus; a committee of fifteen, one from each slave State, was appointed; and a subcommittee of five (two Democrats and two Whigs, with Calhoun as chairman) was designated to draw up an address. Opinion on the wisdom of this step was much divided. President Polk, with Benton, Sam Houston, and other moderate Southern or border Democrats who suspected Calhoun of disunionist schemes, strongly condemned any such action. On the other hands, Secretary Buchanan displayed his leaning toward the extreme Southern side when he declared that it might dispel the greatest danger that had yet threatened the Union. To secure the nation's safety, he wrote privately, "all that is necessary is for the South to act in such a manner as to convince the North that they are in earnest. Let them be united and firm, without being

10 Cf. R. C. Winthrop to Kennedy, January 20, 1849; Kennedy Papers. The conservative Speaker of the House denounced the extreme temper of both Giddings and Calhoun. Though he found Calhoun "fascinating," Winthrop criticized both the Southern leader and the Northern abolitionists for trying "to draw the country from its true constitutional center." For this, Winthrop added, "They almost deserve to be *drawn* themselves, and quartered too."
11 Albert J. Beveridge, *Abraham Lincoln 1809–1858*, I, 481, 482.
12 *Diary*, January 8, 9, 1849; Giddings Papers. *Cong. Globe*, 30th Cong., 2d sess., 212.

violent . . ." [13] The most vital opposition naturally came from the Southern Whigs. While a few of them enthusiastically supported Calhoun's scheme, the majority were against it as essentially a bold stroke to disorganize them and rear a new Southern Rights Party on the ruins of the old organizations.

A stiff battle against the address was inevitable. When Calhoun, who was its chief if not sole author, presented it, a stormy scene ensued in the committee of fifteen. The leading Whig members, Toombs, Stephens, and Clayton, with one Democrat, Rusk of Texas, vehemently opposed it. It was too threatening to be politic, they thought; its bullying tone would arouse the Northern free-soilers to equally belligerent words and acts; and altogether it would do mischief. If they did not say so, they also feared that it would ruin the Whigs in the South and embarrass the incoming Whig Administration.[14] These Southern Democrats, declared Toombs, are ugly-tempered not because Taylor can *not* settle our sectional difficulties, but because he *can* do it. They do not want a settlement.

That was equally the opinion of President Polk, who was left indignant and apprehensive by a call from Calhoun on the morning of January 16. "I anticipated his business the moment he entered my office," wrote Polk, "and I was not mistaken." He came to say that a stop must be put to the aggressions of the North upon the South; that he opposed the admission of California because slaveholders had been prevented from emigrating to that area, and it would come in as a free State; that he equally condemned a plan by Douglas for settling the Texan boundary issue by making the northern boundary of that State the parallel of 36° 30′ and relinquishing to Texas all the New Mexican country on both sides of the Rio Grande and south of that line; that he believed the South must be rallied to resist. "I became perfectly satisfied that he did not desire that Congress should settle the question at the present session," wrote the President, adding: "I was firm and decided in my conversation with him, intending to let him understand distinctly that I have no countenance to any movement which tended to violence or the disunion of the States."

Though the leading Southern Democrats, Calhoun, Jefferson Davis, and Mason of Virginia, argued earnestly for the address, it was returned to committee by a close vote. A milder paper, written by the venerable Georgia Whig, Senator Berrien, was then prepared; addressed not to the South, as Calhoun's had been, but to the whole country. When the two documents were placed

13 To S. L. Gouverneur, December 31, 1849; Buchanan Miss. Papers, L. C. For Polk's opinion see his *Diary*, III, 289–291.

14 T. Metcalfe to Crittenden, January 23, 1849; Crittenden Papers. Rusk explained his views in a long letter of January 30, 1849; Rusk Papers, Univ. of Texas. He thought Calhoun's address "an attempt to create a new political party organization," and a threat to "this glorious Republic."

before the whole caucus of slave State members on January 22, a stormy discussion lasted until two in the morning. As the chairman later put it, the debate was "not only warm, but sometimes red-hot." Wildly but unsuccessfully, the Southern Democrats adjured the Whigs to help them present a united sectional front. First the Berrien address was rejected, 33 to 27, and then Calhoun's, with one section stricken out, was adopted 36 to 19. While a number of men bolted the gathering, the address was handed around for signatures. Only forty-eight Senators and Representatives, nearly all Democrats, appended their names. Twenty-four Whigs and seventeen Democrats flatly refused to sign. Among the recusants were such eminent Whigs as Toombs, Stephens, Clayton, and Henry W. Hilliard, with such well-known Democrats as Howell Cobb and Lumpkin of Georgia and Boyd and Clarke of Kentucky. Representing only a third of the slave State members, the forty-eight signatures made an unimpressive showing.[15]

The manifesto, wrote Buchanan disgustedly, had sunk in the general estimation to a mere party gesture, and was without effect in the North.[16] When it was published, Giddings, supposing that a freesoil reply might be useful, asked many members their opinion, and "everyone appeared to think it of too trifling importance to notice." [17] Cobb, Hilliard, Boyd, and other obstinate dissenters, returning home, published spirited rejoinders to the Calhoun group. Cobb went so far as to ask Buchanan for a certificate of Southern loyalty to show his constituents, and got a statement that no Representative "has been more able and efficient than yourself in advocating and defending, on all suitable occasions, the rights and institutions of the South against the assaults of abolitionists and quasi-abolitionists of every shade and description." The attempt to place the pro-slavery members of Congress behind a Southern Rights Party had failed.[18]

Yet Calhoun's Southern Address was no trifling occurrence, for it was one of his ablest state papers, destined like nearly everything he wrote to take a powerful hold upon the Southern mind. It was published far and wide. Passionately tracing the course of Northern aggression from the days of the Northwest Ordinance and Missouri Compromise onward, he described how it had culminated in the Oregon Bill and the attack on slavery in the Federal District. If this aggression were not arrested, he warned, it would terminate in the creation of sufficient free States to establish a two-thirds majority in both

15 *Ibid.;* Charleston *Courier,* January 27, 30, February 1, 3, 6, 1849. See also Clayton to Crittenden, January 23, 1849; Crittenden Papers.
16 To Howell Cobb, June 12, 1849; Buchanan Papers.
17 MS Diary, January 29, 1849; Giddings Papers.
18 Cobb to Buchanan, June 2, 1849, Buchanan to Cobb, June 12, 1849; Buchanan Papers. Henry Hilliard to Clayton, April 12, 1849; Clayton Papers.

houses of Congress, a reinterpretation of convenient clauses of the Constitution, and an emancipation of all slaves—a calamity immeasurable in scope.

Few passages in Calhoun's writings are more eloquent, and none, read in the light of history, wears a more prophetic tinge, than the paragraphs in which he described the sequel of emancipation—"consequences unparalleled in history." Emancipation could be accomplished only by the overthrow of the Southern whites; the conflict would engender a bitter hostility between them and the North; and in the hour of abolitionist triumph the blacks would be raised to favor, office, and power. The South would then become the abode of disorder, anarchy, poverty, and wretchedness. Calhoun had pierced with the vision of a Hebraic seer to the morrow of Appomattox. To avert this awful dolor, he called on the South to prove its unity and determination without delay. The North might yet turn back. If it refused, "you would stand justified by all laws, human and divine, in repelling a blow so dangerous, without looking to consequences, and to resort to all means necessary for that purpose." [19]

[II]

And Calhoun and his followers were not content with words. They looked to acts as well. After blocking the Douglas bill for admitting California, they used a pliable young Democrat of Wisconsin, Senator Isaac P. Walker, to bring forward an amendment to the civil appropriation bill which explicitly extended the Constitution and the naturally applicable laws of the United States over the area acquired from Mexico, thus abrogating all the old Mexican statutes, including those against slavery; at the same time authorizing the President to make needful rules and regulations, and to appoint civil officials. Northern Whigs and freesoil Democrats leaped to the defense. Webster was a particularly resolute antagonist. He embodied his own plan for a temporary government of the new areas, with retention of the Mexican laws, in another amendment to the civil appropriation bill. As the session drew near its end, the Senate witnessed a memorable collision between Calhoun and Webster.

Senator Walker, gaining the floor, had launched into a callow harangue in which he expressed regret that Webster was absent from his seat, criticized him for contributing so little to sectional concord, and arraigned Massachusetts as responsible ever since Hartford Convention days for treasonable schemes and troublemaking activities. Butler of South Carolina, catching up the theme, expatiated upon it in more mature vein. When Webster, entering late, was told

19 The address was published in the Charleston *Courier*, February 1, 1849. Giddings thought there was "nothing forcible or striking" in it; MS Diary, January 29, 1849.

what had been said, his brow grew black with anger. Interrupting Butler, he emitted one of his thunder peals of defiance. The Senator from South Carolina, he remarked, had declared that the North had disregarded the Constitution; if he would specify in what particulars the Commonwealth of Massachusetts had violated, or had failed to observe, the compromises of the Constitution, "he will find in me on that question a combatant." The sentence was like a roll of drums, with the final "combatant" the blow of a triphammer.[20]

Addressing himself to the attempt to extend the Constitution over the Territories, Webster went on to deny that it could be done; for the cardinal principle of the Constitution was the rule that "all within its influence and comprehension shall be represented in the legislature which it establishes, with not only a right of debate and a right to vote in both houses of Congress, but a right to partake in the choice of a President and Vice-President." It was impossible to give any of these rights to a Territory. "The Constitution is extended over the United *States*, and nothing else." Calhoun, his hawklike eye fixed on Webster, his bony forefinger shaking, rose to the defense of his doctrine that the Constitution *ex proprio vigore* carried slavery wherever the flag floated. The great instrument did apply to the Territories, he said. "Why, the Constitution interprets itself. It pronounces itself to be the supreme law of the land." In this dictum Webster was quick to see the vital flaw. "What land?" he demanded. It was plain to him that a Territory was not part of the land in the sense of the nation—not a part of the United *States*.

The final struggle over the Territorial legislation was marked by scenes of turbulent anger. In an all-night session of the houses on March third and fourth, epithets were exchanged, threats uttered, and even blows struck. Some days earlier the Senate had passed the Walker amendment, but the House would have none of it, and it was clear that if the appropriations were to go through and the wheels of government be kept moving, one chamber or the other would have to recede. The utmost excitement possessed Congress. On the Democratic side of the House, some Southerners were threatening to cut out the hearts of their Northern colleagues if they did not vote for the Walker scheme. "There is no way to manage them but to put them in personal fear," said Meade of Virginia—who was with difficulty kept from assaulting Joshua Giddings when the latter walked over to the Democratic side.[21] At two o'clock in the morning a fistfight broke out. In the Senate several members were grossly intoxicated, and the disorderliness became so shocking that Sam Houston rose to say that, though he was familiar with the license and turbulence of the frontier, the

20 For the scene see Charleston *Courier*, February 28, 1849, Washington correspondence dated February 24.
21 Giddings, MS Diary, March 3, 1849; Giddings Papers. The events of the night are fully described in this journal.

present spectacle filled him with shame.[22] President-elect Taylor was anxious to have California placed under civil rule, but was against the Walker amendment. Seward had just reached Washington to take his seat in the Senate; and after conferring with Taylor, he and Thomas Ewing took a hack and drove to the Capitol to try to get appropriate action. Buttonholing Whig members, they held the line against the Walker amendment, but could do nothing more.[23]

Polk went to the Capitol that evening ready to veto any last-minute action by the House embodying the Wilmot Proviso. Late at night he was told that the House had passed what was substantially Webster's amendment, keeping the Mexican laws in force. The President was ready to veto this, too. "It was a moment of high responsibility," he wrote, "perhaps the highest of my official term." [24] But fortunately the House dropped the Webster arrangement while the Senate abandoned the Walker plan. As the night dragged on, Seward spent part of it chatting with Polk and Cass, hearing from the President, who was deeply embittered and physically exhausted, a long and melancholy history of the insults and injuries he had suffered during the Mexican War. As dawn came the struggle in the hot, murky Senate chamber still went on. But the first rays of the sun, striking between the marble columns and crimson hangings, recalled the members to their senses, and by six o'clock the necessary legislation had been completed. Other business was quickly disposed of; the gavel fell; and the Senators straggled homeward as the bells called Washington to church—for March 4 fell on Sunday.[25]

Congress, to the general disgust, had failed to give California and New Mexico any government. It had merely extended the national revenue laws over these regions. In another direction, the headwaters of the Mississippi north of the Iowa line, it had done better, erecting a Territorial government for what was now definitely named Minnesota. The most important enactment of the session was the creation of the Department of the Interior, or as it was at first popularly called, the Home Department. Robert J. Walker, the bustling, shrewd, farsighted little Secretary of the Treasury, had been the principal advocate of the measure, for particularly since the acquisition of these vast western reaches, his staff had been brutally overburdened by their many internal duties. The new department was to take over public lands, Indian affairs, patents, and pensions. Calhoun, Mason, and other Southerners attacked the bill on the ground that it would augment the centralization of governmental power and

22 *Idem.*
23 Washington *Union*, February 10, 1850; see also Frederic Bancroft, *Seward*, I, 209.
24 See Polk, *Diary*, IV, 362–369, for description of the scene.
25 McCormac, *Polk*, 652ff. Polk left the Capitol at 4 A.M. and returned to his hotel; the Senate adjourned at nine o'clock.

weaken the States, but it was so plainly overdue that it passed the Senate 31 to 25.[26]

At last the wearied and despondent Polk, suffering more than ever from the chronic diarrhea which had troubled him throughout his term and which was soon to end his life, was free to turn toward his Nashville home. A little-known Tennessee politician when he entered the White House, he left an impressive record behind him. He had given the fiscal system a solid new foundation; he had disposed of critical boundary issues with Great Britain in a manner honorable to both nations; carrying on a war of unexpected magnitude in a land of great distances and difficult terrain, and using generals politically hostile to him, he had raised the American flag over the enemy capital; and he had made precisely the right peace, claiming neither too little nor too much. In the difficult issues growing out of the war, he had trodden a just and moderate path between the two sections, and favored a measure of compromise which it was probably unfortunate that Congress did not adopt. Endlessly abused, in most vital fields of public activity he had brought Congress and national sentiment to approve his measures.

Polk had few personal qualities of an engaging character; as F. P. Blair pointed out in a stinging letter to Buchanan, his narrow, rigid mind, ungenerous temper, and frequent pettiness of action alienated sympathy.[27] He owed much to larger-spirited advisers, particularly Benton, who when the Administration was disposed to fight a slow, cautious war against Mexico had insisted upon striking at the heart of the enemy in Mexico City. But he had carried a crushing burden industriously and conscientiously, and though he wore himself to a shadow with detail had nevertheless wrought according to a broad and ambitious design. In 1845 he had laid down a number of statesmanlike objectives, and in 1849 they were all achieved. Leaving office under a dismal cloud of unpopularity, he was destined to suffer in future reputation from historians whose inkwells were filled with corrosive anti-slavery prejudice. "Polk the Mendacious," quoth Von Holst! Actually this truthful, highminded leader had wielded the nation's sword with humanity; he had kept the national treasury full, had avoided war-time corruption, and had striven for internal concord; and he had carried American sovereignty to the sunset ocean, opening illimitable new vistas in commerce, mining, agricultural development, and city-building. An instrument of inevitable if not always creditable forces, he had raised America in the roster of nations.

26 Charleston *Courier*, March 6, 1849.
27 November 22, 1849; Buchanan, *Works*, VIII, 365, 366. Blair denounced Polk's "ungrateful and insidious treatment of the great and good men who gave him his public consequence" and bitterly attacked him for crushing rival candidates even "at the hazard of ruining the Democratic party. . . ."

Twelve weary, jangling years were to elapse before the White House doorsill saw the shadow of a President as great. Grayed hair, short and feeble step, and mien of languid exhaustion were badges of his devotion. He could go to his untimely grave in Nashville with a consciousness of duty done that might satisfy even his exacting Calvinist spirit.

[III]

On a day of gusty cold, flawed with rain and snow, Zachary Taylor was sworn into the presidency by Chief Justice Taney.[28] Polk, riding to the ceremonies with the general, was astounded to hear him drawl out that California and New Mexico were too distant to become integral members of the Union and might probably do best in independent status. Taylor, concluded Polk, was a well-meaning old man, but "exceedingly ignorant of public affairs, and, I should judge, of very ordinary capacity." [29]

Men who had only brief casual contacts with Taylor were likely to overrate his obvious limitations and underrate his sense, integrity, and courage. George W. Julian, paying a call at the White House with Giddings, was pleased by his kindly, honest, farmerlike face, and his old-fashioned simplicity in dress and demeanor, but found his talk awkward, labored, and in point of diction frequently incorrect. He lacked self-possession; his bearing suggested his frontier background; and he seemed "singularly unfitted by training and experience, or by any natural aptitude," for his exalted position.[30] A Tennessee politician, Alfred Balch, after seeing him twice, came to the same conclusion: "He has not one spark of genius in his soul. His mind works slowly—his purposes are honest. His education is exceedingly limited. The mass of his knowledge is indeed small enough." [31] Horace Greeley was outspoken: "Old Zack is a good old soul but don't know himself from a side of sole leather in the way of statesmanship . . ." [32] Those who saw him more intimately formed a better impression. Robert P. Letcher found him in the first week of his Administration "very cool and very deliberate, and very determined to go along regardless of censure or praise." The new Secretary of State, Clayton, became

28 Taylor arrived at Washington on the evening of February 23. A concourse turned out to cheer the new President. Giddings, returning from a walk, heard the crowd's "tuneless huzza," and had "a lower estimate of mankind than I had previously entertained." MS Diary, February 23, 1849, Giddings Papers.
29 Polk, *Diary*, IV, 375–376.
30 Julian, *Political Recollections*, 82.
31 To Buchanan, February 23, 1849; Buchanan Papers.
32 To Colfax, March 17, 1849; Greeley-Colfax Papers. Balch had used the same words in his letter to Buchanan. Taylor's "feelings toward the human family are decidedly kind," he had written, but "he is almost utterly ignorant of civil affairs and has no distinct perception of what the word 'statesmanship' means."

enthusiastic. Six weeks after the inauguration he burst out to Crittenden: "General Taylor is the greatest man, *in truth before God,* I ever knew! He is to a common observer only a kind benevolent man—a sensible man, and a brave man. But he grows greater every day and is the wisest man in *every thing.* You would be astonished if I should tell you what I know about his knowledge both of men and things." [33]

The chief of his many limitations was his total want of political skill. He was helpless as a party leader; and no President can rise to the height of his task, in difficult times, unless he has some political expertness. It was universally and correctly assumed that he would place himself in the hands of chosen advisers. But who would they be? He should have accepted the counsel of Clay and Webster, forgetting their contemptuous treatment of him; most of all of Clay.[34] Above all, a President elected as a moderate should have kept moderates about him. Edward Everett later spoke of his extraordinary delusion that these were times when the government could be administered with the aid of second-rate men.[35] Still more extraordinary was his delusion that he could safely place himself, as he soon did, under the guidance of one of the leading extremists.

The Cabinet was a commonplace body of men, respectable, dull, and very mixed. Greeley privately sketched them with caustic pen: "Clayton is a drunkard, Preston is a weak country lawyer, Meredith is a good commercial lawyer, but no politician at all, Reverdy Johnson a good lawyer and bad politician (which is better than none at all), Jake Collamer an upright, attentive, faithful man of business, but a little too conceited to be popular; Ewing an able man and well informed politician, but overbearing and selfish. Such is the Cabinet. Whenever any one of them shall drop out or be 'hove over,' he will sink like a stone and never be heard of again." [36]

Actually, three of the Cabinet were men of stature. John M. Clayton of Delaware, Yale graduate, attorney of renown, a chief justice of his State, and a thrice-elected Senator, had solid ability of a legalistic type. He declared that

33 Letcher to Crittenden, March 8, 1849; Clayton to Crittenden, April 18, 1849. Crittenden Papers.
34 "General Taylor means well," wrote Daniel Webster, "but he knows little of public affairs, and less of public men. He feels that he must rely on somebody; that he must have counsel, even in the appointment of his counsellors. . . ." Curtis, *Webster,* II, 358, 359. D. R. Atchison made a similar comment to Crittenden, March 8, 1849; Crittenden Papers.
35 February 18, 1850; Everett Papers.
36 To Colfax, March 17, 1850; Greeley-Colfax Papers. The Cabinet, Greeley went on to say, was "a horrid mixture," just what a blind man would have picked if he had been turned loose among several hundred "would-be magnates of the Whig party, and ordered to touch and take." See also Nathan Sargent's description of the Cabinet in his letter to Crittenden, July 15, 1849, Crittenden Papers, and Benton's opinion as described in R. P. Letcher's letter to Clayton, May 8, 1849, Clayton Papers.

in conducting foreign relations he would be as independent of Congress as a wood-sawyer.[37] Yet he had grave defects; not only was he irritable, hesitant, and unstable, but he could be provokingly opportunist, as he had shown in an eager search for the winner during the recent contest for the Whig nomination.[38]

The keenly intellectual Tom Ewing deserved better praise than Greeley gave him. A giant of a man, tall, broadshouldered, and massive-headed, of Scottish descent and frontier Ohio upbringing, he was still familiarly known, from his early calling, as "the Salt Boiler of the Kanawha." His strong principles, granite will, and the command of language which made him unexcelled as a stump speaker, found no adequate outlet in the new Interior Department. He brought to Washington, for schooling in a Georgetown convent, his daughter Ellen, later the wife of General Sherman. More remarkable still was Reverdy Johnson, one of the unquestioned leaders of the American bar, who resigned from the Senate to become Attorney-General. Though his greatest briefs, those in the McCormick Reaper and Dred Scott cases, were still to be written, he was already known as a fit successor to that other lawyer-statesman of Maryland, William Pinkney. Having a marked vein of indolence, he worked by fits and starts. But he was a conservative, sagacious man, who had urged a settlement of the Oregon boundary along the forty-ninth parallel, who had shared Webster's aversion to the annexation of Southwestern territory as certain to plunge the nation into sectional strife, and who objected to the expansion of slavery. Like Clayton, he had held that the status of the institution in the new Territories might well be left to the Supreme Court.[39]

Not much need be said of the genial, likeable William Meredith, a Pennsylvania protectionist who proved quite incompetent as head of the Treasury; of George W. Crawford, a former governor of Georgia who soon showed his want of discretion and of a nice sense of personal honor as Secretary of War; of William B. Preston, of distinguished Virginia family, who took the Navy Department; [40] or of commonsense Jacob Collamer of Vermont, the Postmaster-General. It was unfortunate that John J. Crittenden did not accept a leading place in the Cabinet. He had done as much as anybody to make Taylor President and now he should have taken partial responsibility for his success or failure. But Crittenden had left the Senate to run for the governorship of Kentucky, believing this necessary to carry the State for Taylor, and now he could hardly reject the office he had sought. Moreover,

37 Clayton to Crittenden, August 23, 1849; similarly, Clayton's letter dated April 18, 1849.
38 Toombs to Mrs. Chapman Coleman, June 22, 1849; Crittenden Papers. Gideon Welles also criticized Clayton for being excessively timid, cunning, and showing "time-serving propensities." Undated paper, Gideon Welles Papers.
39 See the sketch of Ewing in the *Atlantic Monthly*, XLVI, 371 (September, 1880); of Johnson by B. C. Steiner in *Life of Reverdy Johnson*, 10–42.
40 Cf. Giddings' praise of Preston; MS Diary, February 7, 1849, Giddings Papers.

he was grieved by Clay's withdrawal, in post-convention sulkiness, of his long-standing friendship.[41] When President-elect Taylor had visited Kentucky to offer Crittenden a choice of posts, the excessively conscientious statesman would take none. This was a misfortune, for if he had brought his sound judgment, knowledge of the law, and lucid grasp of complex situations into the Cabinet, Taylor's course with respect to various measures and his attitude toward the ideas of Clay in particular might have been wiser.[42]

The inclination of the blunt, practical President was naturally to follow the general guidance of his Cabinet. He had declared that he expected this body to be "harmonious, honorable, patriotic, talented, and hardworking," and he was at first much pleased with his associates.[43] It was soon evident that the Northern and border Whig members, Clayton, Ewing, Collamer, Meredith, and Reverdy Johnson, had established an ascendant influence. To Clayton, partly for his own qualities and partly as Crittenden's warm friend, the President naturally deferred, while his relations with Meredith became genuinely affectionate.[44] The fruits of this influence rapidly grew evident. As the President talked in his rough, frank, sententious way with visitors, reports appeared in the press that he was descanting upon the evils of slavery and the undesirability of admitting it into new areas. In one field his actions within six months spoke louder than words. A filibustering expedition against Cuba was fitted out in New Orleans during the summer of 1849. When Taylor learned of it, his soldierly instincts asserted themselves in a sharp proclamation of warning. Two ships were seized, and the expedition disintegrated. With it went into temporary eclipse the bright Southern dream of a quick and easy expansion of American sovereignty into the Caribbean.[45]

But Clayton and Meredith were not sufficiently adroit to maintain their early dominance over Taylor. The President, after his first days of flustration in meeting problems whose elements he did not understand and in dealing with shoals of politicians of whose background, ties, and character he knew nothing,

41 Alfred Balch described Clay's feeling toward Crittenden as "a deadly antipathy." To Buchanan, February 23, 1849; Buchanan Papers.

42 Crittenden suggested to Taylor that ex-Governor Letcher of Kentucky be made Postmaster-General. "The man and his manners are *conciliation* itself," Crittenden had urged; and he also pointed out that Letcher was friendly with many of Clay's friends. But the President rejected his advice. Crittenden to Clayton, February 17, 1849; Clayton Papers.

43 Clayton to Crittenden, August 23, 1849; Crittenden Papers.

44 Weed, *Autobiography*, 589.

45 In the first days of the Administration Taylor seemed so dependent on his Cabinet that the Democratic press charged the country with being ruled by a junta in which the President had only one vote. Crittenden repeatedly urged Clayton to help establish the idea that the President was really the "Grand Agent." Taylor, Crittenden advised the Secretary of State, "must always be presumed to be more popular than any or all of his Cabinet. . . ." To Clayton, July 8, 1849; Clayton Papers. See also Nathan Sargent to Crittenden, July 15, 1849; Crittenden Papers.

gained an almost excessive self-confidence. Lacking finesse and completely un-
tutored in the ways of political manipulators, he readily accepted the flattery of
some of his entourage. They urged him to shake off his timidity, praised his
judgment as wonderfully acute, and encouraged his military instinct for rapid
and irrevocable decisions.[46] Taylor began to formulate "principles" which too
often were mere notions, but to which he clung with bulldog obstinacy. Some
were creditable, like his refusal to appoint that quarrelsome editor James Watson
Webb to office because he fought duels; some were not. Clayton, slipping into
the background, became uneasy and discontented. He corresponded regularly
with Crittenden, sought his advice on many points, and repeatedly offered to
step out that the Kentuckian might take his place.[47] Before the end of 1849
he actually tendered his resignation, which Taylor refused. More powerful
personalities and nimbler brains were required to maintain a grip upon the
President.

[IV]

Would Clay step into the guiding role? Unquestionably Harry of the
West hoped to. He had given every indication of a desire to stand near the
throne if not to lean protectingly over it. He had invited President-elect Taylor
to visit him in Ashland on his way to Washington. Early in 1849 Clay's
Kentucky friends took steps to send him back to the Senate, where his re-
appearance would really be a great national blessing. There was truth in Leslie
Combs' affectionate prediction that he would be the most formidable enemy of
Calhoun ("the Southern Sensibles against the Southern Lunatics—the Southern
Patriots against the Southern Traitors"); that he would frighten the baser
spoils politicians in Washington like the sudden entry of a tomcat into a roomful of cheese-stealing mice; and that he would devote his whole heart to the
prosperity of the country, ready to become the sheet-anchor of the Administration.[48] When a meeting of Kentucky legislators raised the question of Clay's
friendliness to the Taylor Administration, one of his friends presented a written
communication declaring that he would most cordially support it.[49] This
cleared away all obstacles and his election followed. Clay himself assured
Letcher that he would sustain the Administration with all his zeal.[50] Shortly

46 Poage, *Henry Clay and the Whig Party*, Ch. 13.
47 On Crittenden's influence upon Clayton see Poage, *Clay and the Whig Party*, 188, 189;
John Sargent, "Recollections of an Old Stager," *Harper's Monthly*, XL; Crittenden to Clayton, July 8, 20, 1849; Clayton Papers.
48 Combs to Clayton, January 22, 1849; Clayton Papers.
49 Crittenden to Clayton, January 30, 1849; Clayton Papers.
50 Letcher to Clayton, May 8, 1849; Clayton Papers. The thought that Clay would oppose
Taylor's Administration was ridiculous to Letcher.

after the inauguration, he requested that his son be given a foreign post, and Taylor appointed the young man to Portugal, which was as good a place as he deserved. For this favor Clay sent the Secretary of State his cordial thanks.[51] The appointment was well and magnanimously made, commented Crittenden. "Mr. Clay, I am persuaded, is disposed to be General Taylor's friend, and will duly appreciate any mark of the General's favor and confidence—and from my heart I desire as a matter of policy and feeling to see a cordial reconciliation between them." [52]

But there was unhappily little chance for harmony between Clay and the President. They were temperamentally unlike. Both had resentful memories— Taylor of Clay's frigidity during the campaign, Clay of Taylor's success in displacing him. Some of the President's friends in the West were aghast when Clay was reëlected to the Senate. Morbid, irritated, cantankerous, Clay "will play hell," prophesied Bailie Peyton of Tennessee, and unless Old Zack obeys his orders, will make savage war upon him. The Administration should fight Clay like wildcats, he urged; they must regard him as Mad Anthony Wayne regarded the British, for if they didn't kill him, he would certainly kill them. The fact was that in dealing with so powerful a figure as the founder and Nestor of the Whig Party, Taylor could hardly make him chief adviser without making him dictator. Arm's length was the only safety. When Harry was cheered down the Washington streets, Taylor's chief supporters met him with apprehensive hostility, and Taylor himself with suspicion.[53] Nor was Clay himself without fault; he too showed pride and jealousy.

It was a younger Whig chieftain, more tactful, subtle, and inconspicuous, who slipped rapidly into Taylor's right-hand seat—William H. Seward. The President owed so great a political debt to Thurlow Weed that the bland politician-editor, whose long and devious experience enabled him to offer shrewd advice on party management, was cordially welcomed at the White House. At Weed's elbow of course stood his partner Seward, now in the Senate. Those who supposed that Weed was the ruling spirit in their alliance were in error, for Seward had much the stronger mind, the greater vision, and by now the larger public influence. With his long leadership of the New York Whigs to commend him, Seward felt entitled to take a high place in Washington and had been somewhat chagrined that he was not consulted in the makeup of the Cabinet. But, too wise to show pique, he had insinuated himself with diplomatic urbanity into Taylor's pre-inauguration talks with party leaders and was largely responsible for bringing the President-elect and Reverdy Johnson together.[54]

51 Clay to Clayton, June 7, 1849; Clayton Papers.
52 Crittenden to Clayton, June 29, 1849; Crittenden Papers.
53 Poage, *Henry Clay and the Whig Party*, 190–192.
54 F. Seward, *Seward*, II, 101, 103. Taylor perhaps exaggerated Weed's services.

Taylor's gratitude for these good offices was enhanced by a minor incident. After solemnly engaging in the Allison letter not to interfere with the law-making power of Congress, he had acted with Seward on the memorable final night of the session to try to place California under temporary civil govern-ment without embarrassing qualifications. By so doing he brought down upon his head the charge that he had broken his pledge, and the still more unpleasant accusation that he was hostile to the Wilmot Proviso.[55] Seward seized his ready pen and wrote a forcible vindication of Taylor's position on both matters. "It was approved in full Cabinet," he notified Weed exultantly, "the President presiding, in my presence, and ordered printed. All trouble is at an end. I shall have much to tell you." [56] In the distribution of the New York patronage, Seward and Vice-President Fillmore were at first rivals, but the former played his cards so well that he soon controlled the field. The Cabinet decided that in all New York appointments the advice of Governor Hamilton Fish was to be given special weight—and Fish owed his office largely to Seward and Weed. Moreover, Fillmore was handicapped by his modesty, which made him un-willing to press any of his friends' requests for office except under an im-perative sense of duty.[57]

[V]

The policy of the Administration quickly developed along definite lines; some marked out by Taylor alone, some by Taylor and his Cabinet, some by Taylor and Seward, and some simply by events. The President, never a party man, cared little about distributing spoils. But his associates did, and amid pained cries of "Proscription!" from the Democrats, the departmental heads were quickly dismissing the 'locoes' and putting staunch Whigs in office every-where.[58] They defended their course by saying that the new Administration had found not a single Whig collector, first-class postmaster, marshal, diplomat, or bureau head; that for twenty years the Democrats had monopolized Federal office, and that out of about thirty new generals appointed from the citizens at large in the recent war, not a Whig in the wide land had been named. To

55 Frederic Bancroft, *Life of William H. Seward*, I, 215, 216. See also the discussion in the Washington *Union*, February 10, 1850.
56 Frederick W. Seward, *Seward*, II, 107.
57 See Silas M. Stilwell's complaining letter·to Clayton, April 12, 1849. "Mr. Seward is the reverse of Mr. Fillmore in everything," Stilwell lamented. "He forces his opinion in person; and procures hundreds to call upon Gen. Taylor and the Senate to induce them to go against public opinion that he may secure power through a friend. He cares for no interest but his own and regards no means as improper that will secure his object." Much the same view is taken by Washington Hunt to Clayton, April 8, 1849, Clayton Papers, and the N. Y. *Evening Post*, May 29, 1848.
58 Washington *Daily Republic*, June 14, 1849.

strengthen the Administration in another respect, a beautifully printed and well written "organ," the *Daily Republic*, was established in the capital, its first issue appearing June 13th. A wealthy Kentuckian named Albert T. Burnley, ardently devoted to Taylor, supplied most of the funds. The editor, A. C. Bullitt, called "Aleck" in the White House, was regarded highly by Taylor, to whom he had given useful literary aid; while the assistant editor was John O. Sargent, who years later wrote some valuable reminiscences.[59]

"I am for good roads, good harbors, and good laws, and then we can go ahead," the *Republic* shortly quoted the naïve President as saying. Administration leaders talked much of liberal internal improvements. They emphasized the necessity of restoring a fraternal affection between North and South. Bullitt, who had been editor of the New Orleans *Picayune*, and Sargent, who was experienced in New York journalism, made their paper lively and energetic. It admirably supplemented that old Whig sheet-anchor, the *National Intelligencer*, which had not favored Taylor, and which was prosily old-fashioned and conservative.[60] Bullitt and the Southerners who furnished the money for the *Republic* had ambitious ideas for the future of the party. They held that it must drop the aristocratic ideas of Webster and turn its back on the narrow appeal to special interests embraced in Clay's American system, reviving, instead, the broad doctrines of the Republican party in that happy era when Monroe was President and J. Q. Adams Secretary of State.[61] But on one point the editors, speaking for Taylor himself, were determined not to be complaisant. A stern Jacksonian ring characterized one dictum in their first issue: "We regard the dissolution of the Union as an impossibility—a peaceful separation is certainly so."

It was California, where the picturesque gold-rush of '49 was opening a new chapter in American history, which required an immediate formulation of policy, and as the months passed action became more imperative. The mountainous area between the San Joaquin on the south and the Trinity and Klamath rivers on the north had filled as by magic with a boisterous, excited population. Sleepy streams in remote wilderness solitudes saw a few prospectors unload their shovels one day; on the next a feverish camp would spread over the flats and slopes. What had been a poor, ill-governed province of Mexico, with little bodies of apprehensive American settlers living among ten or twelve thousand native Californians, sprang within a year into a powerful commonwealth.

A new American metropolis, San Francisco, had begun to rise on the coast,

59 The first issue of the *Daily Republic* printed a long statement of principles.
60 Orlando Brown criticized the *Intelligencer* for being "too genteel, dignified, and statesmanlike . ." To Crittenden, July 24, 1849; Crittenden Papers.
61 Poage, *Clay and the Whig Party*, 186ff.

changing almost beyond recognition every few months. We have graphic descriptions of its scenes from the pens of famous Americans who visited it in its early days—W. T. Sherman, Bayard Taylor, Bessie Benton Frémont, and others. They tell of the incredible new monetary standards, the soaring speculative spirit, and the reckless disregard for property and life. Porters charged $2 for carrying a bag a few blocks; old New York newspapers sold for a dollar a copy; truckmen made $20 or $25 a day. Taylor reported that the gamblers who occupied the second story of the Parker House paid $60,000 a year in rent, while a canvas tent nearby, called Eldorado, rented for $40,000 a year. A lawyer who wanted an office was shown a dug-out in a hillside and told he could take it or leave it for $250 a month. Commercial transactions were conducted with quarter-dollars as the smallest coin, and if any customer tried to bargain the shopkeeper turned his back. Nearly everybody gambled; Taylor saw a boy of fifteen in one of the gambling dens coolly pocket $500, and watched a fellow passenger on the Panama steamer lose $2,400 in an hour. An Englishman who arrived in January of 1850 thought the city looked enchanting from the bay. But, landing, "on every side I saw filth, misery and wretchedness; in the streets the mud is in some places above one's knees, so that we are obliged to wear long boots, and as every sort of offal is flung into the streets, there will be no doubt much sickness when the warm weather comes on." Everybody was waiting for good weather to usher in a rush to the mines. Meanwhile, hotels charged $80 a week up for board and lodging. "Every other house is a gambling house, and there are few from the merchant downwards who escape the infection. . . ." The city grew like magic.[62]

And Sacramento and Stockton, at the portals of the gold-bearing district, became thriving municipalities almost as rapidly as San Francisco. In April, 1849, the site of Sacramento, on Johann Sutter's domain, had four houses; that fall its population was approaching ten thousand. During the summer months the principal stores took in from $1,000 to $2,000 a day from the sale of mining supplies and provisions.

While lucky men among the placer miners gained almost incredible fortunes, thousands of their less fortunate companions made almost nothing. Since in the first five years after the discovery of gold not less than half a billion dollars was taken out, it is easy to understand that a few men achieved dazzling successes. Nothing was required except strong muscles, a stout heart, a pick, shovel, crowbar, and tin pan. Even the last might be dispensed with if the miner used a cradle or rocker: a wooden box through which the gravel was washed, while the heavy gold stuck to wooden cleats nailed to the bottom. The frenzied,

62 Bayard Taylor, *Eldorado*, offers a vivid picture of this transformation. For the Englishman see J. W. Trutch, January 29, 1850, in British Consular Reports, FO/5, 519.

monotonous work, the hardships of life in tents or crude log cabins, and the constant uncertainties of the struggle all had their effect on the miners' psychology. They became thirsty for diversion. The more excitement they could get the better, and drinking, gambling, and quarreling all prospered. Fiction writers of a later day have overdrawn the picture, for the mining camps numbered many men of puritanical deportment, and they soon boasted of churches, schools, and attractive residences as well as saloons and gambling halls. But after all, a population of young men far from home, toiling week after week at exhausting physical labor, and eager for anything that would break the gray loneliness of their existence, could not be expected to behave sedately. In many communities everybody carried knife and pistol, crime was common, and society became deeply tinged with violence.[63]

There is no more typical story of a forty-niner than that preserved in John W. Audubon's detailed diary of his observations in 1849–50.[64] A strong, alert man of thirty-six, the son of the naturalist, Audubon traveled from New York to Texas, where he joined a large overland company under the command of Colonel Henry L. Webb. The journey was an odyssey of disasters. In the Rio Grande Valley the party were attacked by cholera, coming down one by one, some dying within a few hours. A seizure by the disease was accepted as a death sentence. One sturdy companion was gasping his last when Audubon tried to comfort him. "What hurts you, Ham?" he inquired. "My wife and children hurt me, Mr. John," the sufferer replied. In Rio Grande City the party gave their money-bags, containing about $15,000, into the custody of the hotel barkeeper; the money was immediately stolen, and only about half of it was ever recovered. On the desert journey across New Mexico and Arizona most of their pack mules died, depriving them of a valuable resource, for they might have made large sums on the coast by freighting. Worst of all, they found on arrival that the best placer diggings were exhausted. Audubon, constrained by loyalty to his mates to refuse an offer of $35 a day as architectural draughtsman in San Francisco, made almost nothing in the mines. At typical diggings he learned that while men on rich streams would average $14 a day or more, many got practically nothing for weeks together. Those who fared best were the enterprising fellows who, scraping together some capital, set up as merchants or speculated in lands or claims.

Quasi-military rule in this busy, disorderly area could not be protracted

63 The brutal highwayman, not a romantic or heroic figure at all, was the most notorious violator of the law. But violence did not wait for the highwayman in the mining community; disputes over water rights and claims were as likely to be settled by force as any other method.
64 *Audubon's Western Journal*, 1849–50, edited by Marian W. Audubon and Frank H. Hodder.

without grave injury to the settlers and their material interests. General Bennett Riley, commander on the coast, issued a proclamation on June 3, 1849, declaring that under instructions from the War Department he had assumed the administration of California not as a military governor, but as head of the existing civil government—military government having ended with the war. But California, springing full-grown into equality with some of the oldest members of the republic, wanted something better than the old Mexican framework with a general at the top.

The Administration policy was quickly formulated. Taylor and his Cabinet resolved to invite the early organization of both California and New Mexico as States, and to urge Congress to admit them to the Union as soon as possible. Clayton, laboring from eight in the morning until eleven at night, often without time for dinner, bore an important hand in this decision. "As to California and New Mexico," he wrote Crittenden on April 18th, "I have been *wide awake*. Everything is done as you would wish it. The plan I proposed to you last night will be carried out fully. The States will be admitted—free and Whig!" [65]

Taylor hurried Thomas Butler King, a Georgia Whig of long experience in Congress, off to California as a special agent, with instructions to hasten the work of State making. It was not the President's intent, however, to interfere too openly or drastically. King was to say that he wished California to draw up a Constitution and submit it to Congress with a prayer for admission, but he was not to influence the choice of delegates or the deliberations of the convention. Nor was he to suggest the establishment of any government without consent of Congress. He was soon visiting the important settlements, riding about week after week in the hot sun, the thermometer standing as high as 110° or 113°; forming a close alliance with Generals Riley and Persifer F. Smith; and rallying sentiment against some "demagogues" who hoped to profit by delay and confusion.[66] Riley's proclamation in June had proposed August 1st for the election of delegates, and September 1st for the assembling of the constitutional convention. On the date named a capable body met in Monterey, numbering several men then or later famous—Johann Sutter, William M. Gwin, Henry W. Halleck. It was possible for Taylor to announce in his first annual message of December, 1849, that California's application for entry into the Union would shortly arrive, and that he hoped it would be approved.[67]

65 Crittenden Papers.
66 See King's letter to Clayton, written from King's camp on the American River, July 22, 1849; Clayton Papers. King said that not enough credit could be given to Generals Smith and Riley for their work in carrying through the policy of the Administration.
67 Within six weeks the convention had finished its work. In November the new constitution was approved by a vote of 12,000 to 800. In December the legislature met, General Riley surrendered his civil powers to it, and John C. Frémont and William M. Gwin were chosen Senators.

[VI]

Alas that the placing of the new star in the constellation was to meet with such grave impediment! California to millions seemed a realm of pure enchantment, an Eldorado, a Garden of the Hesperides. Frémont with a happy prolepsis had named the Golden Gate, behind which was now rising a golden city. Men read with wonder of the miners opening their rich lodes and nests of nuggets; of ships laden with gold dust; of the vaults of the Bank of England inundated by the golden stream.[68] While Europe was writhing in revolution, a farther West was springing into aureate vigor. From the chaotic Old World, the strands and valleys of California might soon draw a hopeful population. The Mormons, too—the Hegira of their prophet and the Exodus of their harried people recalling tales of ancient times—had projected a lusty new state in the desert which should also attract its myriads. If the Pactolian stream continued, changes in the standard of value would affect the economy of the entire globe. Then, too, what new links with the Orient might be forged!—for San Francisco was already wooing the commerce of the farther Pacific. With delighted amusement Easterners shortly read of the seal of the new commonwealth: a grizzly bear feeding on a cluster of grapes; Minerva, with Gorgon shield, emblematic of the swift rise of the State to mature stature; a miner, with pick and spade, representing gold; a river with steamboats typifying commerce; and in the distance the snowy Sierras, with the motto "Eureka." It was sad that the knocking of this romantic new sister on the national portal should reawaken the worst passions of the slavery struggle.

For it was glaringly evident that the President's plan would encounter the sternest opposition from the South. Its fears stirred anew by Calhoun's Address, that section would never consent to the unconditional admission of California and New Mexico as free States. The antagonism of most Southern Democrats to Taylor had long been pronounced. By the end of 1849 it was being matched by the antagonism of many Southern Whigs.

As summer passed, the clear ascendancy of freesoil Whig influences over Taylor inevitably excited the bitterest resentment in the Lower South. Here was a Louisiana slaveholder taking Seward to his bosom and allying himself with his section's enemies! A reaction against the Administration would in any event have taken place when the bold war hero revealed himself as a fumbling, uncertain political chieftain. As Greeley put it, his mere election had exhausted the popularity based upon his soldierly achievements.[69] But the disclosure of his

68 See the *Southern Quarterly Review*, July, 1850, for a Southern view of California.
69 Greeley, *American Conflict*, I, 201.

strong Northern orientation furnished more solid grounds for disaffection; grounds which made some Southern Whigs regret that they had not accepted Calhoun's scheme for a Southern Party.

Too late, the pro-slavery Whigs perceived that the most powerful influences in Washington were freesoil influences. The tone of the entire Cabinet, except for Crawford of Georgia, was hostile to slavery expansion. Preston, though a Virginian, had been active in the memorable legislative session of 1831–32 in opposing slavery and supporting Jefferson's plan of post-natal emancipation; just before entering the Cabinet he had spoken in Congress for the admission of California as a free State; [70] and in due time he was to oppose the secession of Virginia. Reverdy Johnson's dislike of slavery was well known. Some commentators pronounced Postmaster-General Collamer an abolitionist, while Secretary Ewing was certainly a determined freesoiler.[71] In the background the great party chieftains Clay and Webster equally objected to any enlargement of the slave area. Robert Toombs believed that political maneuvering was responsible for the Administration's bias. The Cabinet had placed the Northern patronage in the hands of the Seward-Weed element, he wrote, "under some foolish idea of Preston that they would get rid of a Northern competition for 1852, as Seward stood for 1856."[72] But actually more fundamental forces were at work, too strong to be stemmed, and as Taylor responded to them, the Southern alarm deepened.

By midsummer of 1849 the Southern reaction was carrying Congressmen and voters into hostile line from South Carolina to Louisiana.[73] Observers were predicting that when Congress met the President would find both houses against him, for the Senate was already in opposition, and enough Southern Whigs might join with the Democrats to place the House in the same position. Howell Cobb wrote that in Georgia the name of Old Rough and Ready had become almost a byword and reproach.[74] Partly because of resentment against Taylor's bias, partly because of the immense influence of Calhoun's Address, and partly because of the natural demand for some equivalent as it became certain that California would be a free State, the South took a more and more threatening attitude. It is apparent, wrote an astute Georgian in midsummer, "that the slavery question rides insolently over every other everywhere—in

70 *Cong. Globe,* February 7, 1849; see also sketch of Preston in the *Dictionary of American Biography.*
71 Isaac Toucey to Buchanan, July 25, 1849; Buchanan Papers.
72 Colemen, *Crittenden,* I, 364–366.
73 Edmund Burke of the Washington *Union* gleefully reported to Buchanan that the elections in the South and West were favorable to the Democratic cause. "We have got the Administration upon their backs," he wrote, "and if we conduct with any sort of judgment in our policy, we shall keep them there. . ." August 27, 1849; Buchanan Papers.
74 June 17, 1849, to Buchanan; Buchanan Papers.

fact that it is the only question which in the least affects the results of the elections. It is not less manifest that the whole North is becoming ultra anti-slavery and the whole South ultra pro-slavery." [75]

Southern ill-temper was aggravated by the fact that this was a year of distress among many of the cotton growers. Overproduction of the Southern staple had depressed the market. The crop of 1845, according to one authority (for estimates varied widely), had been 1,750,000 bales, which sold at sixteen cents a pound; and the next three years had witnessed three successive increases, until the crop of 1848–49 reached the unprecedented figure of 2,700,000 bales. British agents traversing the country reported this huge yield before it was generally known to the Southerners themselves, with the result that prices sank unexpectedly to a ruinous level. South Carolinians early in 1849 saw the dejected upland farmers waggoning their crop over bad roads to Columbia, eighty or a hundred miles, and getting for it only four and a half cents a pound. According to William Elliott, throughout great Southern areas the planters' incomes did not pay their expenses.[76]

The campaign of Southern publicists to awaken their section to its supposed wrongs and perils, too, was now bearing fruit. The ablest men of letters had taken a hand. Early in 1849 the most famous and prolific of Southern romancers, William Gilmore Simms, began (on the pitiful salary of a thousand dollars) the regeneration of the *Southern Quarterly Review*, rapidly bringing it to substantial equality with the *North American Review*, and making it an organ of crusading power.[77] Its teachings were directed to secession, and one of its most assiduous contributors, Beverley Tucker of Virginia, was a flaming secessionist apostle. Augustus Baldwin Longstreet, who lives in memory as a humorist, but who was also minister, judge, college president, and essayist, had written in justification of slavery on Biblical and other grounds. In 1847 he had published a book of *Letters* addressed from Georgia to Massachusetts, half argument, half defiance. The volume was now running through edition after edition, eight in all; Southern editors were urging every citizen to read it; and it was exerting a potent influence from Virginia to Texas.[78] Longstreet declared that although Georgia loved the Union, if it proved to be a Golden Calf she would overthrow it as boldly as Moses overthrew the calf of Aaron. Of Massachusetts, the seat of puritan fanaticism, he wrote that "by her lust she had engendered a disease, which by her quackery she had turned into a cancer." He urged the South to

75 H. L. Benning in *Toombs, Stephens, Cobb Corr.*, 169.
76 See Elliott's long letter, Charleston *Courier*, August 28, 1849.
77 W. P. Trent, *William Gilmore Simms*, 163ff.
78 While the South acclaimed the book the North ignored it. A package of books sent to a Northern bookstore was immediately returned; this did not tend to increase Long-street's love for the North.

develop its militia and give all its college students military training, and he predicted victory in the field if war ever came.[79]

A sectional propaganda, indeed, was being pressed by pamphleteers and journalists everywhere. Moncure D. Conway, graduating from Dickinson College, went home to Fredericksburg this year and began writing for Southern journals. He was too gifted a man to lose, and the pro-slavery forces at once tried to enlist him. They were carrying on a vigorous crusade in Virginia, promulgating the sociological, cultural, ethical, and economic excellences of slavery. Able pamphlets came from the pens of Beverley Wellford and George Fitzhugh; religious arguments from President William Smith of Randolph-Macon College and Thornton Stringfellow. Young Conway was invited to join a dozen other men, all persons of influence, in forming a Southern Rights Association, which at once proclaimed extreme views. He was taken aback when his father, a man of the old Jeffersonian school, said quietly: "Don't be the fool of these people! Slavery is a doomed institution." [80]

Of practical grievances the chief was the lack of effective legislation upon fugitive slaves. Senator Butler of South Carolina estimated that the annual loss of the South from runaways reached $200,000; Clingman of North Carolina reckoned the total loss since independence at fifteen millions. Southerners read with anger of the meeting of the New England Anti-Slavery Society in Faneuil Hall in the spring of 1849. Wendell Phillips, pointing to two slaves seated triumphantly on the platform, declaimed that Congress might enact its little laws in Washington, but "Faneuil Hall repeals them in the name of the humanity of Massachusetts." [81] Everywhere in the South, too, men were indignantly reading the recent Senate report on the fugitive slave question.[82] This contained the ireful resolutions of the Kentucky legislature on the subject, the text of Massachusetts and Rhode Island laws obstructing the arrest of fugitives, and a flat declaration by the Judiciary Committee: "Laws of the same effect are now in force in all the northern and eastern States, and in some of the northwestern non-slaveholding States."

The Southern propagandists, taking their cue from Calhoun, spoke of meeting ever-growing aggressions and being forced into ever-larger concessions. The North, they said, now proposed to exclude the South from the territory taken from Mexico, though the South had contributed twice as many volunteers to the armies as the North. It proposed to forbid slavery in the District, thus creating a harbor for runaway slaves in the very heart of the Maryland-Virginia area. The next step would be to abolish slavery in the navy-yards, forts, and

79 John D. Wade, *Augustus Baldwin Longstreet*, 283ff.
80 Conway, *Autobiography*, I, 71ff.
81 Garrison, *Garrison*, III, 247.
82 *Senate Report No. 143*, dated May 3, 1848.

arsenals, establishing pockets of abolitionist feeling all over the South itself.[83] Had not Chase of Ohio declared that slavery was to be "localized and discouraged"? In the vast areas extending from Minnesota to Oregon and from Missouri to California, the North would possess enough land for dozens of new States; and when they were admitted, the political power thus created, as Rufus King had long before indicated, would be used to overwhelm the South and extirpate servitude everywhere. "In this alarming situation," warned two leading South Carolina editors, "the South has no hope but in her own firmness." [84]

[VII]

A breakup of parties along sectional lines seemed imminent, with the Southern Whigs deserting the national organization by wholesale. "That the Administration is now amidst rocks, shoals, and whirlpools no one, I think, can be so blind himself as not to see," the journalist Nathan Sargent lamented to Crittenden in early summer.[85] To be sure, he was thinking chiefly of patronage troubles and the incongruities of the Cabinet, but below these surface resentments ran deep sectional animosities. In vain did the Washington *Republic* try to placate the Southern Whigs by declaring that they had received their full share of executive attention and offices.[86] In vain did Burnley and others of the *Republic* clique try to lift the nation's eyes above political squabbling by formulating the new program which they hoped would submerge the slavery issue. A greater crisis than Buena Vista was upon them, declared Burnley, urging Crittenden to enter the Cabinet at once.[87] The party must throw overboard the old Whig doctrines of a national bank, a high protective tariff, and a huge system of internal improvements, for the people did not want any of them. Instead, it must take steps to improve, not repeal, the Sub-Treasury; to revise,

83 Calhoun had made this warning in his speech on the amendment for the Missouri Compromise line in the Oregon Bill. To abolish slavery in those places, he had declared, was much more dangerous than the Wilmot Proviso. "It would open everywhere throughout the entire South, asylums to receive our fugitive slaves, who would as soon as they entered, cease to be so."

84 The editors were Edwin De Leon and W. B. Carlisle. Their arguments are summed up in the Columbia *Telegraph*, April 15, 17, 1849. Gov. John B. Floyd said the same thing in his message to the General Assembly, March 12, 1850. If the Federal Government failed to give equal protection to the South and its slave property, Floyd declared, "then we must take the remedy into our own hands." Governors' Letter Books, No. 26, 130–132; Va. State Library.

85 Crittenden Papers, July 15, 1849.

86 Washington *Republic*, June 15, 1849. The paper pointed out that the State Department had been offered to Crittenden, and the Postoffice to Gentry of Tennessee, while the War Department had actually been taken by Crawford of Georgia.

87 On the dissatisfaction with the Cabinet see Orlando Brown to Crittenden, July 10, 1849, Crittenden Papers, and Poage, *Clay and the Whig Party*, 186ff.

not repeal, the tariff of 1846, of which the iron interests were complaining so bitterly; and to use wisely, not recklessly, the power to make internal improvements. "Let the proceeds of the public lands go to pay the national debt," Burnley urged, *"and above all things, stand by the Union unto death."* [88] But no such neo-Whig platform could persuade the Southern contingent to forget the Territorial issue.

Nor were the Southern Whigs soothed by the President's summer tour to the northward. Taylor left hot, humid Washington in August to travel to Pittsburgh and Erie, making some simple-hearted and, unfortunately, simple-minded speeches along the way. On simple people he produced a pleasant impression, and the Democratic press was driven to ridicule his homely mannerisms and shaky grammar. The Washington *Union* charged him with such expressions as "be them Democrats or be them Whigs!" At Erie he fell ill of what reporters called his old Mexican trouble of dysenteric nature. For some days great alarm was felt, confidential reports reached Washington that his condition was grave, and news of his death would not have astonished a few well-informed people. But, given the best of medical care, he was soon able to proceed. The South did not fail to note that as he traversed New York the Seward-Weed faction kept him in close control.[89]

It was obviously true that, as Benning of Georgia said, the South was becoming more pro-slavery and the North more anti-slavery. Early in the year Calhoun had written elatedly that his area was "more aroused than I ever saw it on the subject," [90] and now, corresponding with leaders throughout the section, he advised them to act with spirit. He had long believed in a Southern convention to unite the slaveholding States behind a common program. Delegates should meet in solemn conclave, he had suggested, and agree upon a frank ultimatum: either the North would abide by the Constitution (as the South interpreted it), or after one year's notice the South should retaliate by such steps as barring Northern ships and goods from its ports.[91] He was now urging this idea in every hopeful quarter.[92] Buchanan, who kept in close touch with William R. King and other Southern leaders, was keenly aware of the seriousness of the situation. "They are preparing for the impending struggle with far more unanimity, determination, and intensity of purpose than they have ever

88 To Crittenden, July 22, 1849; Crittenden Papers. Despite its position on the tariff the *Republic* carried a good deal of protectionist material. It gave a full report of the important meeting of iron-furnace owners in Pittsburgh on August 18, 1849.
89 See the N. Y. *Herald*, Washington *Republic*, and the *Union*, August 20–September 10, 1849.
90 To Mrs. T. G. Clemson, January 24, 1849; *Calhoun Corr.*, 761, 762.
91 To Percy Walker, letter dated Fort Hill, October 23, 1847, and printed in the *National Intelligencer*, June 22, 1855.
92 See Calhoun to J. H. Means, April 13, 1849, *Calhoun Corr.*, 764–766.

yet displayed," he nervously wrote.[93] Buchanan had somehow persuaded himself to accept the whole Southern position (for example, he wrote that the antislavery attempts to provoke a servile rebellion constituted a veritable Damocles' sword), and his timidity as to Southern threats was a positive neurosis; but in this instance he gauged the position clearly.

In the North the same hardening of hearts and of sectional allegiance was visible. Horace Greeley, though no longer worried about the future of California, feared that freesoil would be robbed of most of New Mexico through what he called the swindling claims of Texas.[94] Against compromise in the Territories, against the Texas claims, the New York *Tribune* labored valiantly. It was fast becoming a prime national power. By the end of 1849 it had a daily circulation of 13,400, which much exceeded that of any daily below the Mason and Dixon line; but far more important was the combined weekly and semi-weekly circulation of almost 35,000, which carried the *Tribune's* highly effective combination of news, special articles, and editorials far and wide through the North and West. We have noted that Greeley was much more interested in influence than revenues, and that copies of his weekly were passed from hand to hand until their ideas inseminated whole communities. A new sternness of tone on the Territorial question was animating Samuel Bowles' Springfield *Republican,* Weed's Albany *Evening Journal,* James Watson Webb's *Courier and Enquirer,* Bryant's *Evening Post,* and a long bead-roll of Western sheets. In Connecticut, Gideon Welles was declaring that no honest editor could doubt the necessity of barring slavery from the Territories by positive enactment; that "there is a right in this matter"; and that "it is due to the State, the country, and to ourselves not to shrink from this question." [95]

Highly significant of the crystallization of Northern feeling were the resolutions which the Massachusetts Democratic Convention passed this summer. An unusually large gathering, it met in Springfield. That veteran political organizer, B. F. Hallett, whose ear was always close to any groundswell, presented the platform. Southerners might well rub their eyes as they read it. For these Bay State Democrats declared that "we are opposed to slavery in every form and color, and in favor of freedom and free soil wherever man lives"; that "slavery does not exist by any municipal law in the new Territories, and Congress has no power to institute it"; that "we are opposed to the extension of slavery to new Territories, and in favor of the exercise of all constitutional and necessary means to restrict it to the limits within which it does or may exist by the local laws of the States"; and that "these sentiments are so universal

93 To M. McConnell, September 6, 1849; Buchanan Papers.
94 To Colfax, January 2, 1849; Greeley-Colfax Corr.
95 To John M. Niles, July 20, 1849; Welles Papers.

at the North as to belong to no party, being held in common by all men north of a sectional line, while they are repudiated by most men south of that line, and therefore cannot be made a national party test." [96]

In both sections the mounting discontent and resentment had an irresistible tendency to weaken that party which was regarded as conservative: the Whigs in the South and the Democrats in the North. The fall elections in the cotton States revealed a notable augmentation of Democratic strength. In the free States, meanwhile, the radical Whigs, delighted by the rapidity with which they had brought the President into apparent harmony with their views, began to talk of passing the Wilmot Proviso and persuading Taylor to sign it. They would not only save the new acquisitions from a blighting curse, but bring all the Free Soil Party and many freesoil Democrats into their ranks, and thus establish a lasting domination! Many moderate onlookers began to fear that two sectional parties might actually arise. Fortunately, old party lines have too tenacious a strength to be easily broken and cast aside. In the North, several Democratic organizations saved themselves by executing a bold change of front. The summer of 1849 beheld a remarkable coalition between the Democrats and the Free Soil Party in Massachusetts (as the above resolutions indicate), Vermont, Wisconsin, and to some extent in Ohio. The first fruits of this coalition had already appeared in the sending of Salmon P. Chase to the Senate,[97] and in New England the alliance was soon to produce more astonishing and dubious results. Throughout the slaveholding area, most Whigs were equally anxious to save themselves and their old party banners by conformity to public feeling.

[VIII]

The South, with Mississippi and South Carolina leading the way, swiftly pushed the situation toward a crisis. Calhoun's proposal of a Southern convention and a Southern ultimatum had fallen on especially fertile soil in the State of Quitman and Jefferson Davis. These were what one of her oldtime sons called the golden years of Mississippi, and he accurately indicates the restless, feverish nature of many of her people. Giving themselves up joyously to any popular enthusiasm, "especially did they delight in the excitement of crowds, the fanfare of trumpet and drum, and the appeals of popular oratory." [98] With their rich crops of cotton snowing over the delta country and the higher

96 These reolutions led the Richmond *Enquirer* to admit that a small portion of the Northern Democracy was tainted with abolitionist "fanaticism." See the *National Intelligencer*, September 5, 1854, which reprinted the resolutions and the comment.

97 Chase explained the political factors in his election in a letter to Giddings, March 6, 1849; Giddings Papers.

98 Reuben Davis, *Recollections*, 308.

prairie lands, with their proud planters occupying the mansions of Natchez, Vicksburg, and Jackson, and with their great gangs of blacks (the census of 1850 enumerated 309,878 slaves in a population of 606,526), they felt as good title to leadership of their section as any State.[99]

Calhoun's Southern Address had been fervently applauded by the Mississippi press and by public gatherings. Forty-five leading citizens, both Whigs and Democrats, called a meeting at Jackson on May seventh, and with Chief Justice William L. Sharkey as its most prominent figure, this convention issued a spirited report. It denied the power of Congress to prohibit or restrict slavery in the Territories, and asked for a still larger State convention at Jackson in October.[100] Calhoun was quick to see his opportunity. Mississippi, he wrote, should summon the other slave States to a grand sectional convention. "No State could better take the lead in this great *conservative* movement than yours," he argued. "It is destined to be the greatest of sufferers if the Abolitionists should succeed."[101]

The result was the call of Mississippi, at her October meeting, for a convention of all the slave States at Nashville on the first Monday in June, 1850. Both parties united in this demand. On one subject the Mississippians took a moderate stand: they refused to declare the admission of California a ground for resistance. But they did make it clear that the passage of the Wilmot Proviso, or the abolition of slavery in the Federal District, or the prohibition of the domestic slave trade, would not be tolerated. An address written by Sharkey, full of crisp argumentation, appealed to all the Southern States to appoint delegates to Nashville.

The South Carolinians, though by no means unanimous, were of course strongly in favor of Calhoun's movement. The Columbia *Daily Telegraph* asserted just after the first Jackson meeting that the people must stand firm, "and boldly avow our choice between Submission and Secession, should the issue be forced upon us."[102] Throughout the upper country as well as the lowlands, committees of safety were organized. Governor Seabrook lent impetus to the movement for resistance by spending much of the summer on tours of militia inspection, reviewing muster after muster. A State convention at Columbia in May appointed a central executive committee, and passed resolutions declaring that South Carolina was prepared for concerted action with the other States, and would resist the Wilmot Proviso "at every hazard."[103] These

99 On Mississippi and the Southern Movement see Cleo Hearon, *Mississippi and the Compromise of 1850;* Philip M. Hamer, *The Secession Movement in South Carolina, 1847-1852.*
100 The address also showed that the conservative slaveowners of Mississippi were not eager to dissolve the Union; on the contrary, it expressed a resolute desire to preserve it.
101 To C. S. Tarpley, July 9, 1849; *Southern Hist. Assoc. Pub.* VI, no. 4, 415, 416.
102 May 12, 1849.
103 Columbia *Daily Telegraph*, May 14-16, 1849. On the governor's tour see the issue of September 28, 1849.

sentiments were echoed and reechoed. On July Fourth, an orator in Sumter asserted that while it was frequently said that the Union was stronger than slavery, he could not and would not believe it; and a public meeting at the same place later that month declared that much as the participants prized the Union, they valued their constitutional rights far more.[104] At the second Jackson convention, a South Carolina delegate, David Wallace, was given a seat within the bar.[105]

But other States, particularly of the upper South, regarded Calhoun's course and the call for the Nashville Convention with mixed feelings. Two views, indeed, could be taken of this defiant position. Some conservatives, accepting the statements of Calhoun himself at face value, believed that the movement would save the nation by forcing Northern fanatics to recede. "If the Southern States shall gather around Mississippi and support her," one wrote, "the Constitution and the Union will be rescued from the hands of madmen and traitors." [106] Many, however, adopted the opinion which Polk had long before expressed, that the aged South Carolinian was really plotting the disruption of the Union.[107] Calhoun is our evil genius, wrote Howell Cobb to Buchanan; he is planning to make the Southern Address the test of Democratic fellowship; and by so doing he hopes to establish a sectional party which will supplant the Whig and Democratic organizations throughout the South. He was deliberately refusing to discriminate between Northern abolitionists, and Northern Democrats and Whigs of freesoil views, lumping them all together as objects of antagonism.[108]

No opponent of Calhoun spoke out more emphatically than that stalwart Jacksonian, Thomas Hart Benton. During the summer various politicians suggested that he help promote a general convention of Missouri Democrats to iron out all differences, so that he and the pro-slavery extremists might somehow clasp hands. "I would sooner sit in council with the six thousand dead who have died of cholera in St. Louis," roared Benton, "then go into convention with such a gang of scamps!" His Democracy had nothing in common with Calhoun's, he said.[109] Since he had defied the instructions of the Missouri legislature on the Territorial issue, his fate was precariously in the balance, for his Senate term would soon expire and the legislature of 1849–50 might

---

104 Columbia *Daily Telegraph*, July 6, 27, 1849.
105 *Idem*, October 12, 1849.
106 A. Hutchinson to Calhoun, October 5, 1849; *Calhoun Corr.*, 1207.
107 Polk, *Diary*, IV, 289–291.
108 To Buchanan, June 17, 1849; Buchanan Papers.
109 Letter dated March 8, 1850, printed in the Washington *Union*, May 5, 1850. Calhoun denounced Benton's charges and assailed his character in scathing terms. "He has been false to the South for the last ten years," he wrote a young Missouri friend, "and can do us much less injury in the camp of the abolitionists, than he could in our own camp." To Samuel Treat, July 9, 1849. Judge Samuel Treat Papers, Mo. Hist. Soc.

not reëlect him. But he insisted on a battle without quarter to awaken men to the import of the drama of disunion that he declared was being enacted before their eyes. "Let us have our own party and ticket—no taint of secession and disunion and nullification in it!" he declared. "Let the Calhounites have their own ticket, the important object is to defeat them." In the same spirit, Sam Houston was as doggedly opposed to the Mississippi movement. He made the Texas prairies ring with his denunciation of disunionist schemes, and in midsummer fought a forensic battle at Marshall with fire-eating Louis T. Wigfall.[110]

Yet the last weeks before Congress opened in December, 1849, furnished clear indications that if the sectional deadlock were prolonged, the Nashville Convention might be sufficiently strong and radical to menace the Union. While some Southern newspapers supported Mississippi's call because they hoped for secession (the Charleston *Mercury*, for example), others did so because they believed the mere threat would bring the North to its senses (the Charleston *Courier* was one). As Senators and Representatives from the Cotton Kingdom reached Washington, they evinced a deadly earnestness. Some breathed fiery threats. They were soon being given support, too, by messages which the Southern governors prepared for their legislatures, the executives of Georgia, Mississippi, Alabama, South Carolina, and Virginia all making it clear that their section was in no mood for trifling. Publication of a spirited correspondence between two irascibles, the conservative Foote of Mississippi and the radical Clingman of North Carolina, attracted much attention. Southern reporters, hanging about hotel lobbies, exultantly wrote home that many Northern Congressmen were at last frightened; they had long sneered that the South would kick up a tremendous fuss and then quiet down, but now they were healthfully apprehensive.[111]

By the end of November members had arrived in great numbers, and the National Hotel was full of eager groups chewing, gesturing, and debating. Calhoun came in that day, his eye as bright and his spirit as defiant as ever. Clay, too, had reached the capital, after telling a Baltimore crowd that all true patriots must stand by the Union, and that slavery could never exist in the new Territories anyway, for soil and climate forbade it. Some striking new figures were ready to take their seats in the Senate: Pierre Soulé brought his alert Gallic air, while a combination of Democrats and Free Soilers in the Ohio

110 Shreveport *Caddo Gazette,* July 6, quoted in the Charleston *Courier,* August 9, 1849.
111 See the Washington correspondence and the general news reports in the issues of the Charleston *Courier,* November 28, 30, December 6, 11, 1849. Although Buchanan was not gloomily "apprehensive for the Union," he admitted that it was "in greater danger than it has been at any former period of our history." To Samuel L. Gouverneur, December 31, 1849, Buchanan Miss. Papers, L. C. On the Clingman and Foote correspondence see also "A Chapter of American History: Five Years' Progress of the Slave Power," Boston *Commonwealth,* July–September.

legislature had sent Salmon P. Chase to lend support to Seward. President Taylor, blunt and friendly as ever, was shaking hands with cohorts of White House visitors.[112]

Among the most nervous of the host descending upon Washington were the Southern Whig leaders, who saw the fate of their party and the Union sealed if the Wilmot Proviso should pass. Robert Toombs and Alexander H. Stephens greeted Northern Whigs with determination gleaming in their eyes. Calling at the White House, Toombs frankly asked the President what position he would take if the Proviso were pressed. "I have given and will give no pledges to either the opponents or supporters of the Proviso," responded Old Zack, in effect; "but if Congress sees fit to pass it, I will not veto it." [113] He felt committed to abstain from what he had foolishly called "the coercion of the veto." Instantly Toombs' decision was fixed. He was determined to oppose the Proviso even unto a dissolution of the Union and would forsake his own party if it supported the measure. His first step, with Stephens supporting him, would be to defeat the efforts of Northern Whigs to elect the Speaker and organize the House committees. "I should have gone to any extent to effect that object," he wrote later.[114]

The opening day of December found the three parties caucusing for Speaker, and when they broke up, each had made its choice: the Democrats Howell Cobb, the Whigs Robert C. Winthrop, and the Free Soilers David Wilmot. But various Northern Democrats were bolting Cobb, while Toombs, Stephens, and six other Southern Whigs had indignantly walked out of the Whig caucus when their proposals for dropping the Proviso were rejected. They would never vote for Winthrop.[115]

To Toombs and others the danger that the Northern Whigs would gain control of the powerful House machinery of rules and committees seemed terribly real. The new House would number 112 Democrats, 105 Whigs, 12 Free Soilers, and one Native American. The Southern and Northern Democrats were badly split. If the anti-slavery majority of the Whigs could organize the House and join hands with the anti-slavery Democrats, passage of the Proviso would be in sight. To meet the peril, Toombs and Stephens rallied all their forces. On the first ballot Howell Cobb led by seven votes, but no man had a majority. Day after day the voting went on without result. The first week

112 Washington correspondence, November 30, in the Charleston *Courier*, December 6, 1849.
113 Coleman, *Crittenden*, I, 364–366.
114 *Idem.*
115 Washington correspondence, December 1, in the Charleston *Courier*, December 6, 1849. Winthrop accused Toombs of "personal hostility towards me"; of getting up "a little platform of opposition to screen his own vindictiveness." To Kennedy, December 4, 1849; Kennedy Papers. As early as September, Winthrop fully expected to be defeated.

ended; the second began; then the third week—and still no choice. Americans, some amused, some indignant, all disgusted, saw the wheels of their vaunted government held motionless. The President could not send in his message on the state of the nation. The Senate, adjourning from day to day, could do nothing except transact a little executive business. There hung over the country one of its most appalling crises, for if within six months certain problems were not solved and certain quarrels not composed, the Nashville Convention might recommend steps for breaking up the Union. Yet the fortieth ballot was taken— the fiftieth—the sixtieth—and still the House had no Speaker and was unable to organize.[116]

116 Giddings vividly described the events on one of these days, December 13th. Mead of Virginia made an excited speech favoring disunion and was promptly ridiculed by Root of Ohio. But other disunionist speeches followed and the tempers of the members rose with each. When Duer of New York accused Mead of being a disunionist, Mead denied the charge; and Duer immediately called Mead a liar. Cries of "Shoot him! shoot him!" and "Where is your bowie knife?" were heard. Some Congressmen tensely awaited the outbreak of violence. But Giddings, used to commotions of this sort, laughed at the scene. Clay, who witnessed the incident, was "sober and grave. He sighed, and said he was pained." Giddings to his son, December 14, 1849; Giddings Papers.

8

Clay to the Rescue

FAR ACROSS THE SEA, as the Washington bells rang in the year 1850, an English poet was about to issue a slender volume which would be much read on both sides of the ocean; and some of its most beautiful stanzas might well be taken as applicable to the situation of the young republic. "Ring out, wild bells, to the wild sky," wrote Tennyson. "The flying cloud, the frosty light:

> Ring out a slowly dying cause,
> And ancient forms of party strife . . ."

Never had the slowly dying cause which gave one man right to hold another in bondage, or the ancient strife of parties complicated and embittered by sectionalism, stricken patriotic citizens with such a sense of impending calamity as on this New Year's. The election of Howell Cobb as Speaker, finally consummated when four more Northern Democrats swung over to the Southern candidate, had given members of Congress, as they cleared their desks for Christmas, a momentary sense of relief. A gigantic man, a veritable Falstaff, conspicuous anywhere for his tall figure and broad shoulders, his curly auburn hair and bright blue eyes, Cobb was loved for his geniality and moderation. His frank, open countenance, his prompt, hearty speech, his jolly laugh, made him a general favorite. In aspect and temper he seemed, like his political opponent the portly Preston King, another Friar Tuck. Not ambitious for the Speakership, and realizing the arduous duties of the post, he had stooped to no bargain to gain it. As he wrote his wife, he intended to do what he thought right and leave the result to Providence! The fact that a Southern slaveholder had been chosen to the office by Northern votes was hailed by Buchanan as a propitious omen.

But the real significance of the protracted contest did not escape reflective onlookers. Northern Whigs and Southern Whigs stood glaring at each other with bared knives; a little knot of Northern Democrats had refused to the last to accept Cobb; feelings on all sides were left exacerbated. The sectional chasm seemed deep and wide. It was plain that the House, with Democrats and Whigs so nearly equal that twelve Free Soil members held the balance of power, and with North and South mutually suspicious, would be a chaotic body. While the country needed firm guidance, one branch of Congress was likely to be a bear-garden of contending factions. The President or the Senate must furnish leadership, for the House could not. And guidance was required without delay, for opinion in the two sections was steadily hardening. It would have been easier to settle the grim dispute over the Territories in 1849 than it was in 1850, and by 1851 it might be impossible.[1]

If the struggle over the speakership had any utility, it was in further awakening the North to the gravity of the situation. Night after night the Democratic Representatives had caucussed only to find freesoil and slavery elements more vehemently antagonistic, until Cobb gave way to despair; never again, he wrote, could the party be united on any man. Talk of compromise had been greeted with jeers. "We of the South cannot and will not give an inch to the freesoilers," declared the liberal-minded Frederick P. Stanton of Tennessee. Some Southerners had opposed any organization of the House, asserting that it would be better if Congress never again did any business. R. K. Meade of Virginia, defiantly scanning the benches, announced that if new outrages were to be visited upon the slave States, he trusted that his eyes had rested upon the last Speaker to hold a gavel.

More important were the impassioned outbursts which had come from Robert Toombs and Alexander H. Stephens, whose words derived weight from their well-known love of national unity. When we ask for the simplest guarantees for the future, said Toombs, we are denounced outdoors as factionists, and indoors are met with the cry of "Union, Union!" It was too late for such attacks and such blandishments. "We must arouse and appeal to the nation. We must tell them, boldly and frankly, that we prefer any calamities to submission to such degradation and injury as they would entail upon us; that we hold that to be the consummation of all evil." If the North tried to debar the slaveholders from California and New Mexico, and to abolish slavery in the Federal District, then Toombs was for disunion. As for Stephens, he wrote that if the abolition aggressions were not stopped, "I feel as if I am prepared to fight all hazards and to the last extremity."[2]

Sectional antipathies broke out anew after Christmas in a brief struggle over

1   *Toombs, Stephens, Cobb Corr.*, 181. "Reminiscences of Washington," *Atlantic Monthly*, February, 1881. Stephens, December 2, 1849, in R. Von Abele, *Alexander H. Stephens.*
2   *Toombs, Stephens, Cobb Corr.*, 179. Stanton to Buchanan, December 20, 1849; Buchanan Papers. Giddings to his editor son, December 8, 1849; Giddings Papers. *Cong. Globe*, 31st Cong., 1st sess., December 13, 1849. Toombs with his long black hair, swarthy complexion, and vehement manner, could at times be positively ferocious in aspect. His harsh, unmusical voice rolled out with the force of a hammer. The idol of most Georgia Whigs, who respected his high abilities, he could rally the Southern members about him and excite them almost to frenzy by his passionate declamations upon the rights of the South. Washington *Union*, May 5, 1850, quoting the *Pennsylvanian*.

the clerkship of the House. Since the South had the Speaker, the North felt entitled to the lesser position, and two capable aspirants presented themselves: John W. Forney, a friend of Buchanan, and B. B. French, an intimate of Franklin Pierce. Neither belonged to the freesoil radicals. When a number of Southern Democrats broke over the party line to elect Thomas J. Campbell, a Southern Whig, indignation flamed high. "Forney is beaten by the South," a Pennsylvania observer reported to Buchanan. He added that these Southern gentry, who could never be depended upon in a pinch, had "thrown overboard the very corner-stone of their defence in the North." As for French, a man of talents, he was boiling with rage. He wrote his brother that he had been cheated out of the clerkship, but had learned one lesson: If a Northerner did not "bow and humble and prostrate himself in the dust before their high mightinesses of the South, he must hope for nothing." They were making their bed and could lie upon it. "My Yankee blood is fairly up in this matter, and I will see the South all d—d to everlasting perdition before I will ever . . . open my lips in their defense." [3]

While Washington thus kept feverish, the press of both sections was ablaze; mass meetings were held in both Northern and Southern centers; and new legislative fusillades were being prepared. Already every Northern legislature except that of Iowa, where only one chamber acted, had asserted the power and duty of Congress to exclude slavery from the Territories; while a number of States had urged the abolition of slavery and the slave trade in the District of Columbia. Southern legislatures had placed themselves on record with almost equal unanimity. New manifestoes, however, were—often at the instigation of leaders in Washington—being written. When the New York Senate passed rigorous free-soil resolutions, said to have been prepared by Seward, Southern observers writhed over his supposed influence with the President.[4]

What could be done? The feeling of millions of Northerners was as fixed as chilled steel. California and New Mexico had been free soil under the Mexican flag; word had now reached the East that by unanimous vote of a duly constituted convention, California had determined to remain free soil under the American flag. Few men as yet intended any menace to slavery where it already existed, but the great majority of thinking citizens did intend to see that it should not spread. Not a few Northerners peered into the distant future and took account of moral factors and ideals of civilization. The United States had just fought a war in which it had divested a weak neighbor of an imperial domain, which had already turned out to be one of the richest treasure houses on the globe. To what end? To the greater weal or greater woe of mankind? Was America to

3 To H. F. French, January 20, 1850.
4 See S. P. Chase, *Diary and Corr.*, 189-192, for his wire-pulling in the Ohio legislature, and editorial in Washington *Union*, January 23, 1850, on Seward's influence in New York.

consecrate this far-stretching principality to free enterprise and free institutions, or was it to spread the anachronistic, crippling, and brutalizing slavery system over it? In the right answer to that question, held most Northerners, would lie the justification of the recent conflict, and the redemption of America's promise to the world.

Yet to a majority of Southerners the equities of the situation seemed equally clear. The constitutional equality of fifteen States had been thrown into question. The fate of some sixteen hundred million dollars in slave property was directly involved in the controversy, while a far greater amount of wealth was indirectly menaced. But this was the lesser half of the doom which Southerners felt impending over their heads. Their social forms and institutions, their peace and safety, seemed threatened by powerful Northern elements which regarded it a duty to make war upon slavery. If the attack proved successful, it must terminate in the destruction of everything that Southerners held dear. Conservative slaveholders (and nearly all propertied men were conservative) loved the Union so long as it promised to cherish order and prosperity. But as soon as planters became convinced that the Northern attack would lead gradually to abolition, they turned about and regarded the Union not as a bulwark but as a chain binding them with the destroyer. Hence it was that, as a student of Southern attitudes has remarked, "the 'Union man' was usually just one step behind the secessionist, and that step was simply a matter of evidence and conviction." [5]

[I]

What was needed was some bold appeal to the imagination of men, or some iron enunciation of basic principles, to clear the atmosphere, put an end to petty bickering, and provide a rallying-point for patriots. A Jefferson could have furnished the first, and a Jackson the second. Would Zachary Taylor rise to the challenge of the times? His message, sent to Congress as soon as it organized, was a sad disappointment, received outside the most orthodox Whig circles with vocal disapprobation. He briefly summarized the proceedings in California, and recommended that when that commonwealth applied for admission to the Union, it should receive immediate assent. The people of New Mexico would probably also soon take similar action. Congress, he wrote, would do well to leave the settlement of territorial questions to these spontaneous movements, thus avoiding "exciting topics of sectional character." Taylor's proposals, received with considerable excitement, at once became known as the "no action plan." Since California had declared for freedom and New Mexico was free soil by Mexican

---

5 "Address to the People of the Southern States," privately printed, in Rusk Papers; R. H. Shryock, *Georgia and the Union in 1850*, p. 50.

law, the plan was distinctly unfavorable to slavery, and was regarded by many Southerners as a piece of treachery.[6]

The President's plan was for several reasons quite unrealistic. A great body of Southerners were resolved not to admit California without substantial compensation, and other large bodies in both sections wanted an immediate definition of the status of New Mexico. The Texas-New Mexico boundary line had to be settled quickly, while the position of Deseret or Utah with its now-thriving Mormon community required consideration. Men were preparing to pour bills into Congress not only on these questions, but on the recapture of fugitive slaves, and the slave trade in the District of Columbia. Taylor assumed a readiness to postpone every controversial topic save California when half a dozen were actually irrepressible. Nor were his proposals sufficiently bold. They appealed to the timidity of the American people when their courage needed rousing. They dealt with the moment, when a vision of the farther paths of national destiny was needed.

The realities of the situation were indicated by the speed with which "topics of a sectional character" crowded upon the attention of Congress in the first few weeks of debate. A radical Northern representative named Root introduced a resolution instructing the Committee on Territories to report a bill for the organization of New Mexico and Utah with the Wilmot Proviso attached. For the South, Senator Foote brought forward a bill for the organization of three Territories, California, New Mexico, and Utah, without any prohibition of slavery—thus giving slaveholders an opportunity to settle in them with their human chattels. Douglas offered the Constitution of Deseret with a petition for Statehood. Benton introduced a bill to reduce the boundaries of Texas, carve a State from the ceded area, and pay Texas fifteen millions for her consent. Foote's proposals also comprehended the erection, with the consent of Texas, of a new slave State called Jacinto, being that part of Texas east of the Brazos

6 Taylor's message, the diction of which was clearly recognized as that of his editorial assistants, brought him in for a good deal of ridicule. Would he have used the phrase, "entire elimination of Santa Anna's army"? Would he have spoken of the American people as "an empire of freemen"? And then the sentences! One in the original version (promptly revised) ran :"We are at peace with all of the world, and seek to maintain our cherished relations of amity with the rest of mankind." Here was what the New Orleans *Delta* called the redundant quaintness of Col. Bullitt of the *Republic*. Washington *Union*, January 10, 1850.

John L. O'Sullivan had written Buchanan on December 8, 1849: "I visit the White House pretty generally and find the President very much the same; apparently well content with his position, and not troubling himself much about the organization of Congress—or the doings of his Cabinet—perhaps kindly concluding that they knew better what to do, and that they will perform their duty." Buchanan Papers. Those who dwelt at a distance got the same impression of Presidential inertia. "Unless General Taylor rouses himself and shows that he has a will of his own and intelligence enough to carry it into effect," grumbled Edward Everett, "his Administration will soon be a heap of shapeless ruins." To Winthrop, January 7, 1850; Everett Papers.

River. Senator Mason on January 4, 1850, presented a bill for the rendition of fugitive slaves; a stringent measure, which not only facilitated the recapture of runaways but punished any obstruction by a fine of a thousand dollars. Meanwhile President Taylor was asked to explain his policy with respect to California and New Mexico—whether he had sent an agent to California, how the convention had been chosen, and what he meant by saying that the people of New Mexico would soon present themselves for admission to the Union.[7]

Evidence was appearing that the radical freesoilers and the pro-slavery extremists were eager to join hands in defeating all measures of conciliation, and in pushing the quarrel to an open rupture. Speaker Cobb, in appointing the House committees, had naturally put the Democrats in control of all important posts. But whether through a sense of fair play or not, he had given an astonishingly large place to freesoil members, and even had assigned such radicals as Giddings, Allen, and Wilmot positions where they could keep up their agitation and attack any plan of compromise. While this pleased the Northern irreconcilables, it seemed to give no pain to the Southern fire-eaters! Crittenden's keen-eyed Washington informant, Orlando Brown, commented: "With some gentlemen of the South there is a hypocritical profession of attachment to the Union—an affected horror of Abolition and ardent hope at bottom that the North will pass the proviso to give them a popular reason for the most violent measures." [8]

The President, responding to the request of Congress for information, reiterated his policy in a special message (January 21) describing the turmoil and uncertainty in California, and pleading again for her early admission as a State while New Mexico was left under its existing government. Nothing that he said improved the position. While the great body of Northern Whigs stood with him, the complexities of the situation and the demands of extremist elements made a broad instead of a partial settlement imperative. It was obvious that the unimaginative Taylor did not know what to do. He could not endorse the Wilmot Proviso, for the South would be in instant revolt. He could not assent to the Southern claim of an indefeasible right to take slaves into the Territories, for the North would rise in anger. He could only make some show of neutrality by writing of non-intervention (waiting "the silent effect of causes

7 Alpha in the N. Y. *Tribune*, January 3, 1850; *Cong. Globe*, 31st Cong., 1st sess., December 27, 1849, January 4, 16, 1850.

8 On Cobb's appointments, see Alpha in the N. Y. *Tribune*, January 3, 5, 1850. G. S. Hillard wrote Lieber on January 29: "You ask how the Free Soilers like the proceedings at Washington. I think that they exult at them. They regard Cobb's appointment of Committees as a decided gain and moreover what they aim at is the destruction of both the parties, and I do believe that they would feel an irrepressible jubilation of spirit if Congress should break in wrath without passing the appropriation bills—and political chaos should come again. But then on the other hand I think the party, while it increases in intensity and ferocity, is lessening in numbers." Lieber Papers. Brown to Crittenden, January 11, 1850; Crittenden Papers.

independent of the action of Congress," were his words) in New Mexico and Utah while urging the admission of California with her free Constitution.

To most Southerners the President seemed strongly prejudiced against them and their cause. Not only did he have a predominantly freesoil Cabinet at one elbow and Senator Seward at the other; they heard stories that as a staunch nationalist he was deeply angered by the talk of secession—that he was pounding his desk and talking of Jacksonian measures. He said stubbornly: "If the Union is to go down, I will go down with it." When the instructions which Secretary Clayton had given T. Butler King reached Congress along with Taylor's special message, it was found that they declared that the Mexican laws of California and New Mexico (including those against slavery) must necessarily remain in force until superseded. See that! said many Southerners; while the President had asseverated that he would not interfere in the political affairs of California, these instructions to King proved the contrary. Meanwhile, the radical freesoilers also had their grievance—they complained that Taylor did not maintain a sufficiently bold front against the boundary claims of Texas. He thought precipitate action inadvisable. But such organs as the New York *Tribune* were insisting that he should take firm steps to prevent Texas from subjugating some of the most populous districts of New Mexico to slavery; that he should urge Congress to erect a Territory including the disputed area, and then let Texas contest this inclusion before the Supreme Court.[9]

The harassed President, attacked from all sides and anxious to make his views respected, was handicapped by half a dozen factors: the hostile organization of the House; a hostile majority in the Senate; the coolness, not to say frigidity, of Clay and Webster, who paid as little attention to him as he to them, the fact that his Cabinet possessed no influence, and was indeed a dead weight in Congress; a growing rift between the Administration and its supposed organ, the Washington *Republic*; and his own inexpertness in dealing with politicians and public opinion. He had nothing of Jackson's tremendous ability to command or Polk's patient skill in maneuver. For its Senate spokesmen the Administration, not being *en rapport* with the Whig leaders of the old regime, Clay, Webster, Mangum, and Berrien, had to fall back upon Seward and Truman Smith, two men who showed intimate acquaintance with Taylor and the papers on his desk. Seward was a quick and slashing fighter, but Truman Smith was worse than no spokesman at all, a hesitant figure who struck fear and trembling into the Administration forces whenever he arose. With good intentions and fair ability, he was so slow, tactless, and maladroit that he was a fatal defender. As for

9 *Cong. Globe*, 31st Cong., 1st sess., January 22, 1850; Howard of Texas. N. Y. *Tribune*, January 12, 23, 24, 1850.

the *Republic*, ever since its initial issue the previous June it had disappointed the expectations placed in its heads. They lacked audacity and enterprise.

By this time, though many good Whigs admired Taylor ("The old gentleman grows daily in public esteem by his manly and unyielding honesty of character," wrote John P. Kennedy to his wife), most of Washington had set him down as deficient in personal force. At the New Year's reception in the White House, the most observed and flattered figure was not the President but Henry Clay. As his tall form passed down the East Room, surrounded by a throng eager to obtain notice, the Kentuckian was the idol of the occasion. B. B. French, shortly traveling to Richmond with a Presidential party to assist in laying the cornerstone of the Washington monument, talked at length with Taylor. "He is an honest, plain, unpretending old man," recorded French, "but about as fit to be President as any New England farmer." [10]

[II]

On January 17 Senator Mason's Fugitive Slave Bill was reported from committee and an acrimonious debate began. Mason himself was a pleasing speaker, whose matter and manner gave hearers the impression that they were listening to a deeply-read, widely-traveled, reflective gentleman, his culture somewhat modified by certain prejudices. But hotter men uncorked the vials of sectional wrath. Seward offered an amendment giving the fugitives the benefit of jury trial and the writ of habeas corpus; Foote angrily attacked Seward; and others sprang into the mêlée.[11]

With the President fumblingly stubborn, the House divided and leaderless, and the Senate a scene of rising irritation, the hour seemed dark indeed. Was the nation really on the verge of dissolution? If at this moment the South had firmly united behind a demand for extension of the 36° 30′ line to the Pacific, that simple measure of compromise might well have carried. Buchanan later thought that the Pennsylvania Democrats would have supported the proposal firmly. But Calhoun, insisting on the principle of Congressional non-intervention, had turned many Southerners against the Missouri Compromise line. The general feeling of slavery men seemed to be that they must simply await further Northern aggression, and then retaliate as best they could. William R. King of Alabama, a lover of the Union with forty years of national service behind him,

10 Orlando Brown to Crittenden, April 19, 1850; Crittenden Papers, summarizing Taylor's difficulties, Washington *Union*, January 19, 1850. Crittenden to Clayton, February 18, 1850; Crittenden Papers. Kennedy to his wife, January 22, 1850; Kennedy Papers. *Diary and Correspondence of Benjamin Brown French*, January 1, February 1, 1850. Barnes, *Life of Thurlow Weed*, II, 183.

11 N. Y. *Tribune*, February 2, 1850. Young Jeremiah Clemens took a spirited part in the debate in the Senate on January 17. At one stage it was thought that "coffee and pistols for two" might be needed. John S. Welles to Gideon Welles, January 18, 1850; Welles Papers.

feared that Congress would drive the South to desperate acts. The North could not with impunity continue to violate our rights, he wrote his old mess-mate Buchanan. "They must stop and at once their course of aggression, or nothing but divine interposition can prevent a dissolution of the Union. I am no alarmist, but I cannot be mistaken in this matter . . ." [12]

The floods of oratory rolling forth in House and Senate gave ample support to this despondent view. At the very outset Thomas L. Clingman of North Carolina made a threatening speech which attracted wide attention. A Whig, a man of cultivation and large views, a brilliant debater, he was expected to adopt a soothing tone. But he had lately visited the North, he had for the first time realized the strength of the anti-slavery movement, and he believed that it could be counteracted only by vigorous Southern action. He therefore declared that either passage of the Wilmot Proviso or abolition of slavery in the District of Columbia would justify disunion. The injuries already inflicted by the North on his section, he asserted, far exceeded those which Great Britain had attempted when she drove the colonies into revolt. He believed that secession would give the South many economic advantages—a lower tariff and a large influx of British and other foreign capital to build railroads and erect industries. If war came, he predicted, the slave States, with their six million freemen and their tradition of military leadership—of Washington, Andrew Jackson, Scott, Taylor—need fear nothing from Northern aggression. Incidentally, he suggested that if pressed too far the Southern members might soon act to block all business in the House.

"A comfortable prospect!" wrote former Speaker Winthrop to Edward Everett, and Everett penned a gloomy reply. If the South were disposed to act on such views, conflict would certainly ensue. "I would say let us separate peaceably, as Maine did from Massachusetts, Kentucky from Virginia, and so on. But this is impossible from the very nature of the case, and the impossibility of dividing the territory between the separating parties." [13]

12 Buchanan to King, May 13, 1850, King to Buchanan, January 13, 1850; Buchanan Papers. Some men said later that they believed Calhoun would have accepted an extension of the Missouri Compromise line as a solution of the controversy. Specifically Mrs. St. George Campbell of Philadelphia, sister of Alexander J. Dallas and a close friend of Calhoun, stated that in his last illness, Calhoun said to her: "I think that compromise unconstitutional with my views of the Constitution and I cannot vote for it but for the sake of the Union, if others would adopt it I would acquiesce." MS Memoirs of Hunter, anonymous.

13 Clingman, Selections from Speeches and Writings, 235–254. N. Y. Tribune, January 23, 24, 1850. Winthrop to Everett, January 22, Everett to Winthrop, January 25, 1850; Everett Papers. Ten days later Everett wrote even more gloomily to Nathan Appleton: "With respect to the proper course to be pursued by the North it seems to me to be this: to say to the South, we think you wholly wrong in the matter; that the dissolution of the Union would be the worst thing imaginable both for North and South, but we see you are determined to have it. Let us then go to work like reasonable men, and draw up a plan of a peaceable separation; not rush blindly upon it, and leave the mode of bringing about this great event to chance, which is nearly the same as insuring a civil war."

An excited scene took place on the Senate floor when, resolutions of the Vermont legislature against slavery having been presented, the question of printing them arose. Yulee of Florida opposed publishing a statement so "opprobrious, offensive, and insulting." But Mason of Virginia took a different view; if this issue was to be forced upon the South, he wanted all the evidence of their wrongs and insults recorded. Calhoun, too, was for printing the paper. A younger Senator known for his general moderation, Jeremiah Clemens of Alabama, seized the opportunity to defend his section in ringing terms. The abolitionists, he said, were slandering the South by the foulest libels; they were making terrible appeals to the worst passions of the slaves; they were advocating murder, arson, and rape. He had endured fiery trials in the defense of the Union, but there was a limit to Southern patience. "We do not intend to stand still and have our throats cut." Perhaps the rupture had gone too far to be arrested. At any rate, he thought a continuance of the Northern attack could have but one end; for even the friendliest and most peaceful of Alabamans would soon "scorn your alliance and shatter your Confederacy." [14]

Meanwhile, the same threatening language was heard outside the halls of Congress. Governor John A. Quitman of Mississippi, in the inaugural message he sent the legislature on January 10, spoke bitterly of the loss of fugitive slaves and the attempted closing of the territories. These Northern acts to him plainly presaged a war of extermination against the most sacred rights of the slaveholders, and pointed straight to disunion. Much as the people of Mississippi cherished their ancient ties, they could love no other union than that defined in the Constitution. One dictum by Quitman especially deserved to be marked and remembered. He declared that Congress had power to protect property, but no power to destroy it; a statement in which lay the germ of a far-reaching future demand by slaveholders—the demand for positive Federal protection of slavery in the Territories. This was the germ of ultimate schism in the Democratic Party and disunion in the nation. Quitman exhorted the South to arise in its wrath against Taylor's recommendation of statehood for California. No more concessions or compromises! They simply invited further Northern aggression; grant them, and the spirit of fanaticism would dilate until the Union was rent asunder and the land drenched in blood.

A few days later Henry A. Wise, the Virginia Warwick who had put Tyler in line for the Presidency, delivered a speech at Richmond compact of fire and defiance. He called upon the South to maintain its old constitutional rights, and upon Virginia to sanction the forthcoming Nashville convention. The *National Intelligencer* broke out in an alarming editorial, declaring that the peril of disunion was all too real. Even Maryland seemed preparing to send

14 N. Y. *Tribune*, January 9, 11, 1850; Beveridge, *Abraham Lincoln*, II, 78.

delegates to Nashville. The Philadelphia *Bulletin* sounded a warning to the North:[15]

"During a late visit to Washington, one of the editors of this paper made it his especial business to inquire into the real sentiments of the Southern members, and he found them such that if they are, as is presumable, the echo of those of their constituents, the Union is in the greatest peril of overthrow. The South knows that its weight in the Union grows weaker annually, in consequence of the rapid spread of free States at the North and West; and hence it is determined to make a stand before it is too late."

Beyond question, a great part of the South felt that the section had its back against the wall, and must now resist. Robert Toombs knew that California and New Mexico could never be slave territory. He was aware that probably not another inch of America could be made slave soil. But he fought the Wilmot Proviso tooth and nail, for he was convinced that its passage would so inflame Northern arrogance that the position of the South would become intolerable. Very similar was the attitude of another Georgian, Herschel V. Johnson, who had left the Senate in 1849. He too was aware that California must be a free State. But he did not wish it admitted without price, for such a concession would merely invite further insult and injury. It would leave unsettled the questions of New Mexico, the District of Columbia, and the fugitive slaves; worse than that, it would set a precedent under which, at no distant day, a dozen new free States would be carved out of the West. How powerless would the South then be, swept down by the tide of fanaticism! No, he wrote Calhoun, the only course was to demand a settlement in full—to call for a just compromise as regarded New Mexico, and a total abandonment of Northern encroachments as respected the Federal District and slavery in the States.[16]

These views had an element of soundness: a broad settlement was needed. It was also true that many Northern radicals needed to be taught the importance of certain Southern interests and the necessity for mutual concessions. Their precipitancy even in a good cause might do untold harm. By February the Southern defiance seemed to be producing its effect in Washington. Many free-soil men who had thought it the duty of the North to drive the Proviso through by sheer majority power were turning back. They are shrinking from the trial, Senator Mason exultantly wrote his old friend William C. Rives, "under the conviction that, whether right or whether wrong, the Southern States have determined upon that issue to stake the Union of the States." Never, declared Mason, had he beheld such unanimity as pervaded the people of the slaveholding

15 Philadelphia *Bulletin*, February 1, quoted in *National Intelligencer*, February 2, 1850. For Quitman's inaugural address delivered January 10 and Wise's speech of January 14, see Washington *Union*, January 26, 1850.
16 U. B. Phillips, *Robert Toombs*, 55; P. S. Flippin, *Herschel V. Johnson of Georgia*, 24ff.

area, and he believed their resolution was burying the proviso party fathoms deep and ushering in a brighter day. "I am fully prepared for the issue, if the action of the majority impels us to take it—yet I now believe it will be averted, but averted only by the front which has been presented by the Southern States . . ." [17]

Communities north of Washington, however, did not see the Southern purpose so clearly. In New York, Ohio, and New England many scoffed at the secessionist menace. They deemed it the old gasconade, the familiar vaporing, which would quickly die away after California came in. A few of those who did not scoff hoped secretly that the menace would be made good. When Toombs threatened to bring in a bill at some uncertain period to dissolve the Union, Allen retorted: Introduce it, and it will have respectful consideration! The danger was that the government would simply drift until the session ended— and then find itself on the brink of a cataract. Some leader with imagination, prestige, and tact must give shape to the broad adjustment for which Herschel V. Johnson called, or a fearful penalty might be paid.

[III]

It was to the Senate that men turned as House and President proved helpless; to its elder statesmen, Clay, Webster, and Benton; and above all to the best-trusted and most beloved man in the country, Henry Clay. The Kentuckian had been quick to realize his responsibility. Disturbed on reaching Washington to find disunion feeling so powerful, he had urged his border-State friends to whip up large public meetings to demand fidelity to the republic. Early in January he was deeply apprehensive that the Wilmot Proviso might obtain a decided majority in the House and a small margin in the Senate, for he knew that if it passed, Southern hotheads would demand immediate secession. Already he was meditating upon some comprehensive scheme for the settlement of the whole question in all its ramifications; and as men of both sections came to him for advice and leadership, his desire once more to play the part of pacificator hardened into decision. [18]

Unquestionably Clay's motives were thoroughly patriotic. To be sure, he resented his exclusion from the inner councils of the President and enjoyed the prospect of imposing his will where Taylor had failed to do so. He was glad,

17 February 4, 1850; Rives Papers.
18 Carl Schurz, *Henry Clay*, II, 328. Orlando Brown wrote Crittenden on January 11: "The impression seems to be general that he [Clay] intends to play fair toward the Administration and give it his support. It is said that he intends at the proper time to make a move for adjusting the difficulty between the North and the South but has thrown out no intimation of what his scheme will be. General Cass is also represented as concocting a compromise . . ." Crittenden Papers.

since he could not be President, to close his career with another great stroke of leadership. But above all, he wished to strengthen the threatened fabric of the Union. Coming to Washington with the idea that he need hardly play a major rôle, he had requested excuse from service on any standing committee of the Senate. Now in his seventy-third year, he was still hale and vigorous. To be sure, his cheeks were gaunter than of old, big bright eyes gleamed from a face in which the bones stood out in stark relief, and the fringe of iron-gray hair that encircled his bald skull drooped upon bent shoulders. Living in his old quarters at the National Hotel, kept by a devoted friend, he now saw little of general society, though he liked a quiet game of cards in his room with a glass of toddy from Kentucky whiskey. On the Senate floor, an impressive figure in his well-cut black broadcloth, with gleaming shirt-front, high white collar, and cravat tied in a bow with flowing ends, he displayed his genial, offhand, captivating eloquence less frequently than of old. But his voice was unchanged, as silvery and musical as ever. He still showed grace in every attitude: as he walked with swinging cane down the Avenue; as, entering the Senate, he took a pinch of snuff, picked up the *National Intelligencer*, and sank into his seat; as, straightening his tall form, he rose to speak. The charm of his mobile, expressive features was unaltered. His mind had lost none of its keenness. He was ready to exert himself to the utmost, before some dramatic event could blow the smouldering disunion sentiment of the South into devouring flames.[19]

In his blandest mood, with a conciliatory gleam playing over his visage, he rose on January 29 to offer a series of resolutions which he hoped might exorcise the demon of disunion for long years to come. The separate bills poured in from various quarters had merely confused and irritated Congress. President Taylor's concentration upon California had simply heightened Southern resentment and aggravated the crisis. Clay came now not to plead, but to direct; not to defer to the Administration, but to force it to take a truly national stand; not to conciliate individuals, but to marshal groups and interests into an irresistible phalanx. This was his battle, in which his personal pride was involved. If it were won, the country would be saved, the Whig prestige would be restored, and a brighter luster would burnish his own fame.[20]

His plan, presented with deliberate and impressive emphasis, called for eight steps. They were: (1) that California should be admitted with her free Constitution; (2) that as slavery was not likely to be introduced into the rest of the area gained from Mexico, Territorial governments should be set up there with-

19 "Reminiscences of Washington," *Atlantic Monthly*, February, 1881; Poore, *Perley's Reminiscences*, I, 263.
20 Schurz, *Henry Clay*, II, 329. See F. H. Hodder, "The Authorship of the Compromise of 1850," *Mississippi Valley Historical Review*, XXII, pp. 525–536; George Fort Milton, *The Eve of Conflict*, 47, 52 ff.

out any condition or restriction as to the institution; (3) that the western boundary of Texas should be so drawn as to exclude all of New Mexico; (4) that in return, the national government should assume the public debt of Texas contracted before annexation and hypothecated upon the Texas customs; (5) that the bringing of slaves into the District of Columbia with a view to their sale and delivery at some other time and place should be prohibited, but that (6) slavery should never be abolished there without the consent of the people both of Maryland and the District, nor without just compensation to the owners; (7) that a more effective Fugitive Slave Act should be passed; and (8) that Congress should make formal declaration that it had no power to interfere with the interstate slave trade. Most of the measures which Clay proposed for acceptance as a unit had already been presented separately to Congress, and most of them at the instigation of Stephen A. Douglas. The service which the Kentuckian undertook in his series of eight resolutions was to bind them all together, and place his unrivalled influence behind the whole.[21]

Clay's initial speech was studiously brief and devoid of rhetorical embellishment; a plain businesslike exposition, much less wordy than most of his efforts. Despite its brevity, he was interrupted by Foote and Jefferson Davis. For true Southerners, said Davis, only one compromise was possible, an extension of the Missouri Compromise line to the Pacific, with full recognition of slavery everywhere south of that line. Clay briefly declared that no human power could make him vote to plant slavery anywhere by decree of Congress, and passed on. He refused to be drawn into debate, for he wished the Senate to consider his proposals as a whole, and to make up its mind only after careful meditation. He did hope, he said, that gentlemen would not commit themselves until after studying the suggestions thoroughly and "viewing them as a system—viewing them together." [22]

Before he sat down Clay made it plain that he believed in each proposal; that not one was put in for mere expediency and without conviction of its soundness. California, her delegates voting unanimously, had asked for admission as free soil and should be welcomed to the Union. True, her Constitution had been framed in an irregular manner; but when Michigan had written hers with equal irregularity, she had been admitted without question. The claim of Texas to part of New Mexico he thought plausible, but not valid; and Texas as bounded by the line he proposed would be large enough anyway. As for the debt of Texas, when the United States annexed the republic and possessed herself of the Texas revenues, she had made herself responsible for it. The slave

21 The selling of slaves for use within the District was to go on. See explanation of Jefferson Davis, May 17, 1860, in *Cong. Globe*, 36th Cong., 1st sess.
22 N. Y. *Tribune*, February 2, 1850; *Cong. Globe*, 31st Cong., 1st sess., January 29, 1850.

depots in the District of Columbia, which John Randolph of Roanoke had pronounced an abomination more than forty years earlier, offended the suscep-tibilities of Southerners themselves. Besides, traders could hold their auctions at Alexandria, at Baltimore, and at Annapolis; why should they wish to drive herds of slaves past the Capitol? The abolition of slavery in the District, without the consent of Maryland, from which the District had come, would be a violation of implied faith with that State. As for the confession that Congress had no power to interfere with the interstate slave trade, that simply reaffirmed the verdict of the highest court in the country.

Quite plainly, Clay believed that if his balance was not absolutely fair, it in-clined slightly in favor of the South. For one reason, he held that a new Fugitive Slave Act required no particular sacrifices of the North. The justice and urgency of the measure was "evident." For another, he believed that the erection of Territorial governments in New Mexico and Utah without a word respecting slavery was to the advantage of the South. Some slavery men had clamored for the extension of the 36° 30' line. To what end? "I could show that this is a much better proposition for the South than that of extending the Missouri line to the Pacific unless you couple with it that which the Senator from Mississippi [Mr. Davis] must know to be impossible . . . a declaration for the introduction of slavery south of that line." It was better for the South to leave the slavery question open on both sides of the line, than to interdict it positively north of the line.

Feeling that the South perhaps gained the more, Clay made a moving appeal to the North to be magnanimous. It was by far the richer section, the more populous and powerful. Slavery did not deeply affect its interests; merely its sentiment. But the South had to regard slavery as a cardinal economic and social fact. A great conflagration was raging, dwellings were wrapped in flames, and women and children were fleeing from the peril. Whose homes were being devoured? It was the Southern land which was menaced by the worldwide agitation against slavery. You Northerners, said Clay, "are looking on in safety and security while the conflagration which I have described is raging in the slave States"—a fire to which the North was contributing. Clay was never a Burke or Webster, and only such oratorical masters could have made this image telling. But there was force in the antithesis which he proceeded to draw. "In the one scale, then, we behold sentiment, sentiment, sentiment alone; in the other, property, the social fabric, life, and all that makes life desirable and happy."

After the initial outburst of rapid-fire speeches, Clay's resolutions were made the order of the day for formal Senate debate on February 5th. Mean-while, Washington and the country were buzzing with discussion. The hostility of most radicals on both sides could be taken for granted. What counted was the opinion of the moderates that Clay wished to unite.

In general, the scheme had a favorable reception. The conservative Whig press, led by the *National Intelligencer*, at once rallied to Clay's side. So did some important Democratic journals; Ritchie's Washington *Union* specially commending one feature of the proposal, the attempt to settle all the important questions at once and for good. A few men whose assistance might have been anticipated took an unfriendly attitude. Edward Everett, for example, thought that the compromise would prove a mere palliative and would fail because it did not touch the heart of the issue. "Unless some Southern man of influence has courage enough to take ground against the extension of slavery, and in favor of its abolition in the jurisdictions of the United States, we shall infalliby separate; not perhaps immediately, but before long. This is the only compromise that will satisfy the North; that is, non-interference in the States, exclusion and abolition everywhere else. I am not saying what I think ought to satisfy the North; but I am saying what in my opinion will." Robert C. Winthrop was against Clay's plan and in favor of Taylor's.[23]

But in general Clay seemed assured of moderate support both North and South. The vital question was whether Northern radicals and Southern fire-eaters, the followers of Calhoun and the associates of Seward, could defeat this plan or any like it. Everybody looked to the Senate as the primary arena. If it gave an emphatic decision for compromise, the House would doubtless assent, and the Administration could possibly be drawn into line.

[IV]

The Senate was a fitting battle-ground in this greatest of parliamentary contests since the struggle over the Missouri Compromise. To be sure, the small chamber, with its red carpet and purple hangings, was decidedly stuffy. Even in summer, when the windows were open, the air after a debate of four or five hours became heavily vitiated; and in winter, especially when four or five hundred people jammed themselves into galleries and corners, it was positively mephitic. Smoke from the fireplaces often drifted into the room. But the Senate maintained an old-fashioned dignity. The seats were ranged in four tiers, behind the rearmost of which was a bar to prevent the intrusion of spectators. Great emphasis was placed on oratorical art; apt retorts were eagerly applauded; and

23 Everett to Winthrop, February 1, 1850; Everett Papers. Winthrop wrote to Kennedy in March (no date), 1850, "The true way is to admit California, and let the Territories alone. Any other course will kill Whiggery at our end of the Union. The only reason the Senate opposes this course is because its adoption would enure to Taylor's benefit. That is the reason why you and I should stand up for it." Kennedy Papers.

the members were eager critics of debating skill. Since they were as yet only sixty in number, the body might be called truly deliberative. Dressed usually in somber, long-skirted coats, with tall silk hats, carrying watches in fobs with dangling seals, and using eyeglasses suspended on long ribbons, many of the Senators were gravity incarnate. They frowned heavily on unruly newcomers like Sam Houston, with his panther-skin waistcoat and habit of whittling some piece of wood. They wrote with quill pens, sanded their ink, and frequently resorted to the two great snuff-boxes standing on the Vice-President's desk. Some kept wine or spirits at hand, for that too was a custom of the olden time.[24] Early this year Vice-President Fillmore had thought it necessary to administer a little rebuke. The manners of the Senate were growing lax, he said. "Many little irregularities may be tolerated in a small body that would cause much disorder in a large one. . . . A practise seems to have grown up of interrupting a Senator when speaking, by addressing him directly, instead of addressing the Chair, as required by the rule." The members mended their ways and reverted to a due formality.[25]

As the country studied Clay's scheme, the most mooted question was whether the Administration, which he obviously had not consulted, would accept it. It was obvious that as regarded Utah and New Mexico, it differed materially from Taylor's plan. The President proposed to leave these areas in *statu quo* until they gathered sufficient population to ask for admission as States; while Clay wished to erect Territorial governments over them. In either event the old municipal regulations of Mexico forbiding slavery would presumably remain in force until the time came for statehood. Clay was much more explicit upon this momentous fact than the President, though the two doubtless agreed.[26] The Senator's plan was also superior in that it followed the usual pattern in State-making and would provide a fully adequate government for these western regions if (as proved the fact) statehood had to be deferred for long decades. The boldness with which Clay undertook to solve a whole complex of thorny problems was very different in spirit and fact from the President's restricted approach. Would Taylor sink all personal jealousy to adopt the larger plan? The Washington correspondent of the New York *Tribune* thought that he would gladly see it succeed—but others were not so sure.[27]

A week after he proposed his compromise, Clay rose before a crowded Senate to defend it. Despite the uncertain February weather, such a throng poured into the Capitol and surged at the doors of the Senate that Vice-President Fillmore ordered them shut and the anterooms cleared. People had come even

24 W. E. Griffis, *Millard Fillmore;* H. W. Hilliard, *Politics and Pen-Pictures,* 212ff.
25 *Cong. Globe,* 31st Cong., 1st sess., 631, 632; April 3, 1850.
26 Benton, *Thirty Years View,* II, 740–743; Schurz, *Clay,* II, 348–353.
27 N. Y. *Tribune,* February 1, 1850.

from New York and Boston to hear the great Kentuckian. Every available inch was jammed. Veterans said that the scene had not been matched since the occasion some eight years earlier when he took leave of the Senate. When he rose, the burst of applause within the chamber was answered by a wild roar from the great crowd outside. He was cheered partly as a popular idol, as Harry of the West; but more emphatically as the devoted champion of national unity. Nor did he fail to rise to the grandeur of the occasion. While ascending the Capitol steps, he had taken the arm of a friend with the confession that he felt weak and exhausted, but he refused to defer his effort, saying that the nation was in danger, and "if I can be the means of averting that danger, my health and life are of little consequence." His brief speech the first day was masterly in logic and admirable in temper. He called attention to the awful gravity of the crisis, saying that he had never before addressed an assembly "so oppressed, so appalled, so anxious." The country, he went on, could rid itself of its main differences by the easy method of recognizing facts: the first great fact being that the Wilmot Proviso was unnecessary, for nature and men had already decreed that California and New Mexico must be free soil. Holding aloft a piece of Washington's coffin, he dramatically appealed to the spirit of the nation's founders.[28]

The next day, again facing an attentive throng, he spoke at greater length. This time he dealt with the prohibition of the slave trade in the District of Columbia, with the demand for a new Fugitive Slave Act, and with the right of secession. Once more he said that Congress ought to forbid the slave sales which shocked thousands by the almost daily spectacle of corteges of manacled human beings passing down the Washington avenues. This would be but a mild step, for Mississippi, Kentucky, and other States had already forbidden the importation of slaves for sale. As for the fugitive slave law, here the South had "just and serious cause of complaint"; for many Northern States, in defiance of plain provisions of the Constitution, had enacted laws which obstructed the return of fleeing Negroes.

Finally, Clay pointed out to the Southern States that they had no right to secede and that the step would be ruinous if taken. The Constitution was made not merely for the generation of the Fathers, "but for posterity, undefined, unlimited, permanent, and perpetual"; not merely for the original States, but "for every subsequent State which might come into the Union, binding themselves by that indissoluble bond." If the dissolution took place, the South would not gain a single one of its three main demands—the admission of slaves to the Territories, the retention of slavery in the Federal District, or the return of fugitives. It would lose all three, while secession would mean that where one slave now

28 Schurz, *Henry Clay*, II, 334.

deserted his master, thousands would thereafter flee. Moreover, secession would mean war, for disunion and war were synonymous. Nor would it be an ordinary conflict. It would be "furious, bloody, implacable, exterminating," and free government might sink to ruin in its chaos.

Clay's proposals and his two-day speech produced an immediate effect in a welcome relief of tension. Men plucked up hope. A practicable way had been pointed out of the apparent impasse, and a commanding voice had rallied all the lovers of the Union. It was known that Webster on the Whig side and Cass among the Democrats looked with favor on the plan. When Clay had first spoken, Toombs was reported in perfect ecstasy over the display of courage and oratorical power by the old leader. A general movement to close in behind his standard at first seemed taking place. Speaker Cobb on February 9 wrote his wife in optimistic mood. The excitement was unabated, he remarked, but he now looked forward to a final adjustment of the whole matter. "That such will be the ultimate result I will not permit my mind seriously to doubt. I have great confidence in the virtue and intelligence of the American people and so believing I must look sanguinely to the period when all patriotic hearts can and will unite in saying 'all is well.' " Stephens was equally relieved. He could not foretell the result, he wrote a friend on February 13th, but believed that some adjustment was certain. "I think that the clamor about disunion rather abates," Webster informed Edward Everett. Caucus meetings of the Union men were now frequent.[29]

According to Orlando Brown, the main appeal of the compromise scheme was to the North, for the haughty South would be satisfied with nothing less than the sight of Yankeedom on its knees to beg pardon. But the real truth was that extremists both North and South had been checkmated. The Wilmot Proviso had suddenly become untenable, and Northern radicals forthwith dropped it. On the opposite side, the hopes of various Southern fireeaters for a rapid dissolution of the Union were scattered to the winds. "Southern men," observed Greeley's Washington correspondent, "have been brought to reflect on what would be the consequence to themselves if they carried out their rash acts; and their better judgments have extorted from them thè confession that Mr. Clay *was right* in showing that their last end would be worse than their first. No other Southern man living could have spoken with the boldness that Mr.

29 Orlando Brown to Crittenden, February 1, 1850; Crittenden Papers. *Toombs, Stephens, Cobb Corr.*, 184, 185. Webster to Everett, February 10, 1850; Everett Papers. Webster added: "and I trust that if, on our side, we keep cool, things will come to no dangerous pass." As for the caucuses, Douglas later said, with much exaggeration: "All the Union men, North and South, Whigs and Democrats, for a period of six months were assembled in caucus every day, with Clay in the chair, Cass upon his right hand, Webster upon his left hand, and the Whigs and Democrats arranged upon either side." F. H. Hodder, "Authorship of the Compromise of 1850," *Miss. Valley Hist. Review*, XXII, 524-536.

Clay did, and it is that boldness and fearlessness of speech that has driven the Disunionists in disgrace from the treasonable designs they had partially matured against the integrity of the Union."

Moreover, the launching of the compromise plan gave a signal for the holding of Union meetings all over the country. Such gatherings as Clay had urged in Kentucky were held in other slavery States as well, and proved unexpectedly vigorous. Montgomery Blair, spurred on by letters from Benton urging "no quarter," helped organize a determined gathering in St. Louis. William L. Marcy was soon writing Buchanan from Washington that the skies had brightened. "It is very generally agreed that the aspect of things here is not so menacing as it was some weeks ago. The Union movements at the South have a soothing effect, and I hope much good will come of them." [30]

The most impressive meetings of all took place in the great commercial centers. From New Orleans to Boston, merchants had been terribly alarmed by the increasing antagonism between the free and slaveholding States. In Baltimore all parties united in a gathering which expressed a remarkable degree of unanimity; nobody could be found to avow himself a disunionist. But the greatest demonstration was in New York: a non-partisan meeting at Castle Garden on one of the last evenings of February, to which twenty thousand people flocked, and which expressed a tremendous enthusiasm for the settlement of the controversy and the maintenance of national integrity. The streets about the Battery were blocked with vociferous crowds. Mayor Woodhull presided, while the long list of vice-chairmen included James Gallatin, Peter Cooper, Moses Taylor, George Griswold, and other business and professional leaders. Many ardent freesoilers whom no man but Clay could have induced to support a new fugitive slave law were present. Early in the proceedings the tall form of Winfield Scott was espied, and as the band broke into "Bould Sodger Boy," he was dragged amid uproarious applause to the platform. James Depeyster Ogden, one of the oldest and most respected merchants, made a stirring address. The first mention of Henry Clay's name brought a perfect storm of cheers. Vigorous resolutions were passed, and the meeting was hailed by the press as a complete success.[31]

The compromise found an unexpected ally in Thomas Ritchie, the veteran journalist who after editing the Richmond *Enquirer* for four decades had been brought by Polk to Washington as a larger arena. When Clay first introduced his resolutions, Ritchie disappointed the fireeaters by throwing the *Union* on the side of conciliation. As an ardent Southerner, he disapproved of Clay's

30 Brown to Crittenden, *Idem.* Alpha in N. Y. *Tribune*, February 9, 1850. Marcy to Buchanan, March 3, 1850; Buchanan Papers.
31 N. Y. *Tribune* on New York meeting February 25, 26, 1850; on Baltimore meeting, March 2, 1850.

contention that the old Mexican laws forbidding slavery in the Utah-New Mexico region should be kept in force. This, he declared, gave the Southern people less than justice. But Ritchie's chief editorial assistant, Edmund Burke, threatened to resign when Ritchie asserted that, as Senator Berrien and others maintained, the Mexican regulations were dead, and friends shortly arranged a meeting between Clay and the editor, who had not spoken for years—the *Enquirer* having bitterly assailed Clay when he sought the presidency. On February 10 Ritchie made a dramatic Sunday afternoon call at the National Hotel. Clay received him cordially; they talked over old Richmond days, when they had gone to the same parties and courted the same belles; and then they turned to the compromise. Clay at length consented to recede from his doctrine regarding the Mexican laws and to be content with a provision that the people of the Territories should be allowed to decide for themselves whether they should have slavery. The two parted in perfect agreement.

Thereafter Ritchie and the *Union,* with all their prestige in Democratic circles, fought ardently in the battle for the compromise. The editor attacked Calhoun; he praised Webster; he entreated Taylor to throw the Administration behind the new cause. If necessary to carry the compromise, he declared, he would drain the cup of poverty to the dregs. All the opponents of the scheme—Rhett, Yancey, Calhoun on one side, Garrison, Wendell Phillips, and Seward on the other—he fiercely assailed as disunionists.[32]

[V]

But alas! it was soon plain that the Administration would not support the new plan. Behind it stood most of the great Whig newspapers, led by the *National Intelligencer* and (with reservations) New York *Tribune;* it was approved by Webster and other conservative Whig leaders. But, his own impulses encouraged by Seward and the Cabinet, Taylor made it clear that he was frigidly hostile. The fact was that the President had no great stock of magnanimity. He had hoped, when he brought forward his own limited plan, that Webster and Clay would espouse it. He had been hurt when many Whigs declared they must wait until they learned what these two great Senators proposed. Still more was he hurt when Clay in his initial speech seemed to sneer at his proposals, and went out of his way to compliment the strategic achievement of his military rival, Scott. Some of the men surrounding the President believed that a systematic effort was under way to belittle and injure him—to thrust him to one side. The old general, looking about for defenders, found

32 C. H. Ambler, *Thomas Ritchie,* 280ff. Edmund Burke to Douglas, February 13, 1850; Douglas Papers.

few in Congress, where many Northern as well as Southern Whigs detested
the favoritism shown to Seward, and was mortified when even the *Republic*,
supposedly his organ, refused to speak up for him—for the editors of the
Republic heartily disliked his Cabinet. A morbid jealousy rose in his breast
as he found all the public applause and attention directed toward Clay.
It rankled until at length he believed that Clay had deliberately cut him as the
two passed on Pennsylvania Avenue; the fact being that, as an explanation
promptly disclosed, Clay was in the habit of getting his exercise with eyes
fixed straight ahead to avoid interruption.[33]

"The President called to see me last evening," later wrote Orlando Brown
to Crittenden, "and in a coversation of several hours fully disclosed to me his
feelings and his purposes. He spoke as a friend, a brave and a deeply injured man
alone can speak, of unmerited wrongs and unprovoked persecution. I listened
to his recital of the annoyances by which he has been harassed, of the contumely
that has been heaped upon him, of the contemptuous disparagements which
were showered upon him from high places, till my heart was sad and my eyes
filled with tears. But when, almost with the eloquence, certainly with equal
depth of agony, of Lear, he spoke of his long exposure to this pitiless storm,
I felt like I could now see how keener than a serpent's tongue was the in-
gratitude of our race. But General Taylor is the unconquerable man. When he
was through with the recital of his injuries, the soldier awoke within him, and
he explained that he always kept his flag flying in front of his tent and would
never strike it—that he had never turned his back upon friend or foe, and that
by God he would not do it now. That his station prevented him from righting
his wrongs with his own hand, but it did not prevent him from having his
character rightly defended, and that he meant to do it."

For a time Taylor thought of establishing a new organ, and though this
proved impracticable, his relations with "Aleck" Bullitt and the *Republic* continued strained. Far from doing anything to assist Clay's scheme, he threw his
influence flatly against it. On February 13, he sent the constitution of California
to Congress, and thus precipitated an angry House debate on admission. No
doubt existed that if a vote were permitted, a strong majority of the Representatives would admit California to the Union. But the minority, swearing never
to accept a new free State without a settlement of other issues, were determined
not to permit a vote. By dilatory motions and other obstructive tactics, with

33 Great dissatisfaction with the Taylor administration existed among conservative New
York Whigs, who disliked the favoritism to Seward. Great dissatisfaction existed in Washington. There was no rapport between the Administration and the best Whig leaders—the
giants of the party. Crittenden was so gloomy that he had hesitated to send news because
it would be so exceedingly painful. His conviction of the Administration's incompetence
grew stronger every day. Crittenden to Burnley, March 23, Burnley to Crittenden, March
30, 1850; Crittenden Papers.

Alexander H. Stephens as their leader, the Southerners organized a completely effective filibuster, and thus made good Clingman's threat.[34]

[VI]

Clay, left to fight his battle without Administration aid, had to face an equal storm from the radical North and the fire-eating South. While the extreme Southerners attacked him as an abolitionist, the abolitionists poured all the epithets of billingsgate upon him. When Senator Foote of Mississippi, erratic rather than radical, declared that Clay's initial speech contained more to mortify the South and provoke its resentment than any utterance by Garrison or Wendell Phillips, the Kentuckian retorted that no man in the country was more foully abused by the Garrisonians than he. He added that he was glad to find himself assailed from the two quarters. Northerners said that all the concessions went to the South; Southerners averred that all the benefits would be reaped by the North; and he thought the better of his poor scheme because the fanatics on both sides attacked it in precisely similar terms.

It was to moderate men, lovers of the Union and believers in that principle of compromise which is so essential to the strength of Anglo-Saxon political institutions, that Clay appealed. He represented a slave State. He sympathized with slave-owners. But slavery itself he reprobated. He had never changed his opinion of it. He had said again and again, and he still said, that it was an evil. In his retort to Foote he declared that standing without any earthly goal of ambition before him—standing as it were on the brink of eternity—he would repeat that it was "a social and political evil; that it is a wrong, as it respects those who are subject to the institution of slavery." A year earlier, in a letter from New Orleans to a Kentucky friend, he had sketched a plan for gradual emancipation, for though he knew that it would never be adopted by the people of Kentucky, he wished to keep his record clear for its future effect.[35]

The first strong offensive came from the South. Immediately after Clay had concluded his two-day speech, the Georgia legislature adopted resolutions which, though ostensibly aimed at various separate measures pending in Congress, really struck at his scheme. They threatened secession, declaring that

34 *Cong. Globe,* 31st Cong., 1st sess., February 18, 1850. A. H. Stephens, *Constitutional View of the Late War,* II, 201–202. As to the Southern filibuster, a private letter written in Washington on February 21 reported: "It is understood here that thirty-four members from the Slave States have signed an agreement to persevere in staving off all transaction of business in the House until the Slavery question shall be settled to their liking, by calling the Yeas and Nays, moving adjournments, calls of the House, etc., etc., whenever there shall be an effort to do anything." N. Y. *Tribune,* February 25, 1850.

35 Washington *Union,* February 22, 1850; *Cong. Globe,* 31st Cong., 1st sess., February 20, 1850.

if Congress admitted California with its "present pretended organization," passed the Wilmot proviso, or abolished slavery in the District of Columbia, and if the Northern States continued to impede the return of fugitive slaves, it would be the immediate and imperative duty of the people to meet in convention.[36] And on February 13, crowds again poured up Capitol Hill to fill the Senate galleries as Jefferson Davis, still known chiefly as a military hero—he walked with a cane from his wound and showed a military mien—took the floor to voice the antagonism of radical Southerners to the compromise. Davis, though but forty-three, had already shown intellectual distinction, capacity for command, strong egotism, a quick temper, and a fierce attachment to his section and its institutions. His election to the House in 1845, and his appointment to the Senate two years later, had enabled him to gain skill as a debater. His mind was essentially narrow, arid, and intense; but his keen logic, ample vocabulary, polished classicism of style, and above all, his burning convictions, made him formidable.[37]

Davis's speech was rather a general vindication of the Southern position and an attack upon Northern doctrines than an examination of the specific topics of Clay's compromise. He dismissed the plan with contemptuous brevity. In his eyes, no good could come of it; not even of the new Fugitive Slave Act, for that would never be enforced in States where public opinion was hostile. What was needed was a wholly new attitude on the part of the North, based upon a recognition of the fundamental titles and privileges of the slaveholding States. He spoke particularly of the cardinal right of Southern citizens to take their property into the common domain. Congress could never destroy or abridge that right; the old Missouri Compromise, which was indeed an abridgment, had been valid not because Congress enacted it, but because the States assented to it.

It was the North, pursued Davis, which was responsible for the growing sectional cleavage, for the North was trying to establish a permanent domination over the rest of the Union. The South had done nothing but stand upon the defensive. Northern politicians had made use of the factious, disorganizing, revolutionary spirit of abolitionism for selfish purposes. They were actually animated not by idealism, but by a cold, calculated purpose of mastery; and "I see nothing short of conquest on the one side, or submission on the other." The North had slandered the character of the Southern people and their ancestors, it had attempted to degrade the South in the eyes of Christendom, it had formed powerful organizations to attack Southern institutions, and it was denying the South equality under the Constitution. If its measures were not checked, the North would ultimately gain sufficient power to remodel the

36 H. V. Ames, State Documents on Federal Relations, 259–261.
37 Jefferson Davis, Works (Dunbar Rowland, ed.), I, 263ff.

Constitution and abolish slavery everywhere. For however polite the language of Northerners and however eloquent their protestations, this was precisely their intention. If the slaveholders did not meet the issue at once, they would become "an inferior class, a degraded caste in the Union." But they would meet it!

The manifestations of a stern public feeling in the South by press, orators, and crowded public meetings proved, said Davis, that the people there were amply endowed with the vital spirit which had wrested Magna Charta and the grant of American independence from the oppressor. "That spirit has come down to us. . . . We will not permit aggressions. We will defend our rights; and if it be necessary, we will claim from this government, as the barons of England claimed from King John, the grant of another Magna Charta for our protection." He briefly indicated what he thought might be the vital heart of this new charter. The essential principle of the Constitution was its nice balance of powers. The ideal situation would therefore be control of one chamber of Congress by the South, another by the North; in other words, while the House, representing population, had irretrievably gone into freesoil hands, the Senate, representing States, ought to be kept under slaveholding leadership.

Davis' speech was by no means free from special pleading of a highly dubious sort. At every point he defended the South. Did it want the slave trade reopened? Certainly not, he said; the traffic, which had enriched New Englanders and had been prolonged at their behest, belonged to the past, and was as odious to the Southerners of 1850 as to their ancestors. But the historical fact was that South Carolina and Georgia had been mainly instrumental in continuing the slave trade to 1808, and time was soon to show that a strong Southern element wished to reopen it. Was the South trying to foment disunion tendencies or mainly responsible for the existing situation? "It is not the South! It is not the South!" exclaimed Davis. Northern agitators, societies, and newspapers were the principal architects of disunion, and their attempt to fix the responsibility upon the slaveholding States was "grossly calumnious." Davis recalled that he, the son of a Revolutionary veteran, had been bred to venerate the Union, and that his attachment to its flag had been deepened by years of military service. He looked upon it now with the same ardent affection as of old and was anxious to guard it by a strict adherence to the Constitution. Yet Davis proved later in this debate that he was willing to talk quite openly of disunion. "Let the sections," he said in the Senate, "part, like the patriarchs of old, and let peace and good will subsist among their descendants." Then, he added, the day might come when better feelings would prevail, and the two sections could be reunited! These were specious words. A division could never be peaceable, and if once established, it would certainly prove permanent. Did the South wish to increase the strength of slavery? "We only defend the domestic institution of slavery as it exists in the United States; the extension of which into new territory will not increase the number of the slaves one single person." Actually, expansion into new territory would certainly increase the demand for slaves and the tendency to breed them to meet the demand. It would thus in the long run add to their numbers. But the crux of the issue had nothing to do with numbers; it was concerned with the territorial scope and political power of slavery.

Below Davis' argument lay several fallacies or half-truths which were already familiar parts of the slavery argument. When he said that Congress had no more constitutional right to touch slaves in the Territories than to touch other forms of property, he opened up a question debatable on two main points. First, Congress, or its creature the Territorial government, did have very extensive rights over various forms of property. It could exclude from Territorial limits all salable stocks of intoxicants, or explosives, or banks with bank-bills. If it could prevent citizens from entering with these forms of property, could it not prevent them from entering with slaves? Second, slave property was, as Lincoln shortly maintained, a very peculiar and special form of property, and might well be sharply differentiated from other forms of chattel property. When Davis said that the South was for guarding the Union under the Constitution, and the North was attacking it, he was uttering a sophistry with which Rhett and Yancey were to make great play down to the attack on Fort Sumter. At a hundred points the Constitution was open to differing interpretations. Men had always differed upon them and always would. Conciliation, compromise, and submission to due authority offered the only means by which men could continue to live with one another. For one side to say that its interpretation of the Constitution was the *sine qua non* of maintenance of the Union was to declare that it held the Union lightly.

But perhaps the most remarkable element in Davis' argument was his calm assumption that slaves could be carried into a Territory without giving the area a special character. The fact was that the slave system and free-labor system were antithetical; that if any considerable number of slaves were taken into a given Territory, free labor would stay out of the districts they populated. Full slave entry did not mean just giving the South equal rights in a Territory; it meant dominant or even exclusive rights.

[VII]

But the South had a doughtier spokesman than Davis; a leader of stalwart power, harshness, and determination, for whose views all slavery men were waiting. The influence of Calhoun had become that of some legendary Titan. His lightest word reverberated from the Chesapeake to the Rio Grande. A sage, a prophet, a fighter, he was at the apogee of his Southern fame. The *Southern*

Quarterly Review called him "the moral and intellectual colossus of the age"; an orator "unsurpassed" in either ancient or modern times; a man whose "ordinary talk was wisdom." If his personality was too icy, his mood too impersonally precise, to excite warm affection, he was nevertheless the revered master of the Lower South.[38]

There was something deeply touching in this Southern devotion to Calhoun. A population which loved flamboyant oratory, full of Demosthenian action and colored phrase, somehow found an ideal in his quiet manner and crisp, dry diction. In speaking, he stood straight as a gun-barrel, with head erect, countenance unsmiling and stern, and eyes roving the chamber—often fixing on Webster's responsive face. With his right hand he made a few short, nervous gestures—that was all. His voice was harsh, and though he pronounced some words in the Southern fashion ("pint" for point was one), his intonation might have been a Northerner's. The sociable, hospitable, expressive Southern people somehow regarded Calhoun's rigid manner and repressed emotions, his dour Scottish mien, as admirable. His grim adherence to duty somehow lifted the genial Southern heart. Story after story was told to illustrate his intellectual powers. His friend R. M. T. Hunter of Virginia, who for years in Washington made it a habit to walk and talk with Calhoun, once read Goethe's *Wilhelm Meister*. In the course of a Sunday walk he mentioned the fact, and began to speak of the famous criticism upon Hamlet. To his astonishment, Calhoun interrupted him and in his concise, vigorous style gave the same view of this much-discussed character as Goethe's—which he had never read; his exposition to Hunter's mind being quite as cogent and illuminating. On another occasion, during Dickens' first visit to Washington, Hunter accompanied Calhoun to call on the novelist at his hotel. They found Dickens writing and Mrs. Dickens busy with her needle. The author received them politely. But, Hunter remarked, he did not seem sufficiently impressed by the overpowering honor done him by the visit of the first statesman of the age! Such was the orthodox Southern view of Calhoun's transcendent stature.[39]

38 *Southern Quarterly Review*, November, 1850. The Washington correspondent of the N. Y. *Tribune* wrote on March 2: "There are many of the Southern men who are determined to stand by the course indicated by him, *let it be what it may*. They will regard his admonitions with far more reverence than they ever felt for Washington, and to them it will be a prophetic voice from the tomb, directing the way they shall go in this most difficult of controversies. . . . The hatred of many from the South has become so engrafted upon their very natures that they really look upon the Compromise as the most to be deplored of all evils upon earth. . . . And to Mr. Calhoun, more than any other man living, is the country indebted for this unfortunate state of mind in many of her wisest and best citizens." N. Y. *Tribune*, March 4. On January 20, 1850, O'Brien Snow had expressed concern about Calhoun's health, for "The wild steed of Disunion which he has been training can only be managed by himself." N. Y. *Tribune*, January 22, 1850.

39 O. H. Smith, *Early Indiana Trials and Sketches*, pp. 245-250, for a personal impression of Calhoun's oratory. R. M. T. Hunter Papers, unidentified MS memoir, Virginia State Historical Library, for the anecdotes of Goethe and Dickens.

For more than a year Calhoun's health had been gravely declining. Thrice in the previous session, working beyond his strength, he had fainted in the Senate lobby. On one of these occasions, when he had been borne into the Vice-President's room, Rhett hastened to him and found him sitting feebly on the sofa by the fireside. "Ah, Mr. Rhett," he exclaimed, "my career is nearly done. The great battle must be fought by you younger men." When Rhett protested that never was his life more precious and never were his counsels more needed by the South, his eyes filled with tears. "There, indeed, is my only regret at going," he muttered; "the South—the poor South!" This was his feeling now. Confined during the early weeks of the session to his lodgings at Hill's boarding-house, later known as the Old Capitol, by an exhausting cough, he was slowly mustering his strength to reappear on the floor. He had a firm conviction that the South was about to be struck down and that her cause was almost lost. Indeed, he told Hunter that the section had been "betrayed." During the last week of February he was dictating his speech to an amanuensis. He feared that it would have to be read for him in his absence; but shortly he improved.

On Sunday, March 3, word sped about Washington that he would appear on the morrow—and that it would undoubtedly be his last appearance. Once more the ways to the Capitol were blocked up by eager men and women. Some routine business had been disposed of when a sudden hush fell, and a whisper ran through the assemblage: "There he is!" Supported by Senator Mason and his old friend James Hamilton, Calhoun slowly entered, proceeded to his chair, and seated himself with his cloak draped about him. One by one friends came up to greet him. A long mane of thick, gray hair swept back from his leonine features to fall loosely upon his shoulders. He was emaciated and spectral-looking, his bony hands clasped the arms of his chair like claws, and death seemed plainly written on his brow. But his wild, deep-glowing eyes, from which flashed a peculiar light, his iron jaw, and his massive forehead made him as impressive as some Hebrew prophet, or some chieftain of the old Scottish Covenanters. A member moved that as he could remain only briefly, the order of the day should be waived, and assent was universal. The invalid rose. In a voice of singular clarity, strength, and earnestness, heard distinctly over the chamber, he thanked the Senate for its courtesy and begged its indulgence while his friend behind him (Mr. Mason) read his speech for him.[40]

During the reading Calhoun sat immovable. "Not a change," noted a brilliant young correspondent in the press gallery, Charles A. Dana, "passed over his face; not a movement betrayed any sense of the interest with which every

40 J. P. Thomas, ed., *The Carolina Tribune to Calhoun*, 369, R. B. Rhett's oration. "Reminiscences of Washington," *Atlantic Monthly*, February, 1881. N. Y. *Tribune*, February 25, 1850, quoting Washington correspondent, February 23. Nathan Sargent, *Public Men and Events*, II, 363-365.

Senator listened to his words, but with eyes partly closed and head never wavering from its erect posture, he waited till the last word before he exchanged a glance with the friends around, who listened in satisfaction to the utterance of that intellect which they regard as superior to any other of past or present times."

It was a powerful address; more powerful than Jefferson Davis', which it resembled in ignoring the specific compromise measures and cutting directly to the basic grievances of the South. Men regard it as "very ultra," wrote Edward Everett's vivacious daughter, who was staying with Daniel Webster, "but less likely to produce a prejudicial effect than if it had been spoken with Mr. Calhoun's impassioned manner. It lasted one and a half hours and was listened to with the deepest attention." [41]

He had long foreseen, said Calhoun, that unless the abolitionist agitation were halted, it would end in disunion. He had vainly attempted to persuade the Democratic and Whig parties to adopt some measure to prevent the disaster. Now the crisis was upon them, confronting the Senate with the greatest and gravest question that could ever demand its decision. What had produced the crisis? It was the almost universal discontent of the Southern people. Politicians and parties alike had tried to repress this sudden angry swell of resentment, but it was spontaneous, elemental, and ungovernable. It arose from a complex of forces, some of which had long been maturing; but its immediate cause was the destruction of the balance between the two sections which had existed in 1788 and for long afterward. This destruction was not natural, but artificial and unhealthy. It had been effected by the exclusion of the South from the common territory; by tariff laws which placed a brake upon Southern progress; and worst of all, by a remorseless concentration of power in the central government.

With manifest exaggeration, Calhoun declared that while in the days of Washington and Jefferson the people had enjoyed a Federal republic, now they suffered under a consolidated government "as absolute as that of the Autocrat in Russia, and as despotic in its tendency as any absolute government that ever existed." The rights of the States had been swept under; a great centralized mechanism had been erected in Washington; and control of this dire engine had been seized by the North. Naturally the North would use its ascendency for its own purposes. In ordinary affairs the South could perhaps endure this alien domination. But it could not do so in a matter so vital as the question of the relation between the two races, which touched the very heart of the Southern social organization. One section of Northern opinion called slavery a sin,

41 Julian, *Political Recollections*, 87. Charlie Everett to Edward Everett, March 5, 1850; Everett Papers. N. Y. *Tribune*, March 5, 6, 1850. W. M. Meigs, *Calhoun*, II, 451, finds evidence that Calhoun indulged in "significant gestures."

another termed it a crime, a third denounced it as a blot on the national escutcheon—and all three proposed to annihilate it. Not many years earlier the abolitionist crusade had been a zephyr; it had become a raging storm; and it would yet grow, unless stopped, into an irresistible tornado. Unless something decisive was done, the Negroes would be emancipated. The South thus faced a choice between abolition and secession.[42]

This picture was palpably overdrawn. The American government was still one of the loosest and least centralized of the great governments of the world; the rights of the States were still carefully guarded; and with a Southern slaveholder in the presidential chair, other slaveholders controlling the House, and still others powerful in the Senate, the idea of a hard-riding Northern domination was absurd. No sane man threatened slavery where it already existed.[43]

But Calhoun spoke more realistically when he said that even if the South abstained from a sudden stroke of secession, disunion might still take place. It could be effected, he declared, not by a single blow (for that would be difficult), but by a gradual snapping of the cords which bound the sisterhood of States together. One by one they could part, "until the whole fabric falls asunder." Indeed, they *were* parting. The great Protestant sects had once been national in extent and character, but the slavery issue had rent the Methodist, the Baptist, and the Presbyterian Churches asunder. Only the Episcopal Church stood unharmed. The political parties had once been national. But they too were altering their character, and under the disruptive pressure of the slavery issue threatened to become sectional parties. When all such bonds dissolved, where would the Union be? It would exist in name only, or worse still, as a Union of force, the strong part subjugating the weak.

The whole tenor of the speech was thus disunionist. When Calhoun spoke of the example of Washington and the colonists in resisting British aggression, Southerners in the gallery murmured warm approbation. He declared flatly that neither Clay's plan nor that of the Administration could save the Union. The latter he characterized as simply a modification of the Wilmot Proviso, for it would have the same effect in excluding the South from all the newly-won

42 Men recalled what Calhoun had told Pakenham in 1844, when the British Minister avowed the wish of the British Government to see slavery abolished in the republic of Texas. He wrote that slavery "is in reality a political institution, essential to the peace, safety, and prosperity of those States in which it exists. . . ." See N. Y. *Tribune*, April 3, 1850.

43 The N. Y. *Tribune* commented that the South had had nearly all of the Presidents. At all times a majority of Federal officeholders had been Southerners. It had had its way in the Mexican War. It had had its way, essentially, in dealing with anti-slavery petitions. It had been allowed to pry into the public mails. It had always controlled the action of the Democratic conventions; never but once had a Whig convention overruled a majority of the Southern delegates. And yet Calhoun was now threatening to break up the Union if six million Southerners were not given equal power with fourteen million Northerners! March 6, 1850.

Territories. He thought the action of Californians in forming a new State rebellious and illegal. The South, he said in conclusion, had no compromise to offer and could make no surrender or concession. (Clay had said that neither side need make any.) The only way to save the Union was for the North to give the slaveholding States their equal rights in the new territory; to execute faithfully the constitutional provisions regarding fugitives; and to cease the agitation of the slavery question. In addition, one more step would be necessary: ratification of a constitutional amendment restoring and maintaining the former balance between the sections. If all this were not done, he thought that the States had better agree to separate, and part in peace. But if the North would not admit a peaceable separation, the South would know how to act when faced with the naked alternative of "submission or resistance."

When the Senate adjourned and Southerners surrounded their champion to congratulate him, his eyes sparkled with enhanced brightness as he shook their hands. Dana heard him exhort one group: "At any rate, be men!" He was thinking of the grim eventuality which he had pictured, and which he evidently regarded as no longer escapable.

[VIII]

Yet in this extreme speech Calhoun overshot the mark. Had he made it in January, it might have had a tremendous effect; but coming after Clay's proposals, it was out of key with the situation. His violence of tone, and his ridiculous demand for a constitutional amendment which everyone knew the North would never accept, antagonized all moderate Southerners. The movement toward compromise had proceeded so far that his implacable position was seen to be untenable. A majority of the Southern Senators deserted him; not one seconded his demand for a constitutional change. The Washington *Union*, now cordially behind Clay, condemned his proposal. As the Washington correspondent of the New Orleans *Picayune* wrote, most leaders of the slave-holding States wished to secure protection for their rights and redress for their grievances within the framework of the existing Constitution. "Calhoun has failed to take the South with him in his extreme positions," commented W. L. Marcy. And this shrewd Democrat sounded a reassuring note: "The sentiment in favor of the Union is rapidly strengthening, and consequently the conflicting opinions on the question of slavery are taking a milder type." [44]

By now the more conservative Southern States were raising their voices.

44 N. Y. *Tribune*, March 6, 1850. The same view was taken by the young attorney Montgomery Blair, writing from St. Louis, on March 19. "I begin to think that the shock has passed," he told his father. "Calhoun's speech has produced a reaction which will demolish him and all concerned with him." Blair Papers, Princeton Univ.

Missouri had flatly declined to send delegates to the Nashville convention. Texas had taken similar action. Maryland was standing aloof. The Tennessee legislature had adjourned without appointing delegates, though one reason for selecting Nashville as the meeting-place had been the hope of tolling in the border States. Instead, the lower house passed strong resolutions in favor of the Union. Everybody knew that Kentucky would staunchly align herself with Clay, and a resolution for the legislative choice of delegates was tabled by a vote of three to one. In Louisiana, the House committee on Federal relations had voted against participation in the Nashville gathering, the New Orleans *Bulletin* reported the leaders of both parties opposed to the scheme, and the legislature adjourned without action. Arkansas showed no enthusiasm whatever for disunion proposals. The fact was clear that no border State, and no State along the Mississippi River except that of Davis and Quitman, could be counted on to support a scheme of dissolution or even sharp defiance. A series of powerful editorials in the *National Intelligencer* exposed the real weakness of the Calhoun-Davis forces among the Southern people. As for Congress, it was estimated after his speech that he could not carry with him more than nine Senators and forty Representatives; such was the extent of the faction ready to embrace secession.[45]

Webster, an astute observer of opinion, now thought that the worst of the clamor for disruption was over and that no more trouble would ensue. All the Southern moderates in the Senate—Clay and Underwood, Mangum and Badger, Bell, Rusk, Pratt, Soulé—hastened to repudiate Calhoun's dictum that secession was the only practicable remedy for the grievances of the slaveholding area. So, to the surprise of many, did Foote of Mississippi. His own record was not entirely clear, for he had given notice on February 25 that the nation would hold together hardly a week longer unless the slavery issues were settled, and had privately assured Webster that "if the North did not yield soon, the Union would be dissolved with bloodshed." But the day after Calhoun's speech he rose to answer that leader with force and spirit. The South, he declared, wished no such modification of the Federal compact as Calhoun had demanded. He was ready to defend the present Constitution and "the good old Union, the fruit of the sage counsels of our immortal ancestors." Just as he was closing Calhoun appeared and was stung into reply. A spirited exchange ensued.

"As things now stand, the Southern States cannot with safety remain in

45 N. Y. *Tribune*, March 7; Washington *Union*, March 6; New Orleans *Picayune*, March 11, 1850, quoted in Beveridge, *Lincoln*, II, 121. Marcy to Buchanan, March 10, 1850; Buchanan Papers. Nobody hated Calhounism and all its works more than stout old Benton. He saw Calhoun hurt his cause with ironic satisfaction. "People ask me here, why I do not speak," he remarked. "I tell them that when I was at the bar I never interrupted the adversary counsel while he was proving up my case for me." Letter of March 8, 1850; Washington *Union*, May 5, 1850.

the Union," declared Calhoun. "I think she [the South] may, without any previous amendment of the Constitution," retorted Foote.[46]

Thanks to Clay, the danger of any abrupt national breach was at an end. The principal Southern opponents of his scheme had been heard and had produced little effect. But his chief Northern antagonists were preparing their thunderbolts, while the Administration was throwing in its influence against him. With the success or failure of his plan nicely poised, he and his friends eagerly awaited the voice of Daniel Webster. Would the black knight of Marshfield caper on the margin of the lists, or would he rush forward in fierce onslaught?

46 "Charlie" Everett to Edward Everett, reporting Webster's conversations March 5, 1850; Everett Papers. See *Cong. Globe*, 31st Cong., 1st sess., March 5, 1850, for the Calhoun-Foote exchange. Foote was sometimes called 'Hangman' Foote, for he had declared in the Senate that if John P. Hale came down to Mississippi with his doctrines, he would assist in hanging him to the tallest tree available. Yet in February. 1850, he was ardently in favor of some kind of compromise. Acting on the suggestion of Ritchie of the *Union*, he approached Clay with the proposal that a resolution be offered in the Senate for a committee of thirteen to which all resolutions bearing on the controversy should be referred. Clay agreed to the plan, and asked Foote to introduce the proposal. Accordingly, on February 14 Foote proposed such a committee. See Foote, *A Casket of Reminsicences*, 24–27, for his interesting account.

9

The Great Debate

NO MAN loved the Union more strongly than Webster, and none had done more to instill in Americans a noble spirit of nationality. Clay had known that it was essential to enlist his aid; and eight days before introducing his resolutions, the Kentuckian had rung Webster's doorbell early in the evening to express his anxieties, explain his plan, and ask for help. Impressed by Clay's patriotic fervor, touched by his evident physical feebleness, and sharing his desire to protect the republic, Webster replied that while he was not prepared to concur in all details of the proposal, he could support it as a general plan. To a friend he promptly remarked that Clay's scheme impressed him favorably, and that if his opinions continued unchanged, he would espouse it no matter what might befall him in the North. He knew that he would be hotly assailed, and that abolitionists and radical freesoilers would accuse him of letting slavery into New Mexico. The fact was, he said, that since his Niblo's Garden speech of 1837 he had been squarely on record as opposed to the entry of slavery into any new Territory. If New Mexico were let alone, she would never have slavery, and it was merely irritating to forbid it where it could never exist.[1]

From this determination to give general support to the compromise he never deviated. But for a time he thought silence advisable. "If a moment should come when it shall appear that any temperate, *national*, and practical speech which I can make would be useful, I shall do the best I can," he informed his friend Peter Harvey in mid-February.[2] An explosion in the House on February 18th over the Doty resolution for the naked admission of California convinced him that the moment was near.

As the debate grew fiercer, his harassment became painful. The latter part of February found him arduously preparing to deliver a thunderstroke. "I am nearly broken down with labor and anxiety," he wrote his son Fletcher on February twenty-fourth. "I know not how to meet the present emergency, or with what weapons to beat down the Northern and Southern follies, now raging

1 G. T. Curtis, *Daniel Webster*, II, 397.
2 *Ibid.*, II, 399.

in equal extremes. If you can possibly leave home, I want you to be here a day or two before I speak. As soon as I can guess the time, I will telegraph you. I have poor spirits and little courage—'non sum, qualis eram.'" Reports that the President had confidentially consulted Webster pleased such conservative Whigs as Edward Everett. "I cannot but congratulate him," Everett burst out to Webster, "on recovering from the extraordinary delusion under which he entered office, that these were times when the government of the country could be administered with the assistance of second-rate men." Many hoped that Webster's speech would not only rally moderate opinion, but give Taylor a bridge upon which he could cross to Clay's assistance.[3]

As he toiled over his arguments Webster received abundant warning of the storm soon to burst upon his head. The abolitionists were making their position perfectly clear. Early in the year the Massachusetts Anti-Slavery Society once more adopted resolutions in favor of breaking up the Union, on the ground that this would terminate Northern support of a monstrous evil and leave slavery in a more exposed position. The Rev. W. H. Furness, one of many who pelted Webster with letters, expostulated with him for not taking bolder ground against slavery, and urged a mighty arraignment of its evils. The orator replied in a courteous note, explaining that while he did what he could to restrict slavery, "I cannot coöperate in breaking up social and political systems on the warmth, rather than the strength, of a hope that, in such convulsions, the cause of emancipation may be promoted."[4]

The abolitionists were a small and much-disliked group. But Webster knew that he would have to confront the far more formidable host of freesoilers who were worried over the fate of the New Mexico-Utah country, and anxious concerning a new fugitive slave law. He knew what kind of reports hostile men were spreading: reports that Southern tempters were busy seducing him, and were offering him their support for the Presidency if he would consent to let slavery spread beyond its existing limits. Greeley's *Tribune* was challenging him to live up to his unflinching statement in the summer of 1848 against slavery expansion, when he had said that his opposition bore no reference to lines of latitude. Bryant's *Evening Post* was admonishing him not to waver.[5]

To the last nobody outside Washington knew precisely what he would say. Even former Speaker Winthrop, four days before the speech was delivered,

3 Edward Everett to Webster, February 18, 1850; Everett Papers.
4 For a fervent expression of Webster's moral detestation of slavery, coupled with a firm statement of his unwillingness to break up social and political systems on the chance of furthering the cause of emancipation, see this letter to the Rev. Dr. W. H. Furness in Conway, *Autobiography, Memoirs and Experiences*, I, 226-228.
5 N. Y. *Tribune*, March 7, 1850, quoting Webster in the Senate, August, 1848.

made an utterly erroneous prediction: "I have every reason to think that it will look to the President's plan." [6]

Washington was filled with the keenest expectations and the acutest anxiety. Clay had begun the great debate, Calhoun had lifted it to a grimmer pitch of intensity, and now Webster was to say what many believed would be the decisive word. His forensic powers were unequalled in America and unexcelled in the wide world. Representing that New England area in which anti-slavery feeling was deepest-rooted and most belligerently asserted, and the one American region which through its literature spoke to mankind with strong ethical import, his utterance—if he argued for conciliation and adjustment—would carry a special moral weight. His best orations had become classics. His Reply to Hayne in 1830 was generally regarded as the most eloquent speech ever delivered in Congress. Was the nation now to have a Reply to Calhoun? Webster himself, stimulating his strength by oxide of arsenic and other drugs, living on his last nervous energy after months of insomnia, knew that he was making his great final effort. It is unlikely that he said, as someone reported, that the speech would ruin him, but he certainly knew that it would mean temporary obloquy.[7]

Again, in the crisp March air, crowds blackening the ways to the Capitol; again a buzzing throng filling the halls, again the close chamber crammed with women in silks and bombazines, and with Congressmen, diplomats, and politicians. Walker of Wisconsin was entitled to the floor, but ceded it with the remark that the concourse had not come to hear him. Forthwith Webster launched into his felicitous exordium. "Mr. President," he began, "I wish to speak today, not as a Massachusetts man, not as a Northern man, but as an American . . . I speak today for the preservation of the Union. 'Hear me for my cause.'" His discourse consumed more than three hours, for he pronounced it deliberately and with strange pauses. Great drops of perspiration stood upon his face, and he seemed at first to labor painfully. The fact was that his voice had lost much of its old thunderous power. Edward Everett's daughter was a critical auditor. "He does not charm you by a constant, steady flow of beautiful language as you do, dear papa," she wrote her father, "but he tries you for a long time with his slow, deliberate enunciation and then repays you at once with a burst of rhetoric." The audience enjoyed a moment of drama when, after Webster had spoken but a short time, the gaunt, bent form of Calhoun, wrapped in a black cloak, was assisted into his seat.[8]

It was not its patches of real eloquence which made the speech memorable, but its vigor of thought. Finely architectured, it fell into three main parts. The

6　Winthrop to Everett, March 3, 1850; Everett Papers.
7　Poore, *Perley's Reminiscences*, I, 365.
8　G. W. Julian, *Political Recollections*, 86. "Charlie" Everett to Edward Everett, March 8 (misdated March 7) 1850; Everett Papers.

first was historical, reviewing the forces and events which had brought North and South to such divergent views of slavery and its expansion. The second was an examination of the main sources of crimination and recrimination between the two sections, Webster trying to hold the balance even and to assess every charge at its true worth. The third part was a resolute, intensely earnest, and often thrilling exposition of the needlessness of a rupture, the impossibility of peaceable secession, and the criminality of a conflict so fratricidal. Implying that he supported the great essential measures of Clay's compromise, Webster spoke in particular of his acceptance of the proposals regarding Texas, New Mexico, and—though he said he would press for some amendments—the Fugitive Slave Bill.

His historical review was notable for the realistic emphasis which he placed upon economic and geographical factors as controlling the nation's political and moral ideas. At one time, he said, the South had been even more inclined than the North to criticize slavery. But men's minds had changed with their interests; the North, finding slavery disadvantageous, had come to denounce the slave system as a moral wrong, while the South, profiting from its cotton culture, came to defend it as justified by social considerations and the Bible, and to demand its extension. He went on to argue that the status of every foot of the nation's common territory was already determined. All the lands lying north of 36° 30′ were free under the Missouri Compromise. All the area ceded by Texas to the nation and lying south of 36° 30′ was slave territory by a compact with Texas. All the region taken from Mexico was free by the immutable decrees of nature, which made slavery impracticable and unprofitable. Since no Wilmot Proviso was needed there, why "reenact the will of God?" Why wound the pride of Southerners by a wanton denial of equal privileges, "derogatory to their character and their rights?"

That part of the speech describing the wrongs which the sections had mutually suffered was equally distinguished by courage and candor. The South, said Webster, had just ground for complaint in Northern impediments to the return of fugitives, which made a new Federal law imperative. It could justly complain also of the resolutions of Northern legislatures upon slavery within Southern States. Finally, he declared that Southern repugnance to Abolitionist societies and their practises was quite natural and proper—and he held these societies largely to blame for the accentuation of Southern fealty to slavery. But he did not believe that any or all of the Southern grievances justified action inimical to the Union; for they could all be borne, and the most substantial, that relating to runaway slaves, could be redressed by Congress.

Moreover, declared Webster, the North also had its grievances. That section could rightfully complain that the Southern effort to introduce slavery

into new regions was unwise, unwarranted, and contrary to the general understanding in 1787–88 that slavery should be restricted within its existing limits.
It could also complain of the tone in which Southern leaders treated the free
labor of the North. They often said, even in the Senate, that the slaves were
better off than Northern workers; but this was saying that they were better
off than the great majority of Northerners, for the laboring people were "the
whole North" and held five-sixths of its property. Again, Webster pointed as a
grievance to the Southern laws which kept colored seamen of Northern vessels
in custody while they were in port. A friendly mission by a Massachusetts
citizen to South Carolina had been repelled with insulting asperity. In short,
the orator took and ably enforced the view that the two sections ought to bear
and forbear. So far as their complaints were founded in matters of law, they
could and should be met. But, in so far as they were founded in opinion and
sentiment, the only feasible course was to moderate the agitation and encourage
displays of fraternal feeling.

His final exposition of the impossibility of peaceable secession and the
criminality of civil war was direct and tellingly forcible. "Secession! Peaceable
secession!" he exclaimed. "Sir, your eyes and mine are never destined to see that
miracle. The dismemberment of this vast country without convulsion! The
breaking up of the fountains of the great deep without ruffling the surface!
Who is so foolish . . . as to expect to see any such thing? Sir, he who sees these
States, now revolving in harmony round a common center, and expects to see
them quit their places and fly off without convulsion, may look the next moment to see the heavenly bodies rush from their spheres and jostle against each
other in the realms of space, without causing the wreck of the universe! There
can be no such thing as a peaceable secession." Alas that this axiom was not
reiterated again and again in the next decade!

And Webster gave his reasons. For one, too many interests, social, economic,
cultural, domestic, connected the two sections. For another, no Congress could
draw a boundary between North and South that would be acceptable to five
Americans. For a third, the Mississippi Valley was being so rapidly populated
that it would soon become the main seat of the nation's strength; and what
would happen if an attempt were made to cut the vital river artery in two,
leaving free States along all its upper reaches and slave States at its mouth?
"Can anyone suppose that this population can be severed by a line that divides
them from the territory of a foreign or alien government, down somewhere, the
Lord knows where, upon the lower banks of the Mississippi?"

No speech more patriotic or evincing a higher degree of moral courage had
ever been made in Congress. For once Webster rose to the highest level of
statesmanship. In the fierce light of the history written by events during the

next generation, hardly a line of his address failed to meet the test of truth and wisdom. What he said of the origins of the controversy, of the essential finality of nature's settlement, of the impossibility of separating without blows, all went true to the mark. That his fundamental motive was the salvation of the Union there can be no doubt. Had he been bidding for the presidency he would have trimmed his phrases and inserted weasel-words upon New Mexico and the fugitive slaves. The first precaution of any aspirant for the presidency is to make sure of his own State and section; and Webster knew that his speech would send echoes of denunciation leaping from Mt. Mansfield to Monamoy Light. Human motives are always mixed, and Webster's were doubtless no exception to the rule. Though his course was dictated by public considerations, it may have been strengthened by certain personal feelings. He had always detested the abolitionists, and he had been pained by the general New England drift toward a radical freesoilism not too remote from abolitionist views. Now he was striking a blow against that tendency and proving his independence of wild-eyed reformers. He had been stung, moreover, by a recent discovery that certain Massachusetts men who had professed loyalty to him had actually plotted against his interests—and they were identified with this same radical freesoil movement.[9]

But unquestionably his dominant motives were love of the Union, fear for the Union, ambition to save the Union.

[II]

He had expected a storm—and on his head fell a fiery tempest of wrath. In Washington, to be sure, he was so warmly applauded that Marcy thought his star was in the zenith while Clay's was steadily falling. Moderate Whigs and fair-minded Democrats everywhere in the country praised him. But it was his misfortune that the most vocal elements of the North were precisely those most hostile to the speech. The abolitionists, the venomous Democrats who had always hated him, and the radicals of every type now plied a whip with scorpions. The epithets of the abolitionists were particularly outrageous. Edmund Quincy, son of the old ex-mayor of Boston and ex-president of Harvard, spoke of "the ineffable meanness of the lion turned spaniel in his fawnings on the masters whose hands he was licking for the sake of the dirty puddings they might have to toss to him." A little later, referring to the famous trial of Professor Webster of Harvard for the murder of Dr. Parkman, he sneered at the "other criminal of the same name who is now on trial by God

9 "Reminiscences of Washington," *Atlantic Monthly*, February, 1881.

and his country." Equally unjust was Whittier's famous versified lament over Ichabod—"so fallen! So lost! The light withdrawn which once he wore!"

> Of all we loved and honored naught
> Save power remains;
> A fallen angel's pride of thought,
> Still strong in chains.

Even Longfellow quoted: "Fallen, fallen, fallen from his high estate," while Emerson said that the speech expressed Webster's "profound selfishness." Many Democrats were quick to assail it as a brazen bid for the presidency; Webster was the gamester who at midnight had doubled his stakes and risked all on the turn of the dice.[10]

But these cuts from old enemies were to be taken for granted. What hurt Webster most were the reproachful attacks of a more restrained and thoughtful group, the main body of freesoilers who had followed Van Buren two years earlier. Many of them had hoped that Webster would take a mild but firm freesoil stand; that he would insist on the immediate admission of California, offering no concession to purchase it. Most of these men believed that the Southern threats were mere stage thunder, and leaped to the conclusion that either the redoubtable Daniel had been cowed by these hollow fulminations or was the victim of delusive and unworthy ambitions. His announced determination to vote for an amended version of Mason's fugitive slave bill specially shocked a large section of opinion. This famous tribune of freedom was ready to make slave-catching one of the duties of his Commonwealth of Massachusetts! The Washington correspondent of the New York *Evening Post* wrote of the stir of satisfaction among listening Southern Senators as he spoke, and the exultant gleam on Foote's quizzical visage.

Bryant and Greeley were sternly indignant. "Mr. Webster stands before the public," declared the poet-editor, "as a man who has deserted the cause which he lately defended, deserted it under circumstances which force upon

---

10 Marcy to Buchanan, March 10, 1850; Buchanan Papers. Edmund Quincy's N. Y. *Independent* correspondence, March 15, 1850; Quincy Papers. Daniel Sturgeon, one of Buchanan's friends, thought Webster's speech "a high bid" for the presidency. Winthrop, also, was suspicious of Webster's motives: "Taylor's plan is still the best, and I deeply regret that Webster did not advocate it. Between you and me, he told me he was in favor of it both before and after his speech. Yet in the speech itself he said not a word about it, and is now declaring his readiness for *Territorial Bills*. I think his ambition is rising with the strong afflatus of Southern favor. I should rejoice to have it gratified, and so would you. But—." April 7, 1850; Everett Papers. Sumner spoke of "Webster's elaborate treason," and Theodore Parker of Benedict Arnold. But for his wide array of supporters see C. M. Fuess, *Daniel Webster*, II, 224.

him the imputation of a sordid motive. . . . It is but little more than two years since he declared himself the firmest of friends of the Wilmot Proviso, professing himself its original and incurable champion, and claiming its principles as Whig doctrine." Even Samuel Appleton of Boston termed it a most abominable speech. James Russell Lowell had long before lost faith in Webster's statesmanship, declaring that he had given evidence of great force but not great intellect and had supported no important idea of the age. Outside Boston, only six New England journals approved the speech while seventy criticized it with varying severity.[11]

Yet if hotly attacked, Webster was also strongly defended. That great body of Whig opinion for which the grave *National Intelligencer* spoke was with him. The Boston *Advertiser*, the oldest daily journal in New England and special organ of "the solid men of Boston," approved the speech. Its editor was Nathan Hale, father of Edward Everett Hale. The Boston *Courier*, which had hitherto inclined to accept Taylor's plan, reluctantly moved over to Webster's side. Another Whig journal of weight, the Boston *Atlas*, after printing the speech in full from a corrected copy furnished by Webster himself, became vehement in opposition. It was soon publishing a harsh series of letters by Horace Mann to reinforce its own editorials. Webster, writing from the Senate to his son Fletcher, saw that a prompt and forcible reply was made, and cut Mann on the Washington streets. But the *Bee*, a Whig penny paper of large circulation, gave him unfaltering aid. A majority of the Harvard faculty, a large part of the New England clergy, and a solid phalanx of businessmen stood loyally at his back.[12]

"From what I hear," wrote Edward Everett, "I rather think the majority of the Whig party will go along with Mr. W. The point on which he is least supported is that in reference to which the legal and constitutional authority is perhaps clearest, viz., the surrender of fugitives." Everett was positive that public opinion would never let this act be enforced in Massachusetts. Though not a single other New England Senator during the next three months came to

11 Nevins, *The Evening Post*, 206. Winthrop to Everett, April 7, 1850; Everett Papers. See N. Y. *Tribune*, March 9, for Greeley's well-argued attack. He declared, as Seward did later, that it was not true that an unfavorable soil and climate always forbade slavery. Look at Delaware and Maryland—did soil and climate forbid slavery there? Slavery, more a political than an economic institution, went wherever it was profitable in the remotest degree; and once it found lodgment, was fanatically upheld. "We agree to no compromise," wrote Greeley, "that perils or looks toward perilling freedom in New Mexico." For general Yankee sentiment on Webster, see Godfrey T. Anderson, "The Slavery Issue as a Factor in Massachusetts Politics from the Compromise of 1850 to the Outbreak of the Civil War." (Unpublished Univ. of Chicago doctoral dissertation.)

12 Webster to Graham, September 3, 1850; Wm. A. Graham Papers. Everett to Winthrop, March 14, 1850; Everett Papers. Webster to his son, in Curtis, *Webster*, II, 426ff. Mann, *Life of Horace Mann*, 338. Webster franked out large numbers of a handsomely printed edition of his speech to clergymen, professors at Harvard, editors, members of the legislature, and others; Sumner, Boston, April 9, 1850, to Giddings, Giddings Papers.

Webster's aid, and the attacks upon him continued unabated, a battalion of moderate Whigs did rally to his support. One noted figure who never flinched was Rufus Choate, the acknowledged leader of the Massachusetts bar. He was naturally antagonistic to slavery and had denounced the authors of Texas annexation as land-jobbers and flesh-mongers. But when multitudes forsook Webster, Choate simply lifted higher the banner of a leader he reverenced. The experience rendered him so hostile to the radical freesoilers that he shortly turned down a path which brought him behind Buchanan in 1856. Everett remained quietly loyal; so did the historian George Ticknor; so did many others. At the close of March nearly a thousand Bostonians, of whom about a hundred were persons of real mark, sent Webster an address of formal approval, which enabled him to write a vigorous letter re-stating his views. Ticknor, spending a fortnight in Washington, found the orator's desk flooded with hundreds of commendatory epistles.[13]

Addresses came to him also from Newburyport, Medford, and towns along the Kennebec. In a letter to the people of Kennebec Valley, he argued once more with abundant geographical detail—for he had made a close investigation —that New Mexico was closed by nature to slavery. Much of the country was high, nearly all of it arid, and a great part of it mere desert. On the waterless table-lands slavery was not necessarily excluded by climate; "but all labor, free or slave, all cultivation whatever, is excluded, for all time, by the sterility of the soil, throughout this vast arid region." The future was to prove that New Mexico was neither favorable to predial slavery nor inviting to a large colored population.[14]

Yet even in the expressions favorable to Webster a critical undercurrent was to be detected; for it was widely felt that he had laid an excessive emphasis on the natural factors limiting slavery and had gone too far in support of a fugitive slave law. For two generations the North had extolled the Ordinance of 1787. Nathan Dane and Manasseh Cutler had been all but canonized for their share in that document. Now to have it said that climate and soil settled the matter and that laws were unnecessary shocked many Americans and left them slightly incredulous. They were not certain that in parts of the vast Southwest slavery was really impracticable, particularly as they had heard something of Mexican peonage. As for Mason's bill, it was a sore sticking-point. Even Edward Everett declined to speak for Webster in Faneuil Hall because he objected to it and to part of Webster's Texan position. Indeed, many Bostonians of in-

13 Everett to Winthrop, March 14, 21, 1850; Everett Papers. N. Y. *Weekly Tribune,* July 30, 1859. Curtis, *Webster,* II, 264. Longfellow also took Webster's side and was hotly denounced for his pains. His own better judgment, unaided by influence, led him to this conclusion, wrote Hillard to Lieber, March 9, 1850; Lieber Papers.
14 Curtis, *Webster,* II, 431.

fluence refused on this ground to sign a commendatory address, and some who did later repented of it; the historian Jared Sparks being one.[15]

"I dined in company with Mr. Webster at Frank Gray's last week," Everett

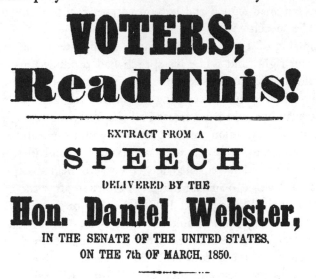

VOTERS, Read This!

EXTRACT FROM A

SPEECH

DELIVERED BY THE

Hon. Daniel Webster,

IN THE SENATE OF THE UNITED STATES, ON THE 7th OF MARCH, 1850.

"If the infernal Fanatics and Abolitionists ever get the power in their hands, they will override the Constitution, set the Supreme Court at defiance, change and make Laws to suit themselves. They will lay violent hands on those who differ with them politically in opinion, or dare question their infallibility; bankrupt the country and finally deluge it with blood."

The Abolitionists Attack Webster.
A Handbill in the New York Historical Society.

informed Winthrop as May opened. "He was in a very calm and happy state of mind, which I was glad though somewhat surprised to see. He alluded to the fugitive slave bill and gave very much the same explanation which is given in the *Courier* of Monday and copied in the *Advertiser* of Tuesday. After he left

15 Everett to Winthrop, April 10, 1850; Everett Papers.

the table, everyone present, and they were Mr. Webster's fastest friends (the Curtises, Choate, Judge Warren, and Ticknor), agreed that he had committed himself very unfortunately on that point; and yet every one, except Frank Gray and myself, had signed the letter expressing entire concurrence in the doctrines of the speech." [16]

The complaint of the milder Northern Whigs was that while Webster was in the main right, and while his speech had produced a generally happy effect, it should for the party's sake have been toned down in certain particulars. "He could have said almost everything which he has said," complained Winthrop, "and certainly could have exerted all the influence which he has exerted in favor of concord and union, and yet, by a few omissions and a few additions and a few qualifications, have left us a safe New England platform. As it is, I think the speech would have killed any Northern man except himself—and we shall have hard work to sustain ourselves under it, after the immediate crisis which called for it shall have passed. If General Taylor had said the same things precisely in his message, we should all have said,—'So much for having a Southern President.' Webster himself would have led off in denouncing him." Another Bostonian of note took the same view. "What a compound of strength and weakness, dust and divinity, Webster is!" wrote G. S. Hillard, the friend of Hawthorne, the editor of Spenser, and the author of a charming book of Italian travels, who knew Webster intimately.

Such critics overlooked the fact which Webster had emphasized in his opening sentences, that he spoke not for a State, a section, or a party, but for the nation. A less resolute tone, a diminution in rugged force, a slight concession to Northern feeling or a hint of bias against Southern views, would have cost the speech half its effect in both sections. Ticknor laid his finger on the essential point when, writing the historian Milman that an adjustment now seemed certain, he added: "This will be mainly owing to the conciliatory tone taken by Mr. Webster, which has much quieted the popular feeling at the North; for if he had assumed the opposite tone, the whole North would have gone with him, and the breach would have been much widened, if not made irreparable. . . ." [17]

Beyond question the Seventh of March Speech marked the great turning point in the history of the compromise. By the end of March, 120,000 copies

16 Everett to Winthrop, May 2, 1850; Everett Papers.
17 Winthrop to Everett, March 17, 1850; Everett Papers. Similarly to Kennedy, March 15, 1850; Kennedy Papers. Hillard to Lieber, September 9, 1850; Webster Papers. Ticknor, *Life, Letters and Journal,* II, 265. G. S. Hillard wrote Lieber that ten days after the speech, still nobody talked of anything else. "In general, it is received with favor in Boston, but with many exceptions, especially among the younger men; but in the country, the dissent is nearly universal." If the Whig Party adopted Webster's views, the State would be thrown into the arms of the Free Soil party. "There is a disposition to be quiet and await the inevitable march of events in Washington." March 18, 1850; Lieber Papers.

had been circulated. Confirming in their views those who had already accepted Clay's proposals, it brought a multitude of new adherents flocking to the compromise standard. No greater error could be made than to suppose that because the abolitionist and freesoil zealots were specially vocal, they were specially important. Even in New England and upper New York the mass of silently reflective citizens probably accepted Webster's main arguments as valid and assumed that a leader usually so right could not now be far wrong. The fierceness of the radical attack was one proof of the power of his influence. Commercial and industrial groups from Portland to Chicago had long felt a peculiar regard for the Senator. Speaking for these substantial businessmen, the *Journal of Commerce* later remarked that Webster "did more than any other man in the whole country, and at greater hazard of personal popularity, to stem and roll back the torrent of sectionalism which in 1850 threatened to overthrow the pillars of the Constitution and the Union." His voice had long been potent in the Northwest, and a large part of the approbatory letters that Ticknor saw heaping his desk were from that area. The readiness of public feeling to rise to Webster's challenge was illustrated by an incident of the same fateful March seventh in the House. Hilliard of Alabama threatened secession and war; he would offer battle at once. When Stanly, a youthful, slender, handsome Whig of North Carolina, reproached him, Hilliard asked what North Carolina would do if the Proviso passed. "If passed," responded Stanly, "I believe the people of North Carolina will stand by the Union Wilmot Proviso or no Proviso"—and galleries and floor broke into a roar of applause. That spirited utterance rang through the Union-loving press.[18]

Disunion feeling from this time, indeed, rapidly subsided—though it might easily rise again. A crisis had been reached and passed, and this blustery week marked a reversion of the tide. The fact that but three days separated Calhoun's and Webster's speeches was of the utmost importance. Tension in Washington and the country sensibly diminished from the hour when Calhoun's bitter words and extreme demands offended many cautious Southerners, while Webster's reasonableness won over doubters of both sections. Fanaticism and statesmanship had been clearly contrasted, and patriotic men could hardly hesitate between them.[19]

"The sentiment in favor of the Union," Marcy reassured Buchanan on

18 Samuel Hopkins Adams, *Webster*, 359; *Journal of Commerce* quoted in *National Intelligencer*, November 6, 1852; on Stanly, N. Y. *Tribune*, March 8, 1850.

19 Foote's subsequent tribute to the Seventh of March speech is noteworthy. Its "mild, conciliatory, and persuasive tone," he wrote, "had penetrated and softened the sensibilities of all patriots." Foote, *War of the Rebellion*, 131. But the correspondence of such hotheads as Floyd, Beverley Tucker, and James H. Hammond still breathed secession and war. "I have no sort of faith in any constitutional compacts with the North," wrote Hammond. "She never has regarded them and never will." March 6, 1850; Hammond Papers.

March 10, "is rapidly strengthening and consequently the conflicting opinions on the question of slavery are taking a milder type. Calhoun has failed to take the South with him in his extreme positions. Yesterday, Webster *was*, perhaps he is today, lord of the ascendent." Still more significantly, William R. King wrote Buchanan on March 11 of divided counsels among Southern radicals and a drift toward compromise. Southern members generally, he thought, would prefer extending the Missouri Compromise line to the Pacific, but knew that this could not now be obtained, and were hence "turning their attention to some other mode of adjustment." They would consent to an arrangement embracing the adjustment of the Texas boundary; the establishment for New Mexico of a territorial government with no provision for or against slavery; provision for future admission of a slave State to be carved out of Texas; and the immediate admission of California. This was reassuring. By March 22 Toombs thought there was "a tolerable prospect" for a proper settlement, while Howell Cobb was highly sanguine. A Western observer, Judge John D. Caton of Illinois, made some shrewd observations in the capital. He was certain that California would be admitted and that a fugitive slave law would probably be enacted. "The disunion fragment seems to be shrinking—falling back on the idea that their potency had coerced compromise—and as this is innocent boasting it is just as well to give it encouragement." [20]

[III]

As March advanced, the debate continued, with many lessening bursts of thunder and lightning. Now and then a bitter utterance evoked bitter replies. An especially mischievous speech by Horace Mann, irritating and inflaming Southern sentiment, was daily mentioned in debate with great rancor. Its concluding assertion was especially outrageous. Than slavery expansion, said Mann, "better disunion, a civil and a servile war." [21] The threat of servile war carried a special horror to Southerners. But the principal new figures in the grand discussion down to April 18th, when the whole subject was referred to a committee of thirteen with Clay as chairman, were Seward and Douglas.

It was Seward who first spoke at length for the anti-slavery North; for the radical freesoilers and the quasi-abolitionists who were determined that slavery should be pent up within its existing limits. On March 11 he rose in an almost empty Senate to make the speech which became historic by its appeal to the "higher law." As yet his reputation was largely confined to his own State,

20 Marcy and King to Buchanan; Buchanan Papers. *Toombs, Stephens, Cobb Corr.*, 184, 188. Caton to Buchanan, March 24, 1850; Buchanan Papers.
21 *Cong. Globe*, 31st Cong., 1st sess., February 15, 1850.

though many knew of the precocious career that had made him governor at thirty-seven. In physical appearance he was unprepossessing. He was of less than middle height, thin, wiry, and alert; his reddish hair already turning gray, though he was only forty-nine; his complexion sandy; his features pointed, quizzical, and keen, with a long nose and a high forehead. His manner was nervous, and his whole aspect spoke of energy and ambition. In private company he moved restlessly, talked readily and frankly, and gestured incessantly. A man of the world, well-travelled and well-read, he showed an easy self-confidence, being equally at home among politicians, professional men, and plain farmers and shopkeepers. Since he was curiously compounded of so many traits, he sometimes seemed all things to all men; and it was his greatest defect that he possessed no really burning convictions and held no passionate principles. Yet an emotional vein gave freshness and warmth to his character, expressing itself in a tender devotion to his family, a marked love for the best English literature, and a strong veneration for the older traditions and leaders of the republic. His brilliancy was married, as is often the fact, to impetuosity, so that his acts were sometimes daring and erratic to the point of folly. He was optimistic, zealous, and quick. Withal, he had a strong bent for political strategy, loving to display his resourcefulness by a devious rather than a direct path to his goal. Most of the party elders distrusted him. "In some respects an able man," was Webster's verdict, "but subtle and unscrupulous, and will make everything bend to the one idea of making himself President." [22]

Seward, disabled by a husky and monotonous voice from the highest oratorical effects, always relied upon a direct conversational delivery, which gave the effect of a simple, sincere man thinking out loud, without rhetoric or reserve. His habit was to pace the floor slowly, his hands thrust in his pockets or locked at his back, pausing for thought, and then ejaculating in carefully-chosen words what had come into his mind. His self-absorption, his earnestness, his lack of pose, struck his auditors forcibly. On this occasion he read his speech; and since there was "no one to approve and no one to admire," as the Washington *Union* acridly remarked, this was just as well. But however critical, Webster, Benton, and Corwin listened attentively, while Clay, after looking at him mournfully from a distant seat, moved closer.[23]

The essence of the speech could have been distilled into four words: No compromises, no concessions! He called for the admission of California as a free State without any compensatory grant. He was against letting slavery into

22 Webster to Peter Harvey. Webster continued: "He has been catering first for Catholic votes and then for Abolition votes; 'tis no matter whose votes they are if they only lift him to the great office." Bancroft, *Life of William H. Seward*, I, 200.

23 N. Y. *Tribune*, March 18, 1850, Washington correspondence of Roger Sherman dated March 12. Bancroft, *Seward*, I, 190-191.

a single foot of the lands acquired from Mexico. He opposed any new fugitive slave law. He was for the abolition of slavery in the Federal District at the earliest practicable moment. More than that, he was for pronouncing a sentence of ultimate extinction upon slavery everywhere; for a policy guaranteeing that it would, "under the steady, peaceful action of moral, social, and political causes, be removed by gradual, voluntary effort, and with compensation." These positions were all buttressed by arguments which involved much refutation of previous speakers.

To Webster's statement that it was unnecessary to reënact a decree of nature, Seward replied that Southerners themselves believed that slavery might flourish in the newly acquired areas; that history showed slavery existing in all climes; and that every just human law is a reënactment of the law of God. To Webster's denunciation of the anti-slavery crusade, he replied that it represented a grand moral upheaval which neither could nor should be halted. "It will go on until you shall terminate it in the only way in which any state or nation has ever terminated it—by yielding to it—yielding in your own time, and in your own manner, indeed, but nevertheless yielding to the progress of emancipation." To the demand for a stringent reclamation of fugitive slaves he offered two replies: first that the South was not entitled to a new statute, and second, that it would be ineffectual if passed. The South assumed that slaves were chattels, and that anybody who helped them escape implicated himself in a larceny; but this view was "unjust, unconstitutional, and immoral." To Calhoun's demand for guarantees of a political balance between the two sections, Seward responded that any such artificial equilibrium between the wealthy, fast-growing North and the more slowly developing South would mean converting the United States from a unified national democracy into an alliance of sovereign States, with the minority enjoying a veto against the majority.

But the most memorable part of Seward's discourse was its almost defiant statement of the doctrine of the higher law. The pending compromise assumed that the Territories were a common possession to be enjoyed by citizens of the States as they liked. Not so, said Seward; they were a trust, a sacred responsibility. The Constitution devoted the domain to union, justice, welfare, and liberty. "But there is a higher law than the Constitution, which regulates our authority over the domain, and devotes it to the same noble purposes. The territory is a part, no inconsiderable part, of the common heritage of mankind, bestowed upon them by the Creator of the universe. We are his stewards and must so discharge our trust as to secure in the highest attainable degree their happiness."

From beginning to end, Seward's speech was animated by a rapt confidence that slavery was doomed, and that its extinction by the advance of moral sentiment and civilization would assuredly take place without long delay. That slavery was interwoven with all the social and economic institutions of the South, he admitted. He had no patience with the incessant demands of the abolitionists for immediate and unconditional extirpation of slavery. He wished to see none but lawful, constitutional, and peaceful means adopted to deal with the problem. Yet he nevertheless felt certain of the final outcome. "I feel assured that slavery must give way, and will give way, to the salutary instructions of economy, and to the ripening influences of humanity; that emancipation is inevitable, and is near; that it may be hastened or hindered; that all measures which fortify slavery and secure it tend to the consummation of violence; all that check its extension and abate its strength tend to its peaceful extirpation."

All in all, Seward's refusal to yield an inch to the South, his appeal to a moral and spirtual law transcending the Constitution, and his bland certainty that slavery was marching to an early doom, enraged Southerners even more than the epithets of Mann and Hale. "Monstrous and diabolical," shrieked the Columbia *Telegraph*.[24]

In both the North and South, Seward's speech aroused the sternest hostility. Mangum and other Southern Whigs swore that if he were the mouthpiece of the Administration they would turn Democrats at once. The speech elicited from Calhoun an expression of withering anger. When Senator Foote remarked that he was on good terms with all his colleagues, no matter what their opinions, Calhoun jerked out: "I am not. I will not be on good terms with those who wish to cut my throat. The honorable Senator from New York justifies the North in treachery. I am not the man to hold social intercourse with such as these." Clay shortly spoke of the higher law with scathing contempt. "Who are they who venture to tell us what is divine and what is natural law? Where are their credentials of prophecy?" He characterized such utterances as "wild, reckless, and abominable theories, which strike at the foundations of all property, and threaten to crush in ruins the fabric of civilized society." Webster, speaking at one of the Virginia springs in June, was equally harsh. This higher law, he sneered, outsoared the mountain-peaks; no common vision could discern it; no conscience that was not transcendental and ecstatic could feel it; it was utterly unsafe—and yet it was the code of the fanatical and factious abolitionists [25]

Even Taylor explicitly condemned his adviser's utterance. Mangum, overflowing with wrath, hurried to the White House to serve a solemn ultimatum upon the President. Taylor, so excited that he stuttered, called the editor of the *Republic* into immediate conference. "Aleck, this is a nice mess Governor

24 Columbia, S. C. *Telegraph*, April 18, 1850. The "higher law" was obviously closely akin to the natural law of Cicero, St. Thomas Aquinas, Coke, and Jefferson.
25 *Cong. Globe*, 31st Cong., 1st sess., March 13, 1850. Webster, *Writings*, XLIII, 435.

Seward has got us into," he sputtered. "The speech must be disclaimed at once, authoritatively and decidedly. Don't be mealy-mouthed about it, but don't use harsh language. We can't stand for a moment on such principles." Thus inspired, Bullitt penned a powerful criticism. Its opening sentence, speaking of Seward as one who proclaimed that he held his credentials from almighty God, authorizing him to reject all human enactment, struck the keynote. The effect was tremendous, and did something to counteract the influence of the speech. But that influence, especially as Greeley, Bryant, and other radical freesoilers reiterated and expounded every part of the address, was not small.[26]

It was soon evident, indeed, that while Seward's speech did not affect the issue in Congress, it was destined to have an enduring effect upon Northern sentiment. Weed's Albany *Evening Journal* printed in its next weekly issue extracts from fifty-two country papers expressing a hearty concurrence in its doctrines. Seward's higher-law indiscretion insidiously appealed to that element of idealists who are quick to fancy themselves above certain laws. Clergymen, religious editors, reformers, and other zealots during the next few years excused a vast deal of illegal and even unconstitutional activity by this dubious abstraction. His attack upon the proposed fugitive slave law fitted handily into the higher law dogma. Later events clearly demonstrated that it was impossible to enforce this statute in communities which universally regarded it as improper and wicked. No enactment, as men learned again in prohibition days, can be made valid in a district whose people regard it as morally indefensible and materially injurious.

Seward's reasoning on this subject was the reasoning of Greeley and thousands more. "Pass a law here in New York that the man who steals a sheep shall be hanged," exclaimed the editor, "and does Mr. Webster suppose he could find a judge or jury to execute it?" Both men were correct upon this particular point. But on all other points Seward might justly be called wrong; and it was fortunate for the country that his discourse—too long, dull, and prosy to compete with Webster's—changed no votes in Washington.[27]

26 "Recollections of an Old Stager," *Harper's New Monthly Magazine,* September, 1873, p. 589.

27 For a typical ministerial utterance, see the 204-page volume by William Hosmer, *The Higher Law in its Relations to Civil Government: with Particular Reference to Slavery and the Fugitive Slave Law* (Auburn, 1852). The author concluded that no man could believe in God without believing in the higher law, or be a Christian without keeping it. See also N. Y. *Tribune,* March 9, 1850. Greeley was filled with enthusiasm by the speech. "Isn't it something?" he asked Colfax. "If he can only maintain that position, he is our hope for 1856." They would probably have to run Old Zack in '52, but four years later they could elect Seward President on a clean, square issue, winning a victory good for something. March 19, 1850; Greeley-Colfax Papers.

[IV]

The great question, in fact, now seemed not whether some kind of compromise should pass, for an adjustment at least roughly similar to Clay's appeared likely, but in what order the compromise bills should be enacted. That issue was even more quickly presented in the House than in the Senate. The middle of February, as we have seen, had found the Northern majority in the House anxious to pass a measure for the admission of California, and the embittered Southerners ready to resist it by determined obstruction. With Cobb in the chair, they had complete power, by dilatory motions and other meaneuvers, to keep the House tied in knots. The contest had become grimly heated on February 18, a day made memorable by the opening of a determined filibuster against the before-mentioned resolution for the unconditional admission of California introduced by Doty of Wisconsin. Foremost among the obstructionists were Stephens, Toombs, and Clingman.

When the tension and irritation became almost unendurable, Douglas had his lieutenant, John A. McClernand of Illinois, chairman of the territorial committee, a man whose courtesy and urbanity made him a general favorite, approach this group to inquire if some way could not be found around the impasse. They replied that they would gladly see California admitted if the questions of New Mexico and Utah were first settled on the basis of no Congressional exclusion of slavery; the people being distinctly empowered to legislate for the admission of slaves, and to frame their Constitutions with respect to slavery as they pleased. This proposal was put in writing and shown to many Northern members to gain their assent. The next night, February 19, a conference was held at Speaker Cobb's house, with Toombs, Stephens, Cobb, and Linn Boyd of Kentucky representing the South, and McClernand, William A. Richardson (another Illinoisan), and John K. Miller of Ohio the North. They agreed to press for a solution of the dispute by three measures: the organization of New Mexico and Utah on the principle named, the admission of California, and the defeat of any attempt to abolish slavery in the District of Columbia. Senator Douglas, who as chairman of the Senate committee on Territories had authorized the two Illinois Congressmen to speak for him, was a party to the agreement. Douglas and McClernand therefore prepared bills for their respective committees. Though some time was required for this preparation, a different atmosphere at once enveloped the House.[28]

It was with a full knowledge of the House arrangement that Douglas rose in the Senate on March 13 to speak for the more militant northern Democrats.

28 Poage, *Henry Clay and the Whig Party,* 212; A. H. Stephens, *War Between the States,* II, 202–205; Shryock, *Georgia and the Union.* 217–232.

Ostensibly hostile to Clay's compromise scheme, he was actually ready to assist it at critical moments. Only thirty-seven, he was already famous, widely popular—and much distrusted. He had first made his parliamentary reputation in a triumphant colloquy with J. Q. Adams in the House in 1846. His readiness and energy in debate, his accurate memory of political details, and his unscrupulous style of fencing made him formidable. While the Young Democracy, particularly on the Western prairies and in the great cities, gave him an ardent personal devotion, sober men disliked his hard-riding ambition, audacity, and a certain brassiness of temper. He stood for vigor, boldness, and enterprise, but his was a rough vigor, a reckless energy, a coarse code of ethics. His speech was regarded as important and was widely reported. But time proved it more momentous than men supposed, for it laid down principles upon which, four years later, Douglas was to base a piece of legislation which raised sectional feeling to fever heat.[29]

Cass had already expounded at prosy length his famous doctrine of the right of each Territory to legislate for itself on all internal questions—the doctrine later famous as squatter sovereignty. He had used both constitutional and practical arguments. Were not the people of a Territory our own people, with all our own intelligence, information, and capacity for managing affairs? Had not the late proceedings in California furnished an admirable illustration of the popular capacity for self-government? The central theme of Douglas' speech was also popular sovereignty, but his arguments were far livelier and more cogent than Cass'. When the people of a Territory applied for statehood, he declared, they could pronounce for or against slavery. This right of self-determination, together with the irrevocable decrees of nature and climate, really settled the whole question. If Congress meddled with slavery in the Territories, it did so without warrant, without real effect on the local situation, and with no result except to irritate national feeling. The Wilmot Proviso had been an outrage against self-government, argued Douglas, for it was an attempt to deprive the people of the Territories, even when they set up new States, of the right to mould their domestic institutions to suit themselves.[30]

29 *Cong. Globe,* 30th Cong., 1st sess., App. 366ff.; Milton, *Eve of Conflict,* 64ff., F. H. Hodder, "The Authorship of the Compromise of 1850," *Mississippi Valley Hist. Rev.,* XXII, 524–536.

30 On January 21, 22, 1850, Cass had made a speech which pleased neither North nor South. Under instruction by the Michigan legislature to vote for the Wilmot Proviso, he announced that he would do nothing of the sort and went on to explain his special doctrines. "I saw Webster scowling at him whilst he spoke with that awful Websterian scowl which portends an earthquake," John P. Kennedy wrote his wife, January 22, 1850; Kennedy Papers. Boston was indignant; Clay laughed at the novelties of the doctrine. As for the Southerners, they almost unanimously renounced him. Brown of Mississippi, Venable of North Carolina, and Seddon of Virginia publicly attacked his views; twenty other Southerners did so privately. He was thought to be trimming his sails to the wind of popularity—and his expedients had recoiled upon himself. L. P. Waldo, Washington, to Welles, February 24, 1850; Welles Papers.

Denying Calhoun's statement that the Missouri Compromise had deprived the South of a fair share of the Territories, Douglas asserted that neither section had any true "share" therein. The Territories, he said, belonged to the whole people and were to be used not for one section or another, but for the general benefit. The Missouri Compromise had declared that no slavery should exist north of a certain line. But this did not really alter the situation in the slightest. Nature had excluded slavery from the area so effectually that Congress was without any true power. Far from restricting slavery, the compromise had neither curtailed nor extended it one inch. Its only real effect had been to allay for a time the sectional excitement on the subject. What really controlled was the local will, dictated by local conditions. Northerners and Southerners alike could go to any Territory just as they pleased, but they could not take certain forms of property there unless the local laws permitted. The owner of a bank could not transfer it to Minnesota, California, or Oregon because of adverse territorial law; the owner of a stock of whiskey could not carry it into Oregon for the same reason. Just so, owners of slave property could not take it into a Territory where local sentiment and law excluded it. Douglas thus explicitly stated the great doctrine of which he was to be the principal exponent during the next decade.

He boldly declared, moreover, that nature made it certain that none of the States to be erected between the Mississippi and the Pacific would be slaveholding. It was useless for Calhoun and others to talk of equilibrium between the free and slave areas, for that was a moral and physical impossibility. Indeed, it had never been contemplated by the founders of the republic. During the early years of the nation practically all men had expected the border States to provide for gradual emancipation. That expectation had been disappointed; but the fact remained that for reasons of soil and climate, slavery could never root itself in the new trans-Mississippi areas. Seventeen States, predicted Douglas, would ultimately be carved out of this domain, and they would all be free whether Congress prohibited slavery or not.

[V]

In the Senate the question of the order of the compromise measures was more difficult to resolve than in the House. The Northern radicals, with the Administration behind them, insisted upon the admission of California divorced from all other legislation. These Northern irreconcilables included nine New England Senators, and the six from New Jersey, Ohio, and Wisconsin, with Seward; making sixteen in all, eleven of whom were Whigs, three Democrats, and two Free Soilers. They were flatly against Clay's scheme or any like it. The Clay-Webster-Cass group of moderates, which by fluctuating and often

inconsistent but generally conciliatory votes and speeches indicated their willingness to work out a scheme of mutual concessions, came to fourteen or perhaps
fifteen Senators in all, the largest single block being the border State men. The
Southern extremists, opposed under all circumstances to the admission of California as a free State and hostile to any other concession—the Calhoun men,
some of them openly hopeful of disunion—numbered perhaps eight Democrats.
All such estimates of strength are merely approximations, for Senators changed
their opinions, they sometimes voted and spoke for temporary effect, and no
clear test of ultimate faith presented itself. The problem of Clay and his supporters was to unite with their fourteen or fifteen avowed exponents of compromise the twenty or twenty-one Senators who, with various opinions, prejudices, and ambitions, and sensitive to a variety of political pressures at home
and in Washington, might somehow be rallied to a practicable scheme. To
muster thirty votes in all from a Senatorial total of fifty-nine was no light task.[31]

The speeches of Clay, Webster, Cass, and Douglas had gone primarily to
an exposition of the feasibility and wisdom of compromise; but a good deal of
supplementary effort was addressed to the task of showing both Northern and
Southern fanatics that they were playing with fire. Webster had been fiercely
emphatic in his indictment of the abolitionists. Mangum was presently arraign-
ing the agitators of the South and the abolitionists and radical freesoilers of the
North as men who would feel "the burning brand of public indignation, that,
if it do not burn into the bone, will leave a mark that they will carry with them
to their political graves." While Cass rebuked Calhoun for calling Washington
an illustrious Southerner instead of an illustrious American, Foote declared that
the course of the South Carolinian, with the Nashville Convention little more
than two months distant, "puts the Union in serious and unnecessary danger." [32]

Others spoke in the same tenor. John Bell of Tennessee warned the Northern
zealots that they were simply dunces when they told each other that the
Southern excitement was artificial, and that it could be traced to party, impulsive
passions, and political ambition. For years, he recalled, he had watched the
whole movement. He had seen a steady and heavy accession of strength to those
who favored extreme measures for resistance and redress. In some Southern
States he had found leading men of both parties coöperating in the cause. "Every
day I hear of some gentleman of intellect and influence, to whom it would be
unfair to impute motives of personal or party aggrandizement, committing himself to these violent resolves. Is it, then, the part of wisdom to say that no consideration is due to these movements? For, though it may be that the great body
of the farming and planting interests repose in quiet . . . yet when leading and

31 Poage, *Henry Clay and the Whig Party*, 212, 213; *Cong. Globe*, 31st Cong., 1st sess.,
passim; data in Crittenden, Buchanan, Douglas, and Chase Papers.
32 *Cong. Globe*, 31st Cong., 1st sess., 481, 517, 520, 950.

sober-minded citizens, one after another, yield to the suggestions of the more intemperate and excited, how soon may a whole population be brought to rally in support of the most violent and dangerous schemes!" This was hard sense.

One gloss upon Bell's statement was an indignant message which Governor John B. Floyd sent to the Virginia legislature early in March. A State agent dispatched to Ohio, to bring home a free Negro charged with crime, had been rudely repulsed. These outrages were of frequent occurrence, said Floyd, and must be remedied. He proposed united action on the part of the Southern States in passing tax laws which would exclude Yankee goods from their markets, and build up either home manufactures or a direct trade with Europe. Another gloss upon Bell's warning was furnished by a large meeting of Southern Senators and Representatives in the Capitol on the night of April 7th. Drawing up a fiery new address to the Southern people upon their perilous situation—a "Calhounical," to use Benton's term—the gathering took steps to establish in Washington a newspaper representing the radical Southern position.[33]

As salutary as Bell's speech were the repeated warnings of Northern leaders that secession would mean the armed and bloody coercion of the South. Webster's statement to this effect was paralleled by others. Bissell of Illinois made a particularly biting argument in the House in late February. He was a Democrat. But he asserted that the Middle West was a unit against the disruption which some Southerners were threatening, and that the plain people of Illinois who had mustered nine regiments for the Mexican War would send four times as many to fight disunionists to the bitter end.[34]

33 Washington *Union*, March 2, 1850, on Bell's speech of February 28. Floyd's message, March 12, 1850; Floyd Papers. "If the Federal Government fail to furnish adequate protection to us touching our slaves and offenders against the laws construing them, then we must take the remedy into our own hands . . . ," said Governor Floyd. "I am of the opinion that a system of taxation under the license law can be so arranged as to transfer entirely the trade from those States which have trampled under foot the Constitution of the United States to those which are still willing to abide by its compromises and recognize our rights under it. This would be a peaceful and efficient remedy . . ." Southern Congressmen in an "Address to the People of the Southern States" asserted: "A great party has grown up, and is increasing in the United States, which seems to think it a duty they owe to earth and heaven, to make war on a domestic situation, upon which are staked our property, our social organization, and our peace and safety. Sectional feeling has been invoked." And the attack, if successful, "must end in our destruction." Copy in Rusk Papers.

34 Some remarks of Bissell on February 21, which were construed as a reflection upon the Mississippi troops in the Mexican War, came near resulting in an affair of honor between Bissell and Jefferson Davis. Meanwhile, many continued to predict physical violence in the House. Some set March 4 as the date for a general mêlée. Washington correspondents sent their papers vivid accounts of the bowie knives and Colt revolvers daily borne in the House, and one suggested that blood would flow like water. Another said that Southern members would withdraw in a block to break up Congress. But the day came and went without violence; the members preferred to draw $8 a day till the end of the session. N. Y. *Tribune*, February 25—March 5, 1850. Later, the Columbia, S. C., *Telegraph*, April 15, 1850, saw in speeches of Bissell and Shields of Illinois, Baker of Indiana, and Chase of Ohio, supporting the New Englanders, an ominous coalition of the Puritans and the Pathfinders, the Bible and the Bowie-Knife.

Meanwhile, the Administration's attitude remained distinctly unhelpful. Taylor, his pique at Clay and Webster unabated, his *amour propre* as sensitive as ever, clung stubbornly to his impossible plan of action upon California and New Mexico alone. In vain did John J. Crittenden, lamenting that the Administration had no friends in Congress and was awaiting rather than making opportunities, urge Secretary Clayton to take a commanding attitude. The excitement of the times required that the *whole* controversy be positively settled, he wrote; the Administration should form a plan, which would make full concession to the South—as the weaker and aggrieved party—of all that she could reasonably demand, and then exert its whole power in supporting and enforcing it. If all that the South asked were granted without stint, thought the sagacious Crittenden, "it would amount eventually and practically to nothing"; but it would soothe and conciliate a section which was playing a losing game.[35] Taylor, however, would not budge beyond his former position.[36]

However brave, the President's stand was wrongheaded. The one contribution which he made to a settlement of the controversy (and even this would have been more effective if coupled with a friendly gesture to the South), was to render it clear that he would meet disunion by force. Late in February, according to a well-informed source, a group of Southerners called at the White House, to inquire if the President had really said that he would maintain the Union at any cost. With blazing eyes, Taylor replied that he had; that he would blockade every Southern port if armed resistance were made to the collection of the customs; that he would call for volunteers, and putting himself at the head of the Northern and Western troops, would pour out his blood in defense of the Union. He was confident, he added, that the people of the Southern States would themselves put down any attempt at a forcible severance of the national ties.[37]

[VI]

It was evident that Administration jealousy and dislike of Clay, coupled with the silly fear of some Democrats that his triumph would make him the next President, constituted the gravest obstacles to his particular plan. Happily, Clay was patriotically willing to step aside and take the substance without the form. A number of slightly varying schemes were taking shape as February passed into March. They found their general basis in the McClernand-Stephens understanding in the House, and the willingness of many Southern leaders, as King of Alabama had noted, to accept an arrangement embracing the admission of

35   April 6, 1850; Clayton Papers.
36   See the steady reports from Clayton and others in the Crittenden Papers; Bancroft, *Seward*, I, 270; C. E. Hamlin, *Hannibal Hamlin*, I, 200ff.
37   U. B. Phillips, *Robert Toombs*, 82; N. Y. *Tribune*, February 25, 1850.

California, the purchase of the Santa Fé area from Texas, the establishment of a Territorial government in New Mexico without slavery restrictions, and provision for carving a future new slave state out of Texas. Senator Bell's compromise plan, offered on the last day of February, embodied precisely these ideas as to the Texas boundary and the future of New Mexico. It proposed, however, that Texas be immediately divided into two States on the line of the Trinity River, and that ultimately a new State, to be slave or free as its inhabitants desired, be made from the area between the Colorado and Rio Grande south of the thirty-fourth parallel. Bell believed this would probably be a slave State, "the last of its race." [38]

Douglas, too, the spokesman of the West, had his plan, the general McClernand-Stephens arrangement. He moved to give it shape by reporting two bills in the Senate, which he was at pains to keep separate. One admitted California with her existing boundaries; the other provided territorial governments for New Mexico and Utah, without restriction as to slavery, and paid Texas a large sum, tentatively set at ten to fifteen million dollars, for the adjustment of her western line. The editors of the *Republic*, who were playing a lone hand with some occasional responsiveness to Taylor and more to Crittenden, endorsed Bell's proposals. Ritchie and the *Union*, still close to Clay though Democratic in allegiance, endorsed Douglas' bills and suggested adding a fugitive slave bill in order to effect a comprehensive settlement of the main issues. The fact was that Clay, Bell, and Douglas, the *Union*, *Intelligencer*, and at times the uncertain *Republic*, were fairly close together on the essential features of a compromise. That is, they believed in a comprehensive arrangement; they desired to couple the admission of California with a generous Texas boundary settlement and with Territorial bills for the New Mexico-Utah country; and they agreed that these Territorial bills should not exclude slavery and should leave the final decision upon that institution to the people when applying for statehood. Washington gossips magnified all the minor differences. They talked specially of Bell's resolutions as rival to those of Clay, and indulged in various conjectures that Taylor might swing around to support the Bell plan—for the President was apparently well disposed toward Bell. However, the essential aims of the Kentuckian were approaching fruition against the fanaticism of the two sections.[39]

Some of the ill-temper which still frothed and boiled in Congress was spectacularly displayed on April 17 in a disgraceful altercation between Benton

38 King to Buchanan, March 11, 1850; Buchanan Papers. Bell's plan in *Cong. Globe*, 31st Cong., 1st sess.; February 28, 1850.
39 Douglas introduced his bills on March 25; *Cong. Globe*, 31st Cong. 1st sess.; Washington *Union*, April 18, 1850. Judge John Catron sized up the situation very accurately when he wrote Buchanan on March 24: "In the few days that I have been here, enough has been seen and heard to satisfy that California will be admitted—and probably a bill passed by which runaway slaves may be reclaimed in the free States, and a Territory established north of Texas." Buchanan Papers.

and Foote. Both these Senators were firm believers of the Union and of an adjustment by mutual concessions. But Foote had associated himself with Calhoun's "Southern Address," which Benton had denounced as sheer treason. The irascible Benton implacably opposed any "omnibus" scheme, though he favored every part of Clay's compromise separately, while the nervous, baldheaded, peppery little Foote was an eager partisan of an omnibus arrangement. Moreover, they were at odds in their fundamental attitude toward slavery, Benton looking forward to its eventual extinction, while Foote defended it. They had exchanged heated words in March when Foote very improperly charged that Benton, in pressing for the immediate and separate admission of California, was actuated by "personal and domestic considerations," his son-in-law Frémont being Senator-elect from the new State. The enmity of the two strutters suddenly produced an explosion which, as a committee later reported, was without precedent in Senate history.

Foote was pressing a motion for referring all the plans of Clay, Bell, Douglas, and others to a select committee of thirteen, which should evolve from them a new master-plan. This, an important step forward, had been suggested by Ritchie of the *Union* and Representative Bayley of Virginia to Clay, who consented on condition that Foote offer the resolution. It was warmly supported by Clay and Cass, and was certain of passage. Benton broke in to charge that the nation was being blackmailed by a factitious and artificial excitement; that the attempt to throw it "into a flame" had been begun by Calhoun's "Southern Address"; that it was being sustained by an incessant cry of wolf, wolf; and that the country had been terrified without reason over a mere abstraction. Foote hotly rose to defend the Southern leaders, declaring them a band of patriots who would be held in veneration when their calumniators were regarded with loathing and contempt. At the word "calumniators" Benton left his desk and strode toward the Mississippian. Foote retreated toward the clerk's table, snatched out a five-chambered revolver, and cocked it. Benton, stopped by a friendly Senator, was turning back toward his seat when he saw the weapon. He instantly tore open his coat and shirt like Governor Berkeley facing Nathaniel Bacon, shouting: "I am not armed. I have no pistols. I disdain to carry arms. Let him fire! Stand out of the way and let the assassin fire!"

Senators in wild excitement surrounded the pair. As order was restored, Benton roared: "A pistol has been brought in to shoot me with—to assassinate me!" "I brought it here to defend myself," Foote shrilled. "I had been informed that I should be fired at." Dickinson of New York caught the pistol from Foote's hand and locked it in his desk. The Senate, its dignity affronted, appointed a committee upon the affray, but this body failed to recommend any action. While some men laughed, the reputation of the country suffered as news of the episode reached Europe. The scene, writes Abbott Lawrence, our minister in London, was "extremely humiliating" to all who represented the republic abroad.[40]

[VII]

Foote's sensible proposal was carried next day, the Senate by a vote of 30 to 22 referring the resolutions of Clay, Bell, and others to a committee of thirteen. Clay was of course made chairman. His associates were six men from the free States and six from the slave States: Cass, Bright, Dickinson, Downs, King, and Mason as Democrats, and Cooper, Bell, Mangum, Phelps, and Webster as Whigs—a large share of the talents and character of the Senate. Only two members, Mason of Virginia and Phelps of Vermont, could be regarded as extremists. Clay congratulated the nation on the prospect of a final and amicable settlement of the question; and when Douglas moved to take up the California bill at once, he warned the Senate that it could not pass alone, and announced his intention of attaching Territorial bills to it. When Benton, holding up four quarto volumes, gave notice that he had parliamentary law to show that his course violated all precedent and propriety, Clay replied that he would answer this "parliamentary law." And so he did.

On May 8, Jefferson Davis made a rasping speech in which he recited the defiant Mississippi resolutions. Then Clay gained the floor. "Mr. President," he announced, "I have risen to present to the Senate a report from the committee of thirteen." He read the report with some brief words of explanation, and a tribute to his committee associates—"I have never been associated with gentlemen on any great and momentous occasion in which a spirit of more kindness, more conciliation . . . was presented." The next day's papers blazoned the recommendations of the committee majority to the country. Another great forward step had been taken.

The committee's proposals were seven in number. First, whenever any new State or States formed out of Texas asked for admission, Congress was to redeem its compact with the Texan people by granting the request. Second, California was to be admitted immediately with her boundaries unchanged. Third, Territorial governments were to be established for New Mexico and Utah without

---

40 *Cong. Globe,* 31st Cong., 1st sess., 748–764; Foote, *Casket of Reminiscences,* 78–80; Lawrence to Rives, May 8, 1850, Rives Papers. Foote remarked about this time that he would write a little book in which his antagonist would figure largely. Benton, hearing of this, told his informant with characteristic pomposity: "Tell Foote that I shall write a very *large* book in which he will not figure at all." In his *Thirty Years View* he did so. *Harper's Magazine,* 1859, p. 569. Foote was the first Southern Democrat to assert in the face of Calhoun and his followers that he would abide by the Constitution and wished no amendments offered to it. He was the first to avow his determination to seek no remedy for Southern complaints outside the agencies provided by the Constitution. For this declaration, which as the *Union* said, "required the utmost firmness and moral courage," he was vehemently attacked. A ready debater, he was a man of integrity and essential kindliness. Washington *Union,* May 3, 1850.

any stipulations for or against slavery. Fourth, the provisions respecting California, Utah, and New Mexico, as constituting the territory obtained from Mexico, were to be bound up in the same bill. This, as a matter of fact, consisted simply of two of Douglas's bills, bound together by a wafer. Fifth, Texas was to be paid for surrendering her jurisdiction over the lands she claimed within the old boundaries of New Mexico, and her northern and western boundaries were to be fixed by the Rio Grande, "and up that river to the point commonly called El Paso, and running thence up that river twenty miles, measured thereon by a straight line, and then eastwardly to a point where the hundredth degree of west longitude crosses the Red River." Sixth, a fugitive slave law was to be passed. Seventh, the slave trade was to be abolished within the District of Columbia, though slavery was to continue therein. The seven recommendations, it will be seen, were much those Clay had made under eight headings in January.

No minority report was made, though Phelps and Cooper on the Northern side, and Mason, Downs, and Berrien on the Southern, expressed disagreement with some of the proposals. When Berrien stated his adverse views at length, Mangum was quick to answer them. The substantive propositions offered much room for disagreement. Apart from them, the report contained one statement of principle which was to prove of the utmost importance. It declared that it was time that the wounds inflicted by the Wilmot Proviso were healed—

". . . and that to avoid, in all future time, the agitations which must be produced by the conflict of opinion on the slavery question . . . the true principle which ought to regulate the action of Congress, in forming Territorial governments for each newly acquired domain, is to refrain from all legislation on the subject in the Territory acquired, so long as it retains the Territorial form of government—leaving it to the people of such Territory, when they have attained to a condition which entitles them to admission as a State, to decide for themselves the question of the allowance or prohibition of domestic slavery."

The attitude of the Administration of course remained one of unrelenting hostility. Rumors had been current throughout late April that Taylor would instantly veto a California statehood bill if it were combined with Territorial bills for New Mexico and Utah. When Benton and Taylor conferred, it was agreed that mischief was brewing. The Washington *Republic* had been imploring all Whigs to rally about Taylor's plan, while Seward's mouthpiece, the Albany *Evening Journal*, made the same plea. "There is nothing but utter wreck ahead for the Whigs of the free States," it predicted, "if the platform of General Taylor on the slavery question is abandoned."

Formal debate on the compromise began May 13, and it was soon plain that it would last for months, for nearly every Senator wished to be heard—and many repeatedly. For some days Washington hummed with wonder, speculation, hope, and fear, the wisest saying the least. Some believed that the omnibus bills would eventually pass Congress, and some that they would be slaughtered. Actually, the rival forces were not ill-matched. Clay, Webster, Cass, Douglas, and Foote, though disagreeing on some details, were squarely behind the general compromise scheme. According to a traditional conversation, Clay had thanked Douglas as "the most generous man alive" for letting him use his bills on California, Utah, and New Mexico. The scheme was opposed from the standpoint of the Southern extremists by Jefferson Davis, Mason, Berrien, and others; from that of the Northern radicals by Seward, Chase, and Hale; and from that of Thomas Hart Benton by Thomas Hart Benton.[41]

But its antagonists could hardly overlook the abundant evidence that majority opinion throughout the nation supported its main features. As the battle rapidly developed, Clay proved a host in himself. Some of his opponents thought with the acid spinster Robert C. Winthrop that he was "dictatorial to the last degree." But dictatorial was never the word for Clay. Despite age and debility, he was indefatigably busy, and his silvery voice presented the arguments of the moderates with beguiling power, while his knowledge of parliamentary practise enabled him to seize every tactical advantage. "Webster is more massive and ponderous in a set debate," wrote Greeley, "but does not compare in winning support to a measure." [42]

One voice that might have taken a powerful share in the debate was stilled. "Mr. Calhoun is a little indisposed, from his exertion in the Senate yesterday," had written his relative, Representative Armistead Burt, on March 14. His strength steadily declined, and it was soon clear that he would hardly outlive the month. His mind remained as luminous as ever. The evening before his death he had his mail read to him, commented upon some of his letters, and directed his son to clear up his table as usual. In the night, aware that he was dying, he gave some simple directions regarding his papers. When speech left him, he still showed consciousness and squeezed his son's hand. He had often quoted the statement that man is protected by the same Providence "on the fatal as on the natal hour." By noon of March 31 the telegraph had carried over the country the intelligence of his death, and in many a Southern town and city the church bells were tolling. It is not too much to say that the news fell on thousands like a thunderclap. He was the Voice of the South, its guardian, its ever-vigilant

41 Orlando Brown to Crittenden, May 15, 1850; Crittenden Papers. "The Capital is at this juncture in a perfect hum of wonder, speculation, and conjecture," he wrote on the 18th. "The wisest know the least . . . Congress is a muddle—opinions as various as the men who entertain them, upon the result of the Compromise Bill—Whig organization nowhere—Democratic harmony equally hard to find—chaos within and chaos without the legislative halls. Old Zach is the only one who stands unmoved." For the supposed conversation of Clay and Douglas see James Sheahan, *Douglas*, 132-134; G. D. Harmon, "Douglas and the Compromise of 1850," Journal *Illinois State Hist. Soc.*, XXI, 453-499.
42 Winthrop to Everett, May 22, 1850; Everett Papers.

champion—and he had passed away in what many thought the hour of its direst peril.[43]

Next day memorial discourses were delivered in the Senate by Rusk of Texas, a friend from boyhood; by Clemens of Alabama, speaking for the Deep South; and by Clay, who, after harking back to the time when the two had been messmates in the opening months of the War of 1812, remarked with emotion that he must soon follow Calhoun on his long journey. On April 2 the Senate gathered in its chamber for the funeral ceremonies. The desks had been removed, and the floor was closely filled with chairs. At eleven-fifteen the members of the House entered; then came the Supreme Court, Taney at its head; and then the diplomatic corps, dressed in black. A voice announced, "The President of the United States," and all stood as Taylor walked down the aisle and seated himself beside Vice-President Fillmore. Finally, at twelve-thirty, a hush descended, and the chaplain slowly entered reading the first words of the Episcopal service: "I am the resurrection and the life." Behind him, attended by six pallbearers—Webster, Clay, Cass, Mangum, Berrien, and King—was borne the coffin. It was deposited in the middle of the center aisle, and an attendant swiftly removed the upper panel, disclosing the pallid features of the statesman. Following the ceremony, a long procession accompanied the body to the Congressional Cemetery, where it was to rest until South Carolina claimed her own.[44]

But from his grave Calhoun still moulded the thought and partisan feeling of millions.[45]

43 Burt to his wife: A. Burt Papers. R. M. T. Hunter to his wife, no date; R. M. T. Hunter Papers. Schirmer MS Diary, March 31, 1850. The brave little band of South Carolina Unionists of course took a different view of Calhoun. "He has been absolute in South Carolina for many years past," B. F. Perry had confided to his journal. "When he dies there are hundreds who will breathe more freely, as was the case in England on the death of Henry VIII." MS Journal, 1849, p. 56. Joel R. Poinsett told Perry that history would deal harshly with the dead leader. Perry, MS Journal, June 10, 1850. And Francis Lieber, who deplored Calhoun's last speech, wrote: "I cannot help thinking that Calhoun's death will be healing rather than otherwise." Thomas S. Perry, ed., *Francis Lieber*, 244.

44 N. Y. *Tribune*, April 3, 1850. "Recollections of an Old Stager," *Harper's New Monthly Magazine*, October, 1873, p. 758.

45 Calhoun had mobilized a devoted group of propagandists, who continued to labor in what they conceived to be his cause. One was Beverley Tucker, who lobbied in the Virginia legislature during January of this year. Another was James H. Hammond, who from his Silver Bluff plantation in South Carolina sent letters flying far and wide through the South. "I would give $1,000 for six hours on the floor of the Senate, to say what no man has dared to say," he burst out on April 18, 1850. A third was Joseph A. Scoville, snugly planted at this time in the N. Y. *Herald* office. He was Calhoun's secretary for a period and close to him till his death. Expressing Calhoun's views, he wrote articles for the *Herald* signed "Patrick Henry," for the Charleston *Mercury* signed "Davis," for the Columbia *Telegraph* signed "Bascombe," for the Macon *Telegraph* signed "George Mason," and for the *North Carolina Standard* signed "Truth." Hammond Papers, March-April, 1850.

10

"The Union Stands Firm"

WEBSTER HAD SAID in his Seventh of March speech that if a convention met in Nashville to concert the overthrow of the Union beside Jackson's grave, Old Hickory would turn in his coffin. Happily, the rapid subsidence of disunion sentiment in Congress during March and April was accompanied by a similar decline throughout most of the South. As a consequence, the Southern attitude toward the convention sharply altered. The New York *Herald*, after a careful study of a hundred Southern journals, found early in April that a quarter of them were either indifferent or opposed to the Nashville gathering, and that with few exceptions the remainder favored it not for disunion purposes, but for consultation and as a warning to the North. According to the *Herald*, Southern opinion was divided into three main parts. A small element wished to proceed to extremities, favoring secession sooner or later. A considerable group desired to set up a Southern political party and hoped to make the Nashville declarations its platform. The most important body of all was in favor of compromising all sectional difficulties at once. Under these circumstances, the Nashville Convention could present no great menace.[1]

The fact was that only two groups of men showed any enthusiasm for the assemblage: the old nullifiers of the 1830's, and the fiery young men who worshipped Calhoun. Most Southern Whigs were either hostile to the convention or contemptuously indifferent. Large numbers of Jackson-Polk Democrats denounced it from the beginning, while after the introduction of the Compromise, others joined them. Public meetings were held at various Southern points to attack it. That old Indian fighter and good Jacksonian nationalist, Cave Johnson, wrote Buchanan from Clarksville, Tennessee, that "to give a counter-direction to public opinion" he had arranged a gathering, and that after harangues by Democratic and Whig leaders, it had voted unanimously for Clay's proposals. "Meetings have since been held in many other counties with like unanimity," he reported.[2]

1 N. Y. *Herald*, April 5, 1850.
2 June 6, 1850; Buchanan Papers. On August 10 Johnson wrote Buchanan from Clarksville, Tennessee, that the Nullifiers "would have shown their hands at Nashville but for the

When the convention opened on June 3rd, only nine States sent delegates; some of them had very dubious credentials, and only those from South Carolina and Mississippi could rely upon strong home enthusiasm. One venerable figure of the past, Langdon Cheves of South Carolina, attended; physically a shadow and a victim of drink, but his name still potent. Beverley Tucker, the learned and equally venerable author of that propagandist novel *The Partisan Leader*, a preacher of secession for thirty years, was present. So were Rhett, Francis W. Pickens, and James H. Hammond, the South Carolina extremists; the last-named bitterly disappointed because he had not succeeded to Calhoun's seat in the Senate. Other delegates included General J. P. Henderson of Texas, who with Louis T. Wigfall had been making fiery speeches beyond the Mississippi; Benjamin Fitzpatrick of Alabama, whose brief hour of fame was to come when he rejected a vice-presidential nomination ten years later; and William L. Sharkey, the former chief justice of Mississippi, who had refused a place in Taylor's cabinet. The tone of the meeting was more moderate than had been anticipated. "From a great deal of conversation with them," wrote Cave Johnson, who spent two days urging delegates to be cautious, "I concluded they were less ultra and factious than I had supposed." The conservative Sharkey, chosen president, strove skillfully to keep the reins in safe hands.[3]

There were three great reasons for moderation: first, precipitancy would alienate the border States; second, rash acts might inflict great hurt upon the Southern Democracy by enabling the Whigs to come forward as friends of the Union; and third and most important, Southern sentiment was plainly unformed and hesitant. It had been understood that the convention would demand the extension of the Missouri Compromise line to the Pacific. This was far less than the radical delegates desired, for as good Calhounites, they wished to insist on Calhoun's terms. Wigfall, in a widely published letter, had urged the gathering to call for a series of amendments to the Constitution. But the Calhounite demand for amendments had always struck most men as preposterous, and the Washington *Union* declared that to press it would mean breaking up the nation. Now all extremist schemes were dropped.[4]

A committee was appointed to draw up resolutions, and it included moderate

---

hope of securing this State, which could only be done by moderation if it could in any way be accomplished. . . . We should unquestionably have adopted the recommended 36° 30′ but for the fact that so many Northern Democrats had committed themselves to an intervention and against the constitutionality of the Missouri Compromise and Calhoun and many of his friends had also committed themselves against its constitutionality that we had no hope of getting anything better than the compromise proposed by the thirteen . . ." Buchanan Papers.

3 Johnson to Buchanan, June 6, 1850; Buchanan Papers. Columbia *Telegraph*, June 14, 1850, quoting the Nashville correspondent of the Augusta *Republican*.
4 Wigfall's letter in Washington *Union*, May 14, 1850.

men like Cass' friend A.O.P. Nicholson, who favored acceptance of the compromise. The principal affirmation, looked upon as the "ultimatum" of the South, declared that as a generous concession, the convention would be willing to see the new Territories divided by the 36° 30' line, below which Southerners should be authorized to take their slaves. It was unanimously adopted. But an accompanying address to the people, drafted by R. B. Rhett, passed only after stiff opposition. This manifesto repeated Calhoun's assertion that passage of the California bill would be equivalent to enactment of the Wilmot proviso, and condemned the compromise proposals before Congress. A great part of the convention actually had high hopes for a satisfactory compromise, and did not wish to embarrass the Southern members in Washington.[5]

The "ultimatum" was generally regarded as a surrender. Some radicals hoped that it could be used to defeat the compromise. But, commented the astute Cave Johnson, "I think there is no *fighting ground* between the Compromise Bill and 36° 30'." He was right. The ultimatum was too late and too weak. When it was adopted, Senator King of Alabama heard in it a requiem note. It will doubtless unite in its support the whole Southern delegation, he wrote Buchanan, "but I still think it will fail." As a matter of fact, it fell far short of uniting the Southerners in Congress. For one reason, Calhoun had implanted too deeply in some breasts his doctrine that the Missouri Compromise line was unconstitutional and the whole principle of slavery restriction wickedly wrong. For another, many Southerners saw that extension of the line through California would do them no good. California was fated in any event to be free soil; cut it in two, and the country would simply have two free States instead of one. The convention passed into history like the far-off rumble of a storm that might have been disastrous, but that had dissolved without loosing a single thunderbolt.[6]

Yet the Nashville Convention was after all destined to have a certain malign influence. If the radicals had been checkmated, they had been given an opportunity to clasp hands, to exchange counsels, and to fortify each other. General Henderson, returning home on the steamboat *Cincinnati*, wrote his Texas friend T. J. Rusk a high-spirited letter. He had exacted of the States represented in the convention a pledge that they would stand by Texas in her boundary dispute with New Mexico; he thought the gathering had exercised a salutary effect upon the Nashville area; and he had made new friends. Reaching Texas, he and the ebullient Wigfall addressed several public meetings in volcanic terms. Other returning delegates took the same line. In the capital of South Carolina, Marcy

5 The address, printed in the Columbia *Telegraph* on June 18, filled more than four columns on the editorial page. On June 21 and 22 the Washington *Union* vigorously attacked the address for misrepresenting the compromise.

6 Johnson to Buchanan, June 6, 1850; King to Buchanan, June 11, 1850; Buchanan Papers. C. P. Denman, *Secession Movement in Alabama*, 30-33.

Gregg and James Chesnut, Jr., made speeches reviewing the work of the convention and reiterating radical doctrines. A large assemblage at Jackson, Mississippi, addressed by Quitman, adopted resolutions unanimously supporting the convention and condemning the compromise.[7]

Particularly noteworthy, for excerpts were reprinted far and wide, were Rhett's lightnings and coruscations at Charleston near the end of July. Asserting that the South would never get its just rights, he declared that secession was imperative. "We are in the beginning of a revolution," he exclaimed. Such fulminations, together with the resolutions and address of the convention, inspired hundreds of new editorial appeals to Southern nationalism, like that of Simms' *Southern Quarterly Review*. What is the Union but a Northern barony? it asked:[8]

"It is their place of pleasant pasturage. There they feed and fatten free of charge. The labours of the South, through this medium, are made to enure almost wholly to their advantage. Our fruits pass into their granaries. The toll which is assessed upon Southern productions pays their taxes, builds their fortresses, crowds their marts with shipping, and clothes their barren hills with marble cities."

Moreover, the secession movement ten years later showed that the radical leaders had learned much from the Nashville fiasco. They saw that a different course was required: not concerted action by numerous States, which was too slow and too likely to play into the hands of the conservatives, but bold precipitancy by two or three. These should lead, and trust others to follow. Of course this was unscrupulous, for the daring States might drag unwilling neighbors into war; but it would be effective. In the speech at Charleston in which he unmasked, Rhett proclaimed his scheme for dissolving the Union by *separate* State action. After picturing the golden delights of Southern independence, he asserted that if all other States deserted her, South Carolina would battle alone for justice and independence.[9]

[I]

Meanwhile, in Washington the endless debate seethed and rippled and roared. It was a relief to have Nashville, which Benton and the *National Intelligencer* had pictured as a foul secessionist plot, out of the way. But the great central question remained. Battle over the omnibus bill had been squarely joined in mid-May; a majority of the committee of thirteen and their moderate

---

7 Henderson to Rusk, June 22, 1850; Rusk Papers. Columbia *Telegraph*, July 2, 1850; July 24 on Quitman's address, taken from the *Mississippian* of July 8.
8 *Southern Quarterly Review*, September, 1850. White, *Rhett*, 108–109.
9 P. M. Hamer, *The Secession Movement in South Carolina, 1847–52*, p. 63.

backers against the two wings of extremists—and against the Administration. For Zachary Taylor, influenced by pride, jealousy, obstinacy, and William H. Seward, had now thrown the full weight of his open influence against the compromise. Indeed, he and Clay had come to an open rupture. The editorials of the Washington *Republic* in support of the compromise had temporarily deluded Clay into believing that Taylor had changed his course, and he had himself used conciliatory language in his speech of May 13, carefully avoiding any criticism of Taylor's ideas. But that very week Washington was electrified to learn that "Alec" Bullitt had been forced out of his editorship; that a new man, Allan A. Hall, a Tennessee journalist acceptable to the Cabinet and President, had taken his place; and that the *Republic* would implacably oppose the omnibus plan. Taylor could hardly hope to carry his own scheme, but he could obstruct Clay's. It was an ironic fact that a President who had pledged himself never to veto measures except on grounds of unconstitutionality was now interposing a virtual veto of the compromise plan.[10]

Pale with anger, Clay on May 21 accepted the declaration of war in a terrific exposure of the inadequacies of the President's scheme. Gesticulating vigorously and stamping his foot, he challenged any Administration man to meet him in forensic combat. "Now, what is the plan of the President?" he asked. "Here are five wounds—one, two, three, four, five—bleeding and threatening the well-being, if not the existence, of the body politic. What is the plan of the President? Is it to heal all these wounds? No such thing. It is only to heal one of the five, and to leave the other four to bleed more profusely than ever, by the sole admission of California, even if it should produce death itself." Taylor's plan failed to establish any civil government for New Mexico and Utah, such as the treaty and constitutional obligations demanded; it failed to fix the boundaries of New Mexico east of the Rio Grande and left the people of that debated area exposed to the incursions threatened by Texas; it failed to adjust the fugitive slave question; it proposed no solution of the burning slave-trade question in the District of Columbia. It would settle only the California issue, and that in a way to flush the Northern extremists with success, while provoking and chagrining the South. The Southern members would return home in exas-

10 Washington *Union*, May 16, 1850, for Benton's letter of March 30. *Ibid.*, April 28, 1850, for the opposition to the compromise on the part of Taylor and Seward organs. J. J. Crittenden felt great solicitude that there should be no breach between Taylor and the Washington *Republic*. "Concession among friends is no sacrifice of independence," he wrote Orlando Brown on April 30. Later, when the break came, he wrote Albert T. Burnley: "I received your letter informing me of your arrangements of all the difficulties of the *Republic*. I do not see how the affair could have been better or more easily settled for all *parties*. Bullitt and Sargent have acted magnanimously in consenting to withdraw, and in the manner of their withdrawal. Nothing could have been better done in style or in spirit." May 25, 1850; Crittenden Papers.

peration to face heated parties, with a heated press, heated stump-speakers, and heated legislatures. When they came back to Washington six months later, the four unsettled questions would be four malignant tumors.

This argument was as wise as it was graphic. The alarmed Crittenden, viewing events from Kentucky, was imploring Taylor's advisers to prevent him from obstructing a settlement. "There is one peril before him that is to be carefully avoided, as it seems to me, and that is the peril of having thrown upon his Administration the responsibility of *defeating* the bill of the Committee of Thirteen, or any other measure of *Compromise*." Personally he would have preferred Taylor's plan, "but the public is *anxious* for a *settlement*, and comparatively indifferent as to the exact terms, provided they embrace anything like a compromise." But Taylor was not to be restrained. Hurt and indignant, he inspired an editorial blast of nearly five columns in the *Republic* of May 27. His editor attacked Clay as vainglorious, dictatorial, and unfair. With pain and amazement, the rank and file of the Whig Party saw the spectacle of Thomas Hart Benton marshaling the Congressional forces of a Whig Administration while Henry Clay and a Whig President were cudgeling each other's heads.[11]

The dissensions of the Whig Party, indeed, had become lamentable. Nobody in Congress or outside had any respect for the Cabinet. One of Bullitt's offences had been to say in the editorial columns of the *Republic* what was daily and hourly said in the lobbies of House and Senate, in the hotels, and wherever else men gathered—that neither the politicians nor people placed any confidence in the various Secretaries. It was to be hoped, he wrote, that the President would not keep what Canning had once said was the greatest possible curse, "a Cabinet insensible to public opinion." For that matter, Bullitt's ejection was itself certain to cause great ill-feeling. A journalist of high character, he possessed a host of friends in Louisiana, Tennessee, and other States; long a devoted friend of Taylor, he had done more for his elevation than all the Cabinet officers togethers. Yet now he was thrown on the scrapheap without a word of regret. As for the language which Taylor privately applied to Clay and Webster, it crackled with expletives peculiar to the army camps in which he had been trained. A fratricidal war had broken out in the party.[12]

Even with the fire-eaters, the Free Soilers, and the Taylor men pitted against it, however, the omnibus bill seemed likely to pass. Clay and Webster were a host in themselves. A cultivated young Virginian who listened to a week of debate, Moncure D. Conway, saw Webster "come down on Yulee as softly and as crushingly as a triphammer." He watched Clay maneuver the handsome

11 Crittenden to Brown, June 7, 1850; Crittenden Papers. Poage, *Henry Clay and the Whig Party*, 233.
12 Washington *Union*, May 14, 15, 1850.

Pierre Soulé into an indignant repudiation of disunionism. The Massachusetts giant was like a ponderous line-of-battle ship, its broadside irresistible; the Kentuckian was like a swift-darting cruiser, quick with its guns and unerring with its torpedo. Though Taylor and Seward carried with them such able Senators as Corwin of Ohio, Hannibal Hamlin of Maine, John Davis of Massachusetts, and W. L. Dayton of New Jersey, the Compromise was still sustained by many of their associates: Greene and Clarke of Rhode Island, Badger and Mangum of North Carolina, Pearce and Pratt of Maryland. Clay was reported in the best of spirits. The sentiment of the country was unmistakably for the compromise, and most important of all, many Democratic leaders were rallying to its support.[13]

For whatever his influence was worth, ex-President Tyler sent a long letter urging passage of the omnibus measure. He was well satisfied with all its provisions. The law prohibiting the slave trade in the District of Columbia was substantially identical with one which he himself had proposed nearly twenty years earlier, as part of a District code! He could find no fault with the fugitive slave bill. As for the territorial settlement, the South would be given a full opportunity to extend her institutions to New Mexico and Utah. He did not believe that Southern planters would ever migrate to that area; he thought that the Wilmot Proviso was a mere abstraction, and that Wilmot could perfectly have trusted to nature to provide for slavery-exclusion. Nevertheless, he wrote, the compromise arrangement would salve the feelings of the South.[14]

Indeed, a host of Democrats were rallying now to the side of compromise. Sam Houston and Foote were indefatigable in the Senate. Influential chieftains outside were laboring with voice or pen: Buchanan and Dallas of Pennsylvania, Louis McLane of Delaware, Levi Woodbury of New Hampshire, James Guthrie of Kentucky, Cave Johnson of Tennessee, Robert J. Walker of Mississippi, and not least notable, Judge Sharkey of Nashville Convention fame. James A. Bayard, soon to become Senator from Delaware, wrote Clay that his plan was the only one which could succeed; if it failed he would despair. Great public meetings were held in May and June to whip up popular sentiment for the omnibus bill. Non-partisan in character, they attracted Whigs and Democrats alike. Near the end of June a monster petition, signed by some twenty-five

---

13 Conway, *Autobiography*, I, 81ff. Washington *Union*, May 5, 1850ff. By early June many Southern extremists were trying to rally on a demand for an extension of the Missouri Compromise, as an alternative to the Clay proposals. But it seemed hopeless. Washington *Union*, June 17, 1850. On June 16 the *Union* quoted the editor of the Richmond *Enquirer* as stating, on June 14 after three days in Washington, that "The great issue in the House is the Missouri Compromise, which is pressed in various forms as an amendment to the California bill. A scrutiny of the movements in that body satisfied us that the Missouri Compromise line, in favor of which we were originally, and would now most willingly accept, is impracticable."
14 See the Washington *Union*, May 28, 1850, for Tyler's letter.

thousand names (many of which represented important firms) was brought from New York to Washington, requesting the New York Senators to vote for the bill. Plans were under way for an impressive meeting in Philadelphia. Outside New England, up-State New York, and South Carolina, the newspapers without respect to party seemed to be in the main for the measure.

When the Washington *Republic* remarked that the Southern Whig press was almost a unit behind Taylor's scheme, the *Union* called this a gross untruth. So did the Savannah *Republican*; the truth was, it asserted, that the leading Whig papers and a majority of the leading Democratic journals of every Southern State united in espousing Clay's compromise. "In Alabama no Whig paper has come out against it; and there is but one in this State which opposes it. In Tennessee and Kentucky, and the Southwest, both parties are emulous in its advocacy. The same is true in North Carolina and Virginia." In an effort to counteract the wide influence of the *Union*, the radical Southerners in Congress were driven to push forward their movement for a special Washington organ; and mid-June witnessed the birth of a gasconading newspaper, the *Southern Press*, edited by two expert tub-thumpers, Ellwood Fisher, a native of Virginia who had practised law in Cincinnati, and Edwin De Leon, a South Carolinian who had been an editor of the Columbia *Telegraph*. Eighteen Senators and forty-six Representatives had agreed to help support this new journal.[15]

The one hope of Clay's opponents was to mutilate the compromise by amendments and paralyze it by delays. They would form a radical block in the House to Clingmanize it; they would brush up the mildewed proposal for extending the Missouri Compromise line; and if worst came to worst, they would get Taylor to repudiate his most solemn pledge by an outright veto of the bill. As they began to fight the battle on these lines, June found the situation grow-

15 Bayard to Clay, July 1, 1850; Bayard Papers. Savannah *Republican*, quoted in the Washington *Union*, June 18, 1850. Robert Toombs and several others, a committee appointed by a large meeting of Southern members of Congress, had reported in favor of the establishment of a Southern daily. "In the contest now going on," they wrote, "the constitutional equality of fifteen States is put in question." In this great contest public opinion was destined to be the most important force. Yet no paper to defend Southern interests existed in the capital, nor was there one which offered a common medium for an interchange of opinions among the Southern States. All moderates, North and South, attacked the undertaking. Southern extremists warmly favored it, and so did many Northern radicals, on the ground that it would give their own Washington organ, the *National Era*, a larger circulation and greater influence. Washington *Union* May 15ff; Howard C. Perkins, "A Neglected Phase of the Movement for Southern Unity, 1847–1852," *Journal of Southern History*, XII, 153–203.

Other sections of the country were stronger than ever for the compromise and the Committee of Thirteen. Former Senator Thomas Metcalfe wrote Clayton on June 18 of his recent trip through Kentucky and Illinois, "If I am not greatly deceived public sentiment is strongly in favor of it. I spent two or three days in Indianapolis and in passing through Indiana to Springfield in Illinois I heard no one individual express any dissent from the views of the committee. . . . In Kentucky there appears to be but one opinion. Whigs and Democrats all go, and go earnestly for the Compromise." Clayton Papers.

ing dangerous again. Confusion increased; sectional passions revived. "We shall have a warm summer," Webster wrote his son. "The political atmosphere will be hot, however the natural may be. I am in for it and shall fight it out." Per-

NOTICE
TO
IMMIGRANTS!!

As there are in our City a number of men with remarkable principles, who go among those who have newly arrived and offer to sell or lease to them the *Public Land* in and about this place—thus imposing upon the unsuspecting. The latter are hereby notified that the vacant land in Sacramento City and vicinity, is open for *ALL*, free of charge ; but, they can make either of the following gentlemen a present of a few thousand dollars—if they have it to spare—Such favors are eagerly sought and ex-ultingly received by them. In fact, some of them are so solicitous in this matter, that, if they are not given *something*, they will *almost not like it*, and even threaten to *sue* people who will not contribute to their support. Those who have made themselves the most notorious, are

Barton Lee,	Prettyman, Barroll & Co.,	Warbass & Co.,
Burnett & Rogers	A. M. Winn,	J. Sherwood,
Hardin Bigelow	S. Brannan,	James Queen,
Pearson & Baker,	Hensley, Merrill & King,	Dr. W. G. Deal,
Thomas M'Dowell,	Conn. Mining and Trading Co.,	Eugene F. Gillespie,
R. J Watson,	Paul, White & Co.,	T. L. Chapman,
J. S. Hambleton,	W. M. Carpenter,	Dewey & Smith,
Starr, Bensley & Co.,	R. Gelston,	E. L. Brown,
	John S. Fowler.	

Sacramento City, June 14, 1850.

"Sacramento Transcript" Print.

By order of the Settlers' Association.

California on the Eve of Admission.
A Broadside used by courtesy of Elmo S. Watson, Northwestern University.

haps the most striking evidence of the renewal of political tension was Toombs' long-remembered speech of June 15. An impassioned advocate of Clay's general plan, the Georgia leader deeply resented Taylor's effort to bring in California as a free State without any concession to the South. He gave the House an arresting exposition of the right of the South to an equal share in the territorial domain. Deprive us of this right, he said, and the government becomes one of Northern freesoilers, not of the nation. "Then I am its enemy, and I will, if I can, bring my children and my constituents to the altar of liberty, and like Hamilcar I would swear them to eternal hostility to your foul domination." [16]

At times it seemed that the committee of thirteen would triumph; at times that the coalition of ill-assorted obstructionists would produce a complete deadlock. Though ailing in health, Clay continued incessantly busy till near the end of June. Webster abetted him by bringing forward an amendment to the fugitive slave bill which distinctly provided for trial by jury, thus mollifying some hesitant Northerners. He also announced on June 17 that he would vote to let the people of the States formed out of the New Mexico-Utah Territories present their constitutions to Congress with or without slavery, as they might see fit to decide. The Toombs-Stephens group coöperated valiantly in the House, blocking all efforts to carry Taylor's separate California bill to a vote. Vice-President Fillmore, a cordial hater of Seward, threw all his influence upon Clay's side. Very early in July he called on Taylor at the White House to explain his stand. "I said to him in substance," he subsequently related, "that, from present appearances, I might be called upon to give a casting vote in the Senate on the Compromise Bill, and if I should feel it my duty to vote for it, as I might, I wished him to understand that it was not out of any hostility to him or his Administration, but the vote would be given because I deemed it for the best interests of the country."

Yet still the outlook remained dubious. Clay, returning to the Senate on July 2 after a short retirement to the country for his health, began to lay plans for strengthening his forces. Since his following among the Northern Whigs was so slender, he felt free—so it was said—to make new concessions to the South in return for some much-needed votes. On July 6, he laughingly remarked that he hoped to get a decision by Christmas. [17]

[II]

At this tense moment, with victory or defeat trembling in the balance, a double crisis invested the White House with clouds of midnight blackness, charged with lurid thunderbolts; and in one of the most dramatic denouements in American history, death placed the control of the government in entirely new hands.

It is seldom that a President has abruptly remade his Cabinet; but that was

16 Poage, op. cit., 228ff. Webster to Fletcher Webster, June, 1850; Everett Papers. Cong. Globe, 31st Cong., 1st sess., June 15, 1850, p. 1216.
17 Cong. Globe, 31st Cong., 1st sess., May 14, June 10–18, 29, 1850. Severance, Fillmore Papers, II, 323. Poage, op. cit., 239.

what Taylor had now determined to do. A dilating scandal, that over the so-called Galphin Claim, seemed to leave him no other choice. This hoary claim dated back to colonial times. In the days of George III certain debts had been due from Creek and Cherokee Indians to George Galphin and other frontier traders, and a treaty of 1773 between these tribes and the British crown provided that Galphin should be paid out of the sale of lands ceded to the crown by the savages. The authorities in Georgia fixed the amount of the debt at £9,791/15, equivalent in the subsequent money of the United States to $43,-518.97. After this adjustment, but before payment was made, the Revolution broke out. Galphin supported the cause of independence. Various committees of the Georgia legislature at different times reported in favor of the validity of his demands; but nothing was done by the State to satisfy them, chiefly on the ground that the United States had succeeded to all the rights and consequently to all the obligations of the British crown in the matter. Finally, Congress itself took this view. By an act of 1848, it directed the Secretary of the Treasury to adjust the claim and to pay the amount due to Milledge Galphin, executor of the estate of George Galphin. Secretary Robert J. Walker decided in favor of paying the principal, and did so, but was uncertain whether interest should be added. His term being about to expire, he prudently left the matter to his successors.

The attorney for the Galphin claimants was George W. Crawford, who was to receive half share for his services; and when Taylor appointed him Secretary of War, he remained attorney and expectant sharer. If the Secretary of the Treasury decided against paying interest, he would have to content himself with less than $22,000. If interest were granted, he would get nearly $100,000! Crawford had sufficient grace to hesitate over the propriety of continuing as attorney, but weakly let himself be persuaded by friends that he would be guilty of no indelicacy; they arguing that the case would not come before the Cabinet, being expressly referred to the Secretary of the Treasury. The demand for interest was vigorously pressed. Secretary Meredith submitted the claim to the comptoller, a shrewd and experienced man, who disallowed it. The question was then put to Reverdy Johnson, the Attorney-General, who decided that the interest must be paid. Thereupon Meredith made out an order for $191,352.89, of which, after payment of a small fee to the attorney of record, Secretary Crawford received one-half.

Inevitably, a blazing light was turned upon this transaction. For one reason, many thought it preposterous that such an antique and worm-eaten claim, dating back to British suzerainty, should be allowed at all. For another, it was hard to believe that Meredith and Reverdy Johnson were totally ignorant of the fact that their decision would give a fellow Cabinet-member a handsome fortune.

The overriding of the comptroller looked suspicious. The Washington *Union*, after some preliminary mutterings, on March 30, 1850, broke forth in a tremendous peal of denunciation. Immediately the New York *Tribune* took up the attack. The New York *Express*, a Whig organ, flatly charged that Meredith knew that Crawford had an interest in his verdict; "kissing goes by favor." An ousted officeholder, one Harriman, who complained that he had been ejected from a minor post because he disliked Taylor's policy, busily agitated the subject. He published numerous articles in the New York *Herald*, rained letters upon Democratic leaders, and campaigned for a committee of investigation. While the *National Intelligencer* defended the Cabinet, the *Herald* and *Express* in New York and the *Union* in Washington conducted a veritable crusade. Meanwhile, they and other newspapers hinted at still more shocking scandals. Secretary Ewing in particular came under fire, the press charging him with improper payment of several large claims, along with employment of several clerks without warrant of law; and Representative Richardson of Illinois asked for an investigation of these allegations.[18]

When the House investigating committee made a report, it proved a damaging document. The majority declared they found no evidence that Crawford had ever used his official position or social relationships to influence the decision upon the claim. They stated their belief that neither Secretary Meredith nor Attorney-General Johnson knew of Crawford's interest until after the matter had been settled. But the committee nevertheless reached some severe conclusions. It found, by a vote of five to four, that the Galphin Claim was not a just demand against the United States, and implied that Crawford and others had shoved it through Congress in suspicious fashion. It found, again five to four, that the act of Congress had authorized no interest payment and that such payment conformed with neither law nor precedent; Reverdy Johnson had made the wrong decision. Johnson and Meredith had denied knowing anything about Crawford's share in the claim. While this ignorance left their honor unstained, it reflected upon their vigilance, for if they had examined the papers with any

18 N. Y. *Tribune*, April 2, 1850. N. Y. *Express*, April 6, 1850. E. Harriman to Caleb Cushing, June 29, 1850; Cushing Papers. Washington *Union*, March 28, April 3–10, 27, 1850. J. J. Crittenden wrote Orlando Brown on April 13: "For the last two or three days we have been startled daily, with telegraphic intelligence that you were upon the eve of great changes in Washington—that there was to be an immediate dissolution and change of the Cabinet, etc., etc., etc. And all this, as I understand, because of the decision of the Secty. of the Treasury upon the Galphin claim, referred to him by act of Congress, and in which the Secty. of War, Mr. Crawford, had an interest long ago acquired. I don't know exactly what the decision, but I presume with entire confidence that it is *right*, and that Mr. Crawford's conduct in relation to the matter has been unimpeachable, as his life and character have always been . . ." Crittenden Papers. Winthrop wrote Kennedy: "Apropos of the Administration, the payment of $190,000 interest on that old Ante-Revolutionary claim under an opinion of Johnson's, and to a party for whom Crawford was agent (if true), is enough to finish what little is left of the present Cabinet." Kennedy Papers.

care, they would have seen that he was involved. Johnson in particular had looked them over with inexcusable haste. It appeared that Crawford had furnished the President an explanation of his connection with the claim, but an incomplete explanation. Clearly, the three Cabinet officers were open to the severest censure. Seward was quick to declare that the Administration could not maintain its character unless Crawford and Johnson—and preferably also Meredith—resigned. As a matter of fact, importing merchants in Eastern cities had for some time been attacking Meredith for his neglect of business, procrastination, and general ineptness.[19]

Old Zack soon came to share Seward's view. Painfully sensitive on all points of honesty, he was cut to the heart by the Galphin scandal. Carefully scrutinizing the papers, he concluded that the three men were compromised; chafed unhappily for several weeks; and then, despite his warm personal attachment for Meredith, decided upon a clean sweep. As it was best to wait until Congress had finished its regular work, and then call a special session of the Senate, at first there seemed no hurry. But to Thurlow Weed on July 3 he divulged his intention of asking everybody to resign and appointing a new Cabinet. Stanly of North Carolina would take over the War Department, Bell or Crittenden the Attorney-Generalship, and Hamilton Fish—so he tentatively agreed with Weed —the Treasury. He was intensely unhappy.[20]

Intensely unhappy for two reasons—for he was now up to his chin in a second terrible crisis, precipitated by New Mexico's application for statehood with boundaries which Texas regarded as a gross infringement upon her own domain. Texas cherished a historical claim to areas east of the Rio Grande which would place Albuquerque, Santa Fé, and Las Vegas within her limits; and Texas desperately wanted not only the land, but the Santa Fé trade, which would offer a rich field for taxation. Much too impetuously, Taylor had urged the New Mexican people, mainly Indians and Mexicans, to follow California's example, form a constitution, and ask for admission to the Union. The fact was that New Mexico had no population justifying statehood, and would not have

19 Washington *Union*, May 18, 1850. Bancroft, *Seward*, II, 130. That Meredith was a highly incompetent Secretary of the Treasury was affirmed by Hugh Maxwell of New York, in close touch with the merchants of that city. They complained that he left letters unanswered; deputed to clerks business that he should have given personal attention; and kept vessels detained at great expense awaiting his pleasure. Maxwell to Robert C. Schenck, July 28, 1850; Tom Corwin Papers.

20 Weed, *Autobiography*, 589–592. "The late Administration," wrote W. A. Graham of North Carolina a little later, after talking with many Washington leaders, "had lost favor with Whigs far beyond what I supposed when I came here, and had they continued, Conrad assures me, there would have been a breach with them, equal to that with Tyler. Clayton seems to have lost character for candor, in a most extraordinary degree, and he was the only man among them who was reputed to have talents, or capacity for affairs." W. A. Graham Papers, U. of N. C.

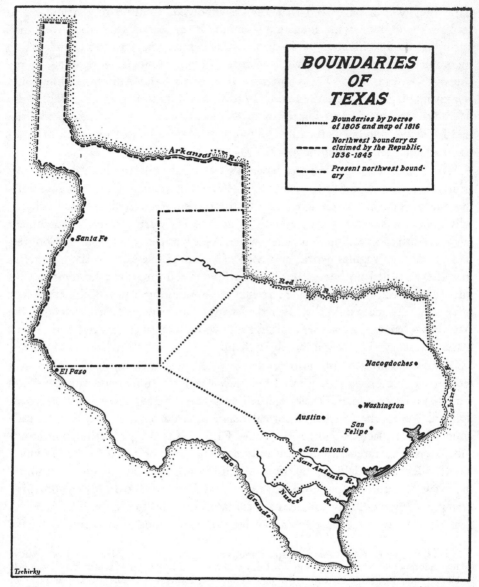

Texas was smallest as a frontier Mexican State. It grew largest when it laid claim to New Mexico east of the Rio Grande. Giving up this area and the lands north of 36° 30', it was paid enough to cancel all its public debts.

one for a long half century. But they took his advice. Colonel John Munroe, commanding the national forces in the area, had called a convention; it sat May 15–25, 1850, drawing up a constitution which excluded slavery; and within a month the people approved its work. It was Taylor's idea that once

New Mexico became a State, the boundary issue could be brought into the Supreme Court for settlement—and meanwhile, New Mexico should hold the Santa Fé district.

But this was not the idea of the Texans and their Southern supporters. In that region of Colts and Bowies, hard-riding cowboys and swaggering planters, two-cent beef and twenty-five-cent whiskey, nobody took orders. Early in the year the bold Texans asserted their control at El Paso and attempted to do so at Santa Fé. They sent a commissioner with full power to extend the civil jurisdiction over what the Texas legislature termed four "unorganized counties" lying in what is now New Mexico. Colonel Munroe quietly helped Santa Fé people thwart this bustling commissioner, who, faced with popular antagonism and military frigidity, returned home with an angry report to his governor. When this report was published, Texas began to buzz like a hornets' nest. Fighting was meat and drink to many people in that land where every settler had to be prepared to cope with rattlesnakes, longhorns, Mexican bandits, Indians, northers, floods, and what travellers called the most terrible diet in the country. Excitement reigned, mass meetings were held, secession was threatened, and demands were made for military action.

Governor Peter H. Bell had already asked the legislature to let him send to Santa Fé for a force large enough to execute Texas laws, saying that if any collision took place, it would be the fault of the United States. This was fire-eating with a vengeance. He now dispatched President Taylor a summary demand for an explanation of his course, and for a disavowal of Munroe's action. Preparing for preemptory measures, Bell called a special session of the legislature for August twelfth. As the news spread across the South, the radicals greeted it with indignant sympathy. Angry editorials blossomed in the "ultra" press, volunteer companies prepared to march to the aid of Texas, and Mississippi made a formal offer of assistance. Sam Houston was reported ready to hasten home from Washington to take command of another army of Texas conquerors.[21]

In Washington, meanwhile, President Taylor on June 17 electrified Congress by a special message on New Mexican affairs. He informed Congress of the Texas designs upon Santa Fé, and while denying that he had ordered forcible

---

21 No claim to Santa Fé or New Mexico, wrote Sam Houston later, "had ever been asserted or pretended, until after the battle of San Jacinto, when in my letter to General Rusk, I asserted our right to it." July 23, 1859; Houston Papers. W. H. H. Davis, *El Gringo*, 110–111. W. C. Binckley, "The Question of Texan Jurisdiction in New Mexico under the U. S., 1848–50," *Southwestern History Quarterly*, XXIV, 1–38. N. Y. *Tribune*, January 26, 1850, for Bell's message of December 26 asking authority (not granted) to send a force to Santa Fé. See Columbia *Telegraph*, August 12, 1850, for Bell's letter of June 14 to Taylor demanding an explanation of Munroe's actions, and Webster's reply. This, penned after Taylor's death, asserted that the late President had repeatedly declared "that he had no power to decide the question of boundary, and no desire to interfere with it, and that the authority to settle that question resides elsewhere."

resistance, declared his conviction that the Federal government should maintain possession until the boundary quarrel was adjudicated. Texas for its part was ready to use its "whole power and resources." The worst of it was that if fighting began between Federal troops and the bellicose Texans, many Southerners would flock to the Lone Star banner. On June 25 St. Louis dispatches informed Congress that the New Mexican constitution was on its way to Washington. Southern members at once began to hold caucusses. This new question had become hopelessly entangled with the general subject of the compromise. Southern radicals were against Taylor's New Mexico proposals as an outrage upon Texas; Southern moderates were against them because he seemed using them to block the omnibus bill! Both opposed Taylor's course, and it was hard to say which felt the more bitterly.[22]

Indeed, Southern advocates of the omnibus scheme were now on the point of a general revolt against the Administration. "Taylor's plan" had been bad enough; his New Mexico policy was the last straw. On July 1, therefore, the Southern Whig members of Congress, at a secret meeting, appointed three men, Robert Toombs, Humphrey Marshall, and C. M. Conrad, to wait on the President and warn him that if he persisted in his recalcitrance, they would be driven to the most hostile measures. They called at the White House separately. Toombs, taking Stephens with him, had his interview on July 3. That morning the *National Intelligencer* had carried a dispatch stating that the forces of the United States and of Texas seemed about to begin shooting in New Mexico. Toombs and Stephens doubtless knew of a scene that had just occurred between the President and their fellow-Georgian the Secretary of War. Taylor had told the Secretary, Crawford, that he wished Colonel Munroe ordered to resist by force any attempt by Texas to exercise sovereignty on the disputed area. Crawford, horrified at the idea of bloodshed, first expostulated with Taylor and then declared that he would never sign such an order. "Then," coolly remarked the President, "I will sign it myself." [23]

At any rate, it was a tensely exciting colloquy that now took place. Toombs and Stephens delivered their ultimatum. Taylor refused to budge an inch. California must come in at once, he said. As soon as the constitution of New Mexico reached him, he would insist on her admission as well. He scoffed at the idea that Texas had any valid claim to the upper Rio Grande valley. No doubt he spoke from a conviction of duty; but he also had some sense of party expediency, for he remarked that if he had to sacrifice one wing of Whiggism for the other, he could not give up the eighty-four members from the North for the twenty-nine members from the South. He was clearly immovable, and Toombs and Stephens strode away in high temper. That day Stephens sat down

22 R. N. Richardson, *Texas*, 181.
23 J. F. H. Claiborne, *Quitman*, II, 33; Phillips, *Toombs*, 83–84.

to pen an open letter to the *National Intelligencer*, whose editorials on the New Mexican situation had exasperated him. "The first federal gun that shall be fired against the people of Texas, without the authority of law," he wrote, "will be the signal for the freemen from the Delaware to the Rio Grande to rally to the rescue." He and Toombs went to see the Secretary of the Navy. They found Preston in front of the Treasury, and a long talk ensued.

"If troops are ordered to Santa Fé," exploded Stephens, "the President will be impeached." "Who will impeach him?" demanded Preston. "I will if nobody else does," rejoined Stephens—and indeed, Ritchie's *Union* was already demanding impeachment.[24]

The Southern defiance would have been met, had not fate intervened, by a still grimmer defiance from the President. Senator Hannibal Hamlin had been waiting outside the President's door when Toombs and Stephens excitedly burst from it. Entering, he found General Taylor in a state of ill-controlled passion. He looked, said Hamlin later, like an enraged lion in his cage, and he paced the room three or four times before he noticed Hamlin's presence. Still striding up and down, he asked what position Hamlin was taking on the omnibus bill. "I am doing what I can to defeat it," rejoined Hamlin. "Stand firm!" exclaimed Taylor. "Don't yield; it means disunion, and I am pained to learn that we have disunion men to contend with; disunion is treason."

Hamlin had no sooner left than Thurlow Weed arrived, to be equally struck by the President's agitation. "Did you meet those traitors?" Taylor demanded, with an oath plainly applied to Toombs and Stephens. He then described what had passed between him and the Southern Whig leaders. When he had stated that he would approve any constitutional bill that Congress might pass, and would execute the laws, they had threatened a dissolution of the Union. "I told them," he said in effect, "that if it becomes necessary I will take command of the army myself to enforce the laws. And I said that if you men are taken in rebellion against the Union, I will hang you with less reluctance than I hanged spies and deserters in Mexico!"

An admirable utterance—if it had been delivered in a better cause. The men Taylor was denouncing were not disunionists, but advocates of a comprehensive plan of compromise to preserve the Union. These Southern Whigs were anxious to prevent disunion by carrying the Clay proposals and taking measures to avoid an unnecessary clash between national troops and Texan volunteers. If Weed's report is correct, Taylor was singularly confused as to the situation. For, according to the editor, he said that he had come to Washington with Southern sympathies; that he had now satisfied himself that the purposes of the South were intolerant and revolutionary; and that he regarded

24 Claiborne, *idem*, *National Intelligencer*, July 4, 1850, for Toombs' letter. M. L. Avary (ed.), *The Recollections of Alexander H. Stephens*, 26.

Davis as the chief conspirator in the scheme which Toombs, Clingman, and Stephens had enunciated. But what were the realities? Davis was a Democrat, Toombs and Stephens were Whigs; Davis vehemently opposed Clay's plan, Toombs and Stephens warmly advocated it; Davis contemplated disunion without pain, Toombs and Stephens with horror. Stubbornly pursuing his own policy, Taylor was failing to view the situation in its larger perspective.

The situation was approaching its crisis, for Taylor was preparing to place before the country an obstinate definition of his position. The morning of the Fourth found on his desk an unfinished message, urging Congress to admit both California and New Mexico, and asserting that he would never permit Texas to seize any part of New Mexico's rightful area. Nearly twenty years earlier, South Carolina had adopted an ordinance of nullification and Jackson had then issued a proclamation denying any right of a State to such interference with Federal laws and courts. For weal or woe, Taylor was prepared to follow Jackson's general line of action.

The press later contained a variety of reports concerning this unfinished message. Some accounts credited Clayton with writing most of it; others Ewing. All agreed that these two men favored it, while Crawford and Preston, as Southerners, were opposed. It seems probable that Senator Bell of Tennessee was consulted and gave his approval. Ritchie must have surmised its nature when he gave warning in the *Union* of July 3 that the slumbering volcano was about to burst into eruption. "The Union is in danger—imminent danger," he wrote. "It is our duty to sound the tocsin." The message fully maintained the right of New Mexico to protection from Texas, and avowed the determination of the President to furnish it to the last extremity. It was to be sent to Congress after Independence Day, and the Cabinet reorganization was to take place forthwith. But the paper was never finished.[25]

[III]

Union-loving people of Washington had resolved to mark the Fourth by an especially impressive ceremony. Henry S. Foote, as a Southerner of staunch loyalty, was selected to deliver an oration at the base of the unfinished Washington monument. A throng gathered to hear his conciliatory address, exhorting all sections to dwell together in harmony.

25 Washington *Union*, July 23, 1850, summarizing reports of this supposed last message. Benton thought that Clayton was the prospective author, for he shortly wrote that gentleman asking for "the purport of that message which you were to draw the Sunday before General Taylor's death." Later he wrote Clayton that he had read in a newspaper that W. M. Meredith had the original manuscript of this "very strong message." He wished to notice the episode in his *Thirty Years*—but he never did. Benton to Clayton, December 8, 1850, August 23, 1852; Clayton Papers. For the colloquies of Taylor and Clayton, and Taylor and Weed, with respect to Toombs and Stephens, see Thurlow Weed Barnes, *Memoir of Thurlow Weed*, 176–181; Wilson, *Rise and Fall of the Slave Power*, II, 259, 260.

"As soon as the oration was brought to a close," Foote relates, "General Taylor and his Cabinet left the well-shaded platform upon which they had been seated, and prepared to return to the presidential mansion." Had they done so, the President might have suffered no ill effects from the burning heat. But a handful of dust from the tomb of Kosciusko was to be deposited in the monument; the President was besought to stay; and he consented, standing for more than an hour under the direct rays of the sun while George Washington Parke Custis and others spoke. He returned to the White House exhausted, drank copiously of iced water and milk, ate some cherries, and was soon prostrated by cholera morbus. Washington, always unhealthful in summer, seemed specially so this year. This attack resembled the one which, recalling a wartime ailment, he had suffered in Pennsylvania. Now sixty-five, he was in poor physical condition. His system had suffered from army hardships, while he had found the confinement of the White House irksome and its cares depressing. The excitement growing out of the Galphin scandal, the Texas threats, the plea of Toombs and Stephens, and the Cabinet quarrel over his message, with the demand of the *Union* for his impeachment, had all caused him great anguish. Thurlow Weed's quick eye had noted on the third that he was "feverish," and Weed had implored his secretary to see that he got rest.[26]

Typhoid fever quickly supervened. The news from the bedside was at first alarming, then so reassuring that the capital burst into a celebration of ringing bells and blazing bonfires, and then gloomy again. Taylor, realizing that his hours were numbered, uttered some sentences betraying the anguish inflicted on him by recent attacks. "God knows that I have endeavored to fulfill what I considered my honest duty," he told his physician. "But I have been mistaken. My motives have been misconstrued and my feelings grossly outraged." The Fourth had fallen on Thursday; on Sunday Taylor predicted that he would be dead in two days; and early on Tuesday the ninth, he told his physicians, "You have fought a good fight, but you cannot make a stand." Later that day he died. The end had been expected throughout the afternoon, and at about half-past ten at night was announced by a general tolling of bells.[27]

The whole city was hung in black. When the funeral was held in the East Room, with President Fillmore standing at the foot of the bier, and when a

26 *Autobiography of Thurlow Weed*, 591, 592. Boston *Post*, July 15, 1850. An epidemic of cholera morbus, which some thought a mild form of cholera itself, was abroad this year. George W. Julian, wandering down Pennsylvania Avenue one night early in July in search of a little air, was startled by the sight of a row of hideous-looking metallic coffins leaning against the wall of a building opposite Gadsby's Hotel. The sign "Undertakers" explained the matter; the coffins had been bought to make a profit from the sickly season. "What an exhibition of hardware!" he wrote his wife. July 9, 1850; G. W. Julian Papers.

27 "Reminiscences of Washington," *Atlantic Monthly*, February, 1881. Rhodes, *History of the United States*, I, 177. Joshua Giddings tersely described the funeral: "There was talking and drinking and any amount of fighting. This latter amusement I thought quite natural for you know that old Zac was a great fighter." July 14, 1850; G. W. Julian Papers.

two-mile procession, in which "Old Whitey" was conspicuous, accompanied the body to the Congressional Cemetery, the country indulged in a deep and sincere expression of sorrow. That Taylor was a statesman nobody believed. But as a soldier and citizen he had impressed the public by his integrity, honesty, and unbending courage. Moreover, many at first felt that his death at the height of the crisis was a disaster; that with civil war threatening, nobody else could do so much to control the passions of the South. "You cannot imagine the shock," John P. Kennedy wrote from Washington to his wife. "Everybody is dismayed—doubtful of what is to come." Seward, who had special reason to feel stricken, declared that "I never saw such grief—public grief, so universal and profound." All Whigs were staggered, and the radical freesoilers were inconsolable. But the South, inimical to Taylor's measures, and those moderate groups of the commercial cities, the border States, and the Northwest who supported Clay's plan, were less lugubrious.[28]

The fact was that, estimable as Taylor's common sense, practicality, and resolution had been, they fell short of supplying the qualities needed for so grave a crisis. Like more than one President who had died in office, he was happy in his hour of exit. What the country needed was not the minatory message lying on his desk, but a calming hand. Even those who thought best of him, like Edward Everett, recognized that his Administration had been fumbling and confused, and his Cabinet ineffective. No secretary had even average popularity, wrote Everett, and the Cabinet as a whole was a perfect non-conductor between the President and the country. He might have spoken in more comprehensive terms. Taylor no less than Clayton, Meredith, and the rest had lacked political acumen, and President and secretaries alike had inspired no sense of high wisdom or deep insight.[29]

Had Taylor lived, his defiant message on the dispute with Texas would have gone to Congress. He would have remade his Cabinet with a decided Northern preponderance. He would doubtless have pushed his quarrel with Toombs, Stephens, and other Southern Whigs to an irreparable party schism. Conflict in the Southwest, coupled with a general Southern revolt against the naked California and New Mexico bills, would have given the country stormy months and perhaps bloody scenes. It may be said that a stern Jacksonian policy in 1850 would perhaps have cowed the secessionists into submission, and thus possibly have averted the civil war which came a decade later. But this seems so unlikely that we may well rejoice that death intervened; that the clash of two civilizations was postponed until the North was relatively much stronger, and a far wiser leader sat in the White House.

28 Kennedy to his wife, July 8, 1850, also July 10, 11; Kennedy Papers. F. Seward, *Seward at Washington* . . . , II, 144. Washington *Union*, July 10, 1850.
29 Everett to Webster, July 16, 1850; Everett Papers.

[IV]

Millard Fillmore, who so unexpectedly took the helm, was a man of dignified bearing, suave manners, conciliatory temper, and limited powers of mind. The son of a poor farmer, he was largely self-educated and self-made. Indeed, it would be difficult to find a more poignant document than his fragmentary account of his early years as a friendless, ill-clad, ill-fed lad in upper New York, apprenticed to toil in succession for two carders and cloth-dressers, both harsh, driving men. He was seventeen before he saw any books beyond a few elementary texts. He then naturally found that he stumbled over unknown words, and bought a cheap dictionary. "While attending the carding machines, I used to place the dictionary on the desk—by which I passed every two minutes in feeding the machine and removing the rolls—and in this way I could have a moment in which to look at a word and read its definition and could then fix it in my memory." A kindly Quaker judge of western New York helped him obtain a legal education. He removed to Buffalo, gained the reputation of a hardworking, safe, efficient lawyer, and completed three terms in the legislature.[30]

Everybody, and especially fellow Whigs, had found this modest, self-made man prudent and trustworthy. As early as 1836, according to the Buffalo *Commercial Advertiser*, people would remark: "Fillmore says it's right; we'll go it." His party saw to it that he spent eight years in Congress. Here he was generally an inconspicuous member, attracting attention chiefly by his conscientious industry, strong freesoil convictions, and support of J. Q. Adams' battle for the right of petition. He did become chairman of the ways and means committee, and was prominent in framing the tariff of 1842. But his speeches were dull, his outlook upon public affairs showed occasional naïveté, and his caution made him seem uncertain. Now in 1850 men found the new President "as calm, as diffident and pretensionless" as before his sudden elevation. Seward caustically remarked: "Providence has at last led the man of hesitations and double opinions where decision and singleness are indispensable." [31]

But on one point his mind was made up. When he had informed Taylor that in the event of a tie on the compromise he would vote in its favor, he had announced an irrevocable decision. Within forty-eight hours after Taylor's death, Webster was rejoicing over the turn of events: "I believe Mr. Fillmore favors the compromise, and there is no doubt that recent events have increased the probability of the passage of that measure." Strange are the chances of politics! Two years earlier Southerners had looked upon Taylor with con-

---

30 F. H. Severance, *Fillmore Papers*, I, 3-15.
31 F. Seward, *Seward*, II, 145. Severance, *op. cit.*, I, XI. Kennedy to his wife, July 12, 1850; Kennedy Papers. Weed, *Autobiography*, 585. Stephens, *War between the States*, II, 198.

fidence and Fillmore with deep suspicion, for they recalled that the latter had acted in Congress with such extremists as Joshua Giddings and John P. Hale. Thurlow Weed had regarded Fillmore as much more aggressive upon the slavery question than Seward or himself. Yet Taylor had been ready to make war against the South, and Fillmore came now tendering it an olive branch! [32]

The Cabinet could at once be remade without private heartburning or party friction. Crawford, Reverdy Johnson, and others were only too glad to get out without humiliation. Fillmore chose a much stronger group than the departing members. For Secretary of State he hesitated between Webster and Robert C. Winthrop. But Winthrop, hearing of the matter, sensibly went to the President, and telling him that he lacked health and strength for the post, insisted that Webster be named. The orator, after waiting until his friends secretly made up a subscription of $20,000 to repay him for his pecuniary sacrifice, accepted the place with alacrity. Beyond question his elevation gave him a sense of triumph over those Whig enemies who had denounced his Seventh of March speech. The attorney-generalship went to Clay's oldtime Achates, the sagacious and conservative Crittenden. The nimble-minded, oaken-hearted Tom Corwin became head of the Treasury, while Fillmore made his law-partner, Nathan Hall, postmaster-general. Three Southerners were chosen to direct the departments of war, the navy, and the interior: Charles M. Conrad of Louisiana, William A. Graham of North Carolina, and Alexander H. H. Stuart of Virginia. The President had taken the advice, among others, of Toombs and Stephens. When the Cabinet met, Fillmore at the head of the table loomed up as the most impressive figure: moderately tall, stalwart and portly in form, with high forehead, strong features, and shrewd gray eyes sparkling in a florid countenance. But Daniel Webster was clearly the dominating spirit.[33]

Seward had of course been ignored, and his chagrin and mortification in being so abruptly hurled from power were intense. His course was not magnanimous. He was scowlingly taciturn. His political partner Weed muttered threats of fierce battles to come unless Fillmore demonstrated his independence

32 Webster, *Private Correspondence*, II, 376, July 11, 1850; Weed, *Autobiography*, 587, 588.
33 Winthrop to Everett, July 19, 1850; Everett Papers. To Kennedy, July 17, 1850, Kennedy Papers: "I am not Secretary of State, nor shall I be. I took so great an alarm, however, that such an honor might fall upon me (and not without reason), that I made a special business of seeing the President today and settling matters *against myself*. I think I have done this conclusively and I have great faith that Webster will have the place before the week is out. I do not know exactly who will be his compeers. I should not be surprised, however, if Dayton were to have a place, and Crittenden, and Graham of North Carolina. Perhaps Corwin will have one also, if he will take it. But I think that nothing will be known certainly until the Compromise Bill is brought to a decision in the Senate . . ." See Fuess, *Daniel Webster*, II, 248, on financial assistance given Webster, and *Recollections of A. H. Stephens*, ed. Avary, 27, on consultations with Fillmore.

of Clay and Webster, and the Albany *Evening Journal* predicted factional strife and crippling schisms. This, Francis Granger resentfully informed Fillmore, was sheer blackmail; Seward and Weed were announcing that if they were not placated, they would raise a mutiny. Nor were the threats entirely empty. Irritated and despondent, Seward quickly concluded that he could do nothing with Fillmore, that he had no immediate future except in the opposition ranks, and that he must find an opposition issue as quickly as possible. It was necessary, he growled to Weed late in July, to arouse the people with a fresh topic of agitation, and "I shall endeavor to make a new one on the admission of New Mexico." In Boston, the *Atlas* adopted the same tone as Weed's paper. The consternation and disappointment of the radical anti-slavery group of Massachusetts over the sudden turn of affairs were so great that the British consul in Boston, Edmund A. Grattan, made a special report to his legation in Washington on the subject.[34]

Equal chagrin and resentment reigned among the Bobadils of the South. The new Cabinet contained only a minority of Southerners; it presaged the speedy adoption of the Compromise. Deep groans and fierce snorts of anger came from such Southern journals as the Columbia *Telegraph*. Crittenden was fond of singing canticles to the Union, it lamented, and Graham was as bad. "Freesoil sits at the Treasury door; Southern soil has not a single champion, known as such." [35]

[V]

In a final Senate speech on July 17, Webster delivered a ringing appeal for the omnibus bill, or at least for the piecemeal passage of its various measures; and his immediate appointment to the Cabinet made it clear that the compromise was now an Administration measure. Webster declared that the Texas boundary was far too pressing a question to be left unsettled. The peace-loving, conservative Fillmore was of the same opinion. Now that pressure from Taylor and the old Cabinet was removed, many Northern Whigs in Congress—not a little alarmed by the grim threat of civil war which had sprung up early in July—could vote for the compromise. It was clear that the unnatural alliance of radical freesoilers with radical slavery men, of Sewardites and Calhounites, now faced a final defeat. Late in the month Seward introduced an amendment to the omnibus bill providing for the admission of New Mexico under her freesoil constitution. It met the opposition of all the Democrats and all

34 Granger to Fillmore, July 16, 1850; Fillmore Papers. Seward to Weed, July 28, 1850; Weed Papers. Grattan to Bulwer Lytton, July 20, 1850; Bulwer Lytton Papers, Duke University. Fillmore's friends gave vigor to an Administration paper in Albany, the *Register*. See Harry J. Carman and Reinhard H. Luthin, "The Seward-Fillmore Feud and the Crisis of 1850," *New York History, XXIV*, 163–184.
35 Washington correspondent of Columbia *Telegraph*, July 25, 1850.

the Fillmore Whigs. In debate it was scornfully ridiculed. Pratt of Maryland called it "the most extraordinary proposition ever submitted to this body," and proposed that the Senate should expel Seward for his higher-law doctrine. The final vote on the amendment was 42 to 1, Seward standing against a solid chamber. Yet this "extraordinary proposition," so contemptuously overwhelmed, was precisely the measure which President Taylor had been contemplating! [36]

The Senate debate on the omnibus bill continued throughout July, and like the weather grew constantly hotter. Butler of South Carolina and Benton of Missouri delivered the two most striking arraignments of the bill. Webster, in his last set speech before entering the Cabinet, joined with a moving appeal to love of the Union a skillful reminder that great business interests were suffering from the deadlock. Pass the bill; get rid of these gorgons, hydras, and chimaeras dire; get back to essential objects of legislation—such was his plea. "Men must live—to live they must work—to work they must be protected in their employment"; businessmen and the laboring community were anxious for action. This gave Horace Mann an opportunity to accuse Webster of appealing to Mammon, and of allying Northern pecuniary interest with Southern slavery; but the argument was essentially sound, and it was effective. That same day Clay gave notice that he wished to be heard in one last rebuttal of the arguments employed against the measure. On July twenty-second he rose to free his breast in a characteristically rambling and disjointed but passionately eloquent address, bad in structure, but truly magnificent in the glow and sparkle of some of its parts. Never had he spoken with greater immediate effect. The crowded chamber was at times exalted to a high pitch of excitement; at times rocking with mirth; at times hushed to an oppressive silence. One retort at Mason drew such a storm of applause from the galleries that the president came near ordering them cleared.

At one point Clay stormed at the Southern disunionists, and ridiculed Rhett's bombastic Charleston defiances. At another point he turned scornfully upon the abolitionists. "They live by agitation. It is their meat, their bread, the air which they breathe." If they saw any measure certain to quiet agitation, would they not oppose it? Would they not *hail* (and he darted a fiery glance at Hale) any measure which increased the agitation? He thanked President Taylor for giving the omnibus bill its appellation. "The omnibus is the vehicle of the people, of the mass of the people." He pointed to the overwhelming peril of a general civil war if the Southwestern boundaries were not settled. "Let blood be once spilled in the conflict between the troops of Texas and those of the United States, and, my word for it, thousands of gallant men will fly from the

36 *Cong. Globe*, 31st Cong., 1st sess., Appendix, 1444; July 25, 1850.

States which I have enumerated [Arkansas, Mississippi, Louisiana, and Alabama], if not from all the slaveholding States, to sustain and succor the power of Texas . . ." He pointed out to the South how much it gained from the compromise. It got nine hundred miles of the best part of the country bordering upon the Rio Grande; it got the abandonment of the agitation over slavery in the District of Columbia. Of the North he asked what real sacrifices it made. The fugitive slave law? That was a constitutional obligation. The Wilmot proviso? It was almost certain that the character and climate of the Southwestern country dedicated every mile of it to free soil.

The great body of the American people, said Clay, ardently desired the passage of the Compromise. Agitators and difficulty-makers declared that the current discontents would persist. To such men he recalled the history of compromise in 1820. "Then, as now, it was denounced. Then, as now, when it was approaching its passage, when being perfected, it was said, 'It will not quell the storm nor give peace to the country.' How was it received when it passed? The bells rang, the cannons were fired, and every demonstration of joy throughout the whole land was made"—with long years of tranquility, harmony, and prosperity to follow. In 1850 the question was peace or war:

Mr. President, what is an individual man? An atom, almost invisible without a magnifying glass—a mere speck upon the surface of the immense universe—not a second in time, compared to immeasurable, never-beginning and never-ending eternity; a drop of water in the great deep, which evaporates and is borne off by the winds; a grain of sand, which is soon gathered to the dust from which it sprung. Shall a being so small, so petty, so fleeting, so evanescent, oppose itself to onward march of a great nation, to subsist for ages and ages to come . . . ? Forbid it God!

When the speech ended, Senator Barnwell, the successor of Calhoun, presumed to rise with a squeal of complaint regarding Clay's reference to Rhett. The orator pounced upon him like an eagle on a fieldmouse. He had said nothing as to the character of Rhett, for whom he had some respect. "But, if he pronounced the sentiment attributed to him of raising the standard of disunion and of resistance to the common government, whatever he has been, if he follows up that declaration by corresponding overt acts"—and Clay's voice rose to thunder—"he will be a traitor, and I hope he will meet the fate of a traitor." The galleries broke into tumultuous applause.

Clay was correct when he said that a clear majority of the Senate was in favor of all the compromise measures in detail; and it would have been a great saving of time and temper if the omnibus bill had passed intact at the beginning of August. But for different reasons different groups opposed this conglomerate. The compromise was stronger in its parts than as a whole. The chief reason was

that numerous Senators, especially at the North, wished to escape the imputation of bargaining—the charge of having sold certain rights of their own
section for concessions from the other. They were ready to accept the fact of
the bargain, but they desired to avoid the form. Men who were disposed to
vote for each of Clay's bills separately, but who would not accept them as a
bundle of fasces, united with out-and-out enemies of the compromise in pushing a series of amendments. Even so, a good chance for passage of the omnibus
bill remained. The last days of July were occupied by much maneuvering,
counter-maneuvering, and counting of noses. On the 27th it was thought that
the bill would pass by a single vote; on the 29th a motion to lay it on the table
was defeated 32 to 25, and Clay believed the battle won.[37]

Yet a fell concatenation of errors, mischances, and opposition hammering
resulted, after an all-day struggle on the thirty-first, in the decisive defeat of
the omnibus bill. The confused details of the battle, which raged about a series
of amendments, centering finally upon the Texas-New Mexico boundary, need
not be rehearsed. At the critical moment James A. Pearce, a quiet, scholarly
country lawyer serving as Whig Senator from Maryland, either deliberately
or stupidly let the bill be maneuvered into a parliamentary corner where it
could be killed. All its sections were stricken out except a provision for the
organization of Utah Territory. Jubilant over their unexpected victory, the
motley opponents of the omnibus gave way to a carnival of joy. John P. Hale,
wrote a reporter for the New York *Express*, could scarcely contain himself.
"Jefferson Davis' face grinned with smiles. Old Bullion's few hairs actually
bristled with delight. *He* had routed *Clay! He* had smashed his Omnibus to
atoms! Seward was dancing about like a little top. Dayton shook his thick
sides with sporadic spasms. Clemens reminded one of a New York B'hoy in an
assembly of admiring G'hals; Yulee looked solemn in solitary glory. Barnwell's
spectacles twinkled, and Butler's gray hairs flourished more than ever. Chase
was shaking hands with Soulé the Frenchman." On the other side, Cass looked
unhappy, Winthrop (who had succeeded to Webster's seat and was champion-
ing the compromise) was a picture of dejection, Foote gave himself up to
despair, and Clay sat "melancholy as Caius Marius over the ruins of Carthage." [38]

But the component parts of the omnibus could be salvaged, and its friends
immediately addressed themselves to the task.

37 Poage, *Henry Clay and the Whig Party*, 244–258; Glyndon G. Van Deusen, *Henry
Clay;* Fuess, *Webster*, II, 236–238; Nathan Sargent, *Public Men and Events*, II, 366–368.
Clay's great final speech is in *Cong. Globe*, 31st Cong., 1st sess., Appendix, 1405–1415. Rhett
in a Charleston speech on July 21 had in effect declared for secession.
38 N. Y. *Express*, August 2, 1850, quoted in Poage, *op. cit.*, 257.

[VI]

On the following day, August 1, after some painful recriminations between Clay and Pearce, the Utah bill or "Mormon mutilation" passed without a roll-call. It was understood that the bill admitting California, and a bill fixing the western boundary of Texas and paying that State ten millions for relinquishing most of the disputed area, would both shortly be enacted.

Indeed, Douglas as chairman of the committee on Territories instantly forced the fighting. He had never fully committed himself to the omnibus bill, doubtless with a view to reserving his strength for the separate items. Now he boldly took the leadership. As Winthrop wrote Everett on August 1, the California bill precipitated a stormy debate on slavery and disunion. "Clay has come out more nobly than ever, and has evidently proved that his courage is of the sort that mounts with the occasion." [39] But as the exhausted Clay shortly left to recuperate at Newport, the brunt of the battle was thrown upon Douglas' shoulders. For some time the Senate devoted a part of each day's work to California, and a part to New Mexico. Since the Texas legislators, with fire in their eyes and six-shooters on their hips, were preparing to assemble in special session on the twelfth, no time was to be lost. "We are of but one determination, resist to the last," a representative citizen of northern Texas was writing.[40] Douglas and Pearce framed a new boundary bill, which it was said that Webster approved, and which fixed the Texas limits as they now stand, giving the State 33,333 more square miles than had originally been contemplated by the omnibus. The sum of ten million dollars was included, a goodly douceur—considering that the Texans had never made any settlements of consequence beyond the Nueces. On August 9 the boundary bill passed. Four days later the Senate voted the California bill. The New Mexico bill, with the aid of a special message from Fillmore, swiftly followed on August 14th, and the Fugitive Slave bill on the 19th.

All these measures met with an embittered last-ditch opposition. "Now," wailed Jefferson Davis as the hour struck for the vote on the California bill, "we are about permanently to destroy the balance of power between the sections of the Union, by securing a majority to one in both Houses of Congress." [41] The familiar coalition of Northern radicals and Southern extremists appeared again on repeated votes. Seward joined hands with Jefferson Davis, Chase with Mason, Hale with Atchison. Yet every measure passed by decisive majorities.

39 Winthrop to Everett, August 1, 1850; Everett Papers.
40 Wm. M. Williams, August 14, to T. J. Rusk; Rusk Papers. John H. Moffatt wrote Rusk from Austin the same day that reluctant as Texas was to strike a blow that would produce unhealable wounds, "she must and will have her rights"; *Ibid.*
41 *Cong. Globe*, 31st Cong., 1st sess., Appendix 1533, August 12, 1850.

The vote on the Texas boundary bill was 30 to 20, and that on the California bill 34 to 18. No fewer than six slave State Senators, to their everlasting credit, voted to admit California. On the New Mexico bill, the Fugitive Slave bill, and the bill abolishing slave-trade depots in the District of Columbia, the adverse vote was purely sectional. Ten Northerners voted against erecting New Mexico into a Territory; twelve Northerners, including Winthrop, voted against the Fugitive Slave bill, which had lost Webster's jury-trial amendment; and nineteen Southerners voted against the District of Columbia bill. Sectionalism, however, was now at a discount.

"The Administration," wrote Secretary Graham, "though quietly, has thrown its whole weight into the settlement of the difficulties . . ." Late August found the compromise forces jubilant after their long Arctic winter of anxiety, for the House was certain to approve the Senate's work. At a meeting of Cabinet members in Webster's cheery parlor on the night of August 24 to compare information, everyone concluded that the bills would pass without amendment and by handsome majorities. Clingman's obstructive faction in the House had dwindled to one-fifth. Corwin was helping to bring the Ohio delegation into line. Massachusetts had sent a compromise man, Samuel A. Eliot (former mayor of Boston, and father of Charles W. Eliot), to take Winthrop's seat in the House, and his strong convictions, tough mind, and weight of character had a happy influence upon New England members. As for the irreconcilable Massachusetts group in Congress, Webster was now quite contemptuous of them. When Winfield Scott, laboring for the compromise, came for advice, Webster told him not to bother about the most bigoted: "Damn John Davis, we'll whip him into hell! Don't trouble yourself about seeing him!" [42]

The House did act rapidly to ratify the Senate's action. Here again a hostile coalition of Northern and Southern extremists took shape, and once more the moderates of both sections overrode it. A little group of leaders—Linn Boyd, impassioned Jacksonian Unionist of Kentucky, Webster's friend George Ashmun, and Douglas' followers McClernand and Richardson—assisted Speaker Cobb in steering the measures to victory. No time was wasted. The initial debate on the combined New Mexico-Texas boundary bills lasted only a week, August twenty-eighth to September sixth. This was the test bill, and it passed easily. Sparks flew in a one-day clash over the Fugitive Slave bill. It also passed by a wide margin, 109 to 76; but numerous Northerners who did not wish to have to make explanations to their constituents absented themselves from the chamber. When the result was announced, Thaddeus Stevens remarked with rasping sarcasm: "I suggest that the Speaker should send a page to notify the members on our side of the House that the Fugitive Slave Bill has been disposed

42 Graham to his brother, August 25, 1850; William A. Graham Papers.

of, and that they may now come back into the hall." The California bill carried by a vote of more than three to one.[43]

Wild jubilation marked the closing scenes of the contest in Washington. On the day that the House passed the California and Utah bills, a general celebration began. Bonfires, processions, serenades, speeches, suppers, drinking, and cannon-salutes filled the next twenty-four hours. At nightfall the principal buildings were illuminated. Exhilarated crowds gathered, shouting, "The Union is saved!" Even the diehards showed good humor. One tipsy Southern radical paraded the National Hotel, saying he wanted to hear no more about Southern chivalry and honor, and asking every man to give him a kick, which he promised to pass around! On that glorious night word was circulated that it was the duty of every patriot to get drunk. So well was the injunction observed that next morning Foote, Douglas, and many others were prostrated, attributing their ailments to headaches, the heat, or over-indulgence in fruit. A great procession roared through the streets, visiting the residences of Webster, Douglas, Cobb, Linn Boyd, and others, and extracting a speech from each. Webster stepped out on the broad doorstep of his house, friends on each side holding candles and lending support, and began his speech: "Now is the summer—no! Now is the winter of our discontent made glorious summer by this sun of York!" He was sufficiently exalted to be in his best form.[44]

"One thing is certain," wrote a Washington observer to Buchanan, "that every face I meet is happy. All look upon the question as settled and no fears are felt in relation to the movements in either the South or North. I can scarcely realize that I am now surrounded and conversing with the same men I heard in warm and angry discussion but a few days ago. The successful are rejoicing, the neutrals have all joined the winning side, and the defeated are silent." [45]

In a triumphant note, Edward Everett congratulated Webster on the final week's work in Congress; probably as momentous a week, he wrote, as any in American political history. "You surely have a right more than anyone else to be congratulated, for it is mainly the consequence of your vision and courage. I trust the country will have the discernment and the gratitude to appreciate and recompense the service." One capable Illinois politician had written Douglas in midsummer that the work he was doing in this session placed his fame upon an enduring basis. "Your highest aspirations will soon be gratified." As the

43 Poage, *op. cit.*, 261, 262, on action in the House. Rhodes, *op. cit.*, I, 183, quotes Stephens (not in *Congressional Globe*). The Columbia *Telegraph*, September 16, quoted the Washington *Union*: "It is time that our countrymen of the North should command fanaticism to stand still, whilst the South should place more confidence in their countrymen in other sections . . ."
44 J. M. Foltz to Buchanan, September 8, 1850; Buchanan Papers. "Reminiscences of Washington," *Atlantic Monthly*, April, 1881. Newspapers, September, 1850.
45 J. M. Foltz, *Idem*.

last bills passed, a New York friend assured the Little Giant: "The way is open to you for high success."

Clay, meanwhile, had been given a series of Northern ovations. At Newport crowds gathered upon the beach to catch a glimpse as he went surf-bathing; he was tendered a formal reception by the Rhode Island legislature; and when he was espied taking a walk, a cheer ran along the street. The great cities, Baltimore, Philadelphia, New York, greeted him with throngs and applause. His return to the Senate on August 27, in good time to give special attention to the District of Columbia bill, brought a host of friends flocking about his seat.[46]

To four men, indeed, the principal responsibility for the enactment of the great compromise must be assigned: Clay, Webster, Fillmore, and Stephen A. Douglas. It was Clay who, when the situation was most gloomily chaotic, gave order and direction to events by his resolutions of January 29, and his speech explaining how they would safeguard the peace and harmony of the Union. It was his speeches, his persistence, his tact, which had kept the compromise alive amid a cohort of enemies. Webster had done far more than anybody else to win over those hesitant Northern elements which were really open to conversion, and by his display of courageous statesmanship had challenged Southern moderates to show an equal generosity. It was Douglas who had framed the provisions of three of the most important bills, who had most forcibly shown that by virtue of climate and geography the Southwestern areas must remain free soil, and who had assumed the captaincy in the Senate when heat and fatigue drove Clay to the seashore. "If any man has a right to be proud of the success of these measures," exclaimed Jefferson Davis, "it is the Senator from Illinois." And it was the influence of Fillmore and his Cabinet, energetically applied, which brought over enough Northern Whigs to make victory certain. No better tribute to Fillmore can be found than in the oft-quoted words of the chagrined Horace Mann: "Here are twenty, perhaps thirty, men from the North in this House, who, before General Taylor's death, would have sworn, like St. Paul, not to eat or drink until they had voted the proviso, who now, in the face of the world, turn about, defy the instructions of their States, take back their own declarations, a thousand times uttered, and vote against it." Chase estimated that Fillmore's first message in favor of the compromise had won six New England Senators to his side.[47]

46 Everett to Webster, September 13, 1850; Everett Papers. S. Breese to Douglas, July 25, and R. H. Gillett to Douglas, September 15, 1850; Douglas Papers.

47 Mann, *Life of Horace Mann,* 322, September 6, 1850; Chase, *Diary and Correspondence,* 217; G. D. Harmon, "Douglas and the Compromise of 1850," *Journal Illinois State Hist. Soc.,* XXI, 453–499. Davis' tribute to Douglas, September 16, is in *Cong. Globe,* 31st Cong., 1st sess., 1830.

But back of the four leaders marched a firm phalanx of other moderate and farsighted men, of whom Northern Democrats like Cass, and Southern Whigs like Stephens and Toombs, constituted the great majority. The courageous Foote of Mississippi must not be forgotten. And behind all these men stood a public sentiment, the weight and firmness of which no fairminded observer could doubt.

Great was the relief of the nation when the compromise became law, and great in particular the exultation of Clay and Webster. That the danger to the nation had been very real, that disunion might easily have been carried to civil conflict, was the sober opinion of both these men. It was the judgment also of two of the nation's most perspicacious editors, Thomas Ritchie and Thurlow Weed. Long afterward, Weed wrote that "the country had every appearance of being on the eve of a revolution"; and that the language and spirit of Southern radicals "were quite as violent and defiant as they were in 1860." Clay, who had at times despaired of victory, turned his face toward Ashland with deep thanksgiving. Webster, who said he had labored for months under a crushing weight of anxiety, journeyed north with the same emotions. "I can now sleep of nights," he wrote Peter Harvey. "We have now gone through the most important crisis that has occurred since the foundation of this government, and whatever party may prevail, hereafter, the Union stands firm. Disunion, and the love of mischief, are put under, at least for the present, and I hope for a long time." [48]

48 Webster to Harvey, October 2, 1850; Everett Papers. Weed, *Autobiography*, 596.

11

Southern Acquiescence—With Conditions

"THE FACE of everything seems changed," wrote Daniel Webster just after the critical House vote. "You would suppose nobody had ever thought of disunion. All say they always meant to stand by the Union to the last." Casting off the despondency that had reduced him to a few hours' sleep a night, the comfort-loving Secretary prepared to eat, drink, and grow fat as an alderman. For years he and Senator Daniel S. Dickinson, who had violently attacked his conduct as Tyler's Secretary of State, had not been on speaking terms; but now, with characteristic magnanimity, he sent the New Yorker a letter saying that "your noble, able, manly, and patriotic conduct" in support of the Compromise "has entirely won my heart and secured my highest regard." It was a letter which Dickinson was not merely to treasure, but in lithographed form to scatter far and wide. To all his friends Webster poured out his joy and relief. Like Clay, he had believed the country in dire peril. Taylor, he thought, would have liked to shoot it out with Texas; he had a soldier's foresight, and knew precisely what would happen if Texas militia marched out to fight United States regulars. What Taylor did not foresee was the possible result, in the existing excitement, if blood were shed in a contest between the national government and a Southern State. But all that was past, and Webster could happily quote Shakespeare, could describe how Samuel Eliot's election as Boston's Representative had helped turn the tide, could plan a trip for relief from heat and hay fever, and could think of New England chip fires, beefsteaks, and codfish chowders.[1]

[I]

The popularity of the Compromise was plainly demonstrated by the events following its passage. Clay's genial foresight was correct; what had happened in 1820 was repeated in 1850; even men previously captious accepted the *fait accompli* with satisfaction. Such an opponent as Greeley had to admit that the great majority in all sections rejoiced in the outcome. The *National Intelligencer* remarked that it could fill a double sheet of forty-eight columns with jubilant

1 Curtis, *Webster*, II, 472–484.

expressions from Southern and Western journals alone. The prosperity of the country and the optimism engendered by the Mexican War and California gold made a hearty acquiescence easy. Capitalists, businessmen, land speculators, railroad builders, farmers, planters, were all glad they could give singleminded attention to developing the nation's resources. Whether they had regarded the threat of civil war as grimly real, or as an insubstantial spectre invoked to frighten each side into mutual concessions, they were glad to see it banished. They had never believed that the slavery issue in far-off, thinly populated Territories justified such anger as would tear down the Union, destroy property wholesale, and consign the flower of the population to battle and death. The Compromise, overriding and rebuking the furious extremists, and imposing no burdens on the taxpayer, opened a magnificent vista of peaceful progress in agriculture, industry, and the arts.[2]

City after city, all over the country, held celebratory meetings. That in New York, called by a joint committee of conservative Whig and Democratic merchants, was more than celebratory; it was designed to encourage Seward's foes, stimulate both parties to endorse the Compromise, and reassure Southerners who were offended by the radical Northern clamor against the Fugitive Slave Act. The committee included such wealthy and influential men as Robert C. Wetmore, George Howland, Moses Taylor, W. H. Aspinwall, and E. K. Collins; ten thousand merchants and firms endorsed the meeting within a week; and the business response was so nearly unanimous that the *Tribune* and the *Evening Post* talked (with some reason) of the "Cotton Terror." A concourse packing Castle Garden on October 23, 1850, heard James W. Gerard denounce the abolitionists and declare that nature had written a proviso against slavery-extension stronger than ten thousand Wilmots could draw. One fruit of the meeting was a Union Safety Committee of a hundred prominent merchants, which for the next two years spent generously of time, energy, and money to bulwark the Compromise and foster a spirit of national unity—concentrating at the outset upon those rural districts where Sewardism was strong. Another result was the organized participation of a large body of merchants in the State election, supporting Horatio Seymour for governor against the Whig candidate Washington Hunt, who was feared to be a Seward man. Largely because of this participation, Hunt came within inches of defeat, running far behind the "safer" candidates. Upstate, countless Union demonstrations left the Seward-Weed faction stunned and apprehensive.[3]

2 Greeley, *American Conflict*, I, Ch. 16. *National Intelligencer*, September 17, 1850.

3 Foner, *Business and Slavery*, 40ff. "Proceedings of the Union Safety Meeting Held at Castle Garden October 23, 1850." At this meeting William M. Evarts wholeheartedly supported the Fugitive Slave Act: "Let us, then, be misled from the plain path of duty by no idle clamor, by no specious sophistry; let us know and feel that he who strikes at *a* law strikes at *the* law; that he who violates or avoids the obligation of one clause of the Constitution, is faithless to the great charter. . . ."

In Boston a meeting had as one spectator W. L. Marcy, who was deeply impressed. "It was a magnificent scene—a vast assemblage of the controlling minds of Massachusetts," he reported to Buchanan. "The voice there uttered was fervent and potential; it was the voice of patriotism and interest combined. The prosperity of New England would pass away along with the Union." In Philadelphia, six or seven thousand citizens met to hear speakers and a long letter from Buchanan. Indeed, enthusiastic assemblages took place all over the country. Franklin Pierce addressed one in Concord, New Hampshire; leading Whigs and Democrats spoke at those in the Middle West; and the border States from Maryland to Missouri were vocal. New Orleans had as vociferous a meeting as any city. The Kentucky legislature on November 15, after unanimously approving Clay's course, tendered him a public reception. It was one of the proudest events of his career, and perhaps its supreme moment. He spoke with such eloquence and feeling that even oldtime enemies were seen openly wiping their eyes.[4] But as good an illustration as any of the largely spontaneous wave of Union sentiment which rolled across the land was afforded by the gathering in New Haven the day before Christmas. For so small a city it had an extraordinary body of sponsors, about eighteen hundred citizens joining in the call. General Dennis Kimberly took the chair; speeches were made by Ralph I. Ingersoll, onetime Congressman and Polk's minister to Russia, and others; and the resolutions were passed for a Union Safety Committee like New York's. Emphasis was laid on the importance of enforcing the Fugitive Slave Act, and Judge E. K. Foster received wild applause for a statement that those who were too conscientious to submit to American law had better betake themselves to Canada.[5]

When Congress met for its short session in the winter of 1850–51, great good feeling was manifested between conservative elements of the two old parties. Webster had remarked that old animosities must necessarily be assuaged, and that he for one could no longer retain hostile feelings toward Cass, Shields, Rusk, and other Democratic Senators who had helped pass the Compromise. Union Democrats for their part went out of the way to praise the Administration

4 Marcy to Buchanan, December 19, 1850; Buchanan Papers. MS Diary of Dr. Jonathan M. Foltz, November 14, 1850. Poage, *Henry Clay and the Whig Party*, 267.
5 "Proceedings of the Union Meeting in Brewster's Hall, New Haven"; privately printed, Harvard Library. These Union meetings, Whigs joining hands with Democrats, did not please some sound party men. They feared that a new Union party might emerge; a conservative party, representing wealth and privilege, and entrenching itself in centers of property. The prominence of commercial leaders, merchants, bankers, and manufacturers in the movement gave some color to this apprehension, which Marcy shared. It gave Southern fire-eaters and Northern radicals a chance to say that these urban demonstrations came from groups who feared they would lose money; from men actuated by pocket interests, not by principle. Marcy to Buchanan, December 19, 1850; Cave Johnson to Buchanan, November 10, 1850; Buchanan Papers.

leaders, Cass extolling Webster's conduct of foreign relations, and Foote making a speech in Philadelphia which included a handsome compliment to Fillmore and his Cabinet. On New Year's Day cordiality abounded. Union Democrats came in throngs to the Cabinet houses, quaffed punch gaily, and slapped Union Whigs on the back. More entertaining was done during the session than for years past. Administration men were in high spirits; so were most Southerners. "I think the settlement of the last session and the firm course of the Administration in the execution of the fugitive slave law," wrote Secretary Graham to his brother, "have given a new lease to slavery, and property of that kind has not been so secure for the last twenty-five years." Fillmore's first annual message, a paper upon which he had expended great pains, receiving Webster's assistance in a long memorandum, was generally praised. He spoke of the necessity for allaying asperities, of the general readiness to defend the Union, and of his confidence that an overwhelming majority would sustain the enactments as "a final settlement." [6]

That phrase, indeed, now became a shibboleth. "I wish to state," Douglas informed the Senate just before Christmas, "that I have determined never to make another speech on the slavery question. . . . Let us cease agitating, stop the debate, and drop the subject. If we do this, the Compromise will be recognized as a final settlement." Early in the session a paper was circulated in Congress which soon gained the names of Clay, Cobb, Stephens, Foote, and many others in both parties. They asserted not only that they intended to maintain the settlement inviolate, but that they would never support for President, Congress, or State legislature any man not known to be opposed to the disturbance of the Compromise and hostile to renewal of the slavery agitation. Outside New England, New York, and the Lower South, most people were content to forget the subject. In many States it faded out of the newspapers. When the editor of the Vicksburg *Whig* went on a Southern tour, he found that men had dropped sectional topics. They would talk about the speed of steamboats, the crops, Benton's bad temper, the Forrest divorce case, and the latest news from Europe, but they would not talk about the Nashville Convention and Southern grievances.

Texas had been placated. Her governor, telling the special session of the legislature that he had called it together because a serious wound was about to be inflicted on the State's honor, had been for seizing Santa Fé first and discussing the title to it afterward. But on September 6 a message had been dispatched by Webster and Crittenden, in hot haste, to the Collector of the Port in New Orleans. "Pierce's bill, Texas bill, has passed, all the Texas delegates

6 Graham to his brother, January 6, 1851; Graham Papers. Webster to Fillmore, November 24, 1850; Everett Papers.

voting for it, and as soon as signed by the President it will be sent to Texas by Express. This dispatch is intended for Governor Bell of Texas and is sent to you to be forwarded to him with the least possible delay by Special Express, the expense advanced and it will be paid by the Department of State." The two Cabinet officers had been joined by Senators Sam Houston and T. J. Rusk in a postscript: "The Legislature ought to continue in session till the bill reaches them." The Southwest could relapse into tranquillity.[7]

[II]

The upheaval had shaken both the great political parties to the core. Northern Democrats who had supported the Compromise felt aggrieved by the course of Jefferson Davis, Mason, and Atchison. To a much greater degree, moderate Whigs were outraged by the conduct of Seward and his radical followers. Three Whig Representatives from North Carolina, who had formerly stood for protective tariffs, let it be known that they had turned sour on that subject. For nine months, they said, most Northern Whigs had done nothing but assault their rights, feelings, and property, and they would henceforth let Yankees look after their own tariff favors. Webster denounced the Massachusetts Whig Committee as a body half-rotten with abolitionism and other isms, and attacked the Boston *Atlas* for bringing the Bay State party to the brink of separation from the truly national Whigs. His strictures upon other radicals were equally violent; there was no estimating the mischief done by the "insane conduct" of Seward, Hale, Chase, and their like; he was out of patience with their littleness, stupidity, and bigotry.[8]

Webster, in fact, was brusquely prepared to read the Wilmot Proviso men out of the party. Now that the Compromise was law, he believed that those who continued to talk about the Proviso, resist the Fugitive Slave Act, or employ any other measures to disturb the country, had no right to consider themselves Whigs or friends of the Administration. This was stern doctrine. But the Secretary of State went even further. He would expel not merely individuals, but entire State organizations. "That can be regarded as no Whig Party, in New York, or Massachusetts, which espouses doctrines and utters sentiments hostile to the just and constitutional rights of the South, and therefore such as Southern Whigs cannot agree to." Fillmore and the Administration as a whole, less intolerant, eschewed threatening phrases and labored toward

7 *Cong. Globe,* December 23, 1850. Johnston and Browne, in their *Life of Stephens,* 258, say Stephens drew up the paper circulated among Congressmen. *National Intelligencer,* January 22, 1851. Columbia *Telegraph,* August 6, 1851, quoting the editor of the *Whig.* A copy of the Webster-Crittenden dispatch to Texas is in the Rusk Papers.
8 Webster to Everett, September 25, 1850; Everett Papers.

one end: a "vindication" in the fall elections in the two worst-inflamed areas, New York and Massachusetts.[9]

It was evident that they had a fierce battle on their hands, and that the Whig schism was too deep to be closed. In both Fillmore's and Webster's States feeling against the Fugitive Slave Act was widespread and embittered. In Massachusetts not merely did such abolitionists as Wendell Phillips and Theodore Parker, supported by many milder men, declare that the law had no moral validity, and was, as Emerson shortly told his Concord neighbors, a statute "which no man can obey or abet the obeying, without loss of self-respect and forfeiture of the name of a gentleman." So moderate a Whig as Abbott Lawrence, who had no patience with abolitionists, thought the enactment far too harsh. "I had hoped that the everlasting question of slavery was settled," he wrote from his London legation, "but when I saw the Fugitive Slave Law, it appeared to me that there would be no peace, if any attempt should be made to execute the law." He supposed, however, that it would remain a nullity like that of 1793. When Lawrence spoke with such energy, there could be little question where Bay State sentiment lay. As for New York, Seward and Weed rallied their forces with indomitable spirit; Greeley, Bryant, and other editors seconded them; and the Whig Convention in Syracuse broke into two warring factions over resolutions which eulogized Seward and demanded a definite exclusion of slavery from all new Territories.[10]

The November elections in both States were highly equivocal. In Massachusetts the Free Soil Party and Democrats, uniting on most legislative candidates, put a dazzling array of speakers into the field: among others Sumner, Palfrey, Henry Wilson, R. H. Dana, Jr., and Anson E. Burlingame. A pending fugitive slave case added to the excitement. Sumner, making the rafters of Faneuil Hall ring, blew up like Mont Pelée. This "legalized outrage," the Fugitive Slave Act, he termed the worst atrocity, the grossest infamy, in all the annals of governmental crime since Assurbanipal, while the President who signed it had plumbed such depths of shame that it were "better for him had he never been born." The unnatural party alliance proved strong enough to overwhelm the old-line Whigs. "Our election is all bad," lamented Webster. "The coalition forces have carried the government of Massachusetts by storm. The Whigs will differ and perhaps quarrel about the causes of this overthrow. I ascribe it entirely to the conduct of the members of Congress from this State, and some of the leading papers, in opposing and denouncing the peace measures of the last session. All this had no effect but to strengthen the hands of the

9 Webster to Peter Harvey, October 2, 1850; Everett Papers.
10 J. E. Cabot, *A Memoir of Ralph Waldo Emerson*, II, 196, address at Concord, May 3, 1851. Lawrence to Everett, October 31, 1850; Everett Papers. Alexander, *Political History of the State of New York*, II, 154–155.

Free Soil people." Still, it was a coalition victory—the Free Soilers alone could never have carried the day.[11]

And in New York the result was almost equally Delphic. The Administration Whigs, led by Francis Granger, whose silver-gray hair gave a name to the faction, joined the Seward Whigs in supporting Washington Hunt for governer, but drew up an anti-Sewardite platform. Upstate, Hunt was generally supported by Fillmoreites and Sewardites alike, but in the metropolis many Compromise Whigs bolted, under the urgings of the before-mentioned Union Safety Committee, to the Democratic ticket headed by Seymour. Seldom has an election been closer; for several weeks nobody knew whether Seymour or Hunt had been chosen. Finally, Hunt's victory, 214,614 to 214,352, was announced; a result which, since Union-Whig candidates ran fully five thousand ahead, might be regarded as an uncomforting victory for the Compromise forces.[12]

The Whig Party, which had done most to win victory for the Compromise, was plainly the worst sufferer from its strains and torsions. Discontent in the Lower South and division in critical Northern States were its lot. The party of compromise always suffers when voters drift toward two extremes. The Fillmore-Webster Administration was entrenched in the Federal patronage; but Fillmore's enemies had gained control of the New York legislature, and Webster's enemies of the Massachusetts legislature. It was a stormy prospect upon which lovers of Whig unity looked. Their hope was that the general acceptance of the Compromise, the unquestioned majority approval, would gradually obliterate all dissenting elements. Voters would rally about the banner of Webster and Clay, Stephens, Mangum, and Toombs; they would forsake Seward, Hale, and Horace Mann. That hope was to be frustrated by several considerations, of which two were especially important: Webster and Clay were about to sink into the grave, while one section of the Compromise could be ignited and brandished like a fiery cross by the Northern radicals.

[III]

The situation of the Northern and Southern extremists was radically different. To resist the Compromise, Southerners had to go the whole hog; they had to attack it all, and threaten or effect secession. In Jackson's day they had been presented with a law which some thought they could nullify. Now they had no such option. The shoe was on the other foot. It was the Northern

11 Webster to Everett, November 13, 1850; Everett Papers.
12 Foner, *Business and Slavery*, 50–51; Alexander, *Political History N. Y.*, II, 156–158.

radicals who had a law to nullify. They could pluck from the Compromise one special section, the fugitive slave law, spurn it, refuse to obey it, and make it a contemptible scarecrow. They would take a partial and easy step, pluming themselves on their moral superiority; while no such facile course was possible for the radical Southerners—they had to march over the precipice or keep still. It was an advantage which anti-slavery men were quick to exploit.

Even while rockets flared and massmeetings roared over the Compromise, a frenetic Northern faction was flatly rejecting the Fugitive Slave Act. In New England, upstate New York, and those parts of the Middle West which were largely an extended Yankeeland, the voice of protest was loud. Meetings were held in Boston, Syracuse, and Chicago. With Charles Francis Adams presiding, Bostonians cheered as Wendell Phillips and Theodore Parker employed their best forensic talents in denouncing the law. The venerable Josiah Quincy, in a letter crackling with heat, threw his influence against the statute. The Syracuse meeting evoked such defiances that it was plain that no fugitive could ever be recovered there. "It would be almost certain death to a slaveholder," declared one abolitionist, "to appear, on his infernal mission, in our streets." Chicago went furthest of all. Her common council declared that the act violated the Constitution and the laws of God; that Northern members of Congress who acquiesced in it were fit to be ranked with Judas Iscariot and Benedict Arnold; and that citizens, police, and all other public officers should refuse to aid in enforcement. While one massmeeting, addressed by Stephen A. Douglas, condemned the councillors and called for a faithful execution of all Federal laws, another upheld the city fathers.[13]

A large part of the Northern pulpit was vehemently opposed to execution of the law.[14] Theodore Parker, typical of militant pastors, published *A Sermon on Conscience* justifying jurors in violating their oath to acquit a man clearly guilty under the act. Writers whose genius touched every Northern lover of literature—Bryant, Emerson, Whittier, Longfellow—were seizing their pens:

> I hear a voice: "Thus saith the Law,
>   Let Love be dumb;
> Clasping her liberal hands in awe,
> Let sweet-lipped Charity withdraw,
>   From hearth and home."

13 R. V. Harlow, *Gerrit Smith*, 289–290. Rhodes, *History of the United States*, I, 196, 197.
14 But not all clergyman by any means. Whittier complained of the ministers who preached obedience to the Fugitive Slave Act. Not a few issued sermons as pamphlets; for example, the Rev. Nathaniel Bonton of Concord, New Hampshire, whose Thanksgiving sermon of 1850, "The Good Land in Which We Live," was a plea for obedience to all laws. What was more significant, he identified radicalism in politics with radicalism in religious thought—with "a bold and blasphemous infidelity."

I hear another voice: "The poor
    Are thine to feed;
Turn not the outcast from thy door,
Nor give to bonds and wrong once more
Whom God hath freed."

[IV]

In contrast, what could Southern extremists do? There was no single section of the Compromise which they could nullify; it was all or nothing—and nothing meant secession and civil war. They saw this clearly enough. But how many would stand up to the alternative?

On the day that compromise triumphed, Representative Holmes of South Carolina declared that his State could no longer remain in the Union, and that he would counsel withdrawal the moment he returned home. Rhett, Yancey, Colquitt, Wigfall, were all breathing fire, disunion, and rash counsels. At a "monster" meeting in Macon, Georgia, in late August ("monster" meaning three or four thousand people), Rhett and Yancey had vied in appeals for immediate secession. "Now is the time for action," exhorted Rhett, explaining that delay would give a fatal advantage to oppressors of the South; Georgia should secede temporarily from the Union and announce that the severance would be permanent unless the rights of the whole South were restored and guaranteed. Yancey was more daring. The North had been victorious, it had trampled every Southern right under foot, and the time had come for revolution. He quoted the "immortal" George H. Troup: "The argument is exhausted and we must stand to our arms!" Colquitt proclaimed the slogan, "Thirty-six-thirty or fight." Ex-Governor C. J. McDonald, chief organizer of the Southern Rights Party in Georgia, who was presiding, nodded approval. These men had a certain bad logic on their side; but could they rally any numbers? [15]

Not on a general Southern scale. When the Nashville Convention held its adjourned session in November, few delegates attended, the radical fire of the leaders had sunk to ashes, and the debates attracted little public attention. McDonald, who had been vice-president of the first session, was now president. The convention issued a *pro forma* protest against the failure to extend the Missouri Compromise line to the Pacific, and condemned seriatim the admission of California, the organization of Utah and New Mexico without protection for slaveholders, the treatment accorded Texas, and the abolition of the slave trade in the District of Columbia. It also called for a Southern Congress, which would either move to restore the constitutional rights of the South or provide for its "safety and independence." But who would heed? Herschel V. Johnson

15 Columbia *Telegraph*, August 30, September 14, 1850.

might call the Compromise a cup of hemlock; Robert Tyler, son of the former President, might declare that it gave Southern institutions an existence of only twenty years, and that he was now satisfied that Southern salvation lay in secession alone, terrible as it might appear. Most of the South was hostile to that policy.[16] And now Georgia spoke.

Upon the passage of the California bill, Governor Towns of Georgia had issued a call for a convention to be elected on November 3 and assemble December 10. A compact was hastily arranged between Union Democrats under Howell Cobb and Union Whigs under Toombs and Stephens. The three began a whirlwind canvass, speaking in every district, while Toombs scattered broadcast a printed argument for the Compromise. The Macon *Journal and Messenger*, commenting upon reports that disunionists had already fixed upon the form of government for a Southern Confederacy, declared that it was astonishing to see how bold the advocates of secession had become. "Some of the presses seem to be edited by infuriated madmen and the public speakers deport themselves like men partially demented." The *Journal*, the Athens *Banner*, the Savannah *Republican*, and other papers poured out cogent arguments for the Compromise and against secession. What of Louisiana? asked the Macon editor. The United States purchased it from France for the benefit of the whole nation; and had Louisiana the right on the morrow to secede from the Union and begin taxing the nation's shipments down the Mississippi? The Unionist campaign bore happy fruit. On election day an unusual number of voters, about seventy thousand, trooped to the polls, and chose an overwhelming majority of Union delegates, including Toombs, Stephens, and Cobb. When the convention met, these leaders saw to it that the famous "Georgia Platform" was presented by Charles J. Jenkins—a Unionist document, through and through.[17]

A Unionist document; but with conditions. It is probable (we have no way of measuring public sentiment) that most Southerners believed that in the great "deal" they had taken the thin end of the bargain. They believed that the Compromise, in Stephens's words, was an agreement on the part of the slave-holding area to remain under the old roof, in consideration of renewed pledges on the part of the free States to abide by the Constitution. They expected these pledges to be kept to the letter. The convention declared Georgia's devotion to the Union, and stated that after mature consideration the people, though not fully approving the Compromise, would abide by it as a permanent adjustment. But the delegates went on to lay down what became the real ultimatum of the

16 Flippin, *Herschel V. Johnson*, 231. Auchampaugh, *Robert Tyler*, quoting letter of November 18, 1850, to Henry Wise. Tyler concluded: "But if the slaveholding States continue to talk without acting, in a few years they will not have even the privilege of talking."
17 N. Y. *Tribune*, November 4, 5, 1850.

South: that if one side breached the new compact, the other would no longer be bound by it. The fourth resolution seemed to many Southerners writ in letters of burning light: [18]

That the State of Georgia, in the judgment of this Convention, will and ought to resist, even (as a last resort) to the disruption of every tie which binds her to the Union, any future act of Congress abolishing slavery in the District of Columbia, without the consent and petition of the slaveholders thereof; or any act abolishing slavery in places within the slaveholding States, purchased by the United States for the erection of forts, magazines, arsenals, dock-yards, navy-yards, and other like purposes; or any act suppressing the slave trade between slaveholding States; or any refusal to admit as a State any Territory applying, because of the existence of slavery therein; or any act prohibiting the introduction of slaves into the territories of Utah and New Mexico; or any act repealing or materially modifying the laws now in force for the recovery of fugitive slaves.

The Georgians would resist to the disruption of the Union any repeal or modification of the Fugitive Slave Act; yet much of New England and the Northwest was preparing to nullify that act. The South would take deep offence if any Territory were refused admission because its people wished to make it a slave State; yet while the South hoped that slavery would go into two Territories, and might yet insist on its introduction into others, a host of Northerners were determined there should never be another slave State. Men had reason for concern, even if they were less timidly pessimistic than one future President of the republic.

James Buchanan, sitting in his study at "Wheatland," was just finishing his letter to the before-mentioned Union meeting in Philadelphia when on November 14 a friend, Dr. Jonathan M. Foltz, was announced. He read it aloud, and Foltz approved it, saying that it was powerful and eloquent, and would help secure his nomination for the presidency. At Foltz's suggestion, Buchanan added a final sentence: "God preserve the Union; I do not desire to survive it." After dinner, as they walked into Lancaster, Buchanan gloomily remarked: "Dr. Foltz, I will tell you now what I have never told to mortal, and what I shall not again repeat. My firm conviction is, after careful and mature deliberation, that in four years from this time this Union will not be in existence as it now exists. There will be two republics, Maryland and Delaware will join the North, and there will be no civil war." As prophecy this was worthless; as evidence of Buchanan's nervous-Nellie character it is interesting; and as proof that even warm supporters of the Compromise thought it might prove but a temporary adjustment it is highly significant.[19]

The decisive result of the Georgia election, and the wide acclaim given the

18 Johnston and Browne, *Alexander H. Stephens*, 258–260.
19 MS Diary of Jonathan M. Foltz, November 14, 1850.

Georgia convention, were destined to bring to the front not the out-and-out Unionists, but a great body of conditional-Unionists. Throughout the Lower South they quickly rose to dominance. Public opinion there could never be summed up as a division between a small body of diehard radicals, and a much larger body of men eager to accept the sectional compact and turn a new page. American feeling is seldom so simple. At least three main groups could be distinguished—two small, one large.

One was composed of the "ultra" Southern Rights men, led by Rhett, Yancey, McDonald, and Quitman. They demanded immediate secession as the answer to the Compromise, which they scarified as a stupendous betrayal of their section. It had cost California to the South, they said, just as surely as if the Wilmot Proviso had been applied to it. It had in effect closed Utah and New Mexico to slavery, for the uncertain status of the institution discouraged slaveholding emigrants. It had torn from Texas a large part of her domain. The abolition of the slave trade in the Federal District furnished a precedent for attacking the interstate slave trade. In short, abandonment of the Union offered the only safety.

Antipodal to this group stood the ultra-Unionists, followers of Clay and Foote. Most parts of the Compromise, they declared, were for the good of the South. Utah and New Mexico, might yet, if climate and soil proved favorable, become slave States. "In comparison with the Union," wrote C. C. Langdon, whose Mobile *Advertiser* was one of the most valiant Compromise papers, "all other objects sink into insignificance." Disunion, declared the Savannah *Republic*, threatens "the total destruction of all that freemen hold dear." Jacksonian Democrats, merchants in the larger cities, some wealthy planters, the non-slaveholding people of hilly areas in North Alabama, Georgia, and upper South Carolina, and above all, the conservative Whigs, were the principal groups who gave this party strength.[20] They joined hands with the staunchly loyal folk of the wide border area, for whom A. J. Donelson had spoken when at Nashville he execrated the unhallowed purposes of the secessionists.

The third and largest element was a body of moderates standing between the other two, who believed both in Southern Rights and the Union, but hoped they could be reconciled. They disliked the admission of California, but thought the Utah-New Mexico settlement fair enough. They objected to any attack upon slaveholding or slave-selling within the States, but placed a strict-constructionist trust in Congress and the Courts. On the whole, they accepted the Compromise—on condition that the North accepted all its parts, too. Yet while this element threw its weight decisively for peace, its attitude was pro-

---

20 Langdon's "Twenty-Seven Letters" in the editorial columns of the Mobile *Advertiser* constituted one of the best expositions of the cause of compromise and Union to appear in the South. Files, Alabama State Department Archives and History.

visional. Feeling the South the aggrieved party, it held that responsibility for maintenance of the Union rested primarily upon the North. If that section dealt in good faith with fugitive slaves, and refrained from striking at slavery where it had legitimate roots, all would be well. If it did not, the probation would be ended. The Georgia phrase, "resistance even to the disruption of every tie," stuck in the Southern memory.[21]

[V]

Disappointed at Nashville, repulsed in Georgia, the fire-eaters were thrown back upon two States, South Carolina and Mississippi, as their ultimate strongholds. Incredible as it may seem, men in each believed that it could secede immediately—and alone.

South Carolina, we must realize, already thought herself almost a little republic, and certainly possessed a more sharply defined character than any of her sisters. The population included several distinctive strains. Most leaders of the State liked to think that the Cavalier influence, dispersed from the early coastal settlement and strengthened by immigration from Virginia, was strongest; but actually the Calvinist element, made up of great numbers of Commonwealth men who had emigrated after the Restoration, of Scots and Scotch-Irish, and of Huguenots, was probably more powerful. It was this Calvinism which did most to give Carolinians their iron tenacity. Nowhere in the South did the great planter families, interconnected by marriage and proud of their lineage, hold a more potent place. They had the gifts, tastes, and strong class feeling of the Virginia planters, while they possessed in addition the guidance which only a considerable city can give—for Charleston was much more a centre of culture and ideas than Norfolk or even Richmond. Much as the South Carolinians loved to talk of planter leadership, actually the Rutledges, Hugers, Legarés, Gadsdens, Middletons, Pinckneys, McDuffies, Lowndeses, and other families held fully as many merchants and lawyers as planters, their resourcefulness and initiative developed in the quick give and take of the bustling little city.

Whether planters or lawyers, the leaders of the State were acutely conscious of several great facts: that the black population decidedly outnumbered the whites; that their prosperity depended upon the overseas market for a few great staples, notably cotton and rice; and that the decay of the cotton lands, the steady if slow sinking and depletion of the rice-fields, and the poor climate for stock-growing, put their agriculture at a disadvantage in rivalry with the new States to the west. They were aware, in short, that on various social and economic fronts South Carolina occupied a hazardous position, and this con-

21 Denman, *Secession in Alabama*, 36ff.

sciousness of danger made them sensitive and gave their bearing a touch of defiance. They had been taught since Revolutionary times to regard their State as one of several which led the country, and their pride was heightened by the deference which younger commonwealths, from Alabama to Arkansas, paid to South Carolina and to Virginia.

It was a State, also, particularly susceptible to foreign influences which strengthened the sense of superiority in the ruling class. Many of the English and a few of the Huguenot families retained close ties with their ancient homelands. The beautiful houses south of Broad Street in Charleston, and the stately mansions of the low country, were full of silver, china, miniatures, paintings, and books brought from Europe. Foreign travel was almost essential to a man of position. Before the Civil War, wrote a highly cultivated Charlestonian, William Henry Trescot, "I do not think any young American of large intellect could have been properly educated without some experience of the Old World." He did not mean knowledge of the London clubs, the Paris boulevards, or the Roman carnival; knowledge even of French picture-galleries, Rhenish castles, or Oxford colleges. He meant acquaintance with the moral atmosphere and historic pulse of Europe, its wealth of traditions and memories. It is certain that those who could afford it went naturally, like Trescot himself, to Europe for lengthy stays. One Charlestonian, J. F. Manigault, was among the pioneer American art-collectors abroad. People of the little city on the Ashley and Cooper read and heard much of Europe. The West Indies, too, were close, and lent their touch to the cosmopolitanism of South Carolina.

Of all foreign influences, the British of course was the strongest; not contemporaneous Britain, but old-fashioned Britain. When William H. Russell visited the leisurely homes of the lowland plantations, he compared them with the old conservative manorhouses of northern England. South Carolinians who grew up on plantations found in the Anglo-Irish society depicted by Miss Edgeworth, or the English society of Miss Austen, some strangely lifelike counterparts of their own experience. But it was politically that British influence was most persistent and powerful. It would be ridiculous, writes the loyal South Carolinian just quoted, to compare the legislature at Columbia with the august Parliament at Westminster. "But it is nevertheless true that in the legislature of this State have been preserved with singular fidelity some of the most striking features of the Parliament of our ancestors. The reverence for the forms of parliamentary law, the influence belonging to that silent body of country gentlemen, the long continuance of individual representatives, the weight given to precedents of former generations, the peculiar respect and dignity attached to the office of Speaker, the antiquated and stately costumes of the presiding officers of both branches of the General Assembly, the unwritten and unbroken law of adjournment so that the parish representatives should be on their estates at Christmas, all were traditions in the habits and thoughts of our English blood."

In every other State, he went on, there was a general legislative conformity to that unhappy model, the Federal House. "But here an unbroken line of Speakers from the colonial days of Jonathan Amory to the Ordinance of Secession, presided over a political assembly which preserved more of the conservatism of the Old World than any other institution on this continent, except, I ought to add, the common law as administered by the judiciary of the same State. Established in colonial times, when the parishes really represented all the wealth and all the population of the State, the parish system, with its intense respect for landed property, its deference to personal connection, its genuine love of culture and its sensitive obedience to the rules of good breeding, gave a character to the legislature which it never entirely lost. The representation sprang from it. Session after session the same men, the natural leaders of the State, the men who represented broad acres and thousands of slaves, the men who had won power and honor by professional labor, the men who, in less conspicuous walks of life, had made for themselves names for industry, honesty, and ability, met to make the laws of the State; and as years went on the boys from the college (as much a part of the State as the legislature) who filled the galleries, and to whom the debates were as much a part of their education as their recitations, came down from the galleries to fill the seats in the House, and to renew and perpetuate hereditary friendships. A member's name was an indication of the district he represented, and the public life of the State was developed in full and fitting sympathy with the personal affections, the traditional associations, the local attachments that made its private life." Such a political structure, like its English counterpart, had manifold defects; it was undemocratic, doctrinaire, and shortsighted; its rotten-borough system of over-representation for lowland parishes implied economic favoritism; but it also had elements of strength. What is chiefly to be noted, however, is that, connected as it was with the social and economic structure, it did much to make South Carolina the self-conscious, independent, proud little nation that it became. The unity of the State was strengthened by the fact that the legislature wielded a unique power over local institutions and the conduct of elections.

One other potent factor in shaping the State needs hardly to be mentioned; the influence of Calhoun, mighty in his lifetime, mighty still when he rested in St. Philip's churchyard. It is almost literally true that for years before his death his will was the law of South Carolina, and his opinions were the decisions that controlled her action. Because he isolated himself from both great political parties, the State isolated itself; because he hated national conventions, the State ignored them; because he moved toward renunciation of the Union, the State so moved. South Carolinians, in justifying their ideal society, could quote Jefferson's letter of 1813 declaring that "there is a natural aristocracy among men," that "the grounds of this are virtue and talents," and that "the natural aristocracy I consider as the most precious gift of nature, for the instruction, the trust and government of society." But above all they quoted Calhoun. He believed that liberty, if forced on a people, was a curse, for men must be capable of self-government before they can enjoy liberty. "No people, indeed, can long enjoy more liberty than that to which their situation and advanced intelligence and morals fairly entitle them. If more than this be allowed, they must soon fall into disorder." By the 1850's the ruling classes of South Carolina had persuaded themselves that they had achieved a perfect mean between the French, who made too much of equality and fraternity, and the English, who made too much of merely hereditary distinctions. By following more natural lines of development, they had attained a better-ordered liberty. With slavery as the foundation of their economic system, yielding full leisure for the aristocratic class to perfect itself in leadership, they could yet reach the high distinction of ancient Greece.[22]

Mississippi had its distinctive characteristics, too, though they were far less complex and remarkable. Her main traits were those of a relatively new country, the wealth of whose millions of rich acres had been seized upon within a single generation by a restless population of planters, merchants, and professional men. The land had been developed, above all, by tens of thousands of small farmers who formed the main population, and who, in the independent, half-wild life of the sun-drenched country, far from city modernities, generated a self-assertive pride. The planting aristocracy was polarized about Natchez in the southwest; the farmers of raw frontier training dominated the northern and eastern sections. Both were keenly aware that in great areas the blacks outnumbered the whites. Freedom for the slaves—that, they passionately declared, would mean the creation of a jungle. With a pattern very different from that of South Carolina, they were equally resolved to maintain their own self-sufficient ways.

Though admitted to the Union in 1817, the State had in large part remained unsettled until in the early 1830's the removal of the Choctaws and Chickasaws threw open the gates to an eager influx. Some came empty-handed; some came with capital and slaves. In the flush days of the great land-boom thousands

22 See William H. Trescot, *Memorial of the Life of F. Johnston Pettigrew*, Charleston, 1870, for an illuminating analysis of South Carolina institutions and ways in a biographical eulogy of a Charleston lawyer who became a Confederate officer.

grew rich; fine mansions sprang up at Natchez, Vicksburg, Jackson, and other points; and many of the features of life in Virginia and the Carolinas quickly reproduced themselves along the Mississippi and Tombigbee—but with a pioneer flavor, a tinge of crudity and violence. Duels, militia musters, barbecues, assassinations, noisy political canvasses, oratorical bouts, legal battles before crowded courts, gigantic feats in clearing land and wastefully mining its fertility—these were the main occupations. If South Carolina was the pinched, proud, uneasy aristocrat, Mississippi was the reckless, exuberant, high-spirited spendthrift among the Southern States. After the Mexican War, writes her most jocund historian, "all the prairie and bottom lands rose at once to seventy-five and eighty dollars"; "our people raised immense quantities of meat and other provisions"; steamboats "bearing 250 bales of cotton" were no uncommon sight; "not a pauper could be found in all the length and breadth of the country." No State at the time made the combination of Negroes, rich virgin soil, and cotton pay better; none flared up more quickly over disturbance of that profitable "domestic arrangement"; none had orators more adept at "fanning the flame of righteous anger." [23]

[VI]

These were the two States which Rhett, Quitman, and others hoped they might get to secede alone—and which might have indulged in that folly had not the Unionists rallied to prevent it. The Compromise had barely triumphed when Governor W. B. Seabrook of South Carolina was inciting Governor John A. Quitman of Mississippi to take action. "Prompt and effective resistance" was imperative, he wrote on September 20th; already the Southern States occupied a position of degradation and inequality; submission would make them weak dependents of the central government forever. South Carolina, with her fire-eating reputation, ought not to lead off. But as soon as the governors of two or more States should assemble their legislatures, or furnish other evidence that determined resistance was in prospect, he would call together his legislature to take steps to "arrest the career of an interested and despotic majority." Quitman, returning an enthusiastic reply, summoned a special session for November 18 on the ground that secession alone could save the State. At this Seabrook was delighted. "Having lately completed a military tour through every District, where a large proportion of the population are non-slaveholders," he jubilantly encouraged Quitman, "I did not meet with one man who was not favorable to the only certain remedy—secession." South Carolina was eager

23 R. Davis, *Recollections of Mississippi*, 103, 110–111, 190, 198. See Herbert Weaver, *Mississippi Farmers, 1850–1860*, for evidence that the farm was the basic rural unit.

for immediate separation, and was prepared, he added, to second Mississippi or any State in any and every effort to halt the despots. He wanted a Southern Congress as soon as possible, for it would be desirable to have a government actually in operation "in the event of a conflict." [24]

Mad as all this seemed, it was nevertheless highly dangerous. The jurist J. S. Petigru, whose unflinching love of the Union was to be given lifelong demonstration, thought the outcome dubious. "Mr. Calhoun and Dr. Cooper," he wrote Tom Corwin, "have succeeded in filling the light heads of the people with the opinion that it is the Constitution of the United States that hinders all their aspirations after greatness; and with such sentiments no wonder that they are disunionists." Of course Seabrook, Rhett, and Quitman did not dream that their two States could long exist as little separate entities. They knew that nothing short of a Southern Confederacy could succeed. Their crusade for immediate and separate secession was launched in the hope of arousing popular sympathy from Mobile to Nashville, and thus carrying other States out of the Union also. This was the hope of the various secessionist newspapers; the Charleston *Mercury*, the Columbia *Telegraph*, the *Mississippian*, and most sinisterly active of all, the *Southern Press* which, so recently established by the Congressional "ultras," was reaching a circulation of 15,000. Buchanan, it is significant to note, was frightened. If one link in the chain was broken, he thought, nobody could predict the result; for if Washington used coercion much of the South might secede.[25]

Into the details of the rapid struggle which checked the immediate secessionists in South Carolina and Mississippi it is unnecessary to go. The Carolinians in particular might easily have taken the bit in their teeth. "Had I convened the legislature two or three weeks before the time of meeting prescribed by the Constitution," Seabrook informed Quitman a week before Christmas, "such was the excited state of the public mind at that time, that I am convinced that South Carolina would not now have been a member of the Union. The people are very far ahead of their leaders and can with difficulty be restrained." But even there better counsels prevailed.[26]

For one reason, a natural breach developed between the immediate secessionists and those who desired to wait for coöperative action with other States. Robert Barnwell and Langdon Cheves, both connected with the Nashville

24 Seabrook to Quitman, September 20, October 23, 1850; Claiborne Papers. Seabrook feared that any delay "may enable Congress and the politicians of the North so to shape their policy as to create the impression among the unreflecting and timid in the South, that every cause of danger to our institutions had been removed." *Idem*, October 23.
25 Petigru to Corwin, November 16, 1850; Corwin Papers. Buchanan, June 16, 1851, Donelson Papers.
26 Seabrook to Quitman, December 17, 19, 1850; Claiborne Papers.

Convention, headed a powerful body of "coöperative secessionists." For another reason, the Unionists asserted themselves with gallant energy. That stouthearted Jacksonian, Joel R. Poinsett, published in the Charleston *Mercury* a letter defending the Compromise and attacking secession. The up-country editor Benjamin F. Perry spoke and wrote indefatigably. "I regard the dissolution of the Union as the most fatal blow which slavery could receive," he declared. Petigru accepted the office of Federal Attorney, vacated by a secessionist, not because he wanted it but because he wished to signalize his loyalty. It was impossible for the peppery jurist to hold his tongue. Arguing a case in a secessionist community, he was warned to be silent on political issues. But as he prepared to depart, a friend proposed a toast. "Petigru," he said, "a health to South Carolina." "With all my heart," rejoined Petigru, "and her return to her senses!"[27]

In the end the legislature, after hesitancies which plunged Seabrook "almost in despair," cast aside the absurd idea of immediate secession, contenting itself with arranging for the election of delegates to a putative Southern Congress, and to a still more putative State convention to be geared to this Congress. It recommended that the Congress be held in Montgomery in January, 1852, and it was understood that the convention should meet thereafter to ratify any measures taken by the Congress. In short, all action was postponed for more than a year. Radicals took comfort in the election of Rhett as Senator, but even this small cup had a bitter drop dashed into it. "There were but two candidates, Rhett and Hammond," ran Petigru's ironic letter to his daughter, "and yet it required four ballotings to get an election. This could not have happened if so many people—about one-third of the whole body—had not thought that neither was fit for the place . . . The whole legislature, with very few exceptions, are declared disunionists, yet they object to Barnwell Rhett because he is so violent. I infer from this that they are not so mad as they affect to be, and that with a great deal of real malice there is also a good deal of acting." If all posturing, North and South, could have been removed from the politics of this era, crisis after crisis would have faded into thin air.[28]

Alas, lamented a South Carolina fire-eater in the first weeks of 1851, "the State is sold to submissionists." Even that oldtime Hotspur, James H. Hammond, who had been eager for a fight in Nullification times, who had urged that abolitionists be put to death, and who had advocated secession when the tariff of 1842 passed, was reported to have written his son: "I have renounced my allegiance to South Carolina, and in future I adopt the Georgia platform." The

27 *Mercury*, December 5, 1850. J. F. Rippy, *Joel R. Poinsett*, 239–240. J. P. Carson, *Life, Letters, and Speeches of James L. Petigru*, 280ff. Lillian Kibler, *Benjamin F. Perry*.
28 C. S. Boucher, *Secession and Cooperation Movements in South Carolina*, 112–114. Carson, *Petigru*, Letter of December 19, 1850.

first wave of the assault had been checked, and the election for the State Convention would bring the next test.[29]

Since Mississippi was so largely a frontier State it had a far stronger federal tradition than South Carolina. Quitman, talking of "degradation and ruin," ex-Governor Albert G. Brown, actively preaching disunion, and the *Mississippian*, claiming a majority of forty thousand for immediate resistance to "the California felony," raised a tremendous clamor all fall. The leading champion of the Union was that pertinacious, explosive bantam, Senator Foote, who had returned from Washington to find editors describing him as a traitor and one town burning him in effigy. According to his own account, he was attacked by two-thirds of the legislative and other officers, his five colleagues in Congress, and a heavy majority of the newspapers. To repel this assault he had nothing but Providence, the good sense of the masses, a few trusted friends, and "my own zeal and activity." Other evidence indicates that Providence and Foote possessed more allies than he suggests. The New York *Tribune* reported that twenty-nine Mississippi papers, Whig and Democratic, stood for the Union, while it listed only fourteen as disunionist or "agitationist." Some rabble-rousers were trying to effect a class-cleavage on the subject. Thus the Vicksburg *Sentinel* appealed to the canebrake democracy by savagely denouncing the large planters, commission merchants, and urban business interests generally for accepting the Compromise. The small planters and farmers, it said, "the genuine sovereigns," were for Quitman and Brown. "They control the cities, and not the cities them." It was significant that while Jefferson Davis, a large planter, was deeply hostile to the Compromise, he did not approve of the immediate-secession scheme. Let Mississippi, he suggested, propose a convention of slave States to demand of the free States a guarantee of equality under the Constitution, and if this were refused, then let the South apply the "last remedy." [30]

Foote, Judge Sharkey, and other Unionists played their hand well. Quitman's call for a special session on November 18 was countered by precisely the right measure. The Unionists gathered a convention of fifteen hundred in Jackson that day to exert their influence upon the legislators. Democrats and Whigs clasped hands, speech followed speech, and a bi-party Union Association was formed. This convention was wholeheartedly for acceptance of the Compromise, on condition that the North duly honored it—that there were no further Yankee "aggressions," such as refusal to admit a new slave State, or repeal or annulment of the Fugitive Slave Act. An enthusiastic Unionist mass-meeting in the hall of the House in Jackson on the 20th also helped take the

29 James Brewer, Columbia, S. C., to John A. Quitman, January 30, 1851; Claiborne Papers.
30 J. B. Ranck, *Albert Gallatin Brown*, 77–79; *Mississippian*, quoted in N. Y. *Tribune*, November 4; Vicksburg *Sentinel*, July 16; Mississippi *Free-Trader*, September 18, 1850; Rowland, *Jefferson Davis*, I, 597–600.

wind out of secessionist sails. Foote addressed it, and whenever he used the word "Union" the roof seemed to lift under the impact of the applause.[31]

The legislature, after listening to a long exhortation from Governor Quitman, meanwhile began a debate which showed that it was in no mood for "intrepid" rashness. The upshot was a decision in favor of a State convention—but one for which delegates would not be elected until September, 1851, and which would not meet until the following November. The New York *Tribune* commented that "Mississippi is riding the high horse," but it had plenty of time to dismount from Quitman's Rosinante.[32]

[VII]

All over the South, in fact, the movement to meet passage of the Compromise by instant forcible resistance broke down. Georgia had done nothing except draw up a conditional-Unionist platform. South Carolina and Mississippi, plied with whip and spur, had simply provided for electing State conventions upon Federal relations in the fall of 1851. Alabama's cautious governor knew that some of the most powerful groups in the State wished to give the Compromise a fair trial. He therefore published a message stating that public opinion was divided, and that if sudden measures were forced upon an unready people, the consequences might be disastrous; recommending that Alabama do nothing until other States had taken action. The result was that Yancey fumed while the State quietly waited. A Southern Rights convention was held at Montgomery early in 1851 and adopted resolutions, but its delegates were mainly restricted to Democrats from the Black Belt counties and no other ripple mantled the lake. In Louisiana, with her strong commercial interests, in Texas, busy with home development and hugging ten million dollars to her breast, and in Arkansas, the dissenters failed to make an impressive showing. The border States, of course, had always been strongly for peace and good feeling.[33]

Virginia's widespread influence, finally, was exerted as Washington and Jefferson, Madison and Monroe, would have wished it to be. Governor John B. Floyd, whose proposal for commercial discriminations against the North now had the support of a "Central Southern Rights Association," met his legislature with a cry of wrath against little Vermont. "The legislature of that State," he snarled, "has virtually abrogated by statute the law of Congress for

31 N. Y. *Tribune*, November 25, 1850.
32 N. Y. *Tribune*, December 3, 1850.
33 Moderate men in Georgia could now afford to smile at the eager haste of the open and avowed disunionists. They wish to do everything in an hour, wrote G. W. Crawford; the eleven o'clock fire-eater is preferred to the twelve o'clock salamander. To Charles Lanman, October 26, 1850; Lanman Papers. On Alabama, see Denman, *Secession in Alabama,* 50–54.

the recapture of fugitive slaves, which alone induced the Southern States to acquiesce in the late Congressional measures. Vermont has thus inflicted upon the whole South at once an injury and an insult. To neither can we with honor or self-respect submit." But unlike Jefferson Davis and the South Carolina legislature, who wanted another Southern Convention, he was for a national convention; a body to assemble not later than May in Baltimore or some other central point. He made it clear that this should be a gathering to commit all participants to honest and cordial enforcement of the Fugitive Slave Act. The idea came to precisely nothing.

No impartial observer could doubt that the Compromise was popular in the Old Dominion, and the opposition to it quickly went to pieces. In vain did R. M. T. Hunter inveigh against it. In vain did Senator Mason continue his intransigent attitude, writing William C. Rives that nothing in the history of the North for the past thirty years led him to expect that its hand would now be stayed—a hand "uplifted for the destruction of a large portion of our population, as an element of political power." The Richmond *Whig*, perhaps the ablest paper in the State, was for the Compromise. Thomas Ritchie (accused of being influenced by his printing contract with the government) was unwearied in its defense. A number of massmeetings, including a great Richmond gathering of legislators, delegates to the Constitutional Convention then sitting, and citizens, endorsed it. In March, the legislature voted its overwhelming approval.[34]

34 Governors' Letterbooks, Virginia Archives, No. 26, pp. 138–140. Mason to Rives, March 31, 1851; Rives Papers. House Journal, March 25, 1851. The Central Southern Rights Association of Virginia, which had organized in Richmond at the end of 1850, proposed to lay heavy taxes on goods from all States which failed to enforce the fugitive slave law. It also proposed to "promote our own mechanics and manufactures, our own institutions and people." On January 10, 1850, it adopted a "Proceedings and Address" which pointed out that Pennsylvania, New York, Vermont, Ohio, and Massachusetts all had statutes conflicting with the execution of the fugitive slave law. After noting the insults and impediments two Georgians had met in Boston in vainly trying to reclaim property known to be theirs, and pointing to the unanimous declaration of the Vermont legislature against the law, "in a form revolting and insulting to an extent beyond endurance," the address went on: "But recently a citizen of Virginia went to New York for the purpose of reclaiming a fugitive slave, and although the proofs were too strong to admit of question, yet the delays and vexations attending the proceedings mark a state of public sentiment resolute and determined to war against our rights and our interests. The determined resistance in this case of Henry Long is in no form satisfactory to any Southern citizen; because a poor man, whose means will not enable him to encounter the expenses and delays . . . must lose his property. It is said the expenses in this case were paid by citizens of New York yet we have no assurance that such will be the result hereafter." Pvt. Huntington Library.

Nevertheless, the moderates in Virginia were early, active, and effective. The first weeks of 1851 saw a Constitutional Convention meeting in Richmond. An influential gathering of members in the Capitol on February 17, 1851, adopted resolutions which in the main were written by Henry A. Wise. The fifth read: "Resolved, that all further agitation of these issues and of their late adjustment, either upon the one hand or upon the other, having no practical end, is now worse than in vain, and is dangerous alike to all that is precious in the Union and that is worth preserving in the States."

The Southern fire-eaters would have done well, in the spring of 1851, to accept the defeat of the secession movement, and to await new issues and new opportunities. Time was telling against them. With every month the sectional temperature fell. But acquiesence is not a trait of extremists. Their bitterness had reached an extreme pitch. As Petigru wrote, they did not wish to see the Fugitive Slave Act executed, for they labored to keep every national wound infected. They saw what might be their last hope of a free Southern republic disappearing. Corresponding widely, and cheering each other on, they resolved to make a final fight in the autumn elections of 1851. They would do their best to carry four States—South Carolina, Mississippi, Alabama, and Georgia. If they gained but two or even one, that might suffice.[35]

In all four States the Southern Rights men, led by Quitman, Yancey, Rhett, and McDonald, flung down their challenge. In all four the natural trend toward a reconstitution of the old Whig-Democratic alignment was checked (though the Whig Party had little vitality in South Carolina), and a struggle between the Southern Rights Party and Union Party substituted. The early weeks of spring found the new battle fully joined.

It was in South Carolina that the situation was most dangerous and the fighting angriest. May found the little knot of disunionist leaders still confident that they could sweep all before them. "There is no temporary excitement here, but a deep resolution and a fixed purpose, which will be steadily carried out," wrote Maxcy Gregg, a leading attorney and Mexican War veteran. He was urging Quitman to maintain an undaunted struggle for secession in Mississippi, so that when South Carolina seceded, the first shedding of blood would raise an irresistible wave of western sympathizers. "In this great struggle, the South wants a great Leader, with the mind and nerve to impel and guide evolution. Be that leader, and your place in history will remain conspicuous for the admiration of all ages to come." Rhett, Seabrook, and others, Gregg added, were laboring to keep South Carolina steadfast. "Very probably there will be no division at all in the ranks of the Resistance Party—and that Party is the State."

For a time William J. Grayson, a Federal officeholder of fine literary talent, B. F. Perry, and Petigru were deeply perturbed. After consulting with friends in Charleston, Grayson pointed out to Secretary Tom Corwin the proper line of attack. If the secession party remained united, it would win. If it were distinctly divided between advocates of immediate secession, and those who although professing disunionist views, would postpone action until other States coöperated or certain remote contingencies were met, then the country would be safe. "Men may be brought to repudiate separate State action, but there

35 Petigru to Corwin, November 16, 1850; Corwin Papers.

are very few who can be brought to do more than that at once." [36] If delay were achieved, the fever would gradually die away.

This line proved easy to take, for the resistance party spontaneously split into two groups. In the fall of 1850 only half a dozen prominent South Carolina leaders had publicly opposed secession, and Grayson, Poinsett, and Perry alone possessed high talents. By the summer of 1851 their ranks had been lengthened by many more; for Representatives Orr and Preston Brooks, Senators Butler and Robert W. Barnwell, with numerous others of influence, demanded a cautious policy. I cannot but believe, Col. John S. Preston told his community, that if South Carolina acts separately, the results will be appalling— and that among these results will be "the consolidation of the Federal power and the consequent early abolition of slavery."

The idea that South Carolina might attain unprecedented prosperity as an independent little republic was showered with ridicule. Even Texas, Senator Butler pointed out, had been unable to maintain herself as a separate nation. A writer in the Charleston *Courier* published a telling exposé of Rhett's vision of commercial wealth as soon as the State became the free entrepôt of the South. He demonstrated that if South Carolina seceded, the best it could hope for would be a commerce of five million a year, paying a revenue of barely half a million in duties. As other writers sarcastically pointed out, the secessionists evidently intended that South Carolina should make money by an illicit smuggling trade with neighboring States; not a proud occupation for her people, and not likely to be long profitable! While the Columbia *Transcript*, a coöperationist journal, pointed to the financial distress which would ensue as soon as other States began sending back for redemption the millions of South Carolina banknotes they held, Representative J. L. Orr touched an even more sensitive nerve. On the day that South Carolina seceded, he reminded citizens, every slave in the State would become immovable, for the laws of the United States would prevent any importation; and how then could South Carolinians dispose of their steadily-growing excess of Negroes? Meanwhile, Robert Barnwell was arguing that South Carolina was already too much divided from her sisters in the South, and that if she went out, contracted a foreign alliance, and began to depend on illicit trade, the division would become irreparable.[37]

36 Gregg to Quitman, Charleston, May 15, 1851; Claiborne Papers. Grayson to Corwin April 16, 1851; Corwin Papers. There could be no question of the ugly temper of South Carolina. Crallé, the literary executor of Calhoun, looking after the publication of his works, came north from South Carolina in the spring of 1851. He reported that the State was "resolute and determined and that she would go out." D. H. London, New York, to Buchanan, April 23, 1851; Buchanan Papers.

37 Columbia, S. C., *Transcript*, August 7, May 22, 30, 1851 on Preston, Orr, Barnwell. *Harper's* Monthly Record, July, 1851. Poinsett made a tart comment on Rhett's scheme for commercial independence: "The Senator tells us that 'safety and honor are on the one hand,

It was well that this uprising of coöperative secessionists took place, for the small Unionist organization alone could never have prevented the separate secessionists from rushing into folly. All reports agreed that lowland South Carolina was the seat of a veritable frenzy. Francis Lieber, deploring the strength of "spouting furibunds," wrote confidentially that "it is a sad thing to know oneself floating on a plank in the midst of a turbulent sea of madness." One of Tom Corwin's Charleston correspondents remarked that he could well understand Corwin's reluctance to believe that an intelligent people could be so insane as to plunge their State without cause into utter ruin. "If however you were as familiar as I am with their foolish and ridiculous *State pride* and their subserviency to the views and ideas of a few artful and designing demagogues" —then he would not be astonished. The novelist J. P. Kennedy, wandering among the Virginia springs this summer, found the visitors from Charleston and Columbia hot for secession. "We have troops of South Carolinians all through these mountains—they are generally rabid and intractable seceders— women as well as men. It is the strangest mania that has ever broke out in this country. . . ." It was not at all strange to those who know the history of South Carolina; nor was Kennedy's hope that the disunionists would get right without having the government set them right shared too confidently by well-informed men.[38]

[VIII]

The crucial decision was made by South Carolina in the elections of October, 1851, for delegates to the State convention—and made with the heaviest poll in many years. The Unionists and coöperationists, joining hands against the separate secessionists, by a vote of 25,045 to 17,710 established a smashing ascendency. Since it was now plain that no other Southern State would coöperate in secession, the vote meant an indefinite postponement. Though unquestionably the coöperationists deserved most of the credit for the victory, the Unionists had made a gallant and memorable fight against heavy odds. W. J. Grayson had remarked in the spring that it would be more proper to call the people thoughtless than faithless, implying that they could be made to

danger and degradation on the other'; and I agree with him except as to on which side lie the danger and degradation." C. W. Dudley, addressing Marlborough District in a broadside handbill, declared for staying in the Union at present and working with the other Southern States for separation. "Let us not drive away our allies, by injudicious haste on our part, but remain and preserve our influence with them, until the auspicious moment arrives to strike the blow that will separate us forever from the hollow hypocrites of the North." S. Caroliniana Library; dated Bennettsville, June 21, 1851.
38 T. S. Perry, *Life and Letters of Francis Lieber,* 249. E. Gamp to Corwin, Charleston, May 18, 1851; Corwin Papers. Kennedy to his wife, Salt Sulphur, Va., August 10, 1851; Kennedy Papers.

think. Undoubtedly he and B. F. Perry, Francis Lieber, Poinsett, and Petigru, by pamphlet, letter, and speech, had done much to make the unreflecting reflect.

Poinsett, speaking and writing, had been ready to sacrifice all his hard-won popularity. Perry, setting up a journal to speak for and to the upland population, the *Southern Patriot*, had declared his willingness to sink every cent he possessed in maintaining it. Grayson had brought out his *Letters of Curtius*, an attack on secessionist ideas which showed something of Tom Paine's epigrammatic touch. He derided the idea that the Southerners had suffered any grave wrongs, saying they paid light taxes and felt no oppression. He sneered at the brown loaf of ugly, sour, indigestible secession bread which its makers pronounced divine food. He ridiculed the braggadocio of South Carolinians, who according to their Fourth of July orators would conquer Fort Moultrie with the Citadel cadets while the older men seized Washington and invaded California. In short, the unionist wing of the opposition had effectively aided Cheves, Orr, Barnwell, Preston, Chesnut, and the other influential co-operationists.[39]

The precise meaning of the election remained a good deal of a riddle. Had the disunionist frenzy been a surface phenomenon, or had it struck deep? Did the vote against separate secession mean that the rich slaveholders, the merchants and bankers, aware that their property was safest inside the Union, were against secession altogether? Did it mean that the poorer whites, so largely disfranchised by the aristocratic constitution, were in revolt against the low-country fire-eaters?—for this optimistic interpretation was offered by some Northern journals. Perry's *Southern Patriot* had consistently asserted that secessionist feeling was waning. Grayson had declared in midsummer that the secessionists were secretly rejoiced to escape the crime of destroying the happiest government the world had ever seen; and though now and then a catamount yell still came from the swamps, he doubted its sincerity. It was the *love of order* that had defeated secession, thought Maxcy Gregg; the same love of order that had been the great obstacle to nullification.[40]

39 Boucher, *op, cit.*, 129. *Harper's Magazine*, December, 1851. *Southern Patriot*, February 28, 1851. Autobiography of W. J. Grayson, ed. R. D. Bass, MS, South Caroliniana Library.
40 On the revolt of the poor whites, N. Y. *Weekly Tribune*, October 25, 1851. B. F. Perry, *Reminiscences of Famous Men*, 288. When the election was over the *Southern Patriot* felt no doubt of its significance. "The recent election *was an anti-secession, and not a cooperation victory*," it said. It added that neither the people of South Carolina nor those of other slaveholding States "are disposed to live in a constant state of excitement and alarm." The last legislature had appropriated $350,000 to buy arms and ammunition, and $150,000 to build a navy. Perry proposed that the State sell or auction them off, pocketing the loss; quoted in Columbia *South Carolinian*, November 5, 1851. Maxcy Gregg believed the conservative "love of order" could be overcome. "I cannot agree with you that the age has passed for maintaining the rights of small communities by force," he wrote on March 29, 1852; Hammond Papers.

And yet there was much in South Carolina's temper to cause continued apprehension. We have few downright submissionists, wrote Maxcy Gregg, and he was right. Even in the speeches of coöperationist leaders throbbed the sullen note of *ultimate* secession. The other cotton States cannot long hold out against the idea of a Southern Confederacy, argued Col. John S. Preston. "They see, and begin to feel, there is no remedy but disunion. That banner is on the breeze, and soon, very soon, its hosts will be beside ours." Orr took the same view. "Five years ago disunion would not have been tolerated in South Carolina," he told a crowd, "but now there is not one union man in this vast assembly. In the other cotton States, newspapers and orators are openly advocating secession and a Southern confederacy, and the party is on rapidly rising ground." Robert Barnwell looked forward to an eventual Southern nation, strong in physical power and in financial resources, which would perhaps sign a British alliance. Even Grayson did not rule out the idea of ultimate secession, and expounded the doctrine of economic nationalism, saying that the South ought to cut off its trade with the North. The Graniteville cotton mills near Aiken had built up among the barren hills, in four years, a well-ordered community of fifteen hundred persons, with growing comfort, intelligence, and refinement. Let the South pursue this path of enterprise, exhorted Grayson, and ten years would do more to make it independent of the world than the previous forty years had done. All this was in reality more threatening than the wild periods of Rhett, delivered under the palmetto flag to a crowd who threw up their sweaty caps for Quitman as the first president of the Southern Republic. Late in September, James Smith Colburn of Charleston sent the Cabinet some advice which there was reason to recall nine years later:[41]

"The Government should keep their eyes on this State and watch all their movements, and in case of secession, the Forts should be defended and kept, the custom house removed to Savannah, and the coast blockaded, which would soon bring them to their senses."

If Calhoun's State offered the most dramatic contest, Mississippi presented the most amusing. Such figures as the volcanic Quitman, the demagogic A. G. Brown, and the icily determined Jefferson Davis were certain to make any political scene interesting. A double battle had to be fought, the election of a governor interacting with the election of delegates to a State convention on Federal relations. While intensely serious, it had its opera bouffe.

The opposing captains, Quitman and Foote, were determined to carry the struggle to a decisive issue; but the governor fought against fortune, and his

41 Gregg to Quitman, May 9, 1851; Claiborne Papers. For Preston's remarks see Columbia *Transcript*, August 7, 1851. *Ibid.*, May 31, 1851, for Orr and Barnwell. P. A. Hamer, *Secession Movement in South Carolina*, 103–104. Colburn to Corwin, September 23, 1851; Corwin Papers.

mischances furnished comedy for the campaign. First he was arrested (February 3, 1851), on a charge of complicity in the Lopez expedition against Cuba. He resigned his seat, and protesting violently, went to stand trial in the Federal court in New Orleans; and when in March a *nolle prosequi* was entered, returned amid acclamations to Jackson. Another striking scene was enacted at the capital in mid-June. The Democratic convention met, and appointed a committee of eighteen to report a nominee for governor. This body favored Jefferson Davis, who had just expounded anew his view that the Southern States ought to meet in convention to try to "battle for our rights from behind the barriers of the Constitution." But Quitman's friends demanded the nomination for him with the utmost vehemence, while Quitman himself visited the committee to make a personal appeal. Since Davis, who was ill in the hotel at the time, was unwilling to accept the nomination if Quitman wanted it, Quitman was chosen! [42]

Thereupon the campaign against Foote, the Union candidate for governor, was launched with terrific heat. All the advantages were with the Senator. Foote was one of the best stump speakers alive, excelling in irony and satire, and possessing a gorgeous imagery and luxuriant diction (Quitman's biographer calls it "a diarrhea of words") which delighted Mississippians. Quitman's style of speaking, on the other hand, was tame and flat. Friends urged him to be more spirited and personal. He took them so literally that at Sledgeville on July 18 the candidates exchanged blows. To the end the campaign went on with unabated fire. When the election for the convention took place on September 1–2, the eyes of the whole nation were fastened on the State; and news that the Union ticket had won, 28,402 to 21,241, delighted all friends of the Compromise. Said the New York *Tribune*: "The peril of disunion, always exaggerated, has ceased to be even a scarecrow." Quitman saw the writing on the wall, and withdrew as a candidate for governor, his place being taken at great personal sacrifice by Jefferson Davis. This was a fitting choice, for the Democratic platform, which disapproved of the Compromise, but declared that secession was inexpedient, precisely expressed Davis's position. But Davis had just begun a six-year term in the Senate which, to meet the party emergency, he resigned.[43]

The November election gave Foote the victory, 28,738 to 27,729—and a

---

42 R. Davis, *Recollections of Mississippi*, 315–316; N. Y. *Tribune*, June 24, 1851; Dunbar Rowland, ed., *Jefferson Davis, Constitutionalist: His Letters, Papers, and Speeches*, II, 111–171.
43 R. Davis, *op. cit.*, 317ff; Claiborne, *Life of John A. Quitman*, II, 144. Many Union Democrats in other States—A. J. Donelson, for example, now head of the Washington *Union*—thought it most unfortunate that Davis had consented to run, for his election would only prolong the secessionist agitation and destroy all hope of a restoration of the old Democratic party on a platform of Compromise-acceptance. It would perhaps even bring about a schism in the Democratic National Convention of 1852. Donelson to Buchanan, October 18, November 2, 1851; Buchanan Papers.

handsomely earned victory it was. First in the Senate battle over compromise and now at home he had shown brilliant talents and indomitable courage. Three of the four Congressional seats went to Unionists, and the official organ of the party, the *Flag of the Union*, commented that A. G. Brown would not have won the fourth had he not paraded himself everywhere as a Union man of the first order. If Quitman had remained at the head of the ticket, he would have been completely crushed. A much larger vote was cast than in September, and the New York *Tribune* commented that the last-hour gains of the State Rights party were attributable to the fact that it had backed out of disunion and gone over to all-potent Democratic appeals, with a very popular candidate for governor. Foote gloated over the spectacle of his hated rival wending his way to "Briarfield" for retirement. Davis, on the other hand, was so deeply mortified that he resolved never to return to public life until the people of Mississippi loudly called him. The humiliation of being beaten by Foote, Fraud, and Freesoil, and by such shallow artifice, he wrote, made defeat doubly galling.[44]

Early in the year ex-Judge Sharkey had written that two-thirds of the people of Mississippi would be satisfied with the Compromise if the Fugitive Slave Act were only honestly enforced. When the State convention met in Jackson on November 10, 1851, it registered the popular reaction against the disunion movement. It expressed confidence in the implementation of the Compromise, voiced its hope for a cessation of all further slavery agitation, and in memorable words, by a vote of 73 to 17, declared that the asserted right of secession "is utterly unsanctioned by the Federal Constitution . . . and that no secession can, in fact, take place without a subversion of the Union established, and which will not amount in its effects and consequences to a civil revolution."[45]

The outcome in other Southern States during the fall of 1851 was equally reassuring. In Georgia the Union Whigs under Toombs and Stephens and the Union Democrats under Howell Cobb united in the Constitutional Union party, which nominated Cobb for governor. His secessionist opponent was Charles J. McDonald, who had the backing of Herschel V. Johnson. The Unionist alliance gained a resounding victory, electing Cobb by more than 18,000 majority. His showing in northwestern Georgia, an upland region of small farmers, was especially impressive. The new legislature, three-quarters Unionist, promptly elected Toombs to the national Senate. Three of the five Congressmen chosen were Union men.

In Alabama, meanwhile, Yancey was striving sleeplessly to keep the agitation

44 *Flag of the Union* quoted in Ranck, *A. G. Brown*, 100. N. Y. *Tribune*, November 24, 1851. Foote, *Casket of Reminiscences*, 355. Rowland, *Jefferson Davis*, II, 121, 334-337.
45 N. Y. *Tribune*, February 11, 1851, on Sharkey. "Journal of the Convention of the State of Mississippi," 31.

alive. Yet the radicals nominated nobody for governor, leaving the race to the out-and-out Unionists and the moderate State rights Unionists—both groups approving the Compromise. Senator Jere Clemens energetically stumped the State for the Union cause, and F. A. P. Barnard, then a professor at the University of Mississippi, delivered a memorable speech at Tuscaloosa in which he blamed the current excitement upon unprincipled agitators, and called upon Alabama to turn her back upon them, set up cotton mills, and develop her own resources. Most old Whig papers joined the Democratic Mobile *Register* in assailing Yancey. The election showed that the great majority of Alabamians acquiesced in the new sectional settlement. Only two Congressional seats were carried by secessionists, while five went to men more or less distinctly opposed to disunionist measures.[46]

[IX]

Peace, prosperity, and Union—all over the South these seemed to be the watchwords of the new era. There had never been any question that the border area, including North Carolina, and the Southwest, full of pioneer nationalism, strongly approved the Compromise. The two old cotton States of South Carolina and Georgia, and the two new cotton States of Alabama and Mississippi, had been the danger points; and even they had uttered a decisive "No." Strong pressure came from national Democratic leaders for reknitting the party fabric and dropping the disunionist clamor. They feared that unless the Rhetts and Quitmans subsided, a permanent Union Party would take root in the South,

46 N. Y. *Tribune*, October 18, 1851. Phillips, *Robert E. Toombs*, 105. L. Dorman, *Party Politics in Alabama From 1850 Through 1860*, pp. 55–60. *Harper's* Monthly Record, August, 1851, on Alabama; November, 1851, on Georgia, Denman, *op. cit.*, 54ff. In Georgia, Herschel V. Johnson, who supported McDonald, declared that secession was coming, for the tone of Northern fanaticism did not abate its frenzy and insolence, and secession was the only remedy. P. S. Flippin, *op. cit.*, 39ff. F. A. P. Barnard, then professor in the University of Alabama, struck a totally different note in a July 4th oration at Tuscaloosa. In this speech, strongly Unionist in tone (later published at the request of the mayor and corporation), he blamed the current excitement upon unprincipled agitators. One of their typical exaggerations, he said, dealt with the losses from fugitive slaves. It was said that organized associations were annually stealing away thousands of the best laborers; that a huge amount of wealth was being lost. The lowest figure for fugitive slaves then in the free States was 100,000—their value $50,000,000. Actually, the census showed that there were not 200,000 free Negroes in all the free States put together, and their numbers had not materially increased in the past twenty years. The agitators shouted about Northern aggressions. But the statesman who had represented Alabama in Washington ever since she became a State said that now "there is less danger of encroachment upon Southern rights than at any time for the last twenty years." Let Alabama turn her back on these false excitements, said Barnard. Let her develop her resources. She could set up a cotton mill on the Warrior River, use raw cotton for four cents less a pound than it cost the English mills, and sell it in the Southern market without costly transportation. She would have to import the first managers of the enterprise, but she could soon be training her own mill officials. Pvt., Huntington Library.

sorely injuring or even destroying the Democratic organization. Douglas and Buchanan were insistent, in their letters to Southern Democrats, that the quarrel must cease, and they were backed by the Washington *Union*, which this year passed under the editorship of Andrew Jackson Donelson, Jackson's oldtime protégé and secretary. In fact, a cohort of Democratic leaders at the North now insisted that the Rhetts and Yanceys keep still; that Howell Cobb and Foote, the chief beneficiaries of the Union Party, return to the regular fold; and that all should rally about the old party tenets.[47]

In retrospect, three main factors could be seen as responsible (beyond a basic love of the Union) for the utter rout of secessionist forces in the cotton States. The first was the general flush of prosperity throughout the region. This prosperity, remarked the *Spirit of the South*, explained the reluctance to undertake resistance; "because there is plenty to live on, because we are out of debt, and cotton brings a good price, many are in so good a humor and so well satisfied with themselves and things around them as to shut their eyes to the future in the consoling reflection that the future cannot hurt them." Men would not fly from affluence to ills they knew not of; ills vividly pictured by the Alabama *Journal*. "Disunion will not give us a better price for cotton—will not increase the value of slave property—will not render them more secure—will not diminish taxation—but will be likely under the best imaginable state of affairs to double taxation, diminish the price of our staples, and reduce the value of negroes and land, fifty per cent." B. F. Perry later stated his conviction that many wealthy South Carolinians who ostensibly backed the secession ticket were delighted by its defeat. He had heard a friend say that the wealthiest rice-planter of the State, who voted for disunion, would at any time have given privately his draft for $100,000 to crush it.[48]

Along with economic factors, the political situation operated against secession in 1850-51. In Alabama and Georgia, as in North Carolina, Tennessee, and other States, the Whigs were still powerful—still nearly equal to the Democrats. Both parties were badly divided on the question. In any clear-cut contest the

47 Files of the Washington *Union*. Donelson to Buchanan, October 18, 1851; Buchanan Papers. In Tennessee an especially interesting campaign was made by Truesdale, a Democratic leader who had fought for his country at sixteen, whose integrity was immovable as a mountain, but who had what Cave Johnson called "a slow and toiling mind." He did not believe that the Compromise had done justice to the South, "and yet he would have suffered death rather than disturb it." Finally Johnson advised him that in order to secure the Hotspurs of the middle and western parts of the State, of whom there were a large number, and to keep the whole Democratic party together for the 1852 campaign, he should criticize the provisions of the Compromise freely, but urge its full and faithful acceptance. He did so, and obtained a large vote—but not large enough. Johnson to Buchanan, Nashville, November 18, 1851; Buchanan Papers.
48 *Spirit of the South*, October 22, 1850. Alabama *Journal*, July 23, 1850. Perry, MS Autobiography.

Unionist majority of the Whigs could unite with the Unionist minority of the Democrats to carry the day; and in some areas it could unite with a unionist Democratic majority! Not until the Whig party was destroyed, permitting a group of secessionists in key States to capture the single party of strength and use its machinery, would revolutionary action be feasible. It might be added that not until the differences between separate secessionists and coöperative secessionists were erased would such capture be easy.

Finally, the social and cultural development of the South as a separate entity was still much too immature to let secessionist tendencies attain vigorous growth. The rise of separate Southern churches, the diffusion of newspapers and magazines preaching an aggressive Southernism, the use of Southern textbooks in the schools, the Southern commercial conventions, Southern poetry and fiction, and above all Southern polemics, were bringing into existence a national spirit; but that is always a plant of slow growth. In 1850, hundreds of thousands who ten years later would think of themselves as Southerners still thought of themselves simply as Americans.

It was significant of the importance of economic factors that Unionist leaders sounded a clarion call for more attention to internal development and less waste of energy on national dissension. The neglect of urgent improvements, said Perry in his *Southern Patriot*, was driving thousands of citizens from South Carolina. Let her extend her railroads and plank roads, build up her manufactories, erect public buildings like the new Statehouses of Tennessee and North Carolina, begin furnishing her own iron, granite, and marble, and above all, develop her schools, academies, and colleges. Let her encourage the direct import and export of merchandise and products. The same cry was raised in Alabama and Mississippi. One of the principal exponents of economic development in Alabama was Daniel Pratt, successful manufacturer of textiles and gins in Autauga County. Saying that incendiary speeches about secession were silly while the State's industries were so primitive, he exhorted Alabamians to go quietly to work to provide their own coal, iron, hardware, farm-implements, clothing, and shoes. Expounding his doctrines in the Alabama *Journal*, he hailed the abolitionist agitation as a much-needed alarm bell to awaken the South to industrial activity. The Alabama legislature in the session of 1851–52 chartered two companies for direct trade between Mobile and Europe, and subsidized them by exempting the sale of direct imports from taxes.[49]

In the political field, strenuous efforts were made during the winter of 1851–52 to reorganize and reknit the Democratic Party. With the Presidential election of 1852 looming ahead, unity was imperative. In Alabama the ranks

49 Perry quoted in *National Intelligencer*, January 17, 1852. Alabama *Journal*, October 21, 24, 1850.

were almost fully closed. Yancey, temporarily putting on the garb of meekness, made speeches advising the people to accept the Georgia platform. Only the sternest Unionists of north Alabama and the wildest secessionists of her rich Black Belt refused to clasp hands. In Mississippi also most of the discordant elements fell into line. Foote, arriving in Jackson on a chill January day for his inauguration, was greeted by cannon, banners, and the jubilant yells of a surging crowd. In his inaugural address he congratulated the country on the fact that the Compromise had commanded the hearty approval of nineteen-twentieths of the American people, saying that in Mississippi not a single voice was now heard in opposition to a series of measures which six months before were assailed by thousands with language of bitter denunciation and caustic ridicule.

In Georgia greater trouble was encountered. "Seeing that the State would be chained to the Car of Whiggery for all future time unless the Democratic party could be reorganized and restored to vigor," Herschel V. Johnson later explained to Franklin Pierce, "a meeting of such Democrats as could be got together was held on the 13th of November, 1851, in Milledgeville, during the session of the legislature, to adopt measures for that purpose. That meeting created a committee . . . to report to a subsequent meeting to be held at the capital on the evening of the 25th of November . . . I hand you a copy of the report and proceedings of that meeting, that you may see for yourself how *formally* and how distinctly, we abandoned the Southern Rights organization and unfurled the old democratic Banner. I beg you to read it, as a matter of justice to the democratic party of Georgia. Does it not breathe the right spirit? Does it contain a word that ought to offend our Union *democratic* brethren? Would it not seem, to any candid mind, that it ought to have resulted in the entire harmony of the party? So far from this, I assure you, not a single Union democrat, united in the meeting; but the whole Union press was out in full cry against us, denouncing us as '*hyprocrites*,' '*secessionists*,' '*fire-eaters*,' '*disunionists*,' etc., etc." Yet even in Georgia ultimate reconciliation took place on the "Georgia platform." [50]

It was the Whig Party which in the end suffered most heavily from the strains of the Compromise. It, too, underwent a process of reorganization in the cotton belt. But the Alabama editor who stated that the election of 1851 had killed the Whig Party dead as a mackerel in his State, and that by the fall of 1852 a Whig there would be a curiosity, hit near the truth. The main reasons were three, and were obvious to all. First, the tendency of the Northern

---

50 L. Dorman, *Party Politics in Alabama, 1850–1860*, p. 76. Editorial and letter from a citizen of Jackson on January 9 in *National Intelligencer*, January 27, 1852. Johnson to Pierce, July 21, 1852; Franklin Pierce Papers.

Whigs to attack Southern institutions made it difficult to remain allied with them without incurring discredit. Second, the Whig Party had lost its chief principles; tariff protection and internal improvements too definitely favored the North to have any appeal to the South. Third, the impending deaths of Clay and Webster would remove the only two Whig leaders of truly national prestige. While the path of the Democratic Party in the South was thorny enough, that of the Whig Party turned definitely downward to obliteration.[51]

Acquiescence had triumphed in the South. But this fatal weakness of the Whig Party was one reason for regarding the future with misgiving. Another ground for apprehension lay in continued recalcitrancy of a bold band of leaders. Yancey continued to watch, wait, and intrigue. One of the organs of his clan, the Dallas, Ala., *Gazette*, said in the fall of 1851 that it was immovable: "For our part when we hoisted the banner of Southern Rights at our masthead, we did so with a determination to stand by it through weal or woe; and come what may, we shall not strike it until the South is independent, or her people sunk so low in the sea of submission as to be forever beyond the hope of resurrection." Rhett closed the year 1851 with a speech saying that he had been a disunionist since 1841, and was a disunionist still. His reasons boiled down to a conviction that the South was steadily being overbalanced and overwhelmed, and that she was being unjustly treated in the distribution of territory. He would fight to the end, he said, to keep his section from being made another Hungary.[52]

But above all, it had to be remembered that Southern acquiescence was conditional. The Georgia Platform was a sufficiently clear warning, and it was underlined in the summer of 1851 by the action of the Mississippi Union Convention in appending to strongly pacific resolutions the emphatic addendum: "Resolved, that it is our deliberate opinion, that upon the faithful execution of the Fugitive Slave law, by the proper authorities, depends the preservation of our much-loved Union." [53]

51 Dorman, *op. cit.*, 60–61.
52 Dallas *Gazette* quoted in Columbia *South Carolinian*, November 8, 1850. N. Y. *Tribune*, December 20, 1851, on Rhett.
53 N. Y. *Weekly Tribune*, July 5, 1851.

12

Northern Acquiescence—With Reservations

THE MORAL IMPULSE which helped rear the anti-slavery movement was of course most deeply touched when a fleeing Negro carried into a Northern community the spectacle of his helplessness, his wrongs, and his anguish. The very act of running away commonly argued moral or physical maltreatment and poignant desperation. Few black men and women faced the hardships of a long and lonely flight, the perils of pursuit, recapture, and punishment, the uncertainties of freedom in an alien land, without heartache and dark misgiving. They began their hazardous journey, usually without a penny, a friend, or a bit of property save the poor clothes on their backs, because they had no decent choice: because their families had been broken up by sale, because they were brutally punished, or because they were threatened with transportation "down the river" to the sugar and cotton fields of the Lower South. And when they crossed the Ohio or Delaware, were the free communities they entered to yield them up to professional slave-catchers, furious in pursuit of their quarry? The great majority of Northerners in 1850 had no desire to interfere with slavery where it existed; possibly a majority would still permit it some little extension. But this same majority would die in its tracks before it would aid the slaveholder to hunt down his harried, panting, wild-eyed bondsman.

Hence it was that the passage of the new Fugitive Slave Act sent a wave of defiant indignation across the North, mitigated only by a strong conviction that it could never be enforced. On this point the demand for conformity stuck in the throats of even the mildest. The conservative Robert C. Winthrop, praising Fillmore's annual message at the close of 1850, wrote that he should not have emphasized so much the word *final*, "as if the Fugitive Slave law was to be as unchangeable as the laws of the Medes and the Persians—which, by the bye, it more resembles in some of its details than any American or European code." Everett agreed. He had already declared that he would never obey the act. "I admit the right of the South to an efficient extradition law; but it is a right *that cannot be enforced*. The difficulty with the old law was that it was against the feeling of the people." Writing to Webster, he had pointed out a certain inconsistency on the part of Southerners. Senator Butler had defended the Charlestonians who in 1846 drove Rockwood Hoar from their city, on the ground that if he had remained he would have been mobbed; but Hoar had gone there merely to argue in the circuit court the second section of the fourth article of the Constitution—the same section which grants the right of extradition. "If such a cause is enough to rouse a mob in Charleston, how can Southern gentlemen expect our mob to assist in arresting their fugitive?" [1]

It was true that the South expected a more precise observance of the Constitution in the North than it was ready to furnish at home. Any Northerner who travelled below the Potomac to announce a lecture on slavery would have been in peril, and any man who scattered an anti-slavery pamphlet in a Southern town would have been lucky to escape with summary ejectment. When black cooks and stewards entered certain Southern ports they were temporarily locked up, though their presence offered no real danger. The excuse of the Southerners for unconstitutional interferences with freedom of speech, the press, the mails, and the person was the state of public excitement and the danger of slave insurrection. Within limits it was a valid excuse; but the South was unwilling to extend to Northern sentiment the same tolerance.

Tolerance was particularly needed because the provisions of the new law were excessively harsh and stringent. Southerners would have been wise if, at the cost of losing a few more slaves, they had satisfied themselves with a milder enactment. The main complaints of the Northern people were four. First, the act allowed no jury trial for fugitives, though the Constitution provided that in suits at common law where the value in controversy exceeded twenty dollars jury trial should be maintained. The claimant's affidavit established his title. Second, the act did not allow the fugitive even a hearing before a judge, but authorized the captor to take him at once before a Federal commissioner, specially attached to the usual courts by the new law, who was empowered to issue a certificate for hurrying the Negro off to slavery without stay or appeal. Third, the commissioner was to get ten dollars if he directed the return of the captive, but only five if he ordered a release. The reason given was that the papers for a return involved more labor, but Northerners were quick to assert that the extra payment was in effect a bribe. Anson Burlingame remarked that the law fixed the price of a Carolina Negro at one thousand dollars, and of a Yankee soul at five! Finally, the marshal or deputies charged with the arrest

1 Winthrop to Everett, December 10; Everett to Winthrop, March 21, to Webster, April 3, 1850; Everett Papers.

of the alleged fugitive were subject to a fine of $1,000 if they refused to execute it; they were empowered to summon all citizens to their aid; and any person who concealed or rescued a fugitive might be fined $1,000, imprisoned for six months, and mulcted $1,000 in civil damages for every slave so lost—all this seeming excessively severe.

These four complaints were iterated and reiterated by the North. What chiefly distressed calm-minded people was the possibility that a Negro who had lived for years in a Northern community, industrious and useful, might now be rapt from home and friends to lifelong servitude on flimsy evidence presented in *ex parte* fashion to a prejudiced Federal placeholder.[2]

It was unfortunate that in a group of laws adopted with conciliatory intent, one should so bristle with offence to a multitude of patriotic Americans. Originally the measure had provided for jury trial. This is, the committee of thirteen had reported a bill which required that the owner or agent reclaiming an alleged fugitive should take him home, bring him before the first court meeting there, and if he asserted his freedom, submit the case to twelve sworn men. This was satisfactory, for as the committee stated, colored persons suing for freedom usually found attorneys quick to defend them, and met with general sympathy. But in the final bill this provision for jury trial was stricken out.

All well-informed people knew that the fifth amendment to the Constitution, stipulating that no person should be deprived of life, liberty, or property without due process of law, and the seventh, safeguarding the right of jury trial, had been carried in response to an overwhelming public demand, and that for centuries the right of jury trial had been one of the proudest of Anglo-American traditions. John Van Buren declared the Fugitive Slave Act flagrantly unconstitutional. On this point the best authorities were against him. But Lincoln was quite right in saying later that the law should have been so framed that a free Negro would be in no greater danger of slavery under it than an innocent man would be of hanging under the murder laws. The deletion of the jury clause saved a few slaves annually to the South at the cost of alienating countless thousands of former friends of the section.

[I]

Theodore Parker had declared that slavery was ringed about by a contracting wall of flame. The harsh character of the new law cast oil upon the circle

---

2 On the provision for jury trial, see Clay's speech in *Cong. Globe*, May 13, 1850; John Van Buren to Massachusetts Convention opposing the Fugitive Slave Act, April 4, 1851, in N. Y. *Tribune*, April 19, 1851.

of fire. While it was pending the religious journals of the North with remark-able unanimity either condemned it outright, or asserted that no humane man could help enforce it. The New York *Evangelist* said that no human compact could bind the conscience of the people to such revolting work as helping re-capture slaves. The New York *Independent* asserted that "the slave catcher shall not budge an inch further than he now does in the North"—that every village would spurn him. The New York *Observer* believed there was "no respectable man, whose feelings would not revolt at the thought of aiding in the capture of fugitive slaves," while the Boston *Christian Register* was for treating the Constitution in this matter as a dead letter. *Zion's Herald,* a Methodist organ, predicted that if Webster compelled men to the odious work of slave catching, the curses of his fellow-citizens would follow him through life and those of their children would fall upon his grave. The Boston *Watchman and Reporter,* the leading Baptist journal, avowed that "even with the alternative of disunion" the North could "sanction no concession." Theocracy was dead in America, but religious interventionism in politics was still powerful.[3]

When morality enters public affairs the general principle has a thunderous voice, and in both morals and economics fear of evils to come is a far greater excitant than any immediate loss. These facts explain why, under the heat generated by the Fugitive Slave Act, mustard seeds sprang everywhere into trees. Had both North and South sat down quietly, appraised the number and value of the fugitive slaves, got at the truth about all reports of the kidnapping of free Negroes, and refrained from emotion and exaggeration, agreement might have been possible. Both sides were equally guilty of hysteria. As Clay pointed out, while his border State of Kentucky, which was most exposed to loss, showed little irritation, the Deep South, from which flight was extremely difficult, lashed itself into fury. No precise figures of the number of fugitives are available. But according to the Census of 1850, only sixteen out of almost 400,000 South Carolina slaves ran away that year. According to estimates embodied in the Census of 1860, the year 1850 saw only about a thousand slaves running away; most of them came from the border area; and by no means all of them got into free States. It was notorious that in Maryland and Delaware many slaveholders thought themselves well rid of runaways, and that many slaves were manumitted to save the trouble of holding them. But many Southerners, relying on wild guesses, convinced themselves that a hundred

---

3 Files Union Theological Seminary. Yet the clergy were much divided. Samuel May later complained that "of the thirty thousand ministers of all the denominations in the United States, I believe not one in a hundred ever raised his voice against the enslavement of millions of our countrymen, nor lifted a finger to protect one who had escaped from bondage." Many ministers insisted on obedience to law. *Recollections of the Anti-Slavery Conflict,* 349–373.

thousand Negroes had escaped, and that the losses ran into tens of millions—the relatively safe Cotton States showing the greatest anger! [4]

Parts of the North, though on the whole small parts, were equally unreasonable. Pursuit and recapture would naturally be commonest along the border, yet it was far-off New England, Michigan, and Wisconsin which evinced the most fury. Webster in 1850 diligently inquired among New England Congressmen as to cases of seizure. He found that (so far as this source of information went) no alleged fugitive slave had ever been seized by a lawful master in Maine; none had ever been seized in New Hampshire; none had ever been seized in Vermont; none had been seized in Rhode Island within the past twenty years; and only one had been seized in Connecticut—that case, some twenty-five years earlier, having terminated in the immediate discharge of the Negro for want of identification. Several seizures had taken place in Massachusetts, but the history of only one was known; that, a capture in Boston in the late 1830's, having ended when the owner accepted a sum which he regarded as less than half the value of the fugitive. Yet many New Englanders talked as if their section was certain to be filled with lawless slavecatchers. While Southerners complained that an honest planter, trying to recover property to which his constitutional title was clear, would be in danger of criminal prosecution for kidnapping, suits for false imprisonment, and even "of being mobbed or being put to death in a street fight by insane fanatics or brutal ruffians," some Northerners cried that brutal gangs of manhunters, running down free Negroes, would compel assistance under penalty of fine, imprisonment, and heavy civil damages.[5]

All explorers of the sociology of agitation will recognize that this situation was ideal for fomenting disorder and strife. In conditions of great public tension the indirect effect of statutes is far greater than their direct results. The Fugitive Slave Act did not accomplish much in the recapture of slaves—though numerous recaptures, and alas! some illegal kidnappings, did take place. But it effected wonders in the stimulation of pro-slavery and anti-slavery agitation. Feeling for and against the law ran so high that every instance of opposition was dramatized

4 *Preliminary Report on the Eighth Census*, 137. N. Y. *Tribune*, July 5, 1851. Channing, *History of the United States*, VI, 94–95; Macy, *Anti-Slavery Crusade*, 128. Estimates of the number of fugitives living in the North varied widely. One observer put the number in 1850 as low as 20,000, another as high as 50,000; W. H. Siebert, *The Underground Railroad*, 236. In 1860 the census recorded only 803 escapes for the previous year.

5 Curtis, *Daniel Webster*, II, 423–426. *Report Virginia House Committee*, February, 1849, on Northern laws. It must be emphasized that Northern opposition was confined to a minority. The chief books on the Underground Railroad—W. H. Siebert's full volume, M. G. McDougall's *Fugitive Slaves 1619–1865*, and Henrietta Buckmaster's *Let My People Go*—all have great merit, but all err in two ways: in making the railroad seem better organized than it was, and in exaggerating the scope and persistency of *active* opposition to the Fugitive Slave Act.

as on a floodlighted stage; every defiance to it resounded as through a megaphone. Senator Mason was given a banquet in Warrenton, Va., to celebrate his victory in writing and passing the law. But had he and such Northern friends as Buchanan, who grew violent in asserting that it was "the only measure of the Compromise calculated to secure the rights of the South," been trying to play into the hands of propagandists and troublemakers, they could have taken no more efficient step. Part of the drive to make the law so drastic had unquestionably come from men who, like Jefferson Davis, wanted to defeat the Compromise, and failing in that, to keep agitation alive.[6]

[II]

Within ten days after the law went into effect a mulatto named James Hamlet, a hardworking Methodist, was seized in New York, hurried before a commissioner on the claim of a Maryland woman, and conveyed to Slatter's notorious slave-yard in Baltimore, while his wife and children were still ignorant of his fate. Before the law had been on the statute books a month, Negroes had been arrested in Philadelphia, Harrisburg, Detroit, and other cities. Some men guessed that during the first year more persons were seized as fugitives than in all the preceding sixty. Most of them had actually fled from lawful masters, but in a number of instances free Negroes were seized. Thus in 1851 Euphemia Williams, averring that she had spent her entire life in Pennsylvania, was claimed by a Marylander who swore that she had fled from him twenty-two years earlier. He also demanded possession of her six children, all born in Pennsylvania, the oldest being seventeen. Great excitement reigned. A hearing was held before Judge John K. Kane, who decided that she was not the person alleged.

In a number of instances violence was used against Negroes before their identity was established, and the first notice some had of their peril was a blow which laid them senseless. Others were subjected to great inconveniences; Adam Gibson was haled from Philadelphia to Maryland, where it turned out that he was not the man sent for, and he was returned. Before many months passed, anti-slavery elements were convinced that the work of pursuing slaves was being made a regular business along the whole border, and that some men engaged in it were eager to decoy free Negroes. Even when a man was proved to have fled from slavery ten, fifteen, or twenty years earlier, the spectacle of

6 Conway, *Autobiography*, I, 86. Buchanan to Whittaker, July 31, 1851; Buchanan Papers. Jefferson Davis rejoiced that by stalling the Compromise, he and others obtained a fugitive law "free from the very objectionable provision" for a possible trial in the slave-owner's State; he seemed to rejoice that the law had received the assent of only 3 Northern Senators and 31 Northern Representatives. *Letters, Papers, and Speeches*, II, 96, 97.

officers dragging him away from family, fireside, and established occupation (like the tailor Boulding of Poughkeepsie, taken to South Carolina and held

FUGITIVE
SLAVE BILL!

HON. HENRY WILSON

Will address the citizens on

Thursday Evening, April 3,

At the

At 7 o'clock, on the all-engrossing topics of the day—the FUGITIVE SLAVE BILL, the pro-slavery action of the National Government and the general aspect of the Slavery question.

Let every man and woman, without distinction of sect or party, attend the meeting and bear a testimony against the system which fills the prisons of a free republic with men whose only crime is a love of freedom—which strikes down the habeas corpus and trial by jury, and converts the free soil of Massachusetts into hunting ground for the Southern kidnappers.

Ashby, March 29, 1851.

White & Potter's Steam Press....4000 Impressions per hour....Spring Lane, Boston.

The Northern Attack on the Fugitive Slave Act.
A handbill in the American Antiquarian Society, Worcester, Massachusetts.

for $1,750) was inexpressibly painful. Aides of Dr. Pennington of the Shiloh Church in New York hastily bought Boulding's freedom.[7]

7 "Five Years' Progress of the Slave Power," anonymous pvt., Huntington Library. Greeley, *The American Conflict*, I, ch. 16. N. Y. *Tribune*, June 28, 1851. Even in 1838 Frederick Douglass had believed that "there were hired men of my own color who would betray me for a few dollars," and had not dared venture upon the wharves or into colored boarding-houses; *Life and Times*, 229, 230.

The first half of 1851 found much of the North in an uproar. A panicky flight of Negroes from dozens of cities into Canada, the frightened folk crowding railroads and steamers, aroused much sympathy. Cassius M. Clay of Kentucky, who though the son of a slaveholder had been converted to abolitionism while attending Yale, where he heard William Lloyd Garrison lecture, and who in 1850 had run for governor on an anti-slavery ticket, was a leader in the revolt. He published articles and scattered throughout Kentucky a circular denouncing the law. Seward issued a long letter under date of April 5 declaring that "constitutional resistance" to the act would not cease until efforts to enforce it were relinquished. From Vermont came news that of the ten leading Whig journals, six were attacking the enactment, three were neutral, and only one upheld it. An anti-slavery convention in Cincinnati denounced the statute as a flagrant outrage. May brought word from Massachusetts that Robert Rantoul, well-known as a Jacksonian Democrat of conservative business connections, was running for Congress in the second Massachusetts district on a platform of stern hostility to the law. Emerson delivered a Sunday evening lecture to his Concord neighbors which attracted attention not only for its arraignment of the act, but for its biting analysis of the character and policy of Webster. When the great orator on May 22 made a speech at Buffalo defending the measure, the opposition press blazed with indignant editorials. The Northern people, stated Greeley's *Tribune*, regard the law as constitutionally and morally of no binding force. "They will not indeed resist it by violence, they will not rise in arms to nullify it, they will not bluster about dissolving the Union on account of it; but they will favor its evasion, they will burden its execution with all possible legal difficulties, and they will help slaves to escape all the more zealously." [8]

Numerically, the instances of resistance to the Fugitive Slave Act were few. They were essentially unimportant—except as fuel for anti-slavery and pro-slavery agitation. But in that light they possessed tremendous gravity.

Resistance instantly sprang up. If the fugitive Hamlet had not been hurried with all speed from New York, a mob might have risen; as it was, a popular subscription bought his freedom. Vigilance committees were formed in numerous cities, sometimes—as in Syracuse—with the aid of the mayor. One June 5, in a crowded courtroom in Chicago, a Federal commissioner discharged a Negro as not answering the claimant's description. "The long-pent feeling of the multitude," recorded the Chicago *Tribune*, "found utterance in shout after

8   N. Y. *Tribune*, April 5, 1851; N. Y. *Weekly Tribune*, April 19, May 17, 31, June 7, 1851. The flight of the Negroes is discussed by F. Landon, "Negro Migration to Canada," *Journal of Negro History*, V, 30ff. Pittsburgh was said to have lost 300 in a few days, while a Baptist church in Buffalo lost 130 members and a church in Rochester 114; see *The Liberator*, October 18, 1850.

shout of exultant applause." The man was escorted to the street, where another jubilant crowd hurried him to a place of safety. In Detroit the first seizure of a Negro precipitated such a riot that regular troops had to be summoned.

As for Boston, everybody knew that it was tinder courting the spark. The fact had been advertised by an indignation meeting at Faneuil Hall in October, 1850, with Theodore Parker as principal speaker. He related that a fugitive in Canada that very day had telegraphed his wife in Boston inquiring whether it was safe to return. "Will you let him come?" demanded Parker. "How many of you will defend him to the worst?" A sea of hands went up. Shortly thereafter, Parker returned from a lecture engagement to find that two Georgians had reached Boston to reclaim William and Ellen Craft, parishioners of his. They were notoriously fugitives; nobody questioned the title of the Georgia owner. But they were a heroic couple, for they had escaped when Ellen personated, in male attire, a young planter travelling with his bodyservant. The strangers were soon given reason to wish that they had never come north. They were arrested for defamation of character, having accused Craft of stealing; advertisements were posted violently denouncing them; Parker, summoning a standing vigilance committee, called with it at their hotel; and he assailed them so furiously that they incontinently fled the city. Meanwhile, the Crafts were hurried aboard a ship for England.[9]

This was rank lawlessness, and equally dramatic instances of obstruction soon followed. The vigilance committee in Boston grew to two hundred members, and obtained funds from Lowell, Palfrey, John A. Andrew, and others of note. When the slave Shadrach was arrested in February, 1851, prayers were asked for him in certain churches. The case came before the commissioner, who adjourned it for two days. Richard H. Dana, Jr., whose law office was across the street, tells us what followed. Suddenly, he writes, "we heard a shout from the courthouse, continued into a yell of triumph, and in an instant after down the steps came two negroes bearing the prisoner between them with his clothes half torn off, and so stupefied by his sudden rescue and the violence of his dragging off that he sat almost dumb, and I thought had fainted; . . . and they went off toward Cambridge, like a black squall, the crowd driving along with them and cheering as they went. It was all done in an instant, too quick to be believed. . . ." Two months later the slave Thomas Sims was delivered to his master in Boston. But a stern display of force was required; he had to be shipped off at four in the morning, and a scheme of rescue failed only because it was anticipated by the authorities. The New York *Tribune* estimated that

9 J. W. Chadwick, *Theodore Parker*, 248–251. Chicago *Tribune* quoted in N. Y. *Tribune*, June 14, 1851.

this recapture cost fully $5,000. Anti-slavery men made the utmost capital out of the incident, Parker a year later preaching an anniversary sermon in which he declared Commissioner George T. Curtis baser than Nero, Torquemada, or Jeffreys! [10]

So far no lives had been lost, but a killing soon took place. In September a Maryland slaveholder went to Christiana, near Lancaster, Pa., where a number of colored people had settled, and, accompanied by an officer with a proper warrant, tried to reclaim two fugitives. A bloody affray ensued. The master was killed, and his son badly wounded. Arrests were made, and for weeks excitement filled the area. Early the following month the famous "Jerry rescue" took place at Syracuse, N. Y., a town which Webster characterized as "that laboratory of abolitionism, libel, and treason." Jerry was a Missouri slave of some education and mechanical skill who many months earlier had fled into upper New York. Quite unexpectedly, an agent of the owner turned up with a warrant on the very day that the Onondaga county fair crowded the city and that the wealthy philanthropist Gerrit Smith and a body of enthusiastic followers were holding an anti-slavery meeting. Word that Jerry had been arrested ran through the town like the wind. Churchbells were tolled, men shouted the news into shops and houses, and the anti-slavery gathering excitedly adjourned. A crowd swiftly filled the office of the Federal Commissioner where the case was being argued. Here a general fracas broke out and Jerry was momentarily liberated, but again captured. As the population poured into Clinton Square and the surrounding streets, the uproar increased. By nightfall it was clear that only an exceptionally strong jail or a powerful military force could prevent a rescue; and the mob soon made a concerted attack with clubs, iron bars, and axes on the building where Jerry was kept. Shots were fired; the crowd surged forward. Jerry was speedily on his way to the Canadian line, while the authorities were left to bring in some futile indictments, and the whole district pulsed with emotion. The simultaneous arrest of a Negro at Jamestown, N. Y., aroused high indignation in the western end of the State.[11]

Yet these episodes, thrown upon a vivid national screen by all the arts of press and politicians, were less significant of public opinion than they seemed. Most citizens, and outside New England most communities, took a law-abiding

10 C. F. Adams, *Richard Henry Dana*, I, 182. Chadwick, *Parker*, 254-255. N. Y. *Tribune*, May 10, 1851. Sumner wrote to Giddings on April 3, 1851: "I have implicit confidence that we shall yet rally the Free States against the Fugitive Slave Bill. Each day discloses its advocates. The persecutions here in Boston will keep them before our public; and our Convention next week will deepen the impression. . . ." Giddings Papers.

11 N. Y. *Tribune*, September 17, 1851, on the Christiana killing; October 4, 1851, on the Jamestown arrest. Curtis, *Webster*, II, 509. W. F. Galpin, "The Jerry Rescue," in *New York History*, January, 1945; R. V. Harlow, *Gerrit Smith*, 297-301.

attitude. The large number of instances in which fugitives were peaceably returned, or their freedom quietly purchased, received little or no publicity. President Fillmore never flinched in his execution of the law, showing himself ready to apply force if necessary. "The North is in a very wholesome state of fermentation, and if the Administration is only backed up by the South and West, the whole country will return to a new observance of the Constitution, and there will be a new lease to slavery"—so Secretary Graham wrote his brother this spring. Such an abolitionist as W. H. Furness feared that the people were getting broken into their office as slave-catchers, to him a bitter idea.

Nor did thoughtful slaveholders feel great astonishment or mortification over the instances of resistance. The fact was that no law could offer them much advantage, because the cost of reclaiming a slave was commonly greater than his value. If a runaway from Kentucky or Maryland was seized in lower Ohio or Pennsylvania, well and good. But to trace men over longer distances cost money; to send out agents and prepare papers cost more; to return the unwilling black to slavery cost an additional sum. Any Negro who reached upper Ohio or New York could usually get on to Canada. Above the border area the business of slave-catching, generally speaking, did not pay even if the law was quietly observed.[12]

The mob outbreaks, half of which would never have occurred under a milder act, simply enabled radicals to keep the pot boiling. The British abolitionist George Thompson, M. P., was revisiting America in 1851. In the larger cities he met a frigid reception, but the towns and villages of the northeastern States' greeted him as an international hero. "The effect of his presence as well as of his public speeches has been everywhere of the most arousing nature," wrote Edmund Quincy. Early in 1851 the annual meeting of the Massachusetts abolitionists centered, at Thompson's suggestion, about a celebration of the twentieth year of the *Liberator*. The speakers included Thompson, Wendell Phillips, Parker, Henry Wilson, and Garrison himself, the indomitable editor receiving a gold watch from his admirers. Abolitionists tossed their hay in the sunshine of the agitation against the Fugitive Slave Act. "In Boston, all is activity," chuckled Wendell Phillips. Public indignation was unprecedented. "The rescue of Shadrach has set the whole public afire."[13]

12 Graham to his brother, April 14, 1851; Graham Papers. Furness to Channing, October 4, 1851; Chamberlain MSS.
13 Edmund Quincy, Press Correspondence, January 13, 28, 1851; Quincy Papers, U. of N. C. Garrison, *Garrison*, III, 313ff. See review of first years of the Fugitive Slave Act, London *Times*, January 7, 1854.

[III]

The embittered discussion of the new law naturally thrust itself into northern politics, boiling up like fiery lava into half the State campaigns of 1851. Massachusetts opened the year with a new demonstration of her intransigent temper.[14] As we have seen, the Free Soil party the previous fall had eagerly allied itself with the Democrats against the detested Fillmore and Webster. The coalition carried the legislature. That body had three important offices to bestow; for since no candidate for governor had received a majority of the popular vote, it must elect one, while it also had to fill the two senatorial seats. After prolonged maneuvering and bargaining, the prizes were divided in a fashion peculiarly painful to Webster and other moderates. George S. Boutwell, an anti-slavery Democrat, was chosen governor. Robert Rantoul, another Democrat whose enmity to the Fugitive Slave Act we have mentioned, took Webster's seat for his short unexpired term. The six-year senatorship fell to Charles Sumner, the eloquent, scholarly, and fanatical leader of the conscience Whigs, just forty years of age.

This was a blow in the face to Compromise men. Rantoul, a leader of intellectual power and business capacity, was hardly to cross the threshold of the Senate before he fell ill and died; but Sumner was destined to a great if dubious place in history. The bargaining in the legislature, with the two long-opposed parties "like pirates sharing the plundered cargo of a merchantman," disgusted many onlookers. But it was the peculiar mental and moral traits of Sumner which excited the most uneasiness. His narrow intensity gave him power, his pedantic learning gave him weight, and his rhetorical eloquence gave him a certain popular appeal; but the witty Boston woman who said that he was "a specimen of prolonged and morbid juvenility" hit near the mark, for he had the bad temper and illogical crudity of a spoiled child. He had already proclaimed that the public conscience would not allow anybody who had trodden the Massachusetts streets as a free man to be dragged away to slavery. Now he began his national career with one of those exasperating peals from Sinai in which he was wont to display his superiority to ordinary mortals. He would be on his guard against efforts "to extend the sectional domination of slavery over the United States." Politics, he added, are simply morals applied

---

14 Webster had energetically pressed his colleagues in the Cabinet to withdraw all patronage from his Massachusetts enemies. He traced such misfortunes as Horace Mann's reëlection largely to the support given Mann by the Boston *Atlas* and other Whig papers, and by certain Custom House officials. Government patronage, he urged, should be given exclusively to such loyal sheets as the Boston *Courier*, *Daily Advertiser*, and *Bee*, and the Springfield *Republican*. Webster to Wm. A. Graham, November 13, 1850; Graham Papers, U. of N. C.

to public affairs, and his course would be determined by those everlasting rules of right and wrong which are a law alike to individuals and communities. All this in an unnecessary letter of acceptance to the legislature. His God-given positiveness that he would always be right and his opponents always morally wrong boded ill for the future.[15]

Massachusetts was shaken to the depths by Sumner's election, half the population rejoicing and half of it embittered. Young Henry Adams was in the gallery of the legislature when the choice was made. He bore the news to his father's dinner-table, where Sumner was a guest, and on his heels came eager groups to congratulate the new Senator. To escape the triumphant crowds, Sumner fled to a quiet evening with Lowell and Palfrey at Longfellow's house. "Throughout Massachusetts, and even in other States," he wrote his brother George, "there have been bonfires, firings of cannon, ringing of bells, public meetings, and all forms of joy, to celebrate the event." Freesoil papers far and wide pointed out, quite justly, that he could have been elected earlier in the session had he been willing to give even a half-pledge to Democratic legislators, and they praised his adherence to the path of duty and manliness. But in State Street, faces were long and scowls were black.

Some of the men who knew Sumner best, like George S. Hillard, were full of forebodings. Robert C. Winthrop had declared that any fate would be better than to be supplanted by Sumner. He would yield with good grace to Adams, Palfrey, or Horace Mann. "But spare me from Sumner, or rather, spare the Commonwealth, spare the country, from him!" Similar emotions animated

15 On the legislative bargaining, see G. S. Hillard to Lieber, January 8, 1851; Lieber Papers. Sumner wrote Giddings on September 11, 1851: "I am not made for a Senator—certainly not for a politician, and wish sincerely another faithful to our cause was in my place. Especially am I disgusted with the intrigue which I see before me in the coming session of President-making." Giddings Papers. When Sumner took his oath of office, it was (as he later confessed) with a mental reservation; he would uphold the Constitution only as he himself interpreted it, and he believed the Fugitive Slave law unconstitutional! Hillard wrote Lieber that "his mind is singularly devoid of original principles in politics, and . . . he is always mistaking hopes for facts and impulses for motives." July 11, 1854; Lieber Papers. It would have been more accurate to say that he was always mistaking prejudices for principles.

The Whigs had hoped and struggled for the election of R. C. Winthrop as Senator. Edmund Quincy wrote on April 28, 1851, from Boston, in his press correspondence: "You should have seen the faces in State Street Wednesday, when the (then unfounded) rumor prevailed that Mr. Sumner had been elected! None but faces made out of dough could have been capable of such preternatural elongation. And if you could have heard the *swearing*, your hair would have stood on end. . . . After so much money had been spent, after all the influences of Whigs and Democrats had been brought to bear on the Legislature, after a nigger (Sims) had been caught and kept and sent back at so great an expense, to find that the whole work was undone, and worse than before it was begun!" The Free-soilers, he added, were in high feather. "It is a fact unparalleled in this State, if not in the country, that a man who had never been a candidate for any, the least, office, and never dabbled in politics at all, should be invested with the highest office in the gift of the State, without solicitation or even wish on his part." Quincy Papers.

Webster, who, paying a short visit to Massachusetts at this very time, expected to make an address in Faneuil Hall (Rufus Choate and other admiring citizens having sent him an invitation), until the board of aldermen refused the use of the hall on the ground that they had denied it to foes of the Compromise. "Was it not a curious concatenation," wrote Edmund Quincy, "that Mr. Webster should have been saluted on the day of his arrival in Massachusetts with the tidings of the election of Mr. Allen, the man who impeached him of corruption, and that he should have been pursued out of the State by the boom of the cannon that announced the election of Mr. Sumner as his successor?" [16]

For Sumner the election was a gratifying personal triumph—and Sumner's egotism was so colossal that it would soon become what Benton's had long been, a national institution. His rise had been rapid. Less than half a dozen years behind him lay the memorable day when his striking gifts and equally striking defects had first been fully revealed to the country. When on Independence Day in 1845 he drew up his six feet four inches of height before the most brilliant audience Boston could muster to deliver his oration on "The True Grandeur of Nations," he was nothing but a promising young man who had failed to get a coveted professorship at Harvard and a coveted reportership for the Supreme Court; when he sat down, he was one of the first orators of New England, his reputation established as a speaker of extraordinary force and a reformer of utter fearlessness. The speech, a flaming vindication of the duty of doing all things possible to keep the nation in the paths of peace, was uttered as the country was hurling itself into a new war, and in the presence of a hundred military and naval officers who felt so directly affronted that they were with difficulty restrained from leaving the hall. Its indictment of the Boston ministers was equally uncompromising. "There were those pro-slavery clergymen," said one abolitionist, "with hearts as black as their coats, and there stood Charles Sumner with a heart as white as his waistcoat."

The oration was a turning point in his career. "The young man has cut his own throat," said Samuel Eliot for the George Apley Bostonians. But he had the singleminded courage to press forward on the course he had marked out, and from that moment was one of the leaders of Massachusetts thought. He could be distrusted; he could be hated; but he could not be ignored.[17]

Now the election seemed to say that his star was rising and Webster's was declining. The Secretary of State was cut to the heart by the shameful charge of Charles Allen's which Quincy had mentioned. This Free Soil Representative

16 Sumner to his brother in Sumner Papers. E. L. Pierce, *Memoir and Letters of Charles Sumner*, I, 244-247. On forebodings about Sumner, see Hillard to Lieber, November 9, December 24, 1850; Lieber Papers. Winthrop to Kennedy, January 7, 1851; Kennedy Papers. Edmund Quincy, press correspondence, April 28, 1851; Quincy Papers.
17 Concerning Sumner's speech of 1845, see *The Nation*, December 3, 1877.

from the Worcester district, reëlected this fall, had accused Webster of corruption in accepting the contribution which a number of personal and political friends made to eke out the Secretary's salary ($6,000) in defraying the heavy expenses of his official station. The fact was, as the diarist Philip Hone wrote, that this gift was "a tribute equally honorable to the donors and the recipient," while the charge was "disgraceful to his villifier, who is not likely to receive such a manifestation of regard." Webster did not even know the names of the donors. Webster was hurt also by the churlish refusal of the Boston aldermen to open Faneuil Hall to the public reception which Whig and Democratic citizens wished to tender him. When the aldermen saw what a storm they had raised, they tried to revoke their action, and waited humbly on Webster as he visited Boston. But he frostily declined their civility, saying that he would not enter Faneuil Hall until its doors were thrown "wide open, 'not with the impetuous recoil, grating harsh thunder,' but with 'harmonious sound on golden hinges moving,' to let in freely and to overflowing" all lovers of the Union.[18]

Along with Sumner another man, also destined to be a thorn in the flesh of slaveholders, was simultaneously elevated to the Senate—Ben Wade of Ohio. Honest Joshua Giddings was passed over for this less famous leader. But he showed no ill-feeling, for Wade was a veteran in the anti-slavery cause, having identified himself with it since the late thirties; and Giddings wrote Chase that he was well satisfied that the legislature's action was determined solely by disinterested consideration of what was best for free soil.[19]

No one could doubt that Wade would make his peculiar mark in Washington. This self-schooled politician, reared in poverty on a Massachusetts farm, had shown a blunt force that carried him from rough manual labor—farmer, cattle driver, canal worker—to the position of lawyer, legislator, and judge. His powerful frame, strong, dark face, deep raucous voice, defiant laugh, and gift for vituperative speech, all stamped him as a man of coarse fibre and brute strength. Yet he possessed better qualities as well. William Dean Howells,

---

18   Nevins, ed., *The Diary of Philip Hone*, II, 914. Edmund Quincy tells of the interview between the aldermen and the Great Insulted:

They . . . where received much as a cross between a bulldog and a mastiff might receive a deputation of spaniels and poodles. After their servile and sneaking resolutions had been read, the Great Panjandrum was begged to vouchsafe an answer.

"I will give my answer in writing," growled out the Expounder. . . .

After a pause, which the Defender showed no inclination to break, His Honor the Mayor . . . ventured to put in:

"Mr. Webster, I hope you enjoy good health, sir?"

"My health's good enough," muttered the Wilmot Thunderer.

The mayor succumbing, one of the worshipful aldermen undertook the conversation.

"We have a fine day after the storm, sir!"   ,

"The weather's well enough," quoth the Defender, and our Civil Fathers sneaked out of the presence. . . . April 28, 1851; Quincy Papers.

19   Giddings to Chase, March 24, 1851; Giddings Papers.

briefly studying law in his office, found him a man of silent dignity who, in talking about the four British reviews which they both read, disclosed not only native power but a considerable degree of cultivation. His Western ideal of oratory was harder, sharper, and more pungent than Sumner's. Once, after listening to a hyper-classic speech by his colleague, he ejaculated: "It's all very well, Sumner, but it has no bones in it." Yet basically the two were in agreement. Wade had delivered a speech at Ravenna, O., the previous fall, which had fairly electrified his audience by the energy of his assault upon the Fugitive Slave Act and his withering denunciation of Webster. The law was the most infamous known to the statute books, he said, and if called up, he would defy fine and imprisonment to give any slave the writ of *habeas corpus*.[20]

New York, too, elected a Senator who disliked the Fugitive Slave Act—but a man of very different type. The patrician Hamilton Fish, who had made a sterling record as governor, was the leading aspirant for the seat which Dickinson was vacating on March 4, 1851. He had rejoiced in the passage of the Compromise, but had suggested that Fillmore, with whom he corresponded cordially, should ask for amendments to the law. Both the conservative Whigs and the Seward-Weed Whigs had tried to extract promises from the grave, quiet, stiff-tempered man, and both had met rebuffs. He made it clear that he believed in the enforcement of all laws, however distasteful they might be to sectional feeling, and this he thought was sufficient. But the Whigs had a majority of only two in the State Senate, one stubborn Whig would not vote for Fish, and a prolonged deadlock took place. The internecine war of the New York party was now raging at its hottest. President Fillmore became satisfied early in the year that the feud with Seward was irreconcilable; he had never expected anything from Seward himself, but he had hoped to win over the mass of Seward's followers by conciliation. Failing in that, he used the Federal patronage as ruthlessly against Seward as the Senator's friends were using the State patronage against the President.

For a time Fish seemed likely to suffer the common fate of men standing between two implacable extremes. But late in March his friends seized a moment when two Democrats were absent, went into an election, and at two o'clock in the morning chose him. Legislators poured cheering into the dark Albany streets. A hundred guns were fired, and "the exultant cannon of the victors," wrote an observer, "startled the city from its slumbers."[21]

20 Howells, *Years of My Youth*, 107–108. For Wade's Ohio speech see the Cleveland correspondence of the N. Y. *Weekly Tribune*, April 5, 1851.
21 Wm. A. Graham to his brother, March 12, 1851, on the New York patronage; Graham Papers. H. B. Stanton, *Random Recollections*, 172. The letters of S. P. Lyman in the Tom Corwin Papers, L. C. (December 28, 1850; January 2, 1851), show that he acted as an emissary of Weed, Blatchford, Grinnell, Draper. and others who wished to have President

There could be no question that majority opinion in the Massachusetts, Ohio, and New York legislatures was adverse to the new law. Nor was there any doubt that the next Whig candidate for President must not be identified with it. A conservative observer in eastern Ohio wrote Tom Corwin that to name either Webster or Fillmore would be insanity so far as that area was concerned. "We can rally on a man pledged to *let the Compromise alone*, but not for one who figured in the enactment of the Fugitive Law. Such is the universal sentiment of this section of Ohio, where 'free soil' has but a feeble hold." [22]

[IV]

But the general trend was against the radicals. Fish was no extremist; a man of constructive instincts, he deprecated, not promoted agitation. Fillmore, who had received private assurances of his support of the Compromise, was pleased by his election. In other States, the Democrats held their own or made gains. Delaware this spring sent James A. Bayard, another patrician of wealth, and a Democrat with a Jacksonian love of the Union, to the Senate. He could be counted upon to uphold the new sectional "deal." The fact was that Maryland and Delaware, like other border States, did not feel deeply about the Fugitive Slave Act one way or the other.

Indiana meanwhile reëlected its crass pro-slavery Democrat, Jesse D. Bright, to the upper chamber. Living on the Ohio River, he owned a plantation with many slaves in Kentucky, and in the tense years to come was to prove that he represented the plantation and not the people of Indiana. Alert, vigorous, and domineering, Bright loved power, knew the art of getting it, and brooked no opposition. He regarded as his foe any man who would not do his bidding. The previous fall a brave editor in Bright's home town of Madison, declaring that the Fugitive Slave Act was repugnant to public sentiment, had said that he would turn a deaf ear and a blind eye to any appeal for help in catching a runaway. With characteristic vindictiveness, Bright not only opened hostilities upon

---

Taylor's appointees left untouched. But the unruly Maxwell proposed a long list of removals! What was worse, the unruly Tom Corwin sanctioned these decapitations.

"Seward and his faction are disposed to apparent peace, and are secretly asking quarter, so far as to be allowed to retain their offices, not a few of them, which they acquired under the last administration. But I think we should not be content with that, although they are observing a cowardly silence, but should eject them from place, and strip them of the influence of office. The President is ready for this, if he can overcome the importunities and counsels of some Northern Whigs." Wm. A. Graham, January 6, 1851, to his brother; Graham Papers. U. of N. C.

The unyielding attitude of the Seward faction in the New York legislature determined Fillmore to fight them implacably. Wrote Graham on March 12: "The President is now satisfied that the feud with the Seward men is irreconcilable. Both Seward and Weed are impudent, and nothing but chastising with a bold hand will check them." Graham Papers, U. of N. C. See Harry J. Carman and Reinhard H. Luthin, "The Seward-Fillmore Feud and the Disruption of the Whig Party," *New York History, XXIV,* 335–357 (July, 1943).

22 J. Medill, Coshecton, Ohio, to Corwin, November 15, 1851; Corwin Papers.

the editor, but arranged the establishment of an opposition newspaper designed to destroy the outspoken sheet. The most striking Democratic victory of all took place in California, where John B. Weller took his place alongside that more fiercely pro-slavery member William M. Gwin.[23]

As spring came on, the Administration prepared to stand up vigorously for its opinions. In May, Fillmore and Webster attended a celebration to mark the opening of the Erie Railroad, and Webster lingered for a few days to deliver at Buffalo, Syracuse, and Albany a series of addresses defending his course. It was not true, he said, that the great recent measures had been dictated by timidity, a taste for appeasement, or a wish to make a neat bargain. The question was whether the Constitution should be so interpreted and executed that all members of the Union could abide under it. He would not give the South a hairsbreadth of improper concession, no matter how much expediency might demand it. He *would* maintain with all his power, and in the face of every danger, the constitutional rights of South as well as North; "and God forsake me and my children, if I ever be found to falter in one or the other." The meaning of the clause providing for the return of fugitives from labor, he insisted, was so plain that no competent attorney could mistake it. Some men appeared to assume that if a Negro came north, it was as a freeman with a freeman's rights; but the Constitution plainly stated that a fugitive from labor was not a freeman and must be surrendered upon just demand.

Once more, Webster declared that the rush of Northern men to California had inevitably made it a free State; that on due investigation, he had seen the emptiness of any threat of slavery on New Mexican and Utah plains; and that since the Wilmot Proviso was needless, he had voted against irritating the South by its passage. He defended his position on the Texas boundary, asserting that without Congressional interposition a civil conflict would have occurred. But it was in dealing with the Fugitive Slave Act that he was most emphatic. Some new law had become imperative, for the old one did not meet the constitutional requirement. He had proposed a very different bill from that which passed, for he believed trial by jury proper and feasible. Nevertheless, he regarded Mason's bill as more favorable to the fugitive than the old act of 1793, for it placed the cases under jurisdiction of a higher authority. For those who urged resistance to the law he had naught but scorn and condemnation.[24]

Indeed, Webster was now, as during the previous summer, a host in himself. Considering his age, his precarious health, and his burden as Secretary of State,

23 W. A. Graham to his brother, March 12, 1851; Graham Papers, on Fillmore's satisfaction over Fish's election. Wm. S. Garber Papers, on Bright's hostilities.

24 Many Southerners did not think that nature would keep slavery out of the new Territories. Significantly, the States Rights Convention held at Jackson, Miss., on June 16, asked the Mississippi legislature to pass laws encouraging the emigration of citizens from the slave States into the new regions.

the volume of his letters and speeches in the twelvemonth after passage of the Compromise was marvelous. He wrote long responses to invitations from New York, Philadelphia, and other cities. He pronounced one of his most impressive orations at the Pilgrim Festival in New York in the last days of 1850. He spoke with great effect at an Annapolis dinner in March. On his fleeting visit to Boston he wrote fresh public epistles and addressed a crowd which gathered before his hotel. He had dreaded the Erie Railroad carnival. He foresaw heat, crowds, limestone water (which upset his digestion), and constant speechmaking. His brain, he said, was as dry as remainder biscuit. But with the Union and the presidency floating before his vision, he rose heroically to the ordeal. He made eleven speeches, apart from mere change-scattering at stations, and Everett, no mean judge, was impressed by the felicity of them all. Though he was in his seventieth year, his mental vigor, courage, and good temper (always argumentative, never denunciatory), were all conspicuous. Garrison's *Liberator* pictured him on this tour as a senile weakling, whose tottering legs were half-hidden by his pendulous abdomen. Actually, he was energy incarnate. At Albany he rose at three in the morning to work on an address, and spent seventeen hours in incessant activity.[25]

Retreating in June to Capon Springs for a little rest, Webster made a long address to the Virginia yeomenry—one Revolutionary veteran walking fifteen miles in the burning sun to hear him. On July 4, when the cornerstone of the Capitol extension was laid, he delivered one of his most eloquent discourses, stating the distinctive nature of American liberty.

He naturally varied the character of his epistles and speeches. But always he maintained that in the crisis of 1850 he had done his precise duty; for "if the chances had been but one in a thousand that civil war would be the result, I should still have felt that one-thousandth chance should be guarded against by any reasonable sacrifice." He always made light of abuse. Was not Washington libelled as a slave-driver? Was not the Constitution assailed as a league with death and a covenant with hell? He always attacked secessionists and disunionists. And he consistently indicted those men, North and South, who refused obedience to any law bound up in the Compromise. "I repeat," he said at Capon Springs, "that if the Northern States refuse, wilfully and deliberately, to carry into effect that part of the Constitution which respects the restoration of fugitive slaves, and Congress provide no remedy, the South would no longer be bound to observe the compact. A bargain cannot be broken on one side, and still bind the other side." [26]

25 Curtis, *Webster*, II, 466–511; Fuess, *Webster*, II, 241 ff., 272 ff.; Everett Papers.
26 Curtis, *Webster*, II, 519. The Capon Springs dinner was on June 28. Some farmers traveled fifty miles to attend. Sir Henry Bulwer also spoke.

Other members of the Cabinet spoke up. To their side rallied great numbers of moderate Whigs. As the new fall campaign came on in Massachusetts, the conservative George S. Hillard threw himself into the struggle. Excitement ran high. "The whole State is like a forest on fire," he wrote Lieber. But going to Worcester, the very den of radicalism, he made a two-and-a-half-hour speech which pointed out a great truth. It was the race problem, he said, which was fundamental. The deepest evils of slavery lay beyond the reach of parties or legislatures, and arose not because slaves were slaves, but because they were blacks. Rufus Choate spoke at the Harvard Law School against 'higher law' doctrines. Let men recall, he said, that Socrates, about to drink the hemlock, pleaded with his disciples to respect the very law which condemned him.[27]

This summer of 1851, indeed, witnessed a clear turning of the northern tide. Majority feeling insisted that the Compromise, in all its parts, be maintained as a bulwark against sectional passion; and men sensed this demand. Rufus Choate and B. R. Curtis reminded Massachusetts that she had made a solemn pledge when she accepted the Constitution. One former doubter after another took an acquiescent posture. Hamilton Fish in an Independence Day address said that he had originally opposed the Compromise measures, the Fugitive Slave Act striking him as especially reprehensible. But the moment they became laws, he accepted them. He hoped for amendments, but he thought that the present was a time for prudent action. When the Whig State Convention of Pennsylvania met at Lancaster, it promised a faithful adherence to the Compromise. The Whig Convention in Ohio gave unqualified sanction to the course of the Fillmore Administration. So did both Whigs and Democrats in other Northern States.[28]

Of the Northern elections this fall, those in New York and Pennsylvania were the most important, New York choosing minor State officers and Pennsylvania a governor. In both the Democrats, pledged to maintain the Compromise, triumphed. The New York Whigs tried hard to avoid divisive issues. Seward relieved everybody by going out to Detroit on prolonged legal business. Greeley devoted himself mainly to the tariff, declaring that Northern feeling against the Fugitive Slave Act "is rather one of abstract principle than of universal, ever-ready interest," and that the issue of fugitives would never have assumed much importance but for the underlying quarrel over slavery extension. Weed descanted upon canal policy. But Whigs lost the canal board, with

27 Hillard to Lieber, November 5, 1851; Lieber Papers. S. G. Brown, *Life of Rufus Choate*, 263-264.
28 Buchanan wrote in the summer of 1851 that the people of the South were seriously divided on the Compromise, and many were advocating secession if its laws were not modified. "In this aspect of affairs, what madness it is for the people of the North to insist upon the repeal or modification of the only measure of the Compromise calculated to benefit the South—and this by simply carrying into effect a clear and explicit constitutional provision in their favor." To Edgar K. Whittaker, July 31, 1851; Buchanan Papers.

most of the other minor offices, and were reduced to a tie in the Senate and a majority of two in the Assembly. Each faction blamed the other. "A noble, glorious party has been defeated—destroyed—by its own leaders," Hamilton Fish wrote Weed. "Webster has succeeded better under Fillmore than he did under Tyler in breaking up the Whig organization and forming a third party." Fillmore, on the other hand, angrily arraigned the Sewardites.[29]

In Pennsylvania the Christiana killing played a vital part in the canvass. When the Pennsylvania Anti-Slavery Society met in October, one element in it actually favored violence in resisting the Fugitive Slave Act. The conservatism of the State properly revolted against such doctrines, and the fact that the Whig governor stood against the Act hampered his run for reëlection. Buchanan aptly summed up the meaning of the result. "The Democracy of Pennsylvania, believing it was their solemn duty to maintain the law, staked the fate of the late election upon this issue. The maintenance and faithful execution of the Fugitive Slave law; the repeal of our unjust and unconstitutional obstruction law; and the suppression of all further agitation on the question of slavery were everywhere proclaimed as essential principles of Democracy. We 'paltered in a double sense' with none of the isms with which our State is infested. The victory has, therefore, been glorious . . . I trust that in our State we shall have no further serious difficulty with the free soil question." [30]

Even in the Northeast the clergy was largely on the side of the Compromise and of adherence to national mandates. Ezra Stiles Gannett, courageously saying that he would bar his door to a fugitive rather than set a law of the republic at naught, found companions in Moses Stuart of Andover, Orville M. Dewey of New York, and many more. Theodore Parker later testified that in 1850–52 the general voice of the New England churches, so far as it was heard through the press, was for the Fugitive Slave Act and its execution. He thought this especially true of the rich and fashionable churches in the commercial towns; the churches whose trinity, he said, were the gold eagle, the silver dollar, and the copper cent. "The great influences of the church, of the more eminent ministers and laymen," reported the Massachusetts Abolition Society in 1853, "are still thrown into the scale of the oppressor." If a moderate spirit was true of the clergy of New England, it was still truer of the ministers of the Middle States and the border. Though the Unitarians were more advanced than other sects, their most influential minister in New York, Orville Dewey, was as emphatically opposed to abolitionism and its extremes as to slavery.

Still another index of the abatement of Northern radicalism lay in the almost complete collapse of the Free Soil Party organization and press. Outside New

29 Alexander, *Political History of New York*, II, 166; Barnes, *Thurlow Weed*, 196.
30 November 14, 1851; Buchanan Papers, N. Y. Hist. Soc.

England, Ohio, and Wisconsin, by the end of 1851 the party was dead. Nearly all its newspapers in the Northwest had disappeared or gone over to the older parties, only a handful remaining. When Congress met at the end of 1851, it was with even fewer animosities and more kindliness than in the previous session. Since in both chambers the Democrats had an overwhelming majority to checkmate the Administration, partisan legislation was impossible.[31]

[V]

In the North no less than the South economic considerations were largely responsible for the trend toward acquiescence. Prosperity bred content. Business interests were insistent that the Compromise be maintained and that troublemaking stop. In Boston, New York, and Philadelphia, in Baltimore, Pittsburgh, and Cincinnati, manufacturers, merchants, and speculators exerted their pressure for peace and quiet. The New York *Daybook* compiled a list of "abolitionist" merchants for Southern distribution, and Southern journals republished it with the advice that these men be shunned like the pestilence. According to the New York *Tribune*, Southern retailers declared that if it were known that they bought goods from "abolitionist" wholesale houses, their shops would be mobbed. But anti-slavery merchants met hostile action nearer home. The Boston *Courier* in the spring of 1851 proposed a systematic boycott of all storekeepers, physicians, lawyers, and even clergymen who resisted the Fugitive Slave Act. The Union Safety Committee set up by the New York merchants not only propagandized rural areas and took part in the fall elections of 1851 but spoke words of sharp warning and earnest suasion to Manhattan businessmen. It was time, most Northern editors asserted, to turn from barren slavery issues to more fruitful questions: to manufacturing enterprises, railroad charters, and tariffs.[32]

So strong was the economic pressure that anti-slavery radicals began to clamor that the money-power was checking all discussion, and that conservative Whig manufacturers had sold their principles for the lure of higher duties. A young merchant, declared one pamphleteer, revolts against slavery. He attends some freesoil meetings. But he soon finds that old-established firms are no longer sending country customers to him. When he wishes to borrow money the banker frowns: "Sorry—credit is very tight." When he asks a shipping favor, the railroad grimaces: "We regret it—but we have no cars." The young trader has to yield or go bankrupt. "The power of the nabob merchants over their less robust brethren is all but crushing." Another chain by which the

31 Theodore Parker, *Works*, XII, 320; Samuel May, *Anti-Slavery Conflict*, 365ff; T. C. Smith, *Liberty and Freesoil Parties in the Northwest*, 243ff.
32 N. Y. *Tribune*, April 5, 1851. Foner, *Business and Slavery*, 55–87; *Courier*, June 9, 1851.

Northern Money Power and the Southern Slave Power bound opinion, said the radicals, lay in the tariff. Had not Berrian, Mangum, and other Southern Whigs suggested that they would grant tariff favors if the South were appeased? Had not Webster told the crowd at the Revere House that Congress could now turn to matters of practical value? "Rejoicing in that consolation, the great city of the Pilgrims licked the dust." In Massachusetts, Edmund Quincy and others wrote reams on State Street control of politics, or rather, control by a golden oligarchy of the Boston, Salem, Lowell, New Bedford, and other merchants and bankers.[33]

Exaggerated though these denunciations were, it was true that business interests North and South hoped that the new sectional concord would prove permanent. The winter session of Congress in 1850–51 made it clear that one era had ended and another was beginning. All the great giants of the past had left the stage. Not only was Calhoun dead, Webster in the State Department, and Clay inactive with his resignation (tendered December 15th) to take effect the following September, but Thomas Hart Benton had been overthrown by a coalition between his Democratic opponents in Missouri and the Whigs. "I am for the country and the Union," he had cried, "and the country and Union require Calhounism to be exterminated in Missouri." But it was Benton who was ousted, while Atchison Democrats ran wild with what he called nullification and high treason resolves. With these men gone, the Senate seemed a tame place. The House chose Boyd of Kentucky, a Democratic supporter of the Compromise, for Speaker. In the appointment of committees, radicals got little comfort in either chamber.[34]

Though the session lasted until the end of August, 1852, thus running into the heart of the presidential campaign, it accomplished little. The Administration, spurred on by Whig editors, urged a revision of the tariff upward and the adoption of specific instead of ad valorem duties, but Congress was deaf to all such proposals. The most it would do was to pass a bill, supported by the Pennsylvania iron lobby and various Western interests, granting three million acres for railroad construction in Missouri. One Southerner, Thomas L. Clingman,

33 "A Chapter from American History; Five Years' Progress of the Slave Power," privately printed. See Edmund Quincy, January 21, 1850, on Massachusetts politics. The lower house, he grumbled, did not give the rural districts sufficient representation. "As it is now arranged, Boston, Salem, Lowell, New Bedford, and a few other cities and populous towns, virtually govern the State. These are sure, as a general thing, to be Whig, and to be under the control of the money power—and thus it is that a handful of men in State Street govern Massachusetts with much more absolute and certain sway, than the old Albany Regency used to govern New York, in the days of its prosperity. For our Oligarchy is compact, and has much fewer wires to pull, and, as the wires are golden ones, they are tolerably sure of a response." Quincy Papers.
34 Washington Union, May 5, 1850, quoting Benton. N. Y. Weekly Tribune, January 31, 1852.

burst out indignantly against the nefarious activities of Thad Stevens's iron interest, which was constantly offering support to Western measures in the hope of rail-orders and tariff favors. A much-needed law was passed for the inspection of steam-vessels. To foreign affairs—that is, to the Hungarian patriot Kossuth, to Webster's brush with Hülsemann, and to British relations—Congress gave prolonged attention. But what most pleased the country was its emphatic support of the sectional settlement. Two Georgia Representatives, Jackson and Hillyer, offered a resolution declaring the Compromise a finality, and by a majority which largely obliterated both party and sectional lines, the House passed it.[35]

This resolution made it clear that a shining new plank, the full acceptance of the Compromise, would be nailed tightly into both party platforms in 1852. Indeed, we have seen that a large body of Congressional leaders in both parties stood pledged against any candidate who would not abide by the Compromise; this excluding such men as Jefferson Davis on one side, Seward on the other. The New York *Tribune* admitted that "we cannot now hope to elect to the presidency . . . an outspoken adversary of the Fugitive Slave Law." Who would disturb the settlement when the skies were so bright? [36]

The world over, Californian and Australian gold were stimulating hope and activity. Placer mining in the West had given way to quartz crushing, in which John C. Frémont among others was a leader. "There is a literally inexhaustible quantity of this quartz in the foothills of the Sierra Nevada mountains," wrote a correspondent of the *Tribune*, quoting a letter from a Grass Valley operator who averaged a $70 yield to every ton of rock. It was certain that unabated quantities of gold were pouring into the markets of the world, and that in all kinds of unforeseen ways it was exciting and enriching business. Merchant shipping had been diverted into new channels by the development of California and Australia. To the old business of equipping miners, which many Easterners in 1849–51 had found lucrative, and the business of building new Western towns and cities, was added a novel industry in the manufacture of mining, crushing, and washing machinery.

Everywhere values were rising. Do not sell your farm for $65 an acre, wrote J. J. Crittenden to his daughter; "my opinion is that the price of real property must in a short time be greatly enhanced by the vast increase of the precious metals and especially by their influx into this country from California." Cotton and wheat were finding a good European market. Railway construction was proceeding apace. Hurrah for boundless speculation! exclaimed the New York *Tribune*; hurrah for giant fortunes made by bond-mongering!—with a hint that

35 *Selections from the Speeches and Writings of Thomas L. Clingman*, 288. Cong. *Globe*, 32d Cong., 1st sess., 825, 976–983, March 22, April 5, 1852.
36 N. Y. *Tribune*, December 6, 1851.

the piper would yet have to be paid, but with full admission of the boom. Slavery could be thrust into the background.[37]

Party battle-lines were thus drawn, as the year 1852 opened, on the dull old field of the tariff, internal improvements, and foreign policy. The Whigs would appeal to the industrial North by demanding higher duties; to the West by promising aid to rivers, harbors, and railroads. They would oppose further acquisitions of territory in Cuba, Mexico, and Central America. The Democrats would deprecate an artificial stimulation of manufacturing at the expense of agriculture, and the levying of taxes to be squandered on dubious schemes of public improvement. They would reassert their time-honored jealousy of national authority, patronage, and interference. But they, and especially their Southern wing, would look with kindly eye upon an expansion of the national domain into tropical regions.

The slavery question would be shelved; on that issue the country would return to its old policy of drift. Neither parties nor government agencies were so organized as to deal constructively with it—to do more than make surface adjustments. Yet the central difficulty remained untouched. The main problem, the triple-headed monster of Slavery, Poverty, and Race-Adjustment in the South, still had to be dealt with, and was growing more formidable every year.

[VI]

At this moment high literary inspiration, amounting almost to genius, suddenly lighted up the division in the American household, and arraigned with burning emotion and true-hearted humanity the institution which was parting a great people. Ideas rule the world, and ideas conjoined with art make the swiftest conquest of men. From the days of Bunyan and Defoe, the writer who can wrap his doctrines in the gay cloak of pleasing fiction has been sure of a large and eager following. In the history of great moral movements the essay, the pamphlet, and the tract have made their deepest impression when endowed with the graces that marked *The Battle of the Books* and *The Story of a Whistle*. Those who thought that the slavery question could be comfortably shelved reckoned only with politicians, editors, and the like; they little thought that a

37 Crittenden to his daughter, November 2, 1851; Crittenden Papers. Ben McCulloch of Texas, who had won fame during the Mexican War with his rangers, and who later became a noted Confederate general, had gone to California. The summer of 1851 found him much excited over the quartz discoveries. "Some of them have proved to be immensely rich," he wrote his friend Senator Rusk. "One has yielded in the two past months over $300,000; one share containing one seventh was sold after that for $100,000; one of the owners had a piece at San Francisco recently weighing 102 pounds containing over fifty pounds of gold. A great deal of machinery has gone and more going every day to the mines. New discoveries are being constantly made, and in truth *these are the mines* of California, and will in my opinion affect the *value* of gold *eventually*. . . ." June 15, 1851; Rusk Papers.

single novel could confound them and exert a far weightier influence than legislators or daily press.

The curious fact that pure literature had as yet taken little note of the slavery question is doubtless partly explicable on the ground of public aversion to so painful and controversial a subject. Robert Montgomery Bird's play *The Gladiator* (1831) had been a sharp if indirect indictment of slavery. With Spartacus its rhetorical hero, it had scored a brilliant success in New York, Boston, and Philadelphia; but Bird thought that if it had been produced in the South he, the manager, and the actors would all have gone to the penitentiary. In 1836 Richard Hildreth, after a Southern sojourn, published a lurid fictional exposé of the darkest side of bondage in *The Slave: or, Memoirs of Archie Moore*. He had great difficulty in getting it published. No reputable house in Boston or New York would take it. It was finally brought out without any publisher's name on the title-page, while with much difficulty a bookseller was found who distributed the first edition in four or five months. "But no review or magazine, or hardly a newspaper, took any notice of it," wrote Hildreth later. Actually, it lacked strength, vitality, and literary art. Herman Melville's *Mardi* had carried several characters to the Southern States, and through their utterances had excoriated slavery, but *Mardi* found few readers. Although the poets, with Whittier in the van, and Lowell, Bryant, Emerson, and Longfellow close behind him, had expressed their hatred of slavery with powerful effect, probably few people in 1851 thought that a popular work of fiction could be written about slavery. But that year a sketch describing the death of a slave named Uncle Tom appeared in Gamaliel Bailey's *National Era*. It aroused so much attention that the author, Harriet Beecher Stowe, set herself to furnish, in weekly instalments, the story which led up to and embodied this scene, *Uncle Tom's Cabin*.[38]

From several points of view the book was almost miraculous. That "Hattie" Beecher, daughter of the famous Lyman Beecher, possessed literary talent was known only to her husband, the stiff, learned, hypochondriac scholar, Calvin Stowe, a teacher successively in Lane Seminary in Cincinnati, in Bowdoin College, and at Andover Seminary. "My dear," he had written her in 1840, after she had confided some of her literary aspirations to him, "you must be a literary woman. It is so written in the Book of Fate. Make all your calculations accordingly." Yet for nearly a decade after this she published nothing but some short stories in the annuals then popular, and a tract or two, showing no great gift. When she sat down to pen *Uncle Tom's Cabin* she was almost wholly untrained as a writer. And of preparation in another sense, thorough study of slavery on its own ground, she was almost equally innocent.

38 C. E. Foust, *Life and Dramatic Works of Robert Montgomery Bird*, 51. Hildreth, *The Slave: or, Memoirs of Archie Moore*, edition of 1840, I, 3.

To be sure, she had lived for seventeen years in Cincinnati, on the borders of slavery. But her first and apparently also her last close inspection of a slave establishment was a short visit in 1833 to a Kentucky plantation which she later pictured as Colonel Shelby's in her story. After her marriage, the Stowes helped succor runaway slaves, while she took some free Negro children into a family school and taught them as her own. She was a woman of quick observation and analytical power, who saw as much in an hour as ordinary folk saw in months. Yet she remained inexpert both as to Negro character and to the institutional aspects of slavery. Her want of special grounding for her book was frankly confessed in a letter to Frederick Douglass in July, 1851, after *Uncle Tom's Cabin* began to appear in the *National Era*. The scene, she wrote him, would soon fall on a cotton plantation, and she needed information from somebody who had been a practical laborer on one. She possessed an able paper by a Southern planter on the practical details of his work, but she needed something from a lowlier standpoint to present a graphic and faithful picture. She supposed that Henry Bibb, a fugitive slave, might furnish the needed information. The wonder is not that Southern critics found the book wanting in home touches and local color, but that its defects were so few.

Of moral preparation for her task she had more, though some abolitionists would have pronounced her record lukewarm and inert. As a child she had sobbed in the pew over her father's groaning prayers for "poor, oppressed, bleeding Africa," and as a woman had been horrified by some sights she saw on Cincinnati streets. It was the Fugitive Slave bill which awakened her to self-expression. Her husband having been transferred to Bowdoin, she reached New England as it was pulsating with anger over the bill and Webster's Seventh of March speech. The press was full of highly colored descriptions of Negroes torn from their homes, or frozen to death as they toiled through the snows to reach Canada. Her heart was aflame when her sister-in-law, sending her a series of letters on the excitement, closed with the appeal: "Now Hattie, if I could use a pen as you can, I would write something which would make this whole nation feel what an accursed thing slavery is." This appeal Mrs. Stowe, standing erect in her little living-room, caught to her bosom with the words: "I will write something. I will if I live." That was her vow, and its redemption is part of American history.[39]

The story of the book is one of the most astonishing in the history of letters. When she began its serial publication neither she nor Dr. Bailey thought of it as much more than a sketch, and it was announced for three months—finally running for ten. Long before it was finished it had made a mild sensation. A Boston

---

[39] Annie Fields, *Harriet Beecher Stowe*, 103ff; Charles E. Stowe, *Harriet Beecher Stowe*, 156–177.

publisher wrote offering to bring it out with an equal division of costs and profits, and the author refused because her husband was "altogether too poor to assume the risk." How the book, finally issued in March, 1852, on a ten per cent royalty basis, brought her ten thousand dollars at the end of three months and another ten thousand at the end of six, how by the end of the year 300,000 copies had been sold and eight power presses were running night and day to keep pace

Manuscript of Mrs. Stowe's Story of Uncle Tom.
From Charles Stowe: *Harriet Beecher Stowe.*

with the demand, how it was translated into half the languages of the world, how it became as universal a household treasure as *Pilgrim's Progress* and *Robinson Crusoe*—this is an old story. In America, Britain, France, and other lands the book did just what Mrs. Stowe had hoped it would do; it inspired a mighty popular enthusiasm for the anti-slavery cause. One reason why it and the plays built upon it gained so tremendous a vogue in America and Britain may easily be overlooked. Novels and plays in both countries were still widely regarded as reprehensible; even Scott and Dickens were often kept under lock and key, while Christian families trembled at mention of the stage. But *Uncle Tom's Cabin* was moral and religious; and countless millions of Yankees and Britons read the novel aloud at the fireside, while multitudes flocked to the play. The deeper reason for its vogue was the universal appeal of the story to the basic human emotions; an appeal so powerful that, read in Russia, it impelled not a few landowners to liberate their serfs.

A lesser novelist than Mrs. Stowe would have indicted the slaveholder, as Hildreth did in *The White Slave*; but with a sure instinct she indicted the institution. Her condemnation was not for the Southerners, unfortunate in inheriting slavery, but for the system. Some of her finest characters, such as the brilliant St. Clare and the splendid Mrs. Shelby, are Southerners, while her basest villain, Simon Legree, is a Yankee by birth. Nor is the indictment of the system crudely drawn. It is given us by implication in an intensely human story; a story animated by a feeling not in the least political or sectional, but humanitarian and Christian. It is the feeling of John Woolman, not that of Garrison. The book attuned itself to the strong philanthropic impulse of the age—the impulse that was opening schools, wiping away slums, passing factory acts, ameliorating the hard lot of the poor and oppressed. It attuned itself no less to the essential spirit of Christianity—the spirit of Him who had died for all who were weary and heavy laden. It was a rebuke to callous materialism, whether Southern or Northern, and to that text-chopping type of Christianity, both Northern and Southern, which justified servitude by Biblical citations. But Mrs. Stowe did not fall into the error of writing a mere tract. Her plot was simple—George Sand was not far wrong when she said that the book dealt only with the life and death of a little child and a Negro slave—but it was gripping. Its characters—Uncle Tom, Little Eva, Topsy, the methodical Miss Ophelia, George Harris and his wife Eliza, the nervous Marie St. Clare—were genuine creations of the imagination, who impressed themselves permanently upon the folk-consciousness of the nation. In far-off lands, where men and women cared little whether slavery remained part of the American system or was rent from it, the trials and triumphs, the crimes and charities, the sufferings and successes, of this vivid knot of human beings had an instant appeal.

The chief defect of the book, as a sociological document, lay in its idealization of the Negro. It did not overstate the case against slavery, which was capable of all the abuses and cruelties she depicted. But it did overstate the contemporaneous case for the slave. Countless Northern readers who had never seen a plantation pictured all Negroes thenceforth in terms of the saintly Uncle Tom, whose soul belonged to God alone, the sturdy George Harris, hugging the free soil of Ohio to his bosom, the devoted Eliza his wife, and the irresponsible but delightful Topsy. These are not the Negroes we see in the pages of

Olmsted, or of the scientific modern students of antebellum Southern life; black folk struggling with many a slip out of barbarism into civilization, with the faults, passions, and limitations of Africa clinging to them as mud clings to a man springing from a slough. That such Negroes as Uncle Tom and George Harris actually lived, that in a free society such men and still better types would

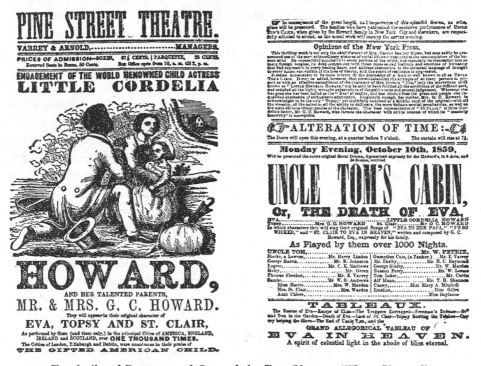

Facsimile of Program of One of the Best-Known "Tom Shows."
Courtesy of the Yale University Press.

become numerous, is of course undeniable; but Mrs. Stowe seemed to teach that all the slaves of 1850 were of that rare fibre. No small part of the incredible over-optimism with which the North later approached the task of converting slaves into voters, self-dependent citizens, and legislators, thinking it could be done overnight, is chargeable to the impression diffused by Mrs. Stowe. Sambo was not Uncle Tom, and Chloe was not Eliza Harris; only education, effort, painful discipline, could make them so, by the slow passage of time.

Some Southern critics of the novel made the error of treating it as a tissue of absurdities. They declared that the dialect was all wrong; that the characters were grotesque and incredible; and that the pictures of slave-maltreatment were grossly overdrawn. As to the first criticism, dialect varied with locality; as to the second, fair Southerners admitted that Uncle Tom, St. Clare, Legree, and the rest were all *possible*; as to the third, Mrs. Stowe promptly supplied a complete answer in her *Key to Uncle Tom*. The really valid criticisms of the book from the Southern standpoint were two.

To begin with, the novel and still more the play presented in Uncle Tom, George Harris, and others not real Negroes or mulattoes, but Anglo-Saxons with dark skins. Particularly when highly trained actors and actresses enacted the story, the audience saw in Eliza, George, and one or two more not the product of slave pens and cotton fields, but white people of refinement and some cultivation simply given black complexions. The book thus confirmed a common Northern misconception. The Bostonian or Clevelander seldom saw any but a highly exceptional Negro, and many people thought of them all as Frederick Douglasses. On the other hand, many Southerners never saw one highly exceptional Negro. The second great fault of the novel was that, presenting the Negro at his best, it quite failed to present the white Southerner in any such light. The South had men as selfish, shiftless, and unprincipled as Shelby, as wavering as the infidel St. Clare, as brutal as Legree; all societies have them. But there was no real Southern gentleman in the book. There was no conscientious, vigilant, benevolent Southern master. There was nothing to show that the South had its Lees, its Dabneys, its Clays, its John Bells, its knightly Pelhams, its gentle Maurys. It might be added that the real arguments of the South for slavery were suppressed, and that the arguments Mrs. Stowe quoted were grotesque caricatures of them.[40]

But the influence of the book was none the less profound for its defects. Longfellow and Lowell thought it one of the greatest triumphs of literary history, and Whittier thanked Providence for the Fugitive Slave Act which had inspired it. If Rufus Choate said, as reported, that it would make two million abolitionists, he made an acute remark. Literally every Northerner was soon reading it. England went through what men called an Uncle Tom fever, the sale in no long time running well above a million copies. Lord Palmerston, who had not taken up a novel for thirty years, read it three times, and spoke admiringly of its statesmanship as well as literary power. In Italy its popularity was such that the Pope debarred it from the papal states. The verdict of Tolstoy upon its merits is well known. It became, in short, a world force, and the young generation just coming of age between 1852 and 1860, particularly in the North and in England, felt the full impact of its emotions and ideas.

At least ten persons, including Mrs. Stowe herself, dramatized the novel

40 See Percy Greg's criticism of *Uncle Tom's Cabin* in *History of the United States*, II, 71–72. George Sand, in an appreciation contributed to one of the numerous French editions, praised Mrs. Stowe as gifted not with literary genius but "the genius of goodness." For an incisive study of Mrs. Stowe see Constance M. Rourke, *Trumpets of Jubilee*, 89–148.

within a few years after its publication. Her version, a three-act play called "The Christian Slave," was never popular. The popular English playwrights Mark Lemon and Tom Taylor produced one dramatization. A Southerner visiting London in 1853 found that Mrs. Stowe had made the Negro quite a lion. Black serenaders with banjoes and bones paraded the streets; Uncle Tom's sable visage looked out from every hoarding; and even wall-paper with scenes from the novel was for sale. "I went of course to see Uncle Tom on the stage," this visitor writes, "where he plays a very subordinate part, the hero and heroine being George and Eliza—people with much fairer complexion than I can boast of. The acting was very good, and I am not surprised that if that is the English notion of the institution, they think it horrible." The most popular American dramatization was by George L. Aiken; and its scenes showing Eliza crossing the ice with bloodhounds in pursuit, the pleasanter side of slavery in the St. Clare home, Little Topsy growing up, the cruelty of Legree, the tragic death of Uncle Tom, and Little Eva borne to heaven amid gorgeous clouds, gripped the Northern imagination and remained popular for decades.[41]

Forming a vivid stereotype and fixing it in the national mind, *Uncle Tom's Cabin* fired alike the indignation of Southerners and the impulsive idealism of Northerners. It aroused a feeling in England that was to be potent when, in years to come, Britain stood the neutral observer of the civil war racking America. One of the direct products of *Uncle Tom's Cabin* was the Stafford House Address, written by the great philanthropist Lord Shaftesbury and signed by many thousands of British women, who pleaded with their sisters of the Southern States for two progressive steps: the preservation of the family life of the Negro, with due provision for the sanctity of marriage and strict interdiction of the forced parting of parents and children, and a systematic education of the colored folk in Christianity. Published at the end of 1852, the address drew applause from Northerners of anti-slavery views, and tart retorts from Southern women. Wherever it went, the novel stirred men's emotions, raised questions, and lifted to notice a basic issue: Was slavery just, and if not, how could its injustice be cured? Its publication gave notice that the slavery problem could not be shelved, and that in dealing with it the nation could not simply drift.[42]

"Every nation that carries in its bosom great and unredressed injustice," wrote Mrs. Stowe, faces the possibility of an awful convulsion. Just what, reflective men asked, was this institution of slavery like, and in what direction was it moving?

41 W. H. Trescot, MS Diary, January 9, 1853; South Caroliniana Library.
42 *Christian Times*, December 3, 1852.

13

The Lot of the Bondsman

TO MOST Americans the word slavery calls up as vivid a series of pictures as any noun in the language, each scene tinged with emotional color. The West African forest, hot, luxuriant, and creeper-tangled; the caravan of manacled blacks, panting under the lash of Ashanti or Benin captors, driven down to the coastal factory for sale; the quick savage murder of all who drop in the path. The murky, feverish hold of the slave-ship, the heartbroken Negroes crammed like herrings in a barrel, wallowing in their own filth and dying as they squirm and gasp. Then, far from all thought of "old moon-mountains African," the gangs of brutish laborers, hoe in hand, creeping slowly across the burning Georgia cotton-fields, the bark of the overseer, the crack of his whip, and the distant cawing of crows the only sounds. The whipping-post, and roped to it an abject black shape, wincing as a bronzed arm swings the lash. A showy, nimble-tongued auctioneer chanting his pitch; a knot of onlookers expectorating, cursing, and squinting at the penned-up human property; a strong field-hand or a woman with a pickaninny turning from side to side on the block.

In contrast with these dark pictures, brighter vignettes will flash before the eye. Smart, well-dressed house-servants of Virginia and Kentucky, as proud of mahogany furniture, silver plate, and dashing equipages as the owner; "mammies" devoted to the white children they guard; gay roustabouts on the Mississippi trotting from bluff to steamboat as they chant "De Las' Sack"; sable congregations exultant in their Christian salvation; Negro mechanics of Mobile or New Orleans patiently earning their freedom; and under the Carolina moon, the happy clatter of a neat slave-quarter as night falls on groups, singing, laughing, gossiping, and munching. Slaves learning to read—slaves mastering intricate crafts.

Slavery was a manysided institution. To name no others, it was a labor system; it was a slow but in some ways efficient process of education; and it was a mode of adjustment between two very differently endowed races. It was also a dynamic institution planted in a dynamic social environment. No valid generalizations regarding slavery can be founded upon emotional impressions, whether bright or grim. Still less can any generalizations be regarded as sound which do not carefully discriminate among its various aspects, and make scrupulous allowance for variegations linked to different times and different places. Any true picture must present slavery in its protean character, with all its local diversities, and all its changes under the impact of new economic forces, new political pressures, and new humanitarian ideas. Southerners liked to think of slavery as static—but it was not. From decade to decade, State to State, it underwent vital alterations, growing, shifting, decaying. Of all false assumptions, the falsest are those which imply even brief unchangeability in any human relationship. Nor, it may be added, can a true record of slavery be written without a strong and equal sympathy for both slave and slaveholder; not emotional bias, but the sympathy which leads to understanding.

[I]

To the Southerners of 1850 slavery was a heritage, for the creation of which they were no more responsible than for their other immemorial heritages—their English speech, their representative institutions, their ideas and customs. It was interwoven with the texture of society. In some seaboard areas slavery by 1850 was well over two hundred years old; as old as the very civilization of the region.[1] Since 1619 black men and white had lived side by side, each in steadily increasing numbers. Some Negroes having back of them a lineage of five or six generations on American soil, had acquired not only the speech but the skills, preconceptions, and religious and social ideas of the white folk. Others were nearer the African village, their grandparents, or even parents having been seized in jungle raids and spirited across the Atlantic. Generation by generation, the slaves acquired a fuller English vocabulary, a larger mastery of tools, and a completer identification with the civilization which encircled them. The hard labor to which they were kept disciplined their character, and the Christian faith which many acquired refined their feelings.

Slavery was the great peculiar *institution* of the South. But the basic *fact* which demarcated South from North lay deeper. It was the fact that in the fifteen Southern and border States the colored population was much more than half as great as the white, while in the North it was an insignificant fraction. That is, the fundamental difference was that while the North was roughly a region of one white race, the South was an area where two races had somehow to live side by side. The single State of Virginia in 1850 had more than two and

---

1 Negroes had however been few during the first two generations of Virginia life, and while the first black comers had been slaves when sold, they were not fully slaves to their buyers; the tenure was vague. U. B. Phillips, *American Negro Slavery*, 75ff; P. A. Bruce, *Economic History of Virginia in the Seventeenth Century*, I, 572-634, II *passim*.

a half times as many Negroes as the sixteen freesoil States. In South Carolina, Mississippi, and Louisiana, the Negroes outnumbered the whites, while in Florida they fell little short of doing so. If slavery was a Southern heritage, so was this stubborn, broadfronted, and profoundly significant necessity for some kind of racial adjustment. Slavery might be abolished. But if it was, on what terms should the 6,184,477 whites and the 3,200,364 Negroes enumerated by the census of 1850 in the fifteen slave States (not to mention the 228,138 free colored people) live side by side? Though slavery appeared the dominant fact of Southern life, what was really fundamental was the problem of race relations.

The distribution of slaves, governed primarily by factors of climate, soil, and transportation, was highly irregular. With its coastal plains, piedmont plateau, and Appalachian and Ozark-Ouachita highlands, its rivers, valleys, sandstone hills, and forest belts, the South was a land of many distinct regions.[2] In the Appalachian highlands, a great plowshare cleaving the section from Maryland down into northern Alabama and Georgia, slaves were so few and widely scattered that some districts found them a curiosity. The same could be said of the Ozark belt running from near Jefferson City, Mo., to the Arkansas River. Here the rough wild terrain was inimical to a slave economy. The interrelations of slavery and transportation were best demonstrated in Texas. At first slavery flourished only in the coastal plain and eastern Texas, but as communications improved and cotton-growing 'spread into central districts, slavery advanced with it.[3] Generally speaking, slavery did not represent an effort to escape the handicap of a fierce sun and high temperatures, for though some Southerners themselves believed that white men could not toil in the severe summer heat of certain areas, thousands of yeomen farmers proved able to work anywhere. Slavery had come into being primarily to meet a labor shortage. It prospered wherever men could establish industrial units, *"agricultural factories"* turning out cotton, sugar, or tobacco, which made slave labor profitable.

The tidewater country of Virginia, the Carolinas, and Georgia offered a broad coastal belt in which the proportion of Negroes to the whole population rose as high as eighty-eight per cent just north of Charleston or eighty-six near Savannah, and rarely sank below forty per cent. But in the uplands of these States the ratios were low. Thus in Virginia the number of slaves about Lexington and other Shenandoah towns sank to thirty per cent or less; those in the mountainous districts were no more than six or seven per cent; and in the panhandle about Wheeling they were almost unknown. In central and southern Alabama, including the so-called Black Belt renowned for its fertile soil, the slave population was generally dense. Nearly two-thirds of the people near

2　Rupert B. Vance, *Human Geography of the South,* Ch. 2.
3　R. N. Richardson, *Texas the Lone Star State,* 211, 212.

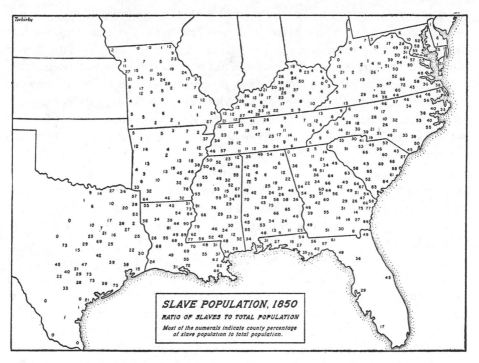

SLAVE POPULATION, 1850

RATIO OF SLAVES TO TOTAL POPULATION

Most of the numerals indicate county percentage of slave population to total population.

In 1820 the country had 1,538,000 slaves; by 1850 the number grew to 3,204,000, and by 1860 it was 3,953,500. The number of manumissions in the year ending June 1, 1860, was just over 3,000; and that year about 800 slaves were reported to have run away.

Montgomery, and more than two-thirds near Selma, were Negroes. But in mountainous northeastern Alabama the proportion dropped to four, six, and ten per cent. Both Mississippi and Louisiana had large valley areas where the slave population was exceptionally large, running in various counties to 89, 90, 91, and even 94 per cent of the whole. But in those districts of northern and western Arkansas given over to small farmers and stockgrowers, and in all of Missouri except along the Missouri River, slave settlement was again fairly sparse.[4]

From the terms used in the angry discussion of slavery, it might have been supposed that almost the whole Southern population had a direct interest in it. Actually, of the 6,184,477 white folk in the slave States, only 347,525 were listed by the census of 1850 as owners, and even this number gave an exaggerated impression of the facts. When a single person owned slaves in different counties, or in different States, he was entered in the returns more than once. Moreover, the census included slave-hirers as well as slave-owners, and unques-

---

4 See the convenient map in Daniel Lord, *The Effect of Secession*, 1861.

tionably there were tens of thousands of hirers. Hinton Rowan Helper, indeed, estimated the true number of slaveholders as "certainly less than two hundred thousand." [5] It would perhaps not be unfair to conjecture the actual number at about 300,000. The immediate families of these owners represented, at an average of five persons each, about 1,500,000 people; and if a generous allowance is made for overseers' families and other white employees on large estates, still those directly concerned with the ownership and management of slaves probably did not exceed 2,000,000. If so, not one-third of the population of the South and border States had any direct interest in slavery as a form of property. This is a fact of great importance when we attempt to estimate the effect of slaveholding upon the culture and outlook of the Southern people. Nor was the proportion increasing; on the contrary, it was falling. If not one-third of the people had any direct interest in slaveholding in 1850, not one-fourth had such an interest in 1860.

Among those who owned or hired slaves, the vast majority possessed fewer than ten apiece, and a clear majority fewer than five apiece. The "big-wigs" of whom Frederick Law Olmsted heard so much while traveling in the lower Mississippi Valley, the nabob planters who figured so largely in the eyes of the North, constituted a very restricted body indeed. Northern readers constantly heard of such men as Wade Hampton, whose family had begun to profit so heavily from cotton on the morrow of Eli Whitney's invention, or the five Hairston brothers of Virginia and Mississippi, who altogether possessed at the beginning of the fifties not far from five thousand slaves. But the census of 1850 listed only eleven persons who owned five hundred or more Negroes, and only 254 who owned two hundred or more each. Indeed, in all the vast range of the slave States from Delaware to Florida and from North Carolina to Texas, there were not eight thousand men who then owned fifty or more slaves apiece. A large auditorium could have held all these "magnates."

[II]

It was true, however, that the richer slaveowners wielded an influence in the South, and particularly in Southern politics, far more than commensurate with their numbers.[6] Their wealth gave them the advantages of leisure, superior education, and social prestige. In large part they were drawn from the old

5 *Impending Crisis*, 147. See Randall's summary, *Civil War and Reconstruction*, 60, 61. The interesting question of Negro ownership of slaves was investigated by the Association for the Study of Negro Life, and the main results are presented in Carter B. Woodson, "History Made to Order," *Journal of Negro Hist.*, XII, 330–348.

6 Ralph B. Flanders, *Plantation Slavery in Georgia*, 280; William E. Dodd, *The Cotton Kingdom*, 118–146; R. S. Cotterill, *The Old South*, 269–272.

families, and countless Southerners subscribed to Dr. Johnson's view that respect for old families was an important element in keeping society healthy. "Now, sir, that respect for authority is much more easily granted to a man whose father has had it, than to an upstart. . . . People will prefer a man for whose father their fathers have voted." Even when "upstarts," the rich men were frequently lent prestige by the recognition of the planter gentry. Throughout the greater part of the South, from the tidewater to the banks of the Missouri and the Nueces, local administration and authority revolved about the county courts. "Co't day" was the shining periodical occasion when county judges, or justices of the peace sitting as a panel of magistrates, became embodiments of the law. These grandees were commonly chosen from the wealthier, better-established families of the countryside. Possessed of stern common sense, some learning in their respective codes, a smattering of the English common law, and a habit of command, they were regarded with respect by all and with positive awe by many. Throughout the lands of cotton, cane, and tobacco (though not in the uplands or on the frontier) these magistrates were almost certain to be slave-holders, and likely to be slaveholders on a considerable scale. They were likely, also, to be churchmen of importance; vestrymen of the Episcopal Church, elders or deacons of the Presbyterian and Methodist Churches. In local affairs their word often had autocratic power—and they represented the slaveholding interest. The picture was steadily changing, so that by 1850 aristocracy counted for far less, and democracy for much more (especially outside Virginia and South Carolina) than a generation earlier; but many of its old outlines remained.

The wealthy planter class, moreover, to a great extent dominated State and sectional politics. In the period of Andrew Jackson's ascendency, to be sure, frontier influences had been strong within the Democratic Party; but even Jackson rather represented the great landowners than the small pioneer farmers, while such aides as Cave Johnson in Tennessee and Robert J. Walker in Mississippi rallied the rich planters behind him. The victorious Mexican War and subsequent annexations, widely accepted as a triumph of planter ideas and interests, added much to the prestige of the slaveholders. The planters easily formed alliances with the merchants and lawyers of the South, whose prosperity depended on that of the slaveocracy. They travelled widely, mingling with men of affairs; if their houses were not what John P. Kennedy called them, "as open as an inn and as rich as a castle," they nevertheless offered a bounteous hospitality. Each was likely to have his retinue of local dependents and admirers, men whom Helper called "sycophants" and "cringing lick-spittles." They imposed their authority upon the great mass of illiterate or semi-illiterate poor whites. To a considerable extent, moreover, they were bound together by inter-marriage, the South making much even of distant degrees of cousinhood, and taking delight in interfamily visitings. The farmers of the South were of course the bulwark of the Democratic party and of slavery, while such men as Jefferson Davis, A. H. Stephens, and Judah P. Benjamin by no means sprang from a planter aristocracy. The patrician type of county court ceased to exist in the cotton States after 1840. Nevertheless, the three hundred thousand slaveholders, and to a large degree the hundred thousand with ten or more slaves each, swayed the policies of the section.[7]

They were assisted in this by the inequalities of representation in many State legislatures, and the undemocratic character of important political mechanisms. In Virginia, for example, the census of 1840 showed that the western counties with 271,000 people outnumbered the eastern with 269,000 people; yet the west had but fifty-six assemblymen and thirteen senators, while the east had seventy-eight assemblymen and nineteen senators. Ten years later the population west of the Blue Ridge was nearly one hundred thousand in excess of that to the eastward. A reform was imperative—yet the new constitution gave the east control of the upper house while the west controlled the lower.[8] Virginia, too, retained the *viva voce* method of voting ("didn' nuttin' but gent'mens vote, an' dee took dee dram, and vote out loud," as Unc' Edinburg in Thomas Nelson Page's story put it), which discouraged any radical forms of dissent from majority opinion. In South Carolina the arrangement by which the low country controlled the Senate and the up-country the House (though even in the House representation was based half on white population and half on taxable property) dated from 1808. Even beyond the Alleghenies gross inequalities existed. Louisville and St. Louis complained of having far too little voice in their legislatures—and both were seats of strong anti-slavery feeling. It was always easier for wealthy planters than for pinched small farmers to find their way to caucuses and conventions.[9]

But above all, the planter-lawyer-merchant patricians took pains to strengthen their grip upon the government by an insistent propaganda upon the identity of interest between slaveholder and non-slaveholder. Had the thought-patterns

7 Charles S. Sydnor, *Slavery in Mississippi*, 247, 248; Cotterill, *Old South*, 272, 273. It does not follow that the rulers of the South sprang from aristocratic old slaveholding families; the opposite was the fact. Jefferson Davis was born in a log cabin. Alexander H. Stephens, son of a poor farmer, did menial chores as a boy. Joseph E. Brown did a day laborer's work until near manhood. Of four of the ablest members of the Confederate Cabinet, Judah P. Benjamin was son of a humble Jewish shopkeeper in Wilmington and Charleston, C. G. Memminger had been brought up in a Charleston orphanage, John H. Reagan was son of a poor tanner, and Stephen R. Mallory helped his widowed mother keep a boarding house in Key West. But planter prestige was a fact. For a good picture of the aristocratic zone of Southern life, see James W. Hungerford, *The Old Plantation* (1857).

8 J. C. McGregor, *The Disruption of Virginia*, 49–52, 61–65.

9 William B. Hesseltine, *History of the South, 1607–1936*, conveniently summarizes the main facts on sectional conflict in Virginia, 249–253.

Classic Grace of the South: The Capitol at Montgomery

The Sentinel of the South: JOHN C. CALHOUN

of the various social classes differed sharply on the principal issues of the time, the dominant group might have faced revolts as fierce as those which Ben Tillman and William Mahone led after the Civil War. But on important national questions, such as territorial expansion, tariffs, internal improvements, and public lands, party opinion cut squarely across social elements, men voting as Whigs and Democrats, not as planters and small farmers. State taxation, education, road building, and various forms of assistance to the underprivileged might have given rise to class conflict. But the well-to-do or rich planter-lawyer groups took pains to see that they did not. In western Virginia, Francis H. Pierpont, a Whig, constantly maintained that the plain Virginia voters had far more important interests to consider than slavery. When the constitution of 1851 exempted slaves under twelve years from taxation and fixed the taxable value of all slaves over twelve at a mere $300, he assailed such favors to the planters as a gross oppression of all smallholders. "I denounced these wrongs in speeches before the people and through the local newspapers," he later wrote—but he got nowhere. A historian who has examined the class struggle in Louisiana finds that the white yeoman farmers and laborers formed about three-fourths of the State's free population, that they were impoverished and essentially powerless, and that the wealthy plantation caste used various devices, but chiefly appeals to race pride and to fears of race conflict, to deflect their class-consciousness and smother their economic grievances.[10]

The maintenance of white supremacy was the theme upon which the planter-lawyer-merchant group played with many a rousing blast and beguiling grace note. Racial unity must be kept intact. J. D. De Bow let a threatening undertone creep into his statement that "the humblest white man feels . . . that where there are slaves he is not at the foot of the social ladder, and his own status is not the lowest in the community." [11] Calhoun touched a more pleasing chord when he told the Senate in 1848: "With us the two great divisions of society are not the rich and poor, but white and black; and all the former, the poor as well as the rich, belong to the upper classes, and are respected and treated as equals . . . ; and hence have a position and pride of character of which neither poverty nor misfortune can deprive them." [12]

This denial that the South had any class lines was paralleled by the assertion of Hammond that *every* freeman belonged to the Southern aristocracy, "an aristocracy of talents, of virtue, of generosity and courage"; by Fitzhugh's avowal that all white men "are equal in privilege, if not in wealth"; and by

---

10 For Pierpont see his autobiographical sketch (in third person), in Pierpont Papers, Brock Collection, Huntington Library; for Louisiana see R. W. Shugg, *Origins of the Class Struggle in Louisiana, passim.*
11 *De Bow's Review,* XX, 622.
12 *Cong. Globe,* 30th Cong., 1st sess., 876; press reports of speech.

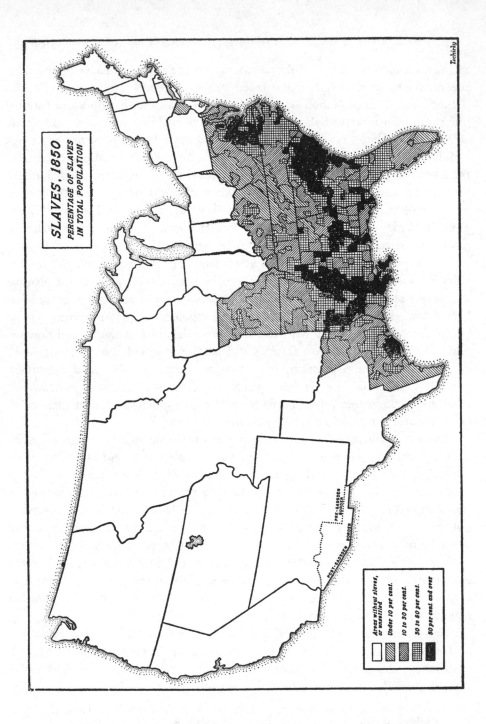

SLAVES, 1850
PERCENTAGE OF SLAVES
IN TOTAL POPULATION

Tschirig

Areas without slaves,
or unsettled

Under 10 per cent.

10 to 30 per cent.

30 to 50 per cent.

50 per cent. and over

PRE-GADSDEN
BORDER

POST-GADSDEN BORDER

420

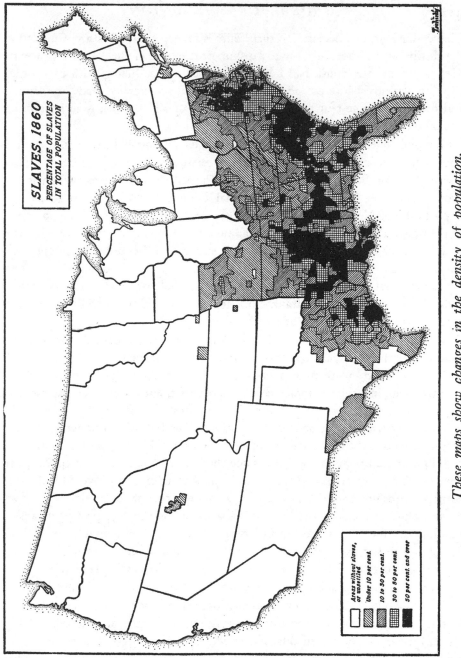

These maps show changes in the density of population.

421

Chancellor Harper's declaration that "ours is indeed an aristocracy, founded on the distinction of races." [13] Judge Upshur proclaimed in the *Southern Literary Messenger* that the South had but one class, all sympathizing with each other, and "but one great interest, and all who possess it are equally ready to maintain and protect it." The true aristocracy, stated Joseph E. Brown, is an aristocracy not of wealth but of color.[14]

Beyond question a majority of non-slaveholding whites accepted this doctrine. Some did so because they were related to planter families, or owed favors to them. Some did so because they hoped to own slaves. When it was proposed in the Kentucky constitutional convention of 1849 to forbid the importation of Negroes, one delegate hotly protested in behalf of the poor men of the State. The laboring folk who had no chance to acquire slaves by marriage or inheritance, he said, would defeat this exclusion scheme by forty thousand votes. "I want to own slaves, and I want the privilege of buying them where I can get them cheapest." [15] But most non-slaveholders swallowed the dogma because they instinctively shrank from any solution of the terrible problem of race-relationship except that offered by slavery.

Here and there a tough-minded agitator might tell the small farmers that they had nothing to gain by slavery, and that it retarded the development of the section. Inarticulate poor whites may have thought this much more frequently than any record indicates. But most of them, even if uninterested in slavery as a form of property, felt a direct interest in it as a labor system and a social arrangement. They shared the opinion of the fellow mentioned by Linton Stephens who said that he wished there weren't no niggers nohow, for then he could get more for his work.[16] But since there were Negroes, they approved of slavery. If it were abolished, the new labor system might prove full of competitive hardship, and the new social arrangement one of great discomfort. As the chief element in the current social stasis, as the one proved means of keeping the Negro on the bottom rung, it seemed indispensable. It is quite misleading to say that the poorer whites supported it only through ignorance and prejudice. If they had read Jefferson, they would have agreed with Jefferson's statement that the South had the wolf by the ears and could not let go.

Throughout the South, an emancipationist movement would have become formidable overnight but for this overshadowing spectre of race-relationship. "If slavery could be voted out of the State of Missouri without having the Negroes set free among us," wrote a Missouri correspondent to the New York

13   Hammond, *Letters and Speeches*, 44; *The Pro-Slavery Argument*, 35, 36, 61–64.
14   *So. Lit. Mess.*, V, 685; *Confed. Records of Ga.*, I, 55.
15   *Debates and Proc. Const. Conv. of Ky.*, 1849, p. 78.
16   James D. Waddell, *Linton Stephens*, 196.

Tribune in 1856, "a majority of our people would be found at any time favorable to such a measure." Olmsted, travelling in Mississippi, heard the same testimony from a poor white farmer who sheltered him overnight: [17]

"Are there many people here who think slavery a curse to the country?"
"Oh, yes, a great many. I reckon the majority would be right glad if we could get rid of the niggers. But it wouldn't never do to free 'em and leave 'em here. I don't know anybody, hardly, in favor of that. Make 'em free and leave 'em here and they'd steal everything we made. Nobody couldn't live here then."
These views of slavery seem to be universal among people of this class. They were repeated to me at least a dozen times.

Governor Collier of Alabama remarked in a message to the legislature that even conceding slavery to be a social or moral evil, still the South was not required to abolish it if by so doing it superinduced greater evils. "I have never heard of any plan for the immediate abolishment of slavery in the Southern States," he went on, "that was at all practicable, or which would not introduce grievances incalculably more prejudicial to society than slavery itself." A fuller statement was made by Senator R. M. T. Hunter of Virginia in a speech at Poughkeepsie in 1856. When white and black were thrown into close proximity, he remarked, slavery afforded the only means yet discovered to secure the happiness and improvement of both races. "The evils which are ascribed to the institution of slavery arise really from the disparity in the natural condition of the two races which circumstances have thus thrown together. To destroy that relation would aggravate and not diminish those evils, so long as two such races are dwelling together." [18] On this dictum a great majority of Southerners, rich and poor, slaveowners and non-slaveowners, agreed.

[III]

Plantation slavery was primarily the slavery of the Lower South. In the cultivation of tobacco large-scale operations by 1850 offered few if any advantages. The same statement held true of hemp, which Kentucky regarded as the crop giving the tiller the greatest remuneration for his investment in Negroes and land. Three slaves, ran the estimate, could cultivate fifty-one acres of hemp. Corn, wheat, and livestock were best managed, east of the Mississippi, in comparatively small units, ranging from 80 to 320 acres. In border slave States like Maryland, Kentucky, and Missouri the word plantation by the fifties was almost obsolete, men speaking of farms instead. By far the greatest number of slaves in this border area were the property of mere farmers. In Kentucky

17 *Journey in the Back Country,* 203.
18 *National Intelligencer,* October 18, 1856.

by 1850 only five persons owned more than one hundred slaves each, while
fully thirteen thousand persons held two, three, or four slaves.[19] But in the land
of cane and cotton the plantation, with its broad acres, mansion, "quarters,"
and gangs of slaves, stood regnant.[20] It held an ancient lordship over the rice
country of Carolina, where the seed from Madagascar rose golden in the swamps
along the fresh-water tidal rivers.

In the Lower South various classes of slaves could be sharply distinguished.
On the smaller plantations and farms the Negroes worked not only under the
direct supervision of the owner, but alongside him. Indeed, boasted Calhoun,
they frequently ate at the same table with the owner.[21] Some slaves worked in
mills and factories, at mechanic employments in town, or on steamboats. Every
mansion had its household servants, a privileged and usually specially intelligent
group—the Jupiter of Poe's "The Gold Bug," the banjo-artist Carey of Kennedy's *Swallow Barn*. These servants, as Representative T. H. Bayly of the
Eastern Shore of Virginia told Edward Everett at a dinner party in Washington, "are more competent; dislike to receive orders from any but the owners;
hate overseers." [22] Finally, there were the fieldhands, who frequently seemed
even to sympathetic observers like Olmsted the very image of cloddish-
ness.

As a labor system, plantation slavery necessarily operated upon a fairly
definite though flexible set of rules. The employment of an overseer; the observance of fixed hours of labor or stints of work for each hand; the issuance of
regular and adequate amounts of food and clothing; provision of sufficient
housing; attention to health and recreation; and the establishment of discipline
by a system of punishments and rewards—all this constituted the typical routine
of a large plantation, though local and temporal variations were numerous.

Over great areas, the overseer was regarded as a necessity whenever twenty
or more slaves were employed, or when the owner of even a smaller number had
occupations which took him from home. To be sure, many highly industrious
planters dispensed with them. An increasing tendency appeared to make well-
trained Negro drivers suffice. Bennet H. Barrow, whose diary of plantation life
in West Feliciana Parish, La., for a full ante-bellum decade, is one of our most
valuable records, hoped for the day when every overseer would disappear.
After 1837 he managed nearly two hundred slaves with the aid of drivers alone.
Overseers, he wrote, "are a perfect nuisance cause dissatisfaction among the
negroes—being more possessed of more brutal feelings—I make better crops

19 J. W. Coleman, Jr., *Slavery Times in Ky.*, 45
20 Sydnor, *Slavery in Miss.*, 193; in 1860, nearly nine thousand persons owned fifteen or
more slaves each, and nearly 1,700 owned fifty or more.
21 *Cong. Globe*, June 27, 1848.
22 MS Diary.

than those Who Employ them." [23] S. Porcher Gaillard of South Carolina, whose manuscript diary is equally illuminating, rose at or before dawn to work in the fields with the thirty-five hands that he managed without aid.[24] But it is little exaggeration to say that the overseer was "central in the (Lower) Southern system," and that upon his abilities depended the success or failure of most larger plantations.[25] Usually recruited from the small-farmer or poor-white classes, he was characteristically an ill-educated, uncultivated man, his narrow nature made harsher by the stern responsibilities imposed upon him. Figures like John H. Reagan, who rose from an overseership near Natchez to the Confederate Cabinet and Federal Senate, were unusual. Socially, the overseer held an inferior status and was never received on an equal footing in mansion, church, or political gathering. Often he was feared as a mischief-maker: "My maxim is, never to have any trading or dealing with an overseer," wrote an Alabama planter. Patrick Henry described the Virginia overseers of Revolutionary days as an "abject, degraded, unprincipled race," and Washington had repeatedly grumbled over their callous brutality. They had not much improved by 1850.[26]

There was general complaint of the difficulty of finding really good overseers, though salaries for the best might reach $1,000 or $1,500 a year. The manager of one of the largest Carolina rice holdings, the Weehaw Plantation, had eight different overseers 1842–1861. He characterizes seven of them respectively as "no planter"; "bad man"; "good man and first-rate planter"; "liar and son of a gun"; "fool"; "good planter"; and "the most incompetent planter ever on Weehaw." [27] James L. Orr, onetime Speaker in Congress, declared that many overseers systematically duped the impractical inheritors of great plantations.[28] Olmsted's numerous vignettes of overseers are usually repellent. He describes most of them as morose, taciturn, ignorant, and hard. An overseer who rode with him north of St. Francis, La., seemed to know absolutely nothing beyond cotton, soil, and slaves, having no idea of the distance to the nearest town and saying that his employer had "gone north to Paris or Saratogy, or some of them places." Another, near Natchez, was more sociable, furnishing much lore about cotton culture, Negro maladies, the best mode of keeping vegetables, and so on; he was obviously intelligent and efficient; but he talked of whippings and of setting the dogs after runaways. At another large Mississippi estate, con-

23 Edwin Adams Davis, *Plantation Life in the Florida Parishes of Louisiana, 1836–1846.*
24 Journal 1856–1858, S. Caroliniana Library.
25 John Spencer Bassett, *Southern Plantation Overseer as Revealed in His Letters,* 1–4.
26 Charles S. Davis, *The Cotton Kingdom in Alabama,* 46–54; William Wirt, *Patrick Henry,* 74; Paul Leicester Ford, *The True George Washington,* 142, 143.
27 Weehaw Plantation Book, Charleston Historical Society. Alabama overseers in the fifties received as little as $185 a year, the norm running $250–$600; Davis, *Cotton Kingdom in Ala.,* 49.
28 Address to S. C. Institute, 1855; *National Intelligencer,* June 5, 1855.

sisting of four adjoining plantations, the five overseers were with one exception frank, honest, temperate, and industrious, though Olmsted observed that "their feelings toward Negroes were such as naturally result from their occupation." [29] Altogether the best overseer Olmsted encountered was one near the Great Pedee in North Carolina, a man deliberate, watchful, efficient, and good-tempered, who seemed not only a good manager, but a firm and considerate master.[30]

Generally speaking, it was the overseer's duty to act as general superintendent of the plantation; to see to the sowing, cultivation, and harvesting of crops; to take care of tools, buildings, and land; and to regulate the whole economy of the place. He was expected to plan and apportion the tasks, punish the vicious and indolent, and maintain strict discipline both in and out of work hours. He weighed out rations, saw to it that fuel was provided, and attended to the wants of the sick. On any well-managed plantation he kept careful records of all expenditures in money, materials, and labor. Various printed record-books and model contracts, which found a considerable sale among plantation-owners, helped hold overseers to a high standard. One prepared by P. J. C. Weston, a South Carolina rice planter, in pamphlet form, laid down the rule that the owner would excuse errors proceeding from want of judgment, "but he never can or will excuse any cruelty, severity, or want of care towards the negroes." [31] The papers of James H. Hammond for his large holdings show that he thought fifty or at most sixty field hands enough for one overseer to control efficiently. They also show that even the best overseer found it hard to draw the line between weak discipline and harsh discipline. On one page Hammond tells of dismissing an overseer who was "a cold, selfish, unfeeling tyrant with very little judgment." On another page he tells of his impatience with another overseer who failed to keep the unruly slaves to their work. "The negroes have no more regard for Rowel than so [many] monkies would have and behave just as they would minding him only for the moment that he is present." [32]

Under each overseer the field hands usually worked in gangs, whose strength varied with their employments—twenty or more being an ordinary number; and for each gang a driver was usually appointed.[33] This was a specially intelligent and masterful slave who saw that the daily task was performed, encourag-

---

29 *Journey in the Back Country*, 12, 44–51, 72ff.
30 *Seaboard Slave States*, 388.
31 Bassett, *Southern Plantation Overseer*, 24.
32 Plantation Records, 1831–1855, S. Caroliniana Library, May 16, 1836; December 31, 1846.
33 Olmsted, *Seaboard Slave States*, 434. The size of hoe gangs, plow gangs, and other groups varied so much under varying circumstances that U. B. Phillips in his two books makes no generalizations. Cf. Sydnor's initial chapter on "Work" in *Slavery in Miss.*, 3–22.

ing the workers with loud exhortations. Large plantations might have a head-driver, the most important of the Negroes. Most Southerners felt that a first-rate driver, securely attached to the place, possessed of long experience, and devoted to his owner, was more valuable than the ordinary overseer. It was important to treat such a man with respect. On no occasion, wrote one South Carolinian in his regulations for plantation management, should he be visited with any indignity likely to lessen his prestige in the eyes of subordinates. On the contrary, he should be given every assistance in seeing that no Negro idled or did careless work, and in punishing errant hands. "He should be permitted to visit the master at any time, without being required to get a card. . . . He is a confidential servant, and may be a guard against excesses or omissions on the part of the overseer." [34] The head driver, ordinarily, blew the first horn for rising and the second an hour later for going to the field, gave the signal for dinner and for quitting work at night, and saw to it that the working-force moved like a little army. It was for the overseer and drivers combined to guard against such calamities as that noted by James H. Hammond: [35]

"December 6, 1856. Yesterday and the evening before two negro children died that perhaps I might have saved had I been apprised of their illness. Last night my mills, gins, and 50 bales of cotton were burned up, by the carelessness of a negro grinding corn at night, without my knowledge that any corn was ever ground at night and contrary to all my rules that no work should be done at night. The Demon who rules my worldly affairs . . . has availed himself of my absence and my ignorance to inflict these damages upon me—Damn him. . . . I have borne as well as I could the merciless slaughter of my negroes for the past 23 years of my planting life and the utter destruction of my crops for the past 14 years. But this has strained my nerve."

[IV]

In food and housing the slaves fared ill compared with workmen and farmers of the Northern States, Canada, and Britain, but were not perceptibly worse off than common laborers or peasants of backward parts of continental Europe. In general, colored families were sheltered in small one-room or two-room cabins, though sometimes better quarters were afforded; for example, a range of cottages with broad galleries in front, affording each family two rooms on the lower floor and a loft above. The worst cabins were windowless, unfloored log structures, dark, dirty, and verminous; the best were of brick or plank-and-

---

34 Edward Spann Hammond, MS "Plans . . . Views of Agriculture," S. Caroliniana Library.
35 MS Journal, S. Caroliniana Library.

clapboard, puncheon-floored and glass-windowed.[36] Even when cabins were well built, the improvidence and slovenliness of the overtasked Negroes in many instances soon reduced them to dilapidation and filth. Fanny Kemble's famous description of the slave-huts of Pierce Butler's Georgia plantation in the thirties as the most miserable human habitations she ever beheld, not fit to shelter cattle, must be taken with reserve, for she had seen little of the rougher side of life. Olmsted found habitations varying from mere cramped huts not more than twelve feet square in inside dimensions, without windows, porches, or shade trees, to brick cabins neatly and comfortably furnished, and, on a South Carolina "show plantation," well-built clapboard houses, whitewashed, twenty-one by twenty-one feet, with fireplaces, cock-lofts, three rooms, and a variety of rude furniture.

In any event, the Negroes of the Lower South lived chiefly outdoors. Care was generally taken to make the housing weathertight, an ample store of fuel was provided, and sanitation received attention. "The Negro quarters must be cleaned up, whitewashed, and scoured," ran the summer directions of Beaver Bend Plantation in Alabama; and every Sunday the slaves must have "clean clothes on for the next week." [37]

Food seems in general to have been sufficient in quantity, but coarse, lacking in variety, and badly prepared. Senator Butler of South Carolina testified in 1856 that field hands in his part of the South were allowed from two and a half to three pounds of bacon weekly, with as much bread as they wished, and that he gave his own hands three pounds of bacon, with all the bread, vegetables, and in summer milk, that they desired.[38] Commenting on this statement, an Alabamian declared that he had found it the almost universal rule on Southern plantations to furnish Negroes with three and a half pounds of bacon and a peck (fourteen pounds) of cornmeal a week. "Besides these rations, the Negroes on ninety-nine plantations in every hundred are supplied with as many sweet potatoes, turnips, cabbages, peas, beans, pumpkins, and other kinds of vegetables as they will consume. To these are generally added rations of molasses twice or three times a week." This was unquestionably a favorable view.[39] The

36 Olmsted, *Back Country*, 74; Phillips, *Life and Labor in the Old South*, 197; C. G. Parsons, M.D., *Inside View of Slavery*, 153, 154. See the interesting summary of more or less trustworthy recollections in John B. Cade, "Out of the Mouths of Slaves," *Journal of Negro Hist.*, XX, 294–337. They unite in saying that furniture was very scanty, with beds usually of planks, covered with hay or shuck mattresses. Cooking was of course done in a fireplace.

37 Fanny Kemble, *Journal of a Residence on a Georgian Plantation* in 1838–39; Olmsted, *Seaboard Slave States*, 396, 421; Phillips, *Life and Labor*, 197. "Something between a haunt for monkeys and a dwelling place for human beings," said Harriet Martineau of the slave village; *Society in America*, I, 224. See Beaver Bend regulations in *Journal of Southern History*, VII, 76–84.

38 *Cong. Globe*, December 4, 1856; see also Butler's letter, *National Intelligencer*, January 3, 1857.

39 Letter of A. W. S., Selma, Ala., December 21, 1856, in *National Intelligencer*, January 3, 1857.

former slave Paul Watts in Virginia testified late in life that his daily food had consisted of fatback, salt herrings, cornmeal, molasses, and in winter blackeye peas.[40] Indeed, herrings seem to have been a common item of diet in the South Atlantic area. On badly-managed plantations the slaves might get little but fat pork, cornmeal, and a few vegetables, and a hard-driving owner might compel them to cook up all the meal on Sunday. But some planters were exceptionally generous (Bennet H. Barrow allowed five pounds of meat a week, with much sugar and molasses, and some wheat flour) and it was obviously as bad economy to underfeed a slave as a horse.

It is to be noted that Olmsted, a highly critical observer, seldom found any evidence of short rations and repeatedly commented on the plentifulness of good food. In the cotton country of Alabama, for example, he noted that the hands on one great estate, eating dinner in the field, had plenty and often more than they wanted of bacon, corn bread, and molasses. Each person on this estate got three pounds of pork, a peck of meal, and in the first half of the year a quart of molasses weekly, with a supplementary allowance of salt and tobacco served every month. In addition, each family had its garden, fowl house, and pigsty, and sold the products or used them to supplement the basic ration. Most of the Negro households bought a barrel of flour every year. The slaves also obtained a good deal of game, setting traps for rabbits, raccoons, and turkeys.[41] In Edward Spann Hammond's set of plantation regulations it is expressly laid down that a rice-field of adequate size should be cultivated for the exclusive benefit of the Negroes, that an orchard should be planted for their use, that they should be privileged to raise fowls, and that they might be allowed garden patches to be tilled in their own time. Moreover, a special garden should be kept in the best condition to furnish vegetables at all times for the children, with a moderate daily distribution to every slave. He and many other planters favored a barbecue at Christmas and at the close of planting or of harvest, with beef or mutton, pork, coffee, and white bread. The oft-quoted statement of a

40 MS recollections furnished me by Mr. Roland McConnell. Andrew Hampton Drew recalls of his North Carolina childhood: "Each Sunday molasses was poured on a long plank for Negro children to lick. Masters from other plantations would come to see the Negro children lick molasses on Sunday mornings." In many instances food for Negro children was poured into a long trough, and sometimes this was even done for adults. "The slaves," writes Dorothy Z. Oldham in her MS life of Jacob Thompson (Univ. of Miss. Library), "were fed in long troughs made of the trunks of trees hollowed out. The life of even the white people was so primitive at this time that no pretense was made to obtain cutlery, etc., for the slaves. The soups, milks, potlicker, and all such food was poured in the troughs and each slave was provided with all the hoecakes he could eat. Occasionally the troughs would be elaborate affairs when partitions of wood were placed at intervals to mark individual places." P. 21. Miss Oldham gathered these facts from Miss Mamie Slate, a niece of Jacob Thompson, who lived in childhood with the Thompsons.

41 Olmsted, Back Country, 75. Rations were ordinarily issued to families; and family cookery done in limited spare time was poorer than that done by plantation cooks. Davis, Cotton Kingdom in Alabama, 83-84.

Louisiana cotton-planter to J. B. D. De Bow that he fed a hundred slaves for $7.50 apiece a year means little if, as was possible, he himself grew the breadstuffs and meat which they consumed.[42]

In evaluating the food, shelter, and clothing of the slaves, we must bear in mind that the standard of Southern white farmers, overseers, and laborers was low. As the slaves wore homespun, coarse cottons, and shapeless cowhide brogans, so did the poorer whites. As corn bread, salt pork, and milk, with vegetables in season, were staple slave dishes, they were also the standard bill of fare for rural Southerners of limited means. Over great areas of the South the majority of houses were of logs, and often without glass windows—as in Spain and Portugal today.[43] Olmsted, like other travellers, was struck by what he called the general destitution of comfort. When told by one rural family that the Negroes fared about as well as they did, Olmsted could easily believe it. Between the Mississippi and the upper James, he writes, in nine instances out of ten he slept in a room with others, in a bed which stank, with but one sheet if any; he washed with utensils common to the whole household; he found no gardens, no flowers, no fruit, no tea, no cream, no sugar, no wheat bread; no curtains, no lifting windows, and no couch; and in the living-rooms no carpets or mats. Many houses were verminous. From the Mississippi to the James he did not see, except perhaps in one or two towns, a thermometer, a copy of Shakespeare, an engraving, a piano, or a sheet of music.[44]

Remembering this widespread squalor, we can understand why Southern and Northern observers took such different views of the same facilities. A Yankee who, after visiting Richmond and travelling across country to Charlottesville, sent his impressions to the New York *Tribune*, was horrified by what he saw. One-room Negro huts, without windows, a sliding board admitting light and air when the door was closed; field hands breakfasting on bacon, corn bread, and milk, dining on the same staples with some vegetables, and supping on bread and milk alone; many slaves sleeping on cabin floors; clothing of the coarsest and most common kind, with no change of undergarments; toil from dawn to dark.[45] But a Mississippi planter, tilling 1,168 acres with 66 slaves, that same year sent the *Tribune* a spirited defense of slavery. His hands, he wrote, worked from daylight to dark, but had a half-hour for breakfast and an hour for

42 E. S. Hammond, MS "Plans . . . Views of Agriculture," S. Caroliniana Library; DeBow, *Resources of South and West*, I, 150. For typical Southern views of plantation management see a Mississippi planter's article on "Management of Negroes," *DeBow's Review*, June, 1851; John Perkins, "Relations of Master and Slave," *De Bow's*, March, 1853; Agricola, "Management of Negroes," *DeBow's*, September, 1855; and J. S. Wilson, "Management of Negroes," *De Bow's*, July, 1860.

43 Olmsted, *Seaboard Slave States*, 384

44 Olmsted, *A Journey in the Back Country*, Ch. 9; Cf. the many caustic observations on Southern discomfort in W. H. Russell, *My Diary North and South*.

45 N. Y. *Tribune*, May 1, 1854.

dinner. They got nearly a half-pound of bacon daily, with unlimited vegetables and cornmeal, all the cooking being done for them by a specially deputed slave. Each slave got two summer suits and a straw hat, two winter suits and a wool hat, and two pairs of shoes annually, while a blanket was served out every second year. The washing was done every Saturday afternoon by the women. Each family was given a house sixteen by eighteen feet, two or three feet above the earth, with a brick chimney. Some had a good deal of furniture, and a few even slept between sheets. This planter, obviously, was describing a situation not very different from that which shocked the Yankee, but he looked at it through different glasses. Stating that holidays were frequent, with two to four days off at Christmas and an occasional dance, he added: [46]

"I saw more destitution in Philadelphia in 1828 than I have seen in the South in forty years. I have seen a negro in Philadelphia buy one cent's worth of wood. I never saw negroes beg for food but those belonging to one man. These are facts. We have hard masters here, but they are more talked against than hard masters are there. I have seen an able-bodied Negro woman in Philadelphia— a good cook, washer, and ironer—work for months for her food only, while here, even if free, she would have been paid $10 to $20 per month. The poor white folks of the South fare worse than slaves."

[V]

Hours of labor were long, but not longer than those of the Iowa pioneer, the New York seamstress, or the Pawtucket factory hand. Olmsted took the road at dawn and left it at dark; he always found the summer-toiling slaves in the fields before him, and heard them trooping home after he put up his horse. But the farmer's boy in the West worked from dawn till after dark, while many a factory hand toiled fourteen hours. On cotton plantations there was seldom an easy season. The planter started his plows in January, and until August waged a laborious struggle with men and horses against the encroaching grass. His hoes were in action as soon as the young crop appeared above ground in March, and were kept busy till the crop matured in late summer. If a good crop, the hands were engaged from August to New Year's in tediously picking it. In bleak December, when most northern farmers clung to their firesides, slaves in the cotton belt were braving all the vicissitudes of the weather and with numbed fingers clutching the half-frozen bolls.[47] Sugar also meant year-round toil. But outside the Lower South slaves had many half-idle days in winter.

46 M. W. Phillips, Lig Hall, Edwards, Miss., in N. Y. *Tribune*, August 1, 1854.
47 Letter by Jefferson County, Miss., planter in *National Intelligencer*, November 17, 1857.

In South Carolina the legal limit of the slaves' workday was fifteen hours. This law, like that of Louisiana requiring a meat ration, was difficult to enforce, but must have had some effect. Elsewhere labor from dawn to dark would have meant sixteen summer hours in the field, but this was shortened by a noonday rest of one to two hours. Indeed, we find E. S. Hammond laying down the rule that "In summer the intermission should increase as the heat becomes more intense to the extent of 2½ hours on the hottest days, diminishing again as the days grow cooler. At fifteen minutes before sunset the plow hands and at sunset the others should knock off work for the day. No night work should ever be exacted." Much the same provision appears in the record-book of Brookdale Farm, a 1,240-acre plantation of Amite County, Mississippi, for 1856–57. A noonday rest-period of one to two and a half hours was to be allowed the slaves during the hot months, no slave was to work in the rain or at night except on essential chores, and none was worked in cold damp weather which might endanger health.[48] Women who suckled children were allowed to leave their work three or four times a day, while on the best plantations women five months pregnant were put in the sucklers' band for shorter hours, and women after confinement were relieved from work for a month.

One Tennesseean told Olmsted that Negroes in many localities "did not work hard, not nearly so hard as many of the white folks"; and Olmsted admitted that this fact, and the general physical well-being of slaves, were incontestable "to a great degree, throughout the country"—though he was convinced that on the large plantation it was necessary to work the slaves with great severity.[49] Perhaps the hardest toil was on the great sugar plantations, where in grinding-time eighteen hours daily of exhausting labor was frequent.

The piece-work or assigned-task system prevailed in eastern Georgia and South Carolina, and was sometimes used elsewhere. The stints were proportioned to strength, children and very old people being regarded as quarter-hands, youths and elderly folk as half-hands, and the mature and able-bodied as full-hands. A full-hand was expected to hoe half an acre of cotton, corn, potatoes, to plow with oxen an acre of mellow soil, to cut and split a cord of pine, to dig a thousand cubic feet of drain in light, clean meadow-land, or to sow two acres of rice, in a day. These tasks were settled by custom, and it was difficult to introduce any speed-up schedule. The driver who marked out each stint had to remain on the ground till it was completed and so had no interest in making it excessive; while overwork resulted in sullen failure to perform tasks well, in

48 "Plan . . . Views of Agriculture, 1857," S. Caroliniana Library; *Journal of Miss. Hist.,* VII, No. 1, 23–31, January, 1945.
49 Olmsted, *Back Country,* 271.

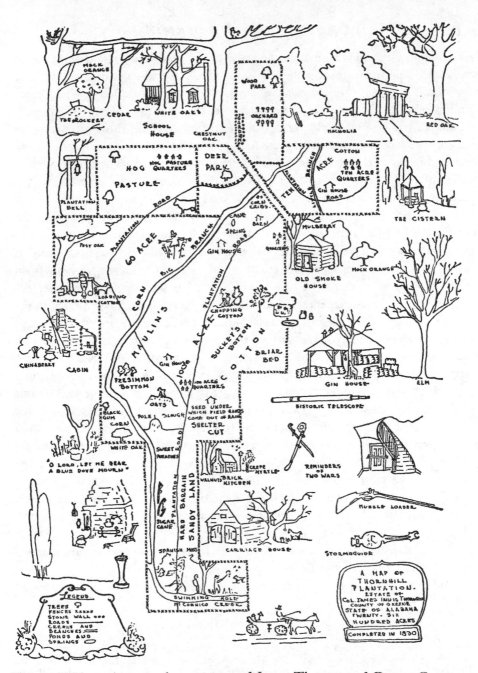

Thornhill Plantation was the property of James Thornton of Greene County, Alabama; a typical large plantation of the so-called black belt.

Reproduced by courtesy of Charles S. Davis, from his *Cotton Kingdom in Alabama* (1939).

433

sickness, or in attempts to escape. Olmsted heard one man boast that he made his Negroes perform double the usual amount of work—but in the long run this would not pay. "These tasks," commented the Northern traveller, "certainly would not be considered excessively hard, by a Northern laborer; and, in point of fact, the more industrious and active hands finish them often by two o'clock. I saw one or two leaving the field soon after one o'clock, several about two; and between three and four, I met a dozen women and several men coming home to their cabins, having finished their day's work"—this on a great rice plantation not far from Charleston.[50]

Considerate planters and farmers allowed a variety of small festivities. On Weehaw Plantation a special supper was given all hands at the close of harvest; when plowing was finished, the plowmen celebrated with a feast; and at Christmas there was a special distribution of rice, molasses, sugar, and fresh meat, with small money gifts—the drovers getting $6 each, the engineer $6, the watchmen, head carpenters, and other mechanics $5, and ordinary slaves smaller amounts. At weddings a special supper was served. S. Porcher Gaillard helped his slaves make merry during their four-day Christmas holiday with tobacco, molasses, apples, and firecrackers.[51] In Virginia and Kentucky, no sight was more picturesque than the slaves streaming on Christmas morning to the "big house" to greet the owners and get their small gifts. On one Alabama plantation the slaves were allowed to cut and haul wood to town, selling it for their Christmas money. The owner's family prepared toys, molasses candy, and other gifts for them. On Christmas eve the Negroes held a prayer-meeting lasting until midnight, when pandemonium broke loose. "After breakfast the yard was filled with laughing, happy negroes, and your father would go to the smoke house to give each family their Christmas provisions, then they came on to the house where I was waiting on the back porch with their presents, which they received with many bows and curtseys and 'thanky mistis'." Bennet H. Barrow built a dance hall for his slaves, and when the rain stopped work would order up the fiddlers.[52]

And yet there was always a darker side; there were plantations where hands

50 *Seaboard Slave States*, 432–438. English visitors reached contradictory conclusions on the question of overwork. Captain Marryat had found that slaves did little and did it badly; James Silk Buckingham, a far more careful observer, found field hands, especially in the Lower South, driven for all that could be gotten out of them. *Southern or Slave States*, I, 133. For the task-system on the Allston plantations, see J. H. Easterby, *The South Carolina Rice Plantation*, 30, 31. That model planter Dr. James R. Sparkman declared that on his rice holdings winter work ran from eight to nine hours, and summer work seldom exceeded ten, while in very cold or wet weather no work was exacted at all. *Idem*, 346.

51 Weehaw Plantation Book, Charleston Hist. Soc.; Journal of S. P. G., December, 1856. S. Caroliniana Library.

52 Ella Storrs Christian, MS "Plantation Life as It Was," Ala. State Dept. of Archives and History. Davis, *Plantation Life in La.*, 51.

were systematically driven to exhaustion, harried by lash and oath, without special holiday and sometimes even without Sunday rest. An Alabama planter used to make sure of a swift morning departure for the fields by whipping the last slave out. The record book of a large Louisiana sugar estate, the Ashland Plantation, for 1852, kept apparently by the overseer, shows that at busy seasons the slaves were worked continuously.[53] The first few Sundays contain no record. Then on Sunday, February 8, we meet the notation: "Give out allowance of pork, planted four loads of corn that we had shucked out last night shiped 12 hhds Sugar and 25 bbls molasses." The overseer had worked the slaves Saturday night and worked them again on Sunday! The record for Sunday, February 15, runs: "Give out short allowance of pork had Jerry Bradocks Madison and Willie cuting a ditch to pay for stealing a sheep." The following Sunday, February 22: "Gave out short allowance of pork. made wharf at the river. Shiped 11 Hhds sugar and 15 Bbls molasses." So the record goes. It lists some Sundays without notation of labor, and others with special tasks, such as Sunday, May 9; "Gave out allowance of pork put all hands to choping wood for stealing wood from woodpile." Sunday was not only the regular day for doling out pork and "taking up" the hogsheads made by the slave-coopers the previous week, but the day on which slaves cultivated the corn grown for their food. On Sunday, October 10, the overseer records: "Negroes gathered their corn made a large crop."

When late that month the cane cutting began, toil had no intermission. "Cuting cane for the mill" is the regular entry seven days a week. We look eagerly for the Christmas holidays. In December the hands finished the standing cane and began work on the "winrow cane." This was especially severe labor. The record runs: "Saturday Dec. 25th. All hands engaged as on Wednesday"—that is, on the windrowed cane. And next day: "Sunday Dec. 26th. Finished 30 acres above the Creek and commenced supply cane." At Ashland it was work, work, work—

> The toiling negro sighed, that Time
> No faster sped his hours.

Many planters and farmers not only permitted, but encouraged, their slaves to earn money by extra labor. They raised poultry and sold the fowls and eggs to the owner, or in town; they cut and sold wood; they made baskets and other small wares; they peddled vegetables. At political rallies, barbecues, and picnics, Negroes both free and slave could be seen vending pies, cakes, and fruit. The author of an essay on "Treatment of Slaves in the Southern States" in the

---

53 La. State Univ. Archives.

Southern Quarterly Review in 1852 declared that every slave should be allowed a little crop of his own. If a family had an acre or acre and a half, the cash product to be its own, it would take an enhanced interest in life. The overseer could ask them to labor diligently, in return for time for their own crops. "So much afraid are they that the grass will take their fields, that they are willing to work night and day to get into them. They have really the same solicitude, and learn to feel as deep an interest in the fate of the main crop, as the overseer and master possibly can. The necessity of quarreling and coercion is thus superseded, to the great gratification of the humane master." [54]

This was a step toward freedom. As such, and because it led to a certain amount of pilfering, some planters opposed it. Bennet H. Barrow was one. He gave his slaves prizes, cash, and special articles of apparel. "I prefer giving them money at Xmas to their making anything, thereby creating an interest with you and yours—if a negro is suffered to sell anything he chooses without any inquiry being made, a spirit of trafficing at once is created to carry this on, both means and time are necessary, neither of which he is of right possessed."

[VI]

All Southerners agreed that discipline was far stricter on the great plantations under overseer management than on smaller holdings where slaves were personally managed by their owners. Many absentee nabobs measured the efficiency of their overseer by one standard only, the number of cotton bales he produced. If he wore out the slaves by overwork, if he tasked Negro women until they miscarried, if he lashed the mules to death, if he exhausted the soil—all this meant nothing so long as he produced large crops. [55] Impersonal management was all too often harsh management, and harsh management sacrificed everything to heavy immediate returns.

This emphasis was unquestionably one element in the manifest tendency toward a concentration of cotton land in large holdings. Rich planters tended to bid for the services of the most efficient overseers, encouraged these men to drive their hands hard, and used the return to buy more land. "If they made plenty of cotton," observed an Alabama tradesman to Olmsted, "the owners never ask how many niggers they killed." A "real driving overseer," determined and relentless, would be paid $1,200, $1,500, and even $2,000 a year, as

54 By N. B. P.; January, 1852. But such plantation experts as N. B. Cloud condemned the practice as leading to overwork, theft, and general dissatisfaction. See files of Cloud's *American Cotton Planter*, established in 1853.

55 Columbia *South Columbian*, quoted in Olmsted, *Back Country*, 60. Sir E. R. Sullivan in *Rambles and Scrambles in North and South America* (1853), 186, declared that many poor planters bought broken-down Negroes cheap and tasked them mercilessly, with little food or clothing, replacing them when dead.

against the average remuneration of from $600 to $1,000. Sauntering in New Orleans or Charleston, taking the waters at White Sulphur or Saratoga, planters boasted to one another of the bales their overseers made. The result was that even a humane owner could not bear to hear how all the plantations roundabout had outstripped him. "He'd think the fault was in his overseer." [56]

Though we have no statistical data upon the number of absentee planters, it was unquestionably large. As a keen-eyed Briton, Henry Ashworth, noted in touring the lower Mississippi Valley, the lot of cotton planters there was unenviable. To the normal discomforts of isolation, summer added stifling heat and clouds of insect pests. Women especially often found plantation life hard. Their houses lacked conveniences. Few visited them, months sometimes passing without sight of a congenial friend. New books, new magazines, and emergency household supplies were hard to obtain. One woman remarked that if she needed a lemon in cookery, she had to send for it by steamer to New Orleans, five hundred miles away. The men fared better, plantation tasks, hunting, and fishing occupying their time, while they usually spent some weeks in New Orleans buying implements and provisions, and selling cotton. But to give their wives company, and to escape the heat and flies, they had to travel a thousand or two thousand miles to cooler resorts.[57] Olmsted concluded after touring the cotton country along the east bank of the Mississippi that more than half of the larger plantations (those with cabins for fifty or more slaves) were without a fit residence for a man of wealth. In more fertile and less healthful districts, he judged that a majority of slaves were left to the nearly unlimited government of hireling overseers for most of the time. Some owners were capitalists normally residing in the North or Europe, some were wealthy Virginians or Carolinians dwelling in their home States, and a still larger number alternated between their estates and places where convenience and luxury were more attainable.[58]

How heavily absenteeism sometimes bore upon slaves is revealed by the papers of F. P. Corbin, owner of two South Carolina plantations, one rice, one cotton, who resided chiefly in Paris and employed a general superintendent, with overseers. These papers show that Corbin lived expensively, giving fine dinners, travelling widely, frequenting costly hotels, and treating himself to the best in food, wines, clothing, and equipages. He invested his surplus funds in railroad bonds paying seven per cent interest and State bonds yielding five or six. His superintendent, with a salary in 1856 of $3,693, which he offered to exchange for a compensation of twenty per cent of the net crop proceeds, also

---

56 *Back Country*, 56, 57.
57 *A Tour in the United States, Cuba, and Canada* (1859), 93ff.
58 *Back Country*, 119.

lived well. But the slaves were held to severe toil and ground down to a minimum in costs. Wrote the superintendent on March 21, 1855: [59]

I shall in a few days send you certified copies of my accounts. . . . I purchase only what is required to keep the plantation in a sound state. I adopt the principle of buying only the best food,—that is, corn, for you will observe that the issue of meat is very small, being on the Hopeton gang 8660 lbs for 1854— not 25 lbs *per annum* each, or 1 oz per day, or ⅛ the usual issue in the south-western states, and upper counties. . . .

The clothing consists of but one winter and one summer suit, from 6½ to 7 yards each for adults. The winter cloth averages about 32 cents per yard, and the summer about 11 cents. One pair of shoes a year at about $1 per pair, and a blanket in 3 years costing about $2 ¼, constitute the clothing; except for a few years when I gave a flannel shirt and petticoat. The clothing purchased is only of good, medium quality. . . .

Exclusive of my charge, you will find that the cost per negro per day is *eight and a quarter cents*,—this includes machinery, tools, buildings, overseer's wages, physicians' fees, etc. etc.,—every thing. . . . The great expense is corn.

Yet this manager spoke with reprobation of another plantation owner of "very penurious character" who "stints his negroes in every issue," buying inferior clothing and half-spoiled bacon. It is to be hoped that over his champagne, truffles, and steak-Chateaubriand, Corbin sometimes thought of those work-worn hands under the blazing Carolina sun who were subsisting, the cost of machinery, buildings, overseer's wages, and doctor's fees included, on eight and a quarter cents a day.

By contrast, many resident owners were models of kindly, watchful, far-sighted managerial energy. They took their responsibilities seriously, and found them incessant and onerous. A great plantation was as difficult to operate as a complicated modern factory, which in important respects it resembled. Hit-or-miss methods could not be tolerated; endless planning and anxious care were demanded. Among the 266 slaves found in 1855 on Weehaw Plantation were a head cooper and under-coopers; a tailor; a head-carpenter and under-carpenters; a supervising nurse ("granny") and under-nurses; drovers; "headmen" specially charged with the care of oxen, of mules, and of sheep; watchmen for the mills and granaries; trunk-minders (the trunk being the master system of sluices and canals for the irrigation system); plowmen; a gardener; a miller; a dentist; skilled dairy workers; and butchers—all beside the ordinary field hands and household servants. The 1,500-acre plantation of Governor William Aiken on Jehossee Island, S. C., had about 700 slaves who included all these categories

59 Francis P. Corbin Papers, New York Public Library; letter signed J. H. Cooper, Hopeton Plantation, March 21, 1855.

and engineers, shipwrights, and sailors as well. Aiken, living in a modest cottage without ostentation or even much comfort, lent more attention to making his people healthy and contented than to making money.[60]

The owner of such a holding had to give careful thought to tasks, discipline, health, and morale. He had to keep each slave effectively at work six days a week and fifty-one weeks in a year. He had to know every detail from the number of skeins of thread (eighty) in a pound and the needles in a paper (twenty-four) bought for the slaves' garment-making to the barrels of rice, six hundred pounds apiece, which each field ought to average. He had to record every hoe bought, every greatcoat given out, every dollar spent for medicines, every calf born, every hog slaughtered. The idea that he lived an idle, comfortable life was a delusion. He was in the same position as the modern factory-manager who must meet a payroll and simultaneously satisfy the stock-holders, and he felt the modern industrialist's scorn for easy moralistic reproaches from amateurish onlookers.[61]

No student of plantation records can fail to be impressed by the multitudinous anxieties which oppressed any conscientious owner. The hands would get sick. The gin would break down. The mules would get snagged and die of blood-poisoning. April frost would nip the young cotton-plants; summer rains would deliver the crop to grass and weeds; August droughts might blast the most promising prospects. On large plantations a nursery for young children, and an infirmary for the sick, had to be maintained and supervised. A midwife had to be kept ready for confinements. Religious instruction was provided; sometimes the master called all hands to the "big house" on Sunday afternoon

60 Weehaw Plantation Book, Charleston Hist. Soc.; *De Bow's Review*, IX, 201–203.
61 "Never did the slightest detail regarding the work on his plantation seem to escape him." So writes Duncan Clinch Heyward in his delightful *Seed From Madagascar* of Nathaniel Heyward, who at his death in 1851 was the greatest rice planter of the country, his slaves being valued at a million, and his other property at a full million more. At the age of eighty he was still ready to give his son minute written directions for the hitching of a yoke of oxen. A good modern picture of the responsibilities involved in the conduct of a large holding worked by Negroes may be found in Patience Pennington's equally delightful *A Woman Rice Planter*.
One of the classic examples of devotion to the well-being of slaves was furnished by Louisa C. McCord, the daughter of Langdon Cheves of Charleston. She had inherited from a great-aunt the beautiful plantation "Lang Syne" on the Congaree about thirty miles from Columbia, and both before and after the death of her husband, Col. David J. McCord, she administered it with skill and energy. The plantation was noted for its excellent housing, its day-nursery for the slave children, and its hospitals. When it was remarked that she wore no diamonds, she answered that she did not see how a woman with more than two hundred children could wear diamonds. James B. Angell, who gives an account of the plantation in his reminiscences, tells how once during his stay Mrs. McCord was up all night nursing a sick Negro baby. The profits were so low that Mrs. McCord said she would prefer $25,000 in good bank stock to $100,000 in a plantation. This busy woman found time to contribute able essays to several Southern reviews. See Jessie M. Fraser, "Louisa C. McCord," Bulletin Univ. S. C., No. 91.

to be taught by himself or a minister.[62] The quarters had to be regularly inspected for cleanliness. Work-oxen, milk-cows, sheep, hogs, horses, and mules had to be watched for special ailments. If the plantation included woodland, pasture, and grain, a wide variety of special labors had to be foreseen and arranged. The seventy-one hands on the Aventine Plantation in Adams County, Mississippi, for example, in 1856 not only planted, thinned, and cultivated a large cotton crop, picked, ginned, and baled it, grew considerable corn, and cared for several hundred head of stock, but cleared stumps, manured the land, cut trees in the woods, made and hauled bricks, trimmed hedges, ground meal, rolled cotton seed, split fence rails, worked on roads, spun cloth, and executed much light carpentry. To see that all this was done with promptness, dispatch, and seasonably, efficiently, and without friction cost the proprietor constant worry. Yet the master might also be active in public life, and was frequently the dispenser of a generous hospitality.[63]

We have abundant literary records of oldtime masters and mistresses who brought a highminded sense of duty to their laborious plantation employments. Thomas Nelson Page has drawn portraits of his parents as heads of the "Oakland" estate with some sixty slaves. His father, a Christian gentleman versed in the ancient and English classics, neglected no responsibility, while his mother was an untiring caretaker; "with her own hands administering medicines or food, ever by her cheeriness inspiring new hope, by her strength giving courage, by her presence awakening faith." [64] Wade Hampton, discovering that his father had left him as eldest child the largest share of the family estates, rejected this bequest, took only an equal portion, and soon carved out a large fortune. Devoting himself to his Mississippi plantations, he gave incessant attention to the well-being of his Negroes, and the crop of five thousand bales of cotton that he garnered in 1861 was produced under a mildly paternal sway.[65] Thomas S. G. Dabney of Mississippi, who is the subject of that most ingratiating Southern classic, Susan Dabney Smedes's *Memorial of a Southern Planter*, was a brave, honest, and generous man. He fed his sick slaves mutton-chops and port wine; he gave generous money prizes to his cotton pickers; he allowed the sale of chickens, peanuts, sweets, mats, brooms, and baskets, by which some

62 Anonymous traveller in western Mississippi, writing in N. Y. *Tribune*, August 30, 1854.
63 Records by Aventine overseers, 1857–59, Miss. Dept. of Archives and Hist. See J. H. Hammond's complaint to W. S. Simms of overwork. "You write your 100 pages a week and I ride my 100 miles. But I hardly get off with writing less than 20 pages a week . . . and I have to think, think, think." He had to think about ways and means, physic, nursing, feeding, mills and water, wheels and machinery, livestock, the whole range of agricultural operations, markets, transportation, ironing, shoeing, clothing, sacking, "and to crown all this damned perversity of all human and animal kind that I have to deal with." November 5, 1855, Hammond Papers.
64 *The Old Dominion*, chs. 8, 9.
65 *Dictionary of American Biography*; Ashworth, *Tour in U. S. and Canada*, 98, 99.

slave women even bought silk dresses; all the slaves were encouraged to come freely to the house for social visits; willing children were taught to read; the cabins were clean and bright and well furnished; marriages were scrupulously performed and family life was respected; only four slaves were sold in Dabney's lifetime, and they only for cause.[66]

But manuscript records suggest that these literary pictures are subtly romanticized. Inevitably more friction, anxiety, irritation, and loss entered into plantation life than such rose-tinted histories indicate. Even Dabney, it is briefly indicated, had his troubles with bad seasons, epidemics, and unruly Negroes. The ordinary honest plantation diary, kept by owner or overseer, is a chronicle of almost constant struggle with the elements, insect pests, livestock maladies, and difficult hands.

Those who supposed that James H. Hammond, whose 12,000-acre Silver Bluff Plantation in South Carolina seemed opulence itself, enjoyed a bed of roses, should have some glimpses into the diary in which year after year that hardworking man lamented fresh calamities. At one time he was threatened with utter ruin, but retrieved his fortunes by using convenient marl deposits to restore his wornout lands. Even so, he was beset by disaster. In 1852, for example, he had to record sickness among the hands, spring cold, June deluges, late-summer drought, and miscellaneous blows from fate. It was too much, he exclaimed on August 27th. "It is a fresh proof added to the thousands I have had before, that I *never* am to make a crop—*never* to have anything like average seasons. I give up entirely. Accused of God and hunted down by man and woman, what a fate is mine. I am very seriously considering now whether I shall ever attempt another crop." Those who supposed that S. Porcher Gaillard lived at ease on his plantation of thirty-five or forty slaves should read his daily account of hard labor and grinding care, with now and then a cry of anguish over his difficulties with a refractory man—though he was a kind master:

May 9, 1856. I rec'd today a letter from Mr. Louis D. Desaussure, of Charleston ac. sale of my man Jacob who was shipped by him and sold in New Orleans. He sold for $900—expenses amounted to $113.07, so I cleared $786.03 which he has turned on to my brother Pete to be invested in bank stock. This villain Jacob has no doubt been the fellow who set fire to my dwelling on the 20 May 1850 and was burnt down. I had a jail and Black smith shop

66 Memorials, Chs. 6–12. For other reminiscent pictures of plantation life and slavery, see Mrs. V. V. Clayton's *White and Black Under the Old Regime* (Alabama); Mrs. E. W. A. Pringle's *Chronicles of Chicora Wood* (South Carolina); Mrs. Lucy Lee Pleasants' *Old Virginia Days and Ways*; Dr. J. B. Avirett, *The Old Plantation* (North Carolina); D. F. Morrow, *Then and Now* (North Carolina); and A. G. Bradley's beautifully written *Sketches From Old Virginia*, which deals partly with ante-bellum, partly post-bellum, days

burnt down since I built here and there is no doubt he committed the act in both instances, he was out last year from 1st May and was caught and brought here made his escape on 5 June last and was out with a gang of runaways all summer, most of all were taken in Jany last near Camden, Jacob made his way up to Charleston and I presume finding the Police regulations so strict there delivered himself up to the Jailer of Charleston I put him in the hands of Mr. Desaussure to ship to New Orleans said scoundrel during the time he was out threatened to burn my dwelling consequently I had to keep up a vigilant watch every night. I ought to have sold him 6 years ago.[67]

[VII]

Though in managing the slaves rewards were much used, praise, extra pay, or small gifts being offered for unusual diligence, the principal basis of plantation discipline was a system of punishments. "At ten years of age," recalled a former slave who had begun life in Bertie County, N. C., "my first task was to pick fifty pounds of cotton. If I failed. . . . I would get a lick for every pound I failed to pick. For every pound over fifty pounds I receive one cent." A man's task on this plantation was a hundred pounds or a hundred rails, with perhaps some additional chores. "If a man failed to do his task he was severely whipped."[68] Frederick Douglass asserts that in his experience of Maryland slavery, fear of whipping was almost the only incentive.[69] Every observant traveller in the South has described the floggings, which were too often viewed as a routine process.

It was generally held, indeed, that whipping was indispensable to the maintenance of order and industry on any large plantation. The childlike character of many slaves, the half-savage character of some others, their opportunities for evading labor or destroying property, their imitative propensities, and the impossibility of making rewards substantial without destroying slavery—these facts, it was believed, necessitated the lash. "They'd never do any work at all if they were not afraid of being whipped," one young master told Olmsted. It must be remembered that flogging was then a commonplace mode of disciplining many groups of whites. It was applied to schoolboys, apprentices, soldiers, sailors, and criminals. "I have no idea of any great effect being produced on British soldiers," Wellington had once told a Royal Commission, "by anything but the fear of immediate corporal punishment." The lash had just been abolished in the American navy. But there is an essential

67 Hammond's plantation records 1831-55, and Gaillard's MS journal, are both in the South Caroliniana Library. Cf. Francis Pendleton Gaines, *The Southern Plantation*, Ch. 9, which compares the literary conception with actuality.
68 MS recollections of Hampton Andrew Drew, July 6, 1938, furnished me by Roland McConnell. Cf. the slave narratives in Library of Congress, *Journal of Current Acquisitions*, November, 1944, and in B. A. Botkin, *Lay My Burden Down*.
69 *Autobiography*, 117.

difference between regulated and unregulated punishments, and much flogging of slaves was excessively harsh.[70]

"We were often whipped severely for any little offense," states the former slave Paul V. Watts. "I have often seen my master poach or roast his whip in hot ashes to make it tough. . . . If a slave did something very displeasing our master would often tie him up with the clothes pulled down and whip the slave until satisfied. Sometimes a paddle with bored holes was used to draw blisters. If a slave attempted to run away, if caught he was often whipped so severely that death came." [71] The British consul in Charleston, Robert Bunch, writing in 1854 of the "frightful atrocities" of slaveholding, told how his next-door neighbor, an aristocrat, himself flogged all his slaves, men and women, when they misbehaved. "It is literally no more to kill a slave than to shoot a dog." [72] The granddaughter of a Louisiana planter, Harrod Clopton Anderson, writes that "he was *very* severe" in whipping lazy or disobedient slaves, while the man's own papers show that he drove his hands hard and exacted high totals in picking cotton, shocking corn, and other tasks. It is not astonishing to learn that one slave woman tried to kill him by putting ground glass in his milk—which he forced her to drink, then giving her an emetic and selling her down the river.[73]

Bennet H. Barrow not only whipped heavily, but punished his slaves in other ways. His diary has such entries as "my hands worked badly—general Whiping": "whipped every field hand this evening"; "a general Whiping frolic." He particularly hated runaways. Of one man he wrote: "ran and trailed about a mile, treed him, made the dogs pull him out of the tree, Bit him very badly, think he will stay home a while." Of another: "dogs soon tore him naked, took him Home Before the other negroes at dark & made the dogs give him another overhauling." The most severe punishment that Olmsted saw inflicted was that of a slave girl who skulked to avoid work, and who got thirty or forty heavy blows across her shoulders with a rawhide whip, and perhaps as many more across her naked loins.[74]

70 Olmsted, *Back Country*, 84; Sir Charles Oman, *The Peninsular War*, II.
71 Watts was reared on the Ewell Plantation near Everett, N. C.; his recollections were sent me by Roland McConnell.
72 Laura A. White, "The South in the 1850s as Seen by British Consuls," *Journal Southern History*, I, 29–48.
73 Anderson Papers, La. State Univ. Archives.
74 Davis, *Plantation Life in La.*; Olmsted, *Back Country*, 87. At the auction of Pierce Butler's slaves at Savannah in 1859, the N. Y. *Tribune* correspondent heard a group of men talking about the management of refractory slaves. Some were for severe whipping, some for branding, some for other punishments. A huge hulk of a man spoke up: "You can manage ordinary niggers by lickin' em and by givin' em a taste of the hot iron once in a while when they're extra ugly; but if a nigger ever sets himself up against me, I can't never have any patience with him. I just get my pistol and shoot him right down; and that's the best way."

One of the worst features of slavery was the temptation which almost unbridled power gave to cruel and passionate men for the exercise of brutality. The anti-slavery press made the most of such reports as crept north, the New York *Tribune* containing frequent items on the killing or maiming of slaves. Atrocities were all too frequent. Now it was a Negro near Natchez, chained to a tree and burned alive for attacking a white man; now a Negro in Jefferson County, Miss., who according to a Methodist minister who had talked with him had committed no worse offense than trying to hold his master's hand while being beaten with a club, but who (though he had a wife and two small boys) was hanged.[75] Slavery is despotism, wrote Mrs. Stowe; and her *Key to Uncle Tom's Cabin*, with Theodore D. Weld's *Slavery As It Is: Testimony of a Thousand Witnesses*, proved the age-old fact that despotism breeds savage excesses. Already burning at the stake, sometimes accompanied by unprintable tortures, was a common penalty for rape.[76] Sometimes a sadist appeared. In 1860 a large body of German-Americans of Beach Island, S. C., petitioned Governor Hammond to protect a slave whom Hammond had hired out to one Charles Axt in Crawfordsville to learn grape cultivation. By beating him, setting dogs on him, and threatening to shoot him, Axt had forced him to run away. When he was caught in Augusta, Ga., Axt tied him hand and foot, dragged him to a tavern room, and beat him so fiercely that outraged citizens intervened. Axt then carried him to a remoter tavern and recommenced his brutalities, until the tavern-keeper ordered him off the premises. Hammond begged Alexander H. Stephens to take immediate action.[77]

That remote plantations witnessed many a dark crime cannot be doubted. The feeling was widespread that a Negro who showed insubordination, struck his master or overseer, or ran away, became an outlaw. Many an overseer would draw his pistol and shoot down a refractory hand. J. W. DuBose relates that his grandfather joined a mounted posse searching the Peedee swamps for a fugitive Negro; the man sprang up and tried to bolt; and Grandfather Witherspoon (who might, as DuBose admits, have shouted a threat to shoot or have fired over his head) coolly gave him a mortal wound with his shotgun.[78] Sometimes justice was done on masters guilty of outrageous offenses, but this was seldom.

The historian of Georgia slavery, after declaring that "many slaves were cruelly treated, and many died as the result of harsh and inhumane treatment," and describing how some slaves were choked, beaten, or even starved to death, adds: "In the great majority of cases of this sort the white man accused of

---

75 N. Y. *Tribune*, February 6, February 14, 1854.
76 N. Y. *Tribune*, June 19, July 11, 1854, for two instances.
77 Petition dated March 20, 1860, letter of J. H. Hammond, March 31, 1860; Stephens Papers, L. C.
78 DuBose Family Papers, Ala. State Dept. Arch. and Hist.

murder or manslaughter was not convicted." The historian of slavery in Kentucky asserts that the slave's right of self-defense in the courts "amounted to nothing more than a legal fiction." The historian of Mississippi slavery refers to the "chance" of a legal penalty for crimes against slaves, citing a seven-year jail sentence for one murder! [79] Henry S. Foote tells of a Mississippi blacksmith who held a slave upon burning coals till he died, but suffered no penalty. Even when a murderous owner was sentenced to death, he frequently got free. A Kentuckian who had helped his brother chop a Negro lad to bits with axes for breaking a pitcher was sentenced to hang, but "escaped." [80] The best diary of ante-bellum life in Charleston contains a summary record of two cases in one year in which the murder of a slave ended in much ado and no punishment: [81]

Jan. 8, 1847.—Jury of inquest was held over the body of a negro woman 'verdict' "came to her death by blows inflicted by another negro, done by the orders of her mistress Mrs. Rowand," the negro has been taken up to be tried and the mistress held to bail. . . .

May 5, 1847.—Mrs. Rowand. Today this lady was arraigned at the bar of Justice to answer to the charge of killing her servant on 8 Jany last, it caused considerable excitement, she pleaded not guilty and challenged 17 Jurors. Bailey for the State Pettigru Hunt and Rhett her counsel Judge O'Neal charged the Jury, that for want of evidence they were compelled to acquit her, Jury retired for about 20 minutes and brought in their verdict of acquittal. The Trial was published. . . .

July 17, 1847.—Mr. Carew lost a negro woman yesterday, caused it is said, by a severe whipping given her by Laurens Toomer on the night of the 5th inst.

The best redress that hopelessly abused slaves could find was in retaliatory vengeance, and many an act of incendiarism, an assault, and even a murder was inspired by the Negro's belief that his wrongs, fancied or real, had no other remedy.[82]

The more enlightened and humane slaveowners, regarding corporal punishment as evidence of a badly-managed plantation, insisted that whipping should never be done in passion, should always be moderate, and should be inflicted in the presence of the highest authority—the owner, manager, or overseer. Punishment, ran the plantation rules of Brookdale Farm in Mississippi, "must always be proportionate to the offense and spirit of the culprit, never cruel, and in all cases requiring punishment, unless immediate punishment be necessary, I must be consulted." The model overseer's contract prepared by P. J. C. Weston

79 Flanders, *Slavery in Ga.*, 241, 242; Coleman, *Slavery Times in Ky.*, 255; Sydnor, *Slavery in Miss.*, 91.
80 Coleman, *op. cit.*, 261.
81 MS Schirmer Diary, Charleston Hist. Soc.; cf. Mrs. Stowe, *Key*, 177–188.
82 Coleman, 263; Flanders, 265.

of South Carolina forbade any punishment beyond fifteen lashes without permission of the owner or his deputy. Never be in a hurry to punish, was James Tait's rule on his Alabama plantation.[83] Perhaps the best of all the books penned by former slaves, Irving E. Lowery's *Life on the Old Plantation*, tells of strict rules against harsh punishment, and gives a picture of but moderate tasks (he wrote of the coastal plain of South Carolina) blended with fun and hilarity.

Enlightened owners and overseers, moreover, found that slave exertions were best awakened by rivalries and rewards. James Lane Allen recalled that when Kentucky hands were given extra pay for special achievement, and divided into competitive squads, they toiled like men possessed. "The hemp-breakers of the neighborhood, meeting in the same field, would slip out long before breakfast, and sometimes never stop for dinner. So it was with cradling, corn-shucking, or corn-cutting—in all work where rivalries were possible." On the Dabney plantation in Mississippi some Negroes who engaged in such contests wished to sleep at the end of their cotton rows to be up the earlier in the morning. Small gifts and prizes had a happy effect. Sometimes even the promise of manumission was held out as a reward for good conduct. Other planters would allow enterprising slaves to earn their freedom; letting them hire their time now and then for a dollar a day to make more in other employments. No Southern prejudice was more vicious than the widespread idea that Negroes would work only under compulsion. This preconception, as much as any other, lay at the root of the belief that slavery must be an eternal and immutable system. It was proved false in almost every instance where special rewards were offered for special enterprise. Time was to prove its utter absurdity, for within a few years after the Civil War, even with many Negro women and children taken out of the fields, the colored folk—so far as we can apply measurements in a different field—were apparently producing larger crops than under slavery.[84]

[VIII]

Whenever Negroes encountered the law, their lot was hard. They had but a slight and precarious standing in court, their testimony was never accepted against whites, and though in some communities public-spirited men took pride in befriending them, the statutes were usually interpreted to their disadvantage. The legal rule was that the Negro or mulatto child followed the conditions of the mother. It was also the rule that every colored person, even if the admixture of African blood was but one-sixteenth or less, was presumptively con-

---

83 *Journal of Miss. Hist.*, VII, No. 1, January, 1945; Bassett, *Plantation Overseer;* Davis, *Cotton Kingdom in Alabama*, 60.
84 Allen, *Blue Grass Region of Kentucky*, 75; Smedes, *Memorials*, 69, 70; Robert Somers, *The Southern States Since the War*, 64, 65.

sidered a slave, and if he asserted his freedom, the burden of proof fell upon his shoulders. In most States provisions for the apprehension and detention of fugitives became progressively more severe as time passed. Arkansas, for example, in 1849 and 1851 enacted stringent laws. Every slave found twenty miles or more from his alleged place of employment was to be regarded as a fugitive; he was to be held by the sheriff and kept at convict-labor for six months while being advertised; and if no owner appeared, was to be sold for the benefit of the State treasury. This law exposed free Negroes to grave perils. In various States colored folk were put to death for offenses not capital when committed by white men, such as criminal assault or crimes against nature. An Arkansas slave convicted of larceny for stealing another slave, a horse, or a mule might suffer death for the second offense.[85]

A Maryland judge, John Thomson Mason of Annapolis, wrote James Buchanan in 1854 that almost a third of all the cases heard by his court related to Negroes as slaves. An ex-Congressman had recently argued, in dealing with a petition for freedom, that a white witness for the Negro should be excluded on the ground of interest, for unless the Negro gained his freedom and mulcted his claimant-master for costs, this witness would never get his per diem! In another case it was shown that a man for years held three free Negroes as slaves. Yet after they had recovered their freedom they had no redress, under the prevailing court interpretation of Maryland law, against this scoundrel who had stolen their labor. In still another case the judges were asked to decide that a will conveying the income (clearly meaning the hire or labor) of certain slaves to a man for life, passed to him full ownership of the children born during the life estate; in other words, that the colored children were the income arising from their parents. This seemed really to be Maryland law!

"Truly," observed Judge Mason, "Negro law is *black law*." He had lately read in a Mississippi newspaper of a man who hired dogs to hunt down runaway slaves. "Mrs. Stowe!" he exclaimed, "*thou almost persuadest me to be an abolitionist!*" [86]

Particularly unhappy was the tendency, as the South grew more militant in defense of slavery, to impede or forbid the emancipation of bondsmen. Liberation, even if it was the act of a white master protecting his child, or rewarding a servant who had saved his life, seemed treason to the "institution" and was increasingly condemned. Mississippi forbade manumission by her revised code in 1859. Georgia allowed no manumission save by act of the legislature, or by will arranging for transportation of the former slaves to some free area; and

85 John C. Hurd, *Law of Freedom and Bondage in the United States; Pubs. Arkansas Hist. Assn.*, III, 179–182.
86 Buchanan Papers.

in 1859 the legislature passed a law prohibiting the post-mortem liberation of slaves directly or indirectly, and within or without the State. Arkansas in 1859 prohibited the emancipation of slaves either by deed or last will. Alabama did so in 1860. Other States took similar action.[87]

Meanwhile, no really adequate safeguards were set up to protect the free Negro. Those who ransack old law reports will find not a few instances, sometimes highly poignant, of the kidnapping of free colored people and their sale into slavery; and for every instance in which such a seizure reached the courts, there may have been five in which it did not. The rising price of slaves added to the incentive. Not a few West Indian Negroes fell victims to kidnappers. G. P. R. James, when consul in Richmond, successfully prosecuted several cases; and the Federal Attorney for Eastern Virginia assured him that he believed that in one year more than two hundred British subjects employed as sailors had been seized and sold in the United States. British consuls took up a number of such cases in various ports, William Mure at New Orleans being especially vigilant; and even a Negro woman from Jamaica had in one instance to be rescued.[88]

Tragic cases sometimes emerged into light from the darker recesses of slavery. Men read in 1859 the sad story of James Oldham, a prosperous planter of Friar's Point, Miss. In the summer of 1857 he brought one of his two daughters by a slave mother, a girl of sixteen, to Oberlin, Ohio, for the double purpose of emancipating and educating her, meanwhile leaving the younger girl in the South. While in Oberlin, Oldham fell mortally ill. Deeply concerned for the freedom of his younger daughter, he made Dr. R. L. Rea of Oxford, Ohio, executor of a will in which he set the two girls free, bequeathing $4,000 for their support and education, and providing that the whole of this sum might be expended to gain the liberation of the younger if the Southern heirs tried to keep possession of her. The heirs did precisely this. Dr. Rea went south to struggle with them. In the end he purchased the girl for $1,000 and brought her back to join her sister at Oberlin.[89]

Yet it was outside the law that the Negro fared worst. We have said that the Northern abolitionist made the most of lynchings and burnings, and though such outrages were admittedly rare, they were numerous enough to trace the

87 Sydnor, *op. cit.*, 248; Flanders, *op. cit.*, 249; *Pubs. Ark. Hist. Assn.*, III, 179–182; Hurd.
88 Laura A. White, *Jour. Southern Hist.*, I, 29–48; Bulwer Lytton to Crittenden, February 6, 1851, Crittenden Papers, Duke Library. I have examined British consular reports in the Public Record Office. James was delighted when Taney and the Supreme Court confirmed the confiscation of the ship *Alvano*, which in 1850 had brought a free Negro from Antigua and sold him into bondage in Virginia; FO5, 677. Mure was angered when a colored British subject was thrown into slavery in 1850 with the connivance of some municipal officials of New Orleans; FO5, 519.
89 *Cleveland Leader*, June 7, 1859.

lines of an appalling pattern. In the House early in 1860 Van Wyck of New York spoke of Southern slave-burnings, which he said seemed to awaken no horror in Southern minds. Reuben Davis of Mississippi interrupted: "I pronounce the gentleman a liar. I pronounce the gentleman's assertion false— utterly false." But a future Senator, George C. Vest, saw a slave burned in the summer of 1853 in Georgetown, Mo.[90] In June, 1854, a Negro accused of rape near Ryalia, Miss., had been seized by a mob whicn castrated him, hung him by the heels tiii he was nearly dead, and then emptied their shotguns into him. The next month another Negro accused of a similar crime in Dandridge County, Miss., was tortured, mutilated, tied to a tree, and burned to ashes in the presence of nearly two thousand people. Late in 1855 a slave was burned at Lexington, Miss., for attempted rape, and another at Mount Meigs, Ala., in the spring of 1856, for murder. It was possible to answer Reuben Davis with details of still other burnings. Two took place just before Christmas in 1858; one near Union Springs, Ala., and one near Troy, Mo., both for the murder of white men.[91]

Such occurrences recalled to well-read Northerners the slave-burnings in colonial New York, and the record in John Woolman's *Journal* of the burning of a Negro at Perth Amboy, N. J.—for nearly every Southern offence against slaves could be paralleled in old Northern annals. Lynching was a frontier practise, but even the worst white criminals were never executed at the stake, and this particular abomination furnished the darkest single page in the history of interracial relations.

[IX]

Yet only less sombre, and in some respects perhaps more heart-rending, is the chapter which records the constant disruption of family life among the slaves by various factors: failure to enforce respect for marriage, white cohabitation with colored women, and forced sales. Many a planter boasted, like Dabney, that he required marriage with proper ceremonies. Edward Spann Hammond thought marriage should be encouraged by awards of five dollars for the purchase of household articles. But how much validity could the family relation possess? Binding ties were not recognized by law, and ran counter to the economic interest of owners, for the value of slave property depended in part on its fluidity. Had the Southern rule been that the child followed the condition of the father, a strong incentive would have existed to make slave

90 *Cong. Globe,* March 8, 1860; Vest, February 2, 1885, to George R. Smith; Smith Papers, Mo. Hist. Soc.
91 N. Y. *Weekly Tribune,* January 15, 1859; March 17, 1860; April 14, 1860.

marriages legal and permanent, while the master would have been less likely to form a passing connection with a slave. But since the child followed the mother, it did not matter whether a marital tie existed or not. A letter by a Memphis woman describing the "marriage" of a pair of favorite slaves illustrates the grotesque uncertainty of any attempt to lift slave relationships to the white level.

"About ten o'clock the Rev. Mr. Collins came in," she writes, "and they [the bridal party] soon followed. First, Lewis and Caroline Lawrence, with two bridesmaids and groomsmen, took their places, and Mr. Collins performed the service beautifully—the whole service of the Methodist Church. . . . But it made me very sad indeed when, instead of the words, 'until death do ye part,' he used the words, 'unless you are unavoidably separated.' " [92]

All the conditions of slavery were inimical to true family life. Since the unions had no legal sanction, were often celebrated without formality, as by simply "jumping over a broomstick," and were sheltered by no vital Negro sentiment, promiscuity was frequent.

"Marriages were no great tie," writes one former slave. "A slave man would ask the master to whom his girl friend belonged for permission. If he consented that would be all that was required to make them man and wife. The slave man was not allowed to take his wife to the master's plantation, but was given permission to visit her. If children were born they still belonged or remained with the mother in her master's plantation." [93]

Among large planters, marriages involving Negroes on two different properties were discouraged, for they interfered with the efficiency of the hands. Among smaller slaveholders, such unions were necessarily common. They were often made and unmade with great rapidity. Some owners punished both fornication and adultery, some adultery alone, and many interfered only when jealousy caused "trouble." The wife of a Montgomery minister, who thought that not one in a thousand of the poor creatures had any conception of the sanctity of marriage, asserted that they were models of conjugal fidelity while the bond lasted, "but to see the coolness with which they throw off the temporary yoke is diverting in the extreme." [94]

The statement of Charles Stewart, a highly capable mulatto born near Petersburg, Va., about 1800, is illuminating. He was sold as a lad to Colonel William R. Johnson, called in Virginia the Napoleon of the Turf, and became a trusted favorite. Shrewd, quick and responsible, he took charge first of one training-stable and then another, while for several years he had entire control

92   N. O. *Crescent*, quoted in N. Y. *Weekly Tribune*, March 20, 1858.
93   MS recollections of Paul Watts, sent me by Roland McConnell.
94   Olmsted, *Back Country*, 112.

Eliza comes to tell Uncle Tom that he is sold and that she is running away to save her Child

Cassy ministering to Uncle Tom after his whipping

Heartstrings Plucked by "Uncle Tom's Cabin"

SLAVE SALE IN CHARLESTON:
A sketch by Eyre Crowe in *The Illustrated London News,* Nov. 29, 1856

THE OLD KENTUCKY HOME: A painting by Eastman Johnson

The South: Realism and Romance

of valuable race-horses and stud-horses as they were carried from town to town in Kentucky. He was sold to a Louisiana judge for $3,500. Always in funds, Stewart bought a Negro girl whom he fancied, one Betsey, for $350, and called her his wife. But he soon took a dislike to her because she lied.

"A woman ought to tell some of de trufe once a day, ef it's only to limber up her tongue," he remarked. He tried 'suasion, finery, birch-rods, and prayer "at de big camp-meetin'." But though she bore him three children, though she cooked excellent meals of hoecake, bacon, hominy, biscuit, and coffee, and though she ironed and washed industriously, she remained a liar. In fine, "it got to be so dat I jes' made up my mind to 'vorce her as quick as eber I could." So he let her previous owner have her back at the price he had paid, adding that "lowin' fur de war and tar of de four year I had done kep' her, I would throw de boys into de bargain." He was never sorry for that 'vorcement. Yet this same Negro proved capable of great devotion to his next wife.[95]

It was commonly said by Southerners that a chaste slave was a rarity, and that sexual promiscuity abounded among the Negroes. To the extent that this was true, it might partly be excused as Jefferson excused the slaves' dishonesty. "That disposition to theft with which they have been branded must be ascribed to their situation, and not to any depravity of the moral sense. The man in whose favor no laws of property exist, probably feels himself less bound to respect those made in favor of others." [96] Where nothing was done to protect chastity, where all children were legally born out of wedlock and all were equally valuable as property, and where innocent amusements were few and intellectual pursuits non-existent, 'immorality' was inevitable. It must be added that many masters set a bad example. Grayson, Harper, Hammond, and other leaders of Southern thought recognized what William Gilmore Simms called "the illicit and foul conduct of many among us." The large and increasing number of mulattoes, the frequency with which slaves appeared who could not easily be distinguished from whites, and the eagerness of many fathers to manumit slave children, were facts which told their own story. "The whole commerce between master and slave," to quote Jefferson again, "is a perpetual exercise of the most boisterous passions, the most unremitting despotism on the one part, and degrading submission on the other." [97] The consequences were certain.

It was a fairly typical plantation nursery, visited by Olmsted, which had among its twenty or thirty children a number who were "clearly the offspring

95 Charles Stewart, "My Life as a Slave," *Harper's Magazine*, Vol. 69 (1884), 730–738.
96 Jefferson, *Writings*, Ford ed., II, 249.
97 Harper and Hammond in *DeBow's Industrial Resources*, II, 219, 245; Grayson in "The Dual Form of Labor," *Russell's Magazine*, October, 1859; Jefferson in *Writings*, Ford ed., III, 266.

of white fathers." [98] Southern youths easily picked up evil lessons from the licentiousness of many plantations. It was notorious that the blood of some of the best Southern families flowed in Negro veins—nor were the slaves unaware of the fact. According to the census of 1860, some 588,000 of the 4,441,800 Negroes in the country were classified as mulattoes, and there is reason to believe that this was an understatement. [99] The responsibility for this population rested almost wholly with the white man, for though more mulattoes were born of white mothers than is commonly supposed, they were comparatively few. [100] That this "amalgamation" often rendered the wives of white farmers and planters miserable is unquestionable. Frequently the marriage of the master broke his connection with some slave mistress, whose mulatto children were embarrassingly in evidence. Not seldom the connection with the mistress persisted. Many of the petitions of Virginia women to the legislature for divorce contain complaints that their husbands were cohabiting with colored women, sometimes couched in language of bitter eloquence. One husband had told his reproachful wife: "Damn you, if that sticks by you, I will bring her here tomorrow in the gig by the side of me in style." In other States a large aggregate of divorces were granted for adultery with slave women. [101]

The human suffering involved in miscegenation—the jealousy of wives, the bitterness of outraged Negro fathers and husbands, the anguish of unwilling slave girls, the frustration of children condemned to slavery while their half-brothers and half-sisters were carefully reared—was not the less real because it found no descriptive pen. Only now and then was a voice lifted against it, as in the measured condemnation of the Rev. J. D. Paxton of Kentucky, writing in Jacksonian days: [102]

"The condition of female slaves is such, that promises and threatenings and management can hardly fail to conquer them. They are entirely dependent on their master. They have no way to make a shilling, to procure any article they need. Like all poor people they are fond of finery, and wish to imitate those who are above them. What now, are not presents and kind treatment, or the reverse, if they are not complying, likely to effect on such persons? And the fact that their children, should they have any through such intercourse, may expect better treatment from so near relations, may have its influence. That the vice prevails to a most painful extent is proved from the rapid increase of

98 *Back Country*, 92.
99 Cf. Census Bureau Bulletin No. 8, 1904, "Negroes in the U. S."
100 J. H. Johnston, *Race Relations in Virginia and Miscegenation in the South, 1776–1860;* MS Dissertation, Univ. of Chicago Library.
101 *Ibid.* See Helen T. Catterall, *Judicial Cases Concerning Amer. Slavery and the Negro,* II, 158ff.
102 *Letters on Slavery*, 129.

mulattoes. Oh, how many have fallen before this temptation: so many, that it has almost ceased to be a shame to fall! . . . Irregular habits are thus formed, which often last through life. And many a lovely and excellent woman, confiding in vows of affection and fidelity, trusting to her power over her devoted lover, has . . . found when too late how incorrigible are those habits of roving desire formed in youth, and kept alive by the temptations and facilities of the slave system."

Fanny Kemble had been filled with horror when she overheard a slave named Joe, the husband of her black maid Psyche, pleading with Pierce Butler not to be sold from her. "Don't make a fuss, Joe," Butler said. "Make up your mind there's no help for it. Keep quiet now; don't fret." Fanny, bitterly protesting, prevented this sordid disruption of a family. The most humane masters prided themselves on never separating members of a household. Impoverished slaveowners sometimes made heavy sacrifices to keep husband and wife, or parents and young children, together. But the common assertion of Southerners that forcible divisions were rare constituted a blinking of the plain evidence.[103]

However reprobated in theory, the breakup of families was all too common in practise. Humane masters, while living, might protect their slaves, but when these masters died, ruthless executors were likely to send them to the auction block. Slave-trading by the 1850's had become a complex and highly organized business, its tentacles embracing the remotest districts, its agents eagerly seeking buyers and sellers, and its leaders manifesting few scruples. Though some dealers met social ostracism, others escaped it. Some, like Louis D. DeSaussure and Thomas N. Gadsden in Charleston, belonged to the best families, while many others held a respectable social position. It became common for them to conceal their vocation by adopting such appellations as auctioneer, broker, and commission merchant, and by mingling the trade in slaves with that in other commodities. Traders often struck a humanitarian pose by talking loudly of their unwillingness to separate families while in fact they never hesitated to do so.

Any examination of plantation records drives home the well-known fact that one Negro man might be the father of children by several women, and that many women were quite uncertain about the paternity of their children. The papers of the Southdown and Waterloo Plantations in Terrebonne and Ascension Parishes, La., for example, contain lists of eleven to sixteen children born annually in the early fifties. Repeatedly the same father is listed for

103 Bancroft, *Slave-Trading in the Old South, passim*; cf. U. B. Phillips, *Life and Labor*, 155. For an early description of the traffic, see E. A. Andrews, *Slavery and the Domestic Slave Trade* (1836).

several mothers, while some "Hester" or "Dulcy" cannot or will not name the father.[104] Such public records of slave sales as exist also show that while creditable efforts were often made to keep mothers and young children together, fathers were usually disregarded. South Carolina's official bill-of-sales books contain interesting evidence on this point. In some instances a female slave with her young children is sold "together with the future increase and issue of the female"—but without mention of a husband. A typical sequence of entries for 1853–54 contains more than a dozen notations for mothers sold with children ("Beck and her three children"; "Minda and her child"; "Rose and her child Ellen"; "Ann and her boy child"; "Salla and her two children 11 and 2"; "Nina and her four children," and so on) before we come to the mention of a true family: "Stephen and his wife Katy and their child Dolly." Many of the married couples mentioned in this book would seem to be elderly, for the entry "two old negroes man and wife" appears more than once. Behind these curt records of sales—"Milesha and her 4 children youngest 8"—in how many instances was a father and husband left bereft? [105]

But even mothers were often disregarded. Louisiana had a law forbidding under severe penalty the parting of mothers from children under ten, but in practise the parting line was drawn at about eight years.[106] Mississippi, Georgia, and Alabama had laws which very slightly hampered the sale, under certain conditions, of children under six, eight, or ten from their mothers, but which allowed owners of unencumbered slave property to do as they pleased. Elsewhere in the South man and wife, child and parent, might be parted at will. All but a small percentage of the slaves put up by interstate traders were sold singly, or were mothers with very young children. The Washington slave-dealer Neal told an inquirer that he had often had owners "take away the infant from the mother's breast, while they sold her." [107] Practically all traders dealt in children from ten to twelve years of age, and many advertised for those from six to nine.[108] A child sold forty or fifty miles away from his mother was lost forever. Writes Mark Twain: [109]

We had a little slave boy whom we had hired from some one, there in Hannibal. He was from the eastern shore of Maryland, and had been brought away from his family and friends, halfway across the American continent, and sold. He was a cheery spirit, innocent and gentle, and the noisiest creature that ever was, perhaps. All day long he was singing, whistling, yelling, whooping,

104   Minor Family Papers, La. State Univ. Archives.
105   "Bill of Sale Book, 1853" (actually 1848–57), S. C. State Archives.
106   Bancroft, *Slave Trade*, 197.
107   E. A. Andrews, *Slavery and the Domestic Slave Trade*, 149, 150.
108   Bancroft, *Slave Trade*, 208.
109   *Autobiography*, I, 101.

laughing—it was maddening, devastating, unendurable. At last, one day, I lost all my temper, and went raging to my mother and said Sandy had been singing for an hour without a single break, and I couldn't stand it, and *wouldn't* she please shut him up. The tears came into her eyes and her lips trembled, and she said something like this:

"Poor thing, when he sings it shows that he is not remembering, and that comforts me; but when he is still I am afraid he is thinking, and I cannot bear it. He will never see his mother again; if he can sing, I must not hinder it, but be thankful for it. If you were older, you would understand me; then that friendless child's noise would make you glad."

An invoice of ten negroes sent this day to John B Williamson by Geo Kremer named & cost as follows

To wit .. Betsey Hackley	...... $410.00
Nancy Aulick	...... 515.00
Harry & Helen Miller	.. 1200.00
Mary Kootz	...... 600.00
Betsey Ott?	.... 560.00
Isaac & Fanny Brent	. 992.00
Lucinda Luckett	..... 467.50
George Smith	... 510.00
Amount of my traveling expences & boarding	5254.50
of lot No 9 not included in the other bills	.. 39.50
Kremers expences Transporting lot N3 to Rich'd	51..00
Carryall hire ..	6.00
	$5351.00

I have this day delivered the above named negroes costing includeing my expences and other expences five thousand three hundred & fifty dollars this May 26th 1835—

John W Pittman

I did intend to leave Nancy child but she made such a damned fuss I had to let her take it I could of got fifty Dollars for so you must add forty Dollars to the above

A Sale of Negro Slaves.
From the original in the Library of Congress.

Nothing aroused the anger even of moderate men like Henry Clay more swiftly than allegations that Southerners undertook slave-breeding for profit;

proof that the business existed was difficult to obtain; and it is certain that the *incidental* profits of slave-increase were far more important. Yet evidence that many owners sought "rattlin' good breeders," and valued early mating and fecundity, anticipating a doubling of population in fifteen years and a quadrupling in thirty or a little more, is abundant.[110] Some unquestionably did make a business of breeding. John C. Reed in his Southern apologia *The Brothers' War* writes that this multiplication "was what the master thought of and talked of all the day long." [111]

Now and then a frank witness could be found. On a railroad train out of Wilmington in 1859 a Southern attorney bound for Georgia, where he meant to make his usual arrangements for hiring out some slaves, was overheard talking of their profitability. He bought girls of sixteen or so, hired them out for $6 a month, and bred them; they lost a month or two for confinement; but the child more than paid for the lost time—for the girls would be worth $1,000 at eighteen, and the boy $1,500–$2,000 at twenty. "So you see, it's a money-making business. Why, our richest men have made their fortunes by it. There's old Squire Brown, who didn't use to be worth a red cent, and always was as poor as could be, now lives in one of the biggest houses in Wilmington, keeps his carriage, and toddles off to the springs every summer; and when people wonder how he got rich so fast, he tells them that they forget that his niggers increase as fast as other people's." [112] As fertility of the soil fell, the temptation to trust to slave-multiplication and high slave-prices for money-making increased.

At the Democratic convention of 1860 Gaulding of Georgia, a particularly crass delegate, when called to order for terming Virginia a slave-breeding commonwealth, also spoke with brutal candor: "Well, I will say the slave-breeding State of Georgia, then. I glory in being a slave-breeder myself. [Loud laughter.] I will face the music myself, and I have got as many Negroes as any man from the State of Virginia." He invited the delegates to his plantation. "I will show them as fine a lot of Negroes, and the pure African, too, as they can find anywhere. And I will show them as handsome a set of little children there as can be seen [laughter], and any quantity of them, too. [Renewed laughter.]" [113]

For many of the scenes in the slave-auction rooms there was no defense, and even traders sometimes had the grace to be ashamed of them. Basil Hall, watching the sale of a chubby shining little Negro in Washington, was so revolted that when the auctioneer asked him for a bid he momentarily lost his good breeding and cried out: "No! no! I thank God we don't do such things

110 Bancroft, *Slave Trade*, 67–87.
111 P. 49.
112 C. in N. Y. *Weekly Tribune*, March 5, 1859.
113 N. Y. *Weekly Tribune*, June 30, 1860.

in my country!" "And I wish, with all my heart," said the auctioneer, in a tone which made Captain Hall sorry for his outburst, "I wish we did not do such things here." "Amen!" said several voices.[114]

As sad as the sale of young children was the disposal of "fancy girls" at high prices for immoral purposes, a traffic which found its chief center in New Orleans. For these girls, ownership of whom was an ideal of thousands of gamblers, turfmen, saloonkeepers, and dissipated young men of wealth, $1,500 to $2,000 was no unusual price.[115] The Anglo-Irish novelist Mayne Reid had ample opportunity to study slavery between his landing in New Orleans in 1839 and his return to England in 1849. Connected for a time with a commission house, he was in charge of the gangs of slaves which it sold at auction. He embodied his special knowledge in a flashy novel called *The Quadroon; or, A Lover's Adventures in Louisiana,* which he wrote when *Uncle Tom's Cabin* was the rage, completing it in 1856. A dramatization by Dion Boucicault had an enduring success. Mayne Reid wrote the London *Athenaeum* that his novel was veracious. "I was an eye-witness of nearly a score of slave auctions, at which beautiful quadroon girls were sold in bankruptcy, and bought up, too, notoriously with the motives that actuated the Gayarré of my tale; and upon such actual incidents was the story of *The Quadroon* founded." [116]

Even when the family tie was respected and no improper purpose entered into sales, they could be callously brutal. An observer at the great sale of Pierce Butler's slaves at Savannah early in 1859 remarked the family of a plantation carpenter; his wife, a girl of three and a newborn baby. The mother and infant were roughly inspected in the chill March wind. Much obscenity was uttered in their presence. It turned out that Daphney's baby had been born on February 14th, that on the sixth or seventh day afterward she had been compelled to rise and take a long railway journey across country to the Savannah race-track where the sale was to be held, had been there exposed for six days to inspection and questioning, and on the fifteenth day was put on the block with her husband and children for sale; the family happily offered as a unit.[117]

Delaware alone made a serious effort to restrict the outgoing trade in slaves, but all the States from Maryland and Kentucky to Louisiana passed laws from time to time to prohibit or restrict the inward traffic. Such laws, however, had no practical effect. In Mississippi, for example, even when the constitutional and statutory prohibitions were strictest, citizens could purchase slaves outside the State for their own use. Nor did the Delaware law mean much. A judicial order could be obtained for a sale into other States, while clandestine

114 Nevins, *British Travellers,* 122, 123.
115 Bancroft, *Slave Trade,* 328–333; Coleman, *Slavery in Ky.,* 121, 137, 159.
116 Issue of December 14, 1861.
117 N. Y. *Weekly Tribune,* March 12, 1859.

transfers were easy. Just before the Civil War efforts were made to repeal the act, Delawareans who believed in emancipation thinking it better to have no statute at all than one which was daily violated.[118] The movement for laws prohibiting the importation of slaves from other States owed something to a desire to strengthen slavery in the border region. When it seemed possible in 1849 that Kentucky might adopt measures for gradual emancipation, a clamor arose in Tennessee to discourage this by statutes which would prevent Kentuckians from dumping their slaves across the line and so escaping financial loss.

[X]

It cannot be too strongly emphasized that the evils of slavery appertained to the institution, and not to any special traits of the Southern people. All of the so-called "barbarities of slavery" had once existed in the North; all had existed in the British, French, and Spanish dominions. The North's own record in the domestic slave trade was darker, and extended down to a more recent date, than is commonly realized. The traffic existed in New York and New Jersey as late as 1818. These States, seats of gradual emancipation, had passed repeated laws prohibiting the slave trade, but speculators were under a strong temptation to run off slave property to the high market of the South and frequently did so.[119] How much Dutchman and Portuguese, Englishman and Yankee, had done in supplying slaves for the American market is common knowledge. New Englanders, Britons, and Germans who settled in slaveholding areas of the South behaved toward slaves precisely like native-born Southerners. It was economic and social conditions, not fundamental moral or humanitarian qualities, which differed from area to area. The South had its full share of American virtues, and more than its share of graces. Since slavery had represented a small money investment in the North and showed tiny profits or distinct losses, Northerners had no right to plume themselves on superior heroism or self-sacrifice in extinguishing it.[120]

118 N. Y. *Tribune,* February 18, 1860.
119 *Nation,* February 16, 1888. In fact, the case of Gibbons *vs.* Morse showed that in 1821 traders were busy buying slaves in New Jersey and shipping off cargoes of them from South Amboy. 2 *Halsted Reports.*
120 Cf. Moore, *Slavery in Massachusetts;* Locke, *Anti-Slavery in America.* In his MS history of the colonization movement (Columbia Univ. Library), Frederic Bancroft points out that what were called the barbarities of slavery had nearly all existed at the North. "It would require a specialist and much study to decide whether, if due weight were given to all the circumstances, the eighteenth century slave codes of New York and Massachusetts were not more needlessly cruel than those of Virginia and South Carolina in the nineteenth. If a historian should pronounce the morals of one section and century worse than those of the other, it would be well to ask for his credentials as a moral philosopher; and if a moral philosopher should especially favor any State, it would be still more important to look into his qualifications as a historian."

"So vile and miserable an estate of man"—such had been the words with which John Locke, in the opening lines of his *Two Treatises of Civil Government*, characterized slavery. It would have taken a bold publicist to declare in 1850 that its essential character had in recent years been much improved, or was susceptible of great improvement. Beyond question the ending of the foreign slave trade in 1808 had opened a new era in the history of American slavery. While it lasted, that trade, pouring annually a large body of Africans, including many freeborn, half-savage, and well-trained warriors, into the South, had given slavery a darker and more ferocious hue. It had kept up in many areas a mutual reaction of truculence and severity. Most of the newcomers were downcast and sullen, while many were ferociously rebellious. Their masters feared the revolt of these half-tamed men—feared arson, outrage, and murder; and they took precautions of the harshest character.

The abolition of the slave trade roughly coincided with the beginning of the great westward movement and the enormous extension of cotton culture. Both changes added to the value of the Negro, and put an end in the United States to any idea that (as many continued to hold in Cuba) "it paid best to use up the niggers and replace them." [121] Much evidence could be cited to show that a distinct amelioration of the attitude of the white man toward the slave, and of the slave toward the master, followed these three great events of the first quarter of the nineteenth century.

But if slavery as an institution thereafter improved in some respects, it deteriorated in others. Slaves acquired more of white skill and culture; more white blood passed into the colored stock; the anti-slavery clamor made numerous masters more sensitive to their responsibilities. Some humane principles of plantation management obtained partial fixity. A great improvement, asserted the *Southern Quarterly Review* in 1853, has taken place in the lot of slaves since 1806. "Of late years they will not work in their own patches or gardens, on Sunday, or perform any other work. They are, assuredly, not required to do any. Besides Sundays, the slaves have ample time to work their own crops; and they generally take up whatever land the planter leaves uncultivated for the year." [122] The influence of agricultural reformers like Thomas Affleck of Louisiana and Texas, and of the model plantation record books which Affleck published, was healthful and growing.[123] The tendency to replace white overseers with Negro drivers, for slaves of responsibility and skill were increasingly numerous, registered progress by the Negro. Plantations

121 Percy Greg, *History of the U. S.*, I, 351, 352.
122 "Life of a Negro Slave," *Southern Quarterly Review*, January, 1853.
123 See T. C. Cole, "Texas Career of Thomas Affleck," MS Dissertation, La. State Univ. Library.

were emerging like that of Jefferson Davis, on which slaves were allowed a large measure of self-government.[124]

Yet if humane and paternalistic principles were gaining ground, discipline was in some respects growing tighter, and emphasis on the immobility of slavery was becoming sterner. The South was taking its stand on the principle that slavery was a positive good and must not be disturbed. It was stirred by resentment of Northern agitation, and fear of the Negro's growing capacity to act for himself—by sabotage, by physical resistance, by running away. Emancipation was increasingly unpopular, and was soon being stopped by positive laws. In some States laws were passed ordering free Negroes to leave. The practice of letting a slave hire his own time, which amounted to semi-freedom, was encountering greater and greater disfavor. Life became more burdensome for the really skilled and intelligent, and their chances of gaining freedom were diminished. Olmsted concluded that in Virginia the physical well-being of the slaves had constantly improved since 1820, while their disciplinary position had rather grown worse. They were not overworked as of old; they were better fed, clothed, and sheltered; and they were punished not with the scoring lash and bruising cudgel but with the pliant strap and scientific paddle. But laws and customs were less favorable than before to their education, freedom of movement, and opportunity for growth. This was obviously because of the opinion that as Negro property increased in intelligence it decreased in security. More attention was paid to health and comfort, but simultaneously efforts were made to suppress the ambition and cramp the mind of the slave.[125]

In the extremes of maltreatment and misery which it permitted, in its hostility to family life, and in its denial of all opportunity to rise above a certain level, lay the three radical defects of slavery. So long as it remained traditional slavery, an institution frozen into an unbreakable mould—what Henry Clay called "interminable, inexorable slavery" [126]—these defects were incurable. The ablest men of the Revolutionary generation, Jefferson, Madison, Patrick Henry, and Washington, thought as Clay did, that slavery should be made an evolutionary, not a static, system. "I believe a time will come," wrote Henry, "when an opportunity will be offered to abolish this lamentable evil." [127] It was easy to suggest means of making it evolutionary. Discipline should be founded upon rewards, not punishments; incentives should be held out to slaves for diligence, energy, and virtue; profit-sharing arrangements for at least the fittest should

---

124 For Davis's experiment see W. L. Fleming, "Jefferson Davis, the Negroes, and the Negro Problem," *Sewanee Review*, XVI, 407–427.
125 Sydnor, *Slavery in Miss.*, 249; Olmsted, *Seaboard States*, 280, 281; W. E. B. DuBois, *Black Reconstruction in America*, 45–47.
126 *African Repository* (the Colonization Society organ), XII, 10.
127 George Morgan, *True Patrick Henry*, 247.

lead first to quasi-independence and then full freedom. Meanwhile, the family should be protected; perhaps, as in medieval villeinage, most slaves should be attached to the land, and the child should follow the condition not of his mother but his father. But all such programs encountered the terrible problem of race-relationship. "I would rejoice to emancipate them all," said Henry. "But is it practicable, by any human means, to liberate them without producing the most dreadful and ruinous consequences?" [128]

Slavery was the greatest misery, the greatest wrong, the greatest curse to white and black alike that America has ever known. Its ultimate abolition was an even greater benefit to the Caucasian than to the Negro. But to most Southerners the prospect of so momentous a revolution not merely in the labor system but the social system seemed fraught with incalculable dangers. The South behaved like a man who, afflicted with some horrible growth but fearful of the pain and peril of its excision, hugs it tightly to his bosom and extols it as after all rather a benefit to his health; knowing all the while that he is self-deluded and walking as in a nightmare. The South needed compassion and help, not condemnation.

128 Elliot's *Debates*, III, 590, 591.

14

The Cash Account of Slavery

ON A BRIGHT day in early spring of 1854, Edward Everett drove from Washington to Arlington to see the venerable George Washington Parke Custis. "The surroundings of Arlington," he wrote, "[are] in a most neglected condition, and the house itself, never finished, is hastening to premature decay. . . . The position of Arlington overlooking the Potomac and the cities of Washington and Georgetown is superb, but it must be highly malarious. The condition of the roads, buildings, and fences bears witness to a social malaria worse than the natural." Everett was simply echoing the words of the Kentuckian Thomas F. Marshall. This nephew of John Marshall had remarked of Virginia that "the clog that has stayed the march of her people, the incubus that has weighed down her enterprise, strangled her commerce, kept sealed her exhaustless fountain of mineral wealth, and paralyzed her arts, manufactures, and improvements is negro slavery. . . ."[1] North and South, a multitude of observers were convinced by 1850 that slavery was economically a ruinous system; while an equally stubborn body of observers maintained that it was profitable and sound.

Of the backwardness, dilapidation, and poverty of much of the South there was no question. Land in Virginia, not twenty miles from Fredericksburg, and lying on both a railroad and a plank road, could in 1856 be bought for $5 an acre. Much land was in fact exhausted, thrown into commons, and abandoned by its old owners.[2] North Carolina, the Boeotia of America, seemed to its own leaders hopelessly full of poverty, ignorance, and conservatism. One citizen wrote early in the fifties that almost every landowner was willing to sell; the newspapers were full of descriptions of a westward exodus. Archibald D. Murphey, after vainly trying for years to obtain the adoption of liberal State policies, had finally exploded: "The Mass of the Common People in the Coun-

---

1 Everett, MS Diary; Marshall (Representative in Congress from the Louisville district, 1841-43) is quoted in G. C. Parson, *Inside View of Slavery*, 168, 169.
2 "The Decay of Virginia" in N. Y. *Weekly Tribune*, February 9, 1856.

try are lazy, sickly, poor, dirty, and ignorant."[3] As for South Carolina, travellers on the railroad running from Charleston to Columbia were astonished to find that most of the regular stopping-places had but two, four, or six houses.[4] Georgia was still full of communities like the Pineville described in *Major Jones's Chronicles*, published in 1843 by W. T. Thompson. It was full, that is, of indolent, good-natured villages marked by a certain charm, but also by illiteracy—stray newspapers had to be read aloud; by squalor—general poverty, poor dress, primitive sanitation, and insufficient diet with much clay-eating; by dirty habits—tipping, tobacco-chewing, and a general distaste for soap and water; and by violence—duelling, lynch-law, and affrays of all kinds.[5]

The evils which afflicted the South were plainly complex. It was an area of widespread illiteracy. The 2,399,651 native-born whites of New England included, by the census of 1850, only 6,209 native-born whites of more than twenty years unable to read and write. The 2,393,101 native-born whites of New York included only 23,240 such persons. But Virginia, with 871,847 native-born whites, had 75,863 native white persons over twenty who could not read and write, while for North Carolina the corresponding figures were 550,462 and 73,226. In Alabama the adult white illiterates were 33,618 out of a native white population of 419,016; in Georgia, 40,794 out of 515,120; and in Arkansas, 16,792 out of 160,721.[6] School appropriations were wretched, and it was said that even penal laws would hardly compel many rural parents to put their children into classes. Anyone could see the omnipresent evidences of this illiteracy.[7]

Everyone could see, too, that the South was an area of rude and wasteful agriculture. The fact that it was almost exclusively a farming region, neglecting its rich minerals, waterpower, and opportunities for secondary industries, was itself one main root of poverty. It lacked the wealth-producing facilities of machinery, accumulated capital, and skilled labor. But the methods of tillage were glaringly deficient in intelligence, providence, and foresight. Slaveowners

3 W. H. Hoyt, ed., *Papers of Archibald D. Murphey*, I, 151; these papers of a North Carolina attorney and reformer who died in 1832 throw light on the early movement in that State for improved public education, amelioration of the criminal laws, resettlement abroad of free Negroes, and internal improvements.

4 *National Intelligencer*, April 23, 1854.

5 Thompson, later the founder of the Savannah *Morning News*, had a full acquaintance with rural Georgia.

6 *Compendium of the Ninth Census* (1870), pp. 458, 459, gives illiteracy statistics for 1850, 1860, and 1870.

7 As Edward Ingle says in *Southern Sidelights: A Picture of Social and Economic Life in the South a Generation Before the War*, illiteracy was by no means equivalent to ignorance; the education of the white Southerner was likely to come by auditory rather than visual channels. He also points out that the South's proportion of illiteracy decreased. In 1840 the South had more than 62 per cent of the nation's white illiteracy; in 1860 less than 48 per cent. Pp. 162–167.

seized upon most of the good land. They exhausted it by heavy crops of cotton, cane, tobacco, and corn, plowing much of the topsoil into the streams. In time they sold out for a song or abandoned their holdings for taxes, moving onward. The poorer whites, in some States three-fourths of the free population, took the hill land, the sterile soils, and the abandoned tracts. Meanwhile, rapid soil-exploitation and Negro-exploitation gave a limited number of landowners temporary wealth at the cost of sectional impoverishment.[8]

Worst of all, any observer could see that the South was an area of appalling human wastes. The pioneer manufacturer William Gregg, addressing the South Carolina Institute in 1851, said that "from the best estimates that I have been able to make, I put down the white people who ought to work and who do not, or who are so employed as to be wholly unproductive to the State, at one hundred and twenty-five thousand." This was nearly one-half of South Carolina's whole white population (274,563)! The eight hundred people he had gathered at Graniteville were industrious and orderly, but deplorably ignorant, three-fourths being unable to write their names. "It is very clear to me, that the only means of educating and Christianizing our poor whites, will be to bring them into such villages. . . ." James H. Hammond had described these poor whites as obtaining a precarious existence by odd jobs, hunting, fishing, plundering fields and folds, and trading with the slaves.[9] The situation was identical in other States. Poor whites in Tennessee and North Carolina could be hired for eighty cents a day, or (with board and clothing included) for $110 a year. "It is not to be disguised, nor can it be successfully controverted," wrote Senator Charles T. James in DeBow's *Industrial Resources of the South and West*, "that a degree and extent of poverty and destitution exist in the Southern States, among a certain class of people, almost unknown in the manufacturing districts of the North. The poor white man will endure the evils of pinching poverty rather than engage in servile labor under the existing state of things . . . Boys and girls, by thousands, destitute both of employment and the means of education, grow up in ignorance and poverty, and too many of them to vice and crime."

8 Lewis C. Gray, *History of Agriculture in the Southern United States to 1860*, II, 908ff, discusses the effects of western expansion on the older slaveholding areas, the widening area of soil exhaustion, and the depressing influence of western competition on eastern agriculture. He cites as responsible for the woes of certain eastern areas not only slavery but government policies "which made land so abundant that expansion and soil exhaustion became prevailing characteristics of Southern agriculture."

9 Gregg's Address published in *DeBow's Review*, August, 1851, XI, 123ff.; Hammond's Address to the South Carolina Institute, 1850, pvt.

[I]

Yet most Southern slaveholders vehemently insisted that slavery was economically sound and profitable. It was the labor system which best fitted the mixture of ethnic stocks, they said, and which was best adapted to the existing stage of economic evolution. It got the most out of the Negro, and was the most efficient means of producing cotton, sugar, and tobacco.[10] These crops, ran the argument, were not really adapted to the labor of small farmers, for they required large bands of laborers working under careful organization. In the 1850's about four-fifths of the cotton used by Christendom was the product of slave labor. This, declared Southerners, represented a natural economic law. The South's monopoly of cotton had given slavery its commercial value, and while the monopoly endured, the institution would continue to spread itself wherever it could find room.

The pro-slavery argument on economic grounds could be compressed into a rough syllogism applicable to the basic situation of the South. The section was yet in that stage of development where cotton, eagerly demanded by the world, was its most economic product; cotton could be planted, cultivated, and harvested only by hand, no machinery being of much use; the best hands were cheap, unskilled labor organized in gangs large or small, and directed by a single mind to a definite end; an abundant supply of such labor was furnished by the Negroes; and slavery kept them efficiently occupied at the lowest cost compatible with health and strength.[11] This syllogism could be varied to suit cane or tobacco. Even observers who, like Olmsted and the British economist J. E. Cairnes, were convinced of the essential fallacy of the argument, admitted that it had partial force.[12] Indeed, it was clear that if ever slavery was economically profitable, it should be so in the Lower South. The staples here were all-year crops, furnishing a maximum continuity of occupation; the simple processes of cultivation were capable of being standardized and reduced to routine for ignorant hands; and the labor force could be concentrated in stable, well-controlled units, minimizing the sullenness and inefficiency of slave groups.[13]

Southerners were quick to point out that the Indian ryot, the free Negro of the West Indies, and the peasant-proprietor of Egypt had shown no ability to compete with their slave system in growing cotton and sugar for the world market. The East India Company had hired several American planters to intro-

10 Gray, *Agriculture in the Southern United States*, II, 939.
11 David Christy, *The Cotton Kingdom*, 56.
12 John Elliott Cairnes, *The Slave Power*, 18; this book, published in 1862, is a penetrating but very onesided analysis of the weaknesses of the slavery system by an economist of the classical British school.
13 Cairnes, *idem*, 43; Frederick Law Olmsted, *A Journey in the Back Country*, chs. 4 and 8,

duce American methods of cotton cultivation. But the chief British importer of Indian cotton said in Parliament in 1857 that the product was so dirty and damaged that no price could be given for it approaching that for the American staple.[14] He said also that his own efforts to establish cotton-growing in West Africa had resulted in failure. Brazilian production was disappointing, while Natal and Australia lacked cheap labor. The fact that early in the 1850's about seventeen-twentieths of the 700,000,000 pounds of raw cotton imported into Britain came from the Southern States was a cause of deep concern to the spinning industry.[15] If war or any great social or physical convulsion shut off this supply, the one-seventh of Britain's population which depended upon cotton-spinning would feel the acutest distress. But no real progress was made in developing other sources.[16]

Southerners were also quick to point out that their slave economy furnished much the largest part of the nation's exports. For the fiscal year ending June 30, 1850, cotton alone accounted for nearly half of the nation's foreign shipments, $71,984,616 out of $144,376,000.[17] Ten years later the situation was from the Southern standpoint equally roseate. The exportation of domestic produce in 1860 was $333,576,000, of which raw cotton represented $191,807,000, as against less than $20,000,000 for wheat. The world's demand for cotton garments, upon which so much of America's and Britain's income depended, was expanding with the wonderful growth of nineteenth-century population. Cotton production must somehow keep pace with it, and—said the Southerners—only slave labor could furnish a uniform and certain supply.[18] In this view of the situation, declared a Southern writer in 1857, the British press and people were abating their denunciation of slave-grown cotton. "They are beginning to think that slavery, after all, is not so bad an institution." [19]

Primary industries usually suffer less from any short-lived panic and depression than secondary or tertiary industries. As in 1857 the South breasted the

14 J. A. Turner, M. P. for Manchester, *Hansard*, Vol. 146, pp. 282, 288, 897; comment in *National Intelligencer*, July 16, 1857. Other members of Parliament were more hopeful of Indian production. Relative production outside the United States was destined in the long run to rise. Average production for 1926–27 to 1930–31 in thousands of bales was 14,834 for the United States; 4,559 for India; 2,090 for China; and enough in other nations to bring the total to 26,320.

15 See address of Chairman Bazley of the Manchester Chamber of Commerce, *National Intelligencer*, April 27, 1852.

16 David Christy, *Cotton is King: or, Slavery in the Light of Political Economy*, 52; Frank L. Owsley, *King Cotton Diplomacy*, 10ff. Christy's book, the work of a Cincinnati believer in colonization as the solution of the slavery problem, was published in 1855 to convince the abolitionists that their plans were an utter failure. It summed up all the statistics and arguments tending to show the world's dependence on cotton, and its very title became a shibboleth of immense influence in the South.

17 *Statistical Abstract of the United States*, 1940, pp. 492, 493.

18 See S. M. Wolfe, *Helper's Impending Crisis Dissected*, 44.

19 *National Intelligencer*, October 3, 1857.

financial collapse much better than the North, a thousand Southerners raised boastful voices. "When the abuse of credit had . . . annihilated confidence," declaimed Senator Hammond; "when thousands of the strongest commercial houses in the world were coming down and hundreds of millions of dollars of supposed property evaporating in thin air; when you came to a deadlock and revolutions were threatened, what brought you up? Fortunately for you, it was the commencement of the cotton season, and we have poured upon you 1,600,000 bales of cotton just at the crisis to save you from destruction." [20] Though the cotton crop for 1857–58 was unusually large, foreign prices remained high. Land, slaves, and crops continued to sell at high rates, and many Southerners became convinced that their slavery economy possessed ironclad stability.[21]

Nor did defenders of slavery fail to point out that many large and even moderate-sized plantations yielded dazzling revenues. Throughout the fifties numerous slaveholders thought themselves highly prosperous. Rising cotton prices, fast-increasing yields, and ever-climbing quotations for slaves, produced a sense of wealth and security. Dixon Hall Lewis, successively Representative and Senator from Alabama, had said in the forties, "give us six cents a pound for our cotton, and we will grow rich"—and in the fall of 1857 cotton reached sixteen cents a pound.[22] It was possible for the enterprising David Dickson of Georgia to amass a fortune of half a million before Appomattox. J. H. Ingraham in *The Southwest by a Yankee* had declared that throughout Southwestern Mississippi annual incomes of $20,000 for planters were common, and that a number made $40,000 or $50,000 a year. His book was published in an era of booming inflation (1835), but statistics down to 1860 can be cited to show that favored men continued to make such incomes. Cotton planters were not alone in their affluence. Southerners read with satisfaction, in the hard days of 1857, of Joshua Phipps of Hawkins County in East Tennessee, who had been comparatively poor twenty years earlier. Now, with more than three thousand acres in wheat, oats, corn, and grass, and with fifty Negroes working his farms, he enjoyed an annual income which fell little short of $20,000.[23]

20 *Cong. Globe,* March 4, 1858.

21 Lewis C. Gray's conclusion is emphatic: "In the last five years of the period (1815–1860) cotton sold at prices that were highly remunerative, especially considering the fact that the average annual product of the five years was much larger than it had ever been before. In the Cotton Belt, therefore, as in other parts of the South, the Civil War brought to a close a period of exceptional prosperity." *Agriculture in the Southern United States,* II, 700.

22 "Cotton," by A. M. of Mississippi, in *National Intelligencer,* November 17, 1857.

23 Ralph B. Flanders, *Plantation Slavery in Georgia;* Charles Sackett Sydnor, *Slavery in Mississippi,* 195. A student of tillers of the soil in twelve representative counties in Mississippi finds evidence 1850–60 of "great prosperity enjoyed by all groups." Herbert Weaver, *Mississippi Farmers 1850–1860.* Poor whites were few.

Where under the sun, asked Southerners, were any agricultural regions as affluent as the aristocratic district about Society Hill in South Carolina, the Yazoo delta, the Alabama Canebrake, or the region of pillared mansions about Natchez? A beguiling picture of the Canebrake, the rich bed of a prehistoric lake, has been drawn by J. W. DuBose. The smallest plantation here was of about 700 acres, the largest of about 2,500. The fertility of the soil, as its primitive growth of dense timber and impenetrable cane had attested, was magnificent. Rearing handsome houses, the planters found the climate so healthy and the society so pleasant that they rarely went away for the summer. They prided themselves on their loyal hands, and Andrew J. Calhoun (son of the statesman), who owned two large estates, once dismissed an overseer for lightly whipping two unruly women without first asking leave. The overseers were exceptionally competent and were highly paid. Every effort was made to bring the working force to the highest expertness. The hoe-hands "moved like a machine"; and "I doubt if in the world," writes DuBose, "agricultural labor executed in quantity and quality the year round as in the Canebrake the last year of slavery." Life in this aristocratic district was pleasant, and profits were large. What was more, land values rose to gratifying levels, and the Negroes increased rapidly.[24]

And where did gentlemen live in more tasteful splendor than those of the best Southern districts? Samuel Hairston, reputed the richest of Virginians, worth perhaps five or six millions, prided himself upon his handsome mansion, furniture, and grounds at Pittsylvania. One observer wrote in the Richmond *Whig* that he had travelled over fifteen States, and seen nothing to compare with his beautifully-kept gardens except some of those in Mississippi. A friend who visited Washington for the first time remarked: "The public grounds are nearly as impressive as Samuel Hairston's." Sprinkling the whole South, in tidewater Virginia and Carolina, the bluegrass parks of Kentucky, along the Mississippi-tributaries, and around such Alabama towns as Eutaw and Greensboro, Selma and Huntsville, Marion and Montgomery, were pillared houses, ancestral mahogany, and well-filled stables which spoke of accumulated wealth.

But of vastly greater significance were the evidences of real if spotty middle-class prosperity. They were not to be seen by those who rode in a hurry. The greater part of the Southern agricultural population were yeomen; and studies based upon census returns, wills, tax-lists, and other data show that land-ownership among both slaveholders and non-slaveholders was high, that it in-

24 For DuBose's picture of this wealthy community, see his MS Recollections in the Alabama State Department of Archives and History. For Society Hill, S. C., which had a valuable community library, and produced a governor, many judges, churchmen, educators, and others of note, see the W.P.A. *American Guide Series, South Carolina*, 304, 305.

creased during the fifties, and that at death many modest farmers disposed of substantial estates. Even the landless whites in such a planting area as Alabama's Black Belt often owned several thousand dollars' worth of slaves, tools, livestock, and furniture. A close student of Alabama's economic structure, denying that its people could be divided into the few very rich and the many very poor, remarks that if its society were charted it would present a gentle curve where small farmers, middle-sized farmers, large farmers, small planters, middling planters, and great planters merged into each other without breaks. In Tennessee, too, where the majority of slaveowners were farmers, not planters, the same student finds a wide diffusion of property. In most Southern regions the segregation of slaveholders upon rich lands and non-slaveholders on poor soil seems to have been exaggerated by superficial students. A broader gamut of economic status, a greater degree of identity among slaveowners and slaveless, a wider diffusion of property, a steady growth of wealth in the fifties—these seem to be facts which superficial observers of the time missed.

Southern poverty, however, remained a real and widespread fact. If in some areas the destitute were but one-twentieth of the whole population, in others they were more. Southern wealth, too, contained some delusive elements. So long as Negroes could be valued at high figures, many owners complacently compared their holdings with those of Northerners. A recent historian of South Carolina has declared that by 1860 the twenty-seven thousand slaveholders had raised that State to such material prosperity that it stood third in per capita wealth, Connecticut being first and Louisiana second. The South Carolinians had attained per capita estates of $779 in 1860 as against an average of $501 for the nation as a whole. Much of this "wealth" represented simply the ownership of one-half the population by the other half, but it seemed as real and profitable as houses and machines. As for the border States of Virginia and Maryland, they realized such increasing sums from the export of Negroes southward that they too were ready to regard slavery as economically profitable.[25]

[II]

If the South was cursed by widespread poverty, declared upholders of slavery, it was primarily because Northerners manipulated government policy to her disadvantage. They robbed her by tariffs which forced up the price of

25 See N. Y. *Tribune*, May 26, 1854, for Richmond *Whig* account of Hairston and four of his wealthy brothers. Frank L. and Harriet C. Owsley, in "The Economic Basis of Society in the Late Ante-Bellum South," and "The Economic Structure of Rural Tennessee" (*Journal of Southern History*, VI, 21–45; VIII, 161–182), maintain with strong evidence that society in the Old South was much more complex than was then or later believed. They have opened up a rich vein of ore in previously unexplored materials. Yates Snowden. *History of South Carolina*, 654.

farm machinery, textiles, and miscellaneous goods; by giving Northern rail-roads an unfair share in the common patrimony of public lands; by heavy spending on other internal improvements; and by fostering an immigration system that did everything for the North and nothing for the South. More-over, Northern factors, jobbers, and merchants leeched the South on every-thing it sold and bought. Northern manufacturers of cotton and tobacco paid prices unfairly low and charged prices unfairly high. Northern speculators rigged the primary markets. The South depended on Northern dealers for most wares consumed on the plantations; it depended on Wall Street money to finance crop-movements, build its railroads, and to set up its factories; and it depended on Northern shipping lines to carry the great staples to market. Profits that should have gone to the South were diverted to Northern pockets.[26]

The most earnest exponent of this view, the New York Democrat T. P. Kettell, found a wide circulation for his vehement *Southern Wealth and Northern Profits* (1860). He had no difficulty in showing that the South possessed a far larger export surplus than any other section, that the value of this surplus was increasing, and that it was one of the chief mainstays of American prosperity. The South not only supplied nearly all Northern wants in cotton, sugar, tobacco, rice, and naval stores, with much wool and hides, but (he wrote) bought the greater part of the imported goods. The North handled both the imports and exports, and did it on exorbitant terms. It could do so because manufacturing, shipping, banking, and the conduct of inter-national trade had been concentrated in Yankeeland.

Shipping his cotton to England, the Southern planter would draw in advance on his British credit to obtain ready cash in New York, which charged a hand-some commission. Cotton paper, most Southerners believed, was subject to vicious speculation in the large Eastern cities. They thought that its value was often outrageously depressed. The North had built the steamers which carried the cotton; they took a share. The North had organized the companies which insured the cargo; they had their premiums. The large cities of the North had the necessary banks, counting houses, warehouses, brokers, clerks, and business-men of a hundred sorts, with commercial connections throughout the globe; they had to be paid for their services. The North had capital for handling trade and charged high rates for its use.[27] Altogether, Kettell, J. D. B. DeBow, and others thought that the urban North took a great part of its subsistence out of

26 Wolfe, *Helper's Impending Crisis Dissected*, 133ff. At different times Federal banking policy was also blamed by Southerners; Gray, *Agriculture in the Southern United States*, II, 910.

27 Congress in the spring of 1857 passed an act to send a special agent to investigate the European consumption of cotton, and the costs of the movement from producer to con-sumer; and the result was John Claiborne's *Consumption of Cotton in Europe*. His estimate that profits of the French industry from start to finish were about four hundred per cent did not lessen the suspicion of producers that their cut of the pie was too small.

the South. It should be more largely understood, wrote Kettell, that the brokers, dealers, bankers, insurance companies, and all those actually employed in receiving and distributing Southern produce, with the long train of persons who furnish them with houses, clothing, supplies, education, amusement, and transportation, are dependent on the active interchange by which a full billion of dollars come and go between the North and the South in a year.[28]

In short, argued many Southerners, the main source of real wealth in the United States was the product of their well-managed slave-system, and if the North was the richer it was because of its parasitic skill. Wrote one Southern publicist: [29]

When we regard the products of the Southern States, and see to what extent their great staples, cotton, sugar, rice, and tobacco, enter into man's consumption; when we consider how much the commercial, manufacturing, and other industrial pursuits of all the great nations are dependent upon them for prosperity and vigor, to how many hands they give employment, and to how much hunger they give food; and then consider to what a vast extent the wonderful development of these great staples is indebted to the system of compulsory labor and the peculiar adaptedness of the constitution of the negro to the climate in which they are produced, it would not be a little difficult to estimate the value to mankind proceeding from that source. Left to its own voluntary selection of employment, labor would never have subdued the rice swamps of Carolina, nor have expressed the juices from the sugar-cane of Florida, Louisiana, and Texas, and but to a small extent would it plough the cotton-fields of Mississippi; for the cultivation of the cereal grains and the production of live-stock are employments more congenial to the freeman.

Wherever slavery prevails capital and labor will be mainly employed in the business of agriculture. In this country it has devoted the immense territory of fourteen States to the growth of raw materials for commerce and manufactures, and converted its inhabitants into consumers of their products. . . . As no inconsiderable part of their earlier gains sprang from the traffic in slaves, so now very much of the present prosperity of the free States proceeds from the labors of that class. Their merchants, mechanics, farmers, lawyers, doctors, in a word, every professional and industrial pursuit among them, in some way, either mediately or immediately, derive profit from that source. . . .

Deprive Great Britain of the fruits of her commerce in our great staples, and she would be almost stricken from the list of independent states; without them she could not clothe and give employment to her thronging masses, nor long stagger under the oppressive weight of her accumulating debt. Deprive the great cities of Boston, New York, and Philadelphia of these fruits, and their huge proportions would fall to decay, and scenes of wretchedness more absolute than words could depict mark their ruin.

The South, rumbled exhorting politicians and editors, ought to revolt against its vassalage. If it refused to remain a hewer of wood and drawer of water for

28 T. M. Kettell, *Southern Wealth and Northern Profits*, 75.
29 R. E. Scott in *National Intelligencer*, April 5, 1854.

the greedy Yankees, it might hold all the wealth it produced. It could readily make itself self-sufficient. It had little debt and disliked speculation. It produced materials upon which the well-being of the globe absolutely depended, and one of which was the very pivot of the world's commerce. All that was necessary was to turn defiantly against the middlemen who appropriated half of the profits, and the speculators and money-changers who took most of the other half. The section should use its wealth for its own aggrandizement and opulence, not that of the North and Great Britain.[30]

The crusade for Southern economic independence was compounded half of a hope to retain the more accessible profits, and half of a desire to promote Southern nationalism. Convention succeeded convention. The most important were a series of Southern Commercial Conventions beginning in 1852 and ending in 1859. They adopted endless resolutions—that the duties on railroad iron ought to be repealed or reduced; that a line of Southern steamers should ply direct from Southern ports to Europe; that a Southern route should be chosen for the railway to the Pacific; that all good citizens should use Southern manufactures; that people should buy Southern books, and visit Southern summer-resorts. Eloquent speeches were made. Banquets were held, where governors and mayors uttered valorous words. Articles of the do-or-die variety were printed in newspapers. Meanwhile, Southern railroad conventions were also held, and Macon, Ga., witnessed in 1852 a convention of planters from all the cotton States dedicated to the worthy cause of making sure that cotton never dropped below ten cents a pound.[31]

But nothing was accomplished by these oratorical gatherings. They steadily lost prestige, until they were dismissed as "a series of humbugs" and as assemblages of "peripatetic politicians and windgalled and spavined political economists." [32] In vain did Dudley Mann push his plan for a line of steamers from Norfolk and other ports which should take the palm away from Northern packets; in vain did G. G. Baylor broach his scheme for making Amsterdam instead of Liverpool and Manchester the great emporium of the cotton trade.[33]

30 Cf. DeBow's Review, XXII, 265ff.; XXV, 220ff.
31 Herbert Wender, Southern Commercial Conventions 1837–1859. For the union of economic and nationalist impulses behind these conventions, see the statement of the New Orleans Picayune of 1859 on the excessive payments for factoring, storage, and transportation, and the Mobile Daily Register's assertion that the Vicksburg Convention of that year was "the Southern Continental Congress"; quoted in Henry H. Simms, A Decade of Sectional Controversy, 1851–1861, pp. 185, 186. But much Southern opinion held the gatherings futile, and the Picayune thought them "a species of escape-valve for sectional patriotism" that left the Union stronger. Cf. R. R. Russell, Ec. Aspects of Southern Nationalism, 123ff.
32 Philadelphia Enquirer, July 31, 1857; Cole, Irrepressible Conflict, 71, 72.
33 National Intelligencer, July 21, August 22, 1857. Liverpool had displaced London as the central European market for cotton late in the eighteenth century. British textile manufacturers employed astute purchasing brokers in the Southern ports. Liverpool methods of grading cotton gradually became dominant in the United States. Gray, Agriculture in the Southern United States, II, 718, 719.

It was true that the South needed more manufactures and better banks, and should have mustered the enterprise to create them. It was true that the profits of middlemen and bill-brokers needed close watching. But the laws of trade were of too immutable a character to be changed by speechmaking in commercial conventions—bodies which represented a high capacity for juleps and rhetoric, but little for business.

The fact was that natural causes led the people of the North toward manufacturing and exchange, as natural causes kept the slaveholders of the South busy with agricultural undertakings. It was also a fact that many Northern undertakings paid scanty returns. The iron manufacturers of whose charges Southerners complained barely made ends meet, while after 1855 the shipping business was in a state of marked decline. The tariff of 1846, largely framed by Robert J. Walker of Mississippi and passed with Southern votes, was so low that Northern industrialists bitterly denounced its inadequacy. Northern and Southern economies were complementary, to the benefit of both sections. Establishment of economic self-sufficiency would simply have cost the South more than it was able or willing to pay. In this sense Willoughby Newton of Virginia was correct in declaring: "The commercial independence of the South will never be secured until her national independence is established." [34]—for triumphant nationalism alone would have been willing to pay the price.

[III]

It was obvious that the rapid expansion of tillage over wide new fertile areas had created a great deal of wealth which could not be attributed to the slave system, for free labor had accomplished precisely the same result in the Northwest. It was also obvious that values fructified in rising land prices and Negro prices could not safely be computed as proof of the routine profits of the system.

Expansion to the Southwest, like expansion to the Northwest, had unlocked the door of a natural treasure-house. The vigorous impulse by which Alabama, Mississippi, northern Louisiana, eastern Texas, and much of Arkansas were filled with an energetic, hard-working body of cotton-planters constitutes one of the impressive colonizing movements of our history. It gave the region the "flush times" that Joseph G. Baldwin of Mississippi so racily celebrated.[35] Alabama, with her inviting prairies and river valleys (and with less inviting pine-barrens), much more than doubled her population in the twenties and almost doubled it in the thirties.[36] Down to the Civil War the restless movement

---

34 *National Intelligencer*, August 8, 1857.
35 *The Flush Times of Alabama and Mississippi* (1853).
36 Population rose 142.01 per cent in 1820-30; by 90.86 per cent in 1830-40; U. S. Census, *Population*, 1860.

never ceased. As Alabama received the overflow from Georgia and the Carolinas, so in the fifties an Alabama surplus moved into Mississippi. From all older parts of the South population streamed toward the sunset. During 1850 there passed through Caddo, La., nearly five hundred wagons and other vehicles bearing 2,359 whites and 1,556 blacks, with long trains of livestock, from the older States into Texas.[37]

The combination of population and virgin land meant a glittering unearned increment. Reuben Davis could point to a small Mississippi town like Pontotoc as full of money; it boasted families of education who had come to seek fortune and had "found it in the increased value of lands," and all its leading citizens had swiftly "realized handsome estates." Ingraham's book presents the region about Natchez, so beautifully placed on its high bluff over the Mississippi, in its era of rising opulence. Everybody was eager to become rich by cotton-planting on the cheap land. Ministers of the gospel bought tracts, looked after plantations during the week and pulpits on Sunday, and gave more attention to slaves than souls. Lawyers practised till they obtained capital to settle on plantations. Some like Robert J. Walker, busily combined law practise, cotton planting, land speculation, and politics. Northerners who had flocked into the area first looked askance at slavery, and then became harder drivers of the blacks than their neighbors. Physicians, gin-wrights, shopkeepers, and overseers all had their eye upon that Ultima Thule, a cotton plantation of seven hundred acres with a troop of slaves to work it.[38]

For shrewd, enterprising men this period of rapid expansion, 1820–1850, offered delightful financial rewards. Whereas the New England farmer was lucky to make three per cent a year, above subsistence, on his investment, the Southern planter frequently made fifteen to thirty. Land was at first cheap; every slave was expected to average six or seven bales of four hundred pounds, selling in the flush years for $48 to $60 a bale. In rich areas of Alabama, Mississippi, Arkansas, and Texas numerous planter-pioneers who had started with nothing achieved within twenty years incomes of $20,000 to $50,000 annually and lived in a style commensurate with their wealth. Even when Ingraham wrote in 1835, however, a peculiar and pernicious system of credit had become deeply rooted. Planters, buying lands on long terms, often commenced with little capital, getting their notes endorsed by some friend. They purchased large tracts and in Davy Crockett's phrase "went ahead," steadily increasing their means but always remaining in debt. Their factors in Natchez, New Orleans, or other cities made advances upon the crops at interest rates

37 M. C. Boyd, *Alabama in the Fifties*, 22.
38 Davis, *Recollections of Mississippi and Mississippians*, 94, 95; Joseph H. Ingraham, *The Southwest by a Yankee*, I, 276, 294ff.

running from eight to twelve per cent, or even much higher; and each advance was conditioned upon an exclusive right to receive and sell the planter's crop. Factors also profited from a concealed interest charge in the shape of credit prices for goods purchased which were distinctly higher than cash prices. Loans were usually made from New Year's to New Year's, and the first of January witnessed a general settlement in every branch of business.[39]

But what of the economics of the slave system in those broad older areas from which population was drained? What of its economics in newer areas after the soil had lost its virgin fertility, and when land cost not $10 an acre but $40, when Negroes which had sold for $700 in 1830 were quoted at $1,500 in 1856, when mess pork which could once have been bought for $10 a barrel commanded $29, and when no speculative increment in land values could be counted upon to help pay the money-lender and commission merchant?[40]

Olmsted at the close of the fifties declared it quite plain that notwithstanding the high price of hands, slave labor was decidedly profitable on the large plantations of Mississippi and other rich lowland cotton regions. Its profits were not only high in comparison with those from slave labor employed elsewhere, but were at least moderately good compared with the return from most investments in the North and in Europe. But the essential question, he pointed out, was not whether slave labor paid at certain times and places; it was whether it was the best-paying form of labor. It had once been profitable to roll Virginia tobacco in casks a hundred miles to market, and to thresh wheat with flails, but it paid still better to employ wagons and threshing machines. Olmsted believed that if it could be certain that in ten years the free-labor system would supersede the slavery system in Mississippi, "twenty years hence the wealth of Mississippi would be at least tenfold what . . . it is likely to be." The slave system, in his opinion, was uneconomic because it mined and depleted the soil, because the slaves gave ignorant, slovenly service, because their use discouraged white industry, and because the sinking of so much capital in Negroes made impossible a proper expenditure on buildings, roads, and implements.[41]

It was not rising land and Negro values alone which deceived many planters as to the profits of the slave system. Failure to institute a cost-accounting system and to analyze income and outgo led to an easy acceptance of the view that all cash surplus meant profit. Agricultural reformers constantly berated planters

39 Alfred H. Stone discusses "The Cotton Factorage System of the Southern States" in the *American Historical Review*, XX, 557ff. See also Gray, *Agriculture in the Southern United States*, II, 712–715. The whole system was inimical to the development of inland concentration markets for cotton.
40 The figures here cited are given by A. M. of Mississippi in the *National Intelligencer*, November 17, 1857.
41 *Journey in the Back Country*, 295, 296.

and farmers for not calculating their expenses. Invisible items, they pointed out, could be uncomfortably real. That shrewd Scot, Thomas Affleck, preached a sermon in the preface to every copy of his much-used plantation account-book: [42]

The plantation is justly chargeable with its own fair cash value at the commencement of the year; and with one year's interest on the same at six per cent. No course of farming can be profitable, which will not pay a fair rate of interest upon the value of the land employed. If, during the year, the planter has expended time and money ditching, hedging, and manuring, or in building and repairing, and in clearing land, the amount stated as its value at the close of the year, may reasonably be more than that alleged at its commencement. If, however, an opposite system has been pursued—crop after crop removed without any return being made in the shape of manure, much of the soil washed away for want of proper tillage, the fencing become poorer and fencing timber scarcer, whilst no improvements of moment have been made—the property cannot be justly valued at as much as it was at the beginning of the year; and thus the difference between the two valuations, is so much out of the year's profits.

And so of negroes, stock, and improvements. It will be readily understood that each year's crop is chargeable with the wear and tear of teams and implements. It is chargeable, with equal justice, with any depreciation in the value of the negroes, occasioned by overwork and improper management. . . . On the other hand, should the number of children have greatly increased during the year; the strength and usefulness of the old been sustained by kind treatment and care; the youngster taught to be useful and perhaps some of the men instructed in trades, and the women in home manufactures, the increased value of the entire force will form a handsome addition to the side of profits.

Those planters who kept detailed accounts usually knew well that they enjoyed no Golconda. The historian of Mississippi slavery concludes that it was by counting the interest on the investment in land and slaves as profit that most planters persuaded themselves that returns were high. On an ordinary six-hundred-acre plantation with fifty slaves, he believes the net profit in the fifties might have averaged $880. This trifling sum, which could be considered the planter's wages for his management, was if anything "too optimistic." [43] Even on the exceptionally fine Polk plantation in Mississippi, worth well over $30,000,

42 *The Cotton [or Sugar] Plantation Record and Account Book.*

43 Sydnor, *Slavery in Mississippi*, 196, 197. No statistics available offer more than precarious support for generalization on the profit or loss of slavery; the census of 1850 was manifestly defective. Moreover, all statistics are subject to varying interpretations. Thomas P. Govan, "Was Plantation Slavery Profitable?", *Journal of Southern History*, Vol. VIII, 513–535, cites authorities on cost-accounting who argue that interest on investment is not expense but profit. He makes other objections to the dark views of U. B. Phillips and C. S. Sydnor. But a planter who borrowed money to invest in land and Negroes (and many did) would find interest on investment a very painful expense.

the average annual income was less than $4,500—from which interest and services had to be deducted. The historian of Georgia slavery cites one wealthy planter, Farish Carter, with fifteen thousand acres, who kept exceptionally detailed records. They show that his return in 1851 was one and a quarter per cent on an investment of $150,000. A fine plantation in the rich Peedee swamplands near Society Hill, S. C., for which we also have full accounts, yielded in 1849 an income of two and seven-tenths per cent on an investment of $161,000. The well-equipped Hopeton Plantation on the Altamaha in Georgia, most carefully managed, returned profits exceeding 3.6 per cent in only four years out of the twelve 1841–1852. According to the *Soil of the South* in 1855, it cost eight cents a pound to produce cotton, and when prices fell below that level planters lost money. The historian of the Georgia institution concludes that slavery was expensive, inefficient, and above all, conducive to wasteful management, for it discouraged proper attention to crop diversification, soil conservation, and scientific methods.[44]

The more thoughtful Southerners deprecated boastful talk of quick and large profits. They insisted that the planter's life had attractions which could not be weighed in money: dignity, leisure, social distinction, an abundant supply of the necessities of life. They maintained that slavery offered the one solution of the race-relations problem. But vaunting assertions about rich plantation returns irritated them as inaccurate, unwholesome, and calculated to put the South in a wrong light. Numerous Southerners, including such ardent believers in slavery as Thomas Cooper, Edmund Ruffin, and Thomas R. Dew, were frankly doubtful whether slave labor had any economic justification save that which the fierce summer climate gave it.[45]

When one Southerner declared in 1855 that a twenty-acre cotton field, growing twenty bales, would yield a profit of four hundred dollars, while a twenty-acre canefield, growing ninety tons of sugar, would yield eighteen hundred dollars, indignant critics sprang up. A cotton-planter of Vicksburg and a sugar-planter of St. Mary's Parish in Louisiana quickly furnished truer figures. The sugar planter pointed out that a twenty-acre field did well, year in and year out, if it produced fifteen or eighteen tons of sugar. A fertile new plantation, in a felicitous season, might yield twenty tons, but this was exceptional. As for ninety!—"your correspondent must have visited Brobdingnag." The price of sugar had for many years past not been above five cents a pound. Altogether, the profits of sugar cultivation were low. They "are less perhaps than those of

44 Flanders, *Plantation Slavery in Georgia*, 221–225; Govan, "Was Plantation Slavery Profitable?" *Journal of Southern History*, VIII, 527–532, for Hopeton Plantation. Once more it must be said that all available statistics leave much to be desired.
45 Flanders, *Idem*, 227.

any other industrial calling in the United States, requiring such an outlay of capital, such heavy expenses, and encountering such constantly recurring risks and vicissitudes attendant on an unsuitable climate; and your correspondent and your readers may be assured that the best we have been able to do of late years has been to provide for the support of our families, the comfort of our slaves, and the education of our children. Those who are much in debt have retrograded, and are likely to continue to do so unless the price improves." [46]

With greater detail, the cotton planter reached the conclusion that the profits of his calling were also modest, considering the risks incurred, and that they by no means achieved the level of twenty dollars an acre described by the correspondent. The only fair estimate, he thought, was based on a fairly improved plantation; "for it is well known to every experienced planter—and how dearly some have purchased their experience!—that the expenses incident to the opening and improving of a plantation, for several years after the undertaking is begun, eat up all the profits and often leave a load of debt behind, sometimes forcing a sale of the whole property." What was the investment in a well-stocked plantation of sixteen hundred acres, twelve hundred of them cleared? The land, valued at the low rate of forty dollars an acre, came to $64,000; the labor force required for cultivating seven hundred and fifty acres in cotton and two hundred and fifty in peas, corn, potatoes, and the like, came to about one hundred and thirty slaves (seventy-five of them effective field hands), which at an average of six hundred dollars apiece would represent $78,000; fifty mules came to $6,500 more; the tools, including a gin, and the miscellaneous livestock reached $4,500; and hence the whole investment could be computed at $150,000. Such a plantation would yield, in an average season, about six hundred bales of cotton, which at eight cents would mean about $18,000 above costs of shipping and selling. [47]

"From this," pursued the Mississippi planter, "must now be deducted the cost of cultivating the place, overseer's wages, clothing and doctoring the Negroes, supplying wear and tear of tools, and losses of mules and stock; altogether, on a place of the size I have named, not falling short of $6,000, many planters estimating their expenses at $100 to the hand, which would make $7,500. Taking it as the former sum and we have the net profits of such a place

46 *National Intelligencer*, July 28, 1855. A successful Louisiana sugar-planter, E. J. Forstall, published in the *National Intelligencer* of February 7, 1854, some interesting statistics on the sugar industry of his State. He computed the cash value of 548 estates at $126,929,000. Three of these estates, he said, had an annual gross return of $350,000 each; two of $325,000 each; and seventy-two at from $200,000 to $300,000 each. We have no estimate of net profits.

47 *National Intelligencer*, July 28, 1855.

as I have described amount to $12,000, being just about an interest of eight per cent on the value of the capital invested." But this planter made no allowance for soil-depletion or his own labor and oversight. In the Northwest money loaned for ordinary developmental purposes often bore ten per cent. Altogether, on such a showing the "opulent" owner of a huge cotton estate, "lord" of a whole village of Negroes, "enjoying" (with much labor and anxiety) an income of $12,000, was not so happily prosperous after all.[48]

[IV]

Growing production-costs, with high prices for slaves always the principal item, made inefficient rule-of-thumb operations more fatal than ever. The fifties, a period of rising values from California to St. Petersburg, brought sharp increases in the price of implements, clothing, and food. But above all, slaves reached unprecedented quotations. In Alabama at the beginning of 1854 vigorous young hands were selling at $1,000 to $1,350, and were hiring at from $80 to $115. A year later, with planters complaining of the extravagant levels, prices had risen again.[49] By 1856 average quotations from prime field hands in Georgia and New Orleans, as computed by U. B. Phillips, had reached nearly $1,600; by 1858, when a "negro fever" was beginning to rage, they had touched $1,700; and by 1860 they had attained the record point of $1,800.[50] Yet at no time in the fifties, save in the one year 1857, were cotton prices so high as in 1839, when slaves had cost but two-thirds of the later quotations.[51] These enhanced labor costs produced an aggressive and growing demand for the reopening of the foreign slave-trade, which projected itself into

48 Yet the wealth of the greater planters impressed the nation. Early in 1859 a paragraph went the rounds of the press describing the 2,100-bale crop of Col. Joseph Bond of Macon, Ga., whose estate was appraised that year at $1,055,000. The Natchez *Free Trader* boasted that the planters of Mississippi and Louisiana did far better. It instanced L. R. Marshall of Louisiana, who grew in that State alone more than 3,500 bales; John Routh of Hard Times, La., who grew fully as much; and Frederick Stanton of Concordia Parish, who had grown 2,800 bales the previous season. Marshall lived in Natchez, owned plantations in Louisiana, Mississippi, and Arkansas, and often produced more than 4,000 bales in all. "The great estate of the two princely planters of this region," said the *Free Trader,* "the late Samuel Davis and Francis Surget, always produced from 3,000 to 5,000 bales each, until their deaths divided the estate among the heirs." Quoted N. Y. *Weekly Tribune,* March 19, 1859.

49 C. C. Clay, Sr., January 9, 1854, H. L. Clay, January 2, 1855, in C. C. Clay Papers, Duke Library.

50 U. B. Phillips, *American Negro Slavery,* table opp. p. 370. One important factor in rising slave prices is stated by Gray, *Agriculture in the Southern United States,* II, 667; by 1860 cotton and sugar were no longer the sole competitors for slaves, for these staples now faced the active competition of a revived and increasingly diversified industry in the border States.

51 Frederic Bancroft, *Slave Trading in the Old South,* 361.

the politics of the period. In the Southern Commercial Convention of 1856 Goulding of Georgia demanded action favorable to this revival, and was warmly seconded by the editor of the Charleston *Standard*.[52]

So marked was the disturbance of the Southern economy by high slave-costs that an Alabama publicist later propounded the view that it promised to bring about the abolition of slavery. The rising generation, he declared, unable to buy slaves, would have been driven into commercial and manufacturing pursuits and into small farming; a free economy would have become paramount over the old slave economy; and emancipation would have followed. "The Negro limited in numbers to the original stock and his offspring had become on his merit too precious an agent of physical development of the country to be longer held as chattel property. The proceeds of his labor were not valuable enough on the market to justify the market value put upon the man as a chattel. He had become more than chattel in the law of co-existent things." [53]

It will be noted that the Mississippi planter whose estimates are given above spoke of the land of a typical 1600-acre plantation as worth but $64,000 while the slaves to work it were worth $75,000. While Francis P. Corbin considered the purchase of a South Carolina rice plantation in 1855, his manager estimated the land, buildings, and equipment at $15,000; the stock and boats at $1,500; and the slaves at $51,200.[54] Yet how many planters accurately computed the costs of their labor? The value of a slave lay in his working years minus his unproductive years. The ordinary slave went to work at ten, became a fully-effective hand at sixteen, and remained highly productive till thirty-five or forty, then slowly declining in value. But if excessively ignorant, indolent, or unruly, his value even in productive years might be small. A slave who injured the roots in plowing cotton, or constantly tried to run away, might be worse than useless. Bennet H. Barrow recognized that there was a right and a wrong way even in cotton-hoeing.[55] Disease might carry a slave off at an early age, accident might maim him, or theft might remove him. Most owners optimistically underestimated the risks attached to slave-owning, and though the insuring of valued servants was by no means unknown, no large-scale insurance systems were attempted. As for procreative capacity, that depended upon factors largely beyond the owner's

52 *National Intelligencer*, December 13, 1856.
53 J. W. DuBose, MS letter to Carl Schurz, "The Southern View," undated, Alabama Department of Archives and History.
54 J. H. Cooper, Hopeton, S. C., March 12, 1855, to F. P. Corbin: Corbin Papers.
55 Edwin Adams Davis, ed., *Plantation Life in the Florida Parishes of Louisiana as Reflected in the Diary of Bennet H. Barrow*, 71ff. Dr. Davis's introduction illuminates every aspect of slavery.

control, and few even of semi-professional slave-breeders studied the problem as a present-day cattleman would study its risks and profits.[56]

The first scientific study of the life-expectancy of slaves based on really adequate data was contained in the Maryland census returns for 1850, published two years later. The conditions of slavery in that border State were mild. Yet the carefully-compiled tables showed that the average life-expectancy of whites was distinctly higher than that of slaves. At birth a white person might expect to live 44.6 years, a female slave 41.3 years, and a male slave 40.3 years. At the age of twenty a white person had a further life-expectancy of 42.2 years, a female slave of 40.6 years, and a male slave of 40.3 years. At forty all three might expect to live about the same period; the white person 28.7 years, the female slave 29.3 and the male slave 27.8. From an economic standpoint the fact to be noted is that even where slavery wore its most beneficent face, the life expectancy of a male slave at birth was but 40.3 years. As until he was ten he certainly did not pay for his rearing, the master in effect obtained an average of thirty years' productive labor from the slave born on his place—though health, temper, diligence, and intelligence might vary from good to bad. [57]

Much less favorable are the statistics given by the registrar whom South Carolina under a law of 1853 directed to compile data respecting births, deaths, and marriages. His returns were admittedly highly incomplete. But he did claim fair accuracy for his statements on the average age of death for whites and blacks, since they were calculated from known and precise data only, excluding all deaths at unknown ages. His tables for 1856 showed one death for every 129.52 whites, and one death for every 54.76 slaves. For the following year, when the statistics were much fuller, they showed one death for every 97.19 whites, and one for every 43.89 slaves. These statistics are dubious. But much greater confidence may be placed in his estimate that the average age of whites and free Negroes at death was 28.03, and that of slaves was 21.13. How many South Carolinians, looking happily at their year's list of newborn slaves, knew that the average Negro would barely reach full maturity? Such considerations made slaveholding a gamble, and at $1,800 a hand, a bad gamble.[58]

Some districts were especially unhealthy, and some groups of slaves especially susceptible to sickness. The Weehaw rice plantation had 266 slaves in the fall of 1855, and during 1857 there were 40 deaths, of which 21 were infants of

---

56 Flanders, *Plantation Slavery in Georgia*, ch. 9.

57 See the elaborate review of the Maryland tables in the *National Intelligencer*, June 12, 1852. It must of course be remembered that the life expectancy of the free Negroes is still below that of whites.

58 The Charleston Society Library has the annual report of Dr. Robert W. Gibbes, State Registrar, for 1856, and the South Carolina State Archives at Columbia, the annual report for 1857. The principal causes stated for deaths among slaves were pneumonia, typhoid, and dropsy; among whites they were diarrhea, pneumonia, and typhoid.

one year or less. The total number of deaths in the six years 1856–61 was 122. Fifteen slaves died of lockjaw, and eleven of diarrhea and dysentery—that is, bad diet.[59] James H. Hammond kept fairly careful vital statistics for his plantations. They show that from the end of 1831 to the fall of 1854 the total slave births were 223 and the total deaths were 235, a decrease of a dozen hands. When he had taken over the property he had found there a stock of 147 slaves, property of his wife's family—"the Fitzsimons Negroes." They had included many elderly slaves, and the deaths among them were 184 and the births only 165. Among the Negroes he later bought the deaths had been 51 and the births 58.

Totalling up these figures, Hammond declared in his journal that they were "awful," and quite apart from the pecuniary loss very distressing to him. For over twenty years he had done everything possible to preserve their health, making ample provision of clothing, food, and housing, permitting no overwork, and keeping the plantation sanitary. But four of the Fitzsimons families had scrofula, syphilis existed in "many others," and one marsh plantation possessed such a bad mortality record that the slaves were utterly panic-stricken. "My purchases have been chiefly of low country negroes, subject more or less to all of the same taints and they also readily become demoralized."[60]

Yet planters insouciantly took the heaviest risks. Records of Alexander F. Pugh of Louisville show that early in 1859, having made a sugar crop which would pay him $27,000, he went to New Orleans and invested $21,000 or $22,000 of this in Negroes. He bought eight women and six men, paying from $1,325 to $1,400 for the women, and from $1,600 to $1,700 for the men, with $2,500 for a blacksmith. "Negroes are high and so are sugar and molasses," he wrote—but the sugar prices might soon fall, while his capital charges for the Negroes would remain exorbitant.[61]

Now and then a conspicuous Southerner would frankly confess his losses.

---

59 Weehaw Plantation Book, Charleston Historical Society.

60 Plantation Records, 1831–55, South Caroliniana Library. In the interesting "Description of Life Among the Slaves, 1858," printed in J. H. Easterby's *The South Carolina Rice Plantation as Revealed in the Papers of Robert F. W. Allston*, 345–350, the writer, a physician of twenty-two years' experience who had been a regular medical attendant on twenty-five or thirty rice plantations of about three thousand slaves, testified to the solicitous care generally taken of slaves' health in this area. "The advice of the Physician is generally sought in all serious illness," he wrote. "Each plantation has its Medical attendant. . . ." Professional consultations over Negroes he had found quite common. "In Surgical cases the advice of the most distinguished and experienced of the profession is frequently had at a pecuniary cost from which the humanity of the Rice planter never shrinks, although I have known it in a few instances to exceed the value of the slave."

61 Pugh Collection, University of Texas Archives. Cf. the entry in the diary of H. C. Anderson in the University of Louisiana Archives, September 24, 1859: "I went to Memphis 22d Sept. and purchased two negroes one 23 years of age the other 12 years the first $1450 the other $1200 likely boys but an enormous price."

Senator Hammond, whose management of his estates deserved the word superb, felt near the end of his career that he would have done far better to remain at the South Carolina bar. At the age of twenty-four he had attained eminence as a lawyer. But his wife then had nearly 150 slaves and ten thousand acres, and loved country life. He relates the unhappy sequel: [62]

Looking over everything and yielding to the wishes of my wife, I left Columbia and my profession, to take charge of an estate whose *nett* income was about $775 as shown by Paul Fitzsimons management for 4 years with the overseer of the highest reputation at that time in the two States—Brooks. Had I learned what I have since learned about planting nothing could have induced me to give up my profession and embark in the *forlorn* hope of making more from a plantation. . . . The negroes had increased during these four years, of which I then thought very little. But I soon found that this increase was owing to their doing so little—that they were utterly rotten from having been physicked for many years at the Marsh and the moment I applied the test—put them to work—they died off like rotten sheep. . . . The lands were no better, I cleared, manured, and ditched, but in three or four years I found it *would not do.* . . . In 1838, I divided the whole into separate tracts and offered it for sale. I then purchased and built in Columbia, where I moved in 1840–41, intending to buy in the West and abandon this worthless property. Give it up to the wilderness—as alas I am about to do now.

But in 1841 I ascertained that there was accessible marl at Shell Bluff, and not wishing to abandon So. Ca. I changed my whole plan and commenced to haul marl. I had already cleared nearly all the land I planted. I marked it with high hopes. As far back as 1834 I had conceived the idea of draining what is now known as Cypress Pond, Green Branch, Long Pond, etc. . . . In 1845 under the stimulus imparted by the *hopes* I had of marl, I went into these operations. I drained and marled these lands. Afterwards I drained (having purchased it) Cowden. I incurred the expenses of the Governor's office for 2 years. . . . I kept open house always. I educated my children in the best manner. . . . But by burying myself in the woods of Silver Bluff, by self-denial and indefatigable labor, I have now at this moment 300 slaves and two plantations comprising over 10,000 acres (exclusive of Redcliffe) that are equal to any in fertility in the Union and am not in debt over and above them more than $10,000 . . .

I must sell everything that can be sold. The slaves who for all my life have been my associates, friends, and faithful co-laborers. Every tie with them must be broken, for no one will perpetuate them as I had fondly hoped. I must let my marled and drained lands, the true labour of my life, go to ruin. Filled up ditches, waste old fields, dilapidated negro houses, barns, stables, mills, and fences are to be the things to be seen below, which I will never see.

Reserving what is required for Redcliffe and my debts, I cannot expect all the rest I own to sell for over $175,000, for the lands I do not propose to sell at all. They are worth $200,000. They could not be sold for $40,000. Let them perish.

62 Hammond Papers, S. Caroliniana Library, date in or near 1857.

[V]

The indictment of slavery by such Northern economists as Francis Bowen of Harvard and such British writers as J. E. Cairnes of Dublin University rested on several main foundations.[63] They argued that slavery was adapted only to agriculture; that it required large capital; and that its inefficiency tended to keep proprietors in debt. They maintained that it degraded and expelled free labor, and discouraged all industrialism. In doing so it kept the section impoverished; for, wrote Bowen, no population chiefly or wholly devoted to agriculture can become wealthy, since it must exchange the product of rude labor for that of skilled labor—must exchange the work of three, five, or ten persons for that of one. The poor men whom it discouraged from undertaking free labor became idle, demoralized, and poverty-stricken. Meanwhile, slave labor, devoted to a few great staples, fastened on the most fertile soil, exhausted it, and moved on. Being wasteful, it had to be expansive, and being expansive, aggressive.

It was true that while slavery did not necessarily involve soil-exhaustion, a fact proved by the Virginia and Maryland planters who used slaves to reclaim wornout fields by soil-replenishing crops and fertilizers, its tendency was strongly in that direction.[64] In flush times most cotton-planters were irresistibly tempted to expand the unit of production. Only intensive or diversified cultivation could preserve the soil. Both small and large planters in the Lower South were guilty of depleting their lands in the most improvident manner. Representative Hiram Warner of Georgia told the House that every slaveholder "knows perfectly well that, when slavery is confined within certain special limits, its future existence is doomed; it is only a question of time as to its final destruction." Take any county largely devoted to cotton and sugar, and confine the existing slave population to its limits. "Such is the rapid natural increase of the slaves, and the rapid exhaustion of the soil from the cultivation of those crops . . . that within a few years it would be impossible to support them within the limits of each county." The same result would follow if slavery were kept within strict State limits; the soil would fail and the master and slave face ruin. Slavery, he declared, constantly "requires fresh lands." Another Representative objected that two-thirds of Georgia was unimproved land, and that the census of 1850 showed that three-quarters of the land in the South was

---

63 Bowen's *The Principles of Political Economy Applied to the Condition, the Resources, and the Institutions of the American People* (first ed. 1856) devotes a large part of its eighth chapter to slavery, as an illustration of the disadvantages in the exchange of rude products for manufactures.
64 Cf. U. B. Phillips, *Life and Labor in the Old South*, 137.

still unoccupied.[65] But this merely bore out the Cairnes-Bowen thesis that slavery seized on the richest acres.

Warner's statement was echoed by hundreds both friendly and unfriendly to slavery. Hinton Rowan Helper summed up one broad section of his indictment of slavery in a sentence: "It must continually be fed by new fields and forests, to be wasted and wilted under the poisonous tread of the slave." [66] C. C. Clay, Jr., expressed alarm in the middle fifties over the rapid depopulation of parts of Alabama. The State was full, he remarked, of sad memorials of soil-exhaustion by ruthless and ignorant cotton-cropping. Of the twenty million dollars realized annually from Alabama's cotton, nearly all that was not required to support the producers was reinvested in land and slaves. "Our small planters, after taking the cream of their lands, unable to restore them by rest, manures, or otherwise, are going farther West and South, in search of other virgin lands, which they may and will despoil and impoverish in like manner. Our wealthier planters, with greater means and no more skill, are buying out their poorer neighbors, extending their plantations, and adding to their slave force. The wealthy few . . . are thus pushing off the many who are merely independent." In some counties white population had fallen and black population risen almost *pari passu*. Clay spoke of Madison: [67]

In traversing that county, one will discover numerous farmhouses, once the abode of industrious and intelligent freemen, now occupied by slaves, or tenantless, deserted, and dilapidated; he will observe fields, once fertile, now unfenced, abandoned, and covered with those evil harbingers, foxtail and broomsedge; he will see the moss growing on the mouldering walls of once thrifty villages, and will find 'one only master grasps the whole domain' that once furnished happy hopes for a dozen white families. Indeed, a country in its infancy, where fifty years ago scarce a forest tree had been felled by the axe of the pioneer, is already exhibiting the painful signs of senility and decay apparent in Virginia and Carolina.

Slavery, observed D. R. Goodloe of North Carolina in a realistic analysis published in 1853, seemed able to bring about the rapid settlement of new

65 Warner is cited and answered by Representative William Cumback of Indiana, *Cong. Globe*, December 17, 1856.
66 *The Impending Crisis*, 112, 113.
67 Quoted in pamphlet. *The Election and the Candidates*, 1856, Huntington Library. The N. Y. *Herald*, in a letter from a Georgia correspondent in August, 1860, described the home of Alexander H. Stephens with remarkable frankness. Crawfordville, about sixty miles west of Augusta on the Georgia Railroad, it thought one of the most miserable, weatherbeaten, unpainted county towns in the country. "The court-house would, in some regions, be deemed rather unfit for a horse-stable. It is very small, dingy, and damp. The doors and windows are so old and shabby that the rain dashes in. All around the wretched old court-house are the signs of decay seen everywhere. There is one institution that flourishes—the grog-shop." Quoted in N. Y. *Weekly Tribune*, September 1, 1860.

districts and States. When it became necessary for the planters of older areas to migrate westward, as those of Virginia and the Carolinas had done, they made whole counties blossom in a sudden rush. "Northern Mississippi and Southwestern Tennessee were almost as densely peopled in this way in the first three years of their existence as they are at the present moment. Towns and villages sprang up with the first influx of population, surpassing in size and beauty the interior towns of the older States." But what caused this migration? It was soil-exhaustion. When the land deteriorated, as it was bound to do under slavery, enterprising, intelligent, and farsighted men sought new homes. A touch of bitterness entered Goodloe's exposition. "It may seem a paradox, and yet it is true," he observed, "that a community of planters may grow rich while they are impoverishing and depopulating their country. Take, for instance, one of the most fertile districts of Alabama or Mississippi. . . . Large planters go in and buy up the best lands, and set their slaves to cutting down the timber and planting. In a few years the soil is exhausted, and the country is actually poorer and has less money value than when the first settlement was made. The planters have invested their large profits not in substantial houses, fences, and other improvements, but in Virginia negroes. They have grown rich and ruined their adopted country . . . and are now ready to emigrate further." [68]

If some parts of the South were prosperous, Goodloe concluded, "it is because the large admixture of free population has given rise to other interests and occupations than planting, thereby retaining some vitality in the body public." This was true of farming areas of Eastern Virginia and the Carolinas, and of many parts of the Southwest.

In districts where the friable soil was specially subject to erosion the consequences of slipshod cultivation were sometimes frightening. A writer who toured the South in 1854 wrote that near Vicksburg he passed several families migrating to Texas. One, with a large gang of Negroes, had settled in northern Mississippi several years before, cut down the forest, and destroyed the best part of the soil in seven crops of cotton. They were now off to ruin more land: [69]

And this is not an individual case, for ten thousand others have done just so before, until all the country south of the Potomac is dotted over and blemished by countless numbers of these old wornout plantations. This particular feature of a 'peculiar institution' is more glaring, more revolting in the western counties of Mississippi than anywhere else, because owing to the extreme uneven surface, and the semi-soluble nature of the soil, it was started on its way to the Gulf quicker and with greater rapidity than any other after

68 N. Y. *Tribune*, August 27, 1853.
69 N. Y. *Tribune*, August 30, 1854.

the arrival of the ruthless destroyer. . . . It is a common thing all through this section to see the corn and cotton stalks of the last crop standing upon ridges with gullies between the rims so deep as to render all future cultivation almost impossible, and rarely if ever undertaken. These gullied fields are innumerable, and eventually the whole plantation ruined and abandoned. . . .

I passed a small stream called Ceolese Creek, which a planter who lives on the bank said he had often crossed in flood time by cutting a small tree to fall across the channel. Now the banks are half a mile apart in places, and going every year down the Mississippi.

From the economic standpoint one of the worst features was the constant enlargement of the scale of operations.[70] In the Lower South particularly planters bought more slaves and land to make more cotton to buy more slaves and land. Georgia, like Alabama, witnessed during the fifties a concentration of attention upon cotton, a centralization of slavery-ownership in a relatively smaller part of the population, and an expansion of the unit of production. Year after year, progressive agriculturists and editors insisted that crops should be diversified, and that Georgia should become more nearly sufficient in meats and maize. They urged the advantages of moderately-sized and carefully-tilled holdings.[71] Yet despite these pleas, the dominant trends were never checked. While population grew by 17 per cent and cotton production rose, Georgia stood still in corn-culture and fell back in some types of livestock. Since both the number and prices of slaves were rising, capital invested in Negroes increased by 84.3 per cent in the decade. But this capital remained narrowly held, for the slaveowners were a smaller proportion of the population in 1860 than in 1850. Moreover, the large slaveholders, with fifty Negroes or more, rose by forty per cent while the general class of slave-

70 See Gray, *Agriculture in the Southern United States*, II, 706ff.

71 Southerners might have remembered that George Washington always emphasized two principles at Mount Vernon. One was that his plantation should be as nearly self-sufficing as possible, a standing order to his overseers being to "buy nothing you can make within yourselves." The other was assiduous experimentation, for he gave careful trial to different fertilizers, to the most improved farming tools and machinery, to various kinds of tobacco, wheat, and other crops, and to different modes of tillage. In inquiring for an overseer he said that the man must be one "who can bring worn out and gullied Lands into good tilth in the shortest time." Paul Leicester Ford, *The True George Washington*, 119–121.

James L. Orr, in his address to the South Carolina Institute in 1855, said that the pecuniary and personal comfort of the people "would be greatly promoted if the planters in this State were all transformed into farmers. That policy is most pernicious which prompts the planter to swell the number of his cotton bales, and sends him into the provision market to buy his provisions, and into the livestock market to buy the animals used and consumed on the plantation." Not merely would income improve, and lands grow more fertile, but the change would better the character of the owners. "The system, order, personal supervision, and care for small matters which this change would initiate will beget economy, a personal virtue which our planters do not in preeminent degree possess." *National Intelligencer*, June 5, 1855.

holders increased by only 6.8 per cent. The big plantations increased their total acreage as compared with the small or moderate holdings.[72]

[VI]

The double thesis that slavery immobilized an excessive amount of capital, and that it meanwhile discouraged the enterprise of non-slaveholding whites, was vigorously upheld by Southern and Northern critics alike. Goodloe argued that while money invested in slaves might often return a handsome profit to the owner, it was relatively unproductive to the community. The Southern planter had to pay $10,000 for ten able-bodied hands, while the same sum bought the Northern farmer several hundred acres, with a comfortable house, fences, and livestock. If the Southerner hired his Negroes as free labor, then he would be able to invest his $10,000 fruitfully. As capital accumulated in Pennsylvania or Illinois, it was devoted to objects of permanent value to the community; to roads, bridges, canals, factories, ships, or banks. They enriched the district, stimulated the demand for free labor, and multiplied production. But in Mississippi or Texas the annual profits of planting were for the most part invested in slaves purchased from outside. "That which induces labor to go to Ohio is the employment of capital in Ohio. That which draws labor to Texas is the investment of capital in Virginia in the form of slaves." [73]

The same argument was given a fuller statement by Cassius M. Clay of Kentucky. The three million slaves of the South did only half the effective work of a similar number of whites in the North, he asserted, because they could not have the skill, the energy, or the stimulus of self-interest. "The twelve millions of capital invested in the slaves is a dead loss to the South. . . . Whatever mechanical talent or intellect there is in the three millions of slaves is lost forever for want of education; whatever mind capable of achieving anything in the laborious departments of human knowledge and mechanism there is in the free five millions, is almost entirely lost because indolence is the fixed habit of the people, industry the exception." [74]

Nobody expounded this double thesis with more ardor than Olmsted. Suppose, he wrote, that a Northern farmer and Southern planter have each

---

72 An interesting controversy raged between Dr. N. B. Cloud of Alabama, and Dr. M. W. Philips of Mississippi, on the optimum size of plantations. Cloud advocated not more than four acres to the hand, half of it in cotton, with careful planting, tillage, and manuring; Philips urged twenty or more acres to the hand, about half of it cotton and the rest corn and small grain, with the use of every possible labor-saving device. For the actual trend, see A. C. Cole, *Changes in Sentiment in Georgia Toward Secession 1850–60*, University of Illinois M. A. thesis.

73 N. Y. *Tribune*, August 27, 1853.

74 *Speeches and Writings of C. M. Clay*, 324.

fifteen thousand dollars to spend. While the Southerner uses the money for more slaves brought from the border area, with a trifle for new tools, the Northerner uses it for buildings, roads, fertilizers, and machinery. The Southerner gains no increase of home comfort or community welfare; the Northerner gains both. Olmsted had found that the Southwest was sprinkled with men who, having begun ten or fifteen years earlier with nothing but half a dozen Negroes, were now quite rich men. Nor was this at all astonishing when the cheapness of the land and the fact that cotton-prices had doubled within a decade were considered. "But in what else besides Negroes were these rich men better off than when they called themselves poor? . . . There was . . . the same bacon and corn, the same slough of a wagon channel through the forest, the same bare walls in their dwellings, the same absence of taste in art and literature, the same distance from schools and churches and educated advisers, and . . . the same makeshift furniture." [75]

That the poor whites, the ignorant, backward people who, wrote Gregg, "live in comparative nakedness and starvation," were a peculiar Southern problem, had long been recognized. White squalor was easily discoverable at the North; in city slums, through the Pennsylvania Appalachians, and in the Indiana backwoods. But in extent, depth, and caste-distinctness, even if allowance be made for the fact that many who *looked* like poor whites were really small farmers and cattle-raisers of some property, Southern poverty was unique.[76]

It is of course erroneous to say that slavery was the main reason for the existence of the degraded poor-white class, which had existed when Byrd wrote his *History of the Dividing Line* and which has survived to fascinate scores of modern sociologists. The poor white of 1850 was in fact not markedly different from the poor white described in books of 1930. Rudimentary education; widespread male illiteracy; skills limited to simple farm operations; pellagra and other ailments of malnutrition common; housing and clothing inadequate; early marriages productive of large families; recreations limited to neighborhood family visitings, community fiddlings, and meetings at the smithy or cotton-gin; caste lines between well-to-do whites and mean whites

75 *Journey in the Back Country,* 323–325.
76 On the poor white, see D. R. Hundley, *Social Relations in Our Southern States* (1860); the paper by Charles T. James in De Bow's *Industrial Resources of the South and West;* the writings of William Gregg; and the five-column article by George M. Weston, "The Poor Whites of the South," in the N. Y. *Weekly Tribune,* February 9, 1856. Walter Hines Page wrote a vivid description of the poor-white area of North Carolina as he saw it with fresh eyes after a New York sojourn. It occurred to him for the first time that "this region is a frontier"; Burton J. Hendrick, *The Training of An American,* 161, 162. On the literary side, see Shields McIlwaine, *The Southern Poor Whites: From Lubberland to Tobacco Road.* But the *destitution* of the poor whites has been exaggerated. See the writings of Frank L. and Harriet Owsley, and W. T. Couch, ed., *Culture in the South.*

closely observed, so that even at political meetings the poor whites kept on the outskirts; knowledge of the outer world ludicrously scant; indolence general— such was the picture in both periods. In both eras, too, the poor whites took an attitude toward the Negroes radically different from that of upper-class whites, showing more jealousy, more fear of Negro "aggression," and less hope of exploiting the blacks, but an equal desire to keep them in their places. Knowing that the upper-class whites were contemptuous of them, and feeling their lives full of frustrations, they were nevertheless prone to identify themselves with their economic and social superiors.[77]

But that slavery was one element in producing the poor-white problem and in keeping it formidable many thoughtful Southerners agreed. By bringing manual labor into disrepute, discouraging diversified industry, cutting off wage-opportunities, excluding poor farmers from the richest and most accessible land, starving education, and restricting governmental action to the interests of the slaveholder, it spread and accentuated that poverty which exists in all lands and times.

Fanny Kemble, vividly describing the Tobacco Road whites she saw, "the most degraded race of human beings claiming an Anglo-Saxon origin that can be found on the face of the earth, filthy, lazy, ignorant, brutal, proud, penniless savages," connected them with slavery.[78] Helper's *Impending Crisis* was written for and to the non-slaveholding Southerners, the "stupid and sequacious masses" whose "unparalleled illiteracy and degradation" he declared were perpetuated by the slave system. It was pointed out in the constitutional convention of Kentucky in 1849 that, according to the second auditor's reports, of the 70,707 white families in the State, 35,540 or about one-half, did not average $100 in property, and 21,783 families had less than $100. One delegate, a physician, spoke of the anguish he had often shared in attending the deathbeds of parents who knew that they left their children destitute of everything; even of a fair education, for the State did not provide it.[79] There was no lack of Kentuckians to connect this white poverty with slavery. Even in Missouri an observer of strong Southern temper, opposed to abolition, wrote in 1852: [80]

Every body knows that no slave state will flourish like a free state. A poor man, or one who does not own slaves, no matter how intellectual or pious he

77 Cf. John Dollard, *Caste and Class in a Southern Town;* Clarence Cason, *90° in the Shade;* and Allison Davis, B. B. Gardner, and Mary R. Gardner, *Deep South: A Social Anthropological Study of Caste and Class.* This last is a rather appalling study of the modern Natchez area.
78 *Journal of a Residence on a Georgian Plantation in 1838-39.*
79 *Debates and Proceedings,* 896, 897.
80 George Patterson, Millville, Mo., Dec. 4, no year, to G. W. Julian; Julian Papers, Indiana State Historical Library.

may be, is despised by the most pious slave holder. Even the children of the slave holder seem to me to shun the children of the poor white man, who does not own slaves. I have often thought that the working men, the mechanics and laboring men of the free states, act like fools in their opposition to abolition lecturers, when if these same white working men were in the slave states, they would be despised (unless they owned niggers). Many of them would be placed along side of a big odoriferous buck negro and would receive about as much respect. I admit that slavery is the hotbed of pride and is a prolific source of castes in society. . . .

I never knew a slaveholder permit his son to learn a trade. They seem to think it disgraceful to work at mechanical vocations. They must all be preachers, merchants, lawyers, or doctors or gentlemen blackguards. True, there are white mechanics and excellent men here, but they acknowledge that there is a coldness shown towards them by the slave holders unless the working man owns negroes.

The before-mentioned correspondent of the New York *Herald*, describing in 1860 the shabby, down-at-the-heels aspect of Alexander H. Stephens's town of Crawfordsville, indulged in a bit of frankness unusual in that very pro-Southern journal. "If the score of idlers who lounge and loiter would set to work," he wrote, "all could soon be changed. The old fields would be cultivated, the old houses renewed, painted, and furnished. But then it is not for white men to do such work, and the negroes are off on the plantations picking cotton." [81]

A hundred travellers and a thousand native observers, indeed, observed the truth of what Jesse Burton Harrison had written of Virginia in 1832, that slavery stigmatized and paralyzed free labor.[82]

[VII]

It was with this human erosion, this waste of labor, brains, and character, in view, that dozens of home reformers urged the development of manufactures and trade in the South. They deplored "the notion of young men that training in handicrafts caused them to lose caste in society." [83] They pointed hopefully to the success of the cotton factories at Prattsville, Ala., founded by Daniel Pratt, a New Englander, at Graniteville, S. C., founded by William Gregg, a Virginian, and numerous other points; to the tobacco factories at Richmond, the bagging-mills of Louisville, the iron-works of Alabama and Virginia, and the abundant tanneries, grist-mills, and saw-mills. But the scarcity of capital and skills was an

81 Quoted in N. Y. *Weekly Tribune*, September 1, 1860.
82 "Review of the Slave Question," *American Quarterly Review*, December, 1832.
83 *De Bow's Review*, XVI, 453; XXIV, 382.

impediment to any sturdy development of industrialism. What manufacturing did attain vigor was chiefly in the primary transformation of raw materials—in mining, tanning, lumbering, and the cruder uses of cotton, flax, and tobacco. Growth from 1840 to 1860 was in most respects slow. The year 1850 found about 164,000 hands employed in industrial establishments in the South, and by 1860 the number had advanced only to 189,500.[84]

Northern observers made much of the extent to which their section, and particularly the Northwestern States, attracted migrants from the Southern area. While a mere trickle of Northerners went into the South to grow cotton, to grind cane, or to establish stores, a veritable flood of Southerners poured across the Ohio to gain free soil. According to the census of 1850, the six Northwestern States contained no fewer than 516,000 persons who had been born in slave areas. This was about five-sevenths of the number (744,000) who had been born in the Middle Atlantic area; it was roughly equivalent to the number (556,000) born abroad; and it was nearly three times as many as the number (176,000) born in New England. Why had this great army of Southerners left the region of the "peculiar institution" to breathe a free atmosphere?

Some, no doubt, were yeomen whites like Thomas Lincoln, who found the society of Illinois or Indiana more congenial than that of any slave State. As a native of Ohio, born of Virginia parents, wrote in the Scioto *Gazette* in 1854, men without property were often "feelingly taught how poor a thing a poor white man who labors for a living is usually considered, both by slaves and slave-owners, in a slaveholding State." Some were men who, like the North Carolina Quakers who sought Indiana to form important communities, wished to rear their children in districts free both from slavery and a perplexing race-problem. But the great majority must have been men who felt not social, nor moral, nor cultural impulses (though all may have been intermingled), so much as an economic incentive. They believed that a poor white man could get ahead faster in Indiana or Illinois than in Alabama or Louisiana.

Were they in error in so believing? The annual value of the great staple crops of the South, cotton, sugar, and rice, was in 1850 more than twenty dollars an acre; the value of the principal Northern crops, corn, wheat, and potatoes, was less than ten dollars an acre. But the costs of cultivation were far cheaper in the Northwest. Railroads, canals, and factories were far more numerous there, so that transportation charges were lower and markets nearer. In 1850 the average value of land in the Northwestern States was $11.39; the average value in the Southern States was $5.34, and in the Southwestern States $6.26. It might be added that much of the Southern land was rapidly becoming worthless, while most of that in the Northwest was steadily augmenting in value. Indeed, no less

84 Edward Ingle, *Southern Sidelights*, 81, 82, 349.

expert an observer of a later generation than William Allen White was to find that a great deal of the prosperity of the Western agriculturist 1850–1914 was built upon the rise in land values—a rise which took place while Southern lands were almost static. A caustic writer, "Northwest," noted that in 1850 the 22,192,000 acres of improved land in Virginia, North Carolina, and Georgia had been worth $380,100,000, while the 19,938,000 acres of improved land in Ohio, Indiana, and Illinois had been worth $590,000,000. So much, he asserted, for the blighting effects of slavery! [85]

Another anonymous writer drew the contrast in even more drastic terms. The free society of the North, he wrote, made constant and huge investments of its surplus in houses, furniture, machine-shops, factories, furnaces, shipping, railroads, and canals, but above all in improvements on the land. In the eight States around New York city (the States touching the coast from Massachusetts to Delaware inclusive), the improvements on the farms—in buildings, drainage, fencing, and soil maintenance—were, he thought, largely responsible for the valuation of $35 an acre set on the cultivated lands. In the five cotton States, with their wasteful system of agriculture, improvements were so few and meagre that the land was valued at only $6 an acre. Meanwhile, the eight Northern States named had invested approximately one and a half billion dollars in furnaces, factories, mills, machine shops and the like, and nearly a quarter of a billion in roads and canals. The South had an unimportant investment in such facilities. In the five cotton States, there was a mile of railroad or canal for every eighty square miles of territory; in the eight Northern States, a mile of transportation for every eleven square miles. "If the 2,060,000 of white population in the five States consume to the value of $50 in clothing and furniture for each person," wrote the author, "we cannot understand how they pay for it—for their surplus for all purposes, except food, is less than $60,000,000, and probably not exceeding $50,000,000." [86]

That the South was economically backward in comparison with the North nobody could doubt. That numerous factors entered into this backwardness, causing and conditioning it, was equally clear. Its soil was less productive than that of the Middle Atlantic or Northwestern States. Its mineral resources were less valuable, and were more difficult to reach. Its harbors were not so good as those of the North, and they lay farther from the European markets. The Southern climate did not encourage energetic year-round labor. Even had the South possessed a free society, all these factors would have handicapped it severely. But slavery undoubtedly constituted an additional disability

85 For the letters of "Northwest" and "Southwest" see *National Intelligencer*, February 17, 1855. See also De Bow's *Statistical View of the United States* (his compendium of the census of 1850).
86 Anonymous, *The Five Cotton States and New York* (1861).

of the severest character. It discouraged industrialism, to which it was indeed sharply inimical. It threw into discredit the labor of the white artisan, and even cast suspicion upon all employments not connected with the soil. Together with the hot climate and the lack of varied industries, it repelled those immigrants who did so much to enrich the rest of America. And in agriculture it tied the South to a slovenly and wasteful staple-crop system, while it fostered a plantation economy which decade by decade squeezed hard the petty tiller of the soil, the independent yeoman in whose hands Jefferson had hoped to see the American future placed.

[VIII]

More and more clearly, defenders of slavery were driven back from economic to social ground. Unable to enter any sweeping defence of it as a business, they could declare that as a way of life it was blessed with high advantages. From the time that Thomas R. Dew described slavery as "the ideal basis of a perfect civilization," [87] and Henry Hughes in his *Treatise on Sociology* defended it with the daring vigor and uncompromising boldness of the Mississippi frontier, intransigent Southerners insisted that it not only offered the one possible solution of the race-adjustment problem, but also the most humane and frictionless solution of the labor problem.

Indeed, celebrations of the social and cultural advantages of slavery can be traced back much further still. The Southern argument from the opening of the nineteenth century, long before the rise of abolitionist propaganda, had a dozen facets: a Biblical exegesis, a clatter of pseudo-scientific 'anthropology' on the supposed racial inferiority of the blacks, an exposition of historical precedents, and so on. But two of the most important were a comparison of the graces, comforts, and patriarchal geniality of slavery with the brutalities and indecencies of industrialism, and a glorification of the opportunities for the development of character and the flowering of a leisurely culture which slavery offered. This gospel had at first to combat the old attitude that slavery was a necessary evil, not a positive good. But it took root and spread like a banyan tree, until the great majoriy of Southerners gave it intellectual assent. Books, pamphlets, and magazine articles expounding it sprang up in a mushroom efflorescence. [88]

Realizing that the combination of labor and capital in one investment was difficult to defend economically, this new school of thought extolled it on

87 *The Pro-Slavery Argument, As Maintained by the Most Distinguished Writers of the Southern States* (1853), 313ff.
88 See William Sumner Jenkins, *Pro-Slavery Thought in the Old South*, especially ch. 7; William B. Hesseltine, "Some New Aspects of the Pro-Slavery Argument," *Journal of Negro History*, XXI, 5ff.

broader grounds. By integrating labor and capital, slavery largely erased the conflict of interests so painful in other economic systems—so the ingenious argument ran. Wherever slavery spread, declared Benjamin F. Stringfellow of Missouri, "the interest of the laborer and the capitalist, the slave and his master, are identical; they cannot conflict." The Northern factory system, growled Southern writers, exploited and exhausted labor. But in the South the capitalist must strengthen, protect, and preserve his worker, for slavery *was* capital. T. R. R. Cobb asserted that perhaps no solution of the great problem of protecting labor and capital from the mutual encroachments of one another "is so simple and effective as Negro slavery." [89] William J. Grayson, in the preface to *The Hireling and the Slave*, declared that if slavery was subject to abuses, it had its advantages as well. "It establishes more permanent and kinder relations between capital and labor. It removes what John Stuart Mill calls 'the widening and embittering feud between the class of labor and the class of capital.' It draws the relation closer between master and servant. . . . The most wretched feature in hireling labor is the isolated, miserable creature who has no home, no food, and in whom no one is particularly interested. This is seen among hirelings only."

In brief, slavery was defended as the socio-economic system which did more than any other to establish an identity of interest between employer and employed. It gave lifelong support to labor, furnished a partial community of property, and embodied some of the essential principles of socialism; so the theme ran. "This union of labor and capital," boasted the *Southern Literary Messenger* in 1857, "counteracts . . . all those social, moral, material, and political evils which afflict the North." [90] Southern society, warmhearted, sympathetic, social-minded, and more interested in self-cultivation than moneymaking, was painted by W. L. Yancey as happier and more elevated than the materialistic Northern society, where, said he, "the masses are day-laboreres, confined closely and unintermittingly to the work shop, the factory, and the field." The Southern system "recognizes that man has a heart as well as a head." [91] And, incidentally, said *Russell's Magazine*, while the hireling-slaves of the North frequently died of starvation, and crime ran riot among them, the bond-slaves of the South were protected from all mischances, and stayed virtuous and orderly because "every master is a conservator of peace and good morals." [92]

The manufacture of this myth was much more than a piece of intellectual diversion. It deluded even its makers, as oft-repeated myths always do. When Representative Holmes of South Carolina helped escort John Quincy Adams'

89 *Inquiry Into the Law of Negro Slavery*, historical introduction, CCXIV.
90 "Slavery in 1857," XXV, 81–94.
91 MS Address to the Erosophic and Philomathic Societies, Alabama State Dept. Archives and History.
92 "The Dual Form of Labor," *Russell's Magazine*, October, 1859.

body to Massachusetts in 1848, he visited the Lowell mills. To the Charleston *Courier* he confessed that this inspection wrought a revolution in his opinions. He had supposed that Yankee money "was wrung from the bone and sinew of these laborers by oppression and exaction. He had the impression that the laborers of the Lowell mills were by dire necessity incarcerated for life; that they never left the occupation which they had entered upon." He viewed the factories, the handsome blocks of houses, the twenty-five churches, the schools, and the alert, well-dressed hands with amazement. The change in his views, he exclaimed, was like emerging from a dark forest upon a verdurous and beautiful plain! [93] The Southern myth naturally excited Northern derision. A note of contempt crept into such refutations as that which Greeley published in 1851. Of course all hireling society had its noisome blots; of course a workman forced by his physical wants to labor without a proper compensation was hardly more free than a slave; of course hirelingism often produced starvation, child-murder, and prostitution. But the true test of human institutions is whether they are progressive and ameliorative. While the festering sores of the slave system remained untreated and must continue to fester forevermore, hirelingism lent itself to activity, invention, innovation, and broadfronted progress, which raised on the evils of one age the bright reforms of the next.[94]

Much of the Southern myth, indeed, contradicted itself in its own terms. To write of slavery, as George Fitzhugh did, as the oldest, best, and most common form of socialism, was a contradiction in terms.[95] The master had everything, the slave nothing—and that was socialism! To condemn free society, as W. J. Grayson did for "its pauperism, rowdyism, mobism, and anti-rentism—its strikes, emeutes, and streetfights," [96] was to condemn it for precisely that ferment which made for progress and betterment. To declare, as even the able John Forsyth of Mobile did, that Massachusetts with 993,400 people had 5,549 paupers while Tennessee with 1,092,000 people had only 531, was to forget that all Tennessee slaves—practically all her laboring force—were not merely paupers, but paupers for as long as slavery endured. To talk of the solidarity of capital and labor, the unity of master and slave, was to deny the dark basic feature of Southern life which made a vast machinery of restrictive laws, patrols, policing, disarming, interdiction of Negro education or general communication, and eternal vigilance, necessary; the sullen, half-slumbering, but always menacing antagonism of interest between the owner and the bondsman. The most significant fact about the Southern myth of the social and moral superiority of slavery was its fan-

93 March 21, 1848.
94 N. Y. *Weekly Tribune*, June 21, 1851.
95 Cf. Fitzhugh's *Sociology for the South, passim.*
96 *Letters of Curtius*, 1851.

tastic character, its divorce from reality; and it was divorced from reality because the realities were too grim to be frankly faced.[97]

97 For an illustration of the extremes to which Southerners sometimes went, hear William D. Mitchell, a lawyer of Oldham, Kentucky, in the constitutional convention of his State in 1849 (*Debates and Proceedings,* 142): "When it is said that slavery is calculated to produce aristocracy, there is more truth in the remark than persons generally allow. But it is general aristocracy—aristocracy of the whole white race. . . . When you institute a comparison between the men of the North and the South, does it not result in favor of those of the South? Has not the South acquired for itself a character for frankness, generosity, high-toned honor, and chivalry which is unknown in the North? Look a little further. Review the history of our government from its first foundations down to the present time. It exhibits a series of brilliant triumphs achieved by the South, illustrating superiority of moral force over mere numerical strength. The voice of its eloquence has predominated in the council chamber. She has displayed her courage and patriotic devotion on every battlefield, and throughout the broad expanse of our country. Her energy and her wisdom have been mainly instrumental in achieving the successful progress of those institutions which were originally moulded by her genius and her patriotism."

15

Slavery, Race-Adjustment, and the Future

THESE IGNORANT black folk, laboring under the overseer's profanity, and wending home at nightfall to the hoe-cake and cabin-pallet—what did they get for all their labor under the sun? Nothing in money; nothing in other material rewards beyond the bare necessities of coarse clothing, primitive food, and crazy furniture; nothing in family security; nothing in hope. They lived rough lives, they encountered a full portion of sorrow and ignominy, and they went to nameless graves.

And yet they were by no means wholly unrequited. They did earn by their toil one bright jewel which their kinsfolk left free in African villages never gained. What they won in the hot cane and cotton of the New World was a brighter heritage for their children. Could they have lifted their gaze from the sordid setting of their drudgery and looked down the generations to come, what would they have seen? Their descendants thronging into schools and colleges; becoming skilled artisans, businessmen, professional workers, and artists; seizing opportunities such as the Negro race in all its errant, thwarted history had never enjoyed; rising to light, laughter, and shining achievement. The hovel and hoe, which seemed to lead to nothing, fell away to a road opening upon wide vistas; and within a hundred years Negro endeavor was flowering into poetry and fiction, song and sculpture, scientific discovery and scholarly achievement. The accomplishments of the Negroes in closing the gap between the white race and themselves have been wonderful, and in one sense those accomplishments have been built upon the foundation laid by the humble slaves.

[I]

Most of the fathers of the republic were sensitively aware of the evils connected with slavery and hopeful of its ultimate abolition. Stern expressions of condemnation are easily culled from their writings. But they perceived that so thorny a problem of race adjustment was involved that emancipation would but dispose of one problem to create others. Franklin, who became head of the

498

Pennsylvania Abolition Society, near the end of his career published an address which described slavery as "an atrocious debasement of human nature." Yet he predicted that "its very extirpation, if not performed with solicitous care, may sometimes open a source of serious evils." On this point Southern leaders naturally felt more strongly still.

Washington, born to a family which had owned slaves for three generations, held them all his mature life, and died possessed of about four hundred Negroes. Never liking slavery, he felt as he grew older an increasing repugnance for it. He wrote Robert Morris in 1786 that no man living wished more sincerely for its abolition, and that his suffrage would never be wanting to support legislative action to that end. Eight years later, addressing Tobias Lear, he expressed an earnest wish "to liberate a certain species of property—which I possess very repugnantly to my own feelings." He spoke elsewhere of his hope that the Virginia legislature might see the wisdom of a gradual abolition. In his will he directed that all slaves held in his own right should be freed on the death of his widow. But he never advocated immediate and general emancipation, for he feared the social dangers of hasty action.

Two more deeply reflective statesmen, Jefferson and Madison, early established their repute as opponents of slavery. But neither believed that abolition should be effected without careful measures for the future disposition of the freedmen. Jefferson suggested that they be transported to a new colony, in Africa or the West Indies, "beyond the reach of mixture." Madison was similarly in favor of segregating the great mass of blacks, but held that the Western country offered the most suitable haven. Both Jefferson and Madison staunchly advocated the diffusion of slavery so long as it existed in America, arguing that its expansion would not add to the whole number of slaves (a very dubious assertion), and would ameliorate the workings of the institution. Both believed also in the principle of state-compensated emancipation, and Madison used spirited language in pointing out that payment of the owners from a national fund would be fair, for the benefits of a general liberation would be national. To the end of his days Madison hoped that farsighted action might be taken. Robert C. Winthrop, visiting Montpelier in 1832, found him elated by the famous speech which James McDowell had just delivered in the legislature. "The recent revolution of opinion in Virginia on the subject of slavery," he exclaimed, "is the most important that had taken place since the Revolution of '76"—adding that almost for the first time he had begun to conceive a confident hope that slavery would yield to a system of gradual emancipation.[1]

1 Matthew T. Mellon, *Early American Views on Slavery*. R. C. Winthrop to Rives, June 24, 1856; Rives Papers. As late as 1859 an anonymous Virginian, Vindex, writing in the *National Intelligencer* of February 23, argued for diffusion of slavery as the best means of

Decade by decade many enlightened Southerners continued to regard con-trolled emancipation as a beneficent goal. But they spoke ever more guardedly. George Tucker, whose life precisely spanned the years between Bunker Hill and Fort Sumter, Virginia's greatest economist and the first chairman of her university faculty, wrote of slavery: "We may say of it as of man: the doom of its death, though we know not the time or the mode, is certain and irrevocable." But he wrote also that various factors might delay emancipation—westward migration, the formation of new slaveholding States, a wider use of slaves in manufacturing, the extension of sugar-growing, or the introduction of such new industries as silk and wine into the South. In later life, when some of those forces had become operative, Tucker became discreetly mild on the subject of slavery. James McDowell, on becoming governor and Congressman, also grew reticent. Winthrop once told him what Madison had said of his great speech. "Oh, Mr. Winthrop, do not mention the subject," he burst out. "I should not dare to make a speech again. It would be burned by the common hangman at the corner of the streets, if this one has not been so already. I have not changed an opinion expressed in it, but your abolitionists have now made it a forbidden topic with us." [2]

Under mighty pressures, the Revolutionary hopes and impulses respecting Southern emancipation died away. Here and there an intrepid figure, like Petigru in South Carolina, John Letcher in Virginia, Cave Johnson in Tennessee, Cassius M. Clay in Kentucky, and Sam Houston in Texas, expressed frank reprobation of slavery. John P. Kennedy of Maryland, whose picture of the institution in *Swallow Barn* seemed superficially mild but was essentially caustic, was unsparing in his private denunciations. Outside the Lower South, he said, slavery was an unmitigated blight. It was an expensive, unprofitable, and slovenly mode of tillage; it impoverished the country by suppressing immigration and manufactures; it impeded public improvements; it begot indolence and debased manners. The sooner it could be thrown off, the better. "Slavery in no community can ever assume the character of a permanent establishment. It is essentially a transitory condition. Not only sound reason demonstrates this *a priori*, but history invariably proves it as the condition of the institution in every clime." [3] Nevertheless, hope for early action died away; and the mightiest of the pressures which killed it was a sense of the frightful difficulties of race-readjustment.

Few careers throw a brighter illumination upon the hopes and fears sur-

lifting Negroes in the scale of civilization. He pointed to the analogy of the immigrant. The alien from Europe remained an alien if he lived in a communty of his fellows; he was rapidly assimilated to the American type when he dwelt among native-born Americans.

2 Rives Papers, *ut supra*; cf. *Dictionary of American Biography* on McDowell.
3 MS Diary, 1848, pp. 78–80; Kennedy Papers.

rounding this question than that of Edward Coles, a figure who well deserves rescue from his obscurity. Sprung of a prominent Virginia family, Coles was reared in the Albemarle County mansion of his father, a Revolutionary veteran, and often saw at the fireside of "Enniscorthy" such guests as Madison, Jefferson, Patrick Henry, and the Randolphs. Private tutoring, followed by attendance first at Hampden-Sidney and later at William and Mary, gave him an exceptional education. A youth of generous impulses, he found his attention drawn to slavery by college experiences, and after long reading and reflection resolved that he would neither hold slaves nor remain in a slaveholding community. The death of his father in 1808 made him owner of a plantation with gangs of hands, but this merely confirmed his determination. For a time he found difficulty in putting it into effect. Accepting President Madison's invitation to become his private secretary, for six years he acted in that capacity. Soon after peace in 1815 he was sent to Russia on a diplomatic mission, and travelled extensively in western Europe. But meanwhile, unwavering in his purpose, he had decided to settle in the Northwest, which he had briefly explored.[4]

His anti-slavery conviction also led to a correspondence with Jefferson which became celebrated. With idealistic ardor, he urged Jefferson to furnish the country a plan of gradual abolition which might at once be put into operation. "In the calm of your retirement, you might, most beneficially to society and with much addition to your own fame, avail yourself of the love and confidence of your fellow-citizens to put into complete practise those hallowed principles contained in that renowned Declaration of which you were the immortal author." But Jefferson shrank from the task. He was too aged, he declared, to respond to an appeal which was like bidding old Priam to buckle on the armor of Hector. He added that he had outlived that Revolutionary generation in which mutual perils and struggles begat mutual confidence. "This enterprise is for the young, for those who can follow it up and bear it through to its consummation. It shall have all my prayers, and these are the only weapons of an old man." Existing laws, he noted, did not permit men to turn their slaves loose, even if it were for the slaves' good. Jefferson's doctrine was not merely that of gradualism, which was sound, but came near that of drift, which was not. Condemning slavery, he believed that men must wait until its extinction was "brought on either by the generous energy of our own minds, or by the bloody processes of St. Domingo."

At last, in 1819, the year after Illinois was admitted to the Union, Coles was able to make good his long-cherished resolve by removing to that State. He loved Virginia, he had many social ties binding him to the Old Dominion, and

4 Cf. E. B. Washburne, *Sketch of Edward Coles, Second Governor of Illinois*, ed. C. W. Alvord; *Illinois Historical Collections*. XV.

he could hope for political eminence if he remained. But he tarried no longer. His slaves, unaware of his wish to liberate them, gladly accepted his announcement of a new home. The whole company embarked at Pittsburgh on two flat-bottomed boats. When well started down the Ohio, Coles marshalled them on deck and in a brief speech told them they were free, and could accompany him or go ashore, as they liked. "The effect on them was electrical," he later wrote. "They stared at me and at each other, as if doubting the accuracy of what they heard. In breathless silence they stood before me, unable to answer a word, but with countenances beaming with an expression . . . which no language can describe. . . . After a pause of intense and unutterable emotion, bathed in tears, and with tremulous voices, they gave vent to their gratitude, and implored the blessings of God on me." They accompanied him to Illinois, where he gave each family a quarter-section of land, and executed for every slave a deed of manumission.

Appointed head of the Land Office at his new home, Edwardsville, Coles soon attained a wide influence in southern Illinois. He found the young State racked by a fierce struggle over slavery. To be sure, the institution was barred from Illinois by both the Ordinance of 1787 and the State Constitution. Yet slavery actually persisted there, the hostility to free Negroes was general, and a large pro-slavery party denied the validity of the Ordinance. How Coles, elected governor, placed himself at the head of the free-soil party, and how after a desperate contest he finally won the victory, is one of the great stories of Illinois history. As the struggle reached its height, the slavery forces invoked methods comparable to those later used in the Kansas struggle. But the scheme for a convention to frame a new pro-slavery Constitution was defeated by a close vote, and rapid immigration from the free States made any renewal of the attempt impossible.

This dramatic story contains much that is instructive. The existence of strong anti-slavery feeling in the Upper South; its essential helplessness as the idealistic impulses of the Revolution spent themselves and new economic conditions appeared; the willingness of many Southerners to make sacrifices to rear their children on free soil; the anti-Negro sentiment common among ignorant folk in the North no less than the South; the existence of an important pro-slavery movement north of the Ohio; its defeat by the combined influences of basic law, climate, immigration, and enlightenment—all this is representative of broad currents in the slavery struggle. Most striking of all is the fact that by 1819 a Southern believer in emancipation had lost all faith in frontal attacks upon slavery, and felt he could achieve his limited personal objects only by evasive action; by removal from the South.

[II]

If the emancipation movement was to revive in the fifties, it would have to be in the border States. Here slavery was numerically weakest and the conviction of its evils strongest. Yet from the Chesapeake to Kentucky, the antislavery movement failed anywhere to attain formidable strength.

In little Delaware, where (as in the Federal District) the number of slaves diminished in every decade after 1820, this failure was partly because freedom seemed gaining an automatic victory. Though at the first census Delaware had 8,887 slaves, by 1850 the number had dropped to 2,290, and was still falling. About two-thirds of the slaves in 1850 were held in the southernmost county, Sussex; and even here many slaveowners believed by 1860 that if left alone, the county would become free soil within a decade. One reason for this conviction was that the underground railroad was easily accessible; through tickets could be had almost for the asking, and it was believed the loss from runaways just about equalled the increment by births. Another reason was that the high prices of slaves induced many holders to sell them outside the State. The late fifties saw speculators roving about, offering from $500 to $1,500 for Negroes, and eager to snap them up. During 1859 a single trader was reported to have sent a hundred slaves out of Sussex, and it was computed that at least six a week or three hundred a year left the county. The institution was thus losing its vitality; gradual emancipation was taking place; and since time would effect the result, no emancipatory law seemed needed.[5]

In Maryland and Kentucky no such automatic solution of the problem was anticipated. Both States kept alive strong movements for gradual abolition, led by such men as Henry Winter Davis and Cassius M. Clay, but in both they were checked by fear of the race-adjustment problem. A slaveholders' convention in Baltimore in June, 1859, debated the best means of regulating the free Negro population. The attendance was large, representative of every part of the State, and determined to repress abolitionist tendencies. It asserted that for the purpose of diminishing "the evils which proceed from the excessive and increasing free negro class," the policy of strict State regulation fixed in 1831 should be reaffirmed, with amendments which "will either prohibit emancipation altogether, or compel the prompt removal from the State of those emancipated. . . ."[6] Kentucky's constitutional convention of 1849 rang the death-knell of all hopes for early steps toward emancipation. Its motives were mixed. Some delegates believed slavery just and profitable, some valued the social dignities it conferred,

5 See survey in N. Y. *Weekly Tribune*, March 3, 1860.
6 N. Y. *Weekly Tribune*, June 18, 1859.

and some felt that hostile action would be a betrayal of the South; but the dominant feeling emphasized the difficulties that would follow abolition.

There were about two hundred thousand slaves in Kentucky, said one delegate; they were valued at sixty-one million dollars; and they produced less than three per cent profit on the capital invested. "That white labor is the cheapest I have no doubt. . . . I have never entertained a doubt that it is the interest of the great slaveholding community of this State, to sell their slaves." [7] But what could be done with the Negroes when liberated? The Kentucky agitation, given the blessing of Henry Clay and Crittenden, and enjoying the leadership of Robert J. Breckinridge, James Speed, and other strong men, rolled on, but achieved nothing whatever.

It was in Missouri that the institution of slavery seemed in most parlous case. The non-slaveholding element was stronger here than in any other slave State except Delaware. Of the 54,438 farms enumerated by the census of 1850, only 8,142 used slaves, while 46,315 did not. Most of the 87,422 slaves were concentrated in the sixteen counties lying along the Missouri River. The steady growth of railroads, manufactures, and cities strengthened the exuberant freesoil sentiment within the State. By 1850 even aristocratic St. Louis, rapidly and healthily expanding, might be called predominantly hostile to the institution. It had nearly six thousand slaves, a few slave auctions, and a sprinkle of slave advertisements, but whenever the auctioneer left his block, the abolitionist could mount it for a much-applauded harangue. Great uneasiness existed among slaveholders, many of whom refused to purchase more hands and advised their children to make no investments in such property. Early in the fifties it was reported that some of the largest planters in Boone, Callaway, Howard, and other counties had sold out and removed to Texas because they felt that a change was overtaking the State, and wanted a safer clime for hands who were currently quoted at twice the Virginia prices. Missouri had too many men from the North, they grumbled, too many foreigners, too many Bentonians, and too many poor whites hostile to slavery. Free labor was clearly more efficient than slave, and according to a common saying in the State, one German worker knocked out three slaves and one Irishman knocked out two.

Were the question of slavery to come up directly in Missouri, trumpeted an observer in 1853, fully three-fourths of the State would vote against the

7 *Debates and Proceedings of the Convention of 1849*, pp. 73-74, statement of S. Turner. James Guthrie, president of the convention, asserted that the Negroes could not be returned to Africa: "Free them, and they will become the Lazaroni of the state. They will crowd to the cities—they will visit the country only on marauding parties—and they will become idle, vicious, and ungovernable. . . . Instead of being productive of wealth, as they are now, they will be destructive of wealth. They will not be advanced in morality, but they will be advanced in crime. They will not be advanced in happiness, but they will be advanced in misery and in degradation." *Idem*, pp. 94-95. Cf. Coleman, *Slavery Times in Kentucky*, 313-325.

institution.[8] No doubt this was true—if getting rid of slavery had meant getting rid of the Negro. But as matters stood, the steady increase in the slaveless population was not accompanied by any marked progress toward emancipation. Though in bustling St. Louis the old 'society' of the city was pro-slavery, the principal businessmen, anxious to outstrip Chicago, were quietly but positively freesoil, and the powerful German-American element felt strongly on the subject. But what could the reformers do? Early in 1857 a resolution was introduced in the legislature declaring that emancipation would be unwise, impolitic, and unjust, and that any movement toward it ought to be discountenanced by good citizens. This passed the Senate 24 to 4, the four St. Louis members voting no; it passed the House 107 to 12, twelve of the fourteen St. Louis representatives opposed. The answer of St. Louis to this demarche was the election of John M. Wimer, heading an emancipationist ticket, as mayor. His inaugural address extolled free labor, denounced the legislative resolutions as intended to bind Missouri to an uneconomic and enterprise-destroying system, and proclaimed: "It is best for the State that it be peopled by white men." The president of the board of aldermen endorsed this principle of "free white labor," and asserted that Missouri would eventually be free. "The heat of the sun does not require an African to stand beneath its rays; none of our agricultural products demands his aid, and certainly our manufactories do not need him." [9]

In fine, these emancipationist city officers were against both slavery and the Negro, and opposed the slave system chiefly because it discouraged white immigration and white labor. The St. Louis *Democrat* and St. Louis *Anzeiger* constantly predicted the eventual extinction of slavery. With the non-slaveholding population increasing thirty per cent every five years, and with the slaveholding population at a virtual standstill, said the *Democrat* in 1857, "Missouri will be a free State during the present generation." But the close of the fifties saw practical measures to effect emancipation seemingly as far distant as when in 1828 a party of about twenty liberal Whig and Democratic leaders in Missouri had met with Benton and Judge Barton to concert plans for a gradual extinction. That lion in the path, race-adjustment, had reared its head then. The bi-party alliance for gradual action had been dropped when Missourians read a highly-colored newspaper story that Arthur Tappan of New York had entertained Negroes at his table and allowed three Negro men to ride out in the same carriage with his daughter! The race-adjustment lion still stood in the road. This fact was advertised to the world when in the winter of 1859–60, following the John Brown raid, a bill passed the legislature by overwhelming majorities to

8 "Letters for the People on the Present Crisis," consisting of letters from an anonymous St. Louis man to a New York friend; pvt., dated October 1, 1853; Huntington Library.
9 *Idem*, Galusha Anderson, *A Border City*, pp. 9–10. N. Y. *Weekly Tribune*, March 7, 1857. *National Intelligencer*, April 14, 1857.

expel all free Negroes from the State. St. Louis had more than a thousand, valued as servants and friends. A thrill of horror ran through the city. For a time the brutal enactment seemed certain to become law—until Governor R. M. Stewart, Bourbon Democrat and pro-slavery man though he was, sagaciously killed it with a pocket veto.[10]

Nowhere, in short, did the emancipationist cause make verifiable and encouraging progress in the slaveholding area between 1840 and 1860. Some liberal men followed Edward Coles's example. Cave Johnson of Tennessee, for example, warmly attached to the sixty-five or seventy colored people whom he had inherited from his or his wife's ancestors, refusing always to sell a Negro except for crime, and never buying one except to unite families, wished late in life to manumit them all. His intention was to buy land for them in Ohio. For this purpose he communicated with Levi Coffin. But the war prevented consummation of his kindly plan. John McDonogh, the wealthy New Orleans merchant who died in 1850, originated a complex scheme by which his slaves purchased their freedom. A determined anti-slavery movement persisted in parts of Virginia. It had the sympathy of more men than dared speak out in its favor. In combination with the pronounced drain of Virginia slaves into the cotton and sugar country, where their labor was far more profitable, it kept alive the dream of emancipation that Jefferson and Madison had cherished. "The causes now in operation," one prominent Virginian wrote in the spring of 1860, "would seem to be sufficient to convert Virginia from a slave State into a free State. The state of *transition* would be a painful one, and might be attended, in *Virginia*, by the irrepressible conflict between free labor and slave labor. . . . The transition has already begun upon the Northern and Northwestern boundaries of the State, and it is a source of surprise to me that it does not go on faster than it seems to do in all parts of the State."

Even in Texas the cause of gradual emancipation had followers. The frontier did not desire slaves. Outspoken and liberal-minded German settlers held a convention at San Antonio in 1854, drew up a broad reform program, and put into it a plank condemning slavery and declaring that if any single State should determine on its abolition, the assistance of the national government might properly be claimed in carrying out the work.[11]

10 *Democrat*, quoted in N. Y. *Weekly Tribune*, March 7, 1857. John Wilson to Thomas Shackelford, January 13, 1866; Slavery MSS, Mo. Hist. Soc., Anderson, *op. cit.*, 12–14; Stewart had been reared in Cortland County, New York. In 1860 St. Louis had a population of 151,780, of which about 1,500 were slaves.
11 W. P. Titus, *Picturesque Clarksville, Past and Present*, 303. W. T. Childs, *John McDonogh, His Life and Work*. John C. Rutherford, Loch Lomond, Va., to W. C. Rives, April 11, 1860; Rives Papers. Cf. G. G. Benjamin, *The Germans in Texas*; R. L. Biesele, *History of the German Settlements in Texas, 1831–1861*; A. M. Hall, *The Texas Germans in State and National Politics, 1850–1865* (U. of Texas thesis).

But where except in St. Louis was a notable victory gained at the polls? When was a strong legislative vote polled for even an exploratory step? Had Delaware boldly abolished her pitiful remnants of slavery, and had Missouri and Maryland both adopted gradual emancipation combined with Negro education, the sharp edge would have been taken off the sectional conflict. Alas that they did not move with the courage which the times demanded! The reasons why they did not could be found in the American tendency to drift, in fear of the effect upon slavery in their sister States farther south, and above all, in the fact that abolition would bring to life a painful race-adjustment problem.

[III]

Precisely what were the anticipated difficulties, and to what extent were they imaginary or real? Many Southerners insisted that only the discipline of slavery could make Negroes work with a steady industry. They argued that in the great districts where Negroes predominated calamitous disorders would follow emancipation. Fallen into barbarian idleness, a prey to agitators, or inspired by hopes of plunder, they would collect in gangs to ravage the countryside. Even if they did not do this, their sporadic robberies and murders would make life unendurable. Doubters were reminded of the massacres of Santo Domingo. It became fashionable for Southerners to say that emancipation would result in a dual struggle; first a contest for political supremacy, and then a life-and-death battle for racial survival.[12]

But above all, Southerners were conscious of a still more formidable possibility. Premature emancipation, wrote a Baltimorean in 1855, would mean that the South would ultimately be peopled by a race of mulattoes. How, in the long run, could a mingling of bloods be avoided? Emancipation meant personal freedom; personal freedom in a democracy means political equality; and political equality is necessarily followed in the end by social equality. The right of blacks to associate with whites on equal terms involved ultimately a deliberate annullment of all distinctions between the two, or an acceptance of the principle that no proper ground for such distinctions ever existed. Once this view was adopted, education of the Negroes would gradually erase all differences in refinement, manners, and intellectual culture.

"What barriers, then, remain to keep those two streams of black and white blood running parallel and level with each other from blending and uniting their currents? They mingle with us in our parlors; why should we exclude them from our chambers? We accept them as partners in the quadrille and the

12 Denman, *Secession Movement in Alabama*, 16ff.

polka; how can our daughters reject their hands for the grand pas-de-deux of matrimony? A well-educated, travelled, refined, accomplished Negro, a Senator in Congress perhaps from emancipated South Carolina (where the Negro vote would be in the majority), and withal, with an income of several thousands a year, would he not be considered a decided 'match' by many a fair-skinned Desdemona in this good time coming of equality and fraternity?" [13]

This might seem an exaggerated apprehension. Yet it struck home to Southerners high and low, gave rise to the ugly label "amalgamationist" for abolitionists, and was not completely met by Lincoln's dictum that it was unnecessary either to degrade the Negro or to marry him; he could just be let alone. The apprehension was founded in part upon the white Southerner's distrust of himself, for abundant evidence existed of a propensity toward one kind of amalgamation. The Southern novelist George W. Cable later wrote a poignant novel, the crux of which lay in a New Orleans quadroon's heroic denial of her own daughter in order that this octoroon might marry a white man; the law forbidding any intermarriage of the races.[14]

In part, the prevalent fear was founded upon the sequels of emancipation in some Latin countries and the British West Indies. It was well known that French and Spanish colonists in the New World intermarried constantly and freely with Negroes. A Bermuda merchant who established himself in Baltimore was quoted as saying that one reason for his migration lay in his disgust over the progress of amalgamation. Negro delegates now represented Negro constituencies in the colonial assembly, and political equality had paved the way for social acceptance. "Instances are not a few where gentlemen moving in the first social circles, particularly Englishmen sent out in the capacity of government officials or agents of commercial houses, have married mulatto or quadroon women, and introduced them and their mongrel children in society." And finally, Southern apprehension was fed by the fact that in various parts of the Southern States themselves certain curious mixtures of blood—Indian, Mexican, French, Spanish, or English with Negro—were already producing some difficult social situations.

Unquestionably not a few mulattoes of very light complexion, decade by decade, passed into the category of white folk and there married. Some States,

13 X. Y., Baltimore, November 21, in *National Intelligencer*, November 27, 1855.
14 George W. Cable, *Madame Delphine; National Intelligencer, ut supra*, November 27, 1855. Amalgamation was a word frequently used sneeringly by proslavery men, who attacked abolitionists as amalgamationists. Once when Douglas resorted to the familiar fling, Henry Wilson replied: "This slang about amalgamationist generally proceeds from men who have the odor of amalgamation strong upon them." (Senate, April 21, 1856.) It was a sharp retort but true. Nearly all mulattoes could trace their ancestry back to slaveholding fathers; Southern cities and towns contained many, while one was rarely born in the North. "Mulattoes," caustically observed the N. Y. *Tribune*, "are generally the offspring of lechery on the father's side, and debasement and dependence on the mother's." N. Y. *Weekly Tribune*, April 26, 1856.

notably Kentucky and Virginia, defined a mulatto as any person who had one-fourth or a *larger* fraction of Negro blood; Georgia's definition was *less* than one-fourth. But in no instance did a State law require that a person having a non-perceptible trace of Negro blood should be deemed a mulatto. More drastic laws would have embarrassed white people with a slight tincture, say one-sixteenth, of Negro blood, and would have been difficult to enforce. A perfectly legal migration from the Negro to the white race was possible. But it seems probable that the greater part of the "passing" went on without reference to courts or legal procedure. The scope of the process cannot be measured, for those who "passed" naturally did everything possible to conceal their ancestry. But an indication of the tendency of light-skinned mulattoes to attempt to establish themselves and their children in the white race is found in the repeated instances in which the attempt was detected and legally checkmated. Everywhere, meanwhile, mulattoes were likely to become a separate caste. Preference was usually given them as house servants, for they were regarded as neater, handsomer, and brighter than full-blood Negroes; many white fathers treated their mulatto children with special consideration; dark-skinned Negroes then (as today) allowed a certain social superiority to the light-skinned. All this was proof that if emancipation triumphed, then "amalgamation" on a broad scale might ultimately—in the course of generations—be no figment of the imagination.[15]

Obviously, the South raised some needless bogies in facing the question of race-adjustment. Its idea that the Negro would revert to savage indolence was utterly belied by time. Though Southerners liked to quote the very Tory utterances by the London *Times* on the shiftless laziness of Jamaica blacks after emancipation, the real story in that island was creditable to the Negroes' industry. Similarly, the bogey of bloody uprisings and massacres was absurd. Let us remind the Southerner, wrote "Ex-Rebel" in the *Nation* long years afterward, that the Negroes had charge of Southern agriculture during the Civil War, and never shirked their task. "Say to him that during all those dreary days of death and destruction the strong arm of the Negro defended the peace and purity of his home, and he cannot deny it. Recall to him the fact that although our fathers asserted with confidence that the Negro without a master would become such a monster that no society could tolerate his presence . . . the history is that he is as docile as when he wore a chain, and a much more useful inhabitant of the earth than when he was driven to work." [16]

15 James Hugo Johnston, *Race Relations in Virginia and Miscegenation in the South*, 1776–1860, p. 250ff.; U. of Chicago dissertation (1937).
16 For Southern bogies, see John Townsend, *The South Alone Should Govern the South*, pvt., 1860. The London *Times* said: "The freed West Indian slave will not till the soil for wages; the free son of the ex-slave is as obstinate as his sire. He will cultivate lands which he has not bought for his own yams, mangoes, and plantains These satisfy his wants; they

But uncertainty, fear, and dark foreboding were altogether natural. Men of liberal outlook and the highest intellectual distinction accepted this view of the impossibility of incorporating millions of liberated blacks into the tissue of a white civilization. Jefferson had used emphatic language. "Deep-rooted prejudices of the whites, ten thousand recollections of the black of injuries sustained, new provocations, the real distinction Nature had made, and many other circumstances will divide us into parties and produce convulsions which will probably never end but in the extermination of one or the other race." Very similar was De Tocqueville's judgment in 1838. Terming the Negro the most perplexing American problem, he could see but two alternatives: to emancipate and intermingle, or to keep the blacks isolated in a state of slavery as long as possible. "All intermediate measures seem to me likely to terminate, and that shortly, in the most horrible of civil wars, and perhaps in the extirpation of one or the other of the two races." [17]

Just before the Civil War, W. T. Sherman wrote from Louisiana in caustic terms. "All the Congresses on earth can't make the Negro anything else than what he is; he must be subject to the white man, or he must amalgamate or be destroyed. Two such races cannot live in harmony save as master and slave. Mexico shows the result of general equality and amalgamation, and the Indians give a fair illustration of the fate of the negroes if they are released from the control of the whites." [18] The general conclusion of Southerners was stated by the Washington *Union*:

"It is clear that the domestic institution of the South cannot admit of a material change without taking some time to effect it. A precipitate policy would inflict the deepest injury upon the South. It took eight centuries to drive the Moors from Spain. Santo Domingo was ruined by the inconsiderate precipitancy of revolutionary France. Jamaica has been seriously injured by the hasty legislation of Parliament. . . . The white men and slaves could not live happily together, if they were all liberated."

---

do not care for yours. Cotton, and sugar, and coffee, and tobacco—he cares little for them. And what matters it to him, that the Englishman has sunk his thousands and tens of thousands on mills, machinery, etc., which now totter on the languishing estate, that for years have only returned beggary and debts. He eats his yam, and sniggers at 'Buckra.' " *Nation*, April 26, 1888, for "Ex-Rebel."

17 Cf. Ballagh, *History of Slavery in Virginia*, 132. E. G. W. Butler, who married a granddaughter of Mrs. George Washington, compared the lot of the slaves emancipated by George Washington with that of Mrs. Washington's slaves, who remained in servitude: "I speak from my own observations and can appeal to citizens of Fairfax County Virginia for the truth of my assertion, when I affirm that the descendants of the latter, many of whom are in possession of the writer of this, have been and are prosperous, contented and happy; while the former—after a life of vice, dissipation and idleness, may literally be said to have disappeared from the face of the earth." To Gayarré, July 16, 1853; Gayarré Papers.

18 W. T. Sherman, *Home Letters*, 178-179, July 10, 1860. Washington *Union*, May 5, 1850.

[IV]

The one apparent means of effecting a simultaneous solution of the problems of slavery and race adjustment was by removal of the Negro to some other part of the world. A later age was to witness wholesale deportations in Europe and Asia as a rough surgical operation to end the friction between diverse national stocks. It was natural that Americans should consider the same expedient. The glittering chimera of "colonization," a bright delusive dream, floated before the eyes of two generations of benevolent men. Jefferson had advocated the idea as early as 1776, had worked out a plan in his *Notes on Virginia*, and had cherished it to his last days. The American Colonization Society, founded in 1817 with numerous eminent men among its supporters, kept the idea nationally prominent. When it held its annual meeting in Washington in 1852 Henry Clay was president, Webster was vice-president, President Fillmore attended, and numerous Senators, Representatives, and Supreme Court justices applauded a hopeful address by the able Frederick P. Stanton of Tennessee. Various State colonization societies lent their assistance. Money came not merely from philanthropic individuals, but from public bodies. Virginia, for example, passed a law in 1853 appropriating $30,000 annually for five years (which was supplemented by about $10,000 annually from the tax laid on free colored folk) for colonization activities. In New York Governor Hunt devoted a large part of his annual message of 1852 to a glowing account of the Society's work and a plea for State assistance. Lincoln's outspoken belief in colonization was maintained to the end.[19]

The colonization dream, despite the heated opposition of most abolitionists and most free Negroes, gave thousands a comfortable feeling that they were doing something practical to attack the menacing national issue. The stated meetings, with a Bushrod Washington, a Clay, or a John H. B. Latrobe in the chair; the beautifully phrased speeches by Everett or Reverdy Johnson; the pleased editorials by W. W. Seaton or Horace Greeley, all made a pleasant stir. The problem was going to be solved without much pain or trouble to anybody. Churchmen like Bishop J. H. Hopkins of Vermont explained how simple it all was. The value of the slaves in the late fifties might be a thousand million dollars. That was not a quarter of the British national debt. By direct taxes which would never exceed an average of $20 for each taxable inhabitant, and would reach that height only for a few years, the government might buy all the slaves, transport them to Africa, and settle them there. Or the public lands, worth twice as much as the slave property, might be mortgaged for the purpose. And

19 *National Intelligencer*, January 13, 1852. May 14, 1853, January 22, 1855. *Annual Reports* of the American Colonization Society. C. H. Wesley, "Lincoln's Plan for Colonizing the Emancipated Negroes," *Journal of Negro History*, IV, 7ff.

what might not this great work accomplish! National stability, Southern prosperity, a regilding of the republic's fame, the regeneration of Africa, the elevation of the Negro race to its highest level—these would be among the fruits.[20]

And yet justice must be done to the American Colonization Society and its work in Liberia. The true significance of its activities is missed if it is regarded as a fully-developed attempt to solve the problems of slavery and racial antagonism. Men like Webster, Clay, and Latrobe, highly practical all, never dreamed that it could perform so staggering a task. In 1848 the Society sent 129 emigrants to Liberia, in 1849 it sent 422, and in the next three years it transported first 670, then 666, and then 783. The republic of Liberia, brought into existence on June 25, 1847, with a Declaration of Independence, a constitution modelled on that of the United States, and a spirited appeal to Christendom for sympathy, was a pitifully weak and staggering colony, whose first president, the Virginia mulatto Joseph Jenkins Roberts, had to contend against hostile native chiefs, internal factions, and economic disasters.[21] It is easy to sneer at such frail and uncertain achievements. But the real objects of the colonizationists were two. They were to carry out a small-scale demonstration of the practicability of a genuine mass migration, and so pave the way toward governmental action of decisive magnitude. They were also to show the people of Africa that such thriving industries could be based upon sugar, cotton, coffee, palm-oil, and ivory that wars and slave-raids ought to be abandoned as unprofitable.[22]

In short, the colonizationists were conducting an experiment—and they believed it successful. They were showing that white culture and a Christian civilization could be planted on the shores of tropic Africa; that former slaves could build up a stable commonwealth; that even free colored people, rescued from their political and social disadvantages in America, could find a fuller liberty in the new republic; that industries of value to the whole globe could

20 John Henry Hopkins, *The American Citizen, His Rights and Duties* (1857). Yet an important element of Southerners opposed colonization. Calhoun, for example, held that separation of the races would injure the blacks, for they would revert to savagery, and the whites, who would lose economically and socially. Cf. W. G. Bean, "Anti-Jeffersonianism in the Ante-Bellum South," *North Carolina Historical Review*, XII, 103ff.

21 Hunt's message of January 6 in *Messages and Papers of the Governors*. For full statement of the objects of the colonizationists, see *National Intelligencer*, July 17, 1852.

22 R. F. C. Maugham, *The Republic of Liberia*, 33–83. President Roberts wrote an old English friend, G. Ralston, from Government House, Monrovia, July 6, 1853: "A few days since an old chief, who had come down with a large caravan from the interior, some eighty or a hundred miles, called on me, and in the course of conversation remarked that he had felt extremely indignant toward the Liberians for interfering with the slave trade. His grandfather and father, he said, for many, many years had sold slaves, and they were rich, but the Liberians had made him poor; he had therefore never intended to visit Monrovia, or have anything to do with the Americans. He was now convinced, however, that the slave trade was very cruel; that it has produced a great deal of distress and suffering among the country people . . . and he was now very glad that the Liberians had interposed to prevent the foreign slave trade. . . ." *National Intelligencer*, October 8, 1853.

be developed; and that the little nation, together with British Sierra Leone, could destroy the slave trade along an important stretch of the African coast. The hope was that once the scheme proved its worth, the national and State governments would unite in a far grander effort. Nobody thought that individual benevolence and scattered State grants would suffice; the Society was to blaze the way, and the United States, with its immense resources, would carry the transfer of the race to a final consummation.

The undertaking unquestionably had elements of hopefulness. In a highly colored volume issued in 1852 Mrs. Sarah Josepha Hale recited the early achievements of the Liberian settlers, some of them truly heroic. The migrants from America numbered eight thousand; they dominated a land of 200,000 native blacks; they had induced tribes aggregating half a million or more to give up the slave trade; and their progress held out hope that "the time will come when all Central Africa will look to Liberia for protection, for instruction, and for laws, as well as Christianity." President Roberts, visiting Great Britain, gained Queen Victoria's sympathetic ear for his moving story, received from Lord Ashley and other philanthropists a thousand pounds toward purchase of Galinhas, a part of the coast where the slave trade still flourished, and was returned to Monrovia on a British warship.

America sent over missionaries, colored physicians, and shipload after shipload of ordinary freedmen or free Negroes. To see a vessel like the *Elvira Owen* take on colored emigrants at Baltimore, at Hampton Roads, and at Savannah, with hymn-singing, prayers, and rapt ejaculations of praise, was a touching experience. By 1854 the Society had settled in Africa 4,549 freedmen, 3,383 free Negroes, and about 1,000 Negroes rescued from slave-traders at various points. Particularly encouraging was the transit of skilled artisans. In 1853, for example, Montgomery Bell, one of the leading iron-manufacturers of Tennessee, sent over thirty-eight slaves and laid plans for adding eighty more, including hands expert in iron-working; while the same year some free Negroes from Pennsylvania went over with a steam-engine and machinery. Although ten thousand American settlers, two regiments, one armed schooner, twenty-three churches, and fifty-odd schools were but the feeble beginnings of a nation, James Beekman told the New York Senate, they were the acorn from which a splendid oak might rise.[23]

By the end of 1856 materials for a college had been sent out. An academy, a high school, and a Methodist seminary for girls had been set up in Monrovia.

23 S. J. Hale, *Liberia; or, Mr. Peyton's Experiments*. Maugham, *Liberia*, 64. *National Intelligencer*, June 26, 1856, quoting Savannah *Republican* of June 21, April 1, 1854, June 17, 1854. Annual Report of the American Colonization Society, 1853. England in 1853 had regular steam lines from Liverpool and Plymouth to West Africa, furnishing a semi-monthly connection with Liberia. Latrobe's address, Washington *Union*, January 18, 1854.

The first Liberian book, a volume of poems, had been published. Roberts and other Liberians, with support from Latrobe, F. P. Stanton, and others in America, were agitating for a direct steamship line to exploit the West African trade, and compete with the regular British steamship lines from Plymouth and Liverpool.

"And there Liberia stands, and has stood for the last six years," exclaimed the Society's annual report for 1853, "a free and independent nation, a bright gem set upon the dark ground of a vast continent, with some two hundred thousand citizens, exerting an undisputed dominion over some seven hundred miles of seacoast."

Visitors told of hopes for large coffee crops, of prospects for livestock growing, of success in producing tropical fruits. They were particularly optimistic over the prospects of a large palm-oil trade. Inspecting the handsome brick residences of Monrovia and the promising plantations scattered about it, they agreed that only capital, managerial energy, more labor, sugar-grinding machinery, and transportation lines were needed; nothing but that! [24]

But however creditable some of the Colonization Society's achievements, in any broad view the experiment gave a triple demonstration of the impracticability of the general undertaking. It proved that Liberia, its lowlands mainly a densely forested country of tremendous rainfall, trackless and unhealthy, its uplands so difficult to reach that a century after the birth of the republic they still remained half-unexplored, its coast lacking in good harbors, its commercial possibilities even harder to develop than those of neighboring British and French colonies, was unfitted to receive a huge new Negro population. It proved that most Negroes free or slave did not wish to return to Africa, and that the South did not wish to give up their labor. It proved that while a few philanthropists and legislatures would give driblets of cash, large-scale financial support was out of the question.

Virginia under her colonization law of 1850 during three years removed 419 free Negroes or freedmen to Africa at a cost of $5,410, and in the first half-year under the new law of 1853 removed 240 at a cost of $5,800. As the governor remarked, this barely sufficed to prevent any increase in the number of free Negroes.[25] But what could be done to reduce the total of fifty-five thousand free colored people already in the commonwealth? If Virginia, earnestly anxious to send its free Negroes abroad, could get rid of fewer than seven hundred in three and a half years of organized effort, what could the national government accomplish with four million Negroes? The fact was that no part of Africa

24 Annual Reports, *National Intelligencer*, May 15, 1855; J. J. Roberts, July 6, 1853, in Buchanan Papers.
25 Governor's message in *National Intelligencer*, December 15, 1853.

then accessible to the United States could absorb any large number of freedmen, and even if fertile South Africa or Australia had been open, still the absorption would necessarily have been by small annual quotas. Housing, transportation, machinery, supplies, and markets would have to be provided concurrently with any wholesale colonization. To settle ten thousand was difficult enough; to settle a hundred thousand a staggering task; to settle a million quite out of the question.

Nearly all free colored people were opposed to colonization, asserting in public meetings year after year that they would never leave America but would fight for their rights. "We intend to plant our own trees on American soil, and to repose in the shade thereof"—so ran the resolution of a national convention of free colored men dominated by Frederick Douglass at Rochester in 1853. They believed that they would gain steadily in strength and power by manumission, the escape of fugitives, and natural increase. Their white friends, including most abolitionists, thought colonization a heartless attempt to get rid of the Negro by taking him to burning deserts and steaming jungles to die. It was only when an increasing number of free States took action to exclude liberated Negroes, while the slave States witnessed a general movement to forbid emancipation except on condition of removal, that a partial change of attitude took place.

Henry Clay stated the dilemma forcibly. If the recent decision of Indiana excluding free Negroes is followed in other areas, he wrote in 1851, what will become of these poor creatures? "In the name of humanity I ask what is to become of them—where are they to go?" James G. Birney dramatically abandoned his twenty years of hostility to colonization. His examination of the Supreme Court decision in *Strader et al. vs. Graham* (1852) concluded with an exhortation to free colored people to remove to Liberia. He declared that the circumstances which had made their presence in the North an encouragement to their enslaved brethren had passed away; pointed to the harsh exclusion laws of various States; and argued that since white superiority would always be asserted to their disadvantage, they should leave. Early in the decade a Liberian Agricultural Association of nearly three hundred Negroes in New York City was actively supporting colonization. Its leader told James W. Beekman that even if he were elected to the State Senate he would have no equality. "When the Senate adjourned, you, sir, would go to Congress Hall, and I, although I have money in my pocket, would go to Dean Street. . . . Here every avenue of distinction is walled up against me, because my skin is dark. I do not choose to submit to this, and for my children's sake I shall go to Liberia." [26]

26 *National Intelligencer*, July 17, 1852; January 17, 1852 for Clay's letter to Abraham Morrison, September 30, 1851; April 1, 1852 for Beekman's New York Senate speech. N. Y.

Instinctively recoiling from colonization as impracticable, Congress refused to be beguiled into any far-reaching measure of support. Representative Edward Stanly of North Carolina proposed in 1852 that the fourth instalment of the surplus revenue which was to be distributed under the old Jacksonian law, amounting to between nine and ten millions, should be paid the several States with a proviso that interest on it be used to transport free people of color to Liberia. But the bill did not pass. Six years later Representative Frank P. Blair of Missouri urged that a House committee should canvass the possibility of acquiring territory in Central America for colonization, this territory to become a dependency of the United States, with guarantees of the civil and political rights of the inhabitants. Again the proposal gained some support, but came to nothing.[27]

Blair's speech was notable for the emphasis with which he stated the basic problem of race-adjustment. Even faraway Oregon, fearing that problem, had placed its interdict upon the admission of free blacks; while the South, apprehensive that an increase of the free Negro population might bring about slave rebellions, was moving to stop manumission and even to reduce previously manumitted slaves to servitude again. In Virginia during the previous summer and fall, large meetings had petitioned the legislature to authorize a sweeping sale of all free blacks. Both races were vassals to slavery, declared Blair, and both ought to be liberated. The slaveholders were not blamable for the arrest of emancipation. "For, whether as slave or free man, the presence of multitudes of the black race is found to be fatal to the interests of our race; their antagonism is as strong as that of oil and water, and so long as no convenient outlet, through which the manumitted slave can reach a congenial climate and country willing to receive him, is afforded, the institution of slavery stands on compulsion.' But suppose Central America were opened to the freedmen? Hundreds of Southerners would instantly send their slaves thither. The border States would

Tribune, July 15, 1853. William Birney, James G. Birney and His Times, pp. 377-399; National Intelligencer, February 7, 1852. Describing Negro opposition to colonization, Charles Lenox Remond of Salem, Mass., told his audience in a lecture at the Broadway Tabernacle, sponsored by the New York Anti-Slavery Society: "The colored people were, with a few exceptions, opposed to the movement. . . . The American Colonization Society has done more to keep up the cruel and absurd prejudice against color in this country than all the other agencies put together." N. Y. Tribune, January 5, 1854.

27 Text of Stanly's bill in National Intelligencer, July 17, 1852; on Blair, see Cong. Globe, January 14, 1858. Private support of colonization did not fall off; on the contrary, it increased. John Stevens of Maryland gave $36,000 for the building of an emigrant ship in 1856, and the next year this vessel, the Mary Caroline Stevens, especially made for the purpose, a comfortable sailing ship of 713 tons, made several trips. In 1867 David Hunt of Mississippi gave the American Colonization Society $45,000. The belief that Central America might be the best scene for large-scale colonization of the Negroes was later held by President Lincoln. Doolittle favored it and said in Congress that he would take Central America "with a friendly hand" and settle the freedmen there to enjoy social and political equality with the natives. Cong. Globe, 36th Cong., 1st sess., April 10, 1860.

soon get rid of the Negroes entirely. And what a change for the better all the way from Maryland to Missouri! The chaotic, jangling condition of the four different classes which in these grain-growing States obstructed each other, the masters and slaves mutually dependent, the free Negroes hanging on their skirts, and the white laborers in great measure excluded from employment and farm-ownership, would pass away. As it did so, the broad border region would become a fertile garden of small freeholders, and a throbbing home of varied manufactures.[28]

That under happier circumstances, and with boldly energetic government support, colonization might have achieved considerable results, few can doubt. Liberia was an unfortunate choice for the transplantation. Central America, or Santo Domingo, which had once been populous and was now almost empty, would have proved a more convenient, attractive, and salubrious site. A sustained national effort, financed by tens of millions of dollars, and directed by men as able as those who were building the powerful mid-century railroads and manufactories, might within a generation have planted a state of several hundred thousand self-supporting Negroes. Such a state within another generation might have attracted several hundred thousand more. But the South was neither willing nor able to give up the labor values represented by the Negro; the country was unready to spend the tens of millions required; and the social and governmental structure of the nation had not attained sufficient organization to make such a tremendous enterprise feasible. Moreover, the subtraction of half a million Negroes from the American total would not materially diminish the problem. The country could not escape its home responsibilities so easily.[29]

28 In a letter to the Sycamore, Ill., *Republican*, September 6, 1858, Frank Blair, Jr. (admitting that he owned a few slaves, "most of them purchased by me in order to prevent them from being separated from their families,") wrote that emancipation was urged by some on religious and moral grounds, by some on economic grounds, and by some on political grounds. All had substance. "For my part I have always given greater weight to the objection arising from political considerations, holding as I do that the institution is hostile to all true Democracy, and that its irresistible tendency is to build up an oligarchy and subvert our Republican Government. The idea of liberating the slaves and allowing them to remain in this country, is one that never will be tolerated." It was because the South always raised this objection that he put forward his proposal for colonizing the Negroes in Central America under American protection and guarantees of their civil rights. But Montgomery Blair wrote his father that emancipation was the only cure. Though "full of immediate trouble and perhaps danger," it would so check the increase of the Negroes that "a few generations would extinguish all but those whose industry would render them useful to the state." February 15, 1850; Blair Papers, Princeton Univ.

29 Jacob Dewees of Philadelphia published a 236-page book in 1854 called *The Great Future of Africa and America; an Essay showing our whole duty to the Black Man, consistent with our own safety and glory.* He believed in compensated emancipation, to be paid for by the proceeds of sales of public lands, and transportation of the Negroes to Africa, a process which he thought could not be concluded in less than a century. While he praised the Colonization Society for the limited work it had done, he thought that nothing less than the whole power of the national government could accomplish this huge effort.

[V]

Nothing better illustrated the impasse reached by the country than the harsh and increasingly harsher lot of the free Negro; a lot darkest in the South, but sad enough throughout the North.

In some salient respects more light is cast upon the race problem by Joel Chandler Harris's short story of "Free Joe and the Rest of the World" than by all of *Uncle Tom's Cabin,* for the pathetic tale better illuminates the central difficulty to be met. Free Joe, liberated in a little town of Central Georgia by a wandering speculator who lost all his other property at cards and committed suicide, remains close by the plantation where his wife Lucindy works. At first the humble black man has a jovial time. Lucindy's master is kind, and the two spend much time together. But the master dies, a hard, mean-tempered fellow named "Spite" Calderwood succeeds to Lucindy, and catching Free Joe visiting her one evening, he tears up the pass from the Negro's guardian, and orders him never to set foot on the plantation again. Poor Joe is crushed. But with the aid of his little dog Dan, he presently finds it possible to arrange clandestine meetings with Lucindy at the home of some neighboring poor whites. When Calderwood learns of this through telltale slaves, he sells Lucindy sixty miles away. For months Free Joe hopefully hangs around the plantation without learning what has happened. But the truth leaks out, and Joe, unable to trace or follow his wife, bereft even of his little dog by Calderwood's fierce hounds, homeless, friendless, and hopeless, dies heartbroken at the foot of the tree where he used to wait for Lucindy, the familiar humble smile still on his face. "His clothes were ragged; his hands were rough and callous; his shoes were literally tied together with strings; he was shabby in the extreme. A passerby, glancing at him, could have no idea that such a humble creature had been summoned as a witness before the Lord God of Hosts."

Many a free Negro both North and South might have been summoned in these years as a witness against neglect, oppression, and outrage. The half-million free colored folk who lived in the United States on the eve of the Civil War should theoretically have been happier, more prosperous, and more secure than their kinsfolk in bondage. Actually they occupied a position which was generally forlorn, miserable, and helpless. That they should have been ill-used in the South, where they held an anomalous position, need not astonish us. But the unenlightened and frequently inhuman treatment accorded them in the North, inspiring Greeley to the bitter declaration in 1852 that they had no future in America and should all be settled elsewhere, was a deplorable blot on the country's shield.[30]

30 N. Y. *Tribune,* June 14, 1852.

The free Negroes of the North were kept in menial positions, debarred from the intellectual professions and skilled handicrafts, denied equal educational facilities in many communities, and subjected to legal and political discrimination. They were in fact little better than outcasts. In New York, where they rode only in public conveyances labelled "Colored people allowed in this car," and in some other cities, a Jim Crow line was tightly drawn. The beginning of the decade found them completely or partially disfranchised in Pennsylvania, New York (where Negroes but not whites had to own $350 worth of realty to vote), Connecticut, New Jersey, Ohio, and Wisconsin; and as the years passed they were excluded from the polls in other States. Indeed, when the fifties ended, only three States allowed Negroes to vote on terms of complete parity with white men—Massachusetts, Maine, and New Hampshire, where their numbers were negligible. It was still true that, as De Tocqueville had said in the thirties, race prejudice seemed stronger in States which had got rid of slavery than in those which retained it. A shrewd student of the subject has concluded that in Illinois local antipathy to the Negro increased *pari passu* with the agitation for Southern emancipation.[31]

One State after another stigmatized the free Negroes by excluding them from its borders. When Illinois drew up its new constitution in 1848 an emphatic clause prohibited the entry of such folk, and the legislature five years later not only made it a misdemeanor for any Negro to enter with the purpose of settling, but provided that the offender might be fined and his time sold for a sufficient period to pay the penalty. Iowa in 1851 severely penalized any free Negro who set foot upon her soil. Indiana had a specially creditable body of free colored people about Newport, descendants of slaves liberated by Quakers in North Carolina early in the century and sent north by the North Carolina Yearly Meeting. It was the State of Levi Coffin. It boasted of one of the best travelled lines of the Underground Railroad, Coffin declaring in his classic

31 See Robert Purvis's protest against his children's exclusion from Pennsylvania schools; *Journal of Negro History,* X, 362ff. Gerrit Smith, speech at Peterboro, N. Y., January 23, 1859. N. Y. *Tribune,* January 17, 1852. N. D. Harris, *History of Negro Servitude in Illinois,* 233. A citizen of Jamaica, Long Island, deplored the condition of the free Negroes there: "The most of them are ignorant, superstitious, and in a state of abject servitude, infinitely worse than the subjects of the hardest taskmaster in the South. . . ." N. Y. *Weekly Tribune,* June 21, 1851. The original New York State Constitution allowed Negroes to vote on the same terms as whites. In early years, the fifth ward of New York City, where free Negroes resided in large numbers, was often carried by their votes. In 1821 the Constitution was revised, and the property qualification of whites was lowered, while that of blacks was raised. In 1826 the property qualification of whites was abolished; that of blacks retained.

Between 1804 and 1849 Ohio had several statutes imposing disabilities upon persons of color. One provided that no black or mulatto might give evidence in court, whether in a civil or criminal case, against a white person. A bill to repeal this came up in 1847 and produced a tempestuous debate. Clement L. Vallandigham undertook leadership of the devious maneuverings and engineerings which it was hoped would defeat the bill. See his explanation in *Cong. Globe,* February 8, 1858.

Reminiscences that some 3,300 Negro fugitives passed through the Newport station. And yet when Indiana placed a Negro-exclusion article in her constitution of 1851, the people approved it by the tremendous vote of more than five to one. Oregon adopted a constitution in 1857 stipulating that no free colored people should enter, that those who came should be forcibly removed, and that anybody who harbored or employed them should be punished. It also forbade the Negroes already there to hold real estate, make contracts, or prosecute suits. Proposals for a general expulsion of free blacks were frequent in the border States and by no means unknown farther north.[32]

Worst of all was the general public assumption in the North that Negroes were inferior creatures who naturally fell into degradation and whom it was hopeless to assist. Dr. Leonard Bacon told his New Haven congregation that of nearly a thousand free colored people in the city, a few families were honest, industrious, and sober, but the remainder, branded with ignominy, were in a condition of dreadful degeneracy. Plainly, the Christian citizens of New Haven were doing nothing to assist them. Even the abolitionists did little. Though William Lloyd Garrison lamented that the free colored people were regarded as an inferior caste to whom liberty was a curse, he gave them relatively little attention. When Edward Everett was asked by Peter Cooper to deliver an address at the inauguration of Cooper Union, he noted in his diary that he was inclined to do so on condition that all the proceeds of the ticket sale were placed "at my disposal, to be appropriated to aid poor Charlotte Ashe, my old cook, in purchasing her daughter's freedom. The daughter is a slave in Mississippi, and Charlotte has for years been trying to effect this object." The alacrity of Bostonians in helping Charlotte was plainly remarkable! Governor Washington Hunt unemotionally pointed out to the New York legislature in 1852 that the free Negroes were excluded from most institutions of religion and learning, were shut out from social intercourse, and were condemned to lives of servility and drudgery; a condition which, as he said, crushed the spirit of manhood and made improvement morally impossible. Uttering not a word of reproach to the white people, and recommending not a single reform of a domestic character, he urged simply that the Negroes for their own good be deported to Liberia.[33]

For a time early in the fifties a movement gained popularity to encourage the

32 On Indiana, see J. C. Hurd, *Law of Freedom and Bondage*, 130–131, 217. The vote was 108,413 to 20,951. N. Y. *Weekly Tribune*, August 23, September 13, 1851, In Ohio, a resolution was introduced in the Democratic State Convention in 1859 advocating the exclusion of free Negroes. Senator Pugh successfully opposed its passage, arguing that public sentiment was not yet ripe for it. He said that annually a thousand slaves were brought into Hamilton County to be liberated. N. Y. *Weekly Tribune*, June 11, 1859.

33 *Life of William Lloyd Garrison* by his children, I, 253–254. B. B. Munford, *Virginia's Attitude Toward Slavery and Secession*, Chs. 23–24. Everett, MS Diary, June 22, 1857; Everett Papers. N. Y. *Weekly Tribune*, January 10, 1852.

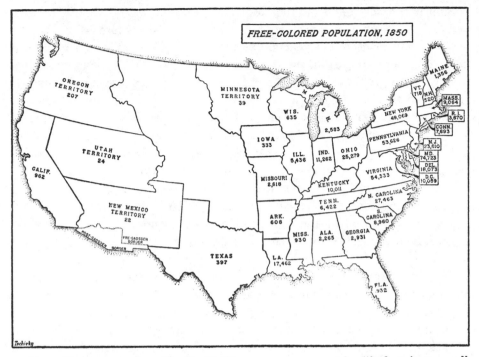

FREE-COLORED POPULATION, 1850

Free Negroes, writes U. B. Phillips, were commonly "industrious, well-mannered, and respected members of society"; and "each locality was likely to have some outstanding figure." But in many areas manumissions decreased and repressive laws grew.

free Negroes (by words, not money) to colonize themselves in detached and self-sufficing communities in the West. It being costly and inconvenient to help these poor people as members of white communities, why should they not look after themselves? A convention of the colored folk of Ohio held at Cincinnati early in 1852 received kindly admonitions from Senator Ben Wade and Representative L. D. Campbell. Did these radical freesoil leaders promise assistance at home? Not at all. Wade exhorted them to withdraw from all menial employments, form their own communities, and by farming, carpentering, blacksmithing, and other crafts attain a sturdy independence, thus overcoming the prejudice against their race. Campbell encouragingly remarked that he thought the existing condition of free colored people "infinitely worse" than it had been ten years earlier, and that he saw nothing hopeful in their immediate prospects. They should prepare to meet an intensified hostility, and he urged them to do so by becoming useful, industrious citizens, setting up their own workshops and their own schools.[34]

34 The convention was held January 15, 1852; New York and Cincinnati press, January 6–20, 1852.

Similar counsel came from the New York *Tribune*, which scolded the free Negroes for their lack of enterprise, dependence on white assistance for executing any project, and general acceptance of a dependent and parasitical position. If, separating from the rest of the nation as the Mormons had done, various Negro groups would set up independent and progressive communities, they would thus do more to advance themselves (urged the editors) than in any other way. Where? Anywhere that land was procurable; a township in New Jersey, a county in the West; just obtain it, settle it, manage it, and improve it. By establishing their own teachers, lawyers, doctors, justices, craftsmen, and expert farmers, they would stride forward as they never could while they insisted on living intermingled with a more powerful, numerous, and ambitious race who repelled them as inferiors.[35] This advice was easy to give, involved no reflection on the chill, aloof whites, required no expenditure by national, State, or local governments, and did not even include a gift of public land. It no more faced the realities of race-adjustment than the abolitionists' demand for immediate emancipation, or the colonizationists' ecstasies over a tiny struggling state in an impossible corner of Africa.

With so little practical assistance given, particularly in the basic economic aid of full employment opportunities, it is not strange that the free Negroes made slow and slight improvement. Here and there exceptional individuals and groups did well. The Negroes of Cincinnati, for example, boasted in 1853 of $800,000 worth of property; of prosperous carpenters, cabinetmakers, barbers, and hotelkeepers; and even of a landscape artist who had been sent to Rome to perfect himself. By 1859 the taxed real estate owned by Negroes in New York City amounted to $1,400,000. The Negro newspapers of New York State, headed by Frederick Douglass' *North Star* (called after 1851 *Fred Douglass's Paper*), were creditable. But the general situation was bad. British readers of Olmsted's pages were shocked by his description of the hard lot of the free colored people of Washington, who constituted one-fifth of the population. Two dozen colored men arrested in the spring of 1855 for holding a private meeting asserted that they had gathered for purely benevolent purposes. Among the objects found when they were searched were a Bible, a copy of Seneca's *Morals*, the constitution of a burial-society, and a subscription-paper for buying the freedom of a young woman. Yet the magistrate ordered one prisoner flogged, sent four others to the workhouse, and mulcted the remainder $111 in fines and costs.[36]

And Edward Dicey, visiting the North in 1861, found his heart wrung by

35 N. Y. *Weekly Tribune*, September 6, 1851, February 7, 1852.
36 N. Y. *Weekly Tribune*, July 15, 1853, on Negroes of Cincinnati. *Idem*, March 22, 1865, for Greeley's long article on the neglect and squalor of Washington Negroes.

the sad lot of the Negroes. Shabby, ragged, downcast, they faced general white antipathy, and seldom gained a post of responsibility. A shrewd, kindly old Ohio farmer, after dilating on the wealth and beauty of his State, concluded: "There is but one thing, sir, that we want here, and that is to get rid of the niggers." He complained of their indolence, illiteracy, and criminality. For such complaints Dicey found some basis of truth, for in every Northern city the free Negroes seemed the poorest, most thriftless, and perhaps most troublesome part of the population. But explained Dicey, if a dog is given a bad name and systematically whipped, he will generally deserve his disrepute. When a resident of Jamaica, L. I., complained that nine-tenths of the free Negroes of that old town, descendants of slaves of the early Dutch settlers, were worthless and dissolute, an illuminating response promptly came from the blacks. Denying the charge, they indignantly retorted that they were refused chances of employment, and their children opportunities of education.[37]

The best excuse which Northerners could make was that their unjust statutes and harsh social attitudes were the work of the baser part of the population, who wished to have somebody to look down upon and feared the competition of the Negroes. In 1854 a mulatto named Allen, announcing that he intended to marry a white girl, was hounded out of up-State New York, finally taking refuge in England. "All such outrages," complained the *Tribune*, "have been the work of the lowest and meanest class of whites, who are . . . particularly furious against 'amalgamation.' "[38] Every loafer, vagabond, and rowdy was indeed violently opposed to any action which would raise the black man toward equality. They had to have somebody to despise, and finding little but the color of their skins to justify a distinction, made the most of that. But it is unlikely that even the most liberal and enlightened people of the North understood how discreditable was their section's callous indifference to the Negroes, and how much doubt it cast upon the sincerity of the anti-slavery movement. Abolition was irrational without some well-studied plan of race-adjustment; yet instead of offering an example of harmony and progress, the North made no real effort to prove that healthy adjustment was even possible!

Southerners were far from blind to this fact. They made much of John Sherman's statement that so far as his observation extended, the relations of blacks and whites were often kindlier in the South than the North. Lucy Stone, traversing a considerable area of the Lower South, found that slaveholders were scornful of such Northern Negrophobes as John Mitchel. Their lips curled with contempt when they spoke of the harsh treatment of free Negroes in

37 N. Y. *Weekly Tribune*, June 14, 28, 1851; Edward Dicey, *Six Months in the Federal States*, I, 65–82.
38 N. Y. *Tribune*, May 13, 1854.

Yankee cities. Even in old Quaker Philadelphia, and in Newport, Ind., she had not been allowed to lecture in public halls except on condition that all colored people were debarred. When she told this to Kentucky slaveowners, they uttered indignant exclamations. In the South, they averred, black people were not crowded into corners; *they* understood the colored folk and Northerners did not—a statement that was to go ringing down the decades long after slavery was dead.[39]

[VI]

In reality, Southern kindliness was chiefly for Negroes in slavery and was that type of amiability always engendered in superior groups by an immutable caste system. It seldom extended to free Negroes, who were regarded with even greater hostility than in the North. Behind this antagonism lay an apprehension of the dangers to the existing order that lurked in the very existence of any large body of freedmen. If they grew numerous, educated, and economically secure, they would arouse the envious discontent of the slaves, become a rallying point against the existing order, and ultimately reduce slavery to atoms. The South therefore took precautions against their rise to strength. Most slaveholders would have said with Spite Calderwood: "Don't want no free niggers 'round here."

For various reasons such Negroes were likely to be of superior type. A good many, evincing unusual enterprise or belonging to specially kind masters, had earned enough money to pay for their freedom. At Fort Smith, Ark., lived a woman, laundress and nurse, who while paying her master ten dollars a month for her time, earned and saved enough in five years to purchase her freedom for $1,000. She then saved another $500 to pay for her aged and ailing husband, and the two continued to prosper pecuniarily. Others had been manumitted; sometimes out of pure kindliness, particularly to superior house servants, and sometimes by reason of blood relationship. A high percentage of free persons of color had white blood. Of the 773 free Negroes in Mississippi just before the war, for example, more than three-quarters (601) were of mixed ancestry, while in the general slave population, fewer than one-eleventh were mulattoes. Not a few slaveholders in signing manumission papers acknowledged their paternity, and case after case of this kind, involving some legal dispute, came before the courts. Strong indications can be found that as a body the free colored people constantly improved their position. This was at any rate true of Virginia, where as against one family in ten holding taxable property in 1830, one family in five had property in 1860. But not only did the number of owners

39 *Cong. Globe*, December 8, 1856; N. Y. *Tribune*, January 25, 1854.

double in these thirty years; the value of the property held increased by about three and a half times. Whereas the 9,000 free Negro families of 1830 in the Old Dominion held $253,000 worth of realty in 1830, three decades later the 9,500 such families were credited with $830,000 worth.[40]

But however superior, the free Negro usually led a hard life. Throughout the South the legal assumption was that any Negro was a slave unless proof to the contrary was presented. For this reason all free Negroes were required to obtain and keep proof of their status, and anyone who lost such proof and could not replace it stood in a perilous situation. Even those who held valid papers could be seized, spirited away, and sold into slavery; and all writers who have investigated the subject agree that illegal reduction to servitude was by no means infrequent.[41] Legal reduction was sometimes all too easy. Maryland laws at the beginning of the fifties, for example, provided that a free Negro convicted of his first penal offense should be sold outside the State for a period of years fixed by the court. At every session of court free Negroes were thus sold for two, four, six, or ten years, as the case might be. But they were bought by slave dealers for just as high prices as if sold for life, and many *were* sent out of the State for life—nobody ever seeing them return. A part of the money from the sale went, under the law, to the officer making the arrest. The result was that any Negro who had ever been in the penitentiary was watched with hawk-like eye, and a small theft or a street affray might mean a lifetime of hard plantation toil. This Maryland law evidently had for one object a reduction of the free Negro population—and other Southern laws were not unlike it.

The free Negro of course had no political rights, and might not vote, serve on a jury, or bear witness in criminal cases for or against a white person. He had limited rights to appear as witness in civil suits, and could of course testify in all cases which involved other free colored persons alone. All free Negroes were sternly restricted in their movements. They must have a local white guardian, and could not wander into another county in search of employment without serious risk of being jailed as vagabonds. They were similarly restricted in their occupations. In Mississippi, typical of the lower South, no free Negro could keep a shop except in an incorporated town; none could keep a grocery or sell liquors anywhere; none could operate an inn or tavern, for this might facilitate clandestine meetings and plots; and none could set type in a printing establishment, for this might permit the circulation of seditious publications. Any printer

40 Boston *Journal*, Fort Smith letter September 13, 1859, C. S. Sydnor, "The Free Negro in Mississippi," *Am. Hist. Rev.*, XXXII, July, 1927, pp. 769ff. Luther P. Jackson, *Free Negro Labor and Property Holding in Virginia 1830–1860*; U. of Chicago Dissertation, 1937.
41 E. G. R. B. Flanders, "Free Negro in Ante-Bellum Georgia," *North Carolina Historical Review*, IX, 1932, pp. 250ff. "Equal Justice," Baltimore, December 30, 1849 in N. Y. *Tribune*, January 1, 1850.

caught with a colored hand was liable to a fine, while the hand was subject to the death penalty.[42] It need hardly be said that free Negroes found hunting difficult, for the possession of firearms, ammunition, or other weapons was forbidden without a license which was instantly voidable.

For various reasons—to find odd jobs, to engage in the vending prohibited elsewhere, to escape planter and farmer hostility—many free Negroes gravitated toward the cities and towns. In Mississippi, for example, Vicksburg and Natchez always contained a large share of the free colored group. In 1840, considerably more than a fifth resided in these two centers, 278 out of 1,366. Ten years later Natchez alone had 213 free colored persons. Besides taking odd jobs, cultivating market gardens, and operating small farms, free Negroes throughout the South found a variety of occupations. Many were smiths, cobblers, carpenters, barbers, cabinetmakers, shoeblacks, housepainters, or small tradesmen. The New Orleans *Picayune* testified in 1859 that free Negroes supplied the great majority of regular settled masons, bricklayers, builders, carpenters, tailors, and shoemakers; that they counted many excellent musicians, jewellers, goldsmiths, and merchants; and that as a whole they were "a sober, industrious, and moral class, far advanced in education and civilization." Some worked on the river steamboats as roustabouts or deckhands, a life so free that it was carefully hedged about by legal restrictions. Many grew prosperous, acquiring not only realty and other goods, but title to slaves, who might or might not be relatives. One Mississippi Negro in 1830 had seventeen slaves and another sixteen. The 360 colored taxpayers of Charleston in 1860 included no fewer than 130 who owned an aggregate of 390 slaves. Naturally the more enterprising free Negroes found means of giving their children schooling, whatever the law, under white or colored teachers, or both. That many of them were highly respected for their industry, ability, and integrity is attested by a thousand pieces of evidence.[43]

One of the most remarkable men of the ante-bellum South was the free mulatto William T. Johnson of Natchez, whose voluminous diaries and personal and business papers are treasured in the archives of the University of Louisiana.[44] Coming to Natchez in 1830 from Port Gibson, he established a barber-shop, married, and grew prosperous. In time he acquired two other barber-shops and a bath-house in Natchez, bought a plantation in that area, purchased at least one town lot, and established business connections with New Orleans. Bright, affable, energetic, and trustworthy, he became a friend of many planters and businessmen of western Mississippi. He performed small services for them, while if any imbibed too freely, his bath-house was at their disposal till they grew

42 Sydnor, "Free Negro in Miss.," *Am. Hist. Rev.*, XXXII.
43 New Orleans *Picayune* quoted in N. Y. *Weekly Tribune*, August 9, 1859. Sydnor, *op. cit.*, 109ff. Phillips, *American Negro Slavery*, 434. Randall, *Civil War and Reconstruction*, 52.
44 The Johnson collection has 58 bound volumes and 1,304 separate pieces.

sober. They gave him business advice, and he lent money to those who needed it, taking the usual high interest-rates. He thus grew rich. Throughout much of the thirties and forties he kept a diary, occasionally illustrated by his own rough sketches, which both furnishes a detailed commentary upon the events of white society, and portrays the mind and activities of an outstanding representative of the more alert, educated, and enterprising free colored people.

It is clear that he led an enjoyable as well as useful life. Like white men of the region, he liked a good horse-trade. He bought and sold oxen, and traded in corn and potatoes. The management of his barber-shops, each of which often took in six or eight dollars a day, and his plantation, where he rejoiced in good crops, did not keep him too busy to enjoy many diversions. He owned horses and raced them under other men's names. He bet on elections and other events, winning many a wager of a dollar or two. He went to the theatre, chafing under his enforced restriction to the Negro gallery. He fished and hunted. Upon the doings of white folk he bent a more sardonic eye than they suspected. Duels, murders, steamboat explosions, lawsuits, fierce political contests, speeches by such visiting notables as Henry Clay, noteworthy marriages, and auctions all find a place in a chronicle so candid that even today publication would require deletions.

Many white men treated him almost as an equal. "I went out this evening near Mrs. Linton's," he writes on one occasion, "and Shot a Mach with Mr. Jacquemine the 3 best in five for One Barrell of Oysters—I won them with ease." He would go shares with whites in small business deals, as in buying a barrel of pork. Many a small gift came to him, and he made gifts in return. When he proudly grew a forty-three-pound watermelon, he sent it off by steamer to a friend. Now and then a distinguished man treated him like the fellow-gentleman that he was. "General Quitman handed me a letter today that was given him at Jackson for me," runs one note. And he adds with touching emphasis: "He did me proud—he did me proud."

Nevertheless, in his almost helpless legal and social position he suffered many injustices. When paper money was depreciated by half, a debtor took advantage of the situation. "Mr. Blank," writes Johnson, "paid me two hundred dollars that he promised me that he would give me good money for it. Such is the nature of mankind." A "Dutch" family threw a cow of his down the steep bank of a bayou, killed her, and stole the meat. In one unfortunate day a scoundrel knocked out the eye of his mare ("Some Outrageous Rascal—oh if I Knew him"), while "Some infernal Thief" stole his skiff. He makes numerous notes upon a worthless and malevolent country neighbor named Baylor Winn. "B. Winns daughter came down to Hard Scrabble without shoes she had just escaped from Irons that her father had Chained her in to keep her from getting

Married to a Mr. Burk the wood Chopper." The girl made good her marriage. In the late forties he became involved in a suit with Winn and a man named Wade respecting the boundary of their plantations. The controversy was carried to the circuit court, which ordered a survey run, and the disputed land was found to be Johnson's. He thereupon proposed a generous compromise; Winn and Wade were to abandon the land improperly occupied and pay for the wood they had cut, while Johnson was to drop all claim for damages.

The last entries of the diary have a quiet pathos. On May 3, 1851, Wade called to say that they accepted the compromise. On May 16, Johnson's ninth child and fourth son was born. On May 18 he wrote that "Shop below made me $10.25 this week." His crops were doing well, and he took pleasure in inspecting them. On a beautiful day in early June he rode out with his children to gather the plentiful blackberries. The final jotting is for June 14th. The weather was mild and pleasant; business had been dull; he could not find two of his horses, and feared that something was amiss, for it was reported that they had been driven out of Lanieres the previous evening; he had bought some groceries, and had treated himself to fifteen cents' worth of soda and cigars. The ink was hardly dry on this record when he was ambushed and fatally wounded, surviving just long enough to name Winn as his assassin. The bullet had slain one of the most remarkable and interesting of American diarists.

Free Negroes slowly increased in number in the United States, rising from 434,000 in 1850 to 482,000 in 1860. They even increased (more slowly still) in the slave States, which by 1860 had about 250,000. But outside the border area, North Carolina, and Louisiana, the totals remained very small. In Mississippi, Texas, and Arkansas the free colored people actually decreased during the decade, while in Florida the population was stationary.[45] The final decade of slavery was unquestionably a black period for these unoffending Negroes and mulattoes. With sectional tension rising, with world sentiment against slavery increasing, Southerners were filled with fear lest the mere presence of free Negroes should excite discontent and insubordination among their fettered brethren. A tremendously forcible demand for repressive legislation rolled like a tidal wave across the South.

From early times a number of States had taken drastic steps to make sure that any increase in this unwanted population would be slow, difficult, and carefully guarded. The favorite measures had been the placing of sharp limits upon manumission, and the stern prohibition of any immigration of free Negroes. Georgia, for example, had halted manumission by deed of gift as early as 1801. In 1818 it forbade manumission by last will and testament, thus forbidding any Georgian to follow Washington's example. For a time slaves

45 Cf. table in Randall, *op. cit.*, 51.

were permitted to purchase their freedom. But kindly masters who permitted Negroes to hire their time and keep the marginal earnings until they had accumulated enough for self-purchase came to be regarded as a menace. They were not only adding to the number of free Negroes but creating a new class of nominal slaves, neither bond nor free, who might conceivably make trouble. Laws were passed to halt the process. The only method of liberating a slave that remained was by special legislative enactment, which was extremely difficult. In some respects Georgia's laws restricting free colored people were more severe than Mississippi's or South Carolina's. They were debarred from certain occupations; they could not hold title to slaves or real estate in their own names; they were never to be taught to read and write; and they might be compelled to labor on public works for twenty days every year. Any free Negro convicted of idleness or immorality might have his labor sold for one year, while the penalty for a second offense was slavery for life. It is not astonishing that Georgia had only 3,500 free Negroes in the year of Lincoln's election, and that their material and cultural progress was pitifully slow.[46]

Yet as if such Lacedemonian laws were not enough, an outcry arose for compelling free Negroes to choose between exile and reduction to slavery. Two legislatures in the midst of the Kansas crisis, when excitement ran high, bowed to this demand. Arkansas in February, 1859, enacted that all free persons of color must sell their belongings and remove from the State by New Year's Day of 1860. If they did not go, sheriffs were to seize them and hire them out for one year to the highest bidder, using the net proceeds of their labor to enable them to leave. Such as wished to remain might choose masters, who under a Pecksniffian clause were to pay half their appraised value into the common school fund. Two months after the law went into effect the Little Rock *True Democrat* rubbed approving hands over its workings, saying that many free Negroes had returned to slavery, and the disposition of the slaves had improved! Yet the idea that Arkansas had been pestiferously overrun by free Negroes, as another newspaper asserted, withers under the test of census figures. In 1850 only 608 had been enumerated! So fearful was Arkansas of being tainted that another law of 1859 forbade steamboats navigating her waters to employ free Negroes.[47]

46 R. B. Flanders, *op. cit.*; Hurd, *op. cit.*
47 Little Rock *True Democrat*, March 7, 1860. Fort Smith *Times*, June 9, 1859. E. L. Harvin, "Arkansas and the Crisis of 1860–1861," MS thesis, U. of Texas. Arkansas Historical Association Pubs. III, 179ff. The Arkansas press carried pathetic advertisements by Negroes trying to sell their property. Henry King of Little Rock, for example, advertised two houses and three lots in that city, with fruit trees, smoke-house, and other appurtenances. The Little Rock *Gazette and Democrat* called attention to this advertisement with the remark that King had been respected since boyhood and that any community to which he removed would be blessed with that noblest work of God, an honest man. February 19, 1859.

Louisiana followed in March, 1859, with legislation which gave all free persons of color not born in the State, upon warning to leave, a choice of exile, a penitentiary term followed by exile, or slavery for life under some self-chosen master or mistress. Its provisions were so complicated that even the native-born were not completely safe. The panic and sorrow among the eighteen thousand free Negroes of the State were indescribable. Newspapers blossomed out with items describing how this or that Negro, giving up well-paid work and independent homes, had selected an owner. Telling of two steamboat cooks, one earning $75 a month and one $100, who did this, the New Orleans *Crescent* added: "From what we hear at present, a great many free negroes, not born in this State, will pick out their masters and become slaves sooner than leave the population and the climate which pleases them so well." Coolly phrased! Behind this smooth, unruffled language, what anxieties, what terror, what agony, as men and women prepared to sell their poor belongings and move northward, or sought for some master whose kindness they could trust! And Louisiana passed another law, under pressure from white stevedores and longshoremen, prohibiting the temporary introduction of free men of color by any ship arriving at the port of New Orleans.[48]

Everywhere in the slave area the feverish excitement of the period and the sense that slavery was on the defensive produced a suspicious and hostile attitude toward Free Joe. Delegates in the Kentucky convention of 1849 murmured against him, saying that vicious whites corrupted him and made him steal, that he was a bad example to slaves, and that he was better off in slavery. In North Carolina his position had long been specially happy. He had once been pronounced a citizen, his right to vote had not been taken away until 1835, he had managed to acquire some education and establish a fairly satisfactory community life, and he practised a wide variety of occupations in the economic system. Yet racial antagonism deepened until in many places it grew intense. Efforts by philanthropic persons to educate the ten thousand free colored people in the District of Columbia meanwhile provoked sharp resistance. They were being instructed far beyond their political and social condition, ran one complaint of 1857; free schools would attract an inundating flood from the surrounding region; and the true course was to prohibit immigration and encourage removals. Tennessee, which until 1834 allowed free Negroes the ballot, hardened its heart; the legislature debated bills late in the fifties to banish these poor folk, and passed a law permitting them to enslave themselves.

48 New Orleans *Daily Crescent*, September 1, 1859, quoted in N. Y. *Weekly Tribune*, September 10, 1859. See Mobile *Register*, November 27, 1859, quoting N. Y. *Journal of Commerce* to the effect that the Louisiana law prohibiting temporary landings of free men of color caused a good many Northern ships to stop at Mobile rather than New Orleans.

Nor were the sixteen thousand slaveholders of Maryland less irritable and apprehensive. They viewed the eighty thousand free Negroes, a body almost as numerous as the slaves, with jaundiced gaze. Many of these black folk had acquired property and standing. Rightly or wrongly, they were connected with the brisk operations of the Underground Railroad running into the very heart of the State. The slaveholders of the Eastern Shore, gathering in convention at Cambridge in the fall of 1858, first blackened the character of Free Joe by accusation of "vicious habits," "refusal to labor," "incapacity for self-government," and then proposed a statewide convention to bring pressure upon the legislature. The proper policy, they declared, was to give all free colored people the choice of leaving Maryland or going into slavery.[49]

Everywhere, North and South, the free Negro offered a demonstration of the fact that the racial problem underlay the slavery problem, and that abrupt action in dealing with the 'peculiar institution' might well complicate the task of race-adjustment. Everywhere, too, the free Negro showed that the colored man's position in American society would be more largely fixed by economic facts, social forces, and inherited attitudes regarding color caste than by laws.

A Southern pamphleteer, Ellwood Fisher, roundly asserted in 1849 that emancipation would fail, because it would leave the Negro's real position largely unchanged. Would the emancipated slave really work as hard as was necessary for competition with the white man, and if he did, would the white laborer welcome such competition? Pointing to the North, Fisher noted some of the rough facts that abolitionists were wont to ignore. Of nearly twelve thousand colored people in the city of New York in 1845, barely a hundred had satisfied the $250 qualification for voting. Throughout the North, despite augmentation by manumissions and escapes, the free Negroes increased more slowly than the slaves of the South. Of all the free persons of color, nearly half preferred to remain in the slave area. The number of Negroes in Boston, the very center of sympathy and agitation for the slaves, had actually decreased during the previous twenty years, while in Massachusetts the percentage of colored persons

49 Debates and Proceedings of the Kentucky Convention, 73ff. John Hope Franklin, *The Free Negro in North Carolina, 1790–1860. National Intelligencer*, May 7, 1857, gives Walter Lenox's denunciation of Miss Myrtilla Miner's Washington school and its enlargement. Wright, *Free Negro in Maryland.* In 1850 Maryland had 74,723 free Negroes; in 1860, it had 83,942. See the Baltimore *American*, November 5, 6, 1858; N. Y. *Weekly Tribune*, November 13, 1858, on the convention at Cambridge. Another Maryland slaveholders' convention met in Baltimore on June 8, 1859. A few members wished to prohibit emancipation and pass laws for the gradual extinction of "Free Negroism." But by an almost unanimous vote, the convention took a more humane view. It adopted resolutions declaring any measure for the general removal of free blacks from Maryland impolitic, inexpedient, and unnecessary, and asserting that for the purpose of diminishing "the evils which proceed from the excessive and increasing free negro class," the policy of the State fixed in 1831 should be reaffirmed with amendments which "will either prohibit emancipation altogether, or compel the prompt removal from the State of those emancipated. . . ." N. Y. *Weekly Tribune*, June 18, 1859.

in the penitentiary was ten times the percentage of whites. The pamphleteer was wrong in concluding that emancipation would be a mistake. But he was right in his demonstration that emancipation would be but one part, and a small part, of a task far heavier and more complex than men realized.[50]

[VII]

With the emancipationist impulse of the fathers dead, with colonization impracticable, with the position of the free Negro tragic in the North and almost intolerable in parts of the South, what was the solution of the great problem? A rising Southern chorus chanted its answer: slavery must be accepted as beneficent, immutable, and eternal. Northerners for the most part held that slavery was a temporary system to be maintained until it could safely yield to gradual emancipation. The abolitionists of course demanded immediate and unconditional liberation. But as they remained a relatively small and uninfluential group, the substantial choice lay between slavery as an immutable discipline, and slavery as an institution evolving toward freedom.

It is a law of history that whenever peaceful evolution fails to effect a needed set of changes, some revolutionary agency steps in and does so. Change and growth are so indispensable in human affairs that whenever an effort is made to erect an immovable dam, the force of the piling waters finally becomes absolutely irresistible. The calamitous error of Southern leadership lay in its refusal to treat slavery as a dynamic institution. By statesmanlike effort reforms could have been introduced (as Robert Toombs advocated in his famous lecture on slavery) to safeguard marriage and the family life of the bondsmen; to give all Negroes fitted for it some education, and to allow those who displayed exceptional enterprise, intelligence, and industry to escape from servitude— in short, to make slavery an educative and transitional labor-system, thus laying the groundwork for a rational permanent adjustment between the races. To be sure, all this would have demanded sacrifice and would have imposed risks. But neither would have been comparable with those incurred when the waters finally broke through with destructive roar.

The great concurrent error of the North was that it did nothing of a practical nature to assist in racial adjustment on a new basis. Merely to rail at the Southerners for holding slaves and to demand instant emancipation was a deplorably barren policy. Why did none of these Northern abolitionists who could easily raise considerable sums of money send agents southward, buy up slaves, and bring them North for settlement? Those who fled from their

50 Ellwood Fisher, "The North and the South" (Lecture, pvt., Richmond, 1849; Huntington Library).

masters were welcomed, but practically nothing was done to purchase any from their owners. Doubtless one reason was that such a course would have raised slave-prices, encouraged slave-breeding, and done little to solve the problem. But another and larger reason was that Northern workers would not have permitted this solution, even had it been valid, for they disliked colored neighbors and colored rivalry. Abolitionists wished to liberate the slaves to compete with the small farmers and workmen of the South; they did not wish to bring them North to compete with farmers, mechanics, and laborers of the free areas. Wealthy Gerrit Smith did distribute an inhospitable tract of land in northern New York among free and escaped Negroes, but that inadequate effort stood alone, cost little in money or care, and demanded no Northern effort at social readjustment. Why did Northern leaders not rally about Webster's proposal that the proceeds of the public lands be used for gradual compensated emancipation, perhaps with some systematic Northern resettlement? Tough-minded men asked these questions. Said the New York *Journal of Commerce* in 1850 of the slaves:

The North first made property of them, and owe much of their gains to them. How many *hundreds* did they ever liberate? On the contrary, when a single individual at the South first liberated sixty, worth as property then at least $30,000, it was found difficult, nay impossible, to raise at the North $3,000 to send them to Africa; and a large proportion of that insignificant sum was contributed from the South. Where is the Northern man, old or young, living or dying, that leaves any bequest of any kind to liberate and restore these people, whom their fathers or themselves have plundered and robbed from Africa, to their homes? [51]

The consequence of these two refusals—the refusal of Southerners to treat slavery as a progressive and evolutionary system, leading by regular gradations to freedom, and the refusal of Northerners to acknowledge that in equity they must share the heavy burdens of racial readjustment—was to place slavery in a position where it became more and more perilous to the body politic. It had to be moved toward a new position, but neither side was willing to move it by gradual plan. Year by year a violent solution of the problem became more probable. The North was quite as much at fault as the South.

Each side could easily rationalize its attitude. Northerners could assert that

[51] O. B. Frothingham, *Gerrit Smith*, 235. N. Y. *Journal of Commerce* quoted in Washington *Union*, May 5, 1850. A Southerner, in a letter in the *National Intelligencer*, August 20, 1857, sardonically congratulated a National Emancipation Convention shortly to meet in Cleveland for adopting, at last, "a practical direction." It intended to seek a way to abolish slavery and remunerate slave-owners. He proposed that it consider the cost of purchasing slaves who steadily would grow more valuable as their number was decreased by manumissions, the costs of the cotton and sugar estates which would be ruined, the losses of Northern cotton mills, labor, ships when raw goods no longer came to market, and so on.

as the South had for two centuries profited from the unrequited labor of the slave, so now it should meet all the difficulties of assimilating them to its own society. They could also declare that no important problem existed, for the Negro possessed such high intellectual and moral characteristics that he could rapidly and painlessly be lifted to equality with the whites. This sentimental exaggeration of the Negro's immediate potentialities (something very different from his ultimate capacities) was particularly common among abolitionists who knew little of the slave at first hand, and who by an easy process of generalization fancied nearly every field hand a Robert Purvis or Frederick Douglass. Southerners meanwhile rationalized their attitude by so exaggerating the dangers and difficulties of change as to pronounce it utterly impossible. More importantly, as we have seen, they could contrast the worst side of industrialism with the best side of slavery. And most fortifying of all to the Southern spirit, they could consciously or unconsciously take the view that the Negro had never been fit for any position but that of bondsman, and never would be. This became a traditional conviction bulwarked by habit, indolence, timidity, and the desire for security.

The assertion that the Negro was an inferior creation, a being of natural incapacity, lent itself to a thought-pattern which opposed all change in slavery. Cultural, democratic, and humanitarian assumptions applied only to man, not brutes, and the Negro was nearer brute than man—so the implicit syllogism ran. The Negro was a creature of great physical strength, of limited intellectual power (scientifically explained by contracted cranial capacity, early closing of the frontal skull-sutures, and special characteristics of the brain-cells), of natural indolence, conquerable only by stern driving, of powerful sexual impulses, dangerous unless rigidly restrained, of innate superstition, and of constant readiness to revert to savagery.[52]

"We recognize the fact of the inferiority stamped upon the race of men by the Creator," said Jefferson Davis in the Senate, "and from the cradle to the grave, our government as a civil institution, marks that inferiority." [53]

52 Cf. John Dollard, *Caste and Class in a Southern Town*. The idea that the Negro was congenitally thriftless and lazy was sharply condemned in the first report of the Virginia Commissioner of Agriculture (1877). The Commissioner, Dr. Pollard, declared white supervision unnecessary. Speaking from his own experience as a farmer under both the slave regime and the free regime, he declared that "the negro, if promptly paid and fairly dealt by, is as good a laborer as he ever was," and that while some would not work, "the majority of them, and enough to till the lands" would. How much work would they do? As much as white men, he thought. He cited the report of Charles L. Flint, secretary of the Massachusetts Board of Agriculture, on the time consumed by labor in performing various farm tasks. "At the time of reading the report we made a calculation, in connection with another farmer, of how long it would take to accomplish the work here in Virginia, and came to the conclusion that our negro hands would do more work per day than the white laborers of Massachusetts." Cited in the *Nation*, February 14, 1878.

53 Davis in *Cong. Globe*, February 29, 1860. Cf. Dollard, Cason, W. J. Cash, *et aliis*.

This supposed biological inferiority, stated by science and the Bible, condemned the Negro to permanent servility. Convenient instances were selected from the mass of evidence at hand to support the defensive generalization. As Cuffy was stupid, and Meg unchaste, so all Negroes were stupid and unchaste; it being forgotten that Joe was very bright and Sally a model of wifely constancy. Beliefs in the mendacity, thievishness, emotional instability, and laziness of Negroes were thus systematically cultivated in order to build up a defensive pattern supporting the slavery relationship—and behind it a fixed caste relation.

Such rationalizations, with clashing economic interests and general divergences of culture, created a greater and greater gulf of misunderstanding. As the two sections faced each other across the chasm, with rising excitement and growing antipathy, each side gave way more and more to irrational emotion; each seemed to catch the far-off note of throbbing drums and sounding bugles.

[VIII]

But it was not the white men alone, North and South, who were to settle the slavery question. The Negro was always a factor, and as the decades passed a more and more active factor. The Southern contention that the Negroes were what "Vindex," writing in 1858, called a debased race of inordinate animality and little intellect,[54] was refuted by the colored folk themselves. The dictum that their condition was and must remain static was being contradicted by steady advances. Slavery, and still more the general contact of whites and blacks whether inside or outside slavery, were steadily if slowly and unevenly raising the Negro toward the cultural level of the more highly developed race. For in one aspect slavery was a school, a channel of education. From the moment they were landed in America, the Negroes in some fashion, and usually in many, were under the tuition of the dominant race. They learned something of a new, more flexible, and more exacting language, of a nobler religion, of a routine of steady industry, of moral principles, and of complex skills.

Unquestionably a primary step in the education of many Negroes was the inculcation of habits of steady settled industry. While the indigenous culture of various Negro peoples in Africa had been on a much higher level than most Americans of 1850 realized, it was not the product of labor as steady and intense as that of contemporaneous white civilizations. We have the testimony of such sympathetic observers as Albert Schweitzer that certain basic conditions of life among the primitive peoples of Africa—the enervating climate, the ease with which a sufficiency of food, clothing, and shelter may be obtained, the lack of

54 *National Intelligencer*, February 23, 1858.

incentive for large accumulations of property—tended to make labor casual and intermittent.[55] But slavery taught the Negro to work without excessive intermissions and with genuine application and method. For some of the most superior slaves brought from Africa such a lesson was superfluous, but for the great majority it meant a valuable toughening of character. Learning that while mere subsistence is possible on a casual labor basis, wealth in volume can be created only by an uninterrupted routine of hard toil, the Southern Negro by 1860 was in countless instances ready to work when he did not please, and for larger ends than mere living.

In the process of working, the Negro acquired valuable new skills. To be sure, very impressive types of craftmanship had existed in Africa. So coolheaded an observer as Sir Harry Johnston calls "wonderful" the culture of one area in metalworking, weaving, pottery, and carving. The Dahomey brasswork, the Benin bronzes, the Ashanti textiles, the iron and basketry of all the peoples, were remarkable. In some districts, as on the lower Congo, a certain differentiation of occupations had grown up; one village devoting itself to fishing, another to palm wine, another to work in iron and copper, and a fourth to trade and brokerage among the rest.[56] But the evidence seems conclusive that the great majority of the black folk brought to America were accustomed to a low stage of endeavor in agriculture, in household management and cookery, in blacksmithing and the mechanic arts, and in the fabrication of clothes and furniture. They grew accustomed to the sight of a much more elaborate and finished set of arts, and to an increasing degree shared in their practice.

Many slaves, to be sure, knew little except the use of the hoe, mattock, and axe. They were constantly and steadily driven up to their work, and the stupid, plodding, machine-like manner in which they labored was painful to witness. So wrote Olmsted of the Old Southwest, and his view that a meaningless drudgery was the lot of most field hands was commonly accepted. But even on the larger plantations of the cotton belt a considerable variety of occupations prevailed. Slaves had to plow, hoe, replant, and pick cotton; to repair fences, houses, and barns, keep plantation equipment in shape, clean wells, and trim trees; to clear new ground, burn brush, and make rails; to manufacture charcoal and bricks; and to look after plantation animals. Most plantations gave some attention to corn, peas, and potatoes. Ginning, baling, and road-repairing all took effort. And then there were the mechanic trades: any ordinary plantation would have a carpenter, blacksmith, shoemaker, shingle-maker, and weaver, or indeed

55 Schweitzer, *On the Edge of the Primeval Forest*, ch. 7; Friedrich Ratzel, *History of Mankind*, II, 380ff.

56 Sir Harry Johnston, *Opening Up of Africa*, 125; cf. Melville J. Herskovits, "Social History of the Negro" in *Handbook of Social Psychology*, ed. C. Marchison, 221-224; W. E. B. Du Bois, *The Negro*, 117, quoting Bucher.

several of each category. A larger plantation would be likely to have a wheel-wright and wagonmaker, with seamstresses, cooks, midwife, and nurses. Crippled Negroes unfit for hard field work would be put to labor in the "loom house" or the cobbler's shop; a boy of great manual skill would be apprenticed to the smith; a lad with a keen eye would be set to laying out the levels for hillside ditches. Of partial Negro self-government on large plantations there were interesting and increasingly numerous examples.[57]

On the smaller plantations and farms the slaves of course had to be master of as many rough crafts as the owner himself; the men carried on all the operations of the place, from breeding livestock and breaking colts to erecting farm buildings and planting orchards; the women spun, wove, sewed, mended, cooked, and cleaned. Plantations or farms which fronted on river or bay offered various water occupations, while those recently cleared from the forest furnished logging and lumbering. In short, it was not merely possible, but indispensable, for hosts of Negroes to acquire nearly as varied a list of skills as those of the frontier or semi-frontier farmer in America, the most resourceful and versatile agricultural worker in the world. One ingenious Maryland slave in 1852 formally applied for a patent on a useful agricultural machine.[58]

The town Negro, it was generally observed, was demarcated from the rural black by superior liveliness and intelligence, but also by a more dubious morality and a slighter sense of duty and responsibility. Both his intellectual superiority and moral inferiority were natural, for while he saw more of life and had fuller opportunities to acquire special training, he was frequently hired out to men who gave his conduct outside working hours no supervision. Town slaves might do almost anything. They might be mechanics, hostlers, carpenters, or shoe-makers. They might work as assistants to white barbers, house-builders, harness-makers, blacksmiths, or wagon-makers. They could be employed in foundries, textile mills, tanneries, brick-making establishments, sawmills, or metal-working shops. Considerable numbers worked in building railroads or as brakemen and firemen, while at least one slave was a locomotive engineer. Others were fire-men, roustabouts, cooks, and stewards on river steamboats. Still others labored in gangs to cut down the firewood which the steamboats burned. Negro janitors for offices and shops were numerous, while most larger hotels and taverns kept Negro servants, sometimes quick, alert, and highly useful, sometimes stupid and inefficient. A number of Negroes even learned such crafts as cigar-making. As

57 Olmsted, *Journey in the Back Country*, 81–82. Sydnor, *Slavery in Mississippi*, 9–11. Woodson, *Education of the Negro Prior to 1861*, p. 210. At the famous sale of Pierce Butler's 436 slaves at Savannah early in 1859, coming from a rice plantation near Darien and a cotton plantation on St. Simon's Island, a number of very passable mechanics were included. "There were coopers, carpenters, shoemakers, and blacksmiths, each one equal in his various craft to the ordinary requirements of a plantation." N. Y. *Weekly Tribune*, March 12, 1859.
58 N. Y. *Weekly Tribune*, December 25, 1858.

for the women, they found employment as seamstresses, cooks, and laundry-women.[59]

Cotton factories, slowly increasing in number, found that white labor was more satisfactory than that of Negroes, and one conspicuous South Carolina mill which depended upon the use of black operatives was soon forced into bankruptcy. Nevertheless, by 1850 the South had abundant proof that the Negro possessed the innate capacity to make not merely a capable mill-hand, but a proficient artisan. Indeed, ten years earlier Savannah had 107 Negroes (slave and free) listed as mechanics, and more who were butchers, barbers, engineers, or pilots. The success of Negroes in handicraft occupations was so great that the Georgia legislature passed a law in 1845 to prohibit colored mechanics or masons, whether slave or free, from making contracts to erect or repair buildings.[60]

White mechanics in Mississippi, as in other States, frequently opposed the training of slaves in their occupations as a degradation of the calling, and a source of competition. When one Mississippi artisan was offered the help of three slaves for half a dozen years on condition that he teach them his craft, he angrily rejected the offer. Wide attention was attracted in 1851 to a memorial by the Mechanics' Association of Portsmouth, Va., protesting against the teaching of crafts and trades to slaves. A convention of four or five hundred delegates which met that same summer in Atlanta, Ga., to consider means of advancing the mechanic arts, proposed among other steps the entire stoppage of the instruction of Negroes in skilled trades. It argued that the admission of blacks to various crafts not only limited the opportunities open to white men, but sharpened their wits, made them restless, encouraged them to run away to the North, and gave them a generally unsettled character. They became ambitious to read and write, mastered these arts in clandestine fashion, and then aroused the discontent of other slaves. "A few Negro mechanics in towns and cities," stated the resolutions of the convention, "have done and can do more practical injury to the institution of slavery and its permanent security, than all the ultra abolitionists of

59 Sydnor, *Slavery in Mississippi*, 5-8; P. A. Bruce, *Plantation Negro as a Freeman*. The New Orleans *Picayune*, quoted in the N. Y. *Weekly Tribune*, August 6, 1859, asserted: "Some of our best mechanics and artisans are to be found among the free colored men. They form the great majority of our regular settled masons, bricklayers, builders, carpenters, tailors, shoemakers, etc. . . . while we count among them in no small numbers excellent musicians, jewelers, goldsmiths, tradesmen, and merchants."

60 Phillips, *American Negro Slavery*, 379. Flanders, *Slavery in Georgia*, 204-205. The Selma, Ala., *Sentinel*, quoted in the *National Intelligencer*, October 30, 1858, described the successful use of slaves in the Scottsville, Alabama, mills. The first profits of the mills—$2,200, paid in 1841—were used to purchase a family of Negroes for work in the factory. "This family has so increased that the company values them at $10,000, and most of them are now working in the factory, and are very useful. The company have made several purchases of Negroes with the profits of the factory, and Negro labor is much employed by them."

the country." No better testimony to the capacity and ambition of the Negro could be found; and the fact that the Georgians attached such importance to the matter suggests that the trained Negro mechanics were becoming numerous.[61]

Everywhere, in towns, on the farms, and on great plantations, the slaves had ample opportunity to acquaint themselves with the tastes, ways, and achievements of the white race. Negroes often went hunting and fishing with the whites; they attended court-days, camp meetings, and carnivals with them; they flocked to look at barbecues and fairs. In the border States and even the Deep South, the white sons played with the children of the slave cabins. James Lane Allen has noted the companionship which a Kentucky youngster, graduating from the lap of his Negro mammy, found among the little ragged black imps of the cabins. He stole away to the duck-pond with them to learn to swim; he and they raced up and down the lane on blooded alder-stalk horses; they told him where the guinea-hen had hidden her nest. "To them he showed his first Barlow knife; for them he blew his first home-made whistle. He is their petty tyrant today; tomorrow he will be their repentant friend, dividing with them his marbles, and proposing a game of hop-scotch." He and they laid upon each other the ineffaceable impression of their different forms of speech, their likes and dislikes, their whole character.[62]

How much of the folklore of the Negroes some youngsters absorbed, the country first realized when Joel Chandler Harris published his tales of Uncle Remus; and simultaneously the Negro children unconsciously picked up nursery rhymes, bits of fairy tales, crude notions of national heroes, and all the folklore of the whites. Thousands of Negroes learned to read with white children—or their white elders. Negro women working in the big houses acquired the tastes of their mistresses in dress and furniture, and white skills in cookery. The author of *The Southwest by a Yankee* reported a conversation between the coachman and footman on a large plantation. "You know dat nigger they gwine to sell, George?" "No, he field nigger; I nebber has no 'quaintance wid dat class." "Well, nor no oder gentlemens would." Amusing as a revelation of class feeling among slaves, the dialogue indicates that these household Negroes felt themselves half white men. And well they might; for in many a planter's house the servants had the same food, clothing (at second hand), and conveniences as the white folk, and took pride in the same dignity and good manners. Visitors to Cuba remarked

61 Olmsted, *Back Country*, 180–181. N. Y. *Weekly Tribune*, July 12, 26, 1851.
62 Allen, *Blue Grass Region*, pp. 61–62. Reuben Davis in *Recollections of Mississippi* describes the pleasure with which Negroes attended political barbecues—nay, presided over the roasting of the meat—happier in them than the whites. The music and songs of the slaves early attracted attention; New Yorkers flocked to hear the "Negro Minstrels" in the 1840's. By 1887 the best collection of Negro songs was a volume called "Slave Songs of the United States." In that year Oliver Ditson & Co. published a volume of words and music called "Jubilee and Plantation Songs."

that American slaves were vastly superior to those of the island, and pointed to the closer communion of the two races on American soil as the principal reason.[63]

The religious activities of the Negro, transferred directly from the practices of the whites, were a powerful though uneven educational influence. In frontier or semi-frontier communities, especially in the border States, church minutes reveal large numbers of slave members, who sat separately (often in the gallery, if one existed), but on whom were enforced as high standards of conduct as on the whites. Evidently the slaveowners frequently used the church as a disciplinary instrument, and greatly valued its influence in checking thievery, lying, impudence, and other offenses.[64] Mason Crum in his delightful book on the sea-island Negroes entitled *Gullah* presents the testimony of one ante-bellum planter after another that churchgoing weakened vicious habits, created cheerfulness, and made the slaves more obedient.

Epecially in towns and cities the slaves often had congregations of their own. In Natchez, Miss., in the middle fifties, three Presbyterian preachers of Northern birth and good education preached to Negroes alone; one of them visiting congregations in Louisiana, one ministering to a large body of colored people in Natchez and to neighboring plantations, and the third ranging the countryside for ten or fifteen miles. In Charleston, S. C., the efforts of the Presbyterian and Episcopal Churches to furnish religious instruction to Negroes aroused in 1849 a bitter discussion. A mob attempted to tear down the Calvary Episcopal Church then in course of erection for colored parishioners. Responsible citizens intervened, and James L. Petigru, rushing from his office, made an impassioned plea to the crowd. Let them deliberate on the issue, he urged, and give it careful study. A committee of fifty was appointed to collect information throughout the South. At a meeting in the city hall in the spring of 1850 it reported that the movement for systematic Christianization of the Negroes deserved support. Petigru made a vigorous supporting speech, and the auditors enthusiastically agreed. The question of a separate church for Charleston Negroes was thus definitely settled.[65]

How much the Negroes valued the right of religious assemblage was repeatedly demonstrated. In a revision of the Mississippi statutes, for example, a provision was introduced into the slave code which made the gathering of any considerable number of slaves for religious exercises, without the presence of an ordained white minister, an unlawful assemblage. The colored folk were in-

63 Woodson, *op. cit.*, 119–120. J. H. Ingraham, *The Southwest by a Yankee*, II, 30. Sydnor, *Slavery in Mississippi*, 4. *National Intelligencer*, January 4, 1859. For an admirable statement of modern Southern attitudes see the expert essays gathered in Edgar T. Thompson, ed., *Race Relations and the Race Problem* (1939).

64 W. W. Sweet, *Religion on the American Frontier*, Vol. I, *The Baptists, 1783–1830.*

65 Sydnor, *op. cit.*, 59–60. Carson, *Petigru*, 280–281. MS Schirmer Diary, July 14, 1849ff; Charleston Hist. Soc.

dignant. One of them went to the Methodist clergyman William Winans, a minister of striking personality and forensic power. Winans was a large, muscular man, a fervent exhorter, a Jacksonian Democrat, and in other respects a notable frontier type. In his manuscript autobiography, a remarkable picture of an itinerant preacher's career kept in the Mississippi archives, he tells how the colored protests touched him. He saw that the law prevented white men from

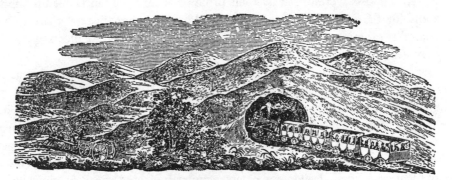

LIBERTY LINE.
NEW ARRANGEMENT---NIGHT AND DAY.

The improved and splendid Locomotives, Clarkson and Lundy, with their trains fitted up in the best style of accommodation for passengers, will run their regular trips during the present season, between the borders of the Patriarchal Dominion and Libertyville, Upper Canada. Gentlemen and Ladies, who may wish to improve their health or circumstances, by a northern tour; are respectfully invited to give us their patronage.

SEATS FREE, *irrespective of color*.

Necessary Clothing furnished gratuitously to such as have "*fallen among thieves*."

"Hide the outcasts—let the oppressed go free."—*Bible*.

☞For seats apply at any of the trap doors, or to the conductor of the train.

J. CROSS, *Proprietor*.

N. B. For the special benefit of Pro-Slavery Police Officers, an extra heavy wagon for Texas, will be furnished, whenever it may be necessary, in which they will be forwarded as dead freight, to the "Valley of Rascals,". always at the risk of the owners.

☞Extra Overcoats provided for such of them as are afflicted with protracted *chilly-phobia*.

Advertisement of the Underground Railroad.
The Western Citizen, July 13, 1844.

praying with their slaves, and slaves from holding informal prayer meetings. Finding that the author of the statute, George Poindexter, was a candidate for Congress, he resolved to make his wrath felt. "My position, as presiding elder of a district embracing a large portion of voters, rendered my opposition more conspicuous than that of any other individual." He brought about the defeat of Poindexter, much to that man's mortification, and the law was modified at an early session of the legislature. Talking with a friend, Poindexter said: "I was not beaten by Rankin, but by an old black man named Winter, belonging to Parson Winans!"

The exact number of Negro church-members in the slave area it is impossible to state, but it was clearly large. Some estimates ran up to 300,000 or 400,000. A more conservative authority in 1854 placed it at about 270,000, of whom the Methodists were credited with 147,000, the Baptists with 100,000, the Episcopalians 10,000, and the Presbyterians 7,000. White leaders in all the important sects constantly urged the importance of attending to the spiritual welfare of slaves, and of carrying out broad missionary programs. All masters, exhorted the *Southern Churchman*, should see that slaves were taught the elements of Christianity, that they were regularly allowed to hear a portion of the Bible, that they were required to attend public worship, and that their children were baptized. Baptists were urged by their principal church organ to set up Sunday schools for the oral instruction of slaves old and young. Special material was prepared for the Negroes, their catechisms and lessons often inculcating duty to the owner no less than to God!

It was unquestionably true that, as white observers often pointed out, the sermons of some Negro preachers were mere burlesques on religion, and had the auditors been less simple and fervent, would have tended to bring it into ridicule. But it was also true that the heartfelt piety of many colored congregations might well have put the cold intellectuality of some white services to shame. Not a few elementary lessons in self-government were learned by these colored congregations. Their deacons or elders, regularly elected in many churches by the members, exercised powers of direction, oversight, admonition, and advice that were quite apostolic in nature and scope. A careful and highly intelligent Southern leader, bearing testimony after the war that the Negroes were deeply imbued with Christianity, attributed to this the fact that they were more orderly and moral than the same class in any other country.[66]

[IX]

The problems of slavery and race-adjustment thus presented an equation in which three main elements, the opinions and wishes of the white South, the views of the white North, and the desires of the colored people, slowly but steadily evolving toward a better status, had to be considered. The third group in the triangle must not be ignored. With every upward step the Negro proved

---

66 *Southern Episcopalian*, June, 1854, pp. 119–123, article by Paul Trapier, a missionary. The Rev. R. G. Curley estimated 300,000 Negro church-members; *National Intelligencer*, November 1, 1853. *Southern Baptist*, December 16, 1856. "Religious Life of the Negro Slave," *Harper's Monthly Magazine*, 1863, XXVII, pp. 479ff., 676ff., 817ff. W. L. Trenholm, "The South: An Address," April 7, 1869 (pvt., Charleston Society Library), in the course of which he said: "These four million descendants of savages were more orderly and moral than the same class in any other civilized country, and they remain so up to the present moment, notwithstanding the temptations and privations of the war, the license of sudden freedom, and the bad advice of political agitators. They were deeply imbued with the principles of Christianity, so much so that since emancipation they have cheerfully devoted their scanty earnings to the building and maintenance of churches and schools, and the establishment of charitable societies; their intellectual powers were stimulated and improved so far as they could be in a condition of slavery, and were sufficiently developed to furnish a stimulus for continued effort, and to constitute the basis of their future self-improvement."

that slavery could not be held a frozen, changeless institution. Every time a Fanny Kemble or Thomas L. Dabney taught a group of slaves to read, the seed of change was sown. Every time a Frederick Douglass lifted himself like Plautus from bondage to the pursuit of culture and letters, proving the possession not merely of talents but of a rare magnanimity, a seed germinated. How could men speak of colored folk as unfit for freedom when they had before their eyes such examples of distinction as James Wormley, who, beginning his career as steward for the Metropolitan Club in Washington, shortly before the war opened a hotel and catering establishment which soon became the best in the national capital? How speak of them as unworthy when the race produced a hero like Bob Butt, who during the terrible yellow fever pestilence which scourged Portsmouth, Va., in 1855, served as gravedigger for eleven hundred and fifty-nine persons, laboring devotedly from morn till dark to give sepulture to the dead, and often making the grave his resting-place.[67]

As the advancing slave learned to know his own worth, he refused to accept the doctrine of an immutable slave system. The old assumption that the vast majority of bondsmen were contented with their lot, or at least passively accepted it, is open to sharp question. Any really penetrating investigation of the institution in the fifties discloses evidence of sharp tension in the Negro-white relation, with indications that countless thousands of colored folk were constantly "fighting back." Some sought to break down the system by insurrection. The list of plots, sporadic outbreaks, and revolts during the decade is long, and it is perhaps significant that the election years of 1856 and 1860, with their pervasive excitement, brought reports of widely-ramified conspiracies. Other slaves resisted servitude by flight, many thousands running away. Still others resorted to economic weapons. Their supposed laziness was frequently a type of passive resistance, while direct sabotage through the destruction of property or maiming of livestock was far from unknown. Slaves who were hard pressed by brutal masters might assert their personalities by impudent language or physical assault. Meanwhile, the colored folk maintained their morale by various devices; by prayer, by hymns and spirituals which emphasized the idea of freedom, by their own interpretation of the Bible, and by clandestine meetings and grapevine communication.[68]

More and more, too, the slaves acquired information about the anti-slavery movement. For example, a mulatto named Sella Martin, who was eighteen in

67 *Journal of Negro History*, April 1935, pp. 268-269, January, 1936, pp. 57-59. Report of Portsmouth Relief Assn., 1855, saying Butt "performed duty beyond all price."
68 Herbert Aptheker, *American Negro Slave Revolts*, esp. chs. 6 and 14; R. A. and A. H. Bauer, "Day to Day Resistance to Slavery," *Journal of Negro History*, XXVII, 388-419. J. H. Johnston, "Race Relations in Virginia," gives 82 instances of slaves condemned to death in Virginia. 1786-1845, for murder of masters or overseers.

1850 and worked as errand boy for gamblers and others in a hotel at Columbus, Ga., learned to read. It was not long, as he later recounted in *Good Words* (May 1, 1867), before the other slaves of the town found this out. One day a knot of them invited him to go to the woods to gather wild grapes. When out of sight one took from his bosom a newspaper and handed it to the youth, saying: "Dere, read dat ar, an' tell us whut him say 'bout de bobbolishinus!" Martin read them an account of Clay's doctrines on emancipation. Thousands of similar occurrences doubtless took place, and helped inspire the growing strictness of laws against Negro literacy and Negro assemblages.

Conflict between North and South; conflict among groups and parties within both sections; conflict between whites jealous of their supremacy and the free Negro; increasing conflict between the bondsman and his master—this was the situation which darkened all the prospects of the nation in the fifties. Nowhere did compromise on any essential issue seem to be gaining ground. The South became more stubbornly determined to maintain the existing status, the North more stubbornly denunciatory, the Negro more stubbornly discontented. The conflict of selfish interests, the provocations of sectional pride, the dull weight of inertia, blocked every hopeful change. With every passing year the pent-up forces were growing more powerful and the dangers of an explosion more appalling.

16

Brother Jonathan Asserts Himself

SMOKE FROM countless cigars wreathed the room; five hundred Democrats, replete with the feast that waiters had hurriedly cleared away, were listening intently; and Senator Douglas hammered home his points to them with forcible gestures. He was making the Jackson Day dinner of 1852 in Washington memorable by a call to action.

"I think," he declaimed, "it is time that America had a foreign policy—(applause and cries of 'Good! Good!')—a foreign policy predicated upon a true interpretation of the laws of nations—a foreign policy in accordance with the spirit of the age—(great applause)—but not such a foreign policy as we have seen attempted to be enforced in this country in the last three years. (Cries of 'Good! Good!') We have been told, and you are told every day, that neutrality is the true American policy; and that plea has been the excuse for the acts which have been performed by the existing Administration in connection with the Cuban question. (Great applause.) They employ the American Navy and Army to arrest the volunteers and seize the provisions, ammunition, and supplies of every kind which may be sent in aid of the patriot cause, and at the same time give free passage and protection to all men, ammunition, and supplies which may be sent in aid of the royalist, and THEY CALL THAT NEUTRALITY!" (Enormous applause.) [1]

The republic which had seized the vast Southwest by a few swift and inexpensive victories, and had then found it filled with dazzling treasures, was intoxicated by its success. It felt the exhilaration of commercial prosperity, rapid growth in population, and boundless opportunities in the exploitation of natural wealth. Far from thinking that it ought to concern itself with internal development alone, it looked abroad to assert what the New York *Herald* called its title to "national glory, national greatness." Why should we not speak out on world affairs? thundered Cass to the Senate: [2]

1 Washington *Union,* January 9, 1852; N. Y. *Weekly Tribune,* January 24, 1852.
2 *Cong. Globe.* 22d Cong., 1st sess., App. 162; February 10, 1852.

545

We have at length reached the condition of one of the great Powers of the earth, and yet we are but in the infancy of our career. That man yet lives, who was living, when a primitive forest extended from the Allegheny to the Rocky Mountains, trodden only by the Indian and by the animals. . . . Then a narrow strip upon the sea-coast, thirteen remote and dependent colonies, and less than three millions of people, constituted what is now this vast Republic, stretching across the continent and extending almost from the Northern Tropic to the Arctic Circle. And the man is now living, who will live to see one hundred and fifty millions of people, free, prosperous, and intelligent, swaying the destinies of this country, and exerting a mighty influence upon those of the world. And why not, Mr. President? Is it not likely to be more beneficially exerted, than the influence now exercised by the despotic Powers of the earth?

The intensified national sentiment of Americans found expression in many ways; in boastfulness, in naval expeditions to far corners of the globe, in a contemptuous attitude toward Latin-American neighbors, in constant attacks upon France, Spain, Russia, and above all Britain. Halleck spoke of the Yankee who

> Would shake hands with a king upon his throne,
> And think it kindness to his majesty.

Even the cultivated diarist Philip Hone could brag, after the Mexican victories, that Brother Jonathan was growing to be a big boy and must be treated with more respect. The Americans, he remarked, had some crude habits, but they were expert with sword and musket. "They eat fast, but they go ahead wonderfully; they use some queer expressions, but in defence of their rights they are apt to talk much to the purpose." National bumptiousness would soon present its worst side in the brutality of Captain Hollins bombarding Greytown into flinders, in the swaggering bombast of Soulé as Minister to Madrid, and in the piratical doctrine of the Ostend Manifesto. Of such manifestations the best Americans were heartily ashamed. The most important tendencies in foreign relations, however, were three: a sharp assertion of American opinion in the Old World struggle between tyranny and liberty; a stubborn maintenance of every supposed right in Central America, Caribbean waters, and along the coasts of British North America; and a strong drive toward new annexations. All three had found reflection in Douglas's Jackson Day speech.[3]

3 *Hone Diary*, Nevins ed., 869, 870; February 5, 1848. A typical crow came from the Washington *Sentinel*, September 30, 1853: "Young America desires to have a voice in the counsels of nations. They found their codes and systems made when they came on the stage of action. They were made to suit the olden times, and the ancient despotisms of Europe. Sensitive to all that touches honor, they will cheerfully submit to what honor requires, but they want to have a voice in the great high tribunal of nations. They want to infuse new ideas and new vigor into the international codes and systems."

[I]

The passionate uprising of one European people after another in 1848–49, a spontaneous ignition of the flame of liberty in land after land, deeply touched most Americans. Of all the struggles for freedom, that of the Hungarians seemed the most heroic and appealing. As the Magyar patriots won victory after victory, and then were crushed by the overwhelming power which the Czar brought to the aid of Austria, the whole western world watched with grief. The brave fighters against such odds seemed like the heroes of a legendary past. Their principal leader, Louis Kossuth, loomed up as a prophet of burning eloquence, his poetic utterances keeping the fire of patriotism alive even amid disaster. The country applauded when in the summer of 1849, the revolt still lustily under way, Secretary Clayton instructed a Virginian then in Germany, Ambrose Dudley Mann, to enter Hungary as special agent to obtain information and offer encouragement. He was virtually empowered to promise recognition if the revolution attained a success which warranted it. "Your readiness to recognize Hungary," Crittenden wrote Clayton, "is a forward and bold step. I like it for the sentiment and resolution it implies. Go ahead!—it is glorious and will please our people to see the Majesty of our Republic exhibiting itself on all proper occasions, with its dignity and fearless front, in the eyes and to the teeth of misruling kings, or despots of whatever make or title they may be." [4]

Later, as the uprising was quenched in bloody ashes, Americans read with interest of the magnificent popular reception which London accorded Kossuth. His picture, with dreamy eyes, thought-oppressed brow, and strong-bearded chin, had become familiar to all freedom-loving lands. As he passed through London streets, standing upright in his carriage in picturesque Hungarian costume, Britons cheered as if he had been a great national hero. [5] When news came that he was about to visit America, enthusiasm rose in a great surge.

On the morning of December 5, 1851, saluting cannon notified New York that Kossuth was coming up the harbor in the ship *Humboldt*; and with military pomp and municipal honors, he received the greatest popular ovation since the visit of Lafayette. Under a brilliant sky, all Manhattan from City Hall Park to Castle Garden was filled with spectators. His face, men said, had a more penetrating intellectuality than they had expected. When he delivered his first public address, in classic English tinged with a soft foreign accent, the audience was delighted. "His manner in speaking is at once incomparably dignified and graceful," declared the *Tribune*. "Gestures more admirable and effective, and a

4 July 20, 1849, Clayton Papers.
5 Carl Schurz, *Reminiscences*, I, 385, 386.

play of countenance more expressive and magnetic, we remember in no other public speaker. . . . Beyond a doubt he is the greatest of orators now living." [6] Foote had already introduced in the Senate a resolution expressing sympathy and admiration for the Hungarian leaders. Leading citizens met at the Astor House on December 15 to organize committees to assist the cause, and wealthy merchants joined George Bancroft, Horace Greeley, Henry J. Raymond, and John Van Buren in pressing a demand for money. "Why can we not raise One Million Dollars before the first of January?" demanded Greeley's journal. "At any rate let us try." [7]

For weeks the Kossuth craze ran rampant from ocean to lakes. The press was full of the movements of the leader. When he attended a dinner given by about 250 members of the House and Senate on January 7, 1852, William R. King presided; Secretary Daniel Webster sat on Kossuth's left, and Speaker Linn Boyd on his right; Cabinet members and judges of the Supreme Court were present. "We shall rejoice," said Webster, "to see our American model upon the Lower Danube and on the mountains of Hungary." Personal sympathy throbbed in Webster's voice, for the guest had confided to him that his property had been confiscated, that his mother was undoubtedly deprived of all means of subsistence, and that his children were prisoners in the hands of the cruellest of all dynasties.[8] Kossuth clubs were organized. Articles on Hungarian history, legends, and literature filled the press. Hungarian music was played in restaurants as people ordered Hungarian wine. Wealthy men wrote checks, women contributed jewels, and children offered their pennies. State legislatures sent resolutions of invitation.[9]

But like all such popular infatuations, the crusade quickly evaporated into nothingness. This Kossuth conflagration, wrote Leslie Combs of Kentucky, was delusive. "It reminds me of the burning of a stubblefield or prairie, high-rising bright flames suddenly dying out, and leaving nought but smoke and ashes in their tracks—not embers enough to scorch the naked bottom of a child's foot." The Ohio legislature took three typical steps: it invited Kossuth to appear, asked him to write out its resolutions, and refused to pay his bill at Columbus. When

6 N. Y. *Weekly Tribune*, December 11, 1851.
7 *Ibid.*, December 18, 1851.
8 Kossuth's letter of January 3, 1852, to Webster, states that of three messengers he sent from England to his family, one was shot. Sending Webster $600, he asked him to transmit it to the American chargé in Vienna for his mother and sisters. Lanman Papers. Moncure D. Conway, listening to Kossuth's speeches, saw many auditors moved to tears. *Autobiography*, I, 111. For an interesting note on the benefits which an independent Hungary would have held out to all Europe from 1850 onward, stabilizing the Eastern situation, see James Creelman, *On the Great Highway*, 242ff.
9 "He has injured his dignity by making speeches for money, and he has injured his respectability by issuing 'Hungarian bonds,' as they were called, down to a dollar, to serve as tickets of admission." Ticknor, *Journals*, II, 276, 277.

the hero called upon Henry Clay, the Kentuckian was frank in saying that little could be done. He entertained the liveliest sympathy with the Magyar struggle for liberty, he said. But sympathy alone was worthless. "You require material aid"—and how could America give it? Even if she went to war, it would be impossible to transport men and arms across the ocean against Russia. Far better, concluded Clay, that "we should keep our light burning brightly on this western shore, as a light to all nations, than to hazard its utter extinction amid the ruins of fallen or falling republics in Europe." [10]

In the end, indeed, Kossuth was the victim of the transient enthusiasm he had aroused. By an early date in 1852 he had sadly reached the conclusion that his mission was a failure. Some abolitionists and radical freesoilers had rallied to the principles he represented—freedom, reform, liberty—to try to make capital out of them. Both Whig and Democratic politicians curtseyed to him in an effort to woo the German vote. But the South was indifferent if not absolutely hostile. Plain hardheaded Westerners like Ben Wade viewed him with suspicion. They wanted no risky intervention in foreign quarrels; and Wade, talking with him in "a private republican way," reached the conclusion that he was "a great enthusiast, and knows but little of equal republicanism, except in theory." While Congressmen and legislators were ready to toast him at dinner, they would not vote a dollar—much less many millions—to aid his enterprise. By midsummer of 1852 Kossuth was aware that he was being humbugged by tricky party leaders. He had hoped for an explicit statement from the Democratic chieftains in regard to American foreign policy on his behalf, and they had proved as guarded as Clay. In time, he sailed back to England, leaving behind him some good friends, a lingering devotion to his cause in the German-American press, and a fashion for Kossuth hats and Kossuth coats. A kind of mild influenza which broke out about the time of his arrival was even called the "Kossuth grip." Beyond collecting about $90,000, he had accomplished nothing.[11]

But the belief that the American republic ought to throw its defiances into the teeth of European despots persisted. Was it true, demanded Cass, that expressions of condemnation for the course of Russian Czar or Austrian tyrant could

10 Combs to Corwin, February 22, 1852; Corwin Papers. Clay's statement is in *National Intelligencer*, February 3, 1852. Martin F. Tupper, writing from England to John P. Kennedy, agreed with Clay. He dropped into verse (January 19, 1852; Kennedy Papers):
> Well thou resolvest, America now,
> Not to be talked into quarrels and wars!
> Olives become thy Minerva-like brow
> Better than blood-begilt laurels of Mars.

11 Wade to his wife, January 25, 1852; Wade Papers. Robert Montgomery Bird wrote the Secretary of State on January 12, 1852, that "while there is much feeling for Kossuth personally, just as there is for any other great poet . . . there is very general dread and horror of his *practical* intervention doctrines." Clayton Papers.

accomplish nothing unless backed by force? He quoted Palmerston, who after asking which were strongest, opinions or armies, had exclaimed: "Sir, my answer is, that opinions are stronger than armies." It was even so, agreed Douglas, Greeley, and many others. Who could tell how often the designs of ambition and injustice had been abandoned in the face of world disapprobation? These men had hold of a powerful bit of truth, even if it was a kind of truth often perverted. "You must not stand still and see the feeble oppressed and the strong triumphant," Cass told a New York audience in 1852. "I do not advocate going to war—going to war now—but the time is coming when the voice of this nation will be potential throughout the world. I trust the time will soon come when not a hostile drum shall roll, and not a hostile cannon be fired, throughout the world, if we say, 'Your cause is not a just and right one.' And a glorious consummation that will be for true democratic principles." It was a spread-eagle sentiment; but it was also an anticipation of the day when Woodrow Wilson and Franklin D. Roosevelt would make the public opinion of America potential indeed against the oppressor.[12]

[II]

In the maintenance of American rights, real or fancied, popular vigilance was directed chiefly toward the Isthmian area. Both Great Britain and the United States had vital interests in Central America. California had no sooner been acquired than a large emigration began to pour across the Panama and Nicaraguan routes. The building of a canal then seemed a much easier enterprise than it actually was, and most Americans inevitably felt that it ought to be under their own control. Great Britain for her part exercised sovereignty over Belize, or British Honduras, asserted a protectorate over the savages who inhabited the so-called Mosquito Coast, and took an interest in islands of the region. The British had the largest ocean commerce in the world, and no small part of it would pass through any Isthmian canal which was constructed.

As the Mexican War came to an end, both the United States and Great Britain took steps to protect their position in the area. The Senate in June, 1848, ratified a treaty with New Granada (Colombia) by which America received transit rights across the Isthmus of Panama, and in return pledged itself to uphold the "perfect neutrality" of that route. In the same year the British, much

12 *Cong. Globe*, 32d Cong., 1st sess., 24ff. 66ff, 72. Cass's speech in Tammany Hall September 2, 1852, was printed as N. Y. *Evening Post* Document No. 10 in the ensuing campaign. Crittenden, aroused by the French occupation of Rome and Russian invasion of Hungary, had written Clayton July 20, 1849: "Whenever there is an opportunity for it, our protest ought to be uttered against these things, and all the organs of the Government made to resound with the voice of Liberty, and of encouragement to all who are striving toward it by rational means." Clayton Papers.

to the annoyance of Washington, took control of the port of San Juan, commanding the best route for any canal crossing Nicaragua, and renamed it Greytown. Their pretext was that they needed the town to protect their dependent tribe of Mosquito Indians, but their real object seemed to be to obtain command over any future canal. A little later (October, 1849), the temporary British seizure of Tigre Island near the probable Pacific terminus of any Nicaraguan canal gave another severe shock to American nerves. Though the island was promptly relinquished, Secretary Clayton expressed himself fearful of a "collision."

The upshot was the negotiation of one of the most famous, most controversial, and most disliked of all American agreements, the Clayton-Bulwer Treaty. An able and tactful minister, Sir Henry Lytton Bulwer, a younger brother of the novelist, reached Washington late in 1849. His manners are perfection, wrote N. P. Willis; "we doubt whether there is a better model of a gentleman in the world." He and Clayton exchanged views in the most candid spirit. "It is no use trying to get around each other, as it is in neither of our characters," the minister wrote the Secretary of State.[13] It was plain that neither the United States nor Great Britain would permit exclusive control of a canal by the other. It was also plain that each wished to restrict the other's territorial pretensions. The Foreign Office was apprehensive that the United States might annex one or more of the five Central American republics—for Clayton declared they would gladly come under the stars and stripes; the State Department was apprehensive that Great Britain might extend its Mosquito Coast protectorate. On April 19, 1850, the two men signed a treaty which embodied a compromise on the canal question and an ambiguity on the territorial issue. It was the only possible road out of an impasse, and the Senate ratified it, after brief debate, by a vote of 42 to 11.[14]

The clauses regarding the canal were sufficiently fair. They provided that

13 April 18, 1850; Clayton Papers. Bulwer spoke appreciatively of Clayton's attitude; he knew "the kindly feelings by which you are actuated, the desire which stimulates, and the good sense which guides you." Clayton Papers. For a brief characterization of Bulwer see N. P. Willis, Hurrygraphs, 194, 195.

14 The subject is discussed in M. W. Williams, Anglo-American Isthmian Diplomacy 1815–1915 (1916); and in R. W. Van Alstyne, "British Diplomacy and the Clayton-Bulwer Treaty, 1850–1860," Journal of Modern History, XI. Clayton was exultant over the treaty. exaggerating its popularity. "I have never witnessed before in this country such an enthusiastic manifestation of kind feeling toward Great Britain as that which has been elicited by the new Convention," he wrote Bulwer. "Men who have heretofore been the bitterest assailants of England now join in the expression of their unbounded admiration of the magnanimity, generosity, and wisdom which have been displayed by her in this negotiation. We have produced a new era in the history of the relations between Great Britain and the United States. We have bound together these two great kindred nations as joint pioneers and partners in spreading the blessings of commerce and civilization. There is not a good man in the world who will not glory in what we have done." Clayton Papers.

both nations would do whatever they could to promote the cutting of a channel, but that neither should ever fortify or exercise exclusive control over it, whenever and however built. More than half a century was to pass before a canal became practicable for either government. But the ambiguity on the territorial question was to prove immediately troublesome. The first article of the treaty soon became famous:

The governments of the United States and Great Britain hereby declare that neither one nor the other will ever . . . occupy, or fortify, or colonize, or assume, or exercise, any dominion over Nicaragua, Costa Rica, the Mosquito Coast, or any part of Central America; nor will either make use of any protection which either affords or may afford, or any alliance which either has or may have to or with any state or people, for the purpose of erecting or maintaining any such fortifications, or of occupying, fortifying, or colonizing Nicaragua, Costa Rica, the Mosquito Coast, or any part of Central America, or of assuming or exercising dominion over the same.

The British Government's view was that this pledged them not to make any *future* occupation or to fortify any places not *already* under their control, but that it left their ownership of Belize and their protectorate over the Mosquito Coast undisturbed. Bulwer had written Clayton the day before he signed the treaty: "The English Government are disposed to do everything they can with honor, but cannot with honor abandon their defensive protectorate of Mosquito, so long as the obligations binding them thereto are not dissolved by the Mosquitoes. . . ." The American view, however, was that the treaty language was retroactive. Attorney-General Reverdy Johnson had been active in the negotiations. He advised the President that the compact effectively disarmed the British protectorate, though it did not abolish the protectorate in terms. That is, it left the British free to succor the miserable Indians, whom some Central Americans wished to butcher, but did not permit the use of any armed forces in the area. By 1852 a merry controversy was raging over the disputed terms, and it grew in heat as the years passed.[15]

The judgment of the best modern critics is that the Clayton-Bulwer Treaty, executed at a time when the United States was a far weaker maritime power than England, constituted a triumph for American diplomacy; for it brought to an end all risk of British expansion in Central America, and terminated the

15 See the review of this dispute by Clayton in the Senate, June 19, 1856; *Cong. Globe*, 34th Cong., 1st sess., 1419–1422. See also Reverdy Johnson's review in a long letter of December 30, 1856, to Clayton, in the *National Intelligencer*, January 31, 1856. Johnson declared that the title to the Mosquito Coast was left uncertain; the United States was free to recognize Nicaraguan or Honduran sovereigny there, as the British were free to recognize the Mosquito king; but neither had the right to compel others to recognize. "The British protectorate was, I repeat, entirely disarmed by the treaty." The British view is stated by an expert on international law, J. D. Harding, in the same issue of the *Intelligencer*.

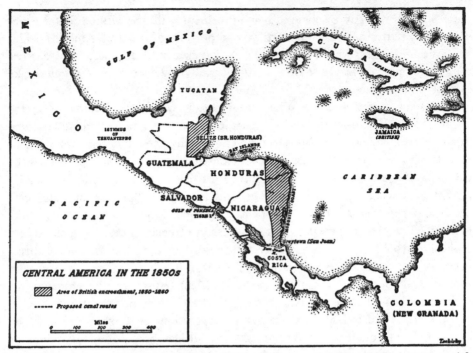

This map shows the area of the filibustering activities of Nicaragua, with the Mosquito Coast and Bay Islands where Britain had claims.

After Thomas A. Bailey, "A Diplomatic History of the American People," by kind permission of Mr. Bailey and F. S. Crofts & Company.

danger that Britain would gain monopolistic control over the Nicaraguan canal route. The accusation that Clayton let himself be outwitted by slippery diplomatists had no truth. He made a fair and for the period a profitable agreement.[16] All the men concerned, moreover—Bulwer, Lord Palmerston, Clayton, Taylor, and Abbott Lawrence at the London legation—acted with exemplary honesty. Lawrence played a larger part in the preliminary negotiations than was realized at the time, while the great Pammy did much to thrust into place the foundations of the treaty. As early as November 19, 1849, Lawrence had written to his friend W. C. Rives: "Lord Palmerston disavows any intention on the part of his Government to colonize or take possession of any portion of Central

16 See T. A. Bailey, *Diplomatic History of the American People*, 292, 293; S. F. Bemis, *Diplomatic History of the United States*, 250–252; sketch of Clayton by M. W. Williams in S. F. Bemis, ed., *Amer. Secretaries of State*, VI. No American government at the uneasy time of the treaty's ratification, with the sectional quarrel over the new acquisitions at its height, could have risked war with Great Britain. Clayton erred in telling Bulwer that he did not adhere to the non-colonization principle of the Monroe Doctrine; and the treaty may in one light be regarded as a British victory over the Doctrine, to which Palmerston yielded nothing. But it did assure peace if not entire harmony.

America, and is ready to come into an agreement with the United States never to 'annex, settle, colonize, or fortify any portion of Central America.' This proposition I was authorized to make which has been accepted, and further these communications are to be open to all the world." Both nations could take just pride in the compact.[17]

But since it was a self-denying ordinance, it was hotly denounced in the United States. Expansionists who saw that it bound America to seize no territory in this region assailed it as an outrage. The Washington *Union* never tired of attacking it. Douglas called it a piece of national cowardice; Buchanan remarked that Clayton and Bulwer both deserved British peerages. Some provoking adventurers were busy in the region, and they joined in the hue and cry. Steamship speculators, transit-company schemers, land-grabbers, and glory-hunters all painted the treaty and its makers in offensive hues. Even so respectable a person as E. G. Squier, who through the influence of the historian Prescott had obtained an appointment as chargé in Central America, and who soon gained fame for his writings on the area, lent himself to the campaign. He had drafted an agreement with Nicaragua which was never ratified, and in private letters and public essays he heaped accusations on Bulwer and scorn on the State Department under Webster. Nearly all Democrats adopted a chip-on-shoulder attitude toward Great Britain in Central American affairs. When in 1852 the British made the tiny Honduran Bay islands, which they had for some time held, into a crown colony, Squier urged Douglas to raise a tremendous row. This, he said, would be "an appropriate time to bring up all these matters in detail, preliminary to a more formal and emphatic affirmation of the Monroe Doctrine than has ever yet been made." [18]

That perennial thistle, the Canadian fisheries quarrel, bloomed again when early in the fifties jealous blue-noses of Nova Scotia and Newfoundland attempted to restrict the inshore rights of Yankees under the treaty of 1818.

17 Lawrence had agreed with Clayton that any ship canal across the Isthmus should "be free to all the world and its neutrality guaranteed forever by every nation that would unite with us." He thought that the Mosquito Indians should "be provided for by annuities or otherwise to the satisfaction of all parties." He refused to *press* upon Great Britain a discussion of the relinquishment of the Mosquito protectorate, although Washington repeatedly urged him to do so. Altogether, Lawrence was one of the chief makers of the treaty. See his letters to Rives October 17, November 19, 1850, February 28, April 13, 1850; Rives Papers.

18 For typical attacks see Washington *Union*, April 28, May 3, 1850. Buchanan's hostility is expressed in his *Works*, VIII, 383. Squier, one of the most distinguished of American archeologists, plied Clayton, Douglas, and others with letters. When he went so far as to publish in the N. Y. *Herald* a letter saying that Bulwer had proposed to the State Department that the United States and Britain should set aside the territorial rights of Nicaragua and jointly appropriate the Nicaraguan Canal route, Bulwer exploded with wrath. He wrote Clayton denouncing Squier's "absurdities, misconceptions, and untruths." See Squier to Clayton, September 2, 1850, Clayton Papers; Squier to Douglas, December 24, 1852, Douglas Papers; Bulwer to Clayton, September 24, 1850, Clayton Papers; etc.

The New Englanders flared up in instant resentment. As a good Bay State man, Daniel Webster was quick to assert American rights, and communicated his spirit in turn to Fillmore. The President then called in John P. Kennedy, who as new head of the navy relished the sense of handling frigates like toys. Kennedy has described the midsummer start of the Codfish War in 1852 in a spirited letter to his wife:[19]

I was very busy in running over a multitude of letters and sundry documents of public concern, when a message from the President was brought to me about eleven o'clock—Mr. F. wishes to see the Secretary. So off I go, and find our Chief looking very grave. "Mr. Secretary, have you got a ship ready for sea?" "Yes, sir, I can give you the *Mississippi* in New York and dispatch her in a day or two." "Put her under orders to proceed to the Bay of Fundy. Prepare a full letter of instructions, in which you will present the whole question of the right to the fisheries. Look up the Treaties of 1783 and 1818, and draw up a statement which shall set the public right on the merits of the dispute." "Very well, sir—when do you want it?" "As soon as possible. No time must be lost. What officer have you for command?" "Commodore Perry." "Tell him to be ready immediately, and telegraph to New York to the commanding officer there to have the ship ready."

So off I go again. I send for Perry and give him his orders—and then the telegraph—and then to prepare my document. I can do little till evening, being engaged to dine at Appleton's at 5. I make a spare dinner and get back to my room at 9. Lock the door and go to work till midnight. Then up at daylight and at it again this morning till near midday when I finish, having written about 30 large pages. I could not sleep last night for the excitement.

At 12 to the Cabinet council. I read my letter of instructions, which is approved, and forthwith I go to work of having it copied—which by the help of several clerks is done by 6 this evening. I sign it—and set Perry on his high-road to Nova Scotia, with a noble steam frigate and a complete equipment for a fight. But I assure you, Puss, this codfish war has given me something approaching a headache.

Happily, headaches in Washington did not lead to broken heads in Canadian waters; but the firmness of the United States did give London a sense of concern which in time was to lead to the important mission of Lord Elgin.[20]

"The present panic about new territory is destined to pass away," Robert J.

19 July 28, 1852, Kennedy Papers; cf. H. T. Tuckerman, *Kennedy*, 220ff., 290ff.
20 The London *Times* pointed out a British dilemma. "It is an unfortunate circumstance in the relations of American politics with this country, that whilst we are naturally inclined, by conviction and tradition, to coincide with the opinions and policy of the whig or federalist party in the Northern States, yet it is in the South, with all its aggressive tendencies, and its connection with slavery, that we find the nearest approach to our own commercial doctrines, and the surest defense of our common mercantile interests."

[III]

Walker, Polk's old Secretary of the Treasury, wrote Douglas in the midst of the Compromise excitement; "and as well might you stop the current of the Mississippi, as arrest the onward march of the American people over the continent—and they will take the Constitution and the flag of the Union, and the free trade between the States with them." [21] The onward march of which he spoke was a dream with many, an appetite with some, and a passion with a few. As the South found that its Mexican conquests had done little if anything to increase its slave area and augment its strength in Congress, many of its leaders turned covetous eyes upon Cuba and Central America. Various Northerners put in an oar to aid this agricultural imperialism. It was John L. O'Sullivan, part founder of the New York *Morning News* and long editor of the *Democratic Review*, who in 1845 had spoken of "our manifest destiny to overspread the continent," thus coining an immortal phrase.[22] He put his doctrine into practical operation, supporting the filibustering activities of the Venezuelan adventurer Narciso Lopez against Cuba in 1849–50, and himself twice being indicted for violation of the neutrality laws. To him, John A. Quitman, William Walker, and thousands of others, almost any method of extending American dominion over this land of sugar wealth and a half million slaves was legitimate.

Polk had tried without success to buy the island. A vote in the Senate late in 1848 on a resolution pertaining to purchase indicated that the North was divided, but the cotton States were a unit in favor of acquisition. When the Whigs came into power, President Taylor showed that while he was favorable enough to commercial expansion northward, he was frigid toward schemes for widening the slaveholders' domain; and at once a powerful impulse toward lawless action made itself felt. The open boat, the unfurled flag, the flashing sword—to these men turned.

It was about the magnetic figure of Lopez that the first strong movement to detach Cuba from Spain by violence gathered itself. Some of his followers were restless veterans of the Mexican War who thirsted for more excitement; some were men with good reason to go abroad, like the Missouri admirer of Quitman who pleaded for an early expedition because he was about to be indicted for murder; some were aspirants for offices or confiscated lands; some believed that Cuba must be saved from British seizure, or from Spanish measures of emancipation that would mean its "Africanization." Checked by Federal authorities in 1849 before he could leave port, Lopez slipped away from New

---

21 May 4, 1850; Douglas Papers.
22 *Democratic Review*, combined July–August issue, 1845, vol. XVII, 5–10. For one arrest of O'Sullivan, see N. Y. *Weekly Tribune*, May 3, 1851. The Washington *Sentinel*, November 13, 1853, exclaimed of Cuba: "She is essential to us in every respect. She must be ours!"

Orleans in the spring of 1850 with several hundred followers. He landed at Cardenas, fired the governor's mansion, and vainly tried to rouse the inhabitants to revolt, but was immediately forced to flee back to Key West. The listless indictments and court trials that followed had no terrors for him and his associates, and they were soon busy conspiring a new descent. One of the men arraigned, ex-Senator John Henderson of Mississippi, took special pride in plotting a second attack while being prosecuted for his share in the first.

A widely-ramified organization supported these lawless activities. Committees or juntas of Cuban rebels sat in New York and New Orleans. Two newspapers, the New York *Sun* and New Orleans *Delta*, were sympathetic organs of the movement. Considerable sums of money were raised, partly through the sale of Cuban bonds and partly as voluntary contributions. With Quitman and O'Sullivan lending encouragement, recruits were gathered, drilled, and armed. Men of some local prominence in the South were induced by the eloquent Lopez—his voice low and musical, his manners mild, but his upright mien and weather-beaten look that of a veteran soldier—to serve as officers.[23] In the articles and letters that promoted the undertaking, the Cuban people were represented as panting for independence and waiting only for help to mount an irresistible revolt. It mattered little to the reckless

Pierre Soulé, Friend of Filibusters and Expansionists. Sketched by Eyre Crowe, During Thackeray's Tour of 1853.

men, chiefly Southerners, who gathered about Lopez for his third attempt, that most of the Northern press were denouncing him. The Washington *Republic* might call the enterprise "a conspiracy for plunder," the Albany *Register* might attack the "marauders," the Baltimore *American* might term the undertaking an "outrage," the New York *Express* might inveigh against the "loose morals" which animated it, and the St. Louis *Intelligencer* might urge the country to "keep faith with Spain"; but all this meant nothing to the thoughtless and misguided young men who believed they could awaken slumbering rebellion. President Fillmore issued a proclamation denouncing the plunder that was being planned, and the authorities in New York temporarily seized two suspicious-looking vessels. Lopez then transferred his headquarters once more to friendly New Orleans, and rallied his hot blooded volunteers. Hearing false reports of a rising in Cuba, he prematurely loosed his blow.

23 Claiborne, *John A. Quitman*, II, 56, 57; cf. R. G. Caldwell. *The Lopez Expeditions*.

The terrible catastrophe that followed should have taught a lesson—but if it did, men quickly forgot it. Landing in Cuba in August, 1851, with perhaps five hundred men, Lopez was quickly overwhelmed. Fifty recruits under a brave young officer of the Crittenden family were captured, taken to Havana, and executed. Lopez, fighting desperately in the jungle, was seized and garroted before a jubilant mob; and numerous others were slain or sent into the slavery of penal servitude. While the best part of the American press rang with condemnation of the intrigues that had made a mockery of American laws, offended the Spanish government, and cost so many youths their lives, the South witnessed a spontaneous outburst of sympathetic anger. Scores of communities there mourned the loss of scions of well-known families. A mob in New Orleans wrecked the Spanish consulate and a Spanish newspaper office, and insulted the Spanish flag; another mob roared through the streets of Key West destroying Spanish property; and in other centres the fiercest indignation was expressed. To multitudes in the Lower South, the "gallant fifty-one" who perished at the hands of their Spanish captors were martyrs. It was not long before letters, articles, patriotic pronunciamentos, and junta appeals were again mobilizing filibuster sentiment. Those sinister execution-grounds, the Morro Castle and the Square of Abrato, said cynical men, were calling for new victims.[24]

One sequel of the Lopez expedition was the proffer of American apologies and reparation ($25,000 for the destruction by the New Orleans rioters) to the Spanish government.[25] Another was the appearance of French and British squadrons in the Gulf with orders to help protect Cuba. When the State Department questioned the French government as to the intentions of these vessels, it replied that they would take measures against "any pirate or adventurers that should attempt to land in arms on the shores of a friendly nation." The British government, similarly interrogated, stated that its warships "have orders to prevent by force any adventurers of any nation from landing with hostile intent upon the island of Cuba." Washington expressed its "grave disapproval" of the action contemplated.[26]

Meanwhile, Madrid was making certain suggestions to London and Paris which in the spring of 1852 resulted in a proposal by the two latter capitals that the United States join Britain and France in a tripartite guarantee of the Spanish possession of Cuba. The suggestion was deeply irritating to most Americans,

24 See article "The Filibusters Again at Work," National Intelligencer, August 24, 1852. Herminio Portell Vilá, Historia de Cuba, I, 457ff.
25 32d Cong., 1st sess., House Exec. Doc. No. 1.
26 The exchanges were reviewed in the Senate by Soulé, with full quotations, March 22, 1852; Cong. Globe, 32d Cong., 1st sess. App. 349–354. Cf. Curtis's Webster, II, 551; Jeronimo Becker, Relaciones Exteriores de España, II.

and to Southerners was decidedly provocative. Why should the United States tie its hands? Though a Whig Administration was in power, and though two conservative Yankees, first Webster and then Everett, were swaying the State Department, the response had a good deal of asperity. Webster, acquiescing in principle, raised political objections. The question was held over till fall so that it would not complicate the presidential campaign. Then, in November, Fillmore and his Cabinet agreed that Everett should pen an emphatic rejection. He did so with gusto. While the President did not want Cuba, he declared, he regarded the status of the island as mainly an American question. No Administration could face the people, he wrote, if it pledged itself under no circumstances to acquire Cuba; for that island "lies at our doors," it "commands the approach to the Gulf," it "bars the entrance" of the Mississippi, it "keeps watch at the doorway of our intercourse with California," and "under certain contingencies it might be almost essential to our safety." [27]

Expansionist sentiment, continuing to run high, expressed itself not merely in new filibustering menaces against Sonora, Lower California, Nicaragua, and Cuba, but in Yankee talk of the acquisition of Canada. Greeley's *Tribune*, for example, beat a steady drum for the annexation of the British provinces. They cost Queen Victoria's exchequer a million and a half pounds a year, it argued; they yielded nothing in return but the name of empire and an asylum for a few politicians and noblemen; they would buy far more British products if placed under the American flag than if kept in leading strings. The liberation of Canada was bound to come, and "Independence is but the precursor of Annexation." The Northern press eagerly caught up the demands of Cobden, Bright, and other Manchester Liberals for the fullest rights of colonial self-government. When Douglas early in 1850 introduced a bill for opening the navigation of the St. Lawrence and its canals to American commerce from the Great Lakes, and at the same time arranging a reciprocity of trade with Canada, he had in mind not only a promotion of the commerce of his beloved Northwest, but a smoothing of the path to eventual annexation. The whole continent for the American dwelling—that was the dream of millions; "its floor shall be the hemisphere, its roof the firmament of the star-studded heavens." [28]

The United States, everyone agreed, was to take a mighty place in the world. But could it first settle the most imperative of its own social and economic problems?

27 British and For. State Papers, XLIV, Howden dispatch, January 9, 1852; 32d Cong., 2d sess., Senate Exec. Doc. No. 13.
28 N. Y. *Tribune*, January 15, 1850; *Cong. Globe*, 31st Cong., 1st sess., 324, February 11, 1850; *National Intelligencer*, June 3, 1852. Bulwer informed Clayton on January 22, 1850, that Great Britain was ready to conclude a general Canadian reciprocity treaty with the United States; Clayton Papers.

A Note on Sources

THE SELECT bibliography for the first fifteen years of this history, 1846–1861, follows the appendices in the fourth volume. A list of the main manuscript sources used in the first two volumes is given herewith. It is far from complete, for it would be profitless to enumerate them all; literally dozens of collections have been consulted in single libraries like those of Duke University or the Massachusetts Historical Society. In this list LC refers to Library of Congress, HS to Historical Society, and PL to Public Library, while L is simply Library.

CHIEF COLLECTIONS OF GENERAL PAPERS

Appleton-Sumner Corr., Boston PL; Nathan Appleton Papers, Mass. HS; Bayard Family Papers, LC; John Bell Papers, LC; William Bigler Papers, Pa. HS; Jeremiah S. Black Papers, LC; Gist Blair Papers, LC; Blair Family Papers, Princeton Univ. L; James Buchanan Papers, Pa. HS and LC; A. Burt Papers, Duke Univ. L; Caleb Cushing Papers, LC; Zachariah Chandler Papers, LC; Chamberlain Papers, Boston PL; J. F. H. Claiborne Papers, Miss. Dept. Archives and Hist. and Univ. of N. C.; Henry Clay Papers, LC; C. C. Clay Papers, Duke Univ. L; John M. Clayton Papers, LC; Moncure D. Conway Papers, Columbia Univ. L; J. J. Crittenden Papers, LC; Jefferson Davis Papers, LC, Miss. Dept. Archives and Hist., and Confederate Memorial Hall, New Orleans; Stephen A. Douglas Papers, LC, Ill. State HS, and Univ. of Chicago L; Edward Everett Papers, Mass. HS; Thomas Ewing Papers, LC; B. B. French Papers, LC; John C. Frémont Papers, Bancroft Library, Univ. of Cal.; Joshua Giddings Papers, Ohio Arch. and HSL; W. A. Graham Papers, N. C. State Archives, Univ. of N. C.; Gratz Family Papers, Mo. Hist. Soc. L; Horace Greeley Papers, N. Y. PL; Greeley-Colfax Corr., N. Y. PL; Allen Hamilton Papers, Ind. State HS; James H. Hammond Papers, LC and S. Caroliniana L, Univ. of S. C.; R. M. T. Hunter Papers, Va. State L and Alderman L, Univ. of Va.; George W. Julian Papers, Ind. State HS; Andrew Johnson Papers, LC; John P. Kennedy Papers, Peabody Institute L, Baltimore; A. A. Lawrence Papers, Mass. HS and Kansas State HS; Francis Lieber Papers, Huntington L and LC; W. L. Marcy Papers, LC; Robert McClelland Papers, LC; C. G. Memminger Papers, Charleston HS and Univ. of N. C.; Wm. Porcher Miles Papers, Univ. of N. C.; Edwin D. Morgan Papers, N. Y. State Archives; Pettigrew Family Papers, Univ. of N. C.; Franklin Pierce Papers, LC; James S. Pike Papers, privately held; James K. Polk Papers, LC; Edmund Quincy Papers, Mass. HS; Wm. C. Rives Papers, LC; Charles Robinson Papers, Univ. of Kansas; Thomas J. Rusk Papers, Univ. of Texas; Schirmer Papers, Charleston HS; Alex. H. Stephens Papers, LC and Manhattanville College of the Sacred Heart, N. Y.; Charles Sumner Papers, Harvard Coll.; Tammany Hall Collection, Columbia Univ. L; Roger B. Taney Papers, LC and Md. HS; W. H. Trescot Papers, S. Caroliniana L, Univ. of S. C., and LC; John Tyler Papers, LC; Martin Van Buren Papers, LC; Ben Wade Papers, LC; Gideon Welles Papers, N. Y. PL and LC.

DIARIES, JOURNALS, AUTOBIOGRAPHIES IN MANUSCRIPT

John Bigelow, N. Y. PL; John W. Du Bose, Ala. State Dept. Archives and Hist.; Edward Everett, Mass. HS; Joshua Giddings, Ohio Arch. and HS; W. J. Grayson, S. Caroliniana L, Univ. of S. C.; James H. Hammond, *Ibid.*; J. D. Hoge, Huntington L; Wm. T. Johnson, La. State Univ.; Benjamin Moran, LC; Edmund Ruffin, LC; George Templeton Strong, Columbia Univ. L.

NEWSPAPERS

The edition of the *National Intelligencer* here used is the tri-weekly; of other journals the daily, save when so identified the N. Y. *Weekly Tribune.* The reporting of debates in the *Congressional Globe* is often so inadequate that it is important to gather supplementary material from the Washington *Union, Republic, National Intelligencer,* and other newspapers.

Index

INDEX

for compromise, 319 ff.; denounces disunionists, 338; appeals for compromise,
339; retires for vacation, 341; honored for
his rôle in effecting compromise, 344,
345; angered by slave-trading, 455; describes slavery, 460; critical of slavery, 504;
elected president of American Colonization Society, 511, 512; concerned for free
Negroes, 515; visits Natchez, 527

Clay, Porter, brother of Henry Clay, 111

"Clayton Compromise," passes Senate, fails
in House, 23

Clayton, John M., in Senate, 15; views on
Mexico, 17; receives letter from Du Pont,
120; United States senator from Delaware,
prefers Senate to Presidency, 164; quoted
by Everett on corruption relevant to Gadsden Treaty, 166; opposes Calhoun's proposal, 223, 224; designated a drunkard, 230;
estimate of, 230–231; influence of, 232;
his plan for California and New Mexico,
239; instructs Thomas Butler King, 259;
urged by Crittenden, 307; favors Taylor's
course, 332; negotiates treaty for isthmian
canal, 551 ff.

Clemens, Jeremiah, on the stump, 184; political career aided by military reputation,
185; in sectional debates, 262; discourses on
Calhoun, 314; in Alabama election, 375

Cleveland, prediction of, by *Hunt's Merchant's Magazine*, 39

Cleveland *Plain Dealer*, quality of, 89

Clingman, Thomas L., estimates loss of
fugitive slaves, 243; in sectional debates,
261; mentioned, 332; denounces Thaddeus
Stevens's iron interest, 402–403

Cobb, Howell, as Speaker of Congress, 170;
secretary of treasury, his view toward
political activity of office-holders, 179; opposes Calhoun's proposal, 224; candidate
for Speaker, 251; elected Speaker, estimate of, 253; gives concessions to freesoilers, 258; optimistic on sectional controversy, 271; optimistic on settlement, 298;
represents South at conference, 303;
supports compromise, 342; as Unionist,
355; in Georgia election, 374

Cobb, Sylvanus, author of *The Gunmaker
of Moscow*, 108

Cobb, T. R., defends slavery, 495

Cobb, W. R. W., his electioneering methods,
184

Cobden, Richard, mentioned, 153; 559

Coffin, Levi, written to, by Cave Johnson,
506; quoted, 519–520

Cogswell, Joseph G., literary advisor to
Astor, 104–105

Colburn, James Smith, warns about South
Carolina, 372

Colby College, founded by Baptists, 72

Coles, Edward, life of, anti-slavery views of,
501–502; mentioned, 506

Colfax, Schuyler, editor of South Bend *Register*, impressed by Illinois, 110–111; receives
letter from Greeley on temperance lecture, 127; written to, by Greeley, on lack
of accomplishment by Congress, 163; informed by Greeley regarding Taylor, 197;
dissatisfied with Taylor's nomination, 203

Collamer, Jacob, Greeley's opinion of, 230;
estimate of, 231; influence of, 232; his abolitionist views, 241

Collins, E. K., celebrates passage of compromise measures, 347

Colonization, plans of, for freed Negroes,
511 ff.

Colorado, diverse population groups in, 49

Colt, Samuel, investigation of influences
affecting extension of his patent on firearms, his agents offer Congressman a bribe,
167

Columbia College, condition in 1850's, 53

Columbia (S. C.) *Daily Telegraph*, quoted,
248; denounces Seward's speech, 301; disappointed at Fillmore's elevation, 337

Columbia (S. C.) *Transcript*, its prediction
in case of secession, 369

Comte, Auguste, influence of, 77

Congregationalists, represented in Home Missionary Society, 71

Congress (House of Representatives), interior of chamber described, 40–41

Connecticut, school system in, 53

Constitutionnel (Paris), mentioned, 44

Cook, Isaac, postmaster in Chicago, builds
machine, 178

Cooke, A. B., & Company, bookstore in Chicago, 103

Cooke, Henry D., editor of *Ohio State Journal*, 88

Conrad, Charles M., attitude toward Texas-
New Mexico dispute, 330; appointed secretary of war, 336

Conway, Moncure D., comments on Carlyle,
81; comments on John M. Daniel, 89; his
description of Cincinnati, 109; writes for
southern journals, 243; observes Webster,
320

Cooper, James Fenimore, influence of, 79;
address on, by Bryant, 84; mentioned by
Seward, 114; his daughter comments on
status of women, 131

Cooper, Peter, admired for his wealth-ac-
quiring and philanthropy, 72; his endow-

573

plains about lack of staff and space, 161; overwork of, 162–163; his debates with Henry S. Foote, 184; political career aided by military reputation, 185; favors Calhoun's proposal, 223; in sectional debates, 266, 276–278, 311; opposed to compromise, 313; in sectional controversy, 331; elated at defeat of omnibus bill, 340; his course disapproved by northern Democrats, 350; mentioned, 367; as disunionist, 372, 373; excluded by compromisers, 403; origins of, 418

Davis, "Honest John," his support of Taylor, 195; supports Taylor and Seward, 321

Davis, Paulina, protests status of women, 135

Davis, Reuben, his electioneering methods, 184; answers critic, 449; on wealth in Mississippi, 474

Dayton, William L., supports Taylor and Seward, 321

De Bow, J. D. B., comments on "white supremacy," 419; views of, 470–471

Delaware, prohibition in, 126; slavery in, 503

Democratic party, loses state elections, 5; splits into factions, 5; northern wing opposed to slavery extension, southern wing in favor of, 6; anti-slavery wing led by Van Buren and Benton, pro-slavery wing by Calhoun, moderate wing by Douglas, 6; opposes Tyler's Texas annexation views, 6; dissension in, 7; its policies, 154 ff.; split in Pennsylvania, New York, and Massachusetts, 174; split in New York, Pennsylvania, Ohio, New England, 190–191; wins state elections, 399

Denver, James W., kills editor, 67

Derby, J. C., publisher of Auburn, locates in New York, 97

Derby, Lord, his policies mentioned, 153

Des Moines Navigation and Railroad Company, involved in investigation of bribery in Congress, 169

De Quincy, Thomas, works of, published by Little, Brown, 100

DeSaussure, Louis D., writes Gaillard, 441; as slave-dealer, 453

De Tocqueville, Alexis, quoted, 33; book creates stir in Europe, 35; quoted, 38; studies American prison system, 123; mentioned, 510

Detroit, prediction of, by *Hunt's Merchant's Magazine*, 39

Dew, Thomas R., pro-slavery philosopher, 148, 477, 494

Dewey, Orville M., supports fugitive slave law, 400

Dicey, Edward, depressed by Negroes' plight, 522–523

Dickens, Charles, avoids cotton states, 37; mentioned by Greeley, 45; observes American customs, 55; receives royalty from Harper, 102

Dickinson, Daniel S., his Senate resolutions, 29–30; "Hunker" Democratic leader, outweighed by "Barnburners," 192; senator from New York, in Benton-Foote altercation, 310; congratulated by Webster, 346

Dickson, David, amasses fortune in cotton, 467

Diplomatic corps, estimate of, 181–183

Dix, Dorothea L., friend of the insane, 114; agitates for prison and asylum reform, 121–123; compared with men, 137

Dix, John A., leader of Barnburners, 190; mentioned for presidency, 192; conservative on slavery, 208

Dixon, James, opposes annexation of Mexican land, 18

Dodd, M. W., publisher, 99

Dodge, Henry, nominated for Vice-President, 205

Donelson, Andrew J., as Unionist, 357; demands cessation of agitation, 376

Douglas, Stephen A., comments on military strategy, 4; leads moderate Democrats, 6; in Senate, 15; views on territorial and slavery issues, 22; offers amendment declaring Missouri Compromise line in force, 24; defends "popular sovereignty" doctrine, 30–31; criticized for tobacco-chewing, 55; effective oratory, 57; visits Europe, 81; mentioned, 137; his views, 155; in Senate, 164; United States senator from Illinois, chairman of Committee on Territories, quoted on judiciary, 170, 171; replies to Wade on judiciary bill, 172; his faction not favored by Buchanan, 175; debates with Lincoln, 183; rejection of, for President in 1856, 187; estimate of, as presidential candidate, 188; comments on condition of Democratic party, 190; his view of sectional controversy, 221; his plan condemned by Calhoun, 223; offers constitution for Deseret (Utah), 257; advocate of compromise, 303–305; mentioned, 309; advocate of compromise, 313; assumes leadership in enactment of compromise measures, 341; celebrates passage of compromise measures, 343; his rôle in effecting compromise, 344; appeals for cessation of